AFRICA'S ANIMAL KINGDOM

A VISUAL CELEBRATION

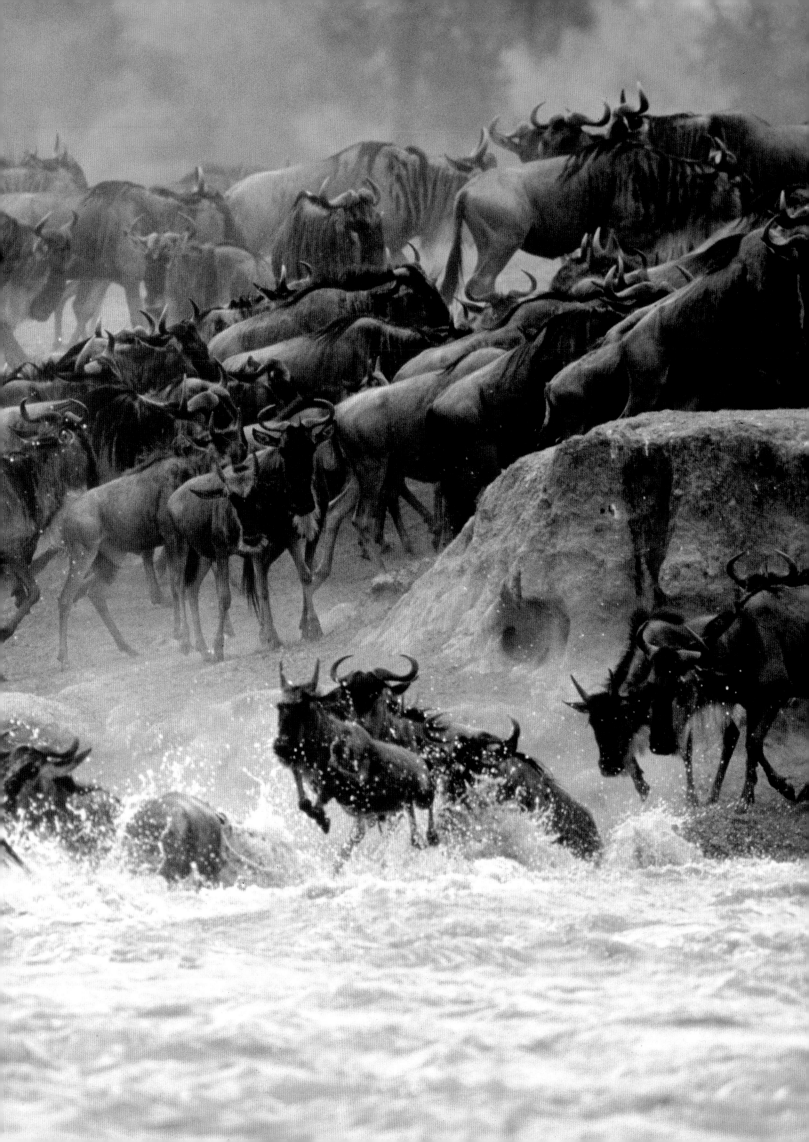

AFRICA'S ANIMAL KINGDOM

A VISUAL CELEBRATION

KIT COPPARD

PRC

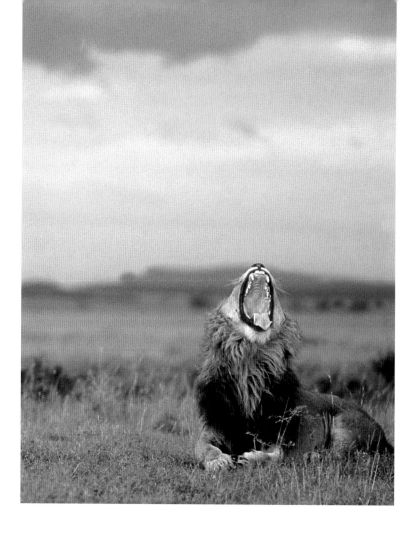

First produced in 2000 by
PRC Publishing Ltd,
64 Brewery Road, London N7 9NT
A member of the Chrysalis Group plc

This edition first published in 2001
Reprinted in 2002
Distributed in the U.S. and Canada by:
Sterling Publishing Co., Inc.
387 Park Avenue South
New York, NY 10016

ISBN 1-85648-590-0

Printed and bound in Taiwan

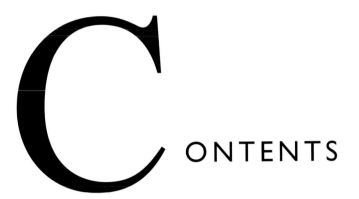

CONTENTS

the CHANGING LANDSCAPE

Africa is the second largest continent after Asia, with an area of about 11,677,240 square miles (30,244,050km²). At one time it formed the core region of a vast super-continent known as Gondwanaland, the other constituents of which included what became South America, Antarctica, Australia, South-East Asia, India and the Middle East. Towards the end of the Paleozoic era, some 275 million years ago, powerful forces within the Earth's viscous upper mantle gradually caused the rigid overlying plates of crustal rock, on which the oceans and continents rest, to begin to split apart. The African continent drifted slowly eastwards, while over a period of some 240 million years the other elements of the supercontinent gradually migrated to their present positions.

THE GREAT RIFT VALLEY

The processes that powered this drifting of continents continue today. On a global scale they are most evident in the vast chains of volcanically active mountain ranges—the mid-oceanic ridges—that rise from the floor of the Atlantic, Pacific and Indian oceans. In Africa the processes can be seen at work in the continent's most striking geological feature, the great Rift Valley system. This remarkable feature runs northwards from near the mouth of the Zambezi river in Mozambique to the northernmost point of the Red Sea, and then onwards through the Sinai peninsula to the Dead Sea—a distance of some 4,200 miles (6,760km).

Right: Part of the eastern Rift Valley in Kenya, with the fault-strewn valley floor several hundred feet lower than the plain at the top of the steep cliffs at left.

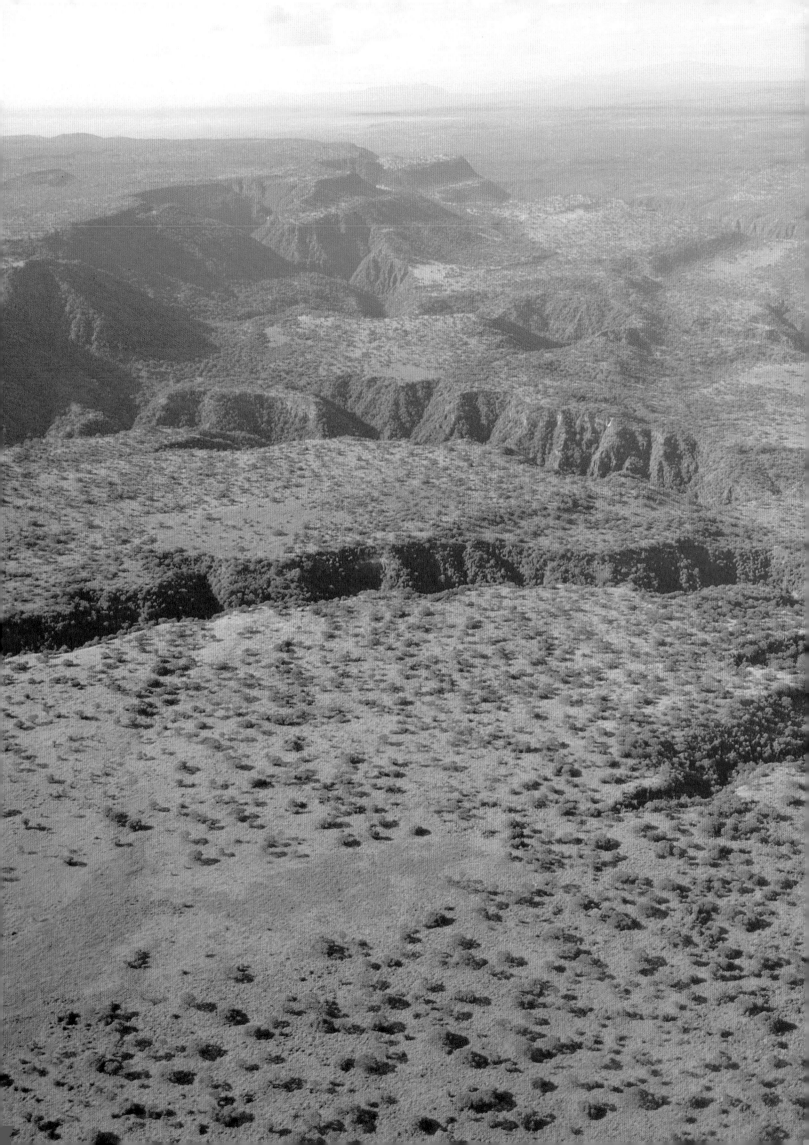

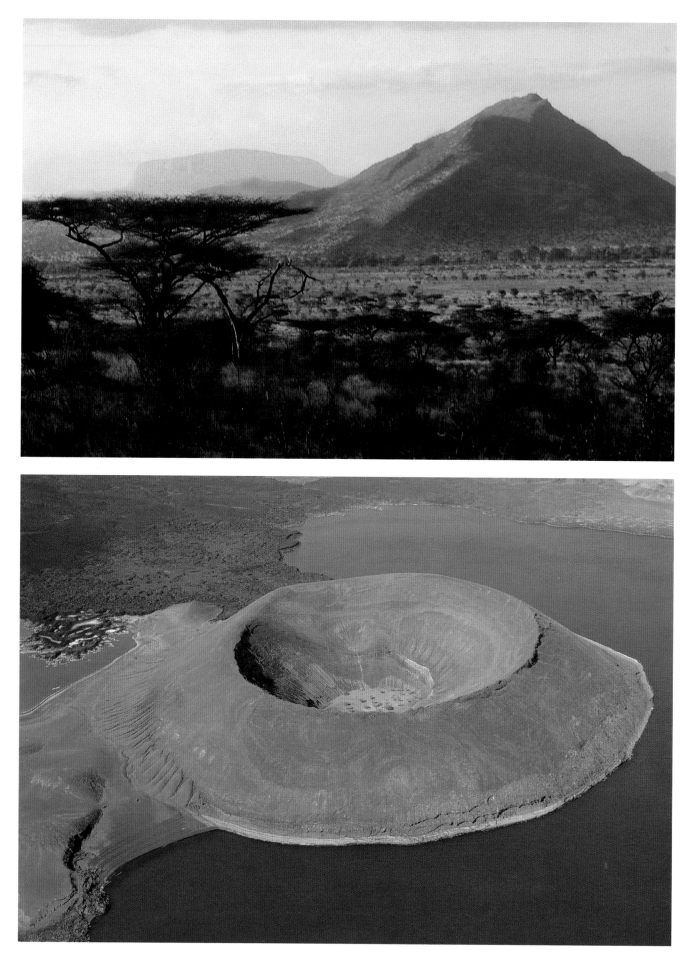

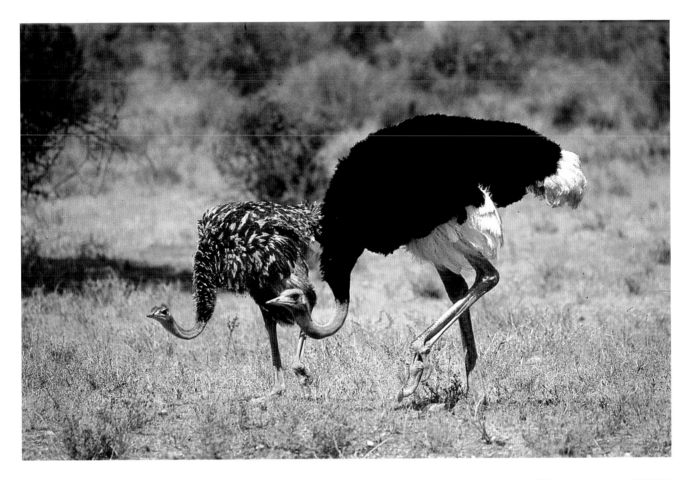

The rift system was formed in the course of several major episodes of sub-crustal movement, the two most recent episodes having occurred some six million and 2.5 million years ago (although the present topography of the system is little more than 50,000 years old). The movement caused uplifting and splitting of the crust at the Earth's surface. The process of uplifting reached its apogee in the immense dome of lava, some 250 miles (400km) wide, in what are now the highlands of Ethiopia. The plateaus on either side of the rift were gradually forced apart, forming valleys that average about 25 miles (40km) in width; elsewhere, as in the Kenya highlands, the rift has created immense gorges whose vertical walls are several thousands of feet high in some places.

South of the Ethiopian highlands the rift splits into two arms. The eastern rift passes through Kenya and Tanzania; the Kenyan highlands section includes the Aberdare range and the Mau Escarpment to the north-west of Nairobi. At many points along the line of both arms the pressure from beneath the crust led to more localised fractures in the form of volcanoes. In the eastern arm the most notable example is Kilimanjaro, in north Tanzania, whose Uhuru peak atop the Kibo cone soars to 19,340ft (5,895m)—the highest point on the African continent. Others include Mt. Meru, some 45 miles (72km) southwest of Kilimanjaro; Mt. Kenya, east of the Aberdares; and Mt Elgon, on the Kenya-Uganda frontier.

The western arm passes through eastern Zaïre and western Uganda, Rwanda, Burundi and Malawi. The edge of the western rift is dominated at its northern end by the non-volcanic Ruwenzori range (the Mountains of the Moon), which has ten peaks 16,000ft (4,880m) or more in height, and which drops steeply to the rift on

Above: A Somali ostrich with young inSamburu National Reserve, Kenya.

Above Left: Much of the northern part of Samburu National Reserve consists, as here, of acacia scrubland that extends northwards into Ethiopia and Somalia.

Left: A volcano on the edge of Lake Turkana, which marks the line of the Rift Valley south of the Ethiopian highlands.

Overleaf: A lioness stalks prey in dense undergrowth in Buffalo Springs National Reserve, whose southerly margin (like neighbouring Samburu's) boasts lush vegetation along the banks of the Ewaso N'giro river.

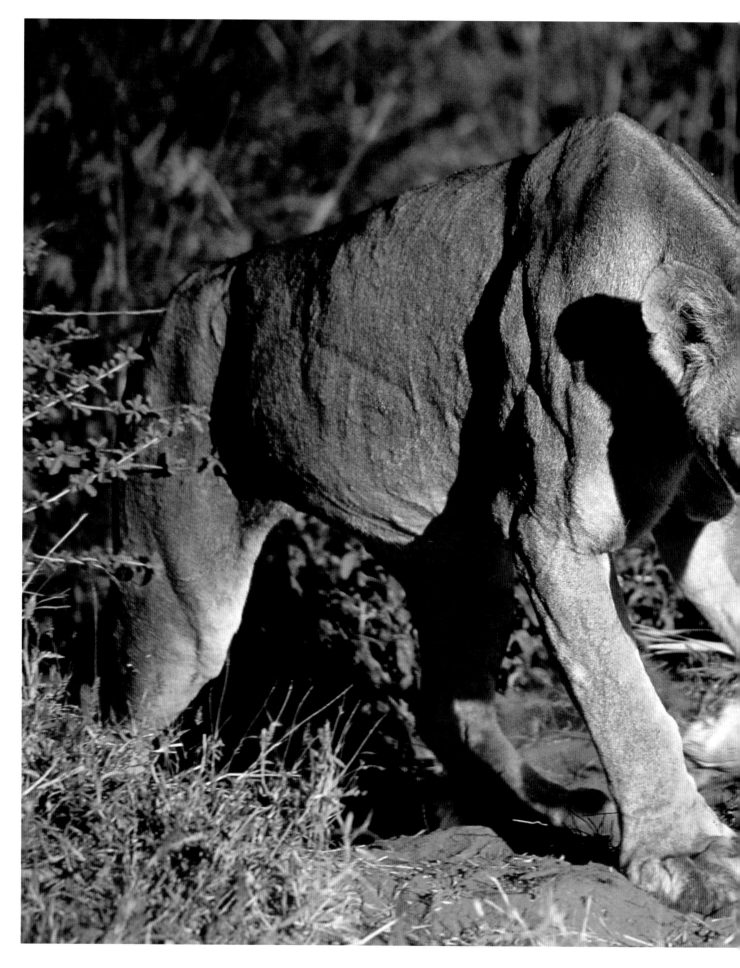

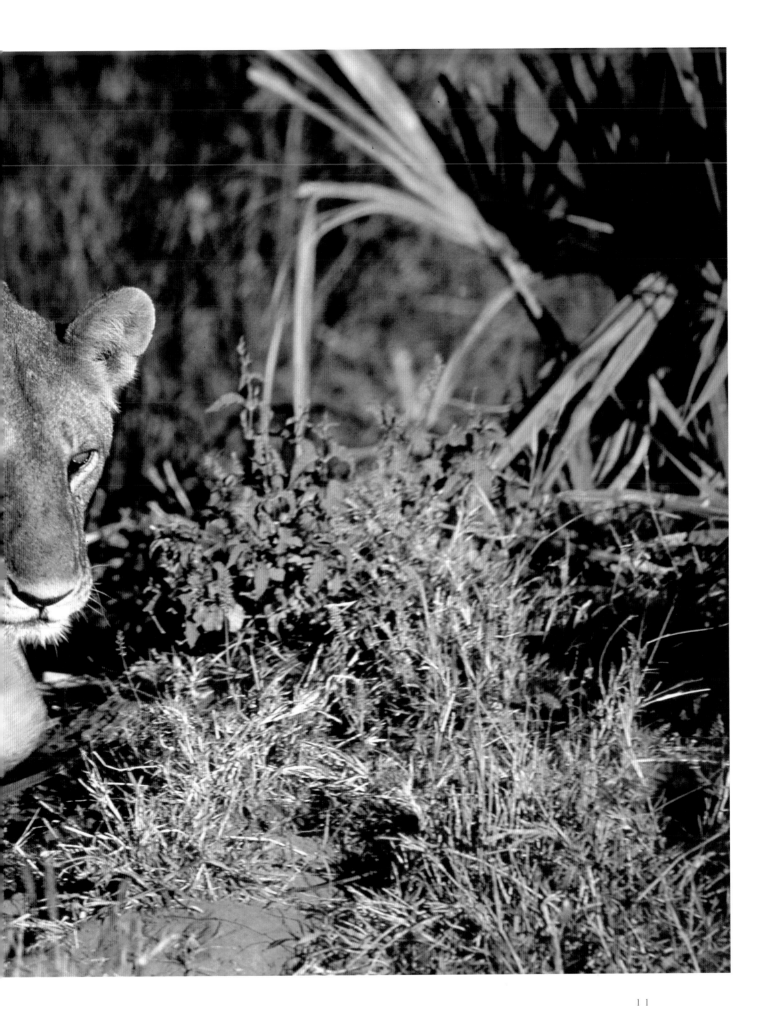

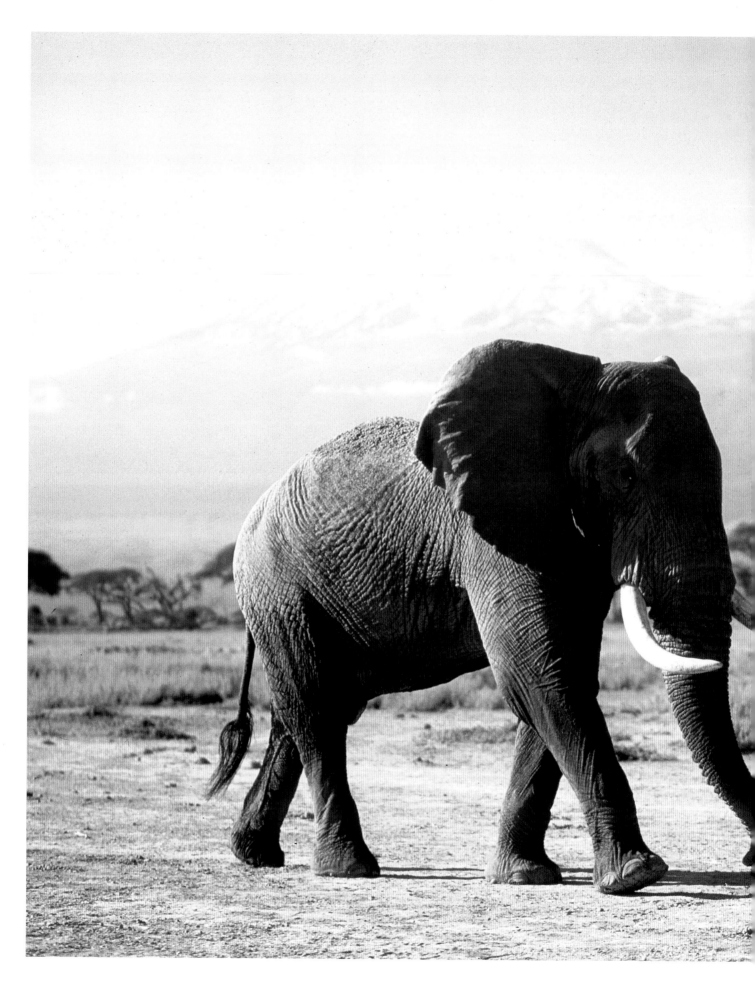

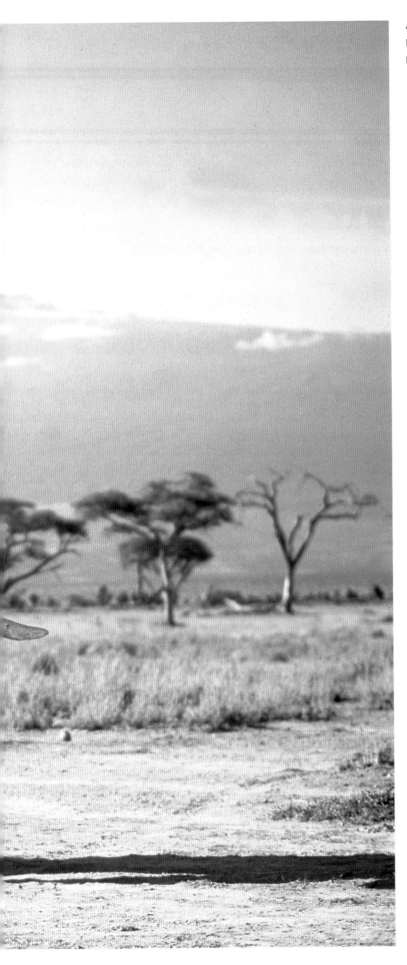

A male bush elephant in the dry savanna of southern Kenya's Amboseli National Park. In the background, just across the Tanzania border, looms Kilimanjaro, an ancient volcano and Africa's highest peak.

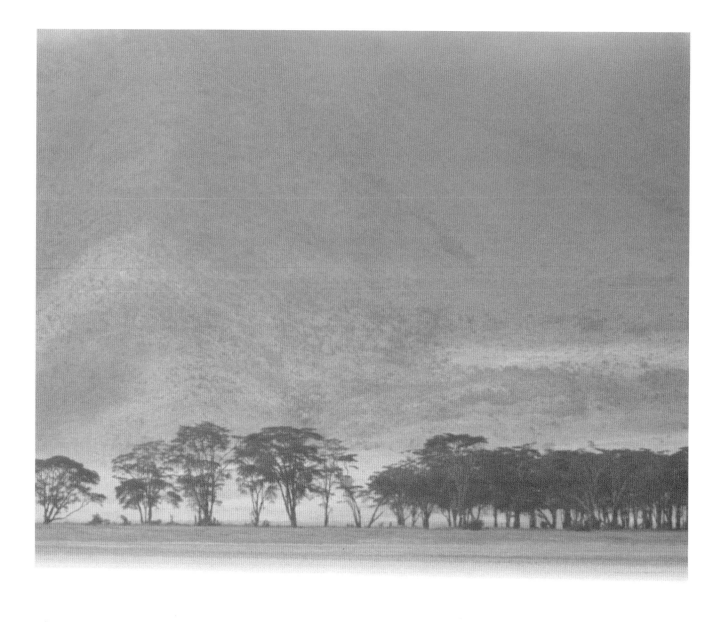

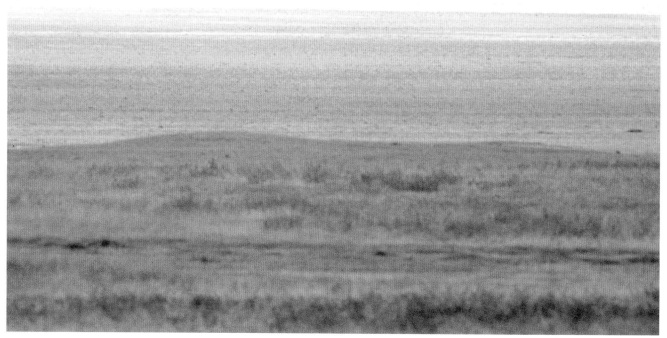

its western side. Like the highest mountains of the eastern rift, the peaks of the Ruwenzori are permanently capped in ice in spite of the fact that they lie almost on the Equator. Farther south much of the floor of the middle section of the western rift is made up of lava flows from the Virunga range, whose still-active volcanoes form the division between the region drained by the Nile to the east and that drained by the Congo to the west.

More-ancient volcanoes associated with the Rift Valley have ceased to be active and have long since been worn away by erosion. To the west of Kilimanjaro and Mt. Mero, for instance, lies the stupendous caldera of Ngorongoro, an oval saucer 12 miles (19km) long and ten miles (16km) wide which was formed when the volcano's huge cone collapsed inward; it is the largest dormant (presumed extinct) crater in the world. Ngorongoro is home to a spectacular range of wildlife.

Above: Soaring on thermals, a fish-eagle searches for prey over the waters of Lake Baringo, most northerly of the larger rift lakes in the Kenya highlands.

Left: A soda lake in Tanzania's immense Ngorongoro Crater. Beyond the trees across the lake the wall of the crater rises to a rim that in this section is some 2,000ft (600m) above the valley floor.

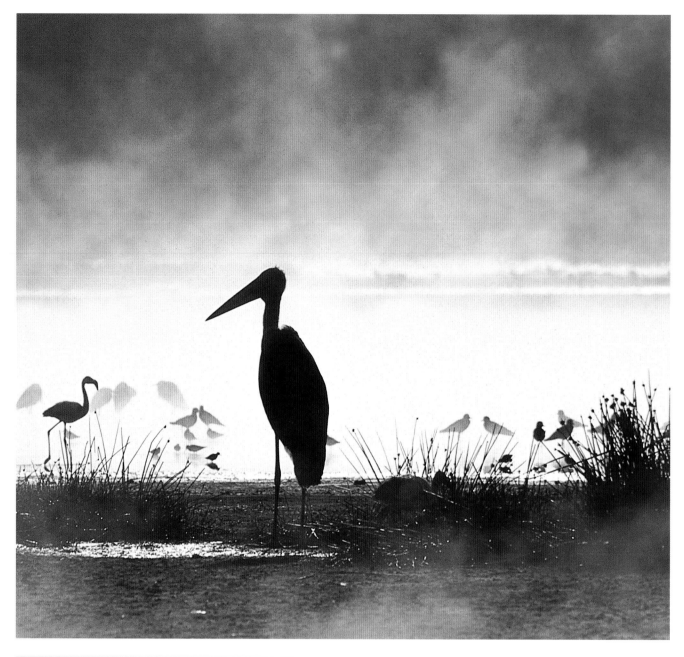

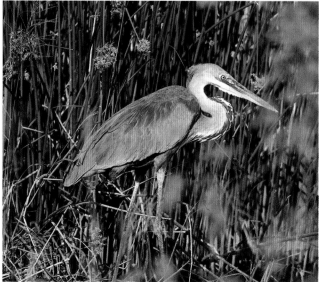

In its deepest sections the course of the Rift Valley is marked by large and small lakes, many of them resembling fjords in their great depth and the steepness of their sides. South of the Ethiopian highlands, in the eastern rift, are Kenya's lakes Turkana (formerly Rudolf), Baringo, Bogoria, Nakuru, Elmenteita, Naivasha and (near the Tanzania border) Magadi. Farther south, in Tanzania, are the soda lakes Natron, Manyara and Eyasi; many others in this region are dry salt beds that are occasionally, and briefly, freshened by seasonal rain.

The largest lakes are to be found in the western arm of the rift. In the north, making part of the frontier between Uganda and Zaïre, is Lake Albert. The Virunga range is bounded on the north by Lake

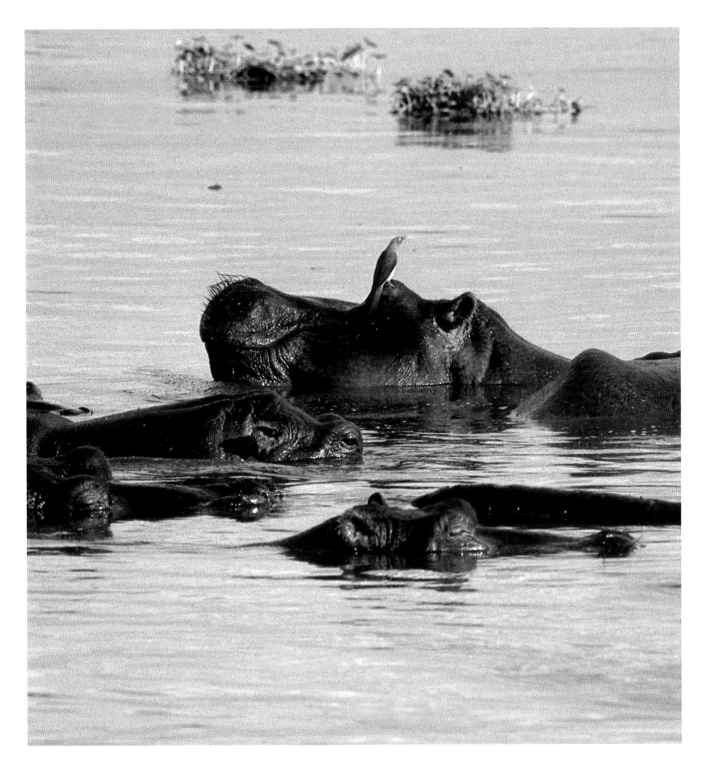

Edward (which is connected to Lake Albert by the Semliki river) and on the south-west by Lake Kivu, which was formed when lava flows from the Virunga volcanoes dammed part of the western rift that had formerly been drained by a tributary of the Nile. Mightiest of the rift lakes is Lake Tanganyika, lying between Tanzania and Zaïre: it is 420 miles (675km) long and up to 45 miles (72km) wide; its maximum depth, 4710ft (1435m), makes it the second deepest lake in the world.

Above: Hippos in Tanzania's Lake Manyara National Park are found in the park's large freshwater pool close to the northern end of the saline lake.

Above Left: A marabou stork and flamingos silhouetted against the hot springs of alkaline Lake Elmenteita, west of Kenya's Aberdare range.

Left: On the lookout for fish, a goliath heron patrols the margins of Lake Baringo.

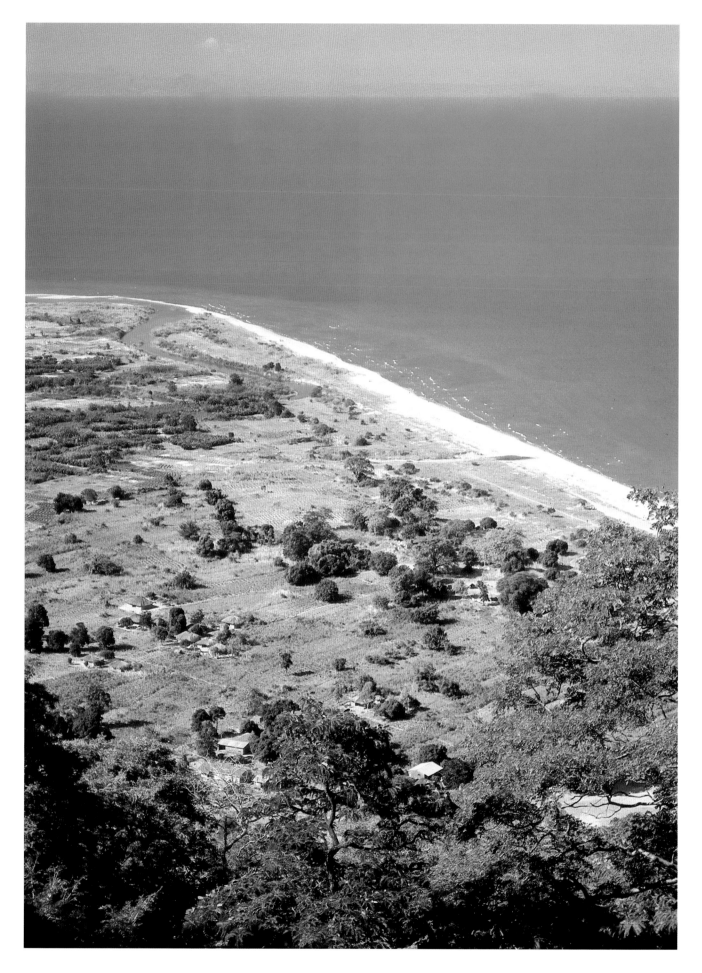

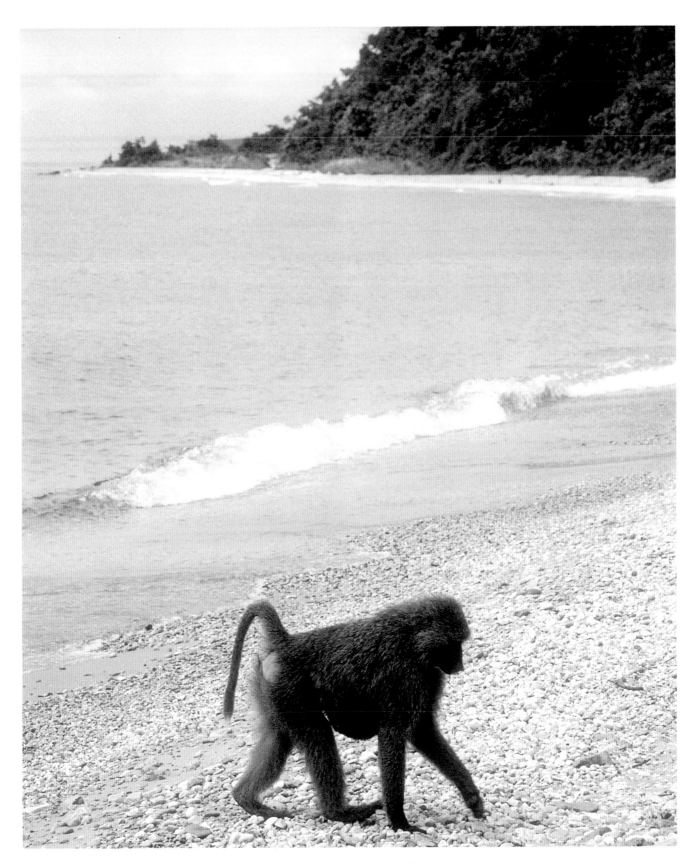

Left and Above: A baboon beachcombs on the shore of Lake Tanganyika (above). The second deepest in the world, this lake and Lake Malawi (seen on the left from the escarpment along its western shore) are part of a chain of mountains and freshwater lakes that mark the line of the western arm of the Rift Valley.

THE PLATEAU LANDS

Between the eastern and western arms of the Rift Valley lies Lake Victoria, which was created about a million years ago when movements in the rift caused downward warping of the crustal surface. Today the lake lies in a shallow depression: it has a maximum depth of only 275ft (84m), but its surface area of 26,830 square miles (69,490km²) makes it the third largest lake in the world.

Although seemingly low-lying compared to the towering ramparts of the rift system to the east and west of it, the surface of Lake Victoria in fact lies about 3,300ft (1,000m) above sea-level. Indeed, Africa as a whole consists mainly of a series of relatively flat plateau surfaces. South of the Sahara desert (which occupies about one quarter of the continent's surface), and especially south of the Equator, almost all the land apart from narrow coastal strips lies more than 1,000ft (300m) above sea level. Huge regions—including the whole of the great Kalahari desert in southern Africa—are above 3,000ft (900m), while large tracts of the Kenyan plateau lie at more than 6,000ft (1,830m). The northern and western regions of Africa south of the Sahara also consist of relatively flat plateau lands, although most of them lie only 500 to 1,000ft (150 to 300m) above sea level.

Relative to its size, Africa has very little land at or near sea-level. In much of the continent the inland plateaus give way on their margins to fairly narrow coastal plains, though more extensive ones are found along the Gulf of Guinea coast and between southern Tanzania to Mozambique. Much of the Indian Ocean coast has coral reefs offshore, while many beaches in the equatorial regions are backed by lagoons with mangrove swamps.

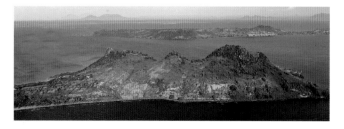

Above: Lake Victoria (the largest in Africa) lies between the eastern and western arms of the Rift Valley. These islands are near the north-eastern (Kenyan) shore of the lake.

Right: Sunrise over the Masai Mara in south-western Kenya. This is the definitive East African grassland savanna: vast open plains punctuated here and there by fever (acacia) trees.

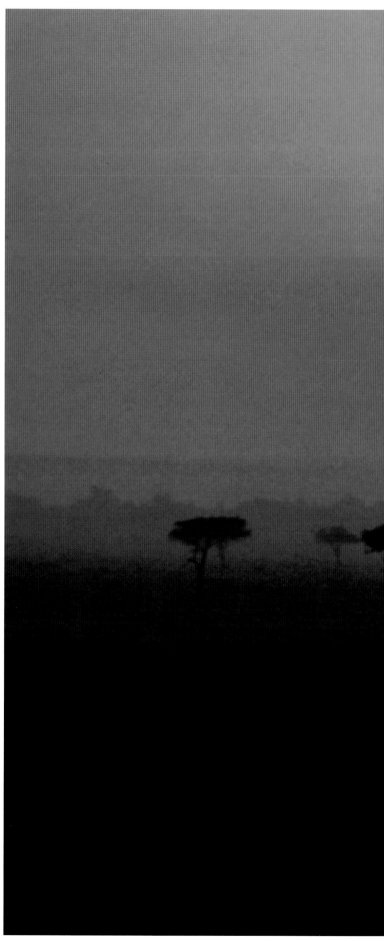

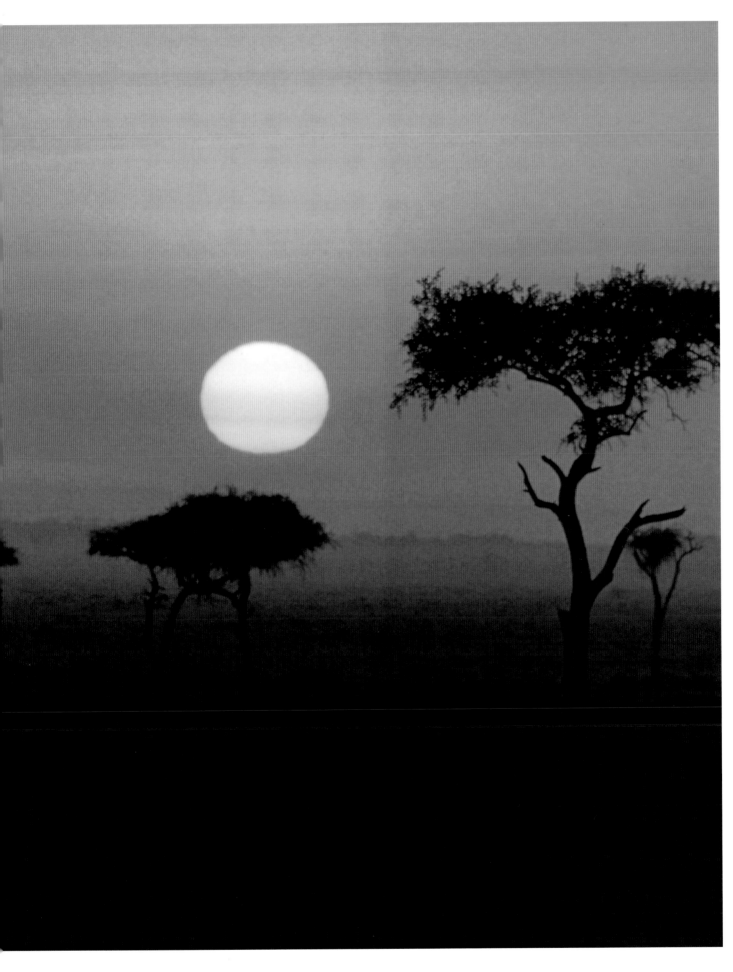

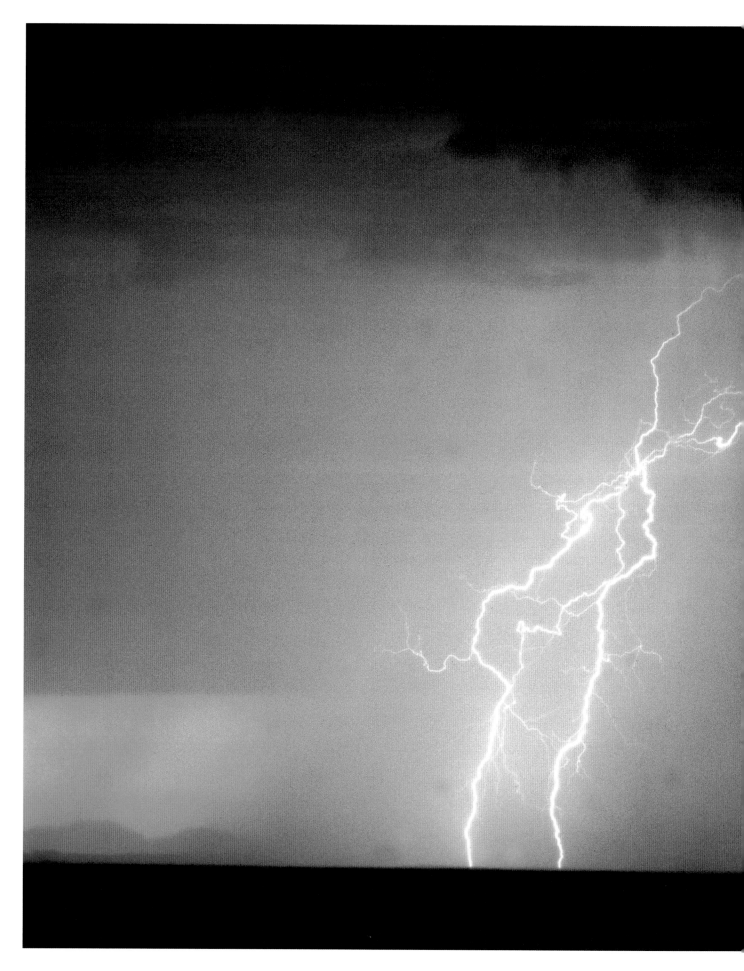

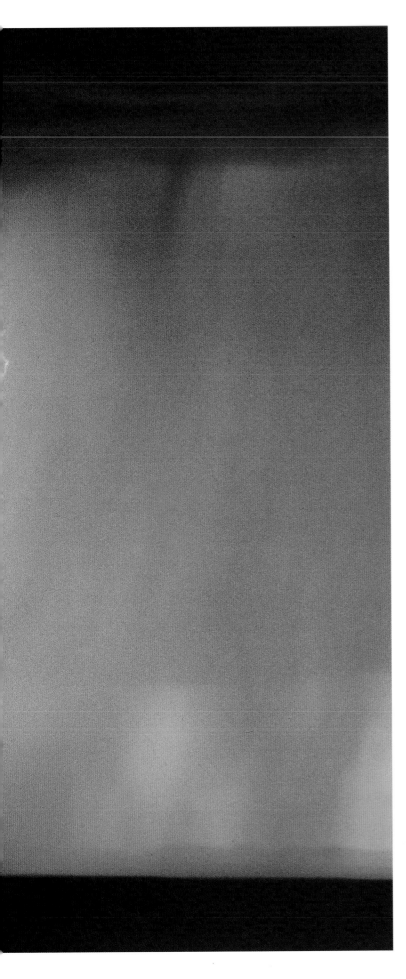

Left: The Karoo, the arid central plain of South Africa's Cape Province, is drier than most grassland savanna. It typically receives only six to 12in (150–300mm) of rain a year, much of it (as here) arriving in the form of violent thunderstorms.

Overleaf: Elephants quench their thirst in the Mara river. Rising in the Kenya highlands, the river flows south-westwards through the Masai Mara and Serengeti plains and is a major factor in the survival of wildlife in this region during the dry seasons.

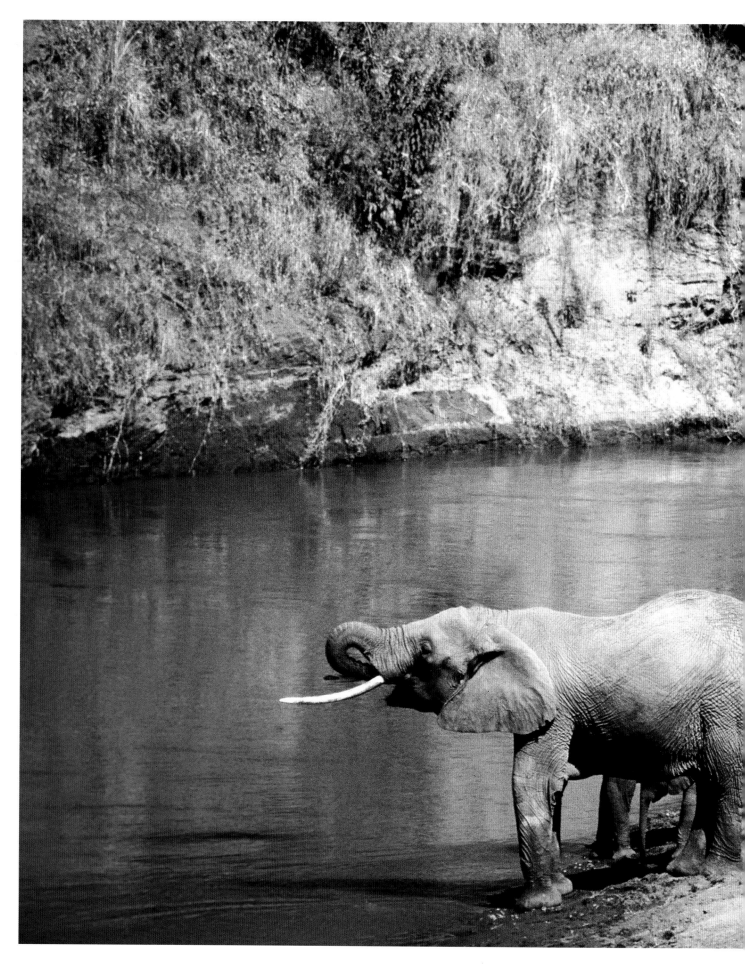

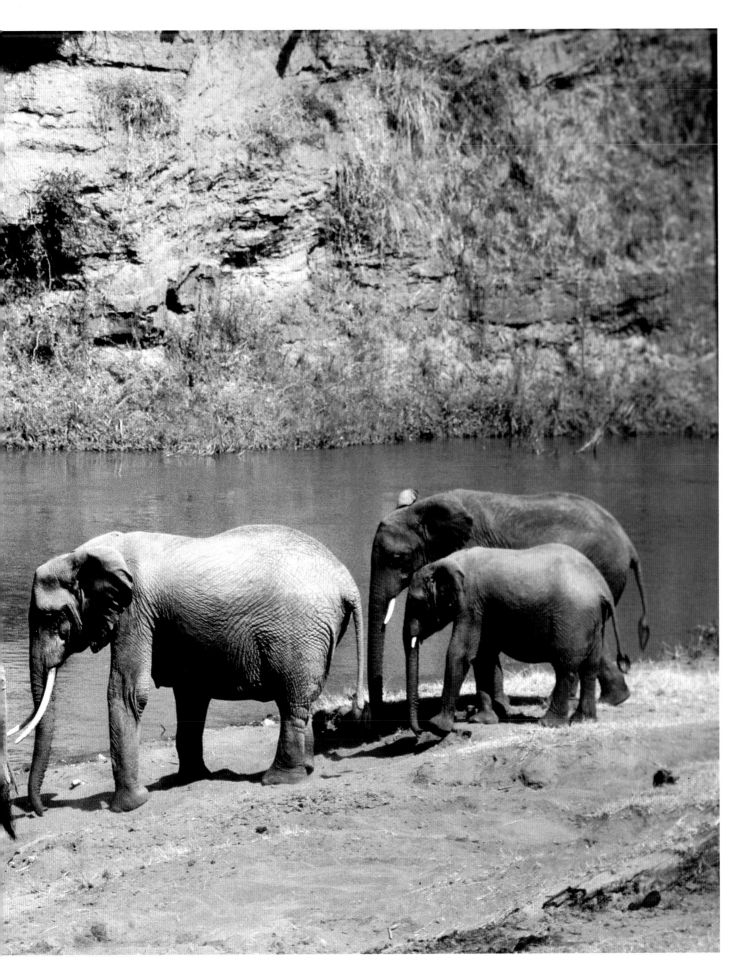

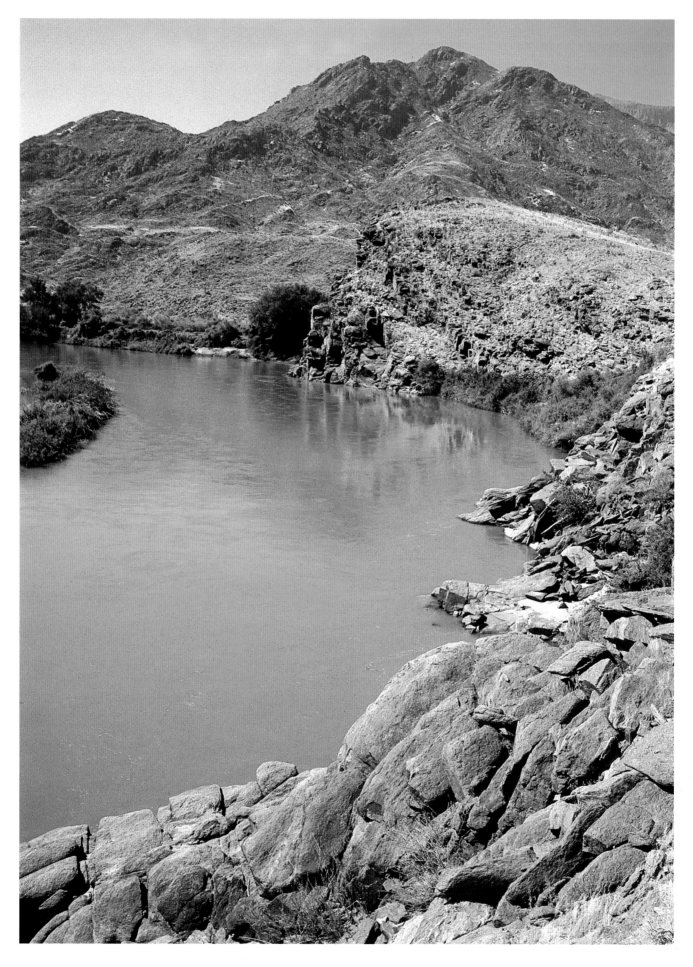

THE GREAT RIVERS

Africa is drained by five major river systems: those of the Nile, the Congo, the Niger, the Zambezi and the Orange. Because they have their headwaters in high plateau lands, and also because in many areas their courses have been affected by upward or downward warping of the Earth's crust, the flow of all these rivers—at least in their upper reaches—is swift and is interrupted, in some cases many times, by falls, cataracts or rapids. On the other hand, the volume of water flowing varies greatly at different times of the year owing to the fact that, away from the Equator, the rain that feeds these rivers is highly seasonal. The exception to this is the Congo, which crosses the Equator twice in its journey from headwaters to sea and has a more or less constant rate of flow throughout the year.

The Nile, at 4,132 miles (6,652km) in length, is the longest river in the world. Its source is Lake Victoria, whence it flows (as the Victoria Nile) into the northern end of Lake Albert, from which (as the Albert Nile) it almost immediately departs northwards into Sudan, where it is known as the Bahr el Jebel. In southern Sudan its course takes it through the swampland of the Sudd. At Khartoum it is joined by the swift-flowing Bahr el Azraq, or Blue Nile, whose source is Lake Tana in the Ethiopian highlands. From Khartoum the great river, henceforth known simply as the Nile (or Bahr el Nil to the Egyptians), flows steadily northward to its delta outlet on the Mediterranean Sea.

The Congo, or Zaïre, is the second longest river in Africa at 2,880 miles (4,630km). A glance at a map of Zaïre and the Congo Republic shows a vast and intensely concentrated network of streams and rivers that flow into this great river. In fact, it drains an area of almost 1,350,000 square miles (3,500,000km), taking in almost all of Zaïre, Congo Republic, much of the Central African Republic, north-eastern Zambia, northern Angola and parts of Tanzania and Cameroon. The Congo's headwater is the Chambeshi river, which rises in the western arm of the Rift Valley between lakes Tanganyika and Malawi. The Chambeshi connects via several increasingly important tributaries and lakes to the Congo's primary tributary, the Lualaba, which rises in the south-eastern corner of Zaïre.

The Niger river, at 2,550 miles (4,105km), is Africa's third longest river and the dominant drainage system of West Africa. It rises in the eastern slopes of the Fouta Djallon highlands of Guinea, flowing northwards and then north-eastwards into Mali.

North-east of the town of Mopti, where the Niger is joined by a major tributary, the Bani, the river flows through a network of lakes

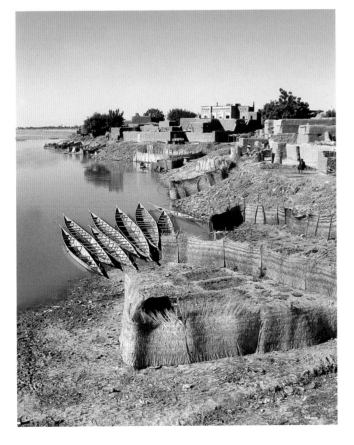

Far Left: The Cunene river, forming the frontier between Namibia and Angola, cuts a land-refreshing path through the northern reaches of the Namib desert.

Left: The town of Djenne is on the Bani river, the major tributary of the Upper Niger in Mali.

Overleaf: At its delta the Niger proliferates into a vast network of streams and channels that extends for 200 miles (320km) along the Gulf of Guinea coast.

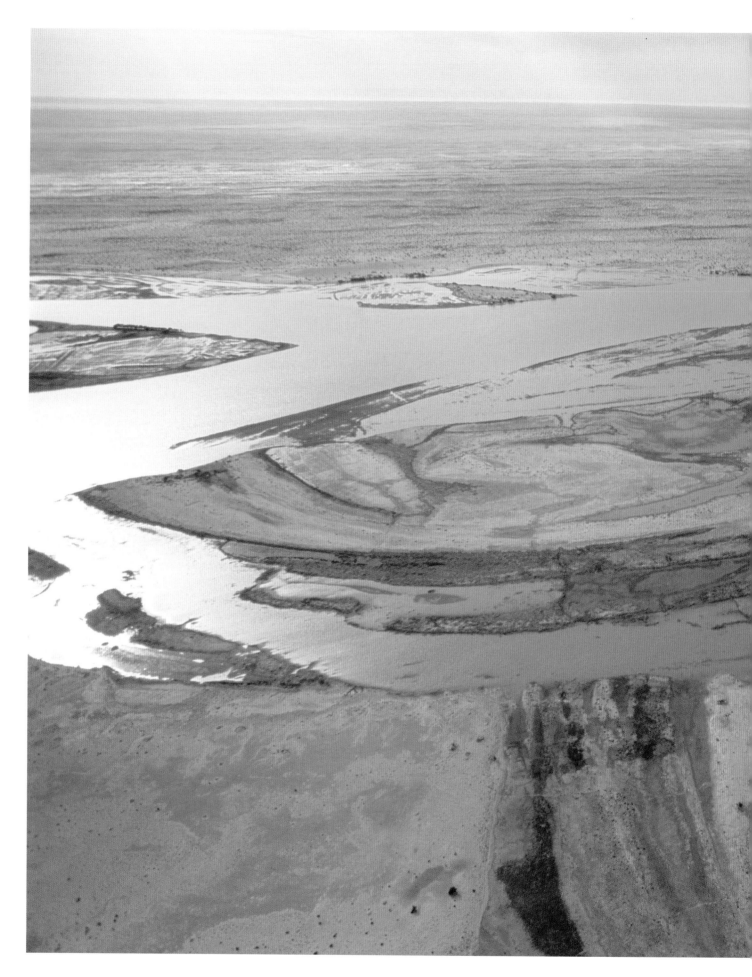

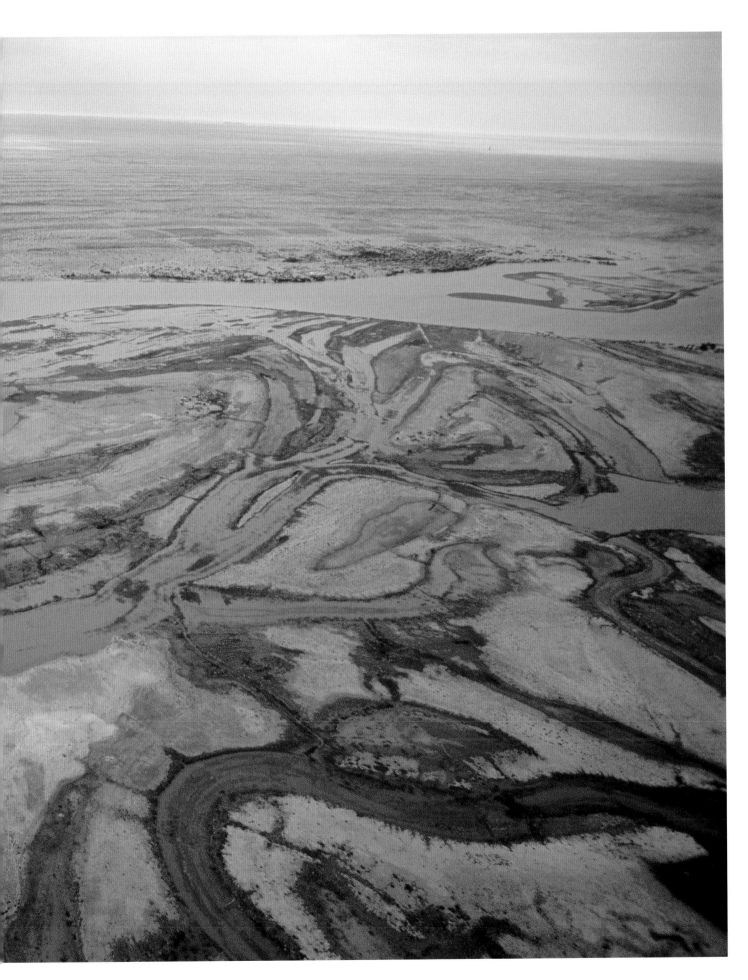

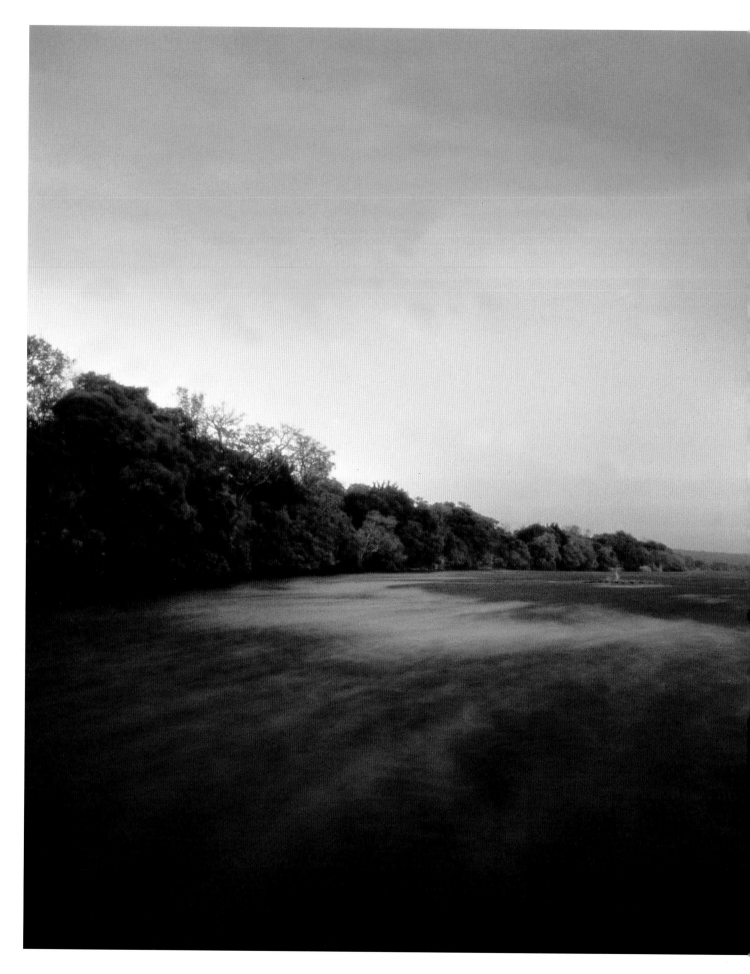

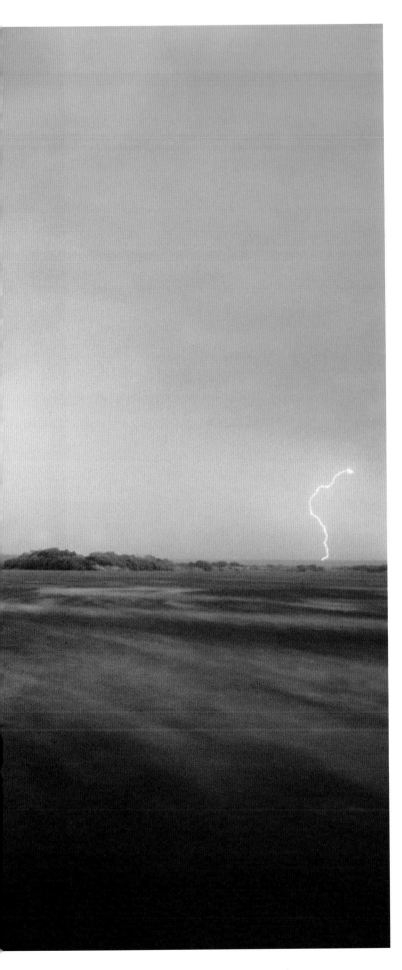

and creeks. After skirting the southerly margin of the Sahara desert the river turns south-eastwards through the state of Niger and finally into Nigeria. At its delta, the largest on the African continent, the river issues into the Gulf of Guinea to the west of Port Harcourt.

Africa's fourth largest river, the Zambezi, is 1,650 miles (2,660km) long and drains an area of more than 450,000 square miles (1,165,500km). It rises near Kalene Hill, in the most north-westerly corner of Zambia, flows south-westward into Angola, where it continues on the same course for about 150 miles (240km) before bending southwards and entering Zambia once more. After skirting the Caprivi Strip on Zambia's southern border the river flows eastward to Victoria Falls, the most spectacular of many falls throughout the river's course. The Zambezi marks the long frontier between Zambia and its southern neighbour Zimbabwe, passing the town of Livingstone (also known as Maramba) and flowing through Devil's Gorge before turning north-eastward and broadening out into the 150-mile-long (242km) expanse of Lake Kariba, with the massive dam at its north-eastern end. At the Mozambique frontier it broadens out once more into a lake formed by the Cabora Bassa dam. Thereafter it turns south-eastward, eventually flowing into the Indian Ocean a few miles south of Chinde.

A stormy sunset on the Zambezi river, which for much of its middle course forms the frontier between Zambia and Zimbabwe. Several major national parks and wildlife reserves are located on or near this section of the river.

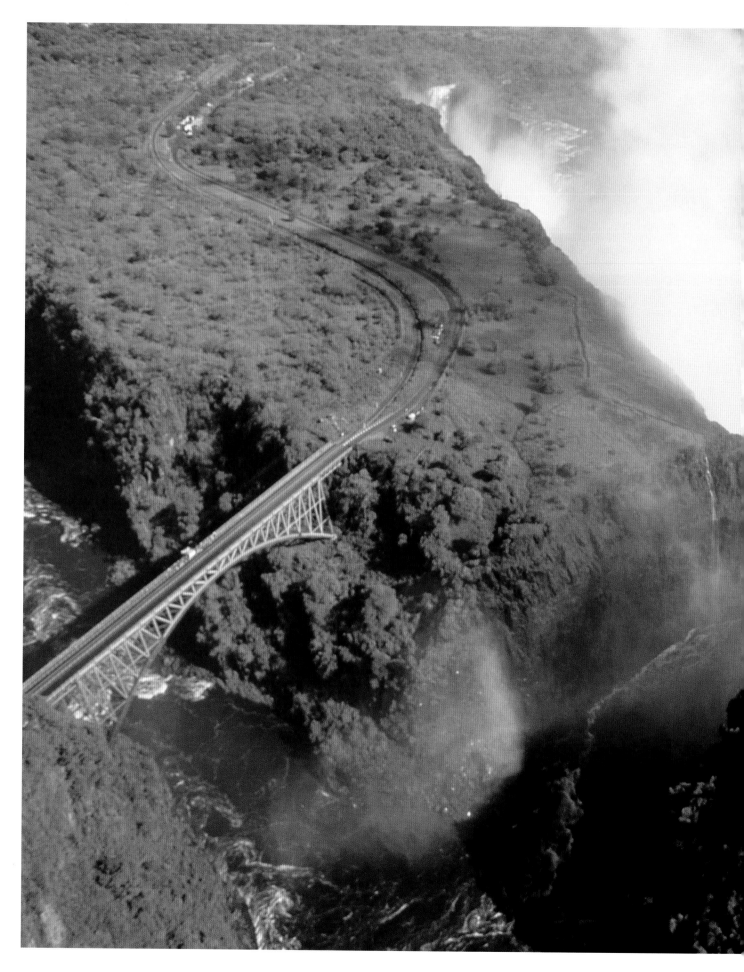

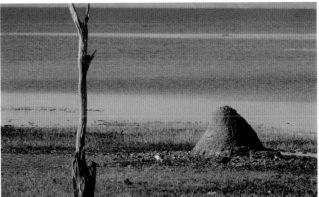

Above: The Zambezi broadens out into Lake Kariba about 100 miles (160km) east of Victoria Falls. This view is from Zimbabwe's Matusadona National Park, on the southern shore.

Left: The Zambezi's most spectacular feature is the Victoria Falls, where the river, more than a mile (1.6km) wide at this point, plunges 355ft (108m) into a narrow chasm before rushing as a white-water torrent beneath the 650ft (200m) long railway bridge.

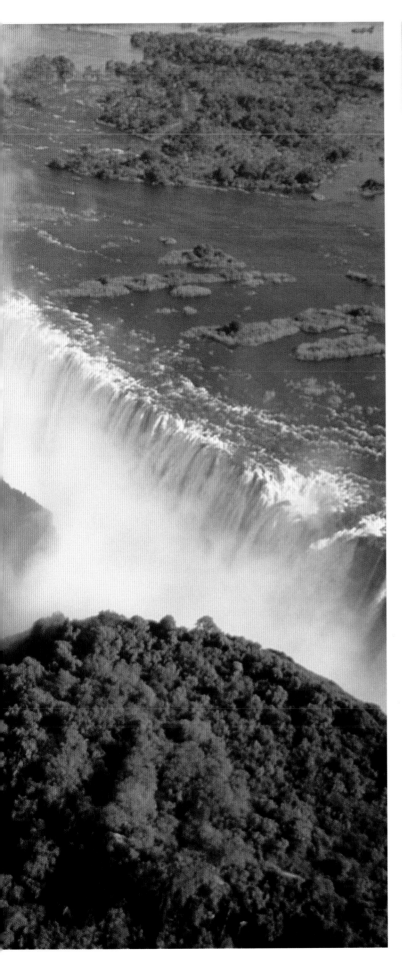

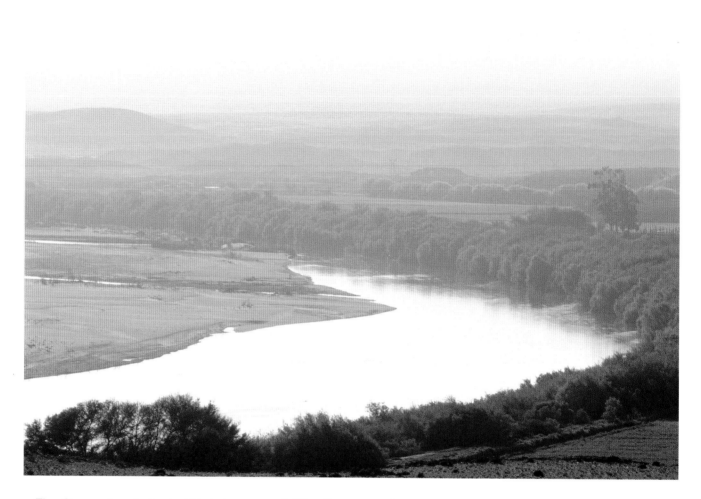

The Orange river is South Africa's longest, at 1,155 miles (1,860km). It has two headwaters: the main one rises high in the Drakensberg range in Lesotho; the other is formed by its major tributary, the Vaal, which rises near Bethal, to the east of Johannesburg, and joins the Orange near Douglas, to the west of the city of Kimberley. From here the Orange flows south-west and then north-west, meanders through the great Kalahari depression, and forms the frontier between Cape Province and Namibia before flowing into the Atlantic at Alexander Bay.

THE CHAD BASIN

Lake Chad, which lies across frontiers shared by Cameroon, Nigeria, Niger and Chad, occupies an upland basin that is the biggest inland drainage area in Africa. In former times this shallow fresh-water lake was much larger than it is today, with a surface area of perhaps 120,000 square miles (310,800km²). By the mid-20th century, however, it covered a maximum of about 11,000 square miles (28,500km²), and today the increasingly dry climate, and the diversion of some of the river waters that feed it, have reduced its surface area to about 4,500 square miles (11,650km²). It has a mean depth of four feet (1.2m) or less, but the water level changes drastically during periodic multi-year wet and dry cycles. The lake is flanked in many places by marshes and papyrus swamps that attract abundant wildlife, notably birds.

Another landlocked water system is the Okavango Delta in northern Botswana. The Okavango river flows into the area from the north-west, then splits into a delta-like network of streams and lagoons which spill over to form flood plains in the southern winter months of June and July. In what is generally an arid region, the delta is immensely important for wildlife.

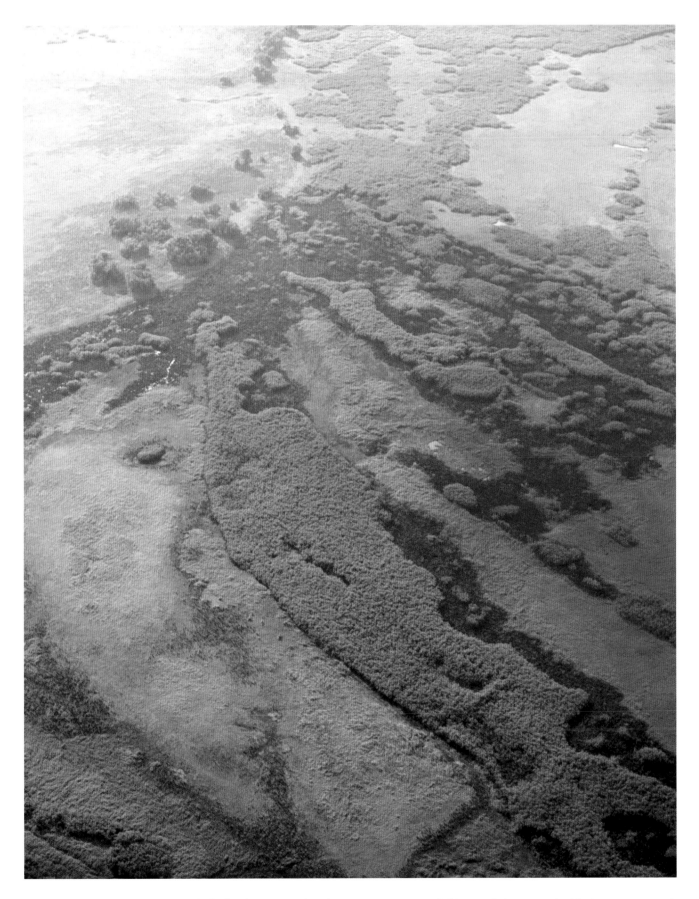

Above Left: The Orange river rises in the Drakensberg range in Lesotho and flows westward to the Atlantic. Here it is seen in its lower course, where it forms a meandering frontier between South Africa and Namibia.

Above: Botswana's Okavango Delta, a network of freshwater streams and swamps that never dries up, is a magnet for wildlife on seasonal migrations in Botswana.

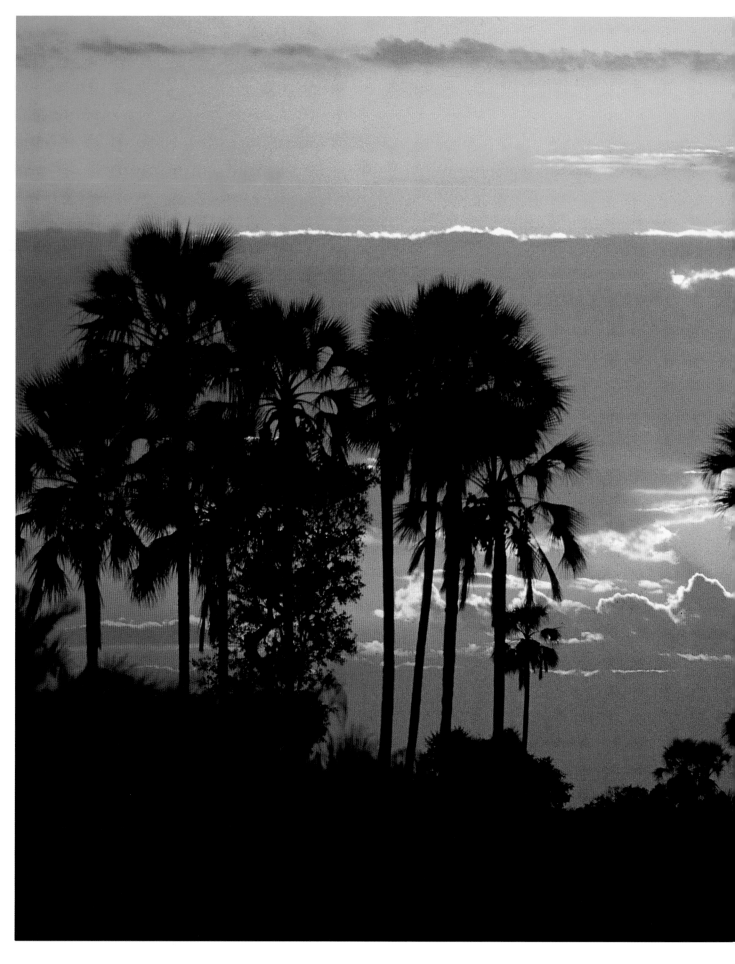

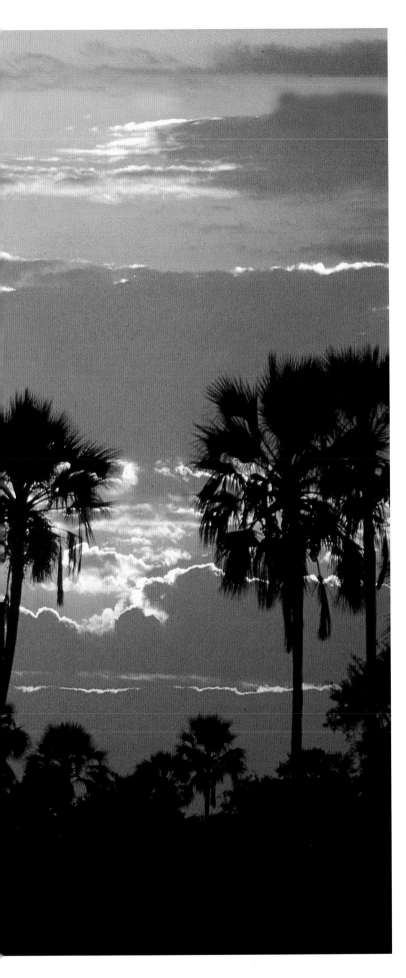

Palm trees and dense shrubbery silhouetted against the setting sun testify to the richness and variety of vegetation that flourishes in the Okavango delta.

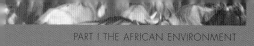

CLIMATE

Africa is cut more or less neatly in half by the Equator: its most northerly point, Cap Blanc in Tunisia, is at about latitude 37°N, and its most southerly point, Cape Agulhas in South Africa's Cape Province, is at almost 35°S. Most of the continent, then, lies within the tropics—the zones that extend 23.4 degrees north and south of the Equator. Africa derives its rain from evaporation of water off, mainly, the Atlantic and Indian oceans, but the seasonal patterns of its rainfall are governed to a great extent by the height of the sun at midday. On about 21 June, the first day of summer in the Northern Hemisphere, the sun is directly overhead at the Tropic of Cancer (23.4°N), which runs from northern Mauretania in the west to southern Egypt in the east. On about 21 December, the first day of summer in the Southern Hemisphere, the sun is directly overhead at the Tropic of Capricorn (23.4°S), which runs from central Namibia through Botswana and northern Transvaal to southern Mozambique. Between June and December, the sun is directly overhead at noon at a point that is farther south on each succeeding day; then, between December and June, the process is reversed, the sun appearing to move farther northward each day.

Right: Semi-arid grassland in midsummer: a giraffe seeks shelter from the sun in the dry plains of Etosha National Park, Namibia.

Overleaf: Mount Kenya straddles the Equator, yet its higher slopes and peaks are snow-covered all the year round.

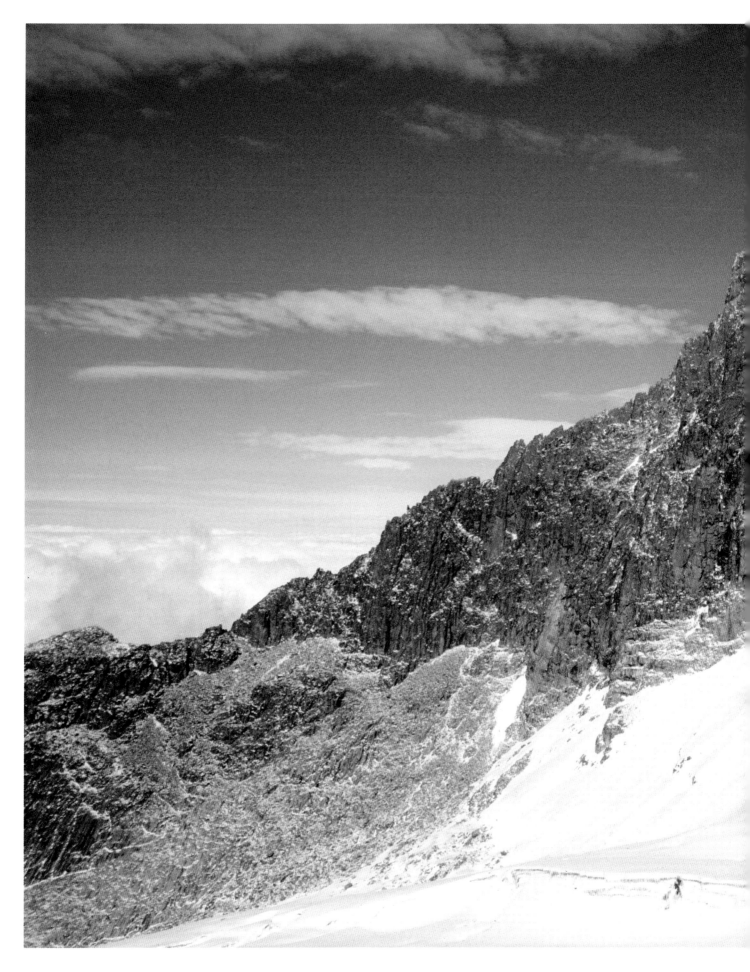

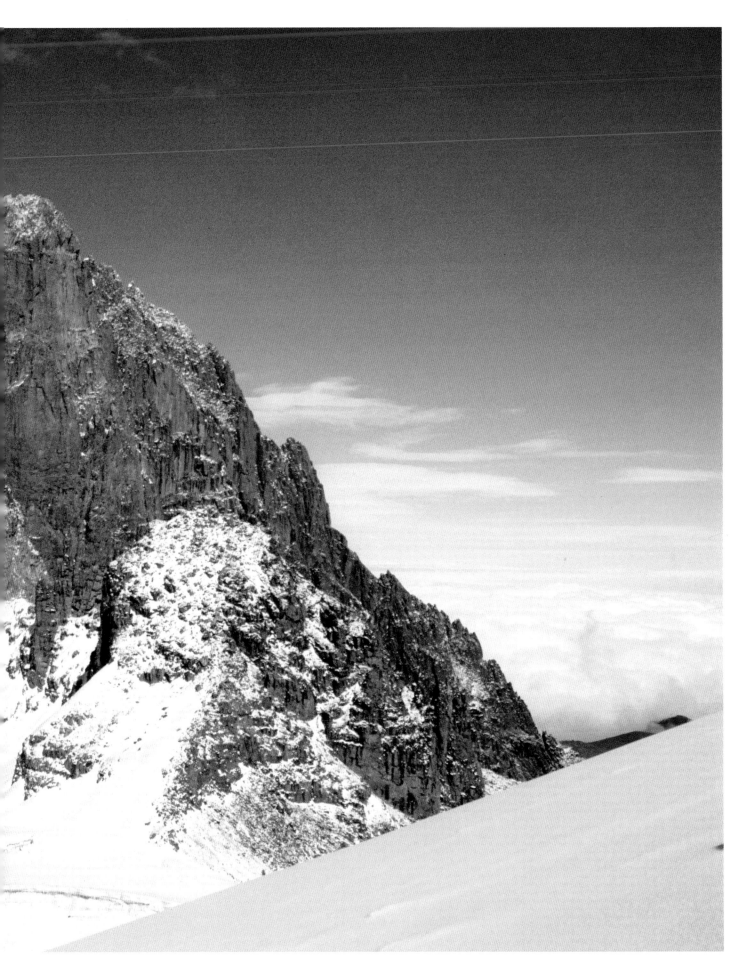

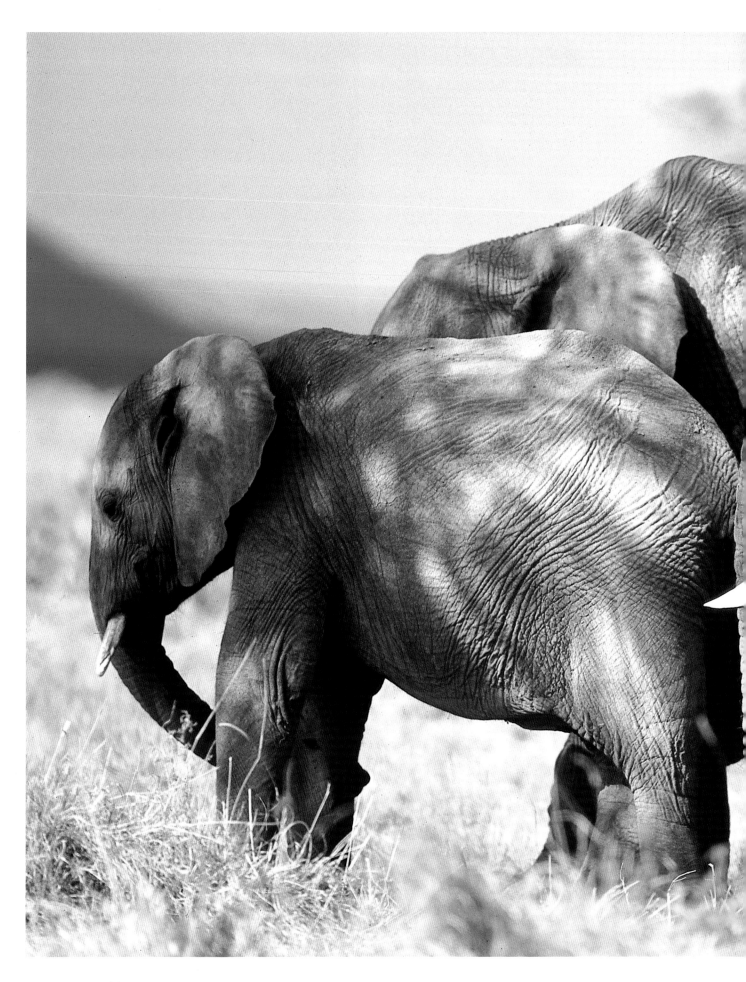

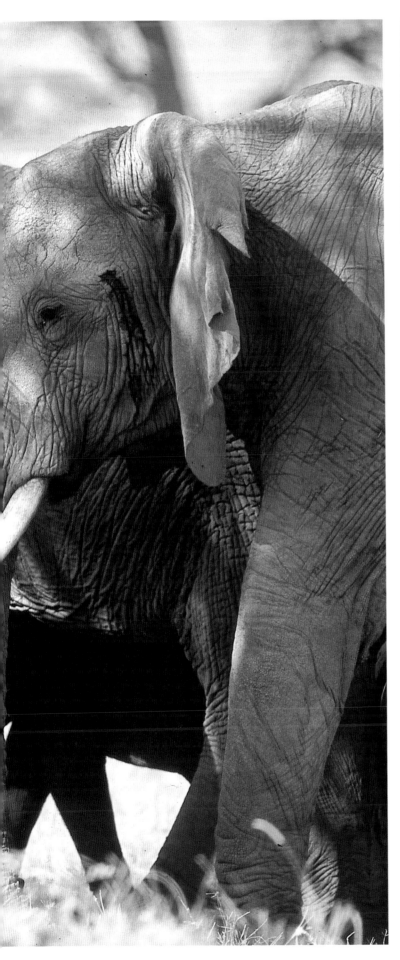

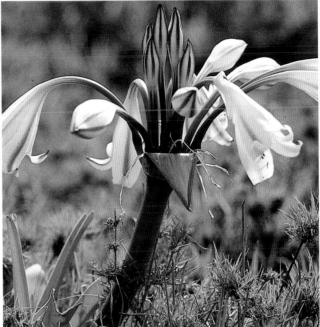

In most parts of Africa lying at or near the Equator there are two rainy seasons—from March through May and from September through November. Farther away from the Equator, but still within the tropics, most rain falls during the six months centred on the summer season: from May to October in the northern tropic and from November to April in the southern. During the other six months of the year, each tropic zone undergoes a dry period that increases in length and severity with distance from the Equator.

That is the general picture. And because the surface of the continent is characterised by extensive plateaus and the absence of very high and long mountain ranges, there tend to be few dramatic climate changes between one region and its immediate neighbours. But there are anomalies and exceptions to the general pattern. In much of the Congo basin that lies at or near the Equator it rains steadily more or less throughout the year rather than in two

Above: After the long rains (March to June) much of the floor of the Ngorongoro Crater becomes verdant pasture dotted with wildflowers such as this pyjama lily.

Left: A group of elephants takes advantage of partial shade offered by a small grove of trees on the blisteringly hot Masai Mara during the dry season in July to October.

Overleaf: Three sub-adult male lions quench their thirst at a waterhole near Savuti, in Botswana's Chobe National Park. Such permanent freshwater sources are critical to the survival of wildlife in the dry season.

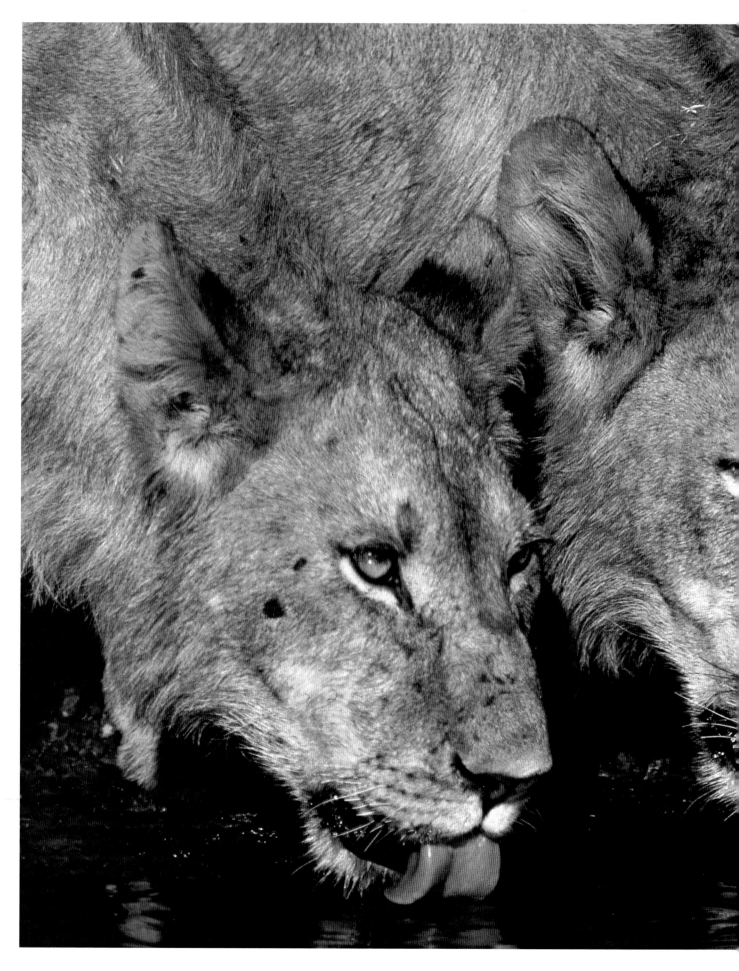

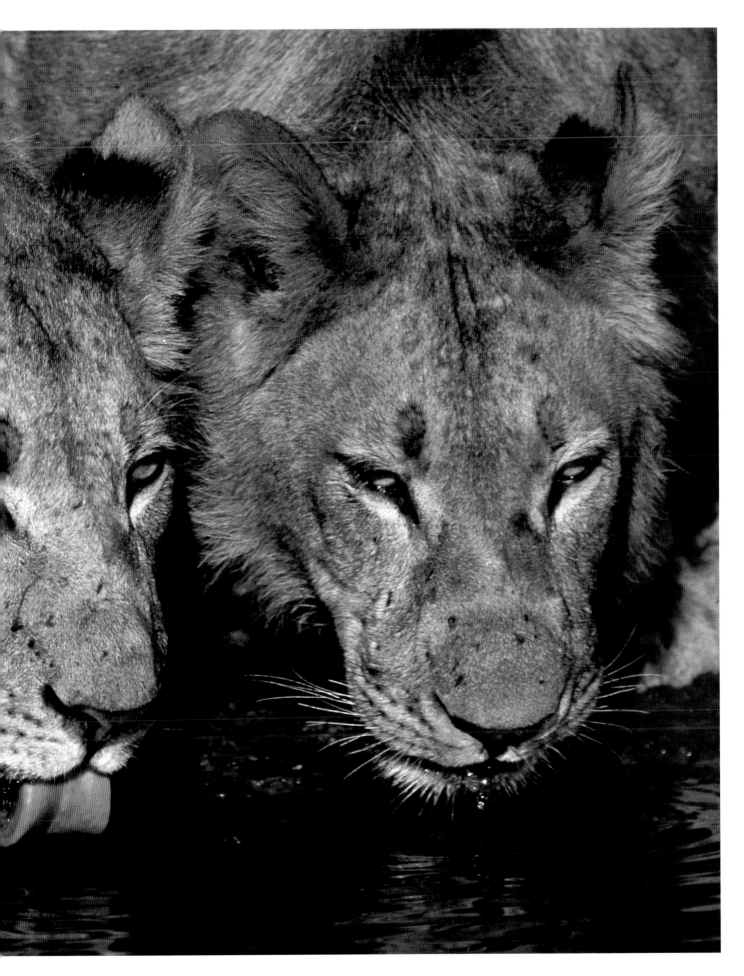

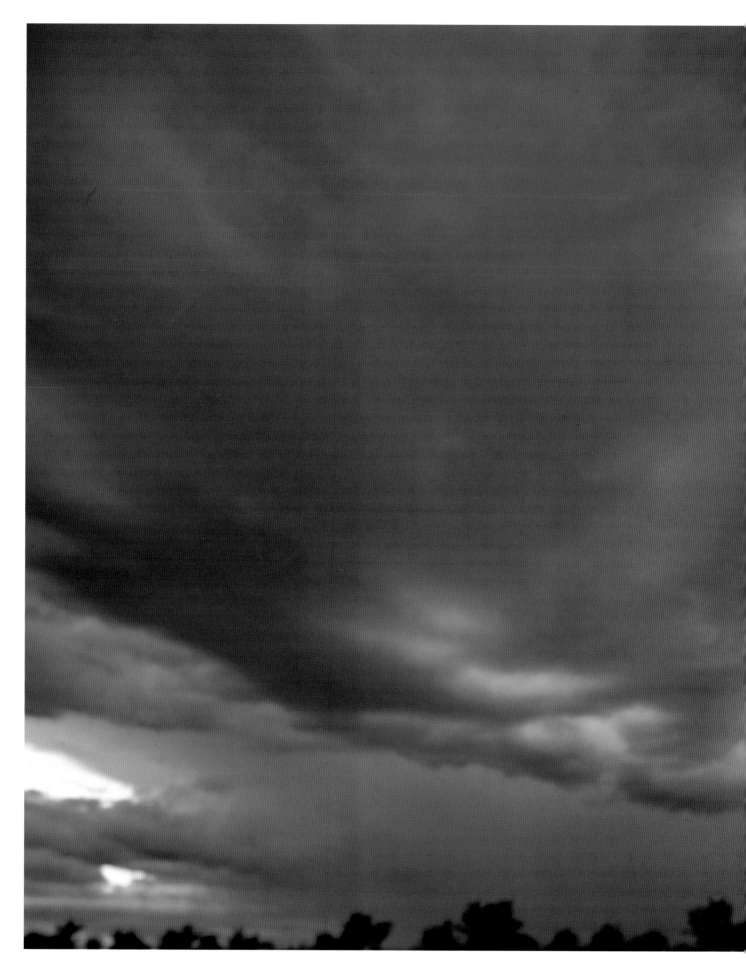

seasons. The same applies to the long coastal margins of KwaZulu-Natal province in South Africa. The high rainfall here is due to the warm Mozambique Current, which flows southwards from equatorial waters along the south-east African coast, leading to a build-up of moisture-laden air masses.

By contrast, many regions within the tropics are dry for much of the year. The Sahara south of the Tropic of Cancer rarely receives any rain at all. It is very hot as well as dry in summer but often cold in winter. In the regions, right across Africa, immediately south of the Sahara, rainfall can be relied upon only in two or three months of the year. In eastern Africa the deserts that cover much of Somalia, eastern Ethiopia and northern Kenya are within four or five degrees of the Equator. Their aridity is due partly to the fact that much of the region is within the "rain-shadow" of the Ethiopian highlands. It is also due in part to a cold-water current that flows along the Somali coast. An Antarctic cold-water mass, the Benguela Current, which flows northwards from the west coast of South Africa's Cape Province, is a direct cause of the Namib desert. This ancient desert, the oldest in Africa, contains the world's highest and longest sand dunes; at the coast and often for several miles inland it is blanketed by fog but rarely receives any rain. Never more than 120 miles (195km) wide, it runs for about 1,250 miles (2,010km) along the Atlantic coast from the middle section of the Western Cape (South Africa), through the length of Namibia to beyond Namibe (formerly Moçâmedes) in southern Angola.

The end of the long dry season (April to November) in Namibia is often signalled by violent thunderstorms. This one is about to break over Etosha National Park.

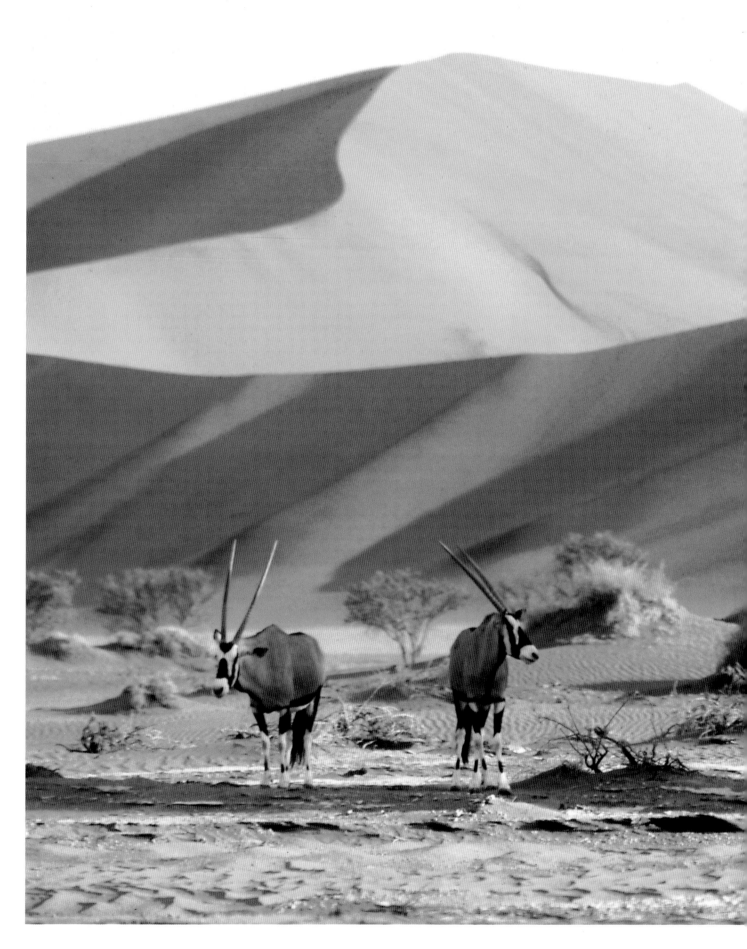

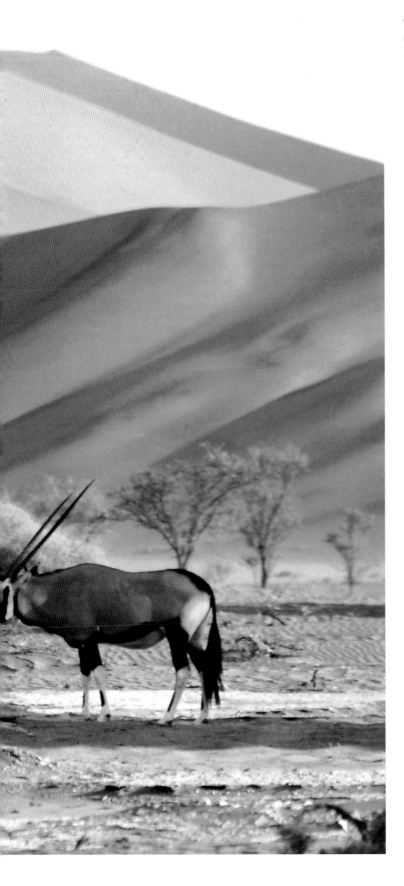

Left: Few antelopes match the gemsbok's ability to survive in desert conditions, where it eats coarse grasses and digs up roots and tubers. These gemsboks are grazing on gravel plains on the southern margins of the Namib desert.

Overleaf: The huge salt pans that lie at the centre of Namibia's Etosha reserve are filled, however briefly, with fresh water during the summer rains from December to March.

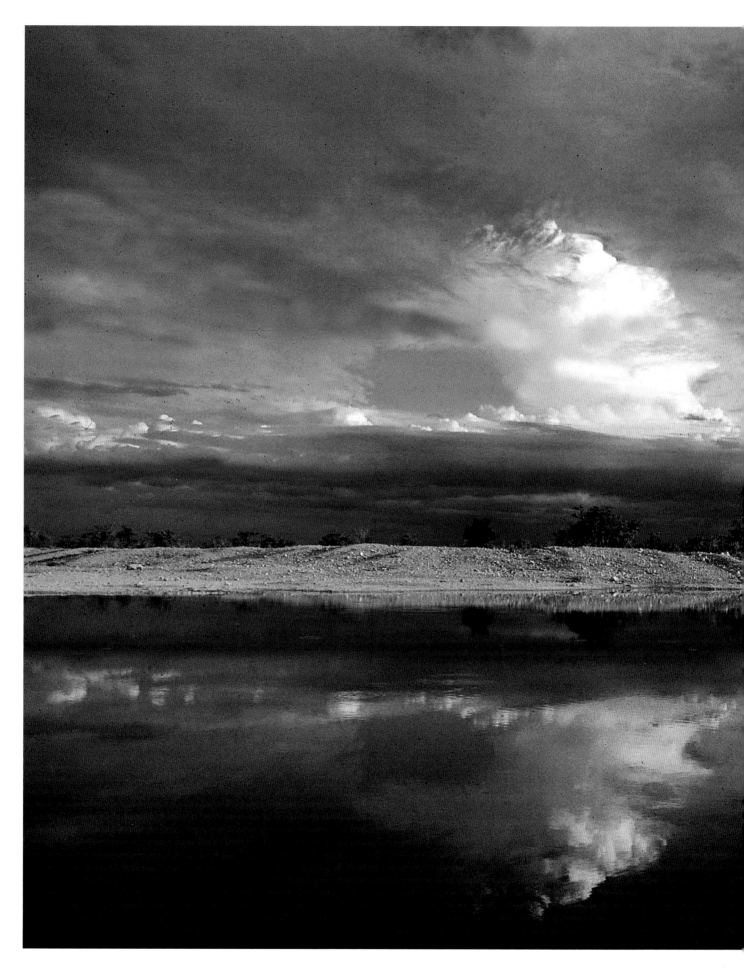

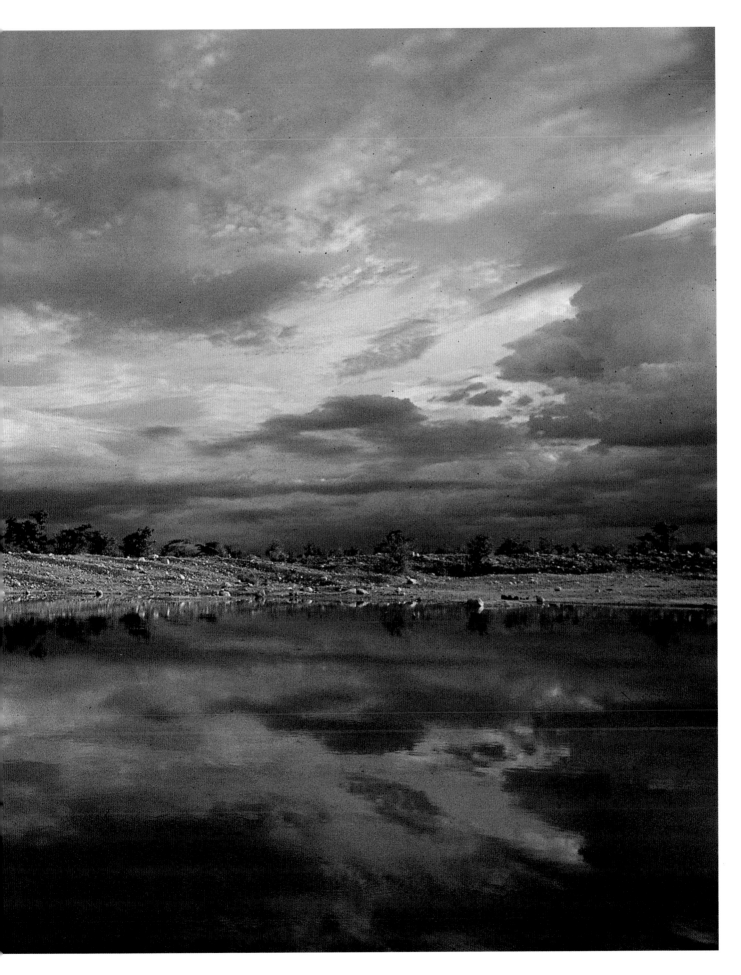

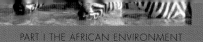

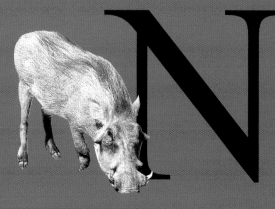

NATURAL VEGETATION

The astonishing abundance, richness and diversity of Africa's wildlife is made possible partly by the continent's variety of natural vegetation, which in turn is a product of its different climatic zones. In this chapter we have a look at six major types of habitat south of the Sahara desert and the range of plant and animal communities that exists in each.

TROPICAL RAINFORESTS

These lowland forests once covered most of equatorial Africa west of the western arm of the Great Rift, typically extending eight to ten degrees north and south of the Equator. In western Africa they covered the coastal region along the Gulf of Guinea as far as Sierra Leone and beyond, interrupted only by the so-called "Dahomey Gap," a drier region along the coasts of Benin, Togo and eastern Ghana. Today, however, only isolated remnants of rainforest remain west of Cameroon, mostly in Ivory Coast, Liberia and Sierra Leone: it has been estimated that 80 per cent has been destroyed as a result of human activities, although in recent years government-funded conservation efforts in several west African states have somewhat slowed the rate of destruction.

Right: Sunrise over rainforest in northern Zaïre. The largest areas of surviving rainforest in Africa are within two degrees north and south of the Equator—a region mainly drained by the Congo river and its tributaries.

Overleaf: An elephant grazes on lush grasses by the edge of a small but dense mixed forest on the floor of the Ngorongoro Crater. Much of the crater rim is cloaked in montane forest.

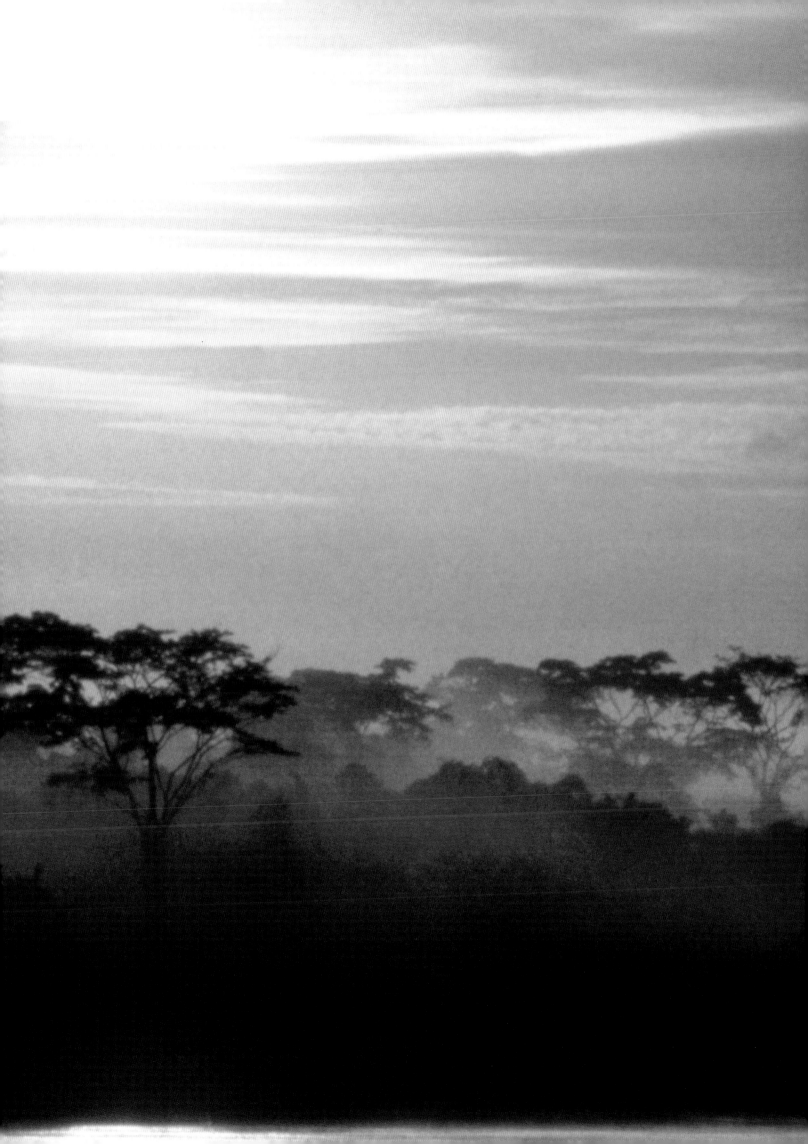

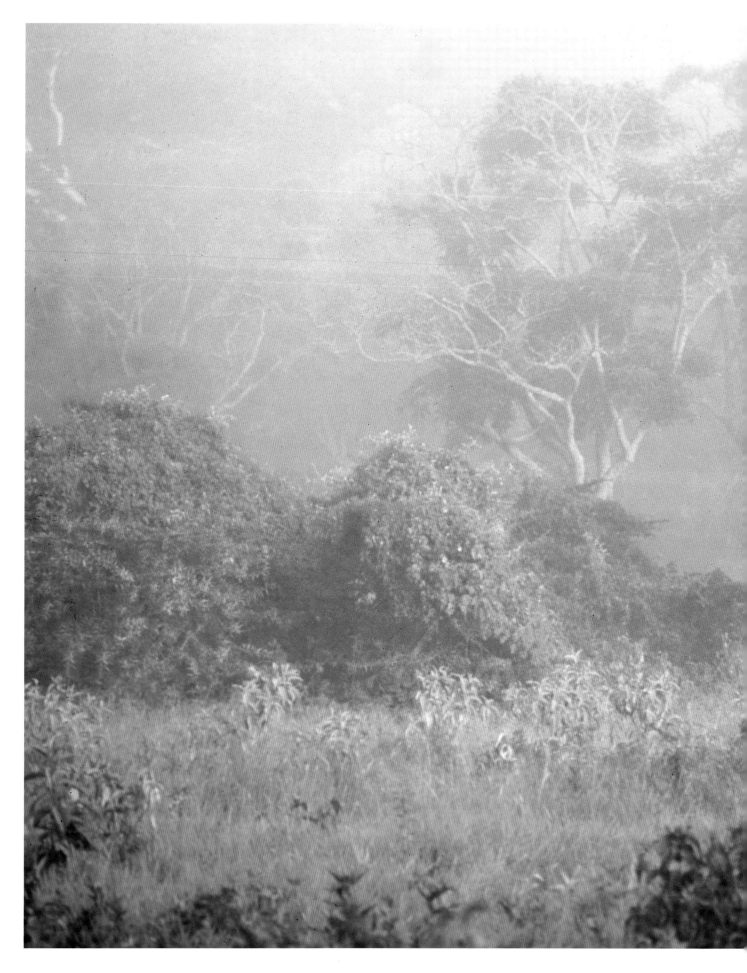

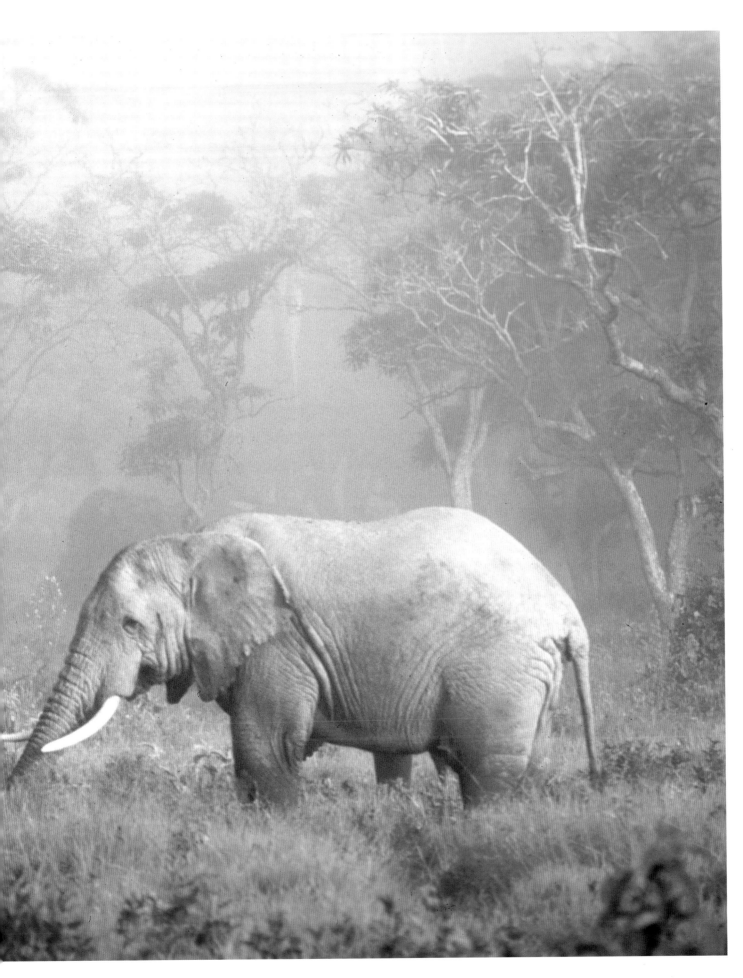

The largest areas of tropical forest remaining in Africa are in Zaïre, Congo Republic and Gabon—essentially the vast region drained by the Congo river. Tropical lowland forests typically receive well over 60in (1,500mm) of rain a year and are one of two types: rainforests within four degrees of the Equator receive rain steadily all the year round, while the basically similar tropical evergreen forests undergo a drier season of two or three months.

The typical rainforest is dominated by a mixture of mature evergreen and deciduous trees between 60 and 100ft (18 and 30m) tall. These produce a dense canopy of branches and foliage at their summits that keeps the forest floor in a state of permanent gloom. Most tree species here, especially the evergreens, have smooth, leathery leaves with pointed tips that readily shed water, and smooth-barked trunks that allow the rain to run rapidly to the forest floor.

On much of the forest floor the undergrowth is sparse owing to the absence of sunlight and also to the fact that the almost constant rain leaches out nutrients from the thin layer of humus at the soil surface. But tree seedlings and some shrubby species manage to eke out a living down below, while epiphytic plants (which obtain their moisture requirements from the air), such as orchids and some ferns, as well as mosses, lichens and the rope-like lianas, grow on the trunks and upper branches of the mature trees. Atmospheric humidity is high and there is very little evaporation of moisture from the ground surface.

The lowland rainforests, especially those of the Congo basin, have a rich diversity of wildlife and are especially well endowed with primates; Zaïre alone has more than 30 species or subspecies and Ivory Coast 17. They include the prosimian bushbabies, the teddy-bear-like potto, many species of "true" monkey (including guenons, some baboons and mangabeys, mandrill and colobus monkeys), and apes (including two subspecies of lowland gorilla, chimpanzee and bonobo).

The largest inhabitant of the lowland rainforest is the forest, or pygmy, elephant, which is substantially smaller than the more familiar bush elephant. An important contributor to the ecology of their habitat, the pygmy elephant's feeding habits help to create and maintain openings and glades in the otherwise dense, dark forest. This may lead to the introduction of a greater diversity of plant

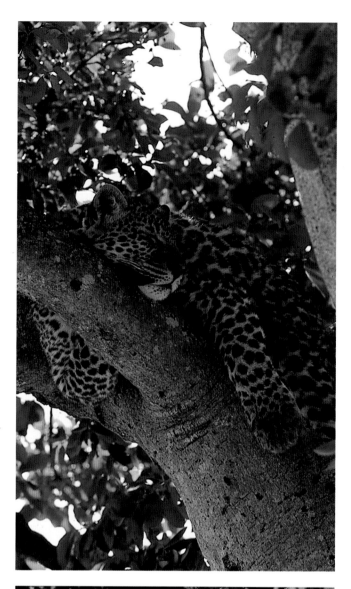

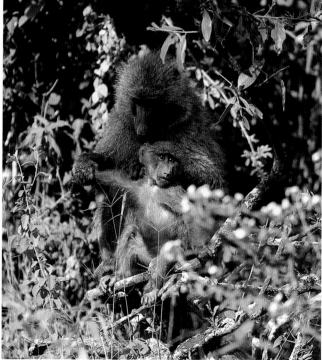

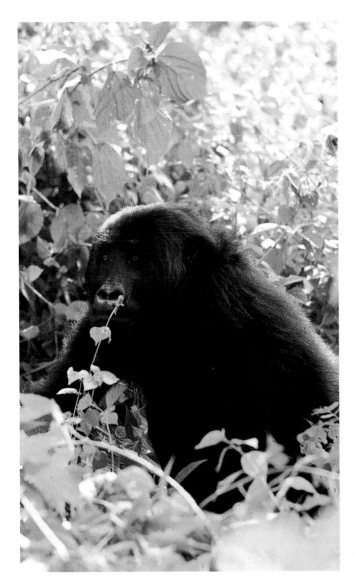

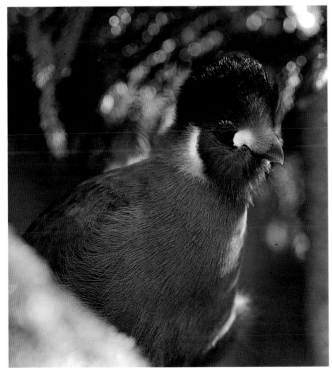

species, many of which depend on better light conditions than are available elsewhere in the forest; and this in turn may encourage a wider range of herbivorous animals, especially browsers, to live there. The same process of plant and animal immigrations also occurs as a result of localised forest clearance by humans.

The largest ungulate to inhabit the lowland forest, albeit in a restricted area, is the long-necked okapi, a cousin of the giraffe. It is confined mainly to the Ituri forest area of the Semliki river valley, north-west of the Ruwenzori range. Among the most numerous ungulates of the rainforest are the duiker antelopes, which vary greatly in size from species to species. Other ungulates found in abundance are the tiny pygmy antelope, the slightly larger dwarf antelope, the bongo and the bushbuck. The largest carnivore in the lowland rainforest, and by far the most formidable, is the leopard, which is found in most African habitats apart from true desert. Among members of the swine family, the giant forest hog—the largest wild pig in the world—is found throughout the Congo rainforest, as are the red river hog and the bushpig. The pygmy hippopotamus is confined to the rainforests of the Guinea coast.

The rainforests are home to a rich variety of birds. The ground-dwellers include guinea fowls, francolins and peacocks. Among larger birds that feed on the ground and in the canopy are hornbills, turacos and parrots. Chief among birds of prey is the crowned eagle, which is large and powerful enough to hunt duikers and bushbuck. Among a diverse population of reptiles are snakes, including pythons and adders, and a number of the largely arboreal chameleons.

Above Left: The lowland gorilla is a true denizen of the rainforest. This female of the eastern lowland race takes her ease in a forest on Zaïre's border with Uganda.

Left: Many of the most colourful bird species live in rainforests. Typical is the crow-sized white-cheeked turaco, native to West Africa.

Far Left, Above: The leopard is found in a wider range of environments than any other large carnivore, making a living in every type of habitat from the margins of true deserts to equatorial jungles. This one naps in the canopy of a broadleaf rainforest.

Far Left: Baboons, in their various races, are also found in a wide range of habitats. This olive baboon and her young live in the upland forest margin of Kenya's Lake Nakuru National Park.

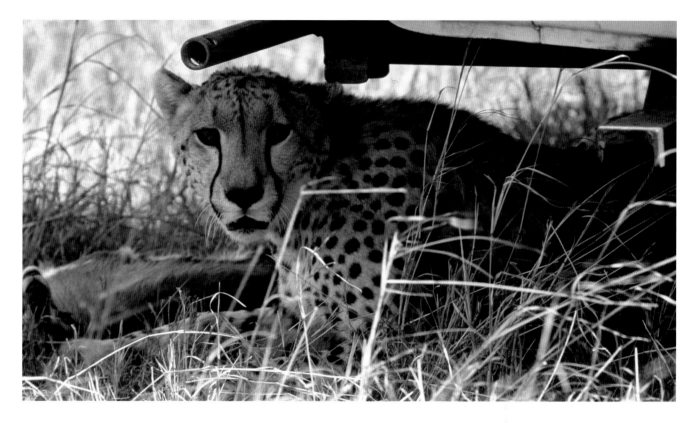

SAVANNA: MOSAIC, WOODLAND AND GRASSLAND

The term savanna embraces a range of habitats that account for more than a third of the African land surface. Their differences are due to climatic factors in general and to rainfall in particular: indeed, they are best regarded as zones that, climatically and in terms of vegetation, are transitional between regions of high and low rainfall.

What is called the forest-savanna mosaic forms a variable boundary between rainforest (or montane forest) and more open mixtures of woodland and grassland. The transition is often most readily apparent along rivers and around floodplains, where dense clumps of rainforest trees stand out against a background of more open woodland and grassy plains. Such mosaics are often formed after areas of rainforest are cleared for human use.

Moist savanna, which is characterised by open woods of mainly broad-leaved deciduous trees, receives 35–60in (750–1,525mm) of rainfall a year, but has one dry period annually (two if close to the Equator). One of the largest regions of moist savanna is the so-called *miombo* woodland, which covers much of Zambia and Zimbabwe and consists of mainly broad-leafed deciduous trees and tall, coarse grasses. A similar pattern, although with different species of dominant trees, is found north of the Equator along the margins of the Guinea rainforests in West Africa.

The drier savannas are regions that receive between 12 and 35in (300 and 900mm) of rain a year and undergo a long dry season. The rainfall decreases and the dry season lengthens the farther one moves north or south of the Equator. North of the Equator the drier savanna belt runs from Senegal in the west through the northern areas of the Guinea coast countries and eastward through the southernmost regions of Chad, Sudan and Somalia; in East Africa it extends south through Kenya and Tanzania. South of the Congo basin it includes large areas of Angola and Zambia, spreading southward to merge eventually with the scrublands of the Kalahari. Between the northernmost areas of the drier savanna and the

Above: Most wildlife tourists get their closest view of the major predators on the East African savanna—but few closer, perhaps, than to this cheetah, which has dragged its ungulate prey into the shade under a safari truck parked on the Serengeti plains.

Above Right: A wildebeest grazes on the Masai Mara (note the pair of ox-peckers looking for ticks on the ungulate's back). Wildebeests gather in hundreds of thousands on their annual migration in search of pasture.

Right: Honde valley in Zimbabwe's Nyanga National Park, exemplifies the moist savanna known as miombo woodland, a mixed terrain of mainly deciduous trees and tall grasses.

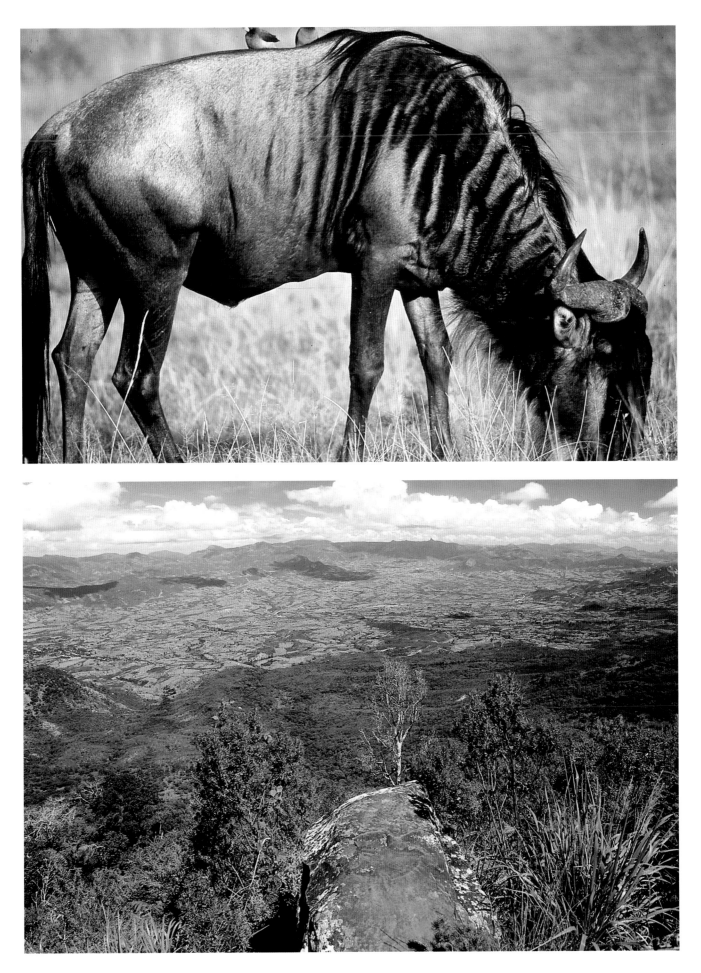

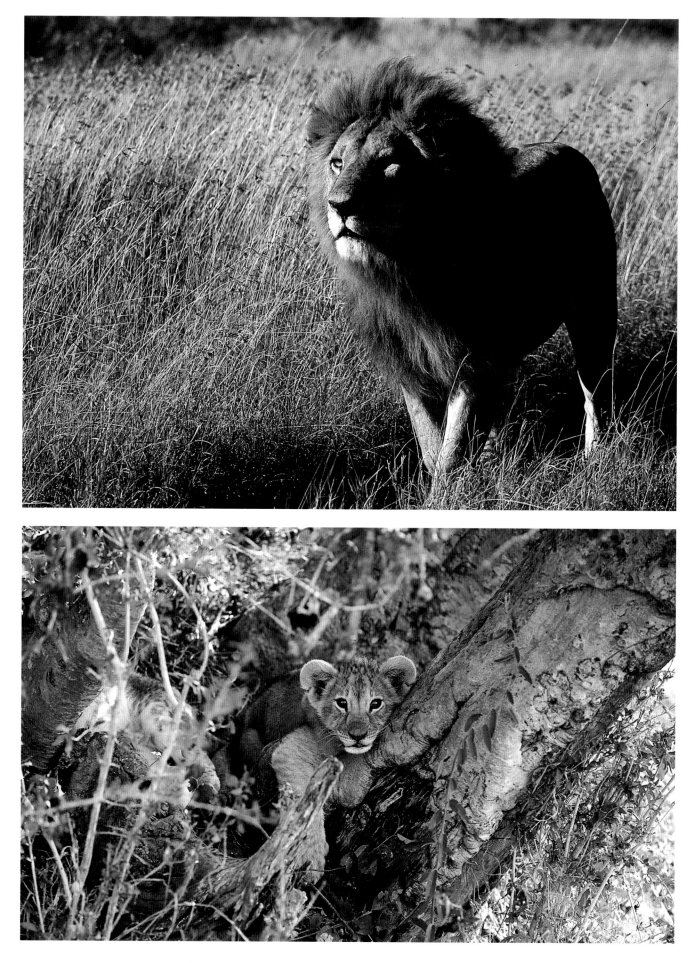

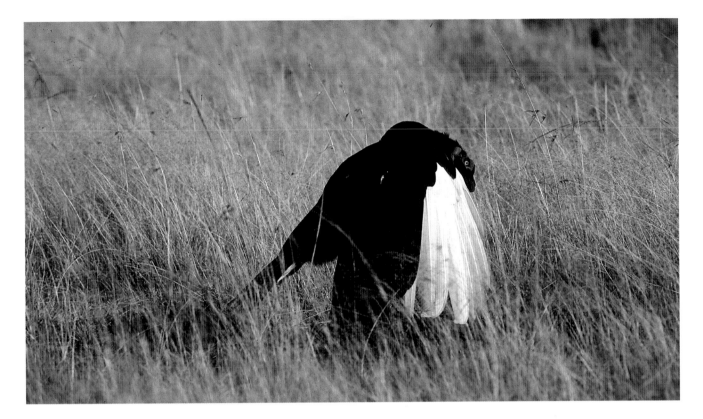

Sahara desert is an intermediate semi-desert zone, subject to prolonged rainless periods, known as the Sahel.

The drier savannas consist, in many regions (and especially in East Africa), of vast, open plains of grassland interrupted here and there by patches of open woodland or elsewhere punctuated by thorn bushes or by isolated flat-topped acacia trees or the occasional granitic rock outcrops known as *kopjes* (pronounced "koppies"). In the hotter areas of the dry savanna the most striking tree is the spectacular baobab (*Adansonia digitata*), with its thick, soft bark, and prodigious girth.

The savannas, and especially the drier ones of eastern and southern Africa, are the continent's most spectacular habitats in terms of wildlife. In the open grasslands of Kenya and Tanzania vast herds of ungulates are forever on the move along their migratory routes; some of their predators follow them on these routes, while others remain in specific areas, preying on different species of migrating herbivores as they pass through their home range. Kenya, Tanzania, Zaïre and Sudan each has more than 30 species of antelope, as well as many other species of plant-eaters. The West African savannas do not have so many species, but many important herbivores are common to both regions. These include buffalo, giraffe, at least one duiker, hartebeest, roan and waterbuck.

The savannas are highly productive in terms of the grasses and other herbage on which the ungulates depend, and each species (or subspecies) will normally feed on a particular type of plant at a particular stage of growth. In this way different species—and in particular those that gather into immense herds of different species—are able to avoid competing for food. For example, some ungulates, such as the zebra of the drier savanna, thrive on coarse, dry grasses; other ungulates prefer younger, softer grasses.

In terms of diet there are three broad types of herbivore: the grazers, the browsers, and those that both graze and browse. The grazers are those that feed on the grasses; the browsers feed on the foliage and smaller branches of trees and bushes. Among browsers, competition is avoided in two ways: first, and most obviously,

Above: By late July, more than two months after the end of the long rains, the once lush growth of grasses on the Masai Mara is beginning to dry out. This southern ground hornbill, here preening its wing, includes many savanna rodents, hares and smaller reptiles in its diet.

Left, Above and Below: The dry savanna of East Africa features immense grassland plains familiar from safari brochures. But even the mainly open Masai Mara includes areas of mixed grassland and bush, patrolled here by a male lion looking for game (above), and even patches of quite dense woodland, affording this young lion cub some cover against potential predators (below).

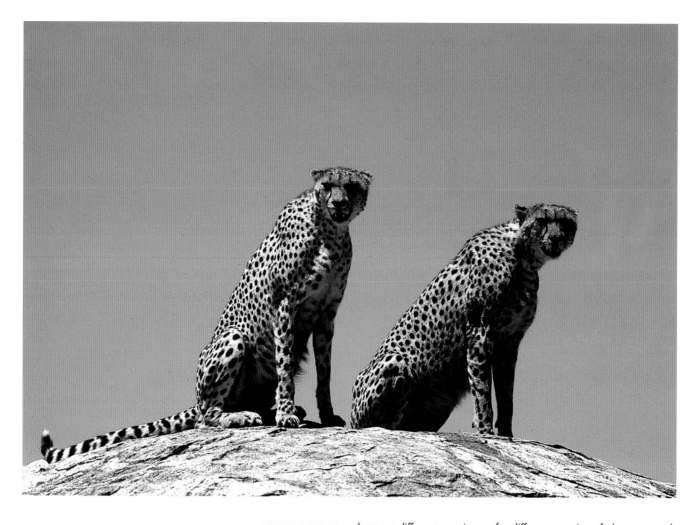

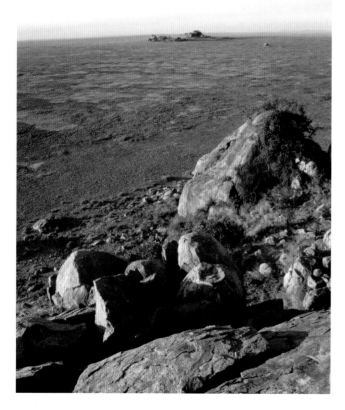

because different species prefer different species of plants; second, because browsers come in vastly different sizes. The giraffe, for example, browses on a much higher part of a tree than, say, one of the browser/grazer gazelles.

Most savanna herbivores are ruminants—animals that chew food (cud) that has been regurgitated after the indigestible cellulose walls of the plants have been broken down by micro-organisms in the gut. When the food is regurgitated, cud-chewing helps the micro-organisms to complete their work, after which it can be swallowed and fully digested.

One of the great sights of the East African drier savanna is the seasonal migration of the blue wildebeest over the vast expanses of the Serengeti plains of north-western Tanzania and their neighbour immediately across the Kenya frontier to the north, the Masai Mara. During the wet season, which extends from December to April, individual herds graze on the short but rich grasses of the volcanic plains close to the eastern arm of the Rift Valley. In May, as the rains cease and the grasses dry out, the herds begin to move westwards,

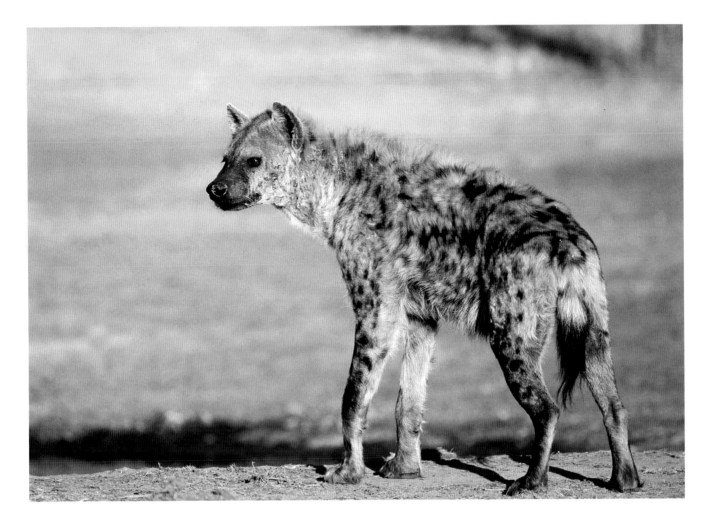

coalescing into ever-larger super-herds by they time they reach the mixed woodland and grassland savanna to the east of Lake Victoria in June and July.

By now the wildebeest have been joined by herds of other migrant ungulates—notably plains zebra, hartebeest, topi, eland, impala and gazelles—while fellow travellers may include small groups of giraffe and families of baboons. Later, as the dry season (August to November) gets into its stride, the grassland pastures of the south become eaten out, the seasonal rivers and waterholes run dry, and the wildebeest move north, into the woodland areas of the Masai Mara. Finally, with the onset of the rainy season, they return to the volcanic plains beyond the south-eastern margins of the Serengeti.

This immensely rich pageant of wildlife moving inexorably on its seasonal round passes by or through the ranges, large or small, of other important denizens of the plains that do not migrate, notably the elephant, rhinoceros and buffalo. It also runs the gauntlet of its most formidable predators: here a lioness acts as lookout from the top of a kopje, while the rest of the pride lies concealed in long grass nearby; there a leopard takes its ease in the branches of a yellow-barked fever tree by a stream, waiting for nightfall—he hunts mostly by night. Elsewhere, smaller prey such as gazelles fall victim to lightning-fast pursuit by lone cheetahs; or a pack of wild dogs brings down and disembowels a wildebeest. None of these major predators pursues an individual target for long distances, since each group—a pride of lions, a pack of wild dogs, a spotted-hyena clan— as well as an individual cheetah or leopard, has its own territory and rarely encroaches on that of others of its own species.

Above: The spotted hyena is second in size only to the lion among African carnivores and, like the lion, hunts collectively in groups.

Above Left: The huge, open Serengeti plains of north-western Tanzania are dotted about with granite outcrops known as kopjes which also serve as excellent look-out posts for predators, such as this pair of cheetahs, scanning the horizon for prey.

Left: Many kopjes are home to a variety of animals, including snakes, rodents, and rock hyraxes.

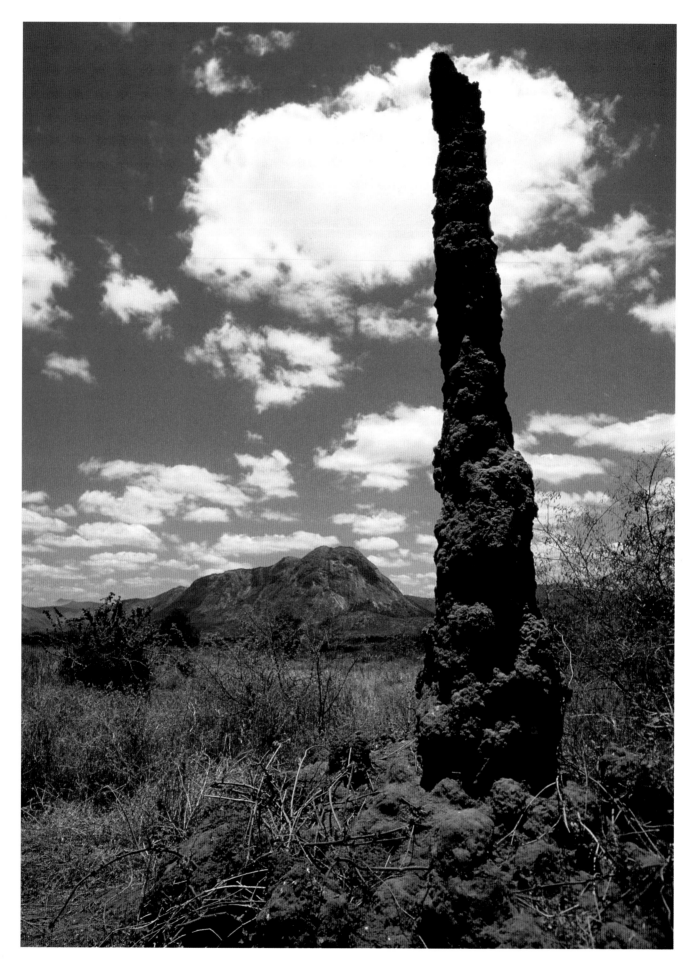

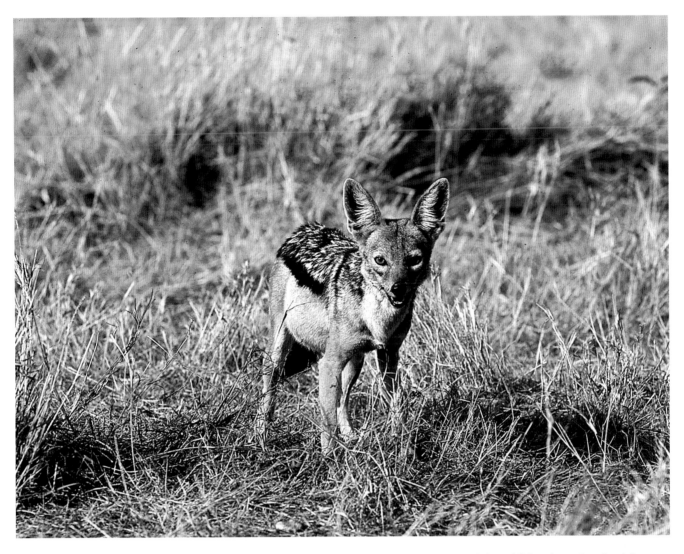

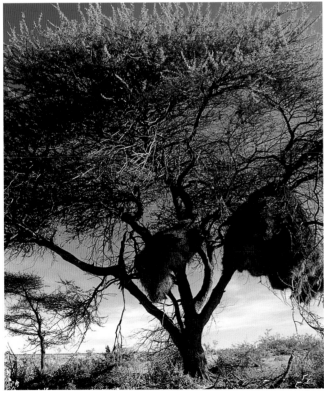

Above: The black-backed jackal is a skilful predator of small or infant mammals, but it also relies, as here, on scavenging scraps of carcasses abandoned by lions or hyenas.

Left: Two huge communal nests of the sociable weaver weigh down the branches of a fever tree on the dry acacia savanna of central Namibia.

Far Left: A 30ft (9m) termite-mound chimney on the northern margins of the Masai Mara. Termites form the main diet of the elusive, nocturnal aardvark and the horny plated pangolin.

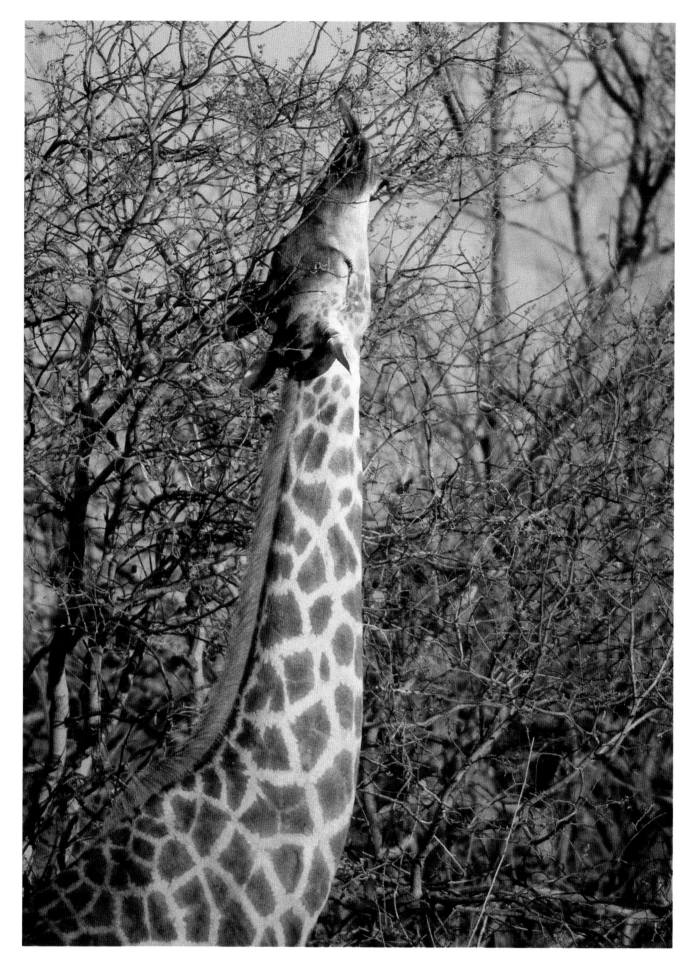

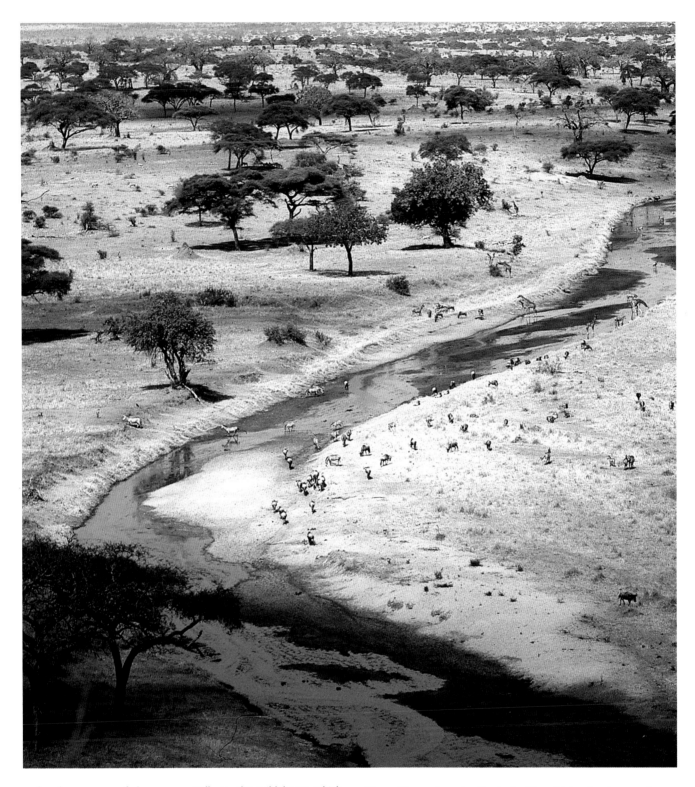

Another source of danger, especially to the wildebeest which adhere relentlessly to their migration routes, is the crossing of rivers, which after the late-December rains may be full and swift-flowing. Thousands of wildebeest drown every year while attempting to ford rivers such as the Mara (which flows southwards into the Serengeti and then westwards to Lake Victoria), and many hundreds of others fall victim to crocodiles.

Above: The ungulate migration begins: blue wildebeest and some zebras arrive at the Tarangire river in late May or June from their breeding grounds on Tanzania's Masai Steppe to the south-east. From here they move steadily westward in ever-larger groups.

Left: Tallest of all browsing ungulates, the giraffe is able to reach the highest branches and foliage of trees, and so does not compete for food with other browsers sharing its habitat.

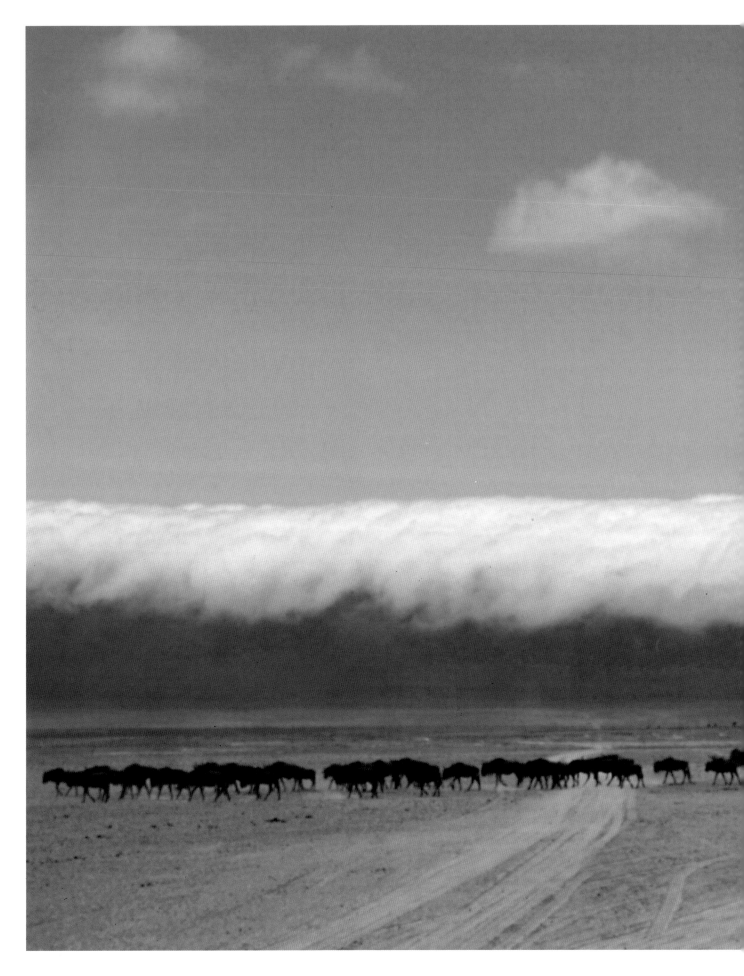

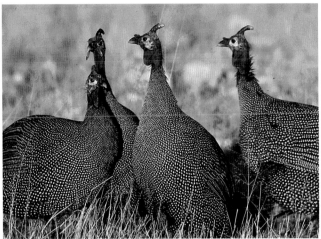

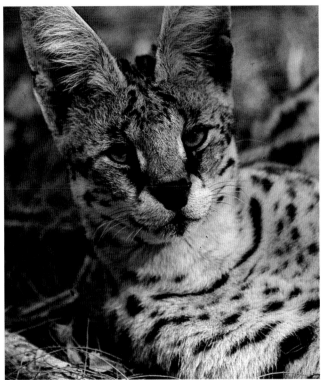

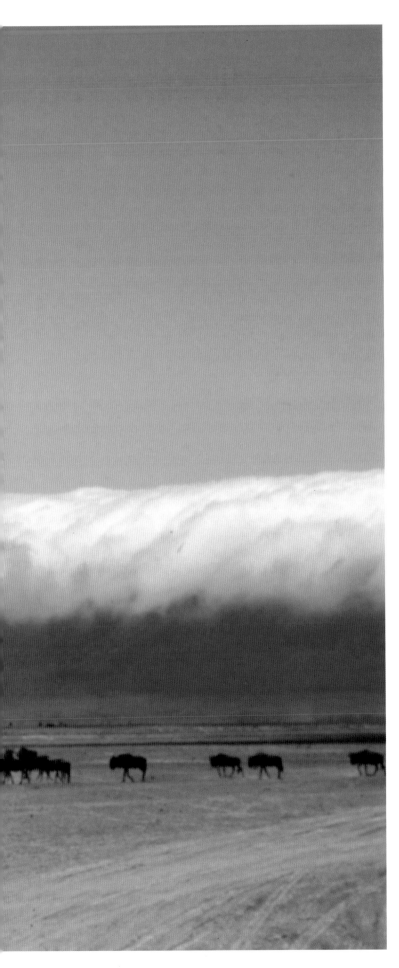

Top and Above: Ground-dwelling birds such as these helmeted guineafowl (above), which live mainly on seeds and insects on the savanna, are preyed on by smaller carnivores, such as this serval (above) and other wild cat species.

Left: Some migrating wildebeest herds make for the Ngorongoro Crater, as here (the clouds in the background clothe the crater rim); others bypass it to the south on their way into the Serengeti plains.

Overleaf: A straggling herd of wildebeest emerges from a river. Ahead of them the dried out Serengeti plains stretch to the far horizon.

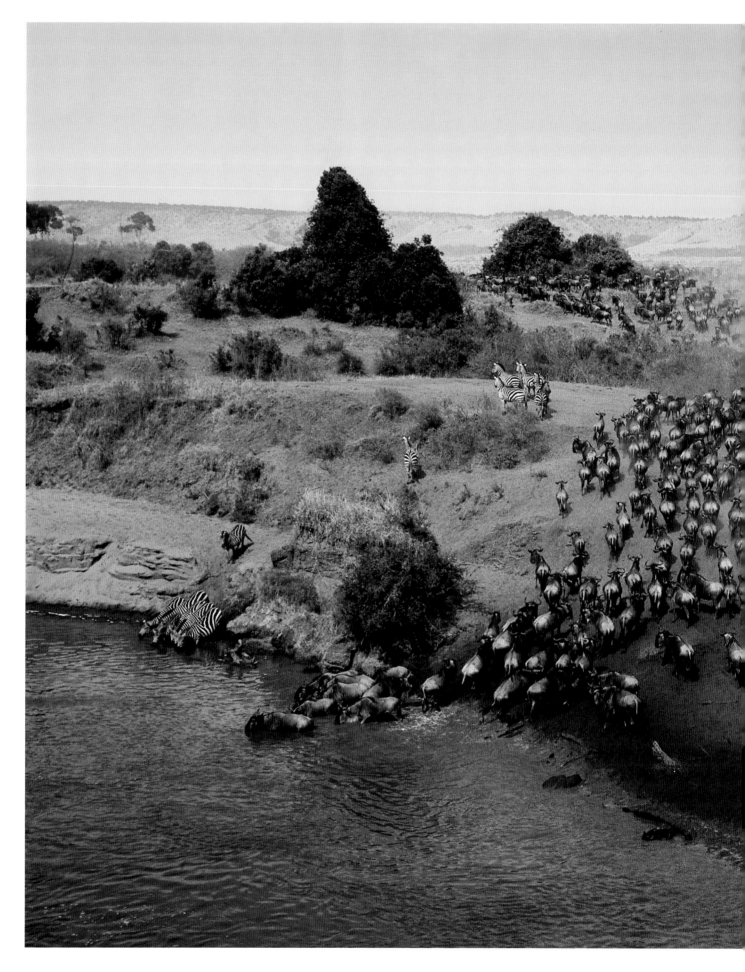

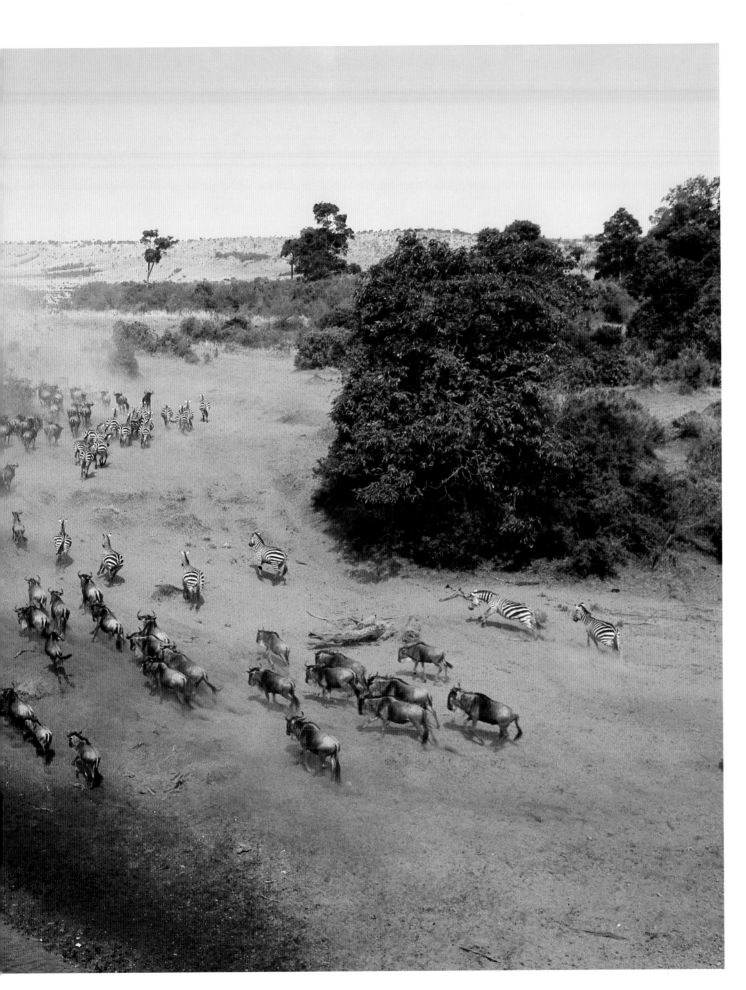

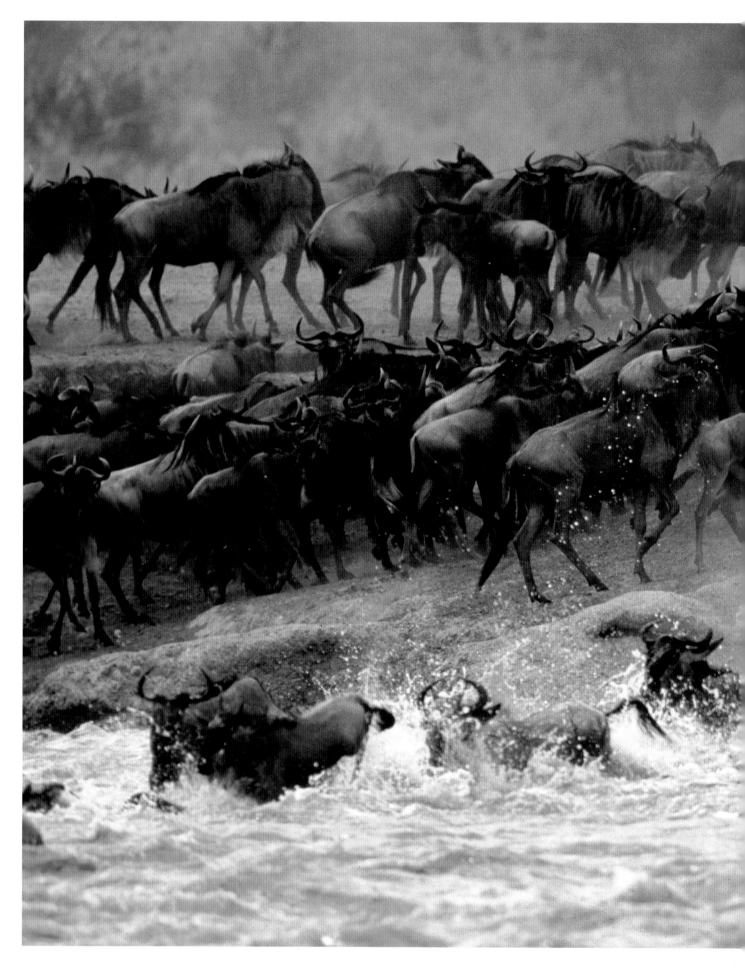

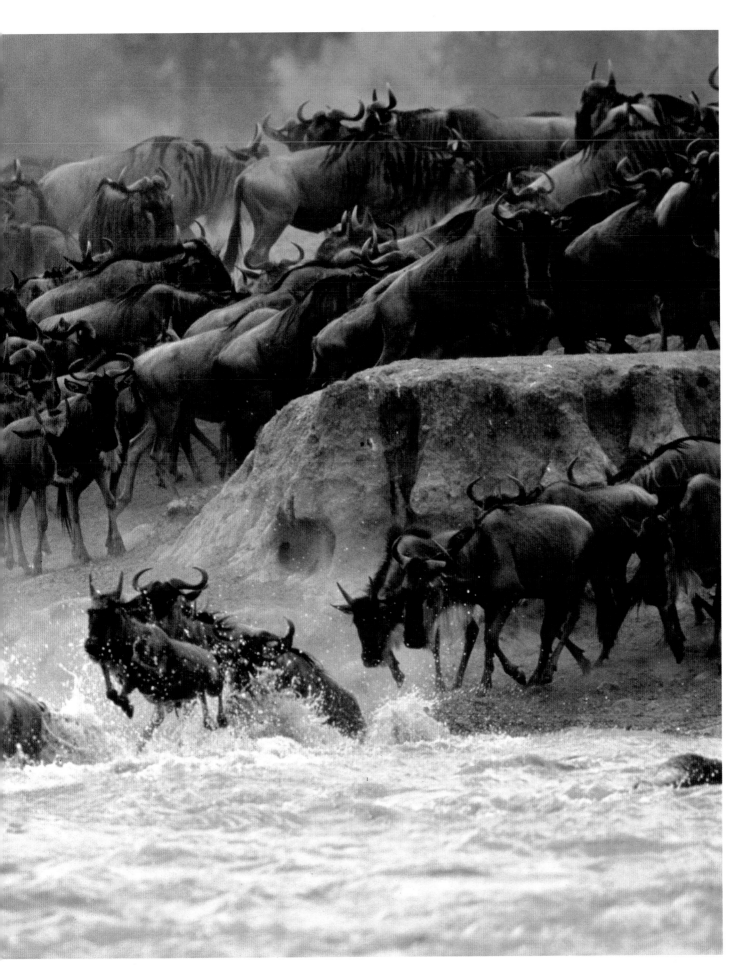

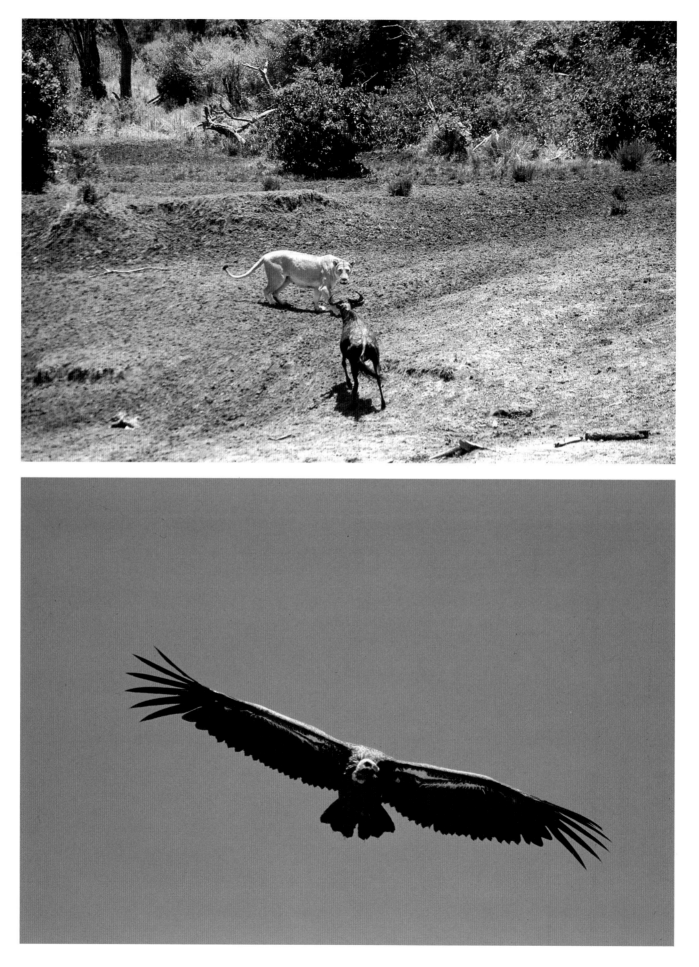

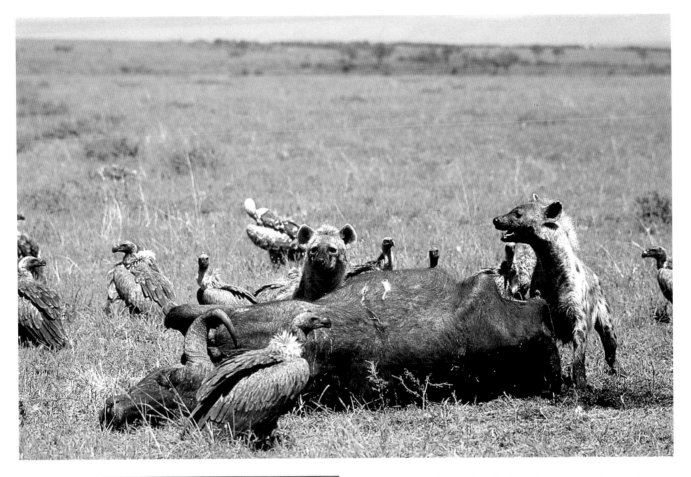

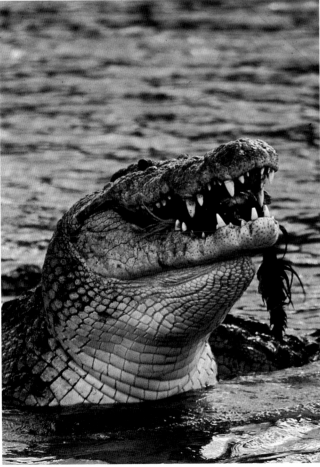

Above: A group of Rüppell's and other vultures await their turn while two members of a clan of spotted hyenas gorge on the carcass of a buffalo.

Above Far Left: Lions, lacking the speed of the cheetah, prefer to hunt where cover—long grass, shrubs or trees—enables them to get close to their target before making their attack. This lion has used open woodland to corner a wildebeest that has become separated from its herd.

Far Left: A Rüppell's griffon vulture patrols the sky above the Serengeti plains in search of carcasses to scavenge.

Left: Many wildebeest fall prey to crocodiles waiting on the banks, or below the surface, of the Mara and other rivers on the migration route. This crocodile has seized a drowning wildebeest's head in its jaws.

Previous Page: Farther upstream, in Kenya, another herd of wildebeest faces the challenge of the Mara. As the huge herd piles down the steep banks into the fast-flowing river, panic sets in: hundreds (sometimes thousands) drown at the many crossing points. Seen here are some of the lucky survivors scrambling out on the far side.

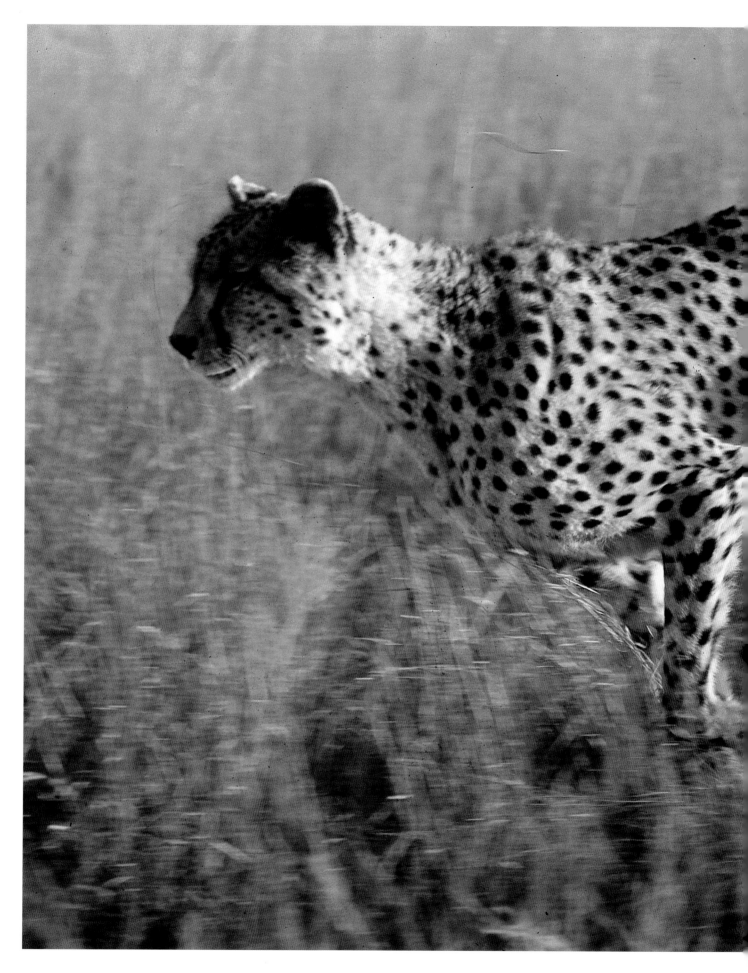

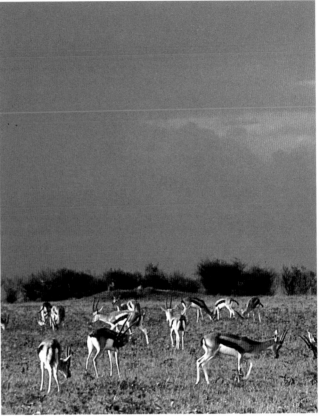

DESERTS AND SEMI-DESERTS

True deserts are generally taken to mean areas that receive less than six inches (150mm) of rain annually (and in some years receive no rain at all) and are more or less destitute of plants. The Sahara desert is outside the scope of this book. But there are many other areas—some of which are called deserts—that typically receive an average of six to 12in (150 to 300mm) of rain that may in places support not only plants but a rich fauna as well. These areas include, for instance, the Sahel, a wide belt fringing the southern margins of the Sahara, which forms a buffer between true desert to the north and the moist forests of West and central Africa; they also include the sub-deserts that cover the lowlands of Somalia, eastern

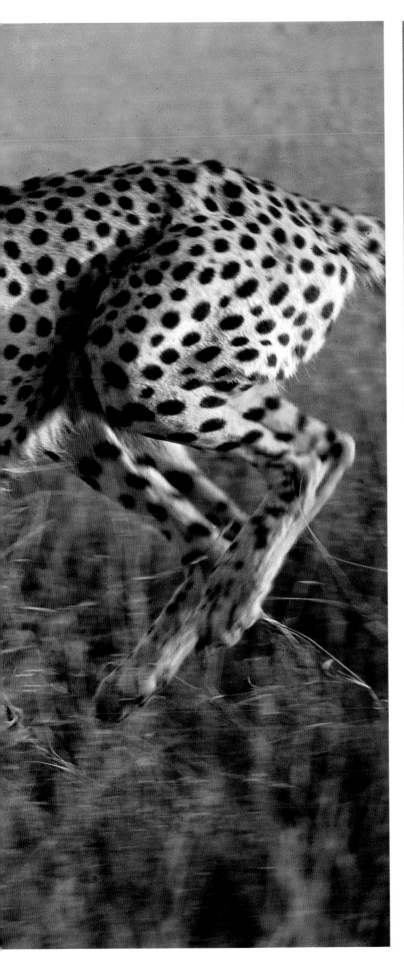

Left and Above: Smaller ungulates, however fleet-footed, are also vulnerable on the open savanna. These Thomson's gazelles (above) grazing on the Masai Mara are a prime target for the cheetah (left). The adult female seen here is breaking out of cover from long-grass at the start of a chase.

Ethiopia, northern Kenya and north-eastern Uganda. In many regions such sub-deserts merge with regions of drier savanna.

The Namib desert of Namibia includes the Namib/Naukluft Park, the largest national park in Africa. It lies to the east and south of the seaside resort of Swakopmund and its larger wildlife residents include gemsbok, springbok, bat-eared fox and ostrich. The Skeleton Coast, between the Atlantic Ocean and the Namib desert, runs much of the way north of Swakopmund to the Angola border. In some parts the shore is patrolled by brown hyenas and black-backed jackals on the lookout for stranded seals. (Until a few years ago lions would ambush seals emerging from the waves; but as they also preyed on local farm stock when the seals were away, the farmers eventually lost patience and killed or drove off most of the local prides.) Occasionally, a few giraffes, zebras and even elephants traverse tracks between the dunes looking for fresh-water channels and waterholes, which are patronised mainly by gemsbok, springbok and other herbivores.

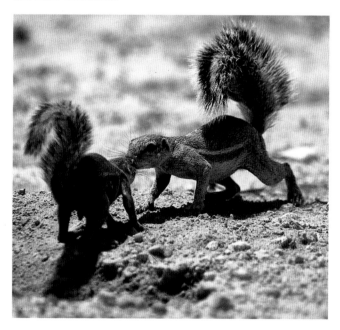

Above: The Cape ground squirrel (*Xerus inauris*) lives in colonies of 20-30 individuals in arid scrubland, along dry riverbeds, and on the edge of salt pans. These two are from the fringes of the Namib desert.

Right: The immense, shifting dunes of the Namib desert offer little scope for wildlife, but its margins may offer a good living for plants and animals. These camelthorn trees thrive in arid scrubland on the edge of the desert and offer a meal to at least some species of ungulate browsers.

Overleaf: A group of ostriches grazes on the flat wastes of the Kalahari desert in south-eastern Namibia, where they live on roots and seeds as well as insects and small reptiles.

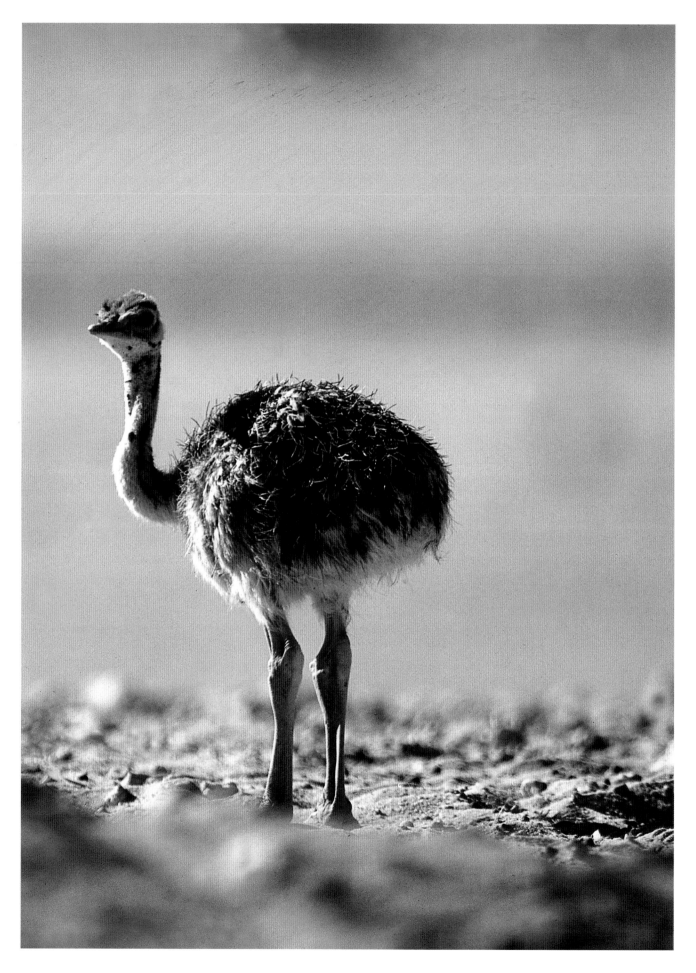

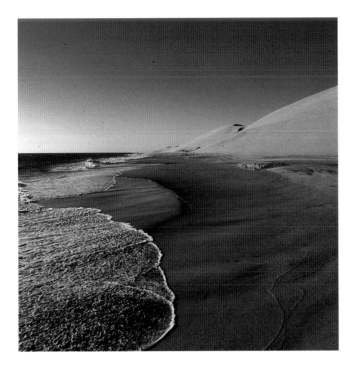

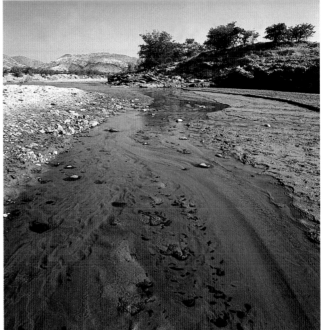

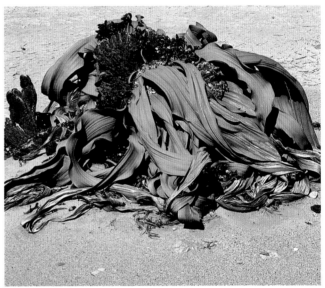

Part of eastern Namibia and most of western, northern and central Botswana are taken up by the Kalahari desert. In fact, only the south-western third of the Kalahari, straddling the Namibia-Botswana border, is true desert: it receives little or no rain and consists mostly of rolling sand dunes cut through by dry river-beds.

The south-eastern third is a mixture of semi-desert and dry savanna grassland, interrupted by salt pans that support little or no vegetation except for stunted acacia bushes, but in some rainy seasons (November/December and March/April) are filled temporarily with water. Much of the northern third is also semi-arid, but it eventually gives way to the extraordinary Okavango Delta, a wetland area of lush vegetation and rich and varied wildlife.

Even the driest areas of the Kalahari contain wildlife. Until about 70 years ago enormous herds of springbok migrated every year across the desert, their timing and itinerary coinciding with the seasonal availability of water and vegetation in each region. Today these vast herds have disappeared but springbok, gemsbok and other ungulates are still found in every part of the Kalahari, as are flocks of ostrich. During the rains the area of Botswana's largest salt pans, the Makgadikgadi, attracts countless thousands of zebra, wildebeest, springbok and gemsbok as well as vast numbers of waterbirds. When the pans dry up, the ungulates migrate westwards towards Lake Ngami, with its reliable water supply, before turning northwards to enter the Okavango Delta.

Top Left: On the Skeleton Coast of northern Namibia the sand dunes of the Namib desert come down to the sea shore.

Top: The bed of the Hoarusib river in Kaokoland, a region immediately to the east of the Namib desert in northern Namibia. The river rises in uplands to the west of Etosha National Park and winds towards an outlet on the Skeleton Coast. The photograph was taken in April, about a month after the end of the rainy season: in another few weeks the bed will be dry.

Above: The welwitschia (*W. mirabilis*), a cone-bearing plant, is commonly found in the Namib desert. In spite of appearances to the contrary, each plant has only two leaves. This medium-sized specimen is several hundred years old.

Left: An ostrich chick on the gravel wastes of the Namib desert.

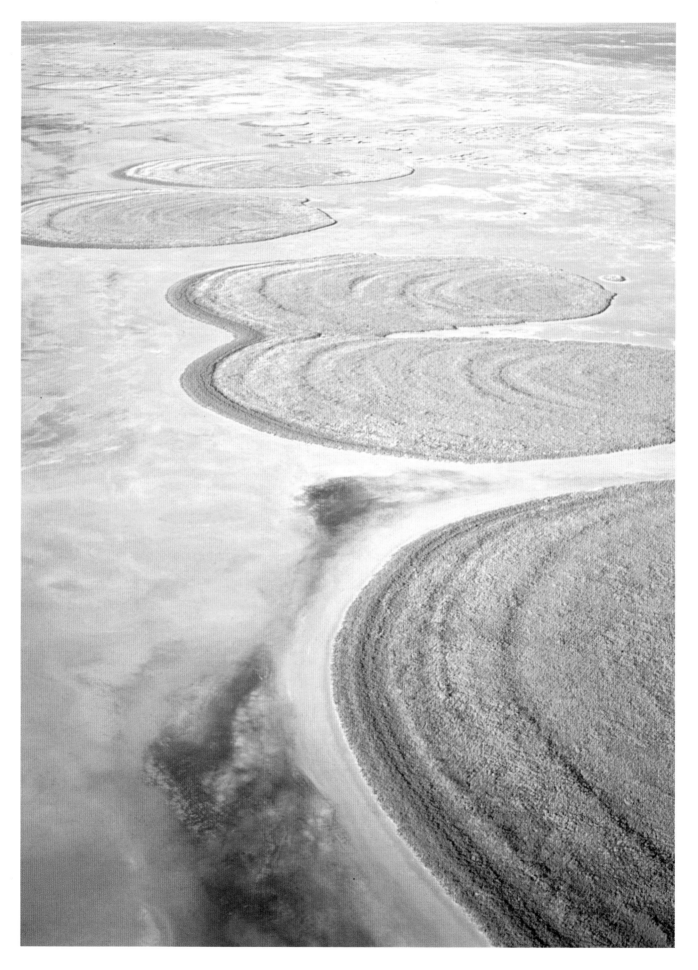

THE MOUNTAINS

Africa has few very high mountain ranges, and these for the most part are widely separated from each other. Each range has a number of vegetation zones, the nature of each zone depending upon both altitude and latitude. The most extensive zonation occurs on the highest peaks and ranges.

In the Ethiopian highlands the lowest zone is a belt of montane forest that tails off at about 10,000ft (3,000m) to be replaced by a moorland zone, dominated by ericaceous plants such as heathers, to an altitude of about 13,000ft (4,000m); the top zone consists of alpine vegetation, mainly grasses. Among ungulates native to these highlands are the mountain nyala (a large antelope) and the walia

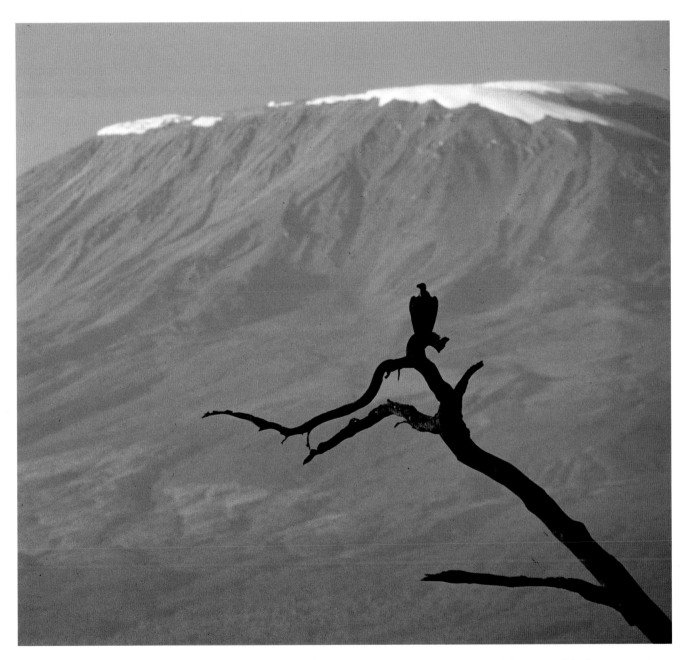

Left: Salt grass growing in Botswana's Makgadikgadi pan. At the end of the wet season the pan's vegetation attracts countless thousands of wildebeest, gemsbok, springbok, eland and zebra.

Above: A Rüppell's griffon vulture silhouetted against snow-capped Kilimanjaro. This species, common on the East African savanna, is also found in mountain regions at altitudes of up to 15,000ft (4,575m).

Overleaf: The high moorlands and alpine zone of the Simen mountains, the most northerly of the Ethiopian highlands, have a rich carpet of ericaceous plants and grasses. They are the realm of the elusive (and now endangered) Ethiopian wolf.

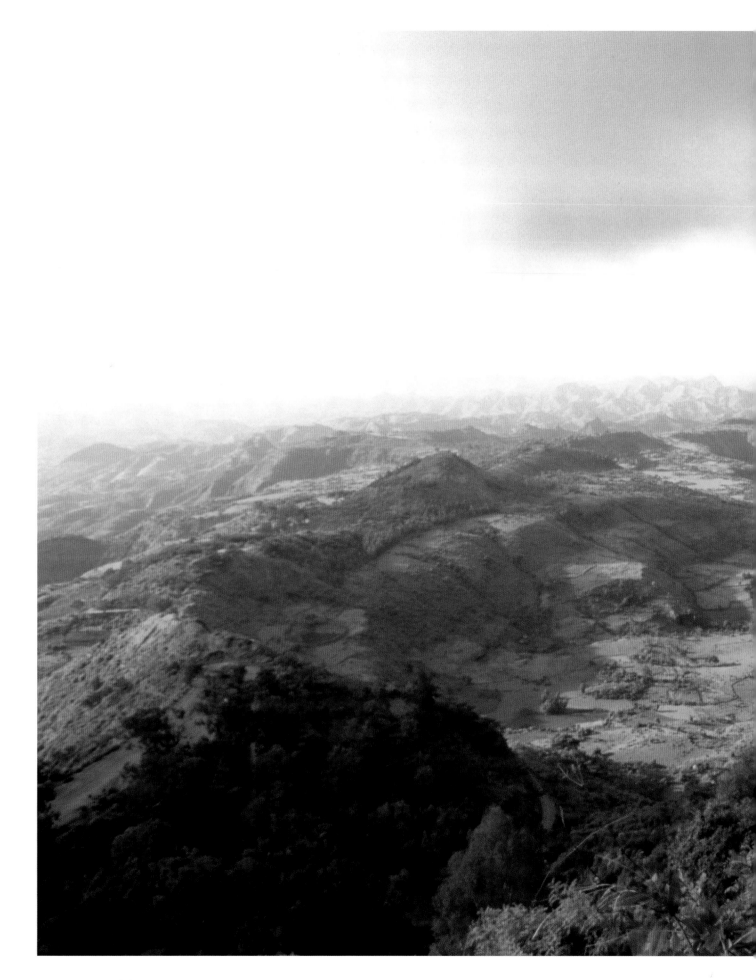

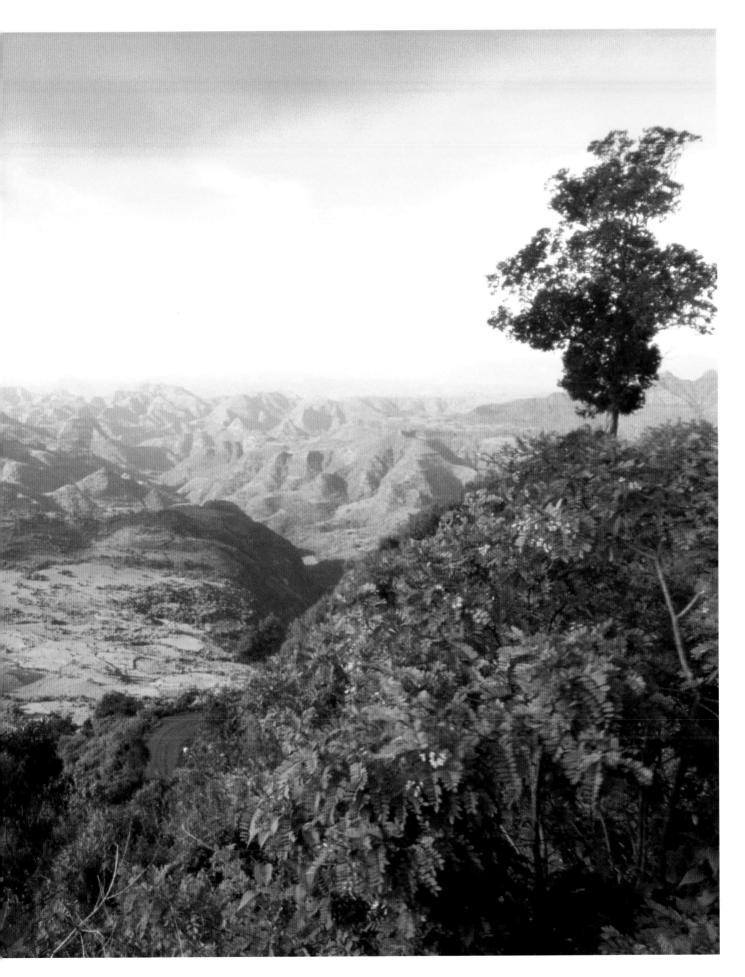

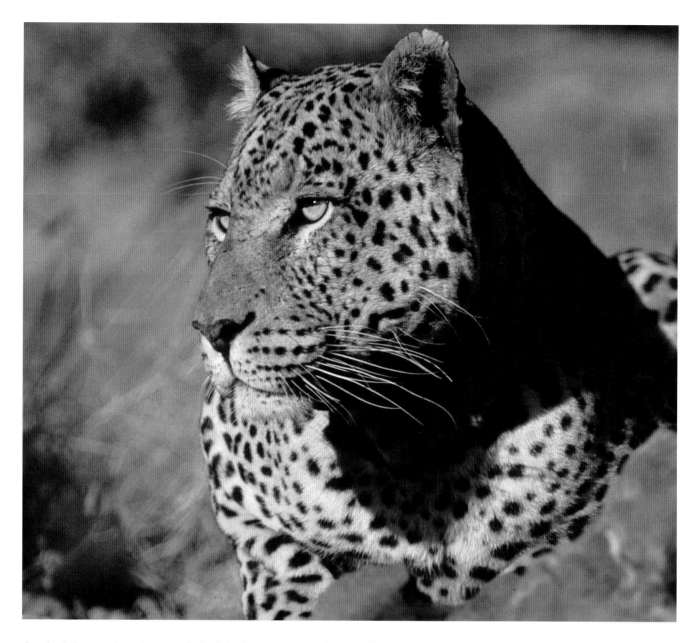

ibex; both live mostly at the upper limit of the forest zone or in the moorland zone (though in different areas of the highlands). Another antelope found here—and in most other mountain regions of eastern and southern Africa—is the klipspringer, which is capable of living at altitudes of up to 15,000ft (4,500m). A primate native to the moorland and high alpine meadows is the gelada baboon, which feeds mainly on grasses and roots.

Although the leopard is sometimes seen in lower parts of the forest zone, the only Ethiopian carnivore that is truly montane in habitat is the Ethiopian wolf (formerly known as the Simien fox), which somewhat resembles a jackal in size and shape. It is virtually restricted to the moorland zone, where it preys on the endemic giant mole rat and other rodents.

Farther south are the ranges and individual mountains of the eastern and western arms of the Rift Valley. All these share somewhat similar patterns of vegetation zones. First, there is a forest zone of mixed evergreen and deciduous species (the latter mainly on the drier slopes in the rain-shadow). Higher up is the cloud-forest zone where smaller, more stunted trees form a dense canopy, their branches festooned with ferns, epiphytes and lichens; and here and there are stands of bamboo. Above the cloud-forest is heath-land, its flora dominated by ericaceous plants. Finally, above 13,000ft (4,000m) is the alpine zone, where mixed scrub and grasses are interspersed with patches of giant shrubs.

Duikers are among the most numerous herbivores found in the mixed forest, cloud-forest and heathland zones in these mountains, different species of these small antelopes occurring in different ranges. The rock hyrax, which resembles a large guinea pig, is found at all levels on the mountains of the eastern Rift. Among the most interesting creatures of this region are the primates. The mountain gorilla is restricted to a small area of the Virunga region and to Uganda's Bwindi forest to the north-east. Various races of blue monkey inhabit montane forests in these ranges, as does the black-and-white colobus. In addition to these and many other permanent inhabitants of the different vegetation zones, the mountains often receive visitors from neighbouring habitats, notably the savanna. The leopard seeks prey on the edges of the montane forests. Bush elephants spend much time browsing not only in the forest zones but in the heathland above, while buffalo often ascend to the alpine zone in search of grazing.

The Cameroon highlands begin in tropical rainforest, which gives way to montane forest and, higher up, to grassland. The ungulate population, found at all altitudes up to 10,000ft (3,000m), includes klipspringer, duiker and mountain reedbuck and the native primates include several species of monkey. There are occasional sightings of the giant forest hog in the montane forest belt. Carnivores include the ubiquitous leopard and spotted hyena.

The volcanic Drakensberg is the most southerly of Africa's major mountain ranges. Most of its areas that lie above 10,000ft (3,000m) are in Lesotho, but the range as a whole extends from eastern Cape Province, through KwaZulu-Natal and northwards into Transvaal (the region of the Highveld). The dominant vegetation on the lower slopes is grassland interrupted occasionally by small patches of woodland, but it also includes a rich variety of herbaceous and shrub species. The common eland, largest of all the antelopes, is found in all the vegetation zones of the Drakensberg, as are the klipspringer and gray rhebok. The savanna baboon is equally at home on the ground or aloft in the canopy in the woods on the lower slopes of the range, while vervet monkeys occur at higher altitudes. Verreaux's eagle patrols the sky above the highest peaks, on the lookout for the rock hyrax (known in South Africa as the dassie) and smaller ungulates on which it preys.

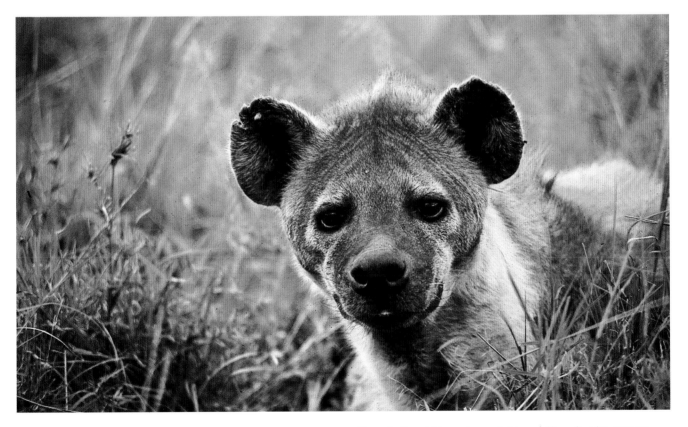

Above Left and Above: Leopards (above left) are found in montane forests, although they prefer to remain on the forest margins at higher altitudes. Spotted hyenas (above is a sub-adult) occur in the montane forests and high grasslands of the Cameroon highlands.

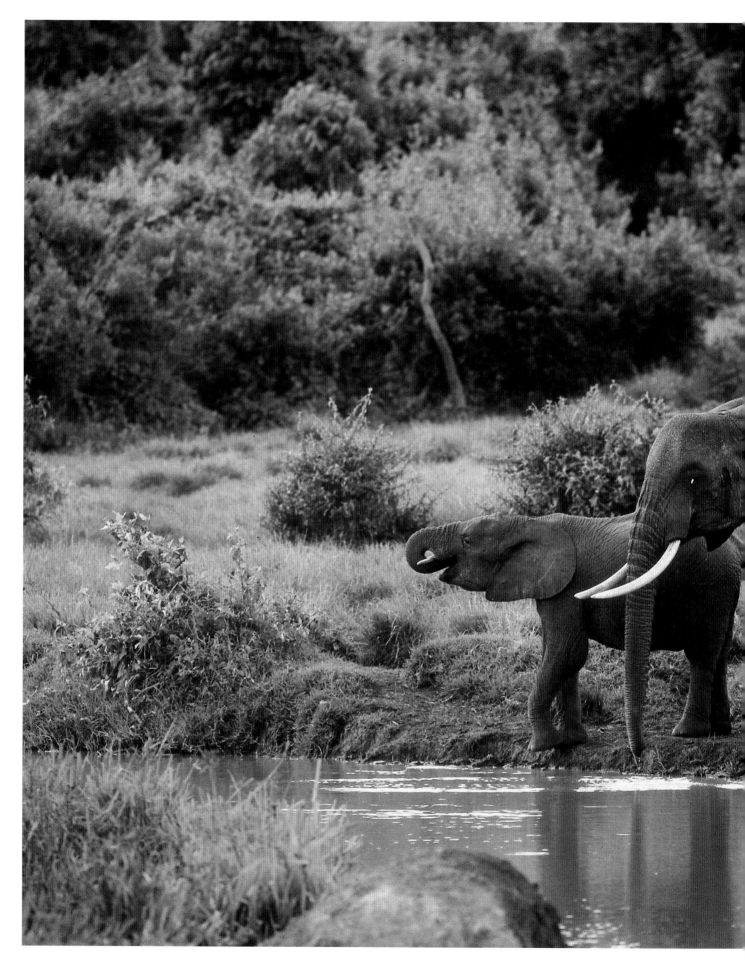

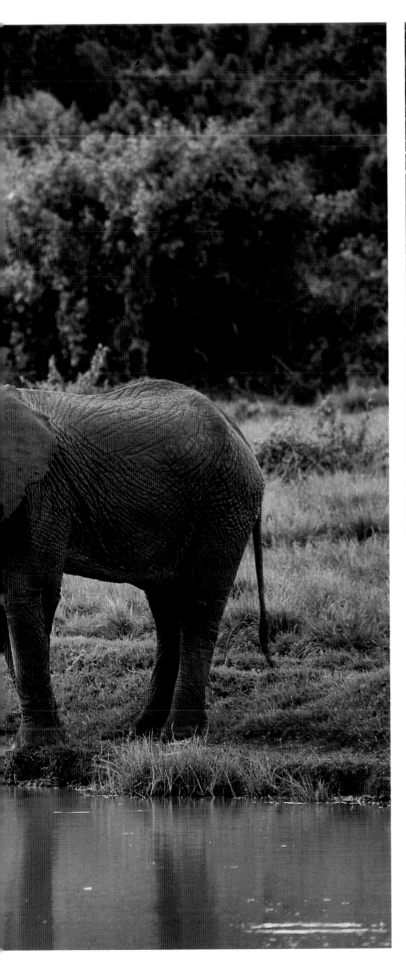

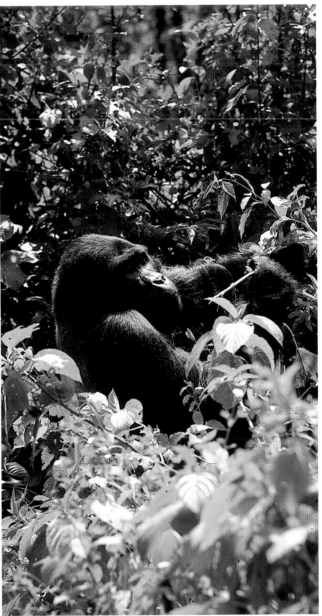

Above: Mountain gorillas occur only in two small areas of the western rift.

Left: More familiar as creatures of woodland and grassland savannas, bush elephants (left) are also found in highlands up to the limit of montane forests. These two are at a waterhole in Aberdare National Park in the Kenya highlands.

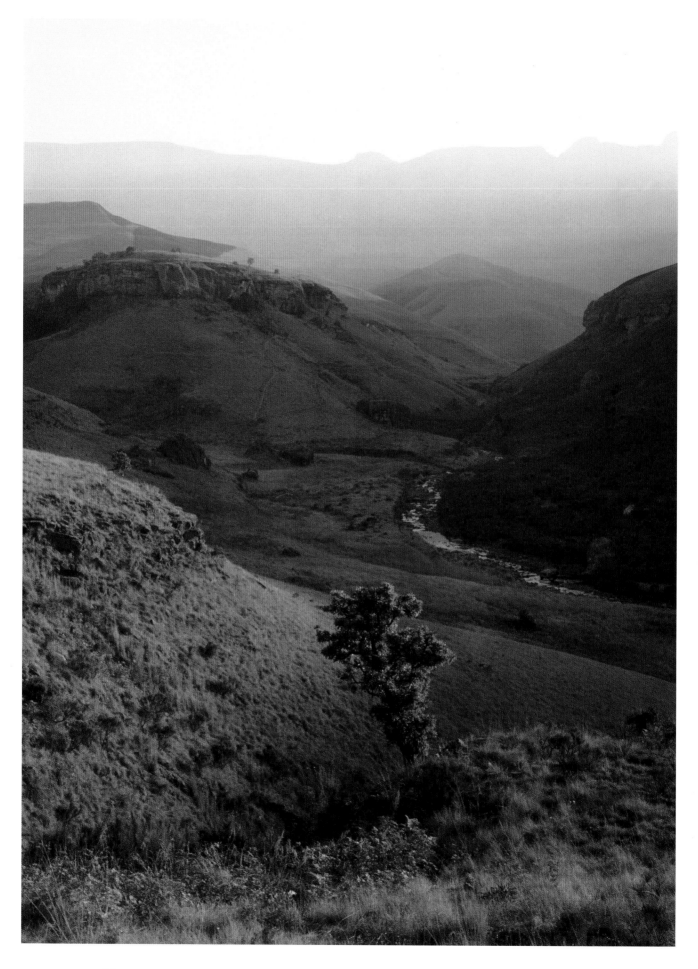

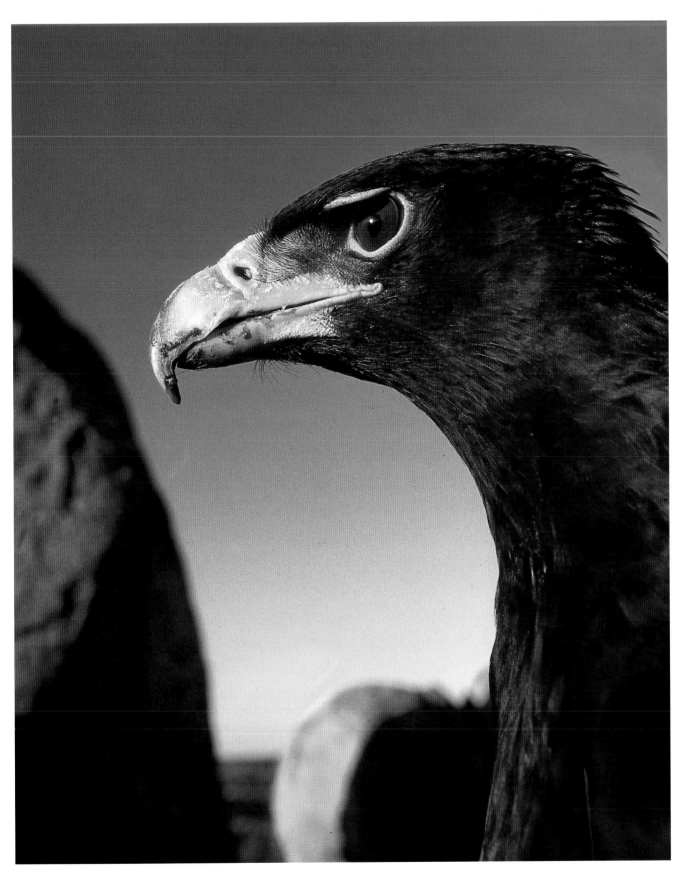

Above and Left: The volcanic Drakensberg range (left) is the most southerly of Africa's major ranges. One of the great wildlife sights of the range is the great jet-black Verreaux's eagle (above) soaring on thermals around the highest peaks.

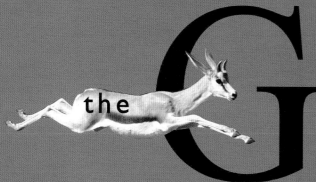

the GREAT NATIONAL PARKS AND RESERVES

Nowadays, it is only in national parks and game reserves that most safari tourists and individual travellers are able to experience the fascination and excitement of seeing Africa's wild animals close up in their natural habitats. In this chapter we identify, region by region, some of the continent's most important game parks and reserves and a few of the animals that make up the characteristic fauna of each. Most of these parks cater to visitors in the provision of guides, lodges, land transport and/or boats. The final chapter of the book contains a more extensive (although not exhaustive) checklist of game parks and reserves in each of the countries. The initials WHS in parentheses after the name of a park indicates that it is a World Heritage Site.

WEST AFRICA: SENEGAL TO NIGERIA

Senegal

Djoudj National Park (WHS), in the extreme north of the country near the Mauretania border, is an important centre for native and Eurasian migratory birds: there is a large resident colony of great white pelicans, and crowned cranes and jacanas are often seen. Mammals include golden jackal, warthog, patas monkey and several species of gazelles. In the far south, in tropical rain forest, is the Basse-Casamance National Park, which has colobus monkeys, duikers and other herbivores including

Right: The Senegal parrot is found in West African rain and riverine forests.

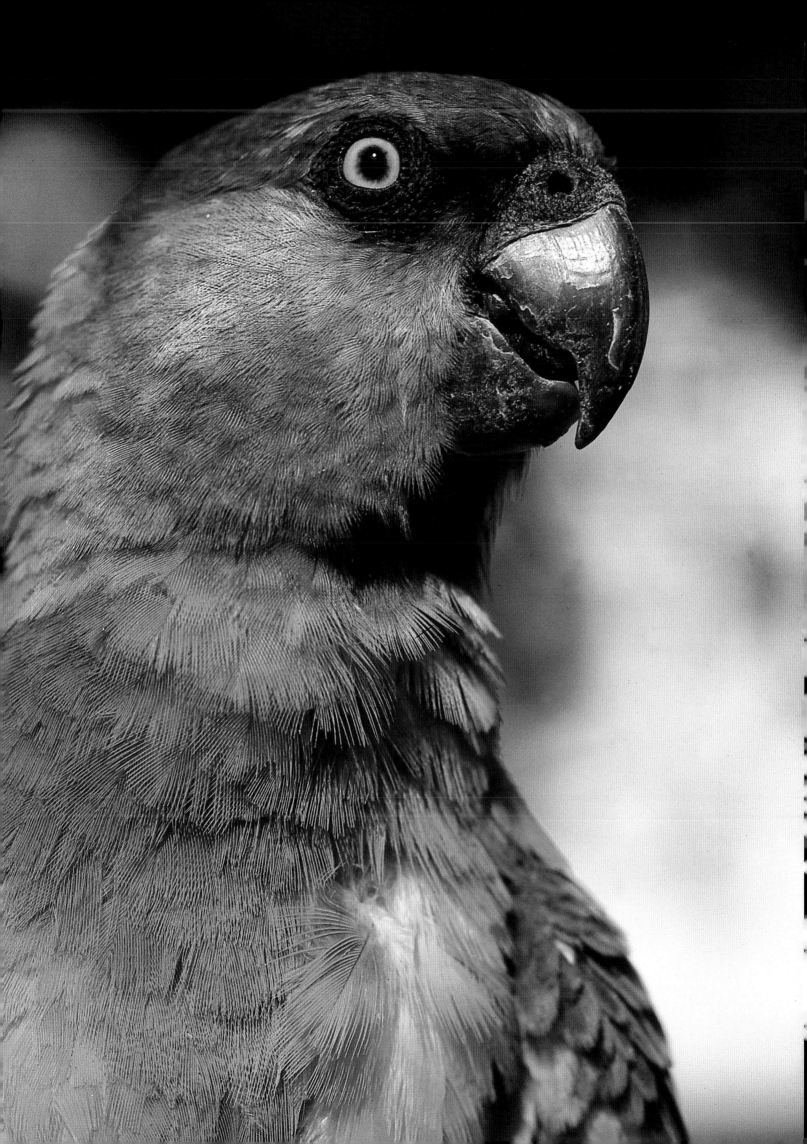

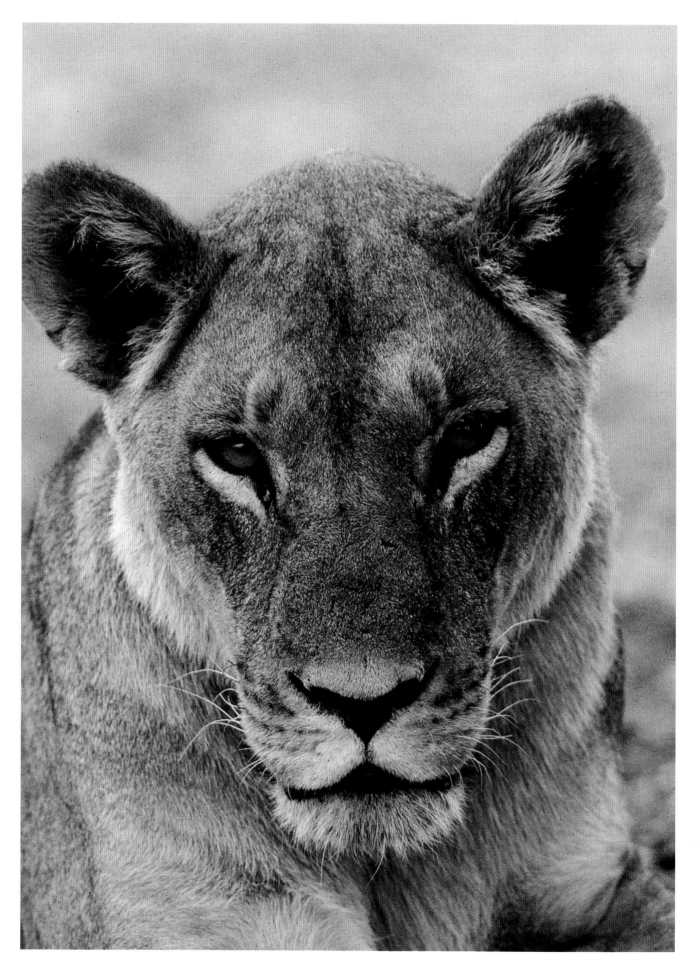

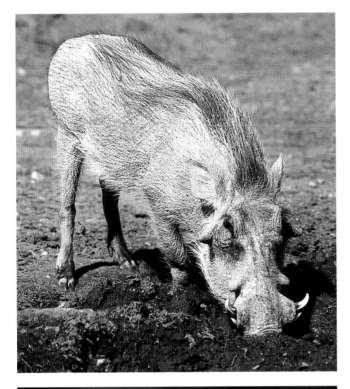

buffalo; among many interesting bird species are crowned eagles and palm-nut vultures. In the south-east the mixed woodland and grassland Niokolo-Koba National Park (WHS), whose northernmost section straddles the Gambia river, boasts numerous hippopotamus and crocodiles; other important residents include elephants, wild dogs, lions and leopards, whose prey species within the park include kob, buffalo, reedbuck, hartebeest and roan.

Gambia

The small Abuko Nature Reserve, a few miles south of the capital, Banjul, is a mixture of savanna and woodland dotted about with streams and ponds. It is a centre for breeding chimpanzees, and it also includes red colobus, patas and vervet monkeys, the water-loving sitatunga antelope and other ungulates. Farther east, near Georgetown, the Gambia River National Park has baboons and hippos, and the islands in the river hereabouts are home to chimpanzees bred at the Abuko Nature Reserve.

Guinea

Badiar National Park, in the north-west corner of the country, has resident populations of elephant and baboons, kob and roan, and leopard and spotted hyena. In the extreme south-east corner the Mount Nimba Strict Nature Reserve (WHS) offers protection to several primates, buffalo, duikers and other ugulates, and pygmy hippo.

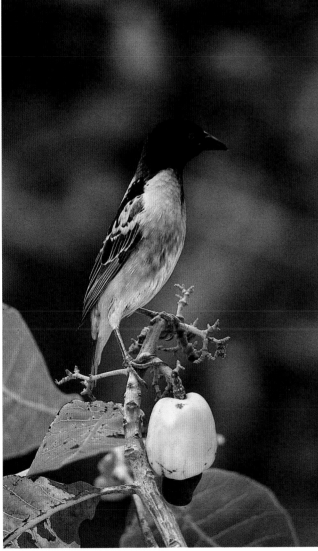

Above Left: Warthogs inhabit the arid woodlands in Senegal's northern reserves.

Left: Common in Gambia, the village weaver builds its spherical nest out of grasses or palm fibre.

Far Left: Big cats, such as this lioness, are more at home in the savanna mosaic farther south.

Overleaf: Hippos are abundant in Sierra Leone's Great and Little Scarcies rivers.

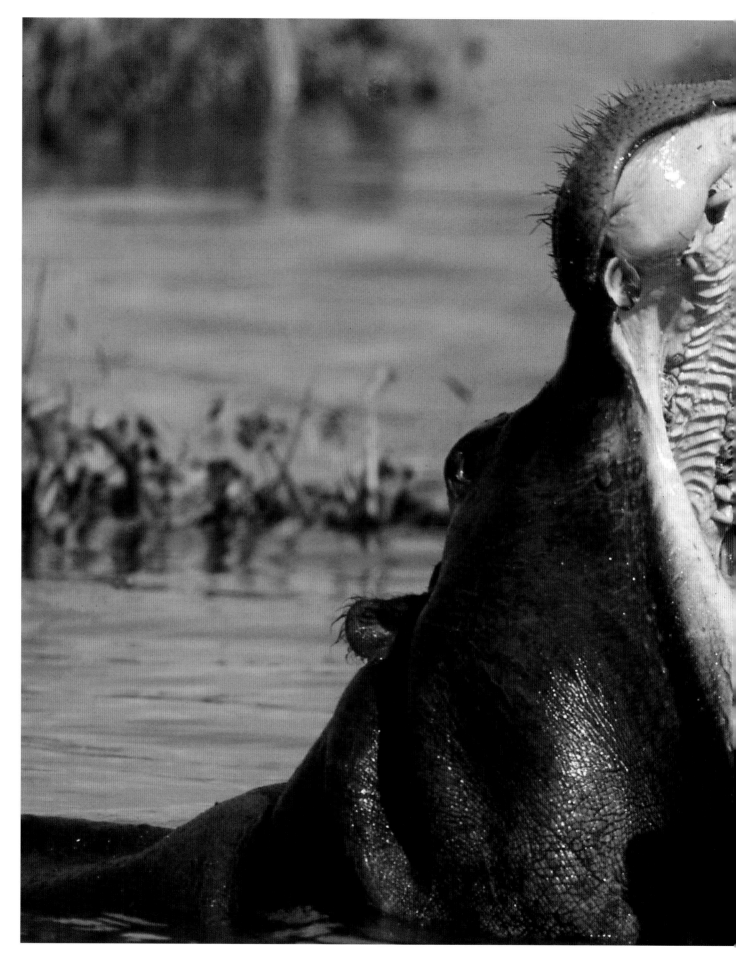

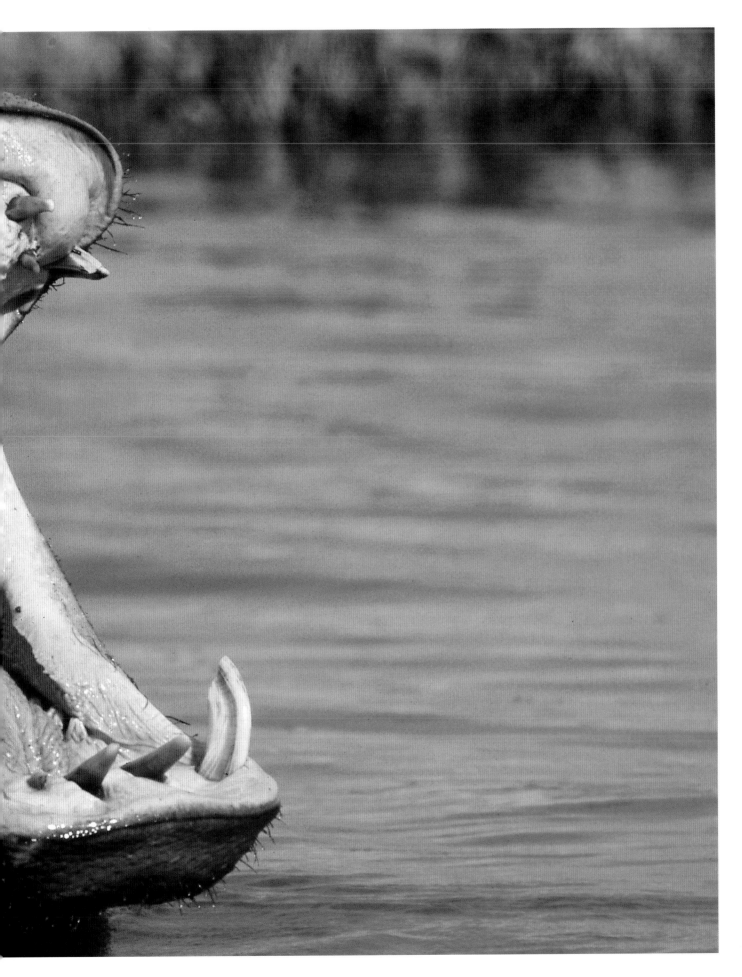

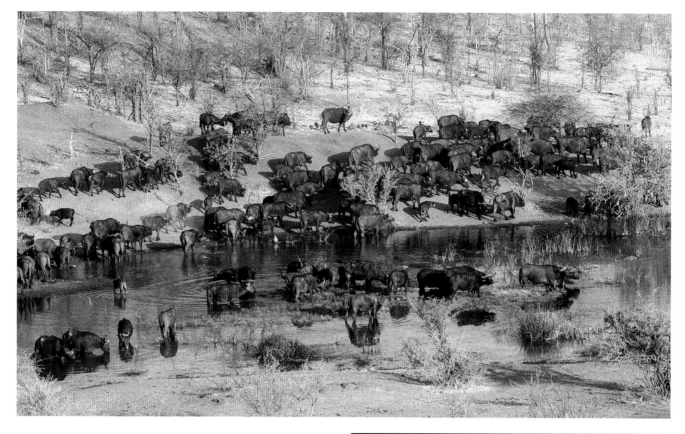

Sierra Leone

The Outamba-Kilimi National Park, in the extreme north on the Guinea border, is divided between forest, more open savanna woodland, grassland and marshy swamps and is home to chimpanzees, waterbuck, the rare forest elephant and buffalo, while crocodiles and hippos are found in the Great and Little Scarcies rivers. Three species of colobus monkeys (the western black-and-white, the western red and the olive), diana monkey and several species of duiker inhabit the Gola Forest Reserve along the Liberia border; but these and other fauna, as well as the integrity of the reserve itself, are threatened by illegal hunting and by logging operations.

Liberia

Almost half of the natural vegetation of Liberia consists of tropical rainforest, and this habitat supports a wide range of wildlife species. In the Loffa-Mano National Park, on the border with Sierra Leone, the forest is cut through by swift-flowing rivers. Among the wildlife residents are forest elephants, many species of antelope, pygmy hippos, and half a dozen primate species. The even denser rainforest of Sapo National Park in the south of the country supports a similar range of wildlife.

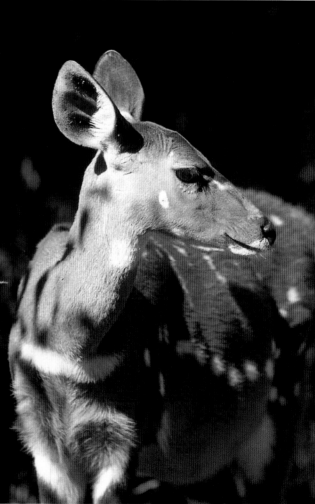

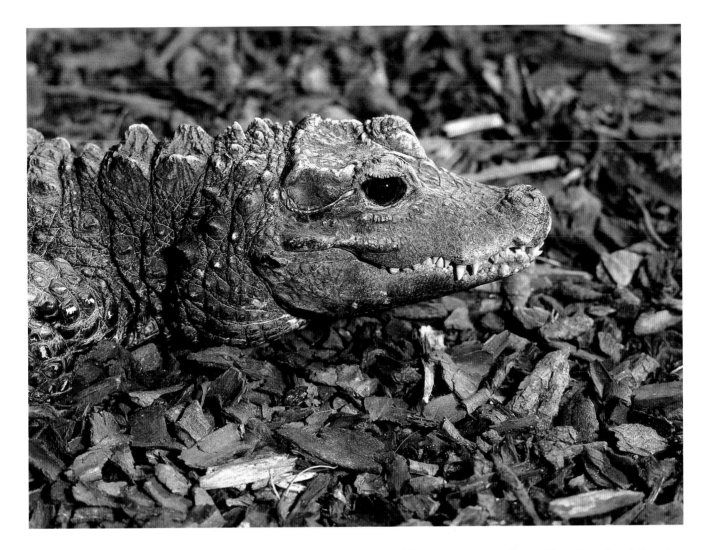

Ivory Coast

The Mount Nimba Strict Nature Reserve (WHS) is dealt with under Guinea (the reserve straddles the point at which the borders of Guinea, Liberia and Ivory Coast meet). In the west, Tai National Park (WHS) is the country's major reserve in the rainforest belt that covers most of the southern third of Ivory Coast. The reserve's fauna include pygmy hippos, six duiker species, water chevrotain, royal antelope, bongo, forest elephant, ant-eating pangolins and several primates. In the woodland savanna that covers much of northern Ivory Coast is the Komoé National Park (WHS), covering 4,450 square miles (12,870km^2) close to the Burkina Faso border. Hippos and the three African species of crocodile are found in the Komoé river that runs through the reserve. In the open woodland are carnivores including lion and spotted hyena, as well as bush elephant, many antelope species, buffalo and baboon. Other primates favour the gallery forests along stretches of the river. The park has several hundred bird species.

Above: The elusive pygmy crocodile, a resident of Ivory Coast's Kamoé river, hunts on land at night.

Above Left: In the north of the country Cape buffalo graze in the mixed savanna grassland and open woodland in Sierra Leone's Outamba-Kilimi National Park.

Left: The bushbuck, a mixed browser and grazer, thrives on the edges of Liberia's rain forests.

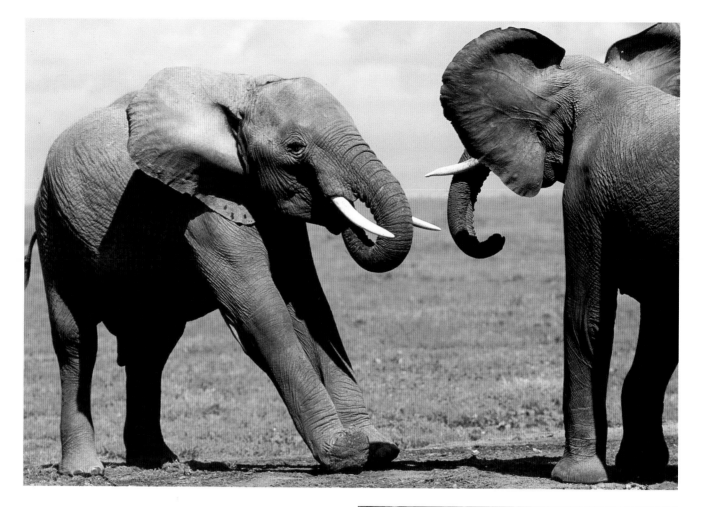

Ghana

The Bia National Park occupies the Ghana's last remaining area of virgin rain forest in the valley of the Bia river next to the Ivory Coast border. It boasts a rich fauna, including forest elephant, giant forest hog, bongo, duikers, chimpanzees and many species of monkeys, and leopard. The many birds species include the magnificent crowned eagle and two hornbills. In central Ghana Digya National Park occupies an area of 1,200 square miles (3,110km²) immediately to the west of Lake Volta. A mixture of forest and more open savanna woodland, it supports elephant, hippo, buffalo, many antelope species and colobus and patas monkeys. In the north, the most spectacular displays of wildlife are found at Mole National Park, which lies just east of the Burkina Faso border along the Black Volta river. Its area of 1,900 square miles (4,920km²), ranging from dense forest to grassland, contains elephant, buffalo, bushbuck, hartebeest, waterbuck, roan, kob, oribi, duiker, colobus monkeys, and baboons, and a range of carnovores including lion, leopard, spotted hyena, wild dog, and side-striped jackal.

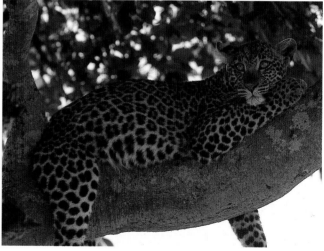

Top: Two young male elephants sparring. Elephants are found in open savanna woodland in Ghana's central and northern reserves.

Above: Usually resting in a tree by day, leopards are night hunters in the woodland and dense forest along the Black Volta river in northern Ghana.

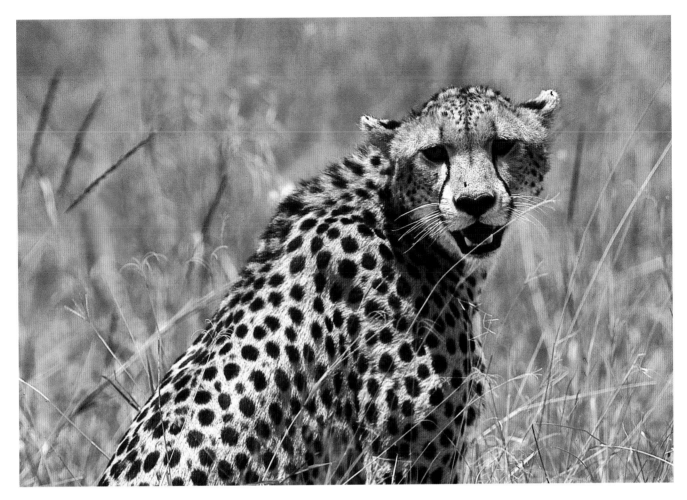

Togo

The best place to see wildlife in this small, narrow country is the Keran National Park, in the wooded savanna of the far north. There are buffalo, many species of antelope, warthogs and baboons, and numerous hippos and crocodiles frequent rivers and streams.

Benin

The W du Benin National Park is in the extreme north of the country. The "W" refers to the shape of bends in the Niger river: the park lies on the river near the point where the borders of Benin, Niger and Burkina Faso meet, and it is run jointly by these countries. The terrain is a mixture of open woodland and savanna grassland and contains many rivers and streams. Wildlife includes hartebeest, topi, roan, bushbuck, reedbuck, kob, gazelles, and duikers, which are preyed on by lion, leopard, cheetah and spotted hyena. There are also many buffalo, warthog, baboon and patas monkey, and hippos and crocodiles in the rivers. The Boucle de la Pendjari National Park to the south-west has a similar range of fauna.

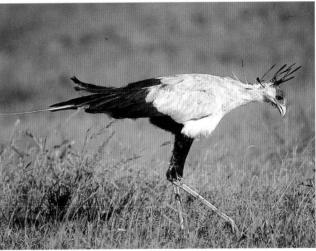

Top: Cheetahs prey on the abundant gazelles and other small antelopes in the grasslands of northern Benin.

Above: The long-legged, crane-like secretarybird of grasslands and wooded savanna lives on insects, rodents and, especially, snakes.

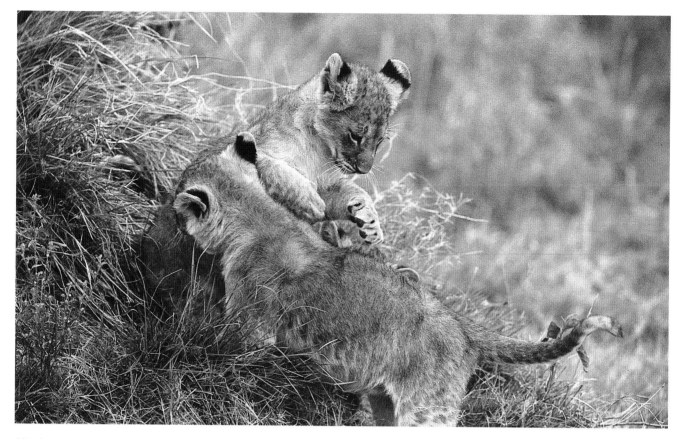

Nigeria

In the south of the country only small, isolated fragments remain of what once was a continuous belt of lowland rainforest. In the extreme south-eastern corner of Nigeria, much of Cross River National Park, north of Calabar between the river and the Cameroon border, and Boshi-Okwango Game Reserve, immediately to the south, consist of remnants of rainforest which are protected and support a small relict community of lowland gorillas and several other primates.

In the western extremity of central Nigeria, between the huge Kainji reservoir and the Benin border, Kainji Lake National Park occupies 2,060 square miles (5,335km²) of mixed wooded savanna and grassland, with patches of forest along the reservoir and river. The park, which has a rich and varied avifauna, is home to several primates, elephant, buffalo, hartebeest, oribi, bushbuck, roan and kob, as well as carnivores such as lion, leopard, wild dog and side-striped jackal. In the centre of Nigeria, about 100 miles (160km) south-east of the town of Bauchi, the Yankari Game Reserve covers 865 square miles (2,240km²) of mixed woodland, grassland and swamp. The reserve supports abundant baboons, elephant, hartebeest, buffalo, bushbuck, waterbuck and duiker,

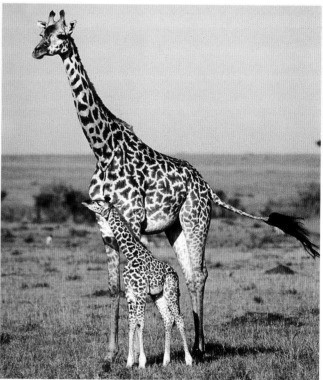

Top: Nigeria's Yankari Game Reserve, with its mixture of grassland and mixed woodland, is host to several prides of lions. These two cubs are playing in swampy ground near a river.

Above: The Yankari also hosts a few giraffe, although the resident population may not be viable in the long term.

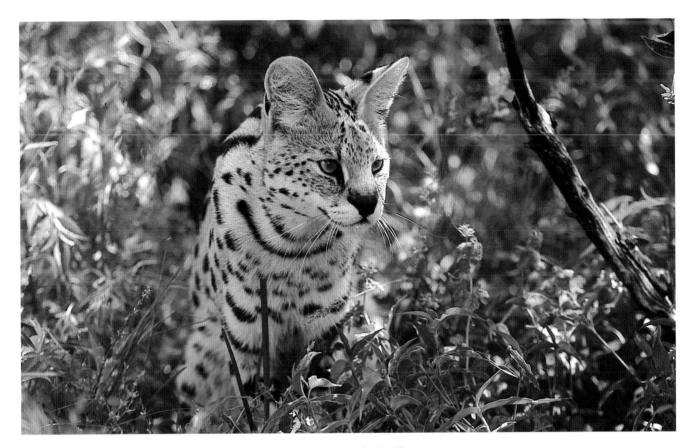

together with lion and leopard and (at least until recently) some giraffe. The many rivers and waterways have hippo and two species of crocodile. In the far north-east the Chad Basin National Park attempts to preserve the swamp and marsh habitats around the large portion of Lake Chad that lies within Nigeria, but most of its once abundant wildlife has gone.

Mali

The country's northern areas reach into the Sahara; south of that is the semi-desert region of the Sahel. Mali is poor in wildlife: drought has conspired with deforestation followed by overgrazing of the cleared areas to eliminate much of the natural vegetation on which the wild fauna depend, while overhunting has devastated most of the remaining mammal and bird populations. Patches of open woodland and grassland, and the remnants of dense forest along the Baoulé river in the Kaarta region north-west of the capital Bamako characterize the country's only national park—the Boucle du Baoulé National Park. However, the large herds of ungulates, the elephants and giraffes, the warthogs, the big cats and the primates that once flourished here have now largely disappeared.

Burkina Faso

The wildlife-viewing prospects in Burkina Faso are limited: the tourism infrastructure is still undeveloped and many ostensibly protected reserves have been almost ruined either by poaching, as is the case with the Biontoli Total Faunal Reserve by the Black Volta river, or by encroachment by stock-raising nomads, as in the huge Sahel Partial Faunal Reserve in the extreme north-east corner of the country. The W du Burkina Faso National Park, at the junction of the borders with Niger and Benin has many wildlife species but is not as well organised for tourism as the equivalent reserve in Niger (see page 107). Perhaps the best area for wildlife tourists is a few miles to the south-west—the cluster of small reserves centred on the Arly Partial Faunal Reserve on the Pendjari river. Maintained ponds and small lakes along the river have hippos and crocodiles, while the grassland supports many species of ungulates as well as lion, leopard, cheetah, and elephant.

Above: One of the smaller predators of Niger's Tamou Nature Reserve is the handsomely spotted serval, which hunts for rodents in tall grass and shrub thickets.

Overleaf: The warthog, like other large mammels, is now rarely seen in Mali's Boucle du Baoulé National Park.

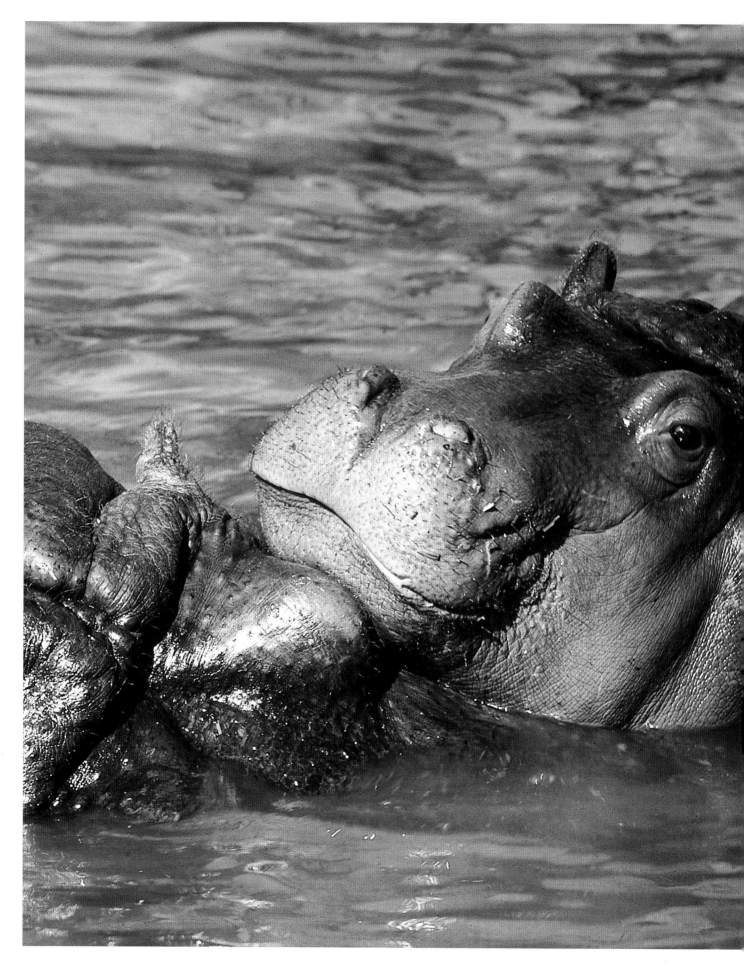

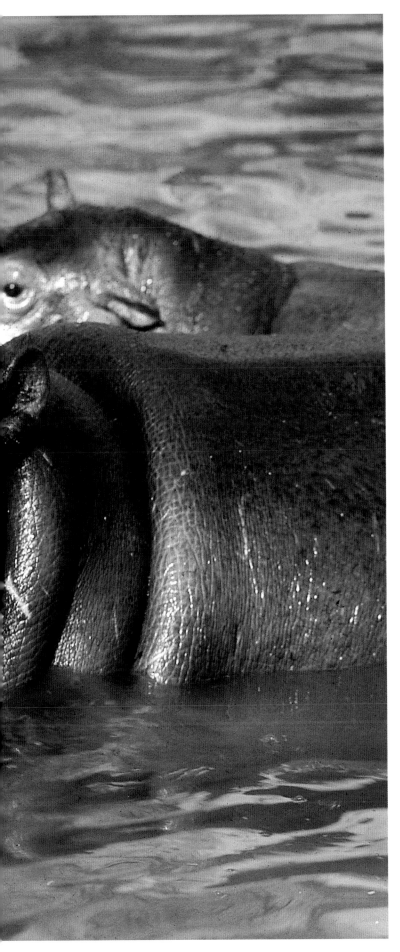

Niger

The northern region of the country is in the Sahara desert, which is expanding inexorably southward; the Sahel belt on its southern margins has degraded grassland which, as one moves south, changes first to scrubland and then to wooded savanna. The most important centre for observing wildlife is the W du Niger National Park, which is part of the large international park region shared with neighbouring Benin and Burkina Faso (q.v.). This park, and its near neighbour, the Tamou Nature Reserve, are on the Niger river south of the capital, Niamey. Rich in fauna, they support flourishing communities of buffalo, hartebeest, bushbuck, waterbuck, reedbuck, topi, kob, roan, and gazelles, as well as elephant, baboon and other primates, lion, leopard, cheetah, spotted hyena, serval and caracal. Hippos and crocodiles are found in the many streams and rivers that flow into the Niger, while there is an abundance of birds, including eagles.

Burkina Faso's most accessible region for wildlife tourists is in the south-west, where the lakes and ponds of the Pendjari river have a thriving hippo population.

CENTRAL AFRICA: CHAD TO ANGOLA AND ZAÏRE

Chad

The country's terrain ranges from the lofty peaks of Tibesti, deep in the stony wastes of the Sahara in the north, to the damp grasslands of the extreme south-west. The two main centres for wildlife are in the south. The Zakouma National Park, south-west of the town of Am Timan, consists mainly of a vast floodplain, fed by the Salamat and Keita rivers, and areas of open woodland. It supports a large and varied population of ungulates as well as warthog, crocodile, lion, leopard, cheetah, spotted hyena and caracal. To the west, the Manda National Park, on the Chari river, has elephant, buffalo, lion, hippo, eland, buffalo and roan. In the centre of Chad is the gigantic Ouadi Rimé-Ouadi Achim Faunal Reserve: with an area of some 30,900 square miles (90,000km²) it is Africa's largest, but its natural vegetation has been undermined by overgrazing by domestic animals and its wildlife population wiped out in many areas by unregulated hunting. Its few surviving scimitar-horned oryx and addax are almost certainly doomed to extinction, as are the once numerous gazelles, the cheetahs that prey upon them and the ostrich.

Central African Republic

In the rainforest of the extreme south-west, where the country's borders with Cameroon and the Congo Republic meet, the Dzanga-Ndoki National Park and its associated reserves are administered jointly by the three nations. Parts of the park are reserved strictly for the hunter-gatherer Pygmies, but elsewhere the reserves support lowland gorillas and a variety of other primates, as well as forest elephant, giant forest hog and buffalo. In the highland country in the north-east, the valleys of the numerous rivers flowing north-westwards towards Chad are clad in dense woods that give way, lower down, to richly grassed floodplains. There are three national parks in this region. The largest and most accessible is the Manovo-Gounda-Saint Floris National Park (WHS), on the border with Chad. Resident wildlife includes forest and bush elephant, giraffe, Derby eland and many other antelope species, gazelles, buffalo, wild pig, black rhino, and many carnivores, including lion, leopard, cheetah, wild dog, and spotted hyena, while there are hippo and crocodile in the rivers.

Sudan

We deal here with the wooded savanna region of southern Sudan. The huge Bandingilo National Park, on the Nile north of Juba, has giraffe, elephant and Nile lechwe antelope. The Bangangai Game Reserve, in evergreen forest on the Zaïre border, has several primates, antelope and wild pig as well as forest elephant and buffalo. The Boma National Park, on the Ethiopian border, has montane forest, wooded savanna and semi-desert, and sees the seasonal migrations of vast herds of ungulates in the early months of the year.

Left: In southern Chad's Zakouma National Park spotted hyena like this trio prey upon a wide range of ungulates that graze on the floodplains and woodland savanna.

Right: In the north-eastern highlands of the Central African Republic the lower river valleys are richly grassed—a food resource exploited by the abundant herbivores, including bush elephants, which are both browsers and grazers.

Overleaf: The Cape buffalo, largest of the African races, forms herds numbering many hundreds. In southern Sudan the herds graze on the wooded savanna in Boma National Park near the Ethiopian border early in the year, migrating south-westwards out of the park in the wet season.

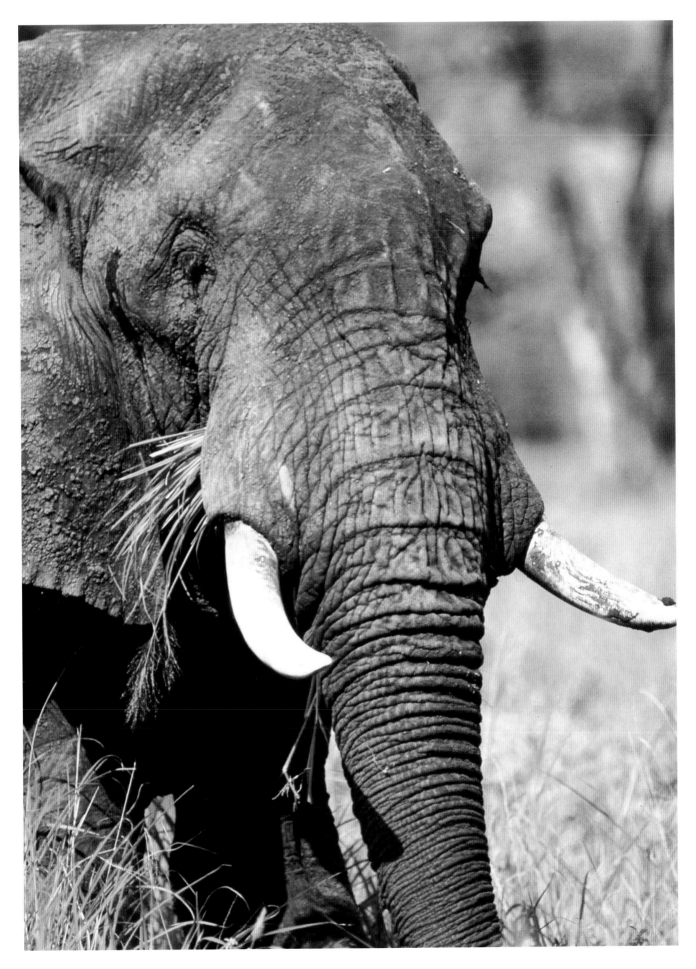

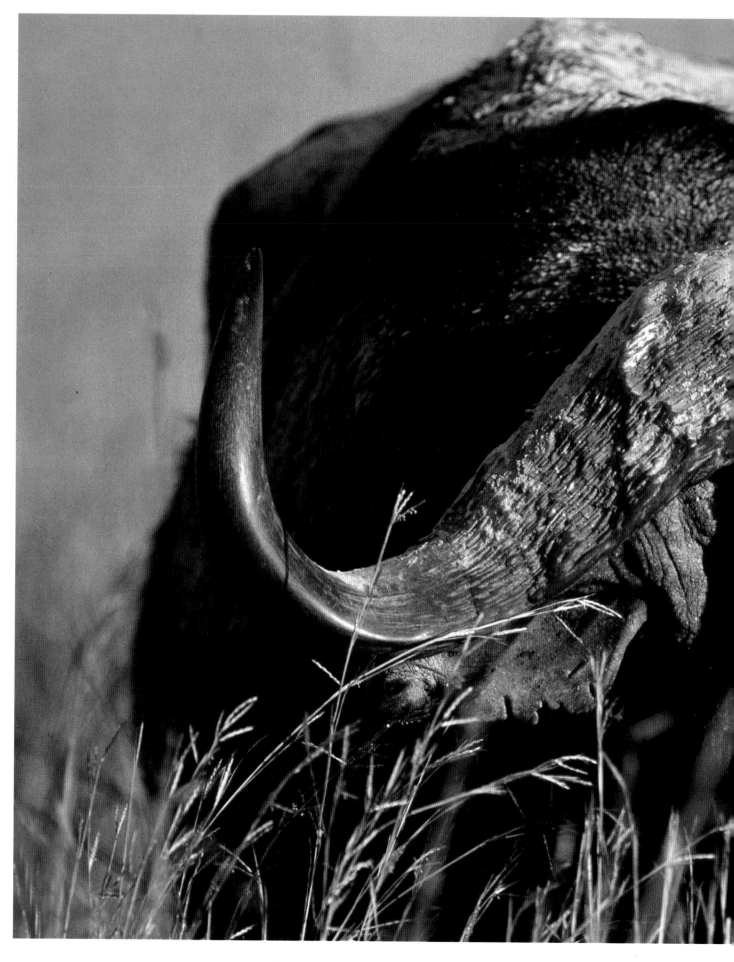

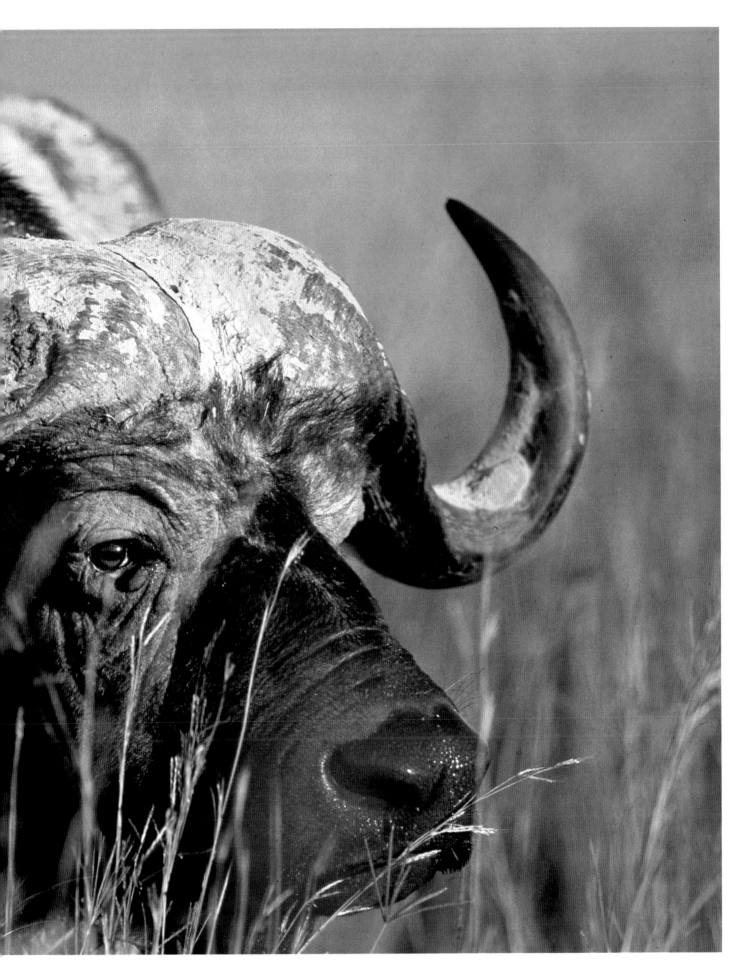

Cameroon

In the south the Douala-Edea Faunal Reserve, near the mouth of the Sanaga river, the Campo Faunal Reserve, near the Equatorial Guinea border, and the Dja Forest and Faunal Reserve, on the plateau south of Yaoundé, support a variety of rainforest species, including antelopes and primates, while the rivers are home to hippo and manatee. The Korup National Park, in rainforest near the Nigerian border, has a number of rare primates. In the Adamoua region in the north are several national parks in the areas drained by the Bénoué, the major tributary of the Niger—a region of wet savanna, woodland and hilly grassland. The Boubandjida National Park, in the hills near the border with Chad, has black rhino, hippo, elephant, a rich variety of antelope species, warthog, lion, leopard, cheetah and spotted hyena. Nearby are the Bénoué National Park and Faro National Park. In the extreme north, in the drier woodlands of the Waza National Park, on the Nigeria border, are giraffe, many species of antelope, some elephant, sand fox, and ostrich.

Gabon

The wide coastal plain south of the capital, Libreville, has remnants of rainforest, moist savanna and, at the coast, lagoons and mangrove swamps. At the Petit Loango National Park there are many primate species including gorilla, forest elephant, manatee, and leatherback sea turtle. In the interior, Lopé Faunal Reserve and nearby Lopé-Okanda Hunting Reserve, where there are elephant, buffalo and mandrill in the forests, lie between the Ogooué river and the hilly country to the south.

Angola

The coast is dominated in the south by the Namib desert. Just north of the Namibia border is Namibe Nature Reserve and Iona National Park (formerly Porto Alexandre National Park), where springbok, gemsbok, mountain zebra, ostrich, elephant and black rhino scratch a living in the valley of the Cunene river (the frontier between Angola and Namibia). In the central coastal area, south of

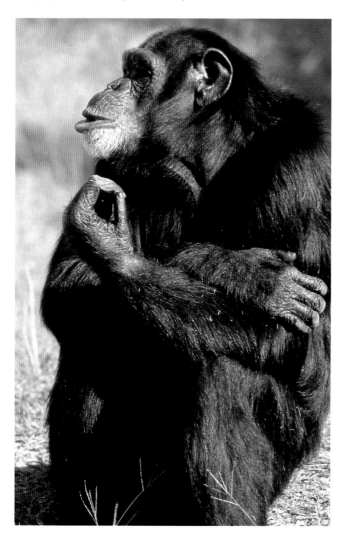

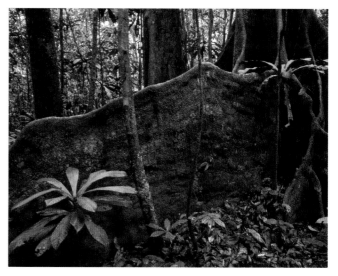

Above: This tall tree in Cameroon's Korup National Park has massive buttress roots that help to anchor it in the thin rainforest soil.

Left: The chimpanzee (and other primates, some endangered) are resident in rainforest areas in Cameroon's southern faunal reserves.

Above Right: The Gabon viper is fat and no more than 48in (1.2m) long with beautiful geometrical markings. Concealed in leaf litter on the forest floor, it lies in wait for rodents, ground-feeding birds and other prey.

Right: A female springbok and young. Springbok and other ungulates are found in the valley of the Cunene river on either side of the Angola/Namibia border.

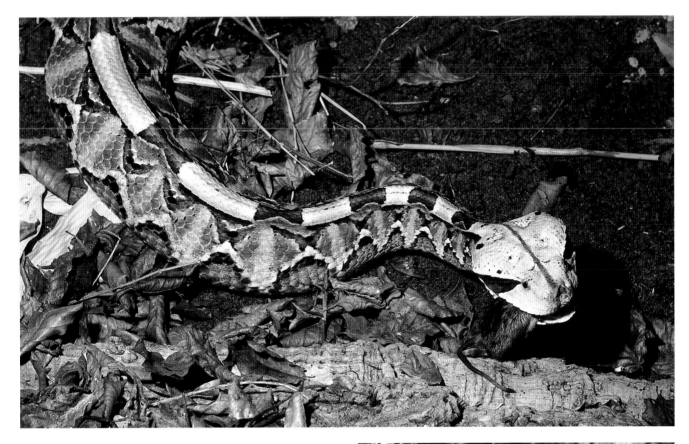

the capital, Luanda, Kisama (Quiçama) National Park includes flood-plain, savanna and woodland that support a wide range of fauna including the big cats and their ungulate prey, elephant, crocodile, manatee and several species of monkey. In the far east of the country, lying between the Luena river and the headwaters of the Zambezi (here the Zambeze) is the Kameia National Park, where elephant, giraffe, ostrich, many ungulates and lion can be seen.

Congo

The country's 100-odd miles (160km) of Atlantic coast is partly taken up by Conkouati Faunal Reserve, which inland also includes grassy lowland that gives way to steep, densely wooded hills. Its wildlife includes manatees in coastal lagoons, several species of ungulate on the grassland, and forest elephant, gorilla and chimpanzee in the woods. Inland, in a mountainous area close to Gabon's south-western border, more gorillas are found in Mont Fouari Faunal Reserve, while in neighbouring Nyanga Nord Faunal Reserve, hippos live in a river running through the remnants of a lowland rainforest. In the north of the country, in Sangha province close to Gabon's north-eastern border, are Odzala National Park and Lekoli-Pandaka Faunal Reserve in an area of mixed rainforest,

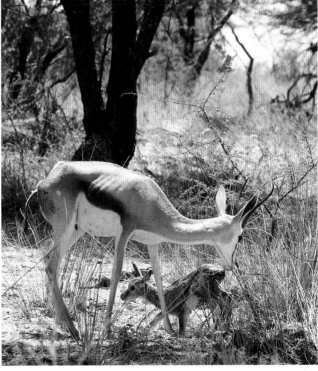

degraded savanna and salt pans. The rich variety of wildlife includes a few small prides of lion, spotted hyena, elephants, bongo, sitatunga and duiker, and, in the forests, gorilla, chimpanzee and other primates. Ndoki National Park has lowland gorilla, elephant, buffalo and leopard.primates. Farther north still, north-west of Impfondo on the Central African Republic border, the Nouabale-Ndoki National Park supports lowland gorilla, forest elephant, buffalo, leopard, and several species of antelope.

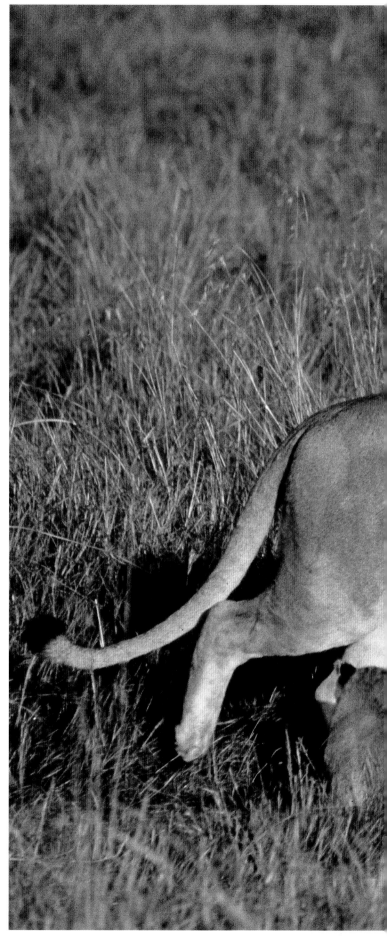

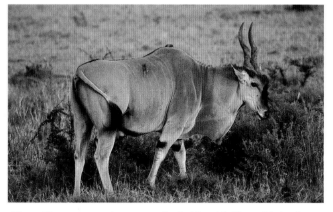

Above: The savanna and open woodland of Angola's Kisama National Park, south of the capital Luanda, are rich in big predators and their prey, including the eland, largest of the antelope species.

Right: A lioness carries one of her cubs back to their den in Kisama National Park.

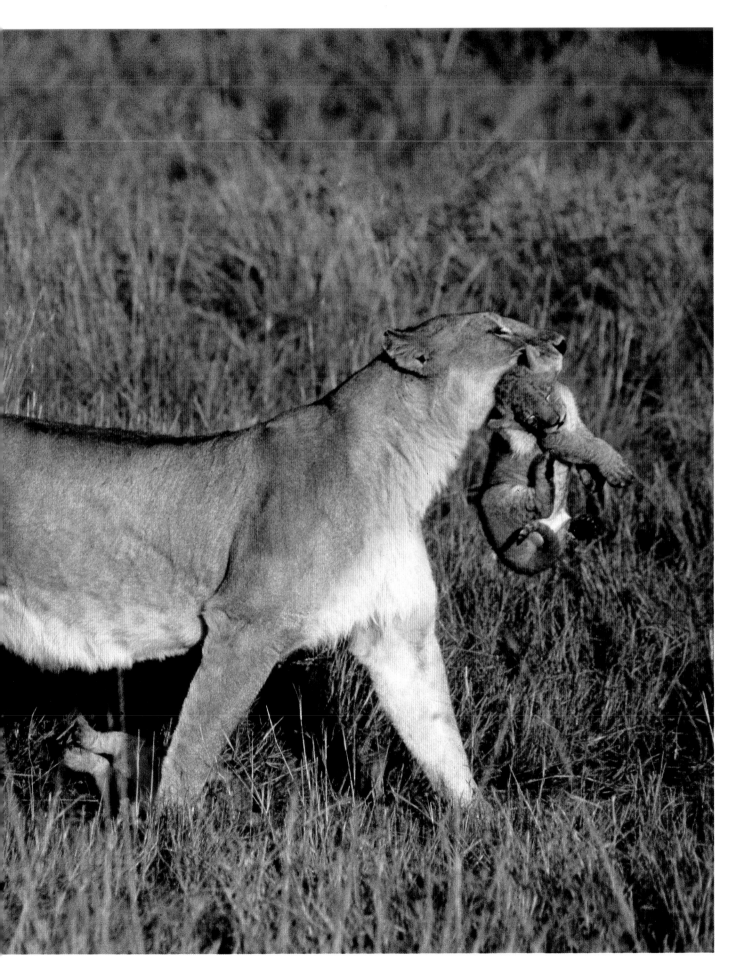

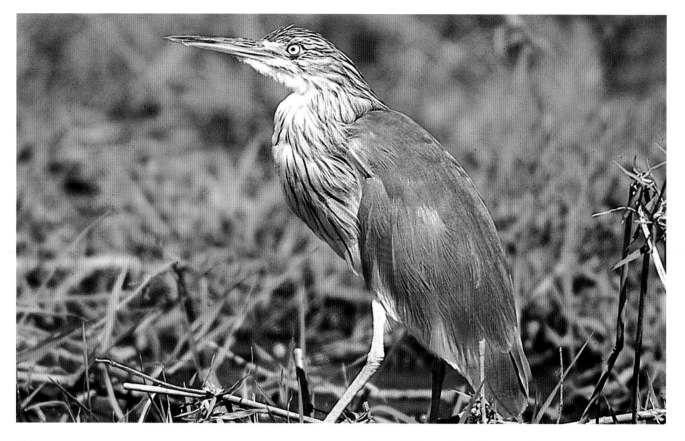

Zaïre

The second largest country in Africa, Zaïre's topography is dominated by the Congo (Zaïre) river: almost the entire country is drained by the river and its numerous tributaries. The dominant vegetation is tropical forest, but almost half the country has a mosaic of wooded savanna and savanna grassland. The main exception to this occurs on Zaïre's eastern borders, which are formed by the mountains and lakes of the western arm of the Rift Valley. Although rich in wildlife, the western areas of the country and the vast central region south of the Congo river have few facilities for safari tourists. In the north-east the Okapi Wildlife Reserve, in the Ituri Forest about 50 miles (80km) south-west of the southern end of Lake Albert, has okapi, elephant, and chimpanzee. Some 200 miles (320km) to the north, in on the Sudan border, is the Garamba National Park (WHS), in mainly savanna grassland. The great draw here is the very rare northern white rhino; other herbivores include buffalo, eland, hartebeest, roan and elephant, while the rich community of carnivores includes lion, leopard, wild dog and serval.

Zaïre's finest wildlife reserve is Virunga National Park (WHS), which runs along the western side of the western rift from Lake Kivu northwards to include the Ruwenzori. Mountain gorilla live on the forested slopes of the Virunga volcanoes, and there is a chimpanzee sanctuary near Rutshuru farther north. Grassland south of Lake Edward supports elephant, buffalo, many antelope species, lion and black-backed jackal, while there are abundant lakeside hippo and pelican. Another fine park, rich in wildlife including many primate species, in Zaïre's western rift region is Kahuzi-Biega National Park (WHS), west of Lake Kivu; while Luama Valley Reserve, west of Lake Tanganyika, has abundant ungulates. Finally, in the extreme south-eastern corner of the country, in the upper reaches of the Congo, Upemba National Park, and Kundelung National Park support varied populations of primates, antelope, zebra, buffalo, elephant, hippo and carnivores. Both parks are accessible from the city of Lubumbashi.

Above: The squacco heron, a bird of freshwater marshes, is a common sight on the edge of Rift Valley lakes in Zaïre.

Right: Greater kudu and many other ungulates graze grasslands in the upper reaches of the Congo in Zaïre's extreme south-east.

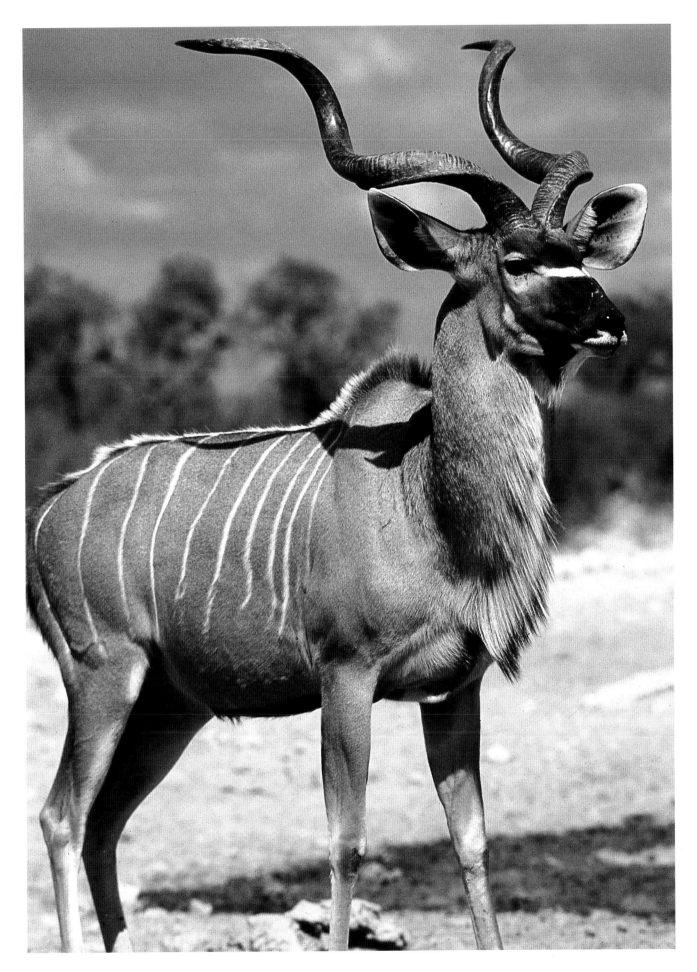

EASTERN AFRICA: ETHIOPIA TO TANZANIA

Burundi and Rwanda

Both countries have been disrupted by Rwanda's appallingly brutal civil war of the past few years, and the survival, let alone integrity, of their wildlife reserves is a matter of conjecture. The two countries' western borders run along the line of the western rift. Burundi's border with Zaïre runs through the middle of the most northerly 90 miles (145km) of Lake Tanganyika, continuing northwards along the Ruzizi river until about 30 miles south of Lake Kivu. Rwanda's border with Zaïre continues northward from there, through Lake Kivu and onwards through the Virunga range until a few miles north of the town of Ruhengeri, where the Zaïre/Uganda border begins. Both countries are mainly mountainous in the west but feature wooded savanna in the east, where they have borders with Tanzania. In Burundi the main wildlife centres are Ruzizi Nature Reserve, north-west of the capital, Bujumbura; Kibira National Park in the north; and Ruvuvu National Park in the east. And, in Rwanda, Volcanoes National Park, near Ruhengeri; Nyungwe Forest Reserve in the south-west; and Kagera National Park, running along the border with Tanzania.

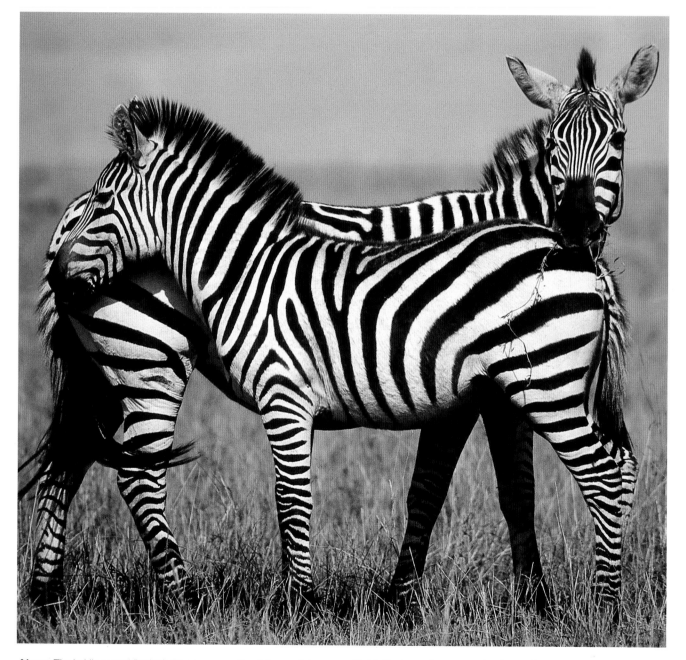

Above: The boldly striped Boehm's (also known as Grant's) race of the plains zebra is a familiar sight on the East African savanna.

Right: The leopard was once abundant in the wooded savannas of eastern Rwanda and Burundi and in the mountains of the western rift.

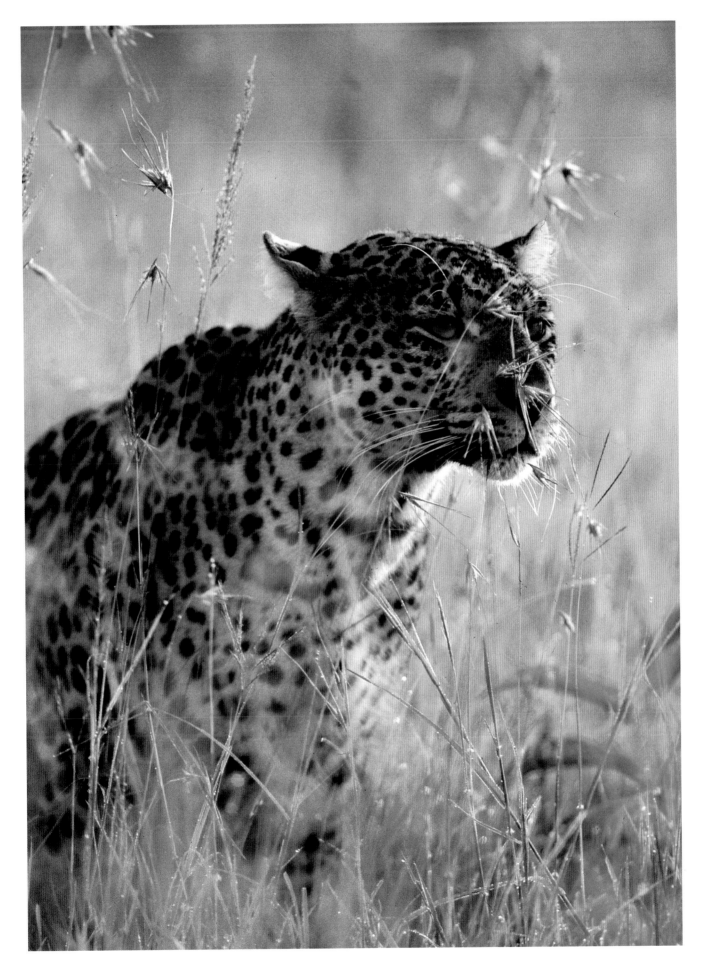

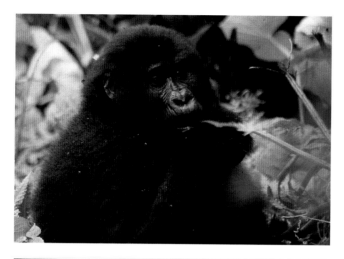

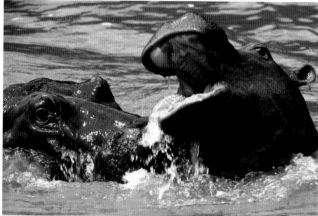

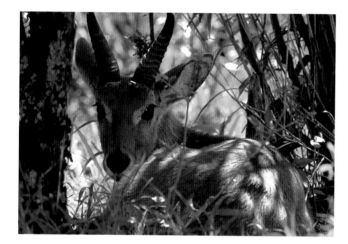

Top: The mountain gorilla, seen here in Uganda's Bwindi National Park, is also found on the forested slopes of the Virunga range farther south.

Above, Centre: Uganda's lakes Edward and George are home to thriving populations of hippos.

Above: Kirk's dik-dik, which obtains all its moisture requirements from the shoots, berries and fruit on which it browses, lives on the arid uplands of Uganda's extreme north-east.

Right: A male lion cub watches as an elephant slowly rises to its feet. Both species are found in Uganda's Kabalega NP, north of Lake Victoria.

Uganda

Bounded by Rwanda and Tanzania to the south, Zaïre to the west, Sudan to the north and Kenya to the east, Uganda (like many countries of central Africa) consists mainly of plateau land lying between 3,500 and 4,500ft (1,070 and 1,370m) above sea level. In the west are the folded and volcanic ranges and lakes of the western rift, with rainforest and montane forest interspersed with wooded savanna. The country becomes progressively drier from south-west to north-east, where dry savanna is interspersed with semidesert. In the south is the vast expanse of Lake Victoria, source of the Nile.

Lake Mburu National Park, in the south near the Tanzania border, is in open savanna, and is a good place to see many antelope species, zebra, buffalo, leopard and spotted hyena. To the west, close to the Rwanda border, is Mgahinga National Park, with its montane forest on the northern slopes of the Virunga range; it is an important habitat of the mountain gorilla. Close by, to the north, is Bwindi National Park, which also has mountain gorilla, chimpanzee and other primates. Farther north, Queen Elizabeth National Park lies across lakes Edward and George and Kazinga Channel that joins them, and both lakes are home to many hippos. Other attractions are elephant, buffalo, lion, leopard and several antelope species. North again is the Ruwenzori Mountains National Park, with several primates and many species of colourful birds. To the east, south of Fort Portal, is Kibale National Park, the best centre in Africa to see a range of smaller primates: mangabey, several colobus species, bushbabies, potto, red-tailed monkey, and others. Another primate centre is Semliki National Park, along the Semliki river, which forms the border with Zaïre to the south of Lake Albert.

Kabalega National Park sits astride the Victoria Nile, which flows from Lake Victoria to Lake Albert and includes Kabalega Falls (more widely known as Murchison Falls) near the Lake Albert end of the river. The river is home to crocodile and hippo and the park is home to elephant, buffalo, many antelope species, lion and leopard.

Finally, in the extreme north-east, close to the Sudan and Kenya borders, is Kidepo Valley National Park, a plateau area of semidesert and seasonally dry rivers hemmed in by mountains. Its wide range of ungulates includes kudu, oryx, Grant's gazelle, dik-dik and mountain reedbuck. Other residents include cheetah, bat-eared fox, zebra, elephant, ostrich and giraffe.

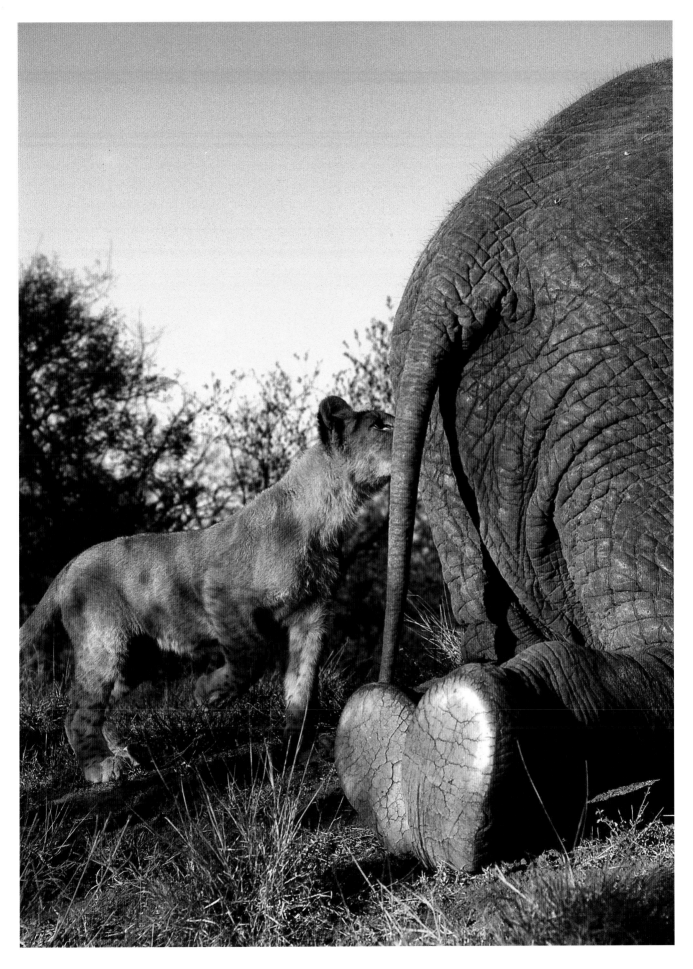

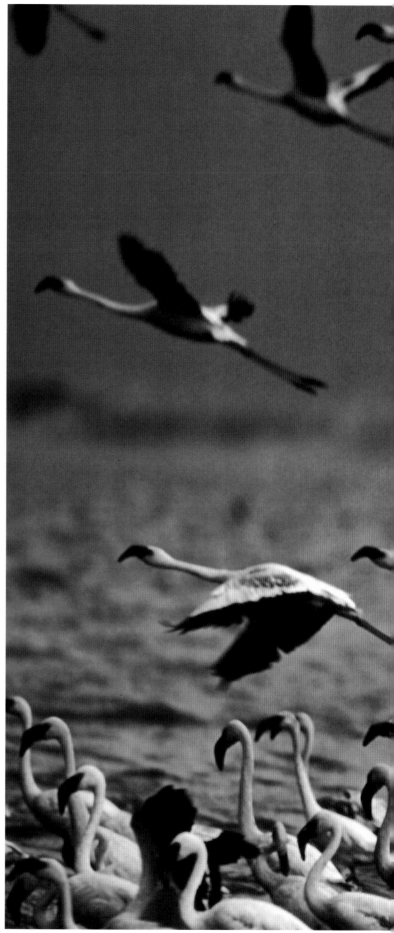

Ethiopia

The Ethiopian highlands are split by the Rift Valley, which follows the north-east to south-west course, first of the Awash river and then of a series of fresh and saltwater lakes that finally culminate in Lake Turkana (also known as Lake Rudolf) on the Kenya border. East of the highlands the rift underlies an arid tableland with many soda lakes. Awash National Park, some 75 miles (120km) south-east of Addis Ababa, follows the Awash river, which has many waterfalls and rapids and runs through lush grassland. The park has zebra, water-buck, gazelle, oryx and many other antelope species, and two species of baboon. Abyata-Shala Lakes National Park is in a deep depression overlooked by steep cliffs. Lake Abyata, a few miles west of Lake Langano, is a fresh-water lake that attracts immense flocks of waterbirds. Lake Shala, to the south-east, is a deep salt lake with teeming colonies of flamingo and pelican. Lake Turkana receives its water from the Omo river, which has two national parks along its banks; Mago National Park has many antelope species, elephant, giraffe, buffalo, lion, and leopard, while crocodiles and hippos are found in the river.

In the north of the western arm of the highlands, Simen Mountains National Park (WHS) is home to the northern race of Ethiopian wolf, ibex, serval, and baboon. In the eastern highlands, Balé Mountain National Park includes Mount Batu, which is 14,131ft (4,307m) high, and large tracts of wooded, lake-strewn tableland to its north. Resident wildlife includes the southern race of Ethiopian wolf, mountain nyala, and other antelope species, as well as leopard and caracal.

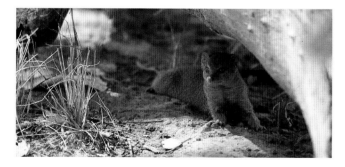

Above: The slender, or black-tipped, mongoose, seen here taking shelter from the midday sun, occurs in most of sub-Sahara Africa from rainforests to semi-deserts.

Right: Lesser flamingos taking off from the salty waters of Lake Shala in the Ethiopian rift.

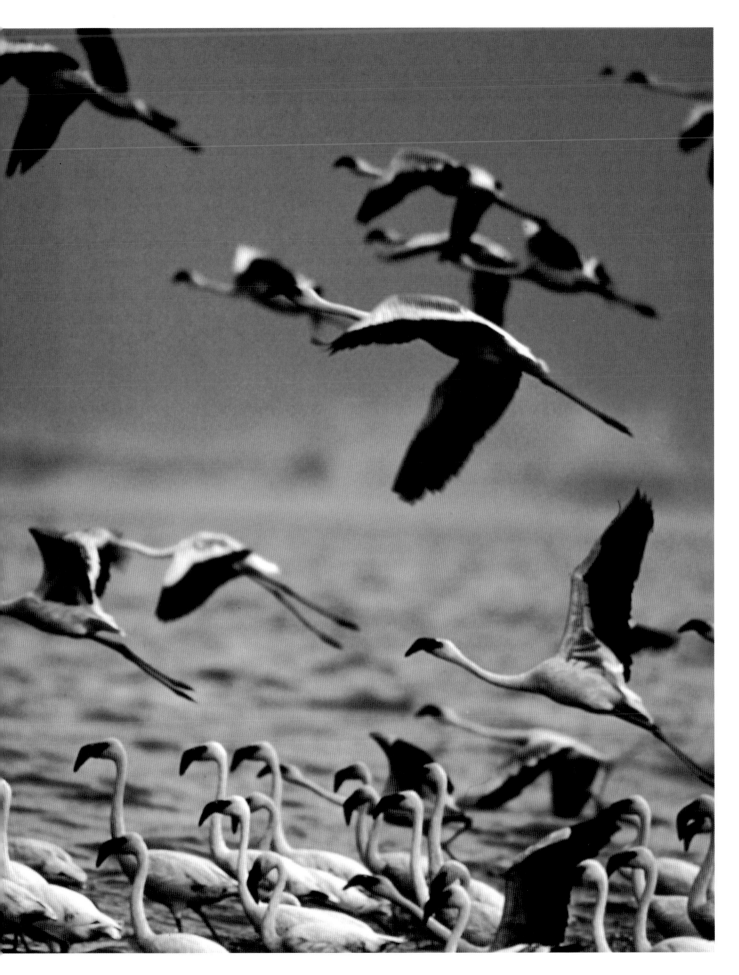

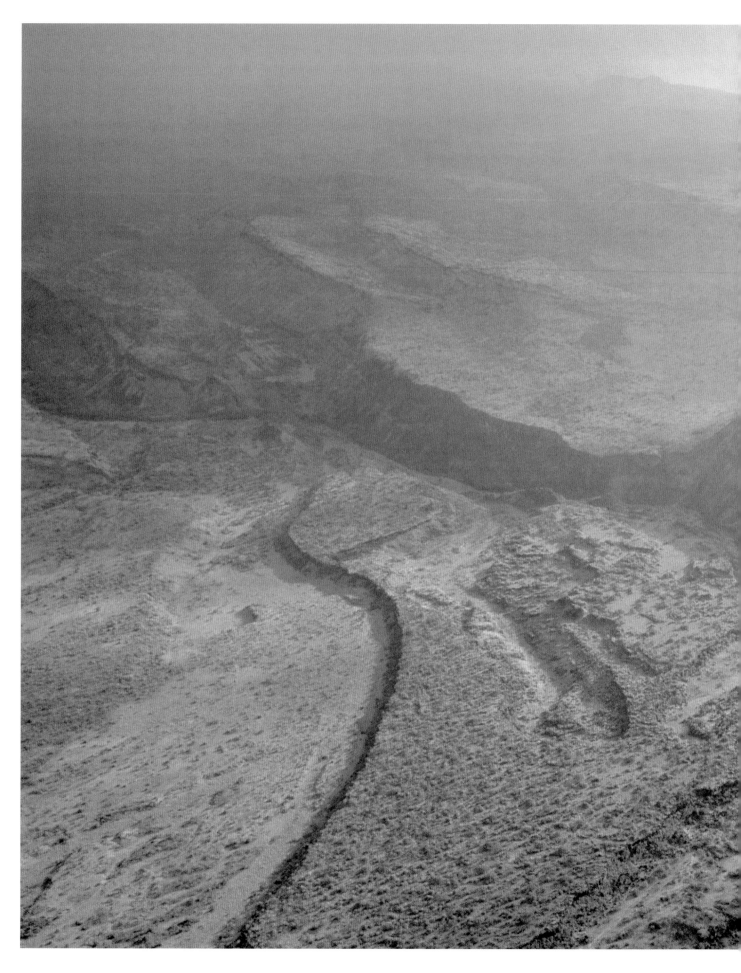

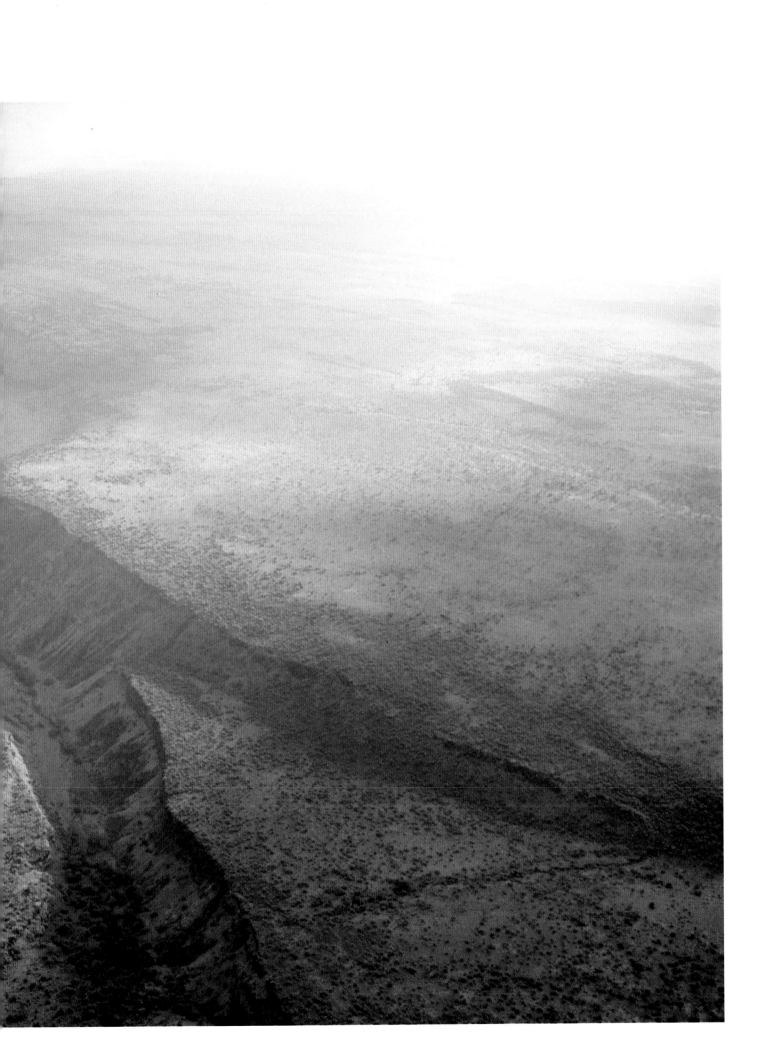

125

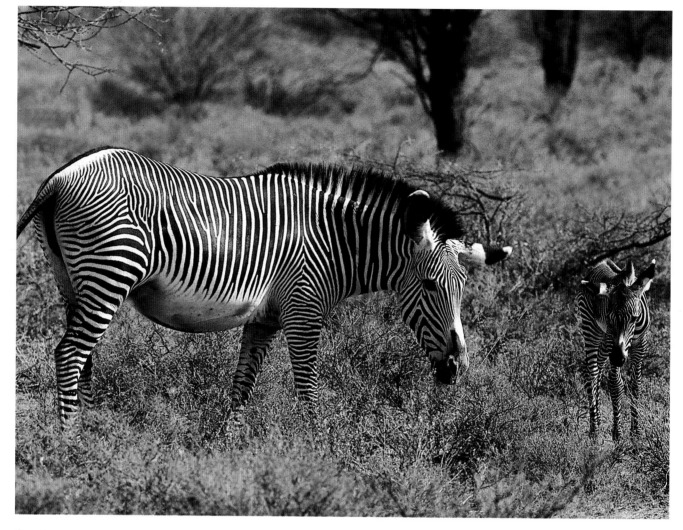

Somalia

War and civil strife in recent years have disrupted life in most parts of the country and the status of the national nature reserves has been problematical. Two of the most attractive reserves are situated along the Scebeli river, which rises in the eastern highlands of Ethiopia close to Balé Mountains National Park, whence (as the Shibeli) it flows south-eastwards to the Somali border. The small Balcad Nature Reserve along the river a few miles north of the Somali capital, Mogadishu, covers an area of grassland and riverine forest and is frequented by several hundred species of birds. Some 100 miles (160km) farther upstream in a marshy section of the river is Alifuuto Nature Reserve, which may still support its old-established populations of elephant, buffalo, many antelope species, ostrich and hippo.

Kenya

This country, with 18 national parks and more than 30 national or nature reserves, offer perhaps Africa's richest rewards for the wildlife tourist. In northern Kenya, to the north and east of Mount Kenya, a semi-desert region of scrubland, dry grassland savanna and occasional open woodland continues all the way to the Ethiopian and Somali borders. Three national reserves are grouped together along the palm-lined, permanently flowing Ewaso Ng'iro river some 50 miles (80km) north of Mount Kenya's snowy peaks: Samburu, Shaba and Buffalo Springs. Wildlife throngs here, especially during dry periods, from the arid regions to north and east. Visitors and permanent residents include oryx, giraffe, zebra, dik-dik, gazelle, elephant, lion, leopard and cheetah; crocodiles sun themselves on sandbars in the river. To the south-east is Meru National Park, sited on the headwaters of the Tana river, which has abundant buffalo, elephant, gazelle, zebra, oryx, giraffe, leopard and hippo.

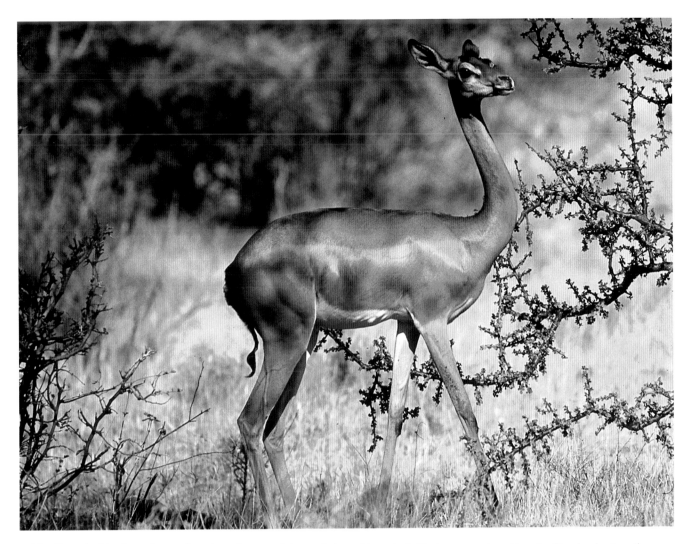

The Kenya highlands to the north and north-west of the capital, Nairobi, have a much higher rainfall and an altogether lusher natural vegetation than the northern plateau lands. Mount Kenya National Park is a conservation area for the higher regions of the mountain. Wildlife in the forest that clothes the mountain up to about 11,000ft (3,350m) includes the tiny suni and other antelopes, several species of monkey and giant forest hog. To the west of Mount Kenya, Lesatima, the highest peak in the beautiful Aberdare Range (which lies on the eastern margin of the eastern rift), soars to 13,104ft (3,994m). It lies within Aberdare National Park, an area of dense forest and moorland. Wildlife includes elephant, black rhino, buffalo, a few lions and several antelope species, and a richly colourful avifauna.

The north to south course of the eastern rift, hemmed in on either side by steep cliffs in some sections, is punctuated by a series of lakes, some fresh-water, some alkaline. The most northerly (and by far the largest) is alkaline Lake Turkana (formerly Lake Rudolf) on

Above Left: The largest member of its tribe, Grevy's zebra is easily recognisable by its immaculate narrow stripes (absent from the belly and around the tail) and the ass-like braying of the territorial male. These were photographed near the Somali border in south-eastern Ethiopia.

Above: The gerenuk, seen here in Kenya's Samburu National Reserve, north of the highlands, is purely a browser, feeding on fresh green foliage.

Previous Page: The Kenya section of the eastern rift is marked by numerous ravines, most of them caused originally by movement in the Earth's crust, some of them subsequently enlarged by rivers and/or by rainwater run-off from escarpments on either side.

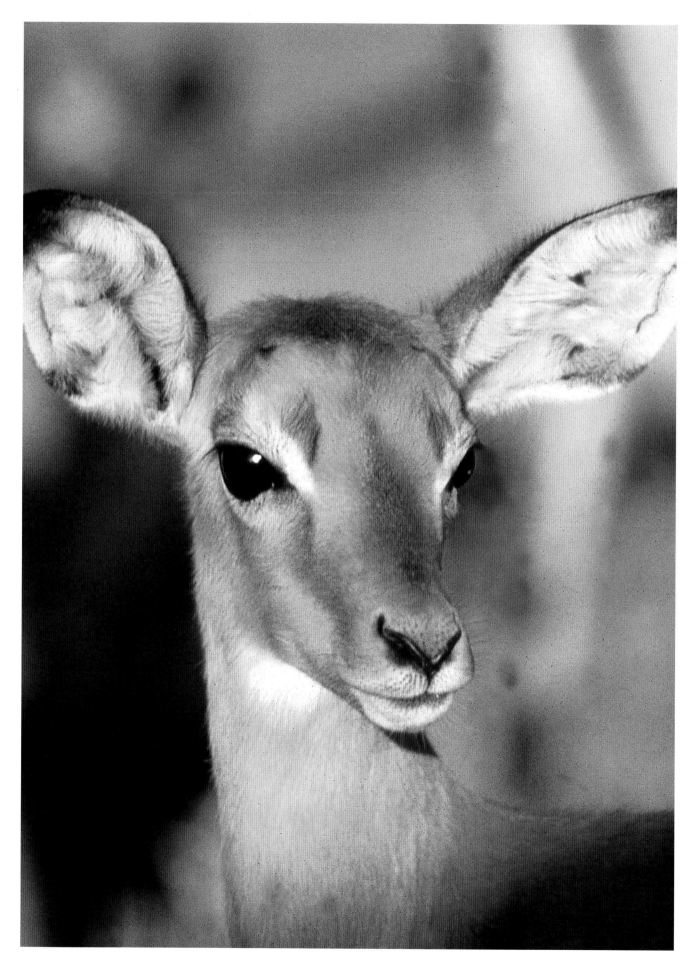

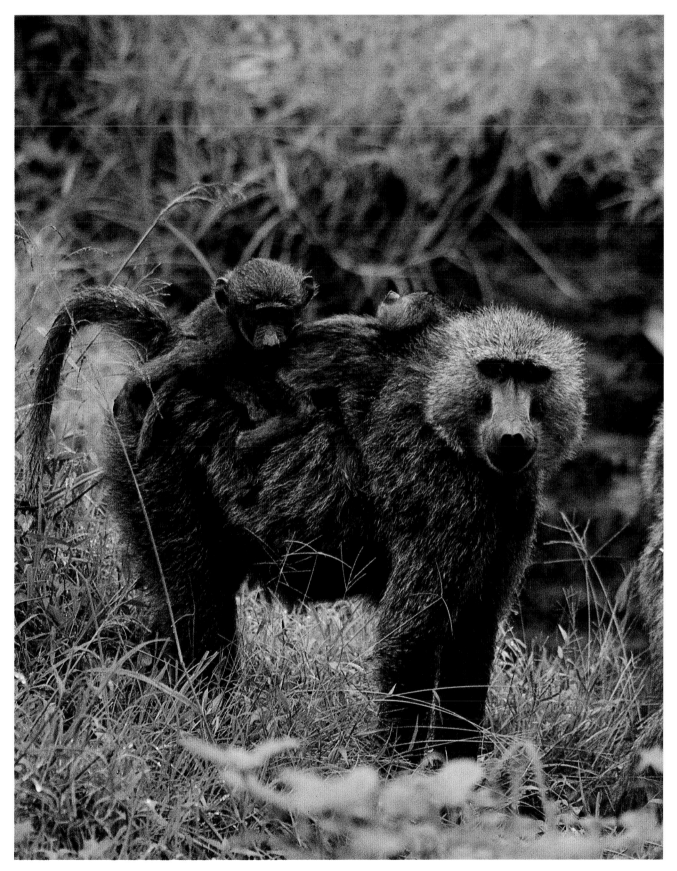

Left: The graceful impala—seen here in Samburu National Reserve—is found from Kenya, through woodland savannas in both arms of the Rift Valley, southward to the northermost fringes of South Africa.

Above: The olive baboon, one of the races of the savanna baboon, is found widely in East Africa from Somalia to northern Tanzania. This group is from Kenya's Lake Nakuru National Park.

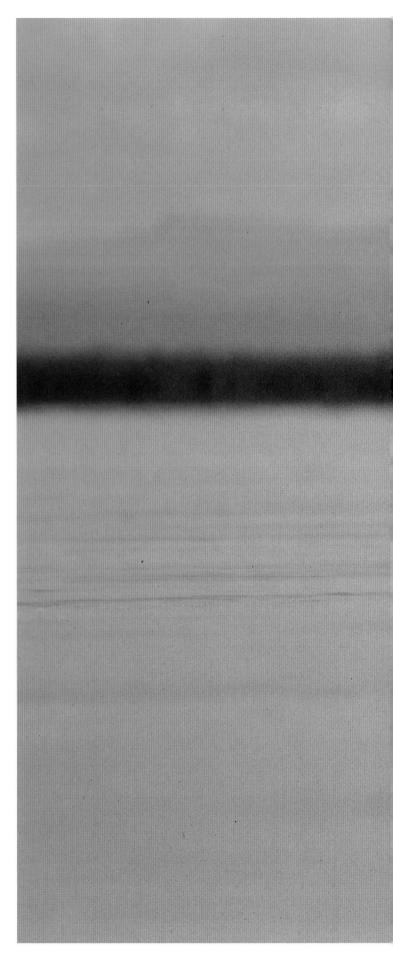

Right: Farther north, beyond the highlands, fresh-water rift Lake Baringo attracts a multitude of birds—though this white pelican has a corner of the lake to itself.

Overleaf: Lake Baringo also has a thriving population of Nile crocodiles, by far the largest and most widespread of the three African species.

the Somali border; then follow lakes Baringo, Bogoria, Nakuru, Elmenteila, Naivasha and, some 25 miles (40km) from the Tanzanian border, Magadi (salty, but sometimes dry). Sibiloi National Park (formerly East Rudolf National Park) lies along the eastern shore of Lake Turkana. The main wildlife interest in this bleak and arid region are the immense numbers of crocodiles that breed on Central Island in the lake opposite the park. Lake Bogoria National Reserve is notable for its noisily eruptive hot springs and for the flamingos that trawl its shallows. Fresh-water Lake Baringo, a few miles to the north, attracts countless thousands of native and exotic birds. Lake Nakuru National Park, lies south of the town of Nakuru and between the lofty Aberdare Range to the east and the Mau Escarpment to the west. It is a sanctuary for black and white rhino and its other residents include many species of antelope, giraffe, hippo and leopard; but it is famed primarily for the countless thousands of birds—flamingo, pelican, heron, ibis, cormorant, stork and others—that cram the salty shallows. Fresh-water Lake Naivasha, about 45 miles (73km) north-east of Nairobi, has hippo, many birds including fish-eagle, and colobus monkey in woods that come to the water's edge.

Kenya's capital, Nairobi, is about 45 miles (73km) south of Aberdare National Park, and Nairobi National Park, just beyond the southern outskirts of the city, is an area of undulating grassland. The Athi river flows eastwards out of the Ngong Hills and through the park, where its banks are forested. Hippos and crocodiles are in the river, while black rhino, zebra, giraffe, many species of antelope, ostrich, lion and the occasional cheetah and leopard roam the grasslands.

About 90 miles (145km) south-east of Nairobi is Amboseli National Park, which not only has a magnificent array of wildlife but offers stunning views of Mount Kilimanjaro, a few miles away across the Tanzanian border. In this semi-arid region alkaline Lake Amboseli rarely has much if any water, but reliable supplies are available in

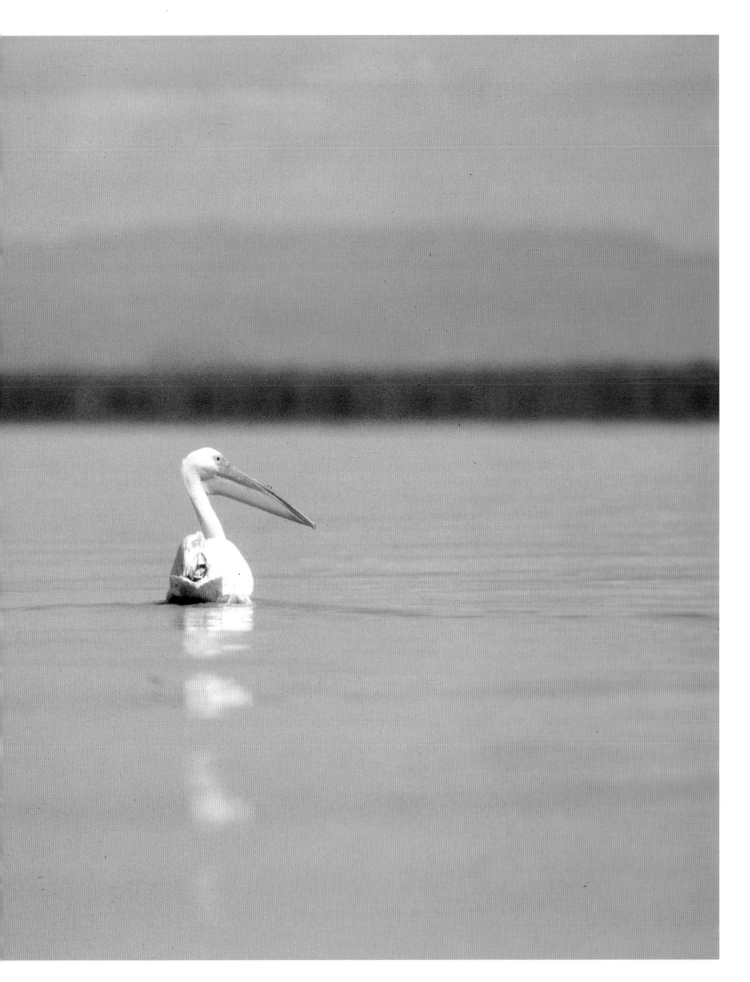

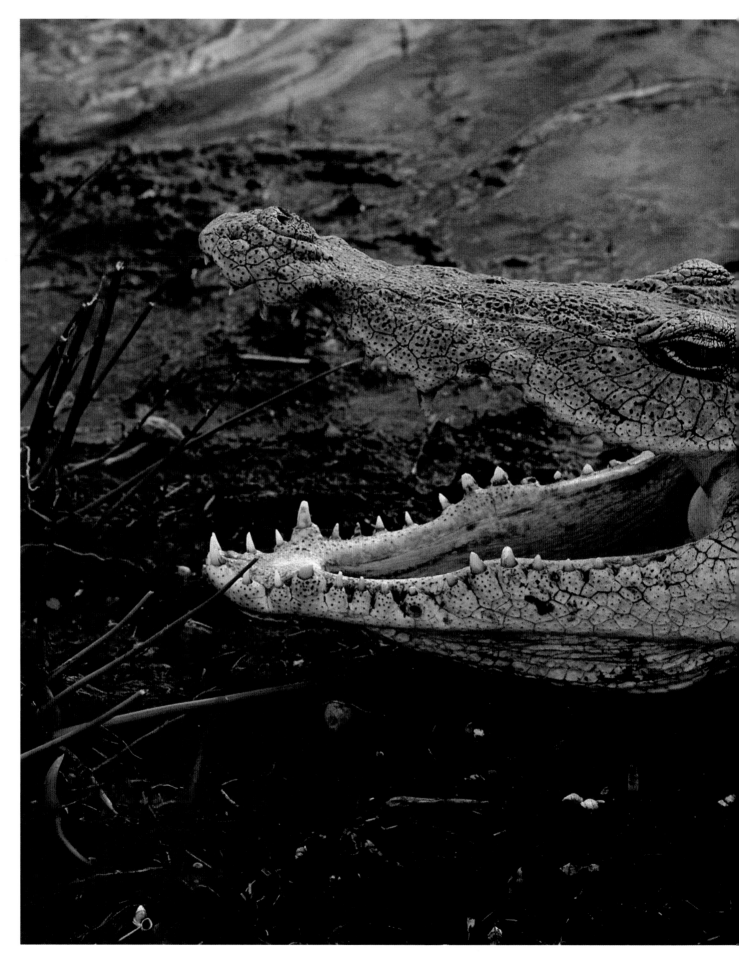

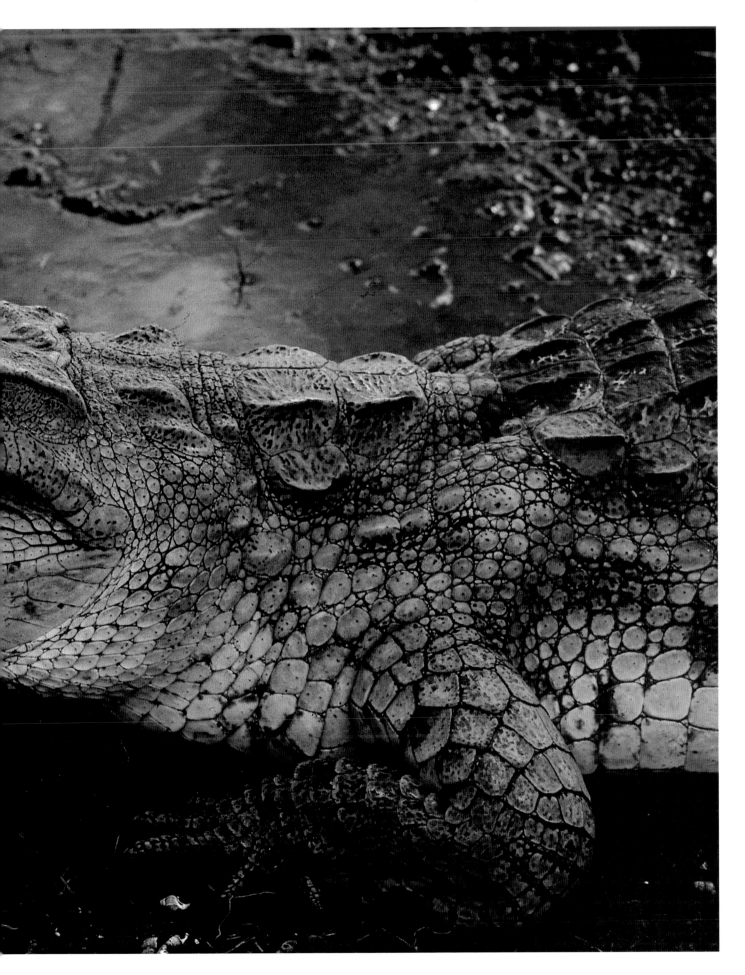

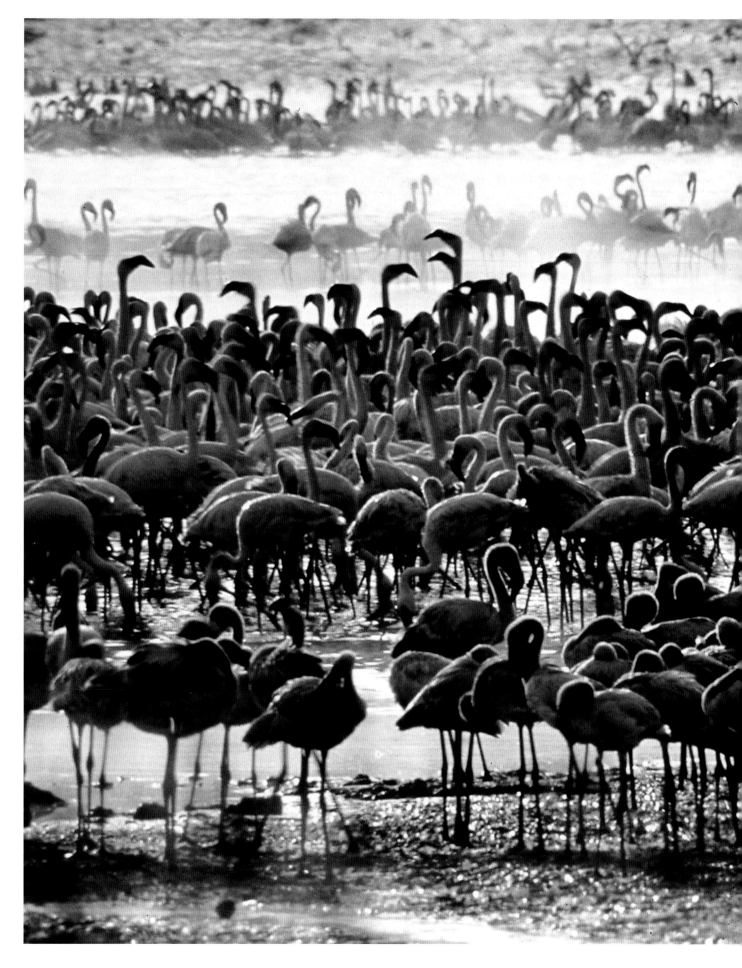

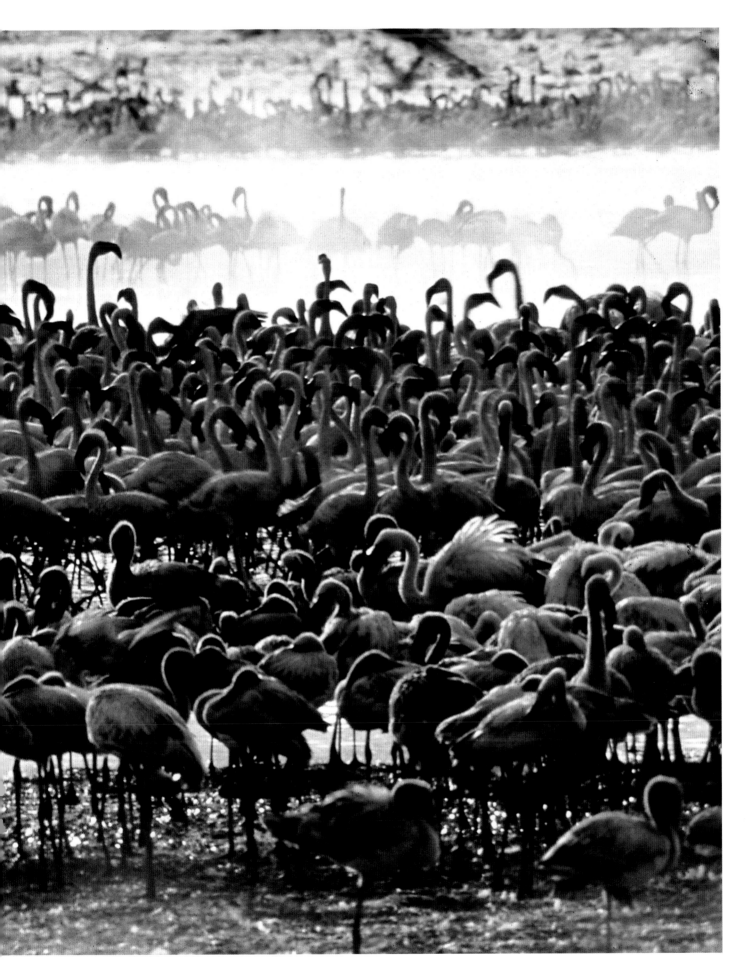

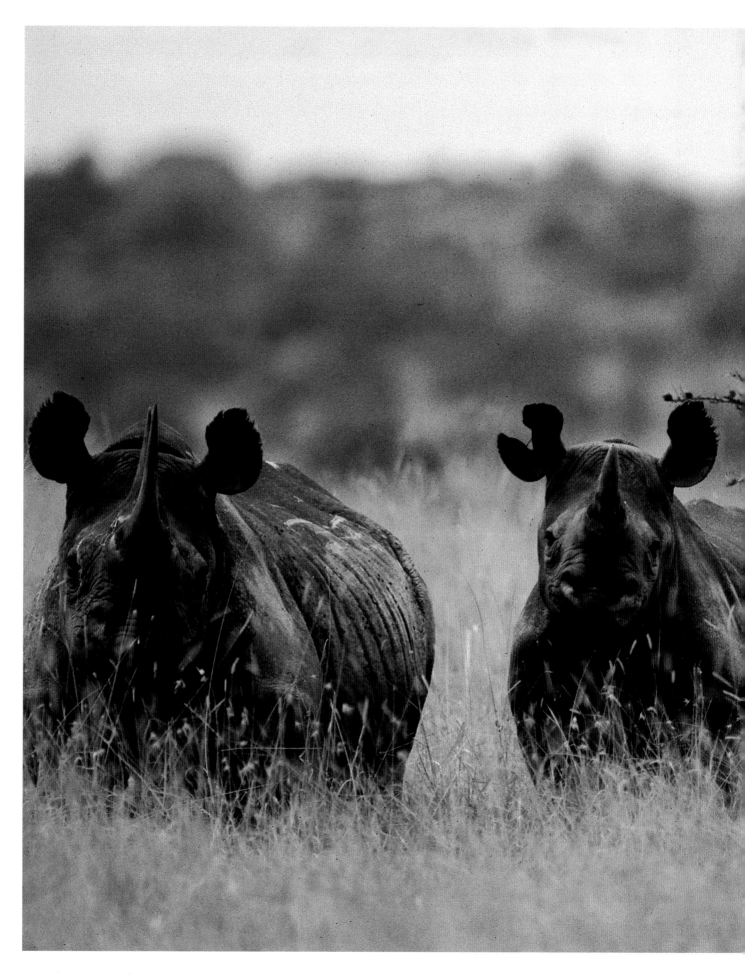

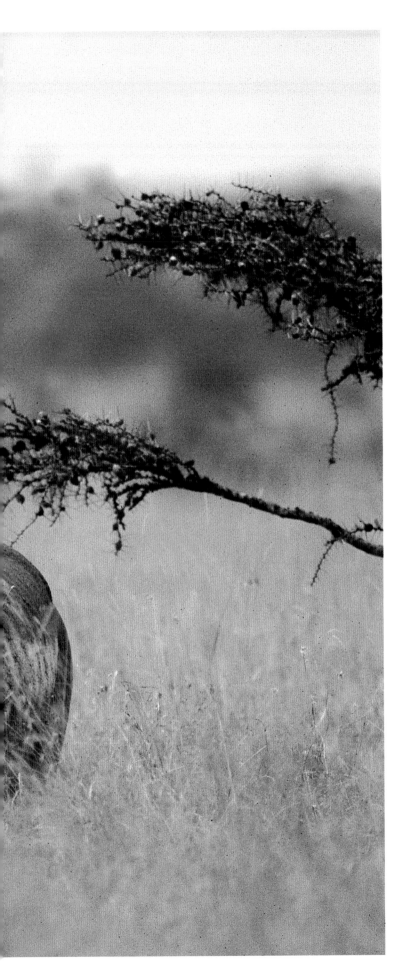

two large swamps fed by underground springs, where the lush vegetation attracts large numbers of elephant (about 700 are more or less permanently resident in the park). Among the many other species of mammal to be seen are lion, leopard, cheetah, buffalo, black rhino, many antelope and gazelle species and hundreds of bird species including ostrich, eagles and vultures.

A further 90 miles (145km) to the south-east, separated by the main highway and railway linking Nairobi and the port of Mombasa, are Tsavo West National Park and Tsavo East National Park. Both parks are watered by the Galena river, which is forested along its banks, offering good browse for elephant; and here and there are spring-fed pools that attract breeding hippo. Many lions have territories within both parks, preying on a number of antelope species as well as giraffe, buffalo and gazelle. Among several reserves on or near the coast are the Tana River Primate Reserve north of Malindi; Arabuko Sokoke Nature Reserve south of Watamu; and Shimba Hills National Reserve, south-west of Mombasa.

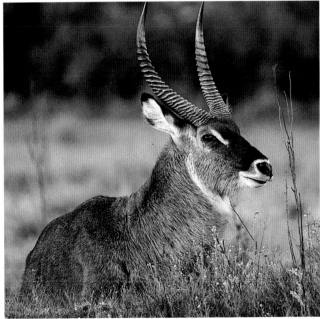

Above: South of Nakuru, fresh-water Lake Naivasha is the large eastern rift lake closest to Kenya's capital Nairobi. This male common waterbuck grazes lush grasses close to the lake.

Left: A black rhino and juvenile graze in Nairobi National Park. A mixture of grassland and riverine forest, the park is only a few miles from the centre of the city.

Previous Page: Greater and lesser flamingos cram the alkaline shallows of Lake Nakuru, one of the finest and most scenic places in Africa to view a remarkable range of water birds.

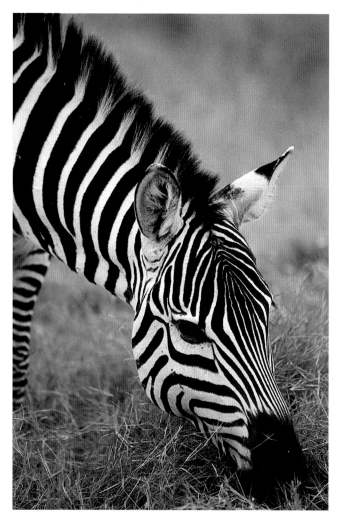

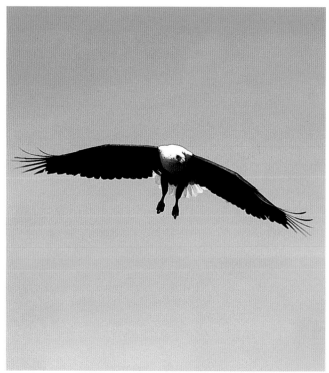

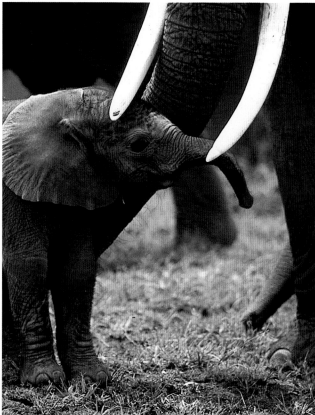

Finally, there are three important national parks to the west of the Rift Valley. In the dry region near the Ugandan border north-west of Kitale is Mount Elgon National Park, which occupies much of the forest and moorland that clothe the south-eastern slopes of the mountain and which supports elephant and other wildlife. Kakamega Forest National Park, north of Kisumu (an important port on Lake Victoria), consists of a remnant of wet tropical jungle that is home to several primates, giant flying squirrel and hundreds of species of birds. The Masai Mara National Reserve is continuous with the even larger Serengeti National Park across the Tanzanian border, the two combining to form an immense region of mainly

Above: A fish-eagle homes in on a target over Lake Amboseli. This eagle will take young flamingoes, ducks, monitor lizards and turtles if fish are unavailable.

Above Left: A plains zebra (also known as common or Burchell's zebra) in Amboseli National Park. This species, of which there are five recognised subspecies, is by far the most numerous and widespread of the three African zebras.

Left: Amboseli National Park has a large resident population of elephants, including this youngster which was one day old when caught on camera.

Right: A small group of elephants gathers at a waterhole near the town of Voi in Tsavo East National Park. Although the grass is eaten out around the waterhole, the park offers good browse for elephants and ungulates, especially along the densely wooded Galena river.

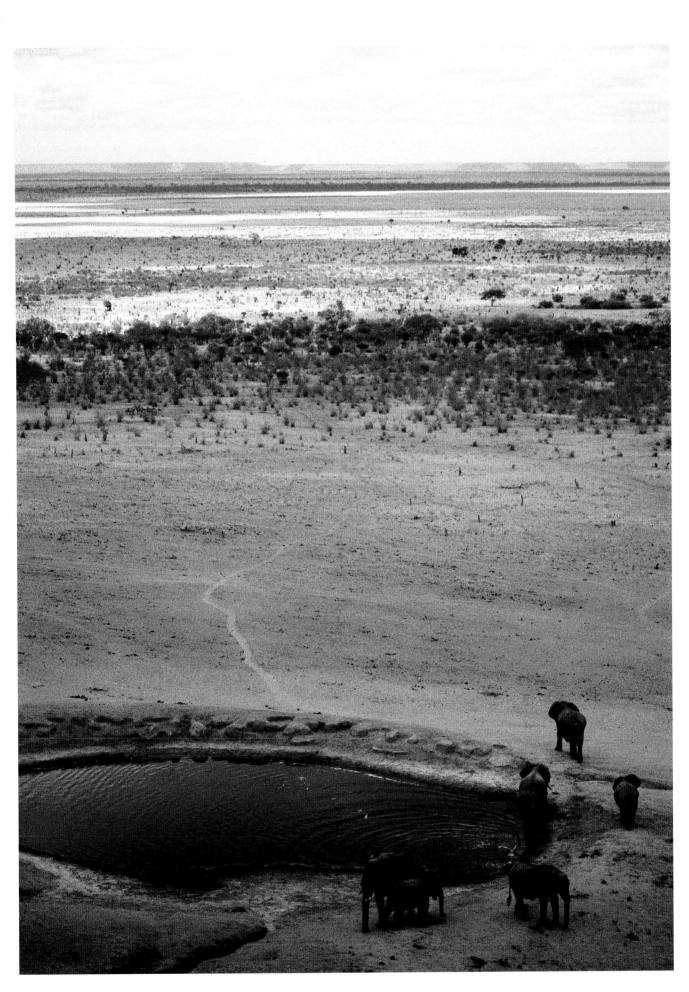

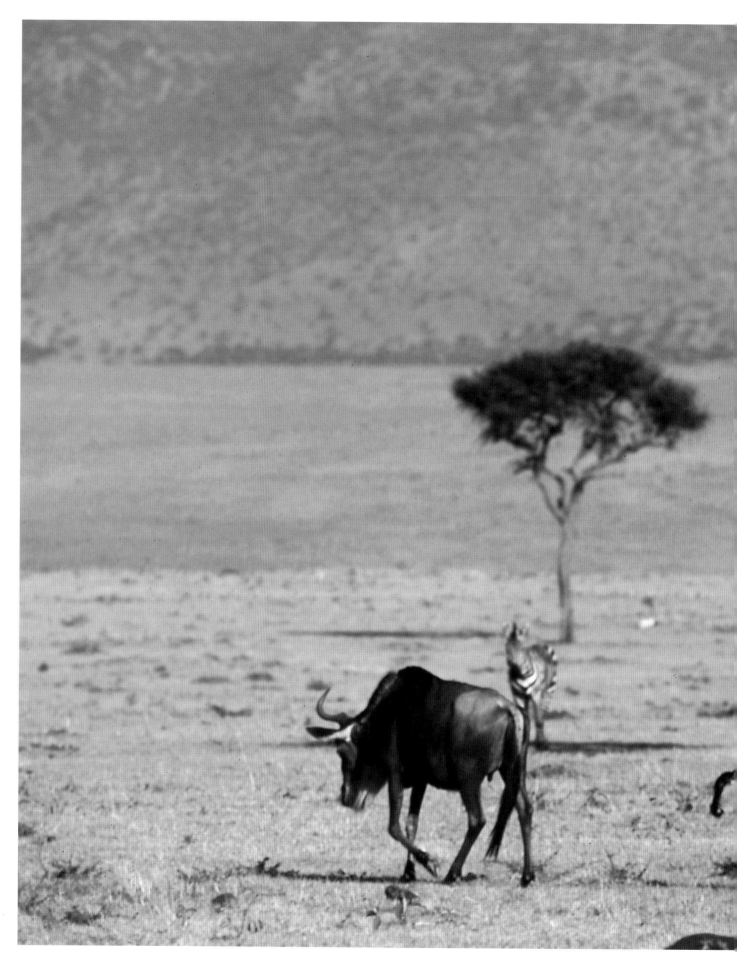

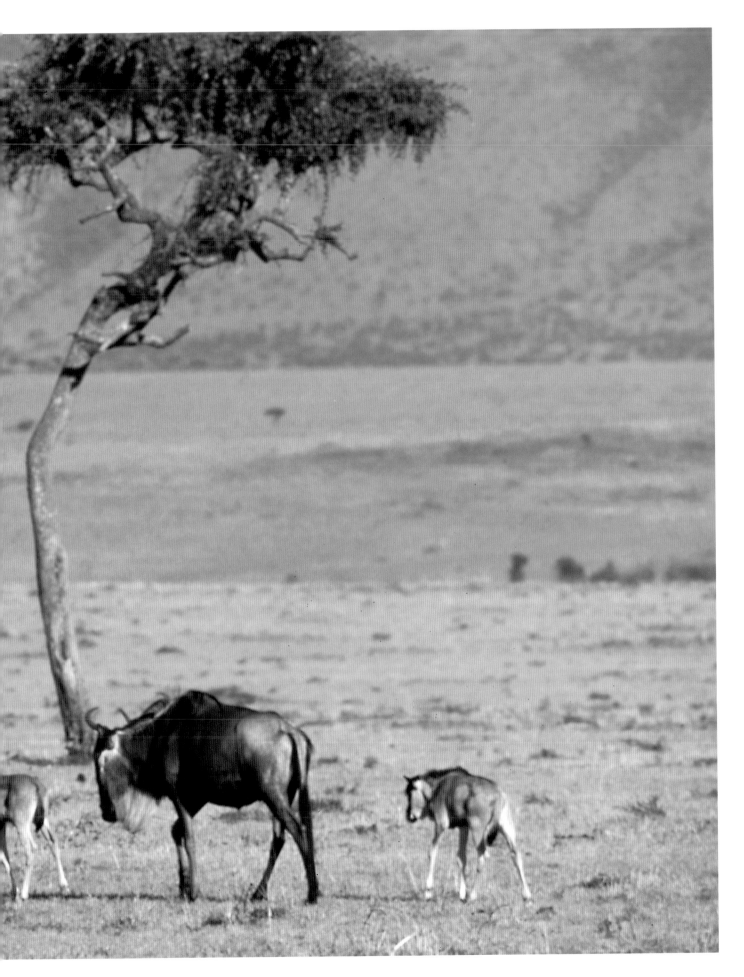

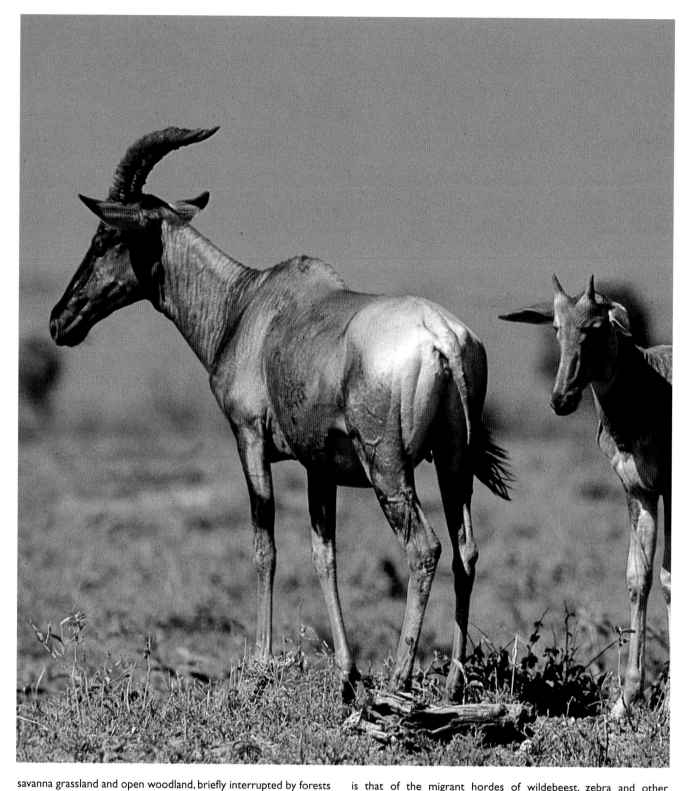

savanna grassland and open woodland, briefly interrupted by forests and marshlands associated with the two main rivers of the region, the Mara and Talek. Because of the openness of the much of the terrain, with stunning views over gently undulating grassy plains towards seemingly limitless horizons, the Mara (as the locals call it) affords the finest opportunities for seeing wildlife in Kenya, and tourists are especially well catered for. The greatest sight, of course, is that of the migrant hordes of wildebeest, zebra and other ungulates on their seasonal journey (July to October in the Mara) in search of grazing. There are predators in plenty—lion, leopard and cheetah—hunting the migrants as well as other species of antelope and gazelle, and there are also elephant and black rhino, as well as hippo in the rivers, and birds of prey among hundreds of other species.

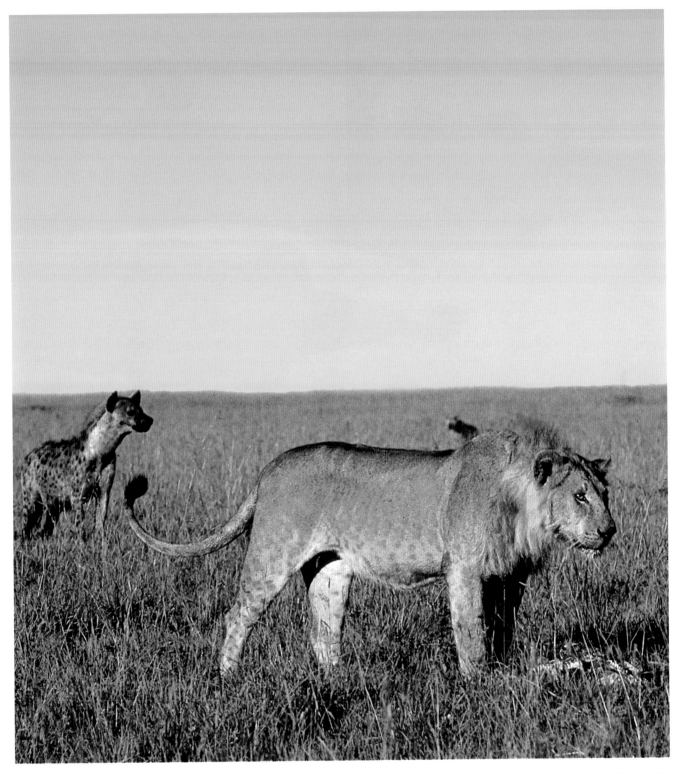

Previous Page: Two wildebeest adults and their calves traverse the eaten-out Masai Mara at the end of the dry season in October. By now hundreds of thousands of ungulates will have grazed the Mara on their migration northwards from the Serengeti plains.

Above Left: A female topi and calf on the Masai Mara. The species is closely related to the wildebeest and hartebeest

Above: A male lion with prey on the Mara, watched by spotted hyenas. A determined hyena clan can usually force a lone lion to abandon its kill.

Overleaf: Hippos half submerged in a river in southern Kenya. Here and in northern Tanzania rivers and specially maintained pools in the reserves offer excellent breeding sites for hippos.

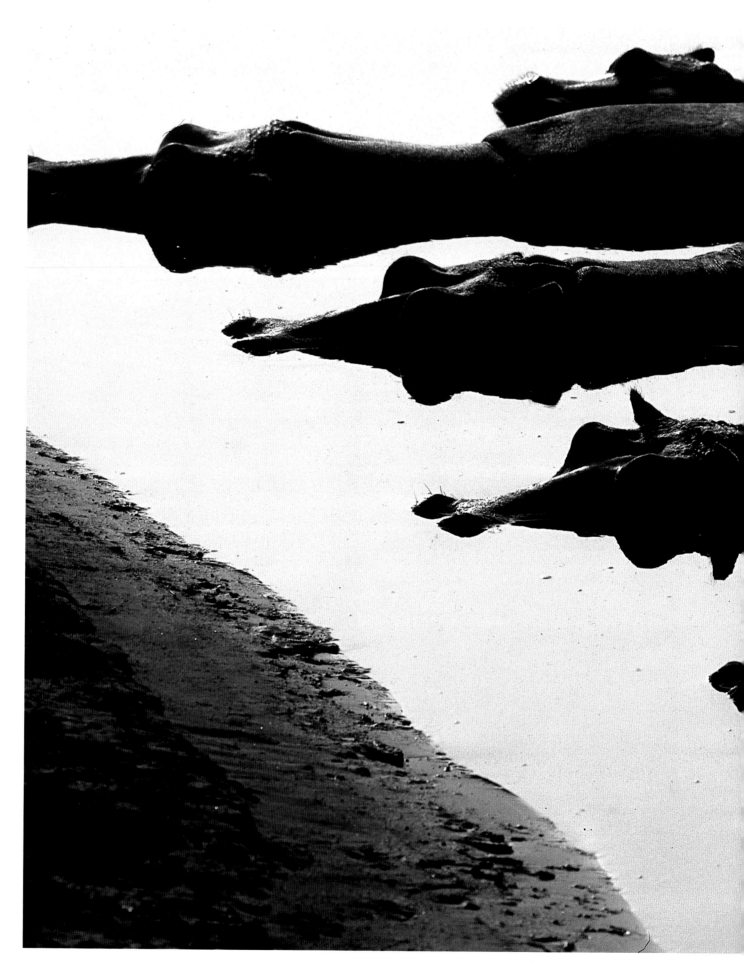

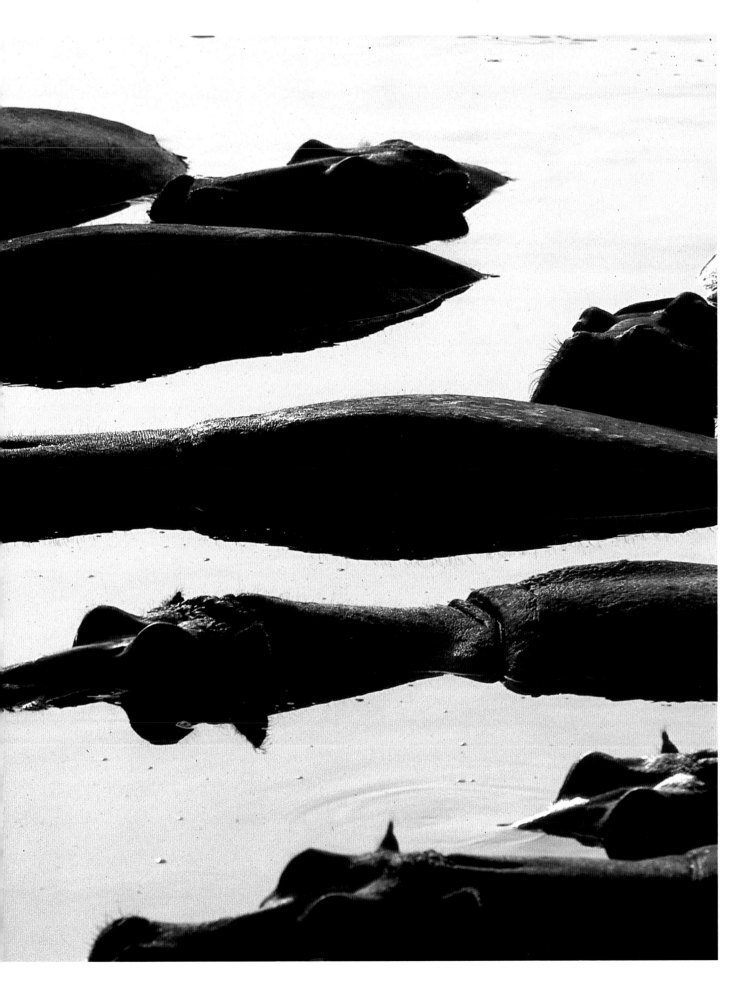

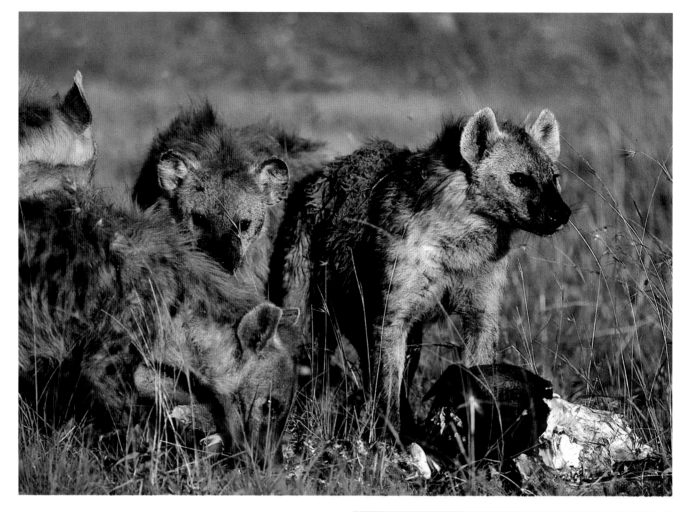

Tanzania

Serengeti National Park (WHS) lies within the immensity of the Serengeti Plains, which are bounded in the west by Lake Victoria, in the south by lakes Eyasi (soda) and Kitangiri, in the east by the Ngorongoro Crater, and in the north by the Masai Mara. It is a region of grassland, the dominant grass species being tall in the west, where here and there it is mixed with open woodland, and short grass in the drier east, where granite kopjes occasionally dot the mostly treeless plain. The courses of many of the rivers—some perennial, some seasonal—are delineated by groves of fever trees that line their banks and enclose their pools. The great migration of millions of herbivores, mostly wildebeest, but including many other species including zebra, begins beyond the Serengeti's south-east margins in the region known as the Masai Steppe, south of Arusha, in May. Over the next four months or so the vast herds move steadily westwards and then north-westwards until they reach the dry-season grazing and year-round water, such as the Mara river, in the northern Serengeti and Kenya's Masai Mara. The Serengeti offers

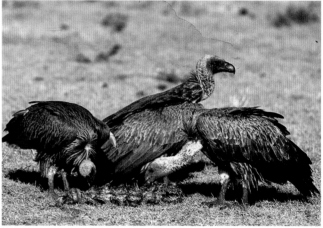

Top: Spotted hyenas are efficient killers as well as scavengers. This group is gorging on the remains of a topi.

Above: White-headed vultures pick over the remains of an abandoned carcass on the Mara. These birds often chase a cheetah away from its kill.

Above Right: A female olive baboon with young in Serengeti National Park. Troops of baboons are often to be seen among herds of migrating ungulates on the open savanna.

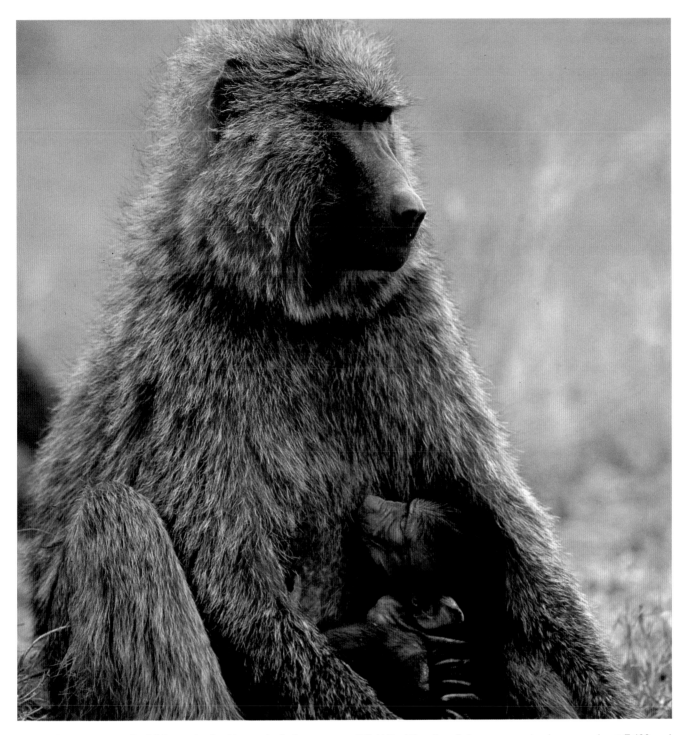

a magnificent pageant of wildlife species: herbivores, including many species of antelope and gazelle, giraffe, topi, buffalo and elephant; carnivores such as lion, leopard, cheetah, spotted hyena and two species of jackal. Hippos live in the permanent rivers and pools; troops of baboon are often seen among the migrating herds; dwarf mongoose and hyrax live on the kopjes.

The gigantic 12 mile (19km) long oval bowl of Ngorongoro Crater, the remains of a volcano whose towering cone collapsed some two million years ago, lies athwart the eastern arm of the Rift Valley. The rim of the crater varies between about 7,400 and 8,000ft (2,255 and 2,440m) above sea level; its floor is more than 2,000ft (610m) below the rim. The Ngorongoro Conservation Area (WHS) includes this and two other large craters and much of the immediately neighbouring countryside. Within the crater the vegetation is surprisingly lush for what is a relatively dry region—a product of a micro-climate that is somewhat cooler and with more, and more evenly spread, rainfall throughout the year than the surrounding area. The vegetation is mainly grassland, but there are

The solitary leopard hunts mainly at night, though this female is out hunting on the Mara in the early evening. Immensely skilled stalkers, leopards are known to approach from downwind so that their prey cannot catch their scent until it is too late.

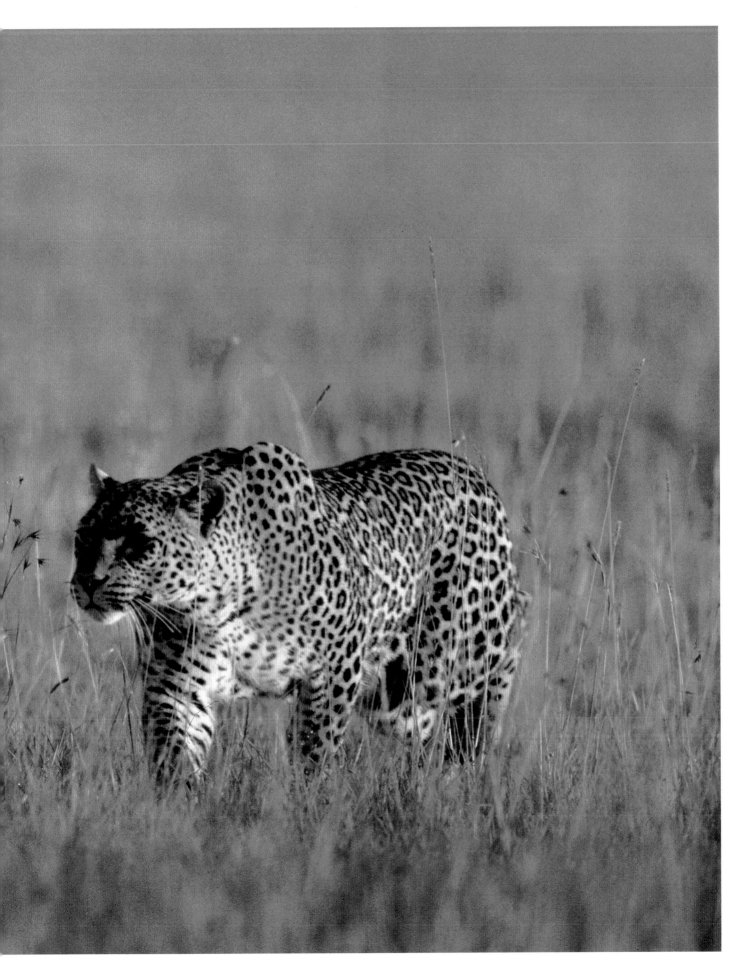

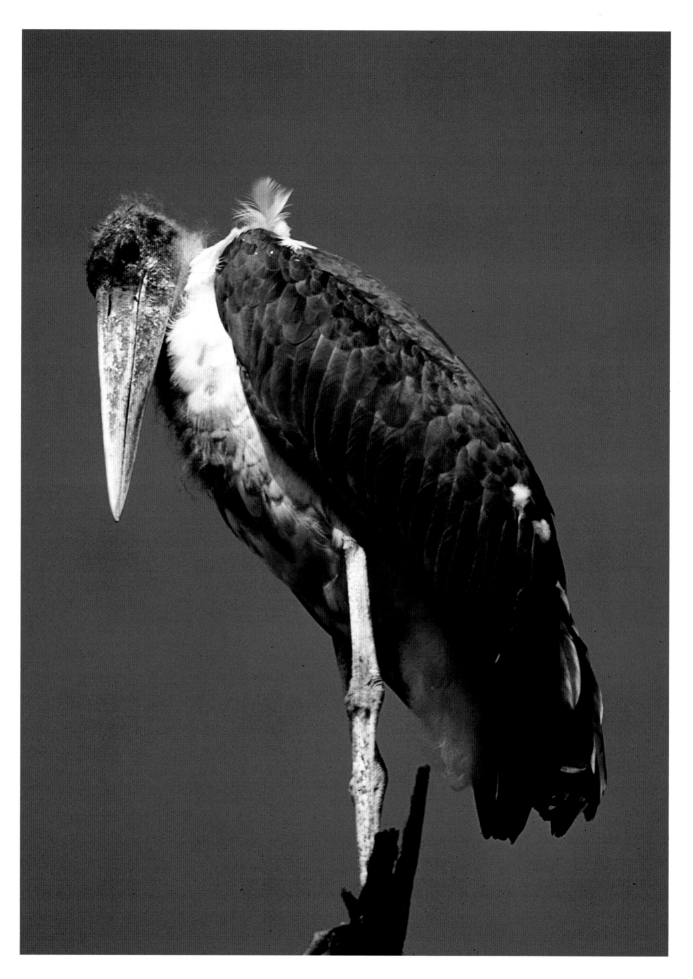

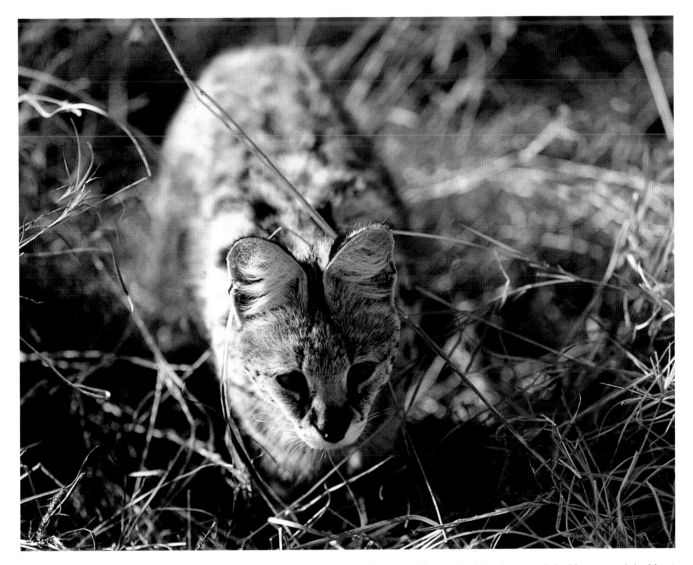

several quite dense woods, extensive marshes, fresh-water ponds and a soda lake. Wildlife residents include black rhino, zebra, buffalo, several species of antelope and gazelle, lion, cheetah, spotted hyena, jackal and serval. Hippos wallow in the ponds; elephants browse the foliage in the woods.

Some 20 miles (32km) south-east of Ngorongoro Crater the western wall of the eastern rift descends steeply to the northern and western shores of salty Lake Manyara. This area is taken up by Lake Manyara National Park, which consists partly of acacia-dotted open grassland and partly of dense forest fed by underwater springs. Buffalo, many antelope species, zebras, giraffe, leopard and tree-climbing lions roam the grassland, while primates (including baboon), elephant, bushbuck and waterbuck inhabit the forest; the lake (like salty Lake Natron, to the north of Ngorongoro) is often crowded with flamingo, pelican and stork, while hippo live in fresh-water streams and pools around the lake.

Tarangire National Park lies between Lake Manyara and the Masai Steppe. The seasonally reliable water of the Tarangire river attracts the huge herds of herbivores on their migration westwards; permanent residents include elephant, giraffe, oryx and other antelope, lion and leopard.

Arusha, the largest city and chief centre for wildlife touring in north-east Tanzania, lies some 80 miles (130km) east of Ngorongoro. Mount Meru Game Reserve and Arusha National Park are on either side of Mount Meru, some 10 miles (16km) north-east of the city. Lakes on the eastern flank of the mountain attract thirsty

Above: This serval, in scrub on the edge of open woodland on the Mara, is stalking more modest prey such as small rodents.

Left: The huge marabou stork, seen here using a dead tree trunk on the Mara as a lookout post, is a fierce scavenger that may force even the largest vultures to give way at a carcass.

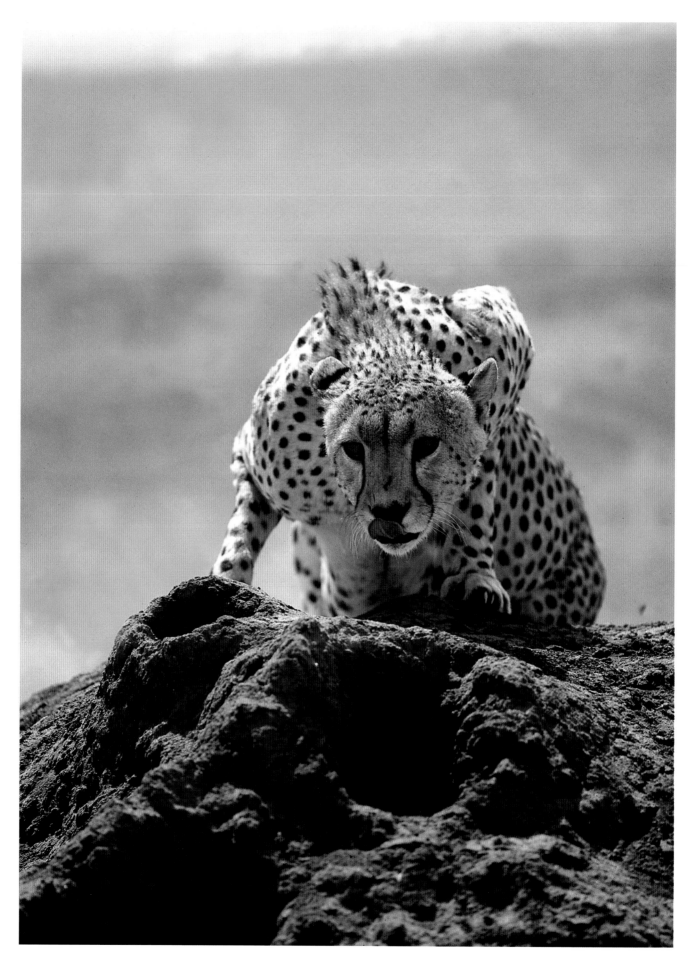

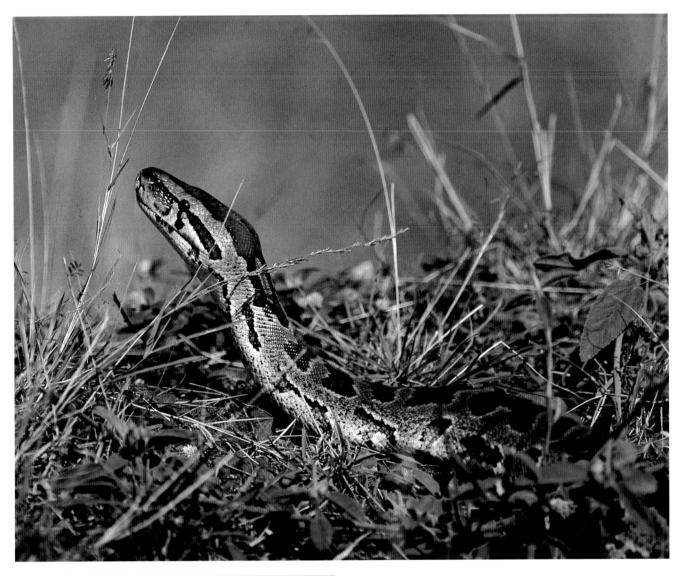

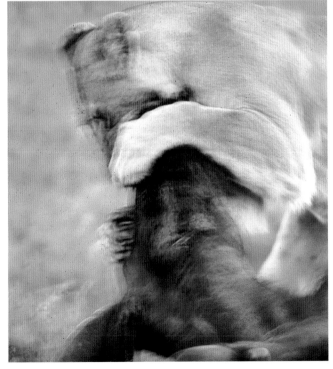

Above: The rock python, Africa's largest snake (seen here on the Mara), preys on gazelles, jackals, monkeys, waterbirds and monitor lizards.

Left: A lioness attacking a sub-adult Cape buffalo on the Serengeti plains. It would normally take more than one lion to kill an adult male buffalo.

Far Left: This cheetah, atop an earth mound, has just sighted potential prey on the Serengeti plains.

Overleaf: Pelicans face into the wind before a thunderstorm breaks over alkaline Lake Manyara, south-east of Ngorongoro Crater.

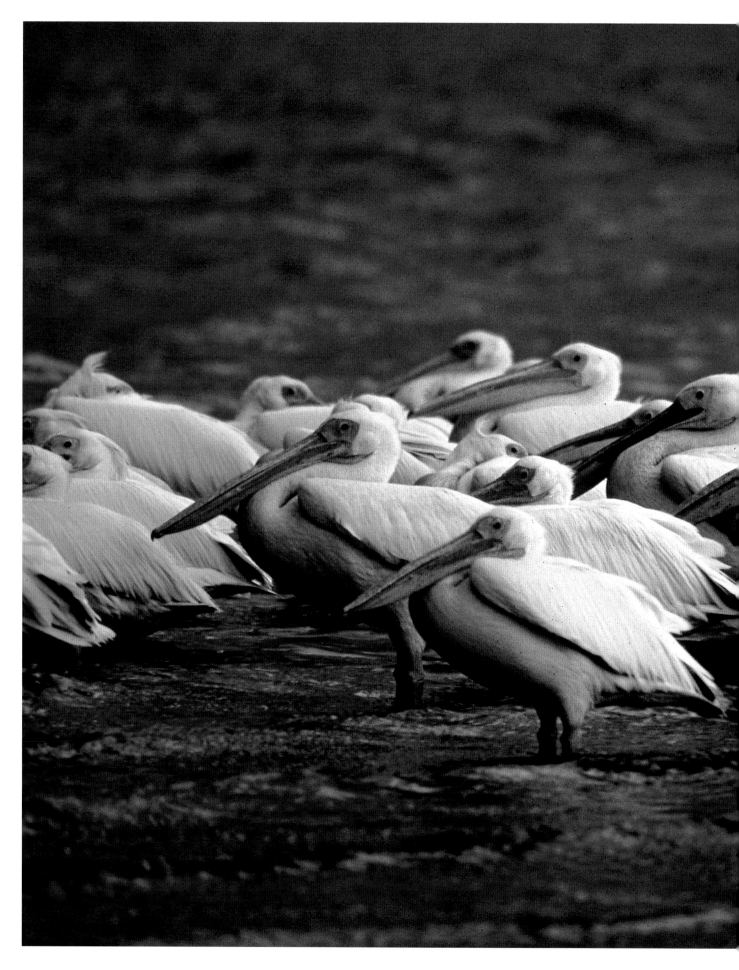

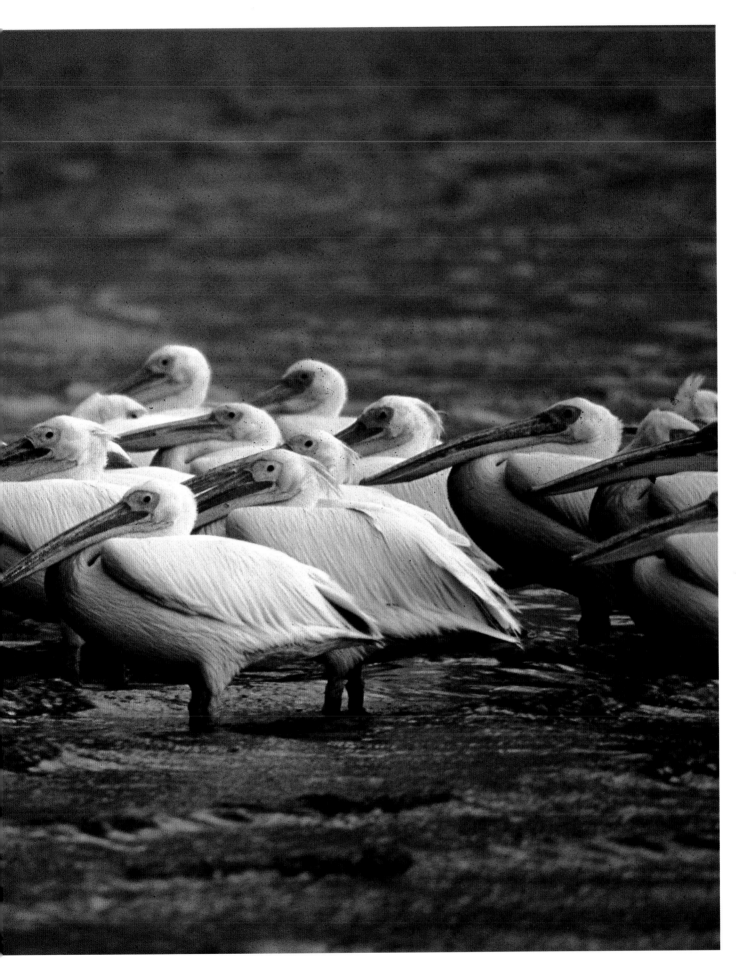

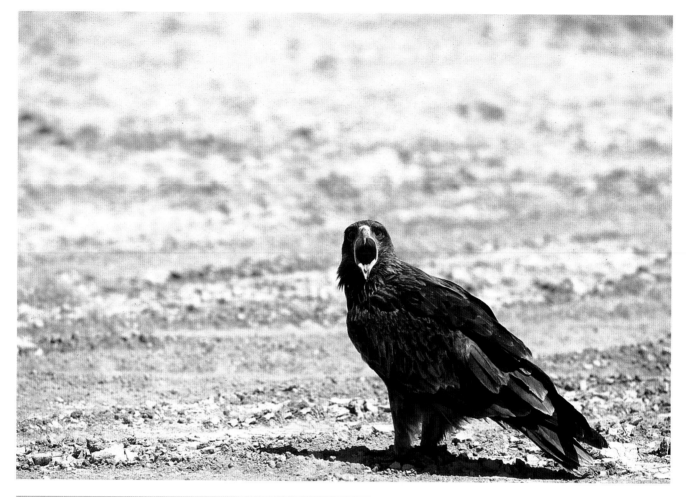

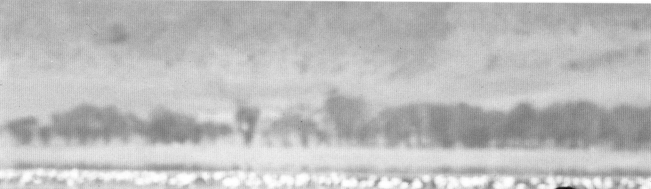

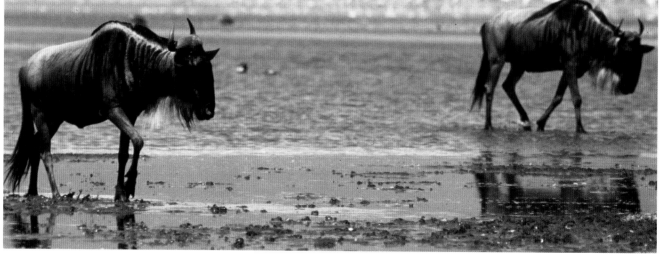

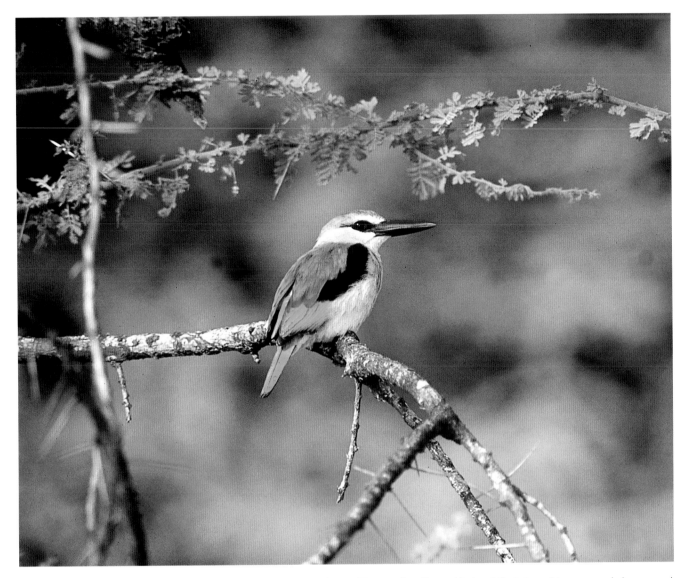

giraffe, waterbuck and bushbuck. A few miles to the east is the crater of extinct Ngurdoto volcano, frequented by buffalo, elephant and many antelopes. Some 30 miles (48km) north-east of Ngurdoto loom the snow-capped peaks of Kilimanjaro near the Kenya border. The higher slopes of the mountain, above about 9,000 feet (2,750m), are now the protected area of Kilimanjaro National Park (WHS). At lower altitudes, in montane forest, there are antelope and the colourfully named white-bellied go-away-bird, a member of the turaco tribe.

The western regions of Tanzania have interesting parks associated with the two great lakes, Victoria and Tanganyika. On Rubondo, the largest of the many islands in the south-west corner of Lake Victoria, Rubondo National Park has colonies of introduced black rhino, elephant and chimpanzee as well as resident hippo. A few miles north of Kigoma, Tanzania's main port on Lake Tanganytika, Gome National Park has chimpanzees, baboons and other primates and an attractive avifauna; while 100 miles (160km) south of the city, the Mihale Mountains National Park has chimpanzees, elephant, giraffe, antelope and lion.

Above: A woodland kingfisher on the lookout for insect prey in lush woodland fringing Lake Manyara. It is absent from this region during the dry months.

Above Left: This tawny eagle is a powerful killer, preying on anything from young gazelles, mongooses and wading birds to snakes, locusts and other flying insects. This one is being subjected to "dive-bombing" by a flock of plovers defending their nestlings in the Ngorongoro Crater.

Left: A pair of wildebeest paddle in the shallows of Lake Makat, Ngorngoro Crater, in the stifling midday heat. In the background wading birds are visible through the haze.

A lioness washes one of her cubs after feeding. One of the best places to see lions in the extreme west of Tanzania is in Mahale Mountains National Park overlooking Lake Tanganyika.

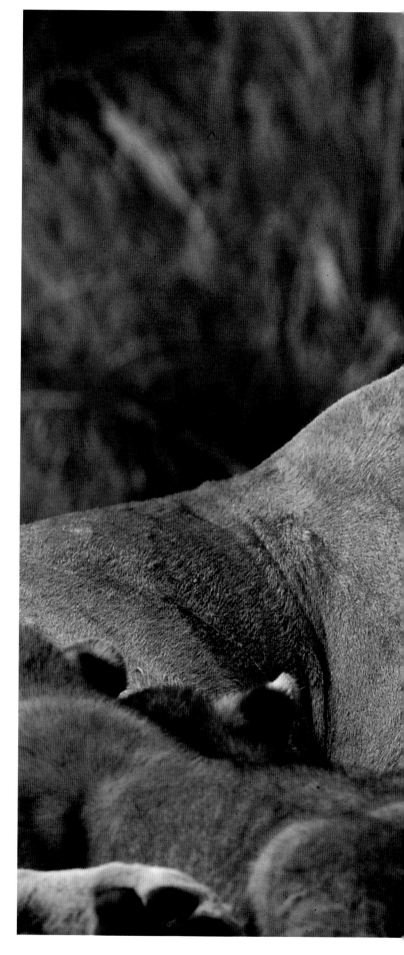

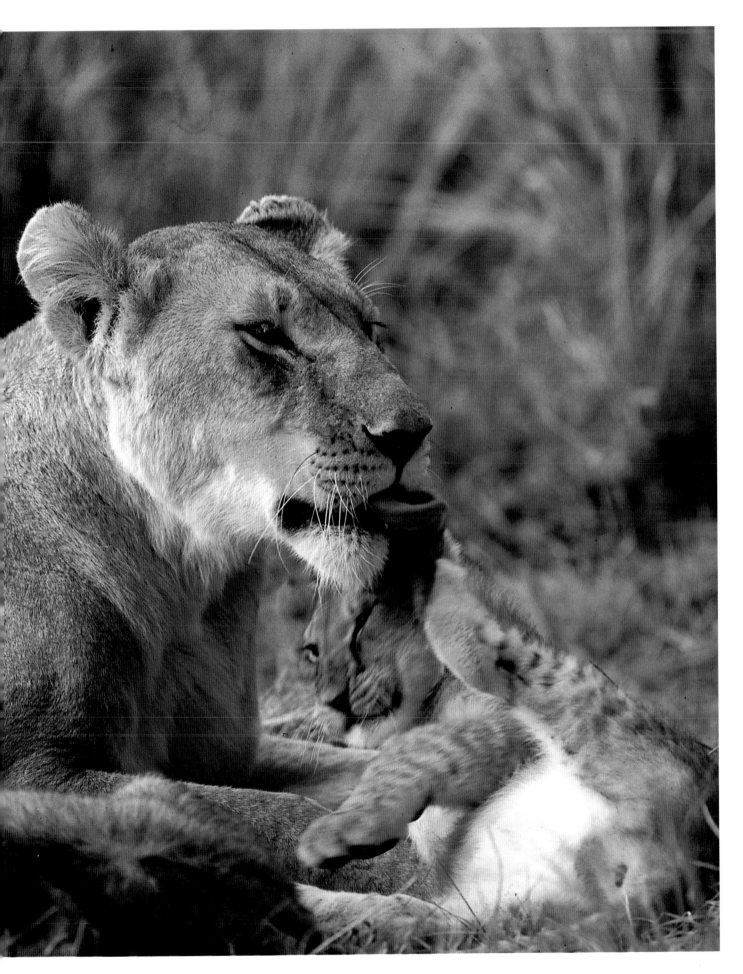

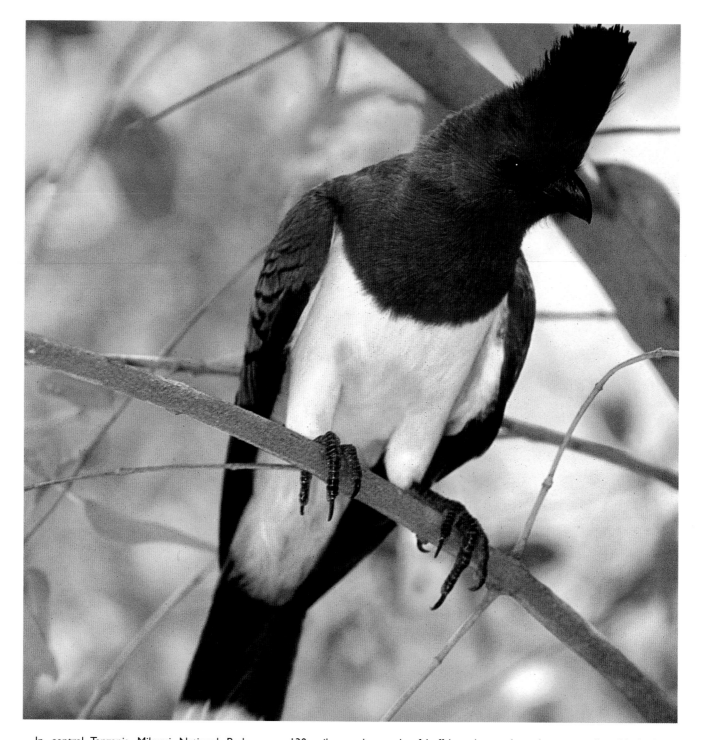

In central Tanzania Mikumi National Park, some 130 miles (210km) south-west of Dar es Salaam, is an area of grassland and open woodland framed by mountains to the north and west. Attractions include elephant, giraffe, zebra, buffalo, many antelope species and carnivores such as lion, leopard and the increasingly rare wild dog. Immediately to the south is Selous Game Reserve (WHS), the largest wildlife sanctuary in Africa, with an area of 19,300 square miles (49,990km²), and one of the finest in which to see the wildlife. Its grasslands and open woodlands are host to thousands of buffalo, zebra, and antelope, as well as black rhino, elephant, wild dog, and lion, while hippo and crocodile inhabit the inland delta created in its north-east corner by the Rufiji and Great Ruaha rivers. Finally, Ruaha National Park, near the city of Iringa in south-central Tanzania, includes the gorges of the Ruaha river as well as high plateau woodlands. The park boasts several thousand elephant, abundant antelope of many different species, buffalo, lion, leopard, cheetah, and some smaller felids.

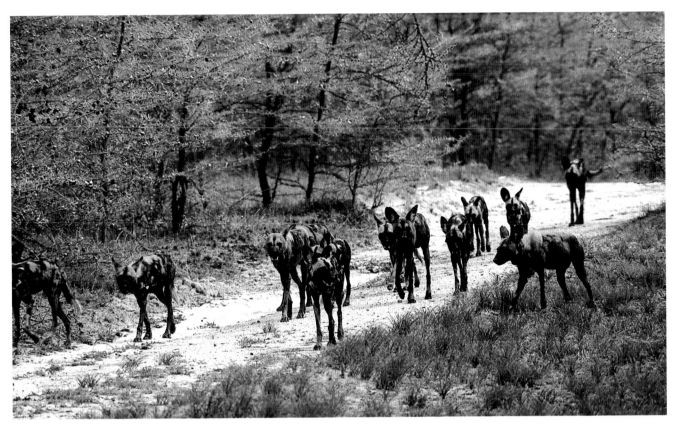

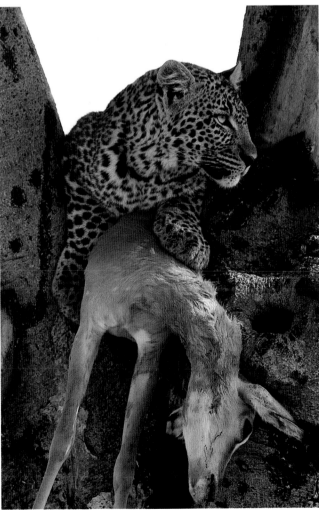

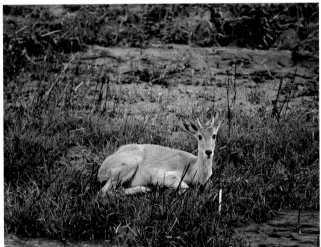

Top: A pack of wild dogs on the trail in Selous Game Reserve, Tanzania. The species has been ruthlessly hunted throughout its once-extensive savanna and semi-desert ranges in sub-Sahara Africa. This reserve is now one of the few locations where safari tourists are likely to get a glimpse of it.

Above: A common reedbuck—one of many antelope species to be seen in Tanzania's Ruaha National Park—near the northern limit of its range.

Above Far Left : The white-bellied go-away-bird, seen here on the lower slopes of Kilimanjaro, eats the fruit and flowers of acacia and other trees.

Left: Ruaha National Park hosts a thriving population of leopards. This one has cached its ungulate kill in the fork of a tree, out of the reach of lions and scavenging hyenas.

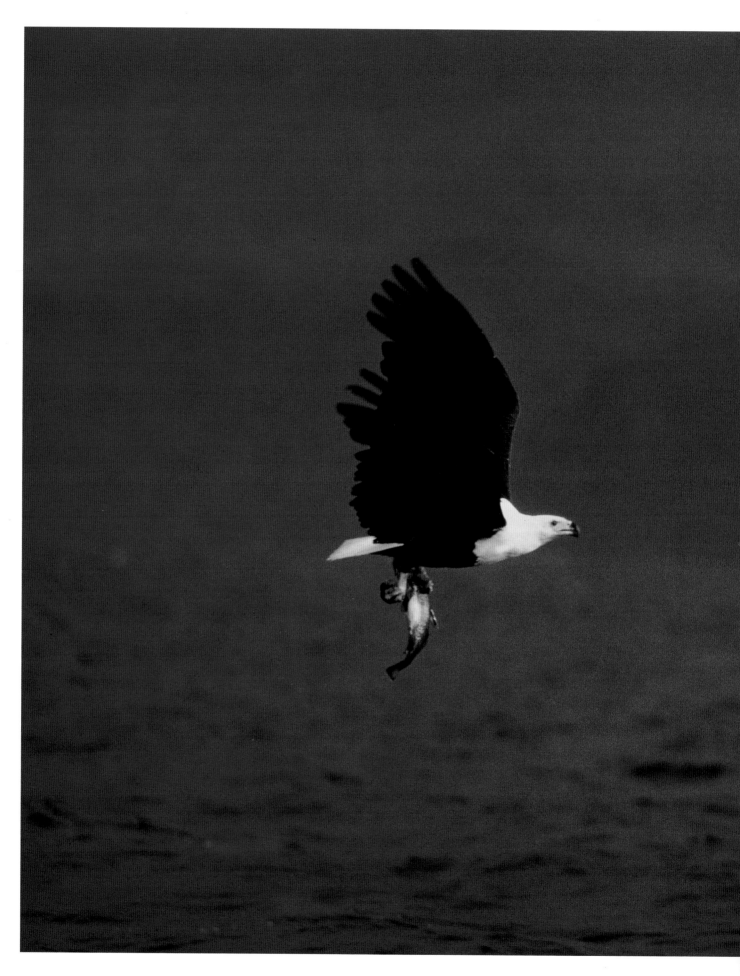

A fish-eagle rises from Lake Malawi with a large fish in its talons.

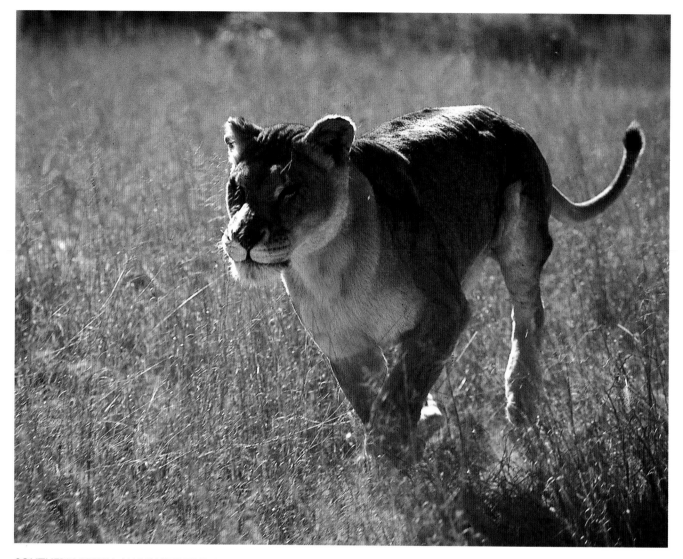

SOUTHERN AFRICA: MALAWI TO THE CAPE OF GOOD HOPE

Malawi

This long, narrow country extends for most of its length along the western shore of Lake Malawi (formerly Lake Nyasa) and lies near the southern end of the Rift Valley. Lake Malawi National Park (WHS), to the east of the capital, Lilongwe, includes the peninsula around Monkey Bay and neighbouring islets towards the southern end of the lake. Wildlife includes hippo and crocodile as well as fish-eagles and other birds of prey. North-west of Lilongwe, in the mixed woodland and grassland of the plateau region along the Zambian border, Kasungu National Park includes elephant, buffalo, black rhino, cheetah and many antelope species. Farther north, on the Nyika Plateau north of Rumphi, Nyika National Park, parts of which lie at more than 8000 feet (2440m) above sea level, consists of open grassy plains hemmed in by mountains and cut through, here and there, by deep, heavily wooded gorges. The spectacular scenery supports herds of eland, many other antelope species, zebra, leopard, side-striped jackal and spotted hyena. In the far south, Liwonde National Park lies along the east bank of the Shire river (which drains water from Lake Malawi and eventually joins the Zambezi). The park's woodland, noted for its baobab trees, is home to elephant, lion, hippo, several antelope, and a rich avifauna. Still farther south, between Blantyre and the Mozambique border, Lengwe National Park is in drier woodland; its wildlife includes blue monkey, many antelope species, lion and leopard.

Above: A lioness in pursuit of prey in Liwonde National Park in the far south of Malawi.

Right: Three adult plains zebras and a colt in the open woodland setting of Malawi's Lengwe National Park.

Overleaf: Bush elephants quenching their thirst in a river in southern Mozambique.

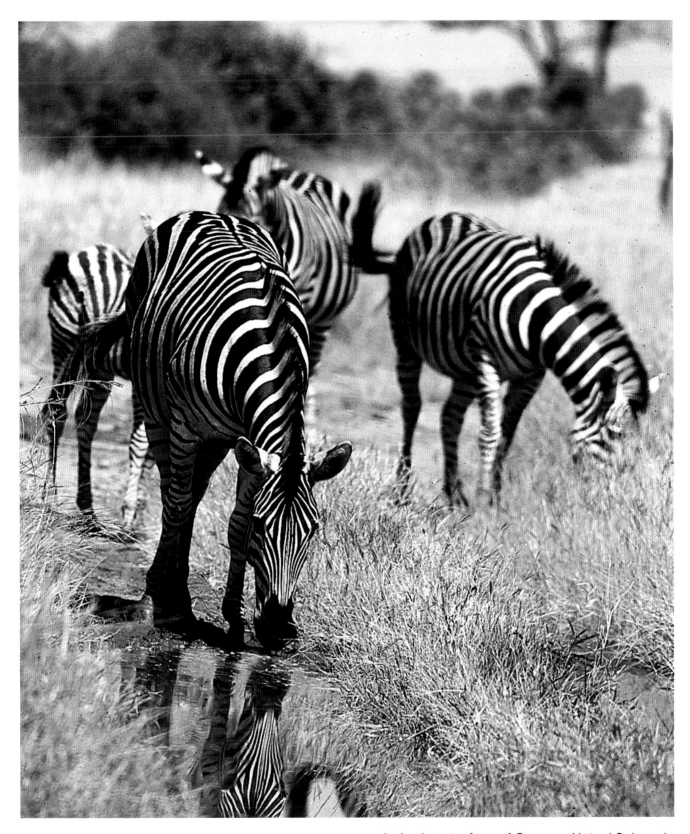

Mozambique

Civil war in the 1980s and 1990s severely disrupted the management and threatened the very existence of wildlife in what had been a number of excellent national parks and reserves, of which the following were among the best. The mixed open woodland, savanna grassland and riverine forest of Gorongoza National Park, northwest of the port of Beira (also known as Sofala), featured hippo, elephant, black rhino, buffalo, many antelope species, leopard and lion. In the extreme south, Maputo Reserve, on the KwaZulu-Natal border, was notable for its large population of elephants.

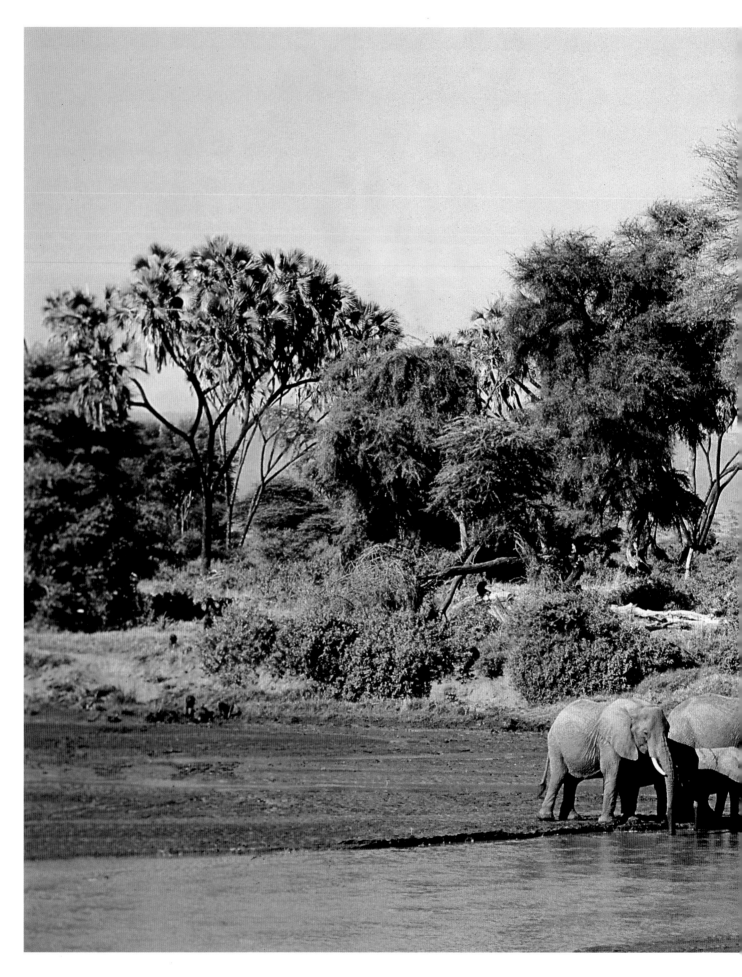

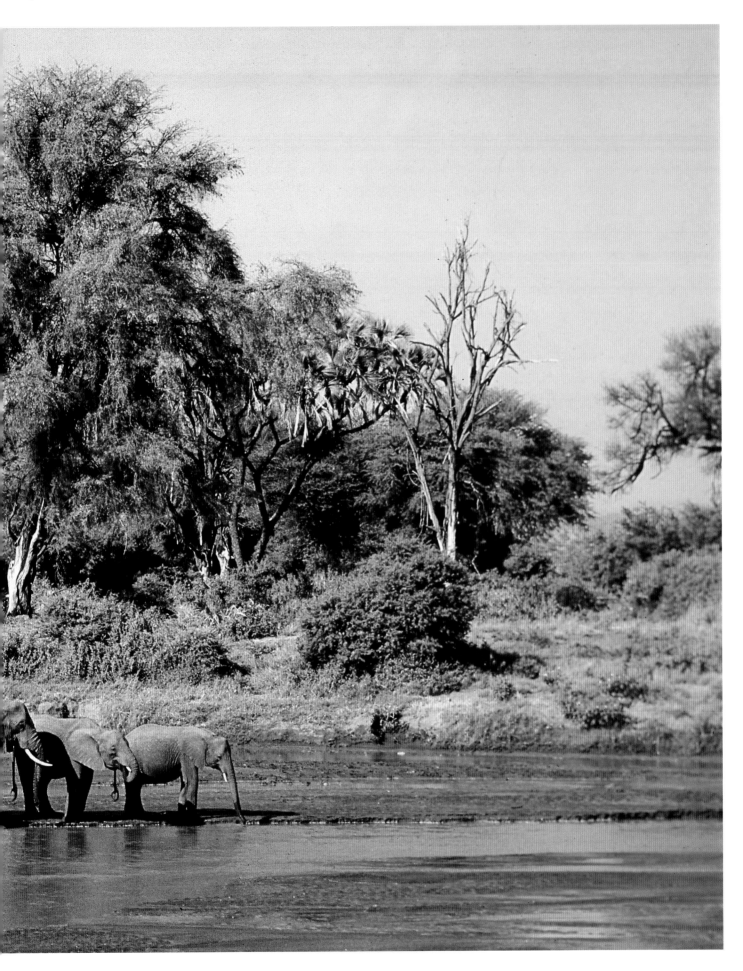

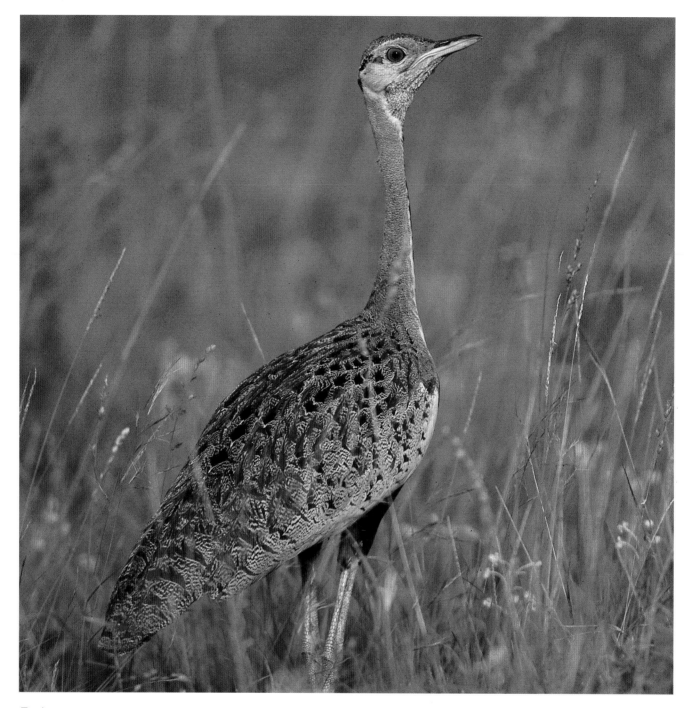

Zambia

There are many fine national parks in Zambia, although some are difficult of access for wildlife tourists. In the far north-east, Sumbu National Park, near the southern end of Lake Tanganyika, consists mostly of grassland and is home to many elephant, buffalo, and many antelope species. Lusenga Plain National Park, lying along the Kalungwishi river east of Lake Mweru, has elephant, antelope and a few leopard. Farther south, Zambia's finest national parks are in the middle reaches of the Luangwa river valley, which meanders south-westward along an arm of the rift valley, eventually joining the Zambezi at Feira on the Zimbabwe border. The North and South Luangwa National Parks, mainly on the western side of the river, consist of wooded savanna, with forest along the river banks; there are floodplains in the rainy season. The abundant resident wildlife includes black rhino, giraffe, elephant, buffalo, many antelope species, zebra, lion, leopard and jackal, with hippo and crocodile in the river.

From the confluence of the Luangwa and Zambezi, the Lower Zambezi National Park follows the north bank of the river west-wards to the Kariba dam. Canoe safaris offer good views of hippo and elephant. Three national parks to the south-west and west of

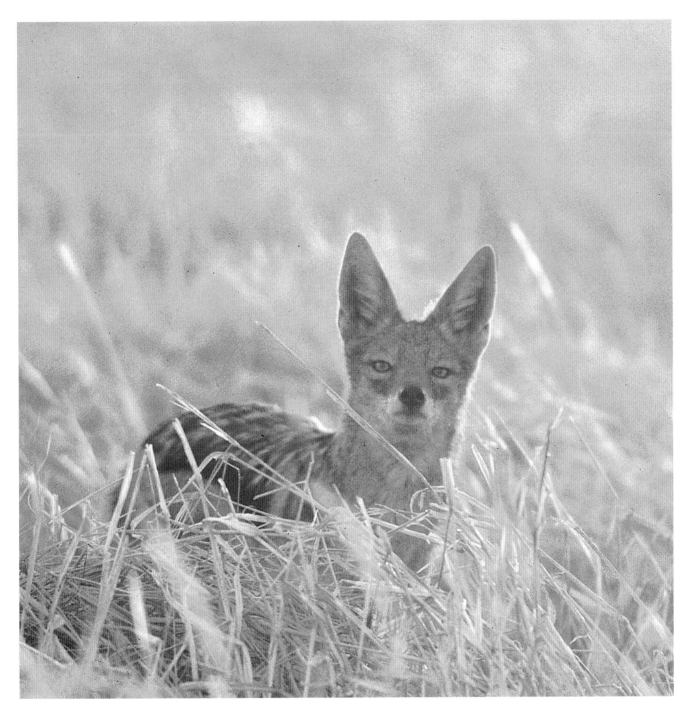

the capital, Lusaka, feature the local subspecies of an antelope, the Kafue lechwe, named after a major tributary of the Zambezi. Kafue National Park, one of the largest in Africa, also has many other antelope species, hippo, elephant, zebra, buffalo, lion and leopard. Lochinvar National Park, on the Kafue river 85 miles (137km) south-west of Lusaka, and nearby Blue Lagoon National Park both have large numbers of various antelope species, zebra and hippo, while the latter also has wild dog. Mosi-Oa-Toenya National Park, on the Zambezi's north bank west of Livingstone, has a rich and colourful avifauna, but its oustanding attraction is the Victoria Falls.

Above: A black-backed jackal takes advantage of good cover while hunting for prey. This jackal is one of the southern race, found from Zambia to South Africa and Namibia.

Above Left: A black-bellied bustard (also known as korhaan) in lush grasses in southern Mozambique—one of 18 bustard species in Africa.

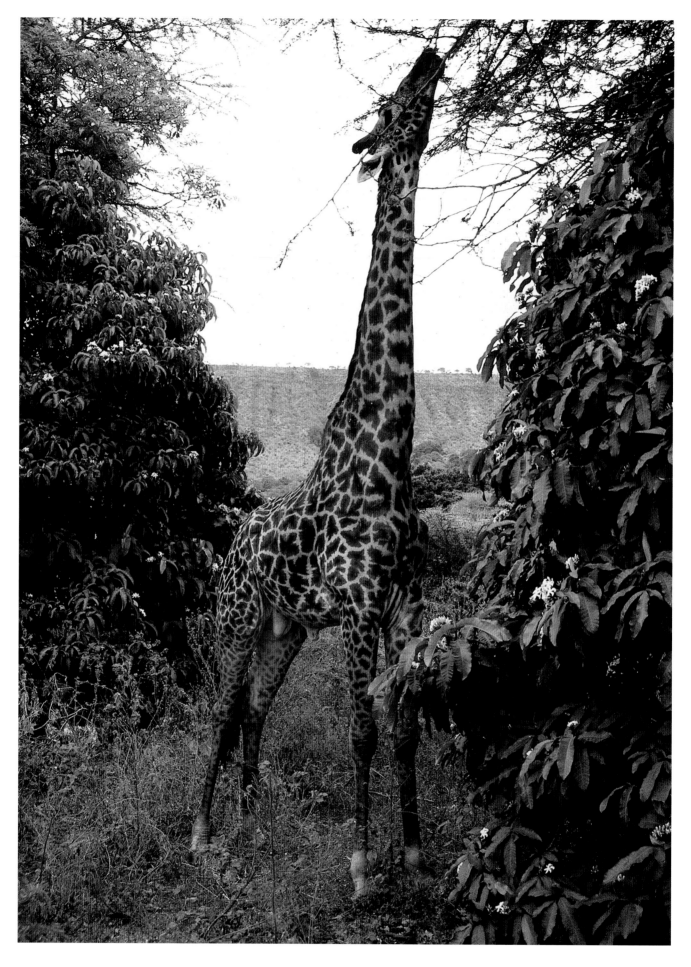

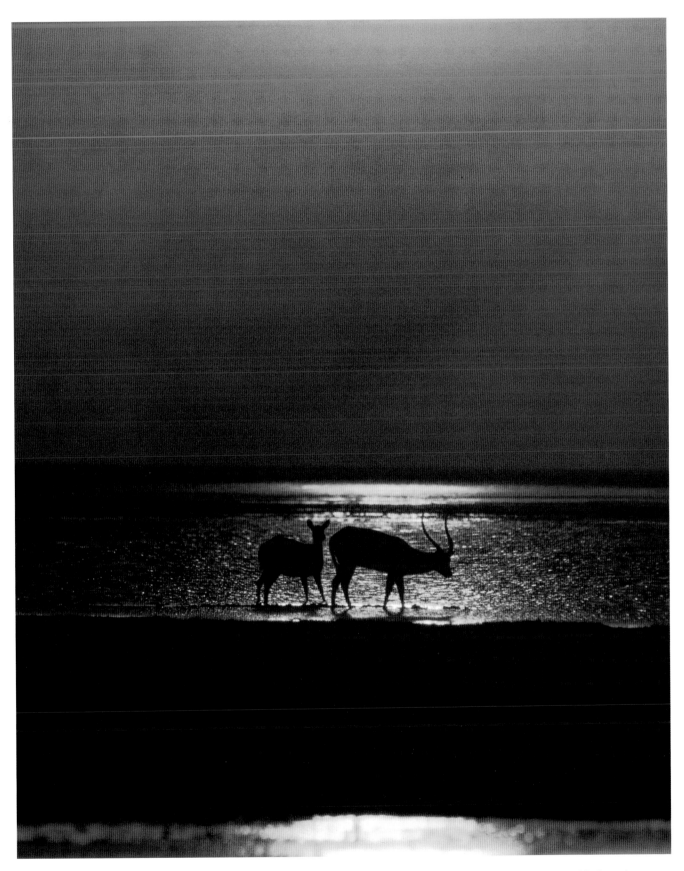

Left: A giraffe takes advantage of its great height to browse the upper branches of trees. Giraffes feature in several of Zambia's national parks in the Luangwa river valley.

Above: Kafue lechwe at sunset in Lochinvar National Park, south-west of Zambia's capital Lusaka. This subspecies, one of three lechwe races, is named after the Kafue river, a tributary of the Zambezi, and occurs naturally only in this part of the country.

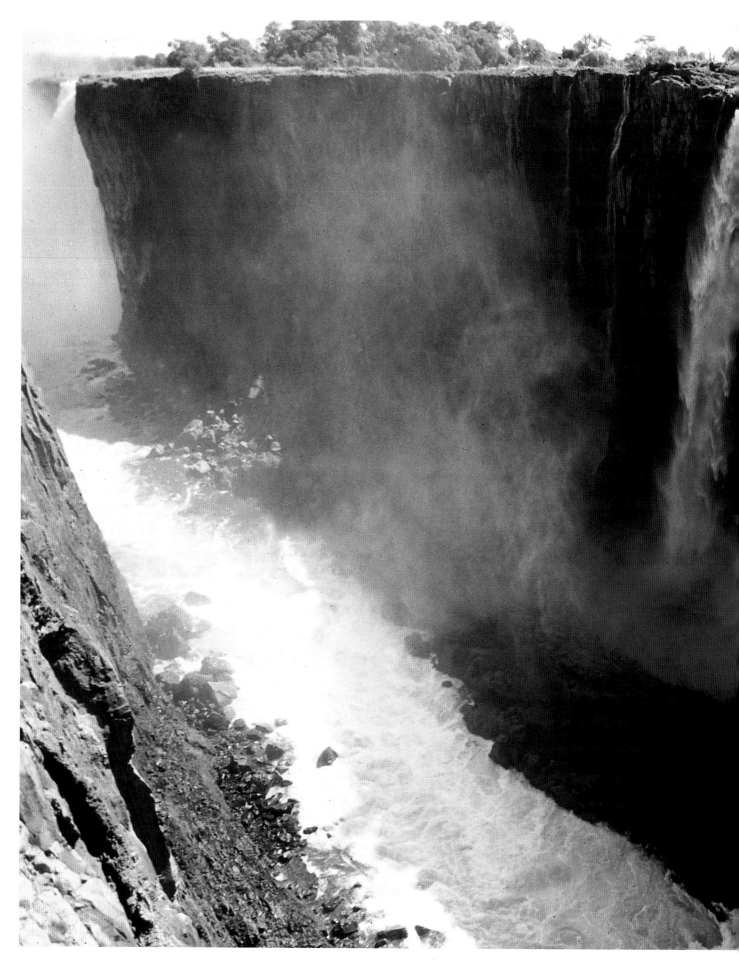

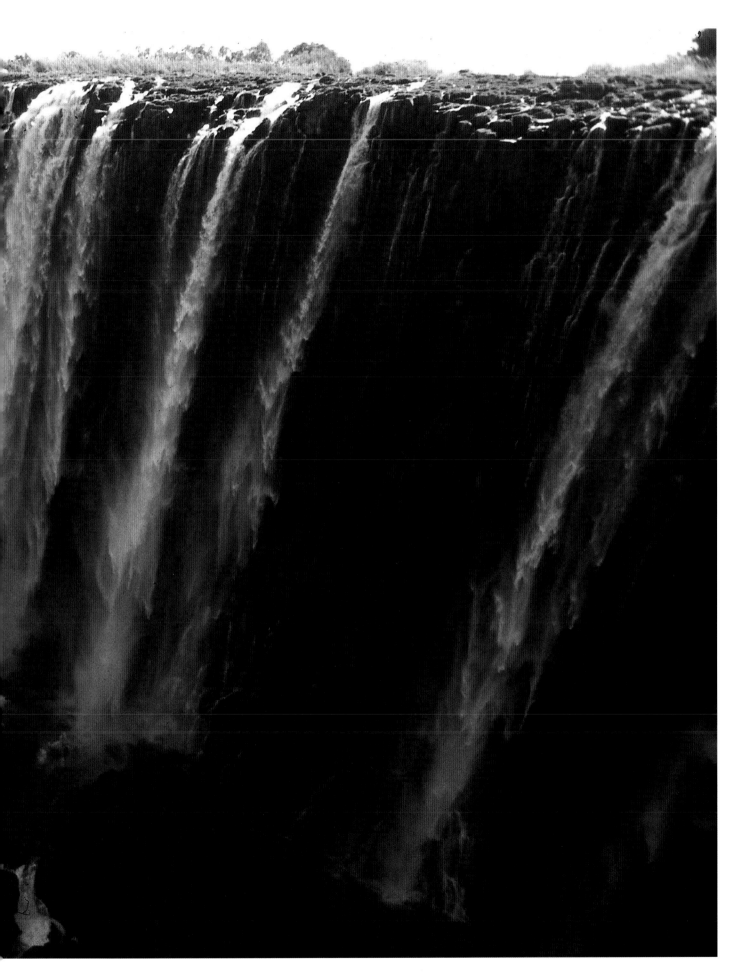

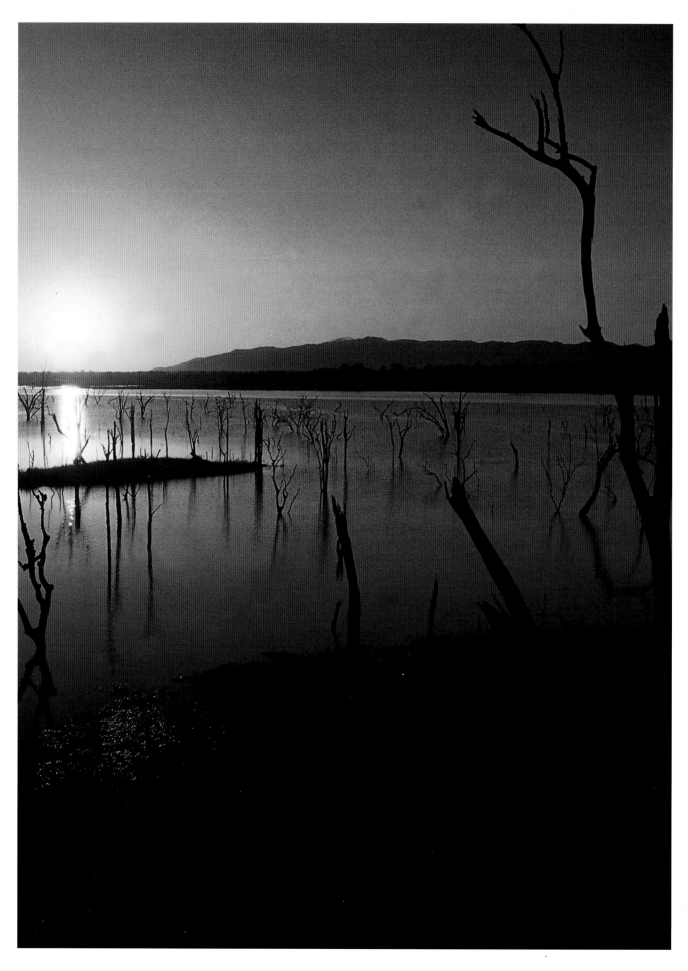

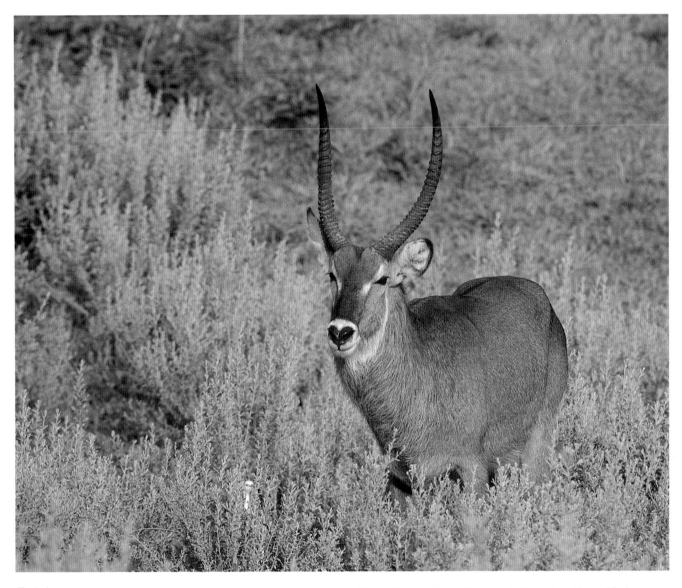

Zimbabwe

Much of this country lies at 4,000ft (1,220m) above sea level, especially the high plateau that runs south-west to north-east through the centre of the country. North-west of the plateau the rivers drain to the Zambezi; south-east of it most of the streams and rivers are tributaries of either the Sabi (also known as Save) river or the Limpopo, which runs along the South African border in the extreme south. Mana Pools National Park (WHS), lies across the Zambezi from Zambia's Lower Zambezi National Park; wildlife includes hippo, elephant, buffalo, half a dozen antelope species, leopard, lion and spotted hyena. Farther west, Matusadona National Park runs along the southern shore of Lake Kariba. Here there are hippo, many water birds, buffalo, elephant and many impala. There is a black rhino sanctuary in the Chizarira (also known as Sizarira) hills south-west of Matusadona; it also hosts elephant, lion, and several

Above: The waterbuck—this one is in Matusadona National Park—favours mixed grassland and open woodland close to water.

Left: Lake Kariba at sunrise, viewed from Zimbabwe's Matusadona National Park. The dead trees were drowned when the Zambezi's Kariba Gorge was dammed to create the lake in 1958.

Previous Page: Batoka Gorge, where the Zambezi plunges over the Victoria Falls. The river divides Zambia from its southern neighbour Zimbabwe, and there are numerous excellent national parks and wildlife reserves on both banks.

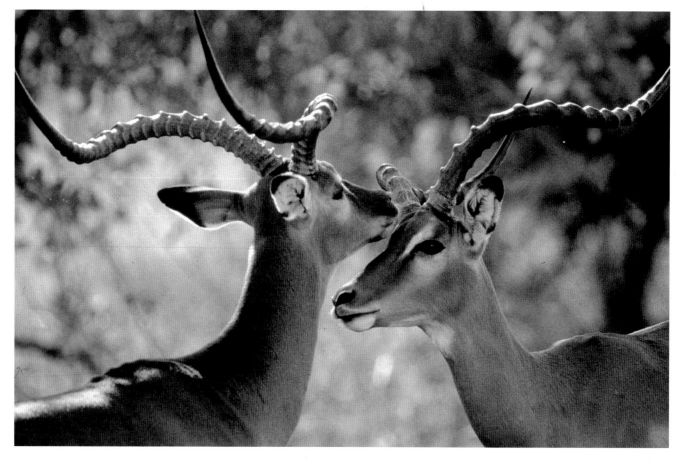

species of antelope. Hwange National Park, south-east of Victoria Falls and extending west to the Botswana border, is mainly woodland in the north and grassland in the south. A tremendous array of wildlife can be seen at the many waterholes in the park's Nyamandhlovu pan, including large herds of elephant, buffalo, thousands of impala and other antelopes, giraffe, lion, leopard, wild dog, jackal, ostrich, and a few highly protected black and white rhino. Big cats as well as giraffe and elephant can also be seen in Zambezi National Park on the river's south bank west of the falls.

In the kopje-strewn Matobo Hills south of Bulawayo in the south-west, Matobo National Park has white rhino, impala, kudu, klipspringer and other antelope, leopard, rock hyrax and, most notably among its avifauna, Verreaux's eagles. In the north-east highlands on the Mozambique border, Nyanga National Park includes Nyangani, at 8514 feet (2595m) the highest peak in Zimbabwe, and also the Mtarazi Falls, which has a drop of 820 feet (250m)—almost two and a half times as high as Victoria Falls.

The most interesting wildlife species here are the birds, including crowned eagle and wattled crane, but there are also duiker, kudu, and other antelope, and the occasional serval can be seen. Finally, in

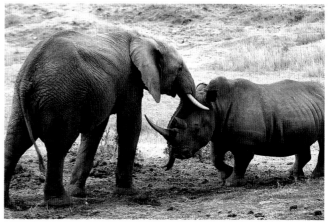

Top: Hwange National Park, a mixture of woodland and grassland in north-westernmost Zimbabwe, is renowned for its thriving population of impala. This pair of mutually grooming males belongs to the East African race.

Above: A bush elephant and white rhino standing head to head in Hwange National Park. Such confrontations seldom lead to serious injury to either party.

Right: Giraffes are present in both Hwange National Park and its neighbour immediately to the north, Zambezi National Park.

Overleaf: The most notable scenic feature of eastern Zimbabwe's Nyanga National Park are the Mtarazi Falls. They scarcely compete in grandeur with Victoria Falls but are more than twice as high.

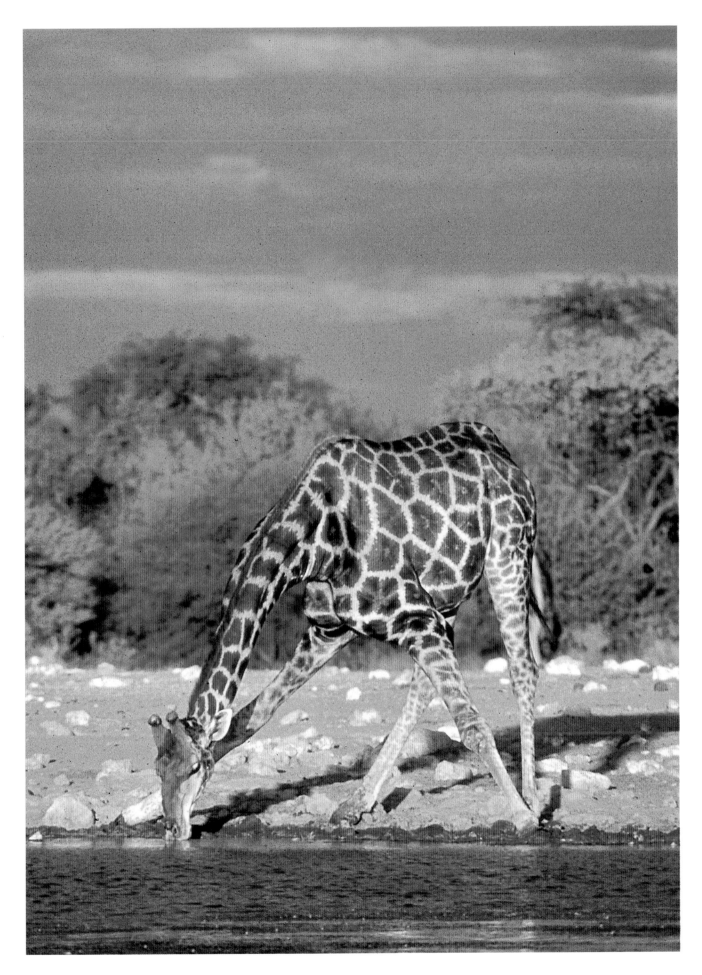

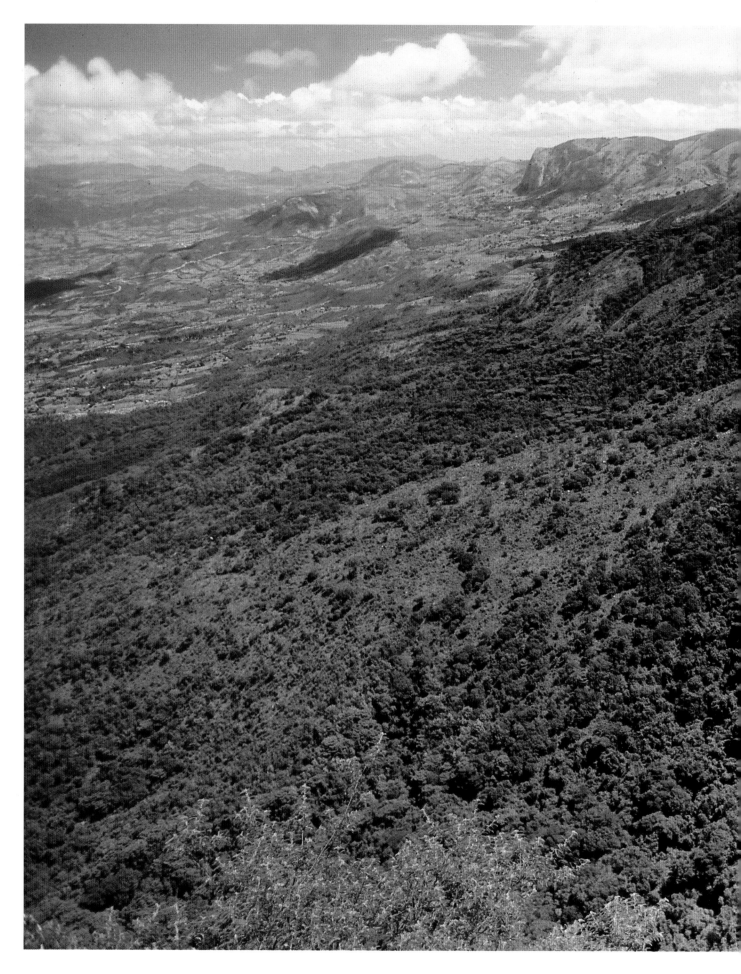

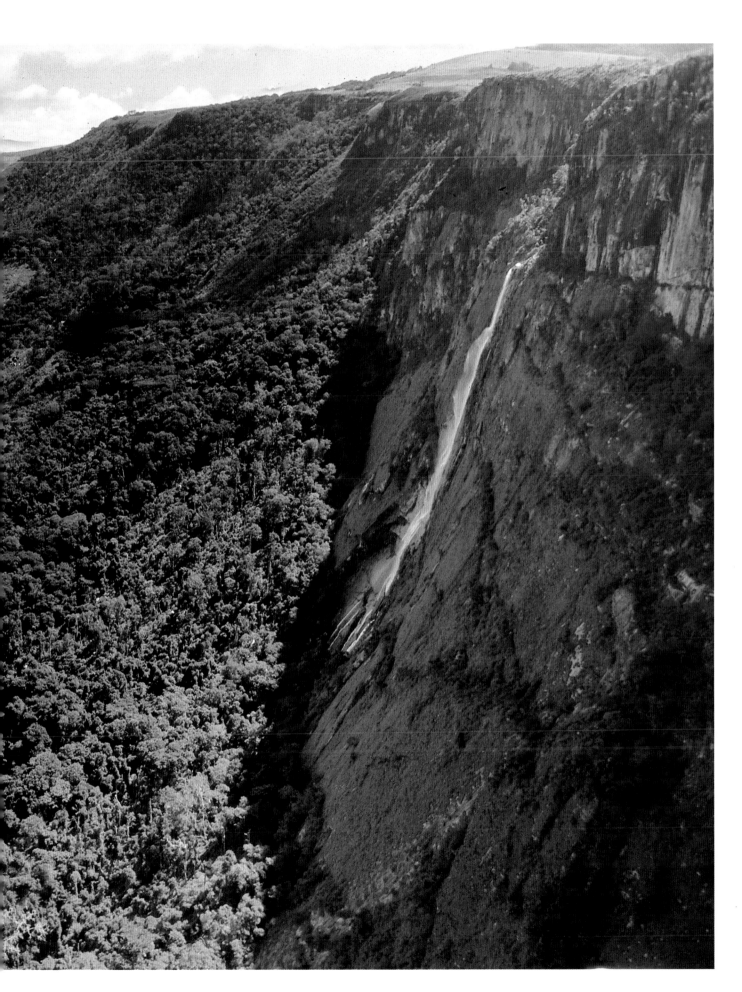

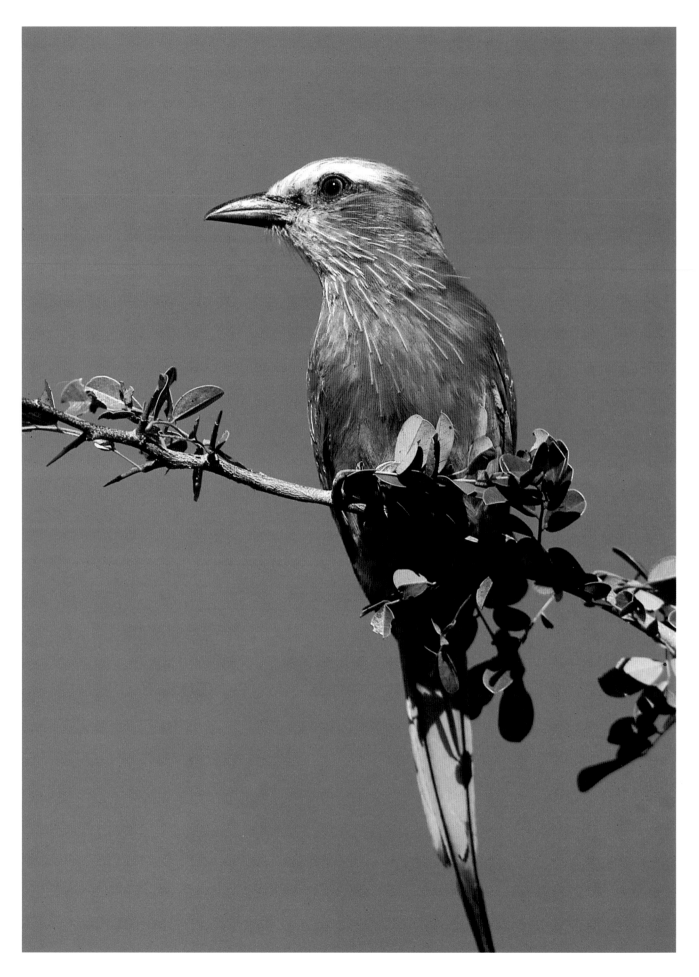

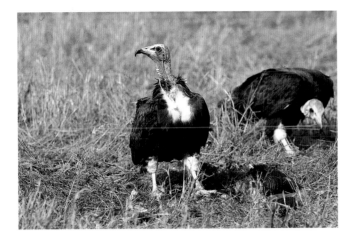

the extreme south-east, just across the border from South Africa's Kruger National Park, Gonarezhou National Park is set in woodland and open grassland and features the massive red sandstone Tjolotjo cliffs lining the Lundi river. Resident mammals include elephant, buffalo, hippo, zebra, giraffe and many antelope species. The abundant avifauna includes hooded vulture and Pel's fishing owl.

Botswana

A landlocked country like Zambia and Zimbabwe, Botswana is on plateau land averaging more than 3,000 feet (915m) above sea level. Relatively dry in the north and north-east, it is more arid in the south and south-west, where even in a good year the Kalahari desert rarely receives more than 8in (203mm) of rain.

Botswana has four regions in which the opportunities for viewing a broad range of wildlife species compare with any available elsewhere in Africa. Chobe National Park, in the north-eastern corner of Botswana, is next door to the Caprivi Strip, the long Namibian "corridor" that runs between Angola and Botswana. The northern part of the park is watered by Angola's Cuando river, which crosses the Strip and, after passing through the Linyanti swamp, runs north-eastward along Botswana's border as the Linyanti or Chobe river and eventually joins the Zambezi to the west of Victoria Falls. The Linyanti river is well stocked with hippo and many waterbirds. Farther south there are abundant migratory elephant and buffalo herds as well as several antelope species, baboon, giraffe and lion.

To the west of Chobe National Park another important river from Angola, the Cubango, flows into Botswana and, as the Okavango, proliferates into a network of rivers, channels and swamps to form the Okavango Delta, where there is permanent water. Patches of forest, open woodland and grassland occur between the waterways, offering grazing and browse to a variety of antelope species, buffalo, zebra and elephant, as well as good hunting for lion, leopard, wild dog and smaller carnivores. Storks and other waterbirds are found in abundance, as well as fish-eagle and fishing owl. Most of these animals can be seen in Moremi Wildlife Reserve in the north-eastern corner of the delta.

Between the delta and Francistown, away to the south-east near the Zimbabwe border, is the Makgadikgadi Pan Game Reserve, set on the northern margins of an enormous area of salt flats. Dry for

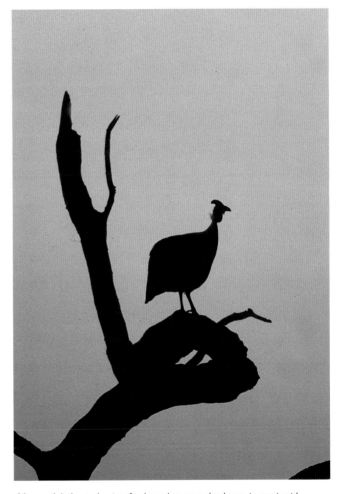

Above: A helmeted guineafowl perches on a dead tree in semi-arid grassland in northern Botswana.

Above Left: Hooded vultures, a feature of Zimbabwe's Gonarezhou National Park, are smaller than most other vultures of the savanna and tend to be last in the queue at carcasses.

Left: The vividly coloured lilac-breasted roller occurs in many national parks and reserves in south-central and East Africa. This one was photographed in Zimbabwe.

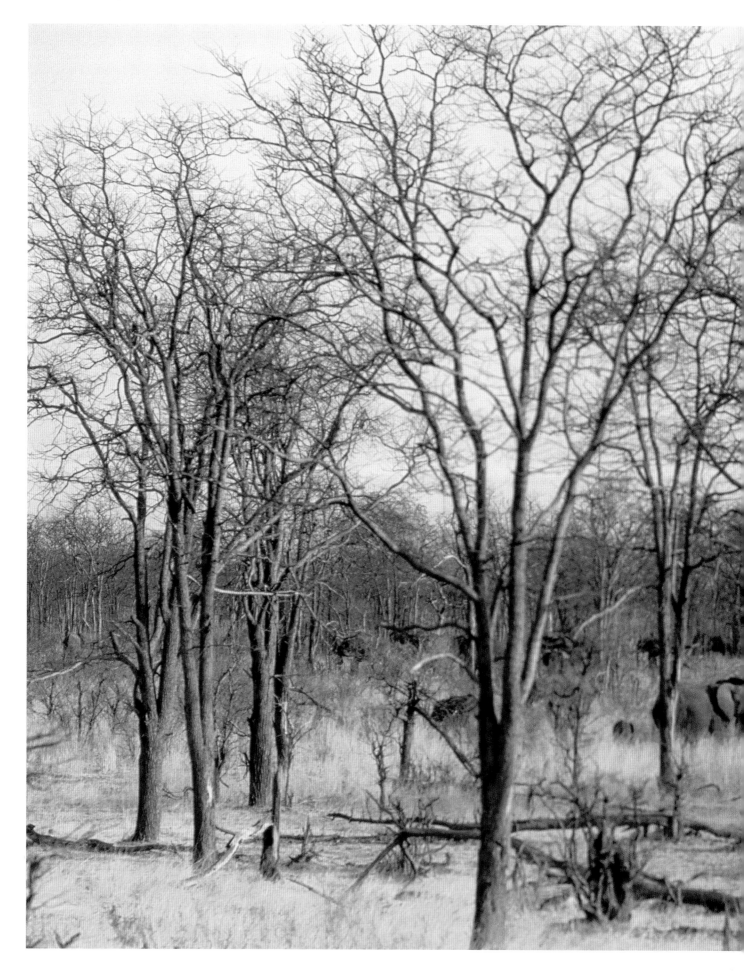

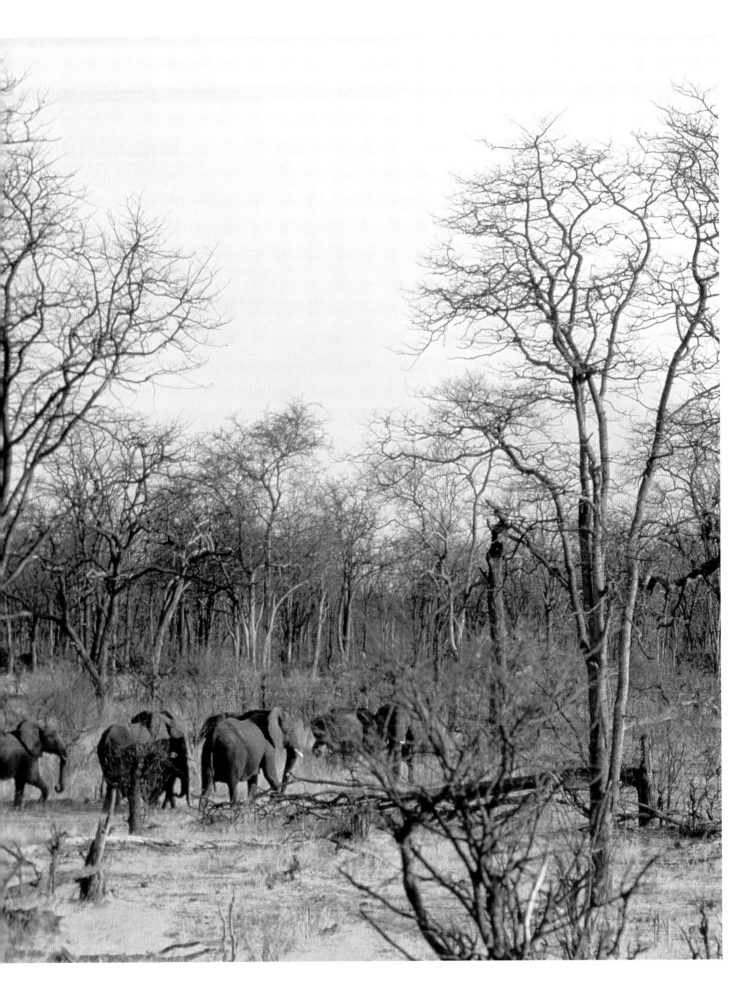

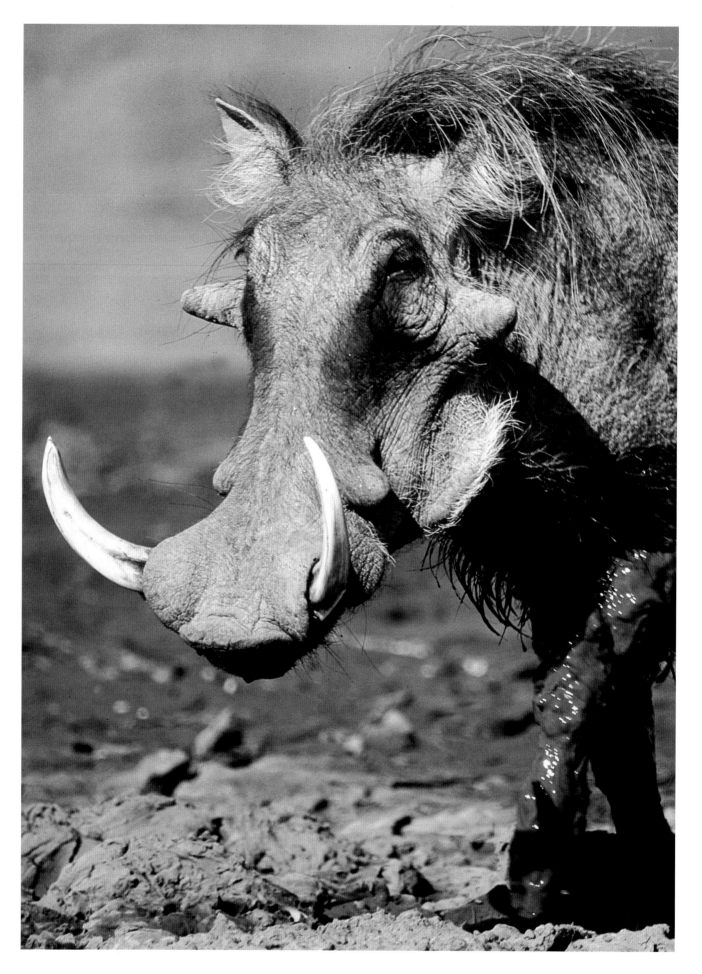

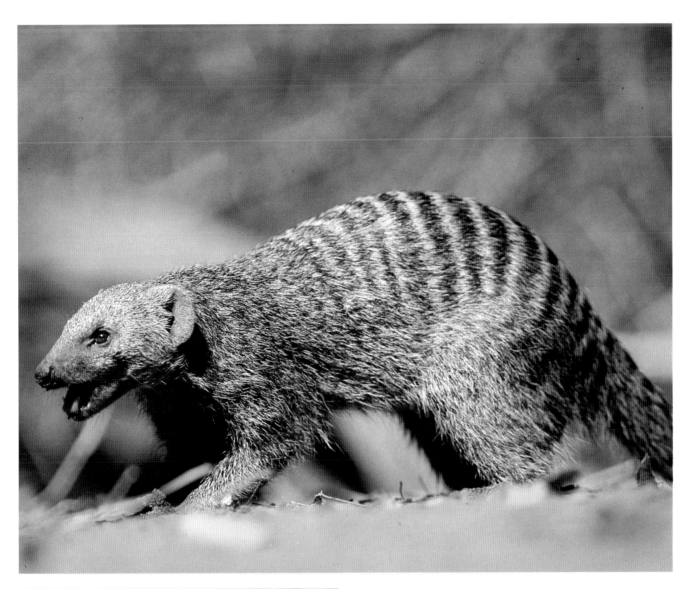

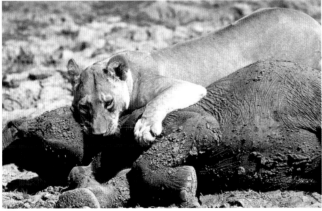

Above: A banded mongoose searches through leaf-litter in search of invertebrates in Botswana's Chobe National Park. This species also eats mice, snakes and other reptiles, as well as ground-nesting birds and their eggs.

Left: A lioness with a baby elephant kill in Chobe National Park. It is only in their first few months of life that elephants are vulnerable to predation other than by human hunters and poachers after their ivory tusks.

Far Left: A male warthog displays its superb upper tusks after taking a mud bath in northern Botswana's Savuti marshes, between the Okavango Delta and Chobe National Park.

Previous Page: A party of elephants makes its way through dry mopane woodland in the southern reaches of Chobe National Park.

most of the year except occasionally in the rain season, the pan sometimes also receives water if the Okavango Delta overflows. The pan provides May-October grazing for huge herds of ungulates—mainly antelope species and zebra—that migrate northwards to the Nxai Pan National Park, which offers reliable grazing in the November-April wet season.

The Kalahari desert consists of semi-arid grassland in the north, becoming increasingly arid towards the south and south-west, and with areas of true desert in south-eastern Namibia. Kgalagdi (or Central Kalahari) Game Reserve covers 20,000 square miles (51,800km^2) in central Botswana, and just to the south is the smaller Kutse Game Reserve. In the far south Mabuasehube Game Reserve is next door to Gemsbok National Park, which is on the border with South Africa. Immediately on the other side of the border is the Kalahari Gemsbok National Park. The two great parks are now combined, the removal of frontier fencing allowing free passage for migrating animals. In all these areas there are abundant antelope species—wildebeest, hartebeest, gemsbok, springbok, kudu and others—as well as their predators, including lion, leopard, cheetah, wild dog, and hyena. Smaller carnivores include the suricate, or meerkat.

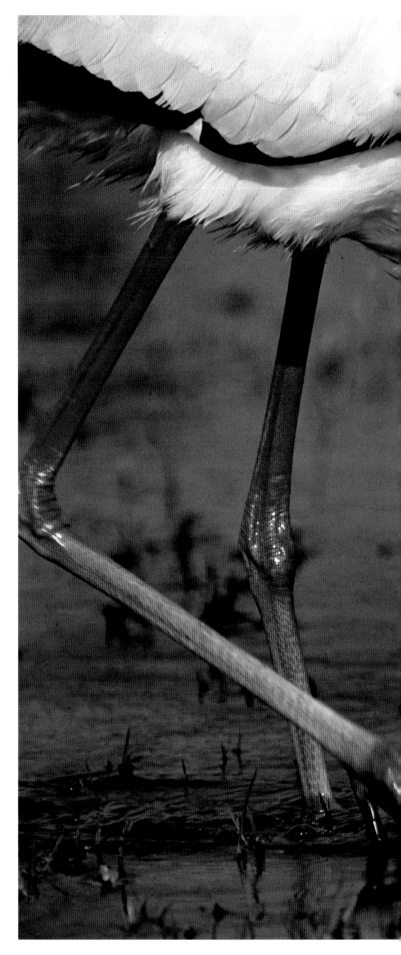

Right: A yellow-billed stork probes muddy swamp water for frogs, fish and other food in the Okavango Delta.

Overleaf: Taking turns at a waterhole in the delta: greater kudu drink their fill while impala pace up and down on the bank; a pair of giraffes waits patiently in the background.

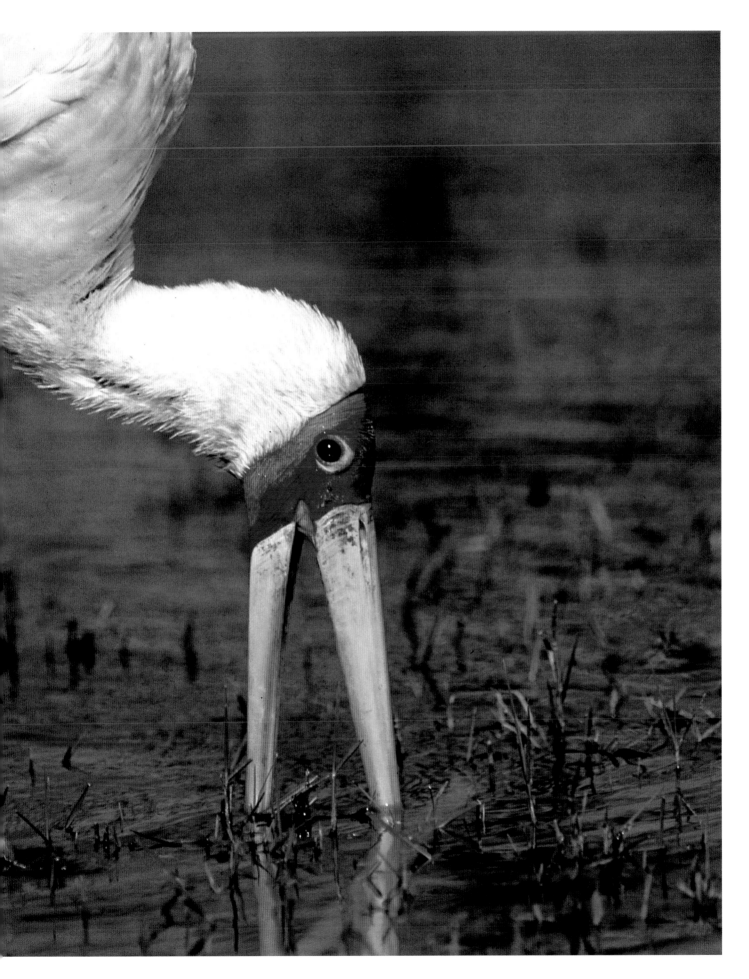

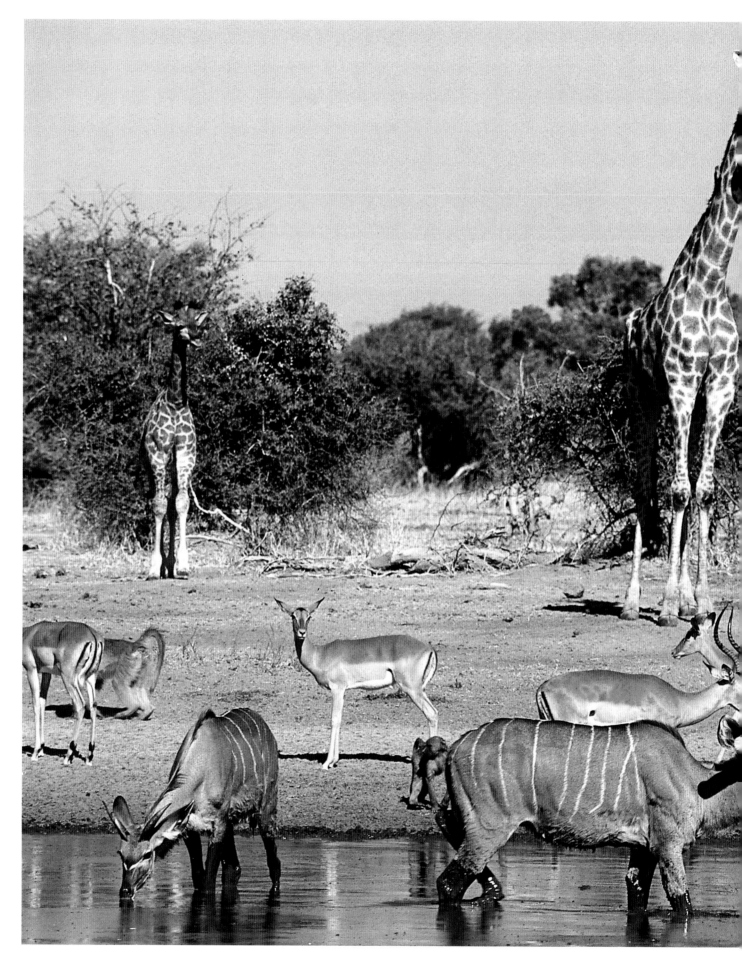

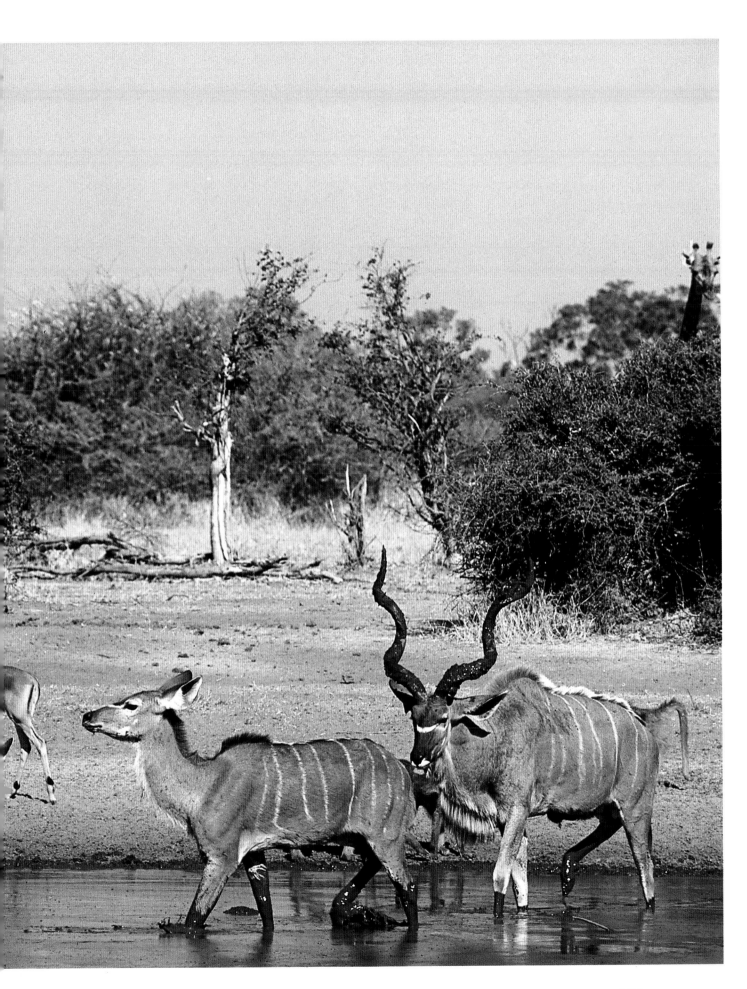

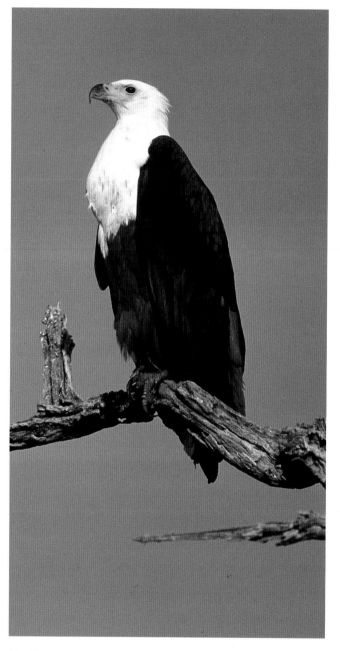

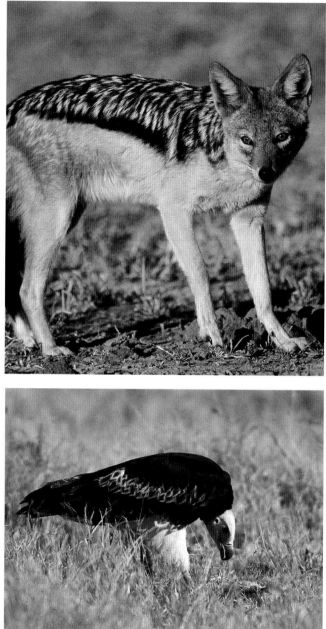

Namibia

The finest centre for viewing wildlife in Namibia is Etosha National Park, which is some 250 miles (400km) north-west of the capital, Windhoek. The park, which has an area of 8,600 square miles (22,275km^2), consists of grassland and dry, open woodland enclosing a huge salt pan, which turns into a series of shallow lagoons in wetter-than-average summers. Waterholes—some natural, some man-made—help to extend the period of available water, which attracts a wide variety of antelope species as well as a large number of black rhino and elephant, lion, leopard, cheetah, jackal and Cape fox. Flamingo and pelican breed in the area when the pan has water.

Top: A black-backed jackal on the lookout for food in Botswana's Gemsbok National Park. A clever and persistent scavenger, this species is often seen at lion and hyena kills, snatching food from under their noses.

Above: A white-headed vulture picks at the remnants of a carcass in Kgalagdi Game Reserve on the northern fringes of the Kalahari desert.

Above Left: Scanning the water for large fish swimming near the surface of deeper pools and streams, an African fish-eagle perches on a dead tree in the Okavango Delta.

Right: The Namib desert, which has the world's largest sand dunes, runs from the South African border in the south into southern Angola in the north, and at many points in Namibia its dunes rise from the beaches on the Atlantic shore.

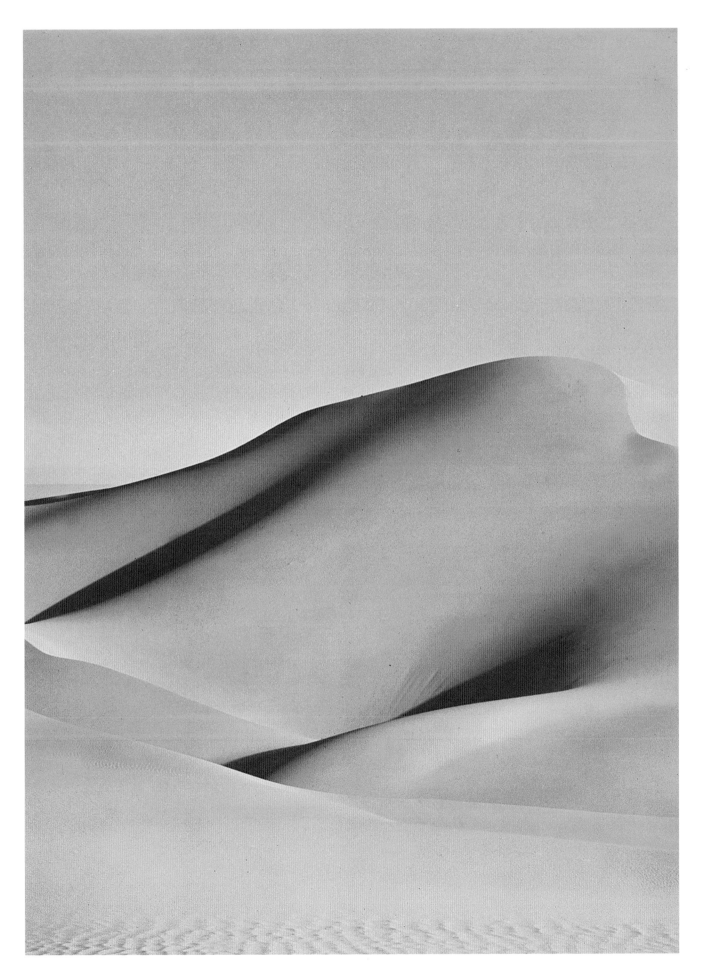

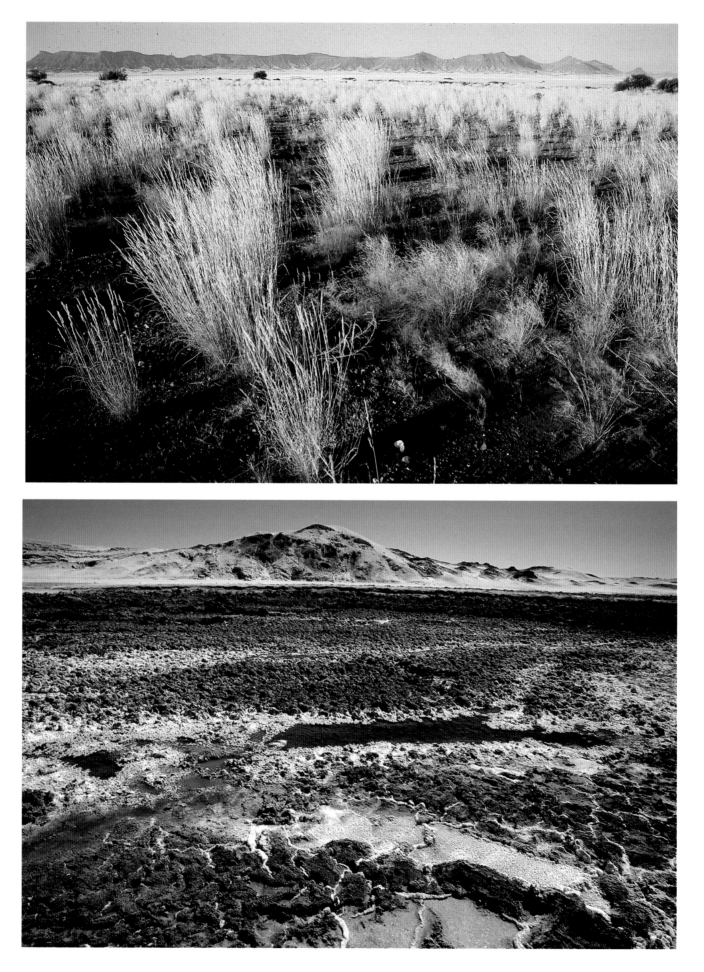

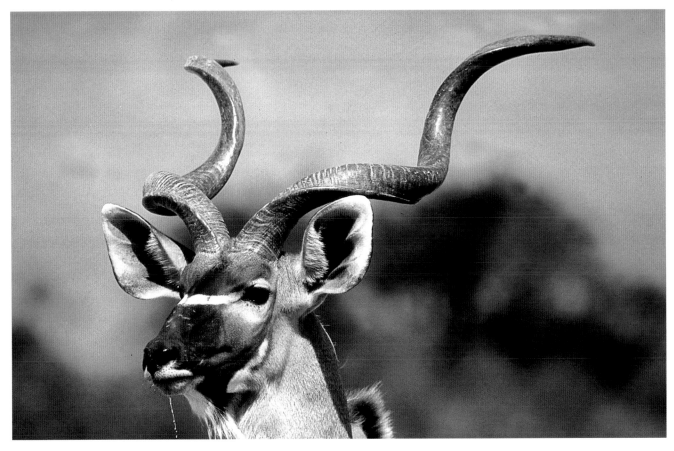

Away to the east the Caprivi Strip is largely open woodland with extensive riverine wetlands. The Strip has four reserves, the largest of which is Mudumu National Park, which has hippo, crocodile, waterbuck and sitatunga in the rivers and wetlands, with elephant, buffalo, giraffe, antelope, zebra, lion, leopard and wild dog in the woodland areas. West of Etosha National Park, Skeleton Coast National Park extends for about 300 miles (480km) from the Angola border southwards to the Ugab river north of Cape Cross. Never more than 25 miles (40km) wide, it includes the western margins (with the massive sand dunes) of the Namib desert as well as the fogbound and always rainless coast. Beach scavengers include brown hyena and black-backed jackal. Elephants that have adapted to semi-desert conditions are frequently seen in the northern areas of the park, while a few black rhino graze along the riverbeds; other wildlife in the park includes springbok, gemsbok, kudu, mountain zebra, lion, and cheetah. South of the park, Cape Cross Seal Reserve has tens of thousands of Cape fur seals.

Some 150 miles (240km) north of Windhoek, Waterberg Plateau Park sits on a flat-topped plateau that rises abruptly from the surrounding plains, deriving its name from the fresh-water springs that

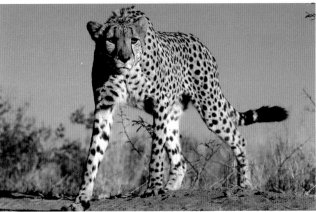

Top: A greater kudu in Namibia's Etosha National Park. Only the male of this species has horns, which make two full turns of an open spiral. Note the huge, cupped ears.

Above: A cheetah stealthily approaches game in Etosha National Park.

Above Left: Kaokoland vista: lying between the Namib desert to the west and Etosha National Park to the east, this region is one of the last of the country's true wildernesses.

Left: An area of salt pan in Etosha National Park. In a good rainy summer (December to March) the vast pan at the centre of the park will be temporarily filled with water, attracting waterbirds and herds of ungulates and other game.

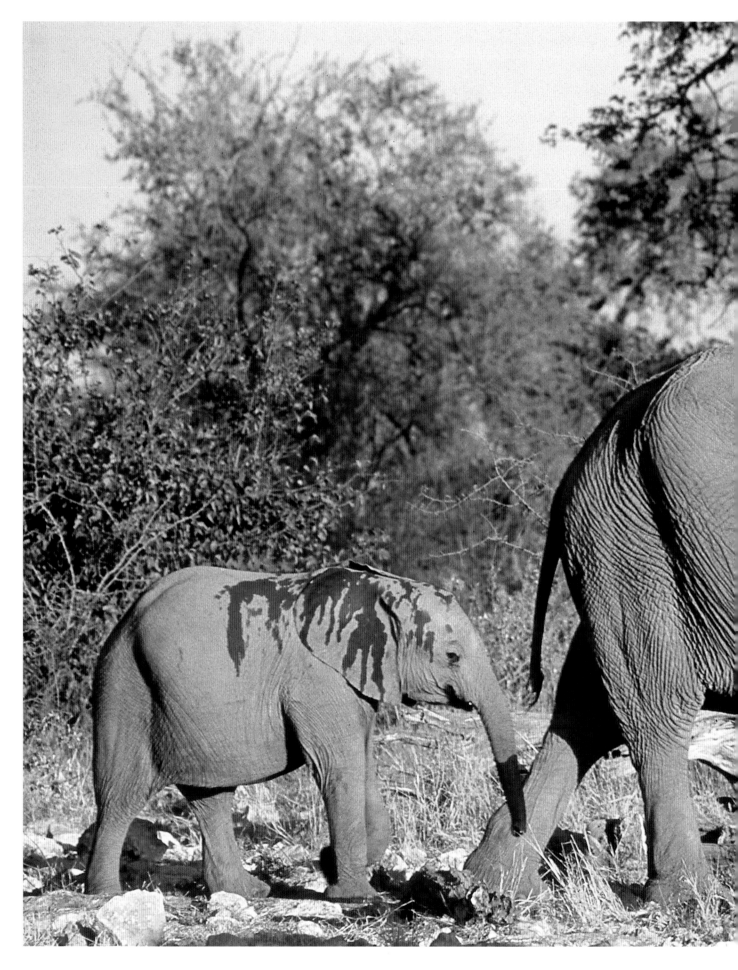

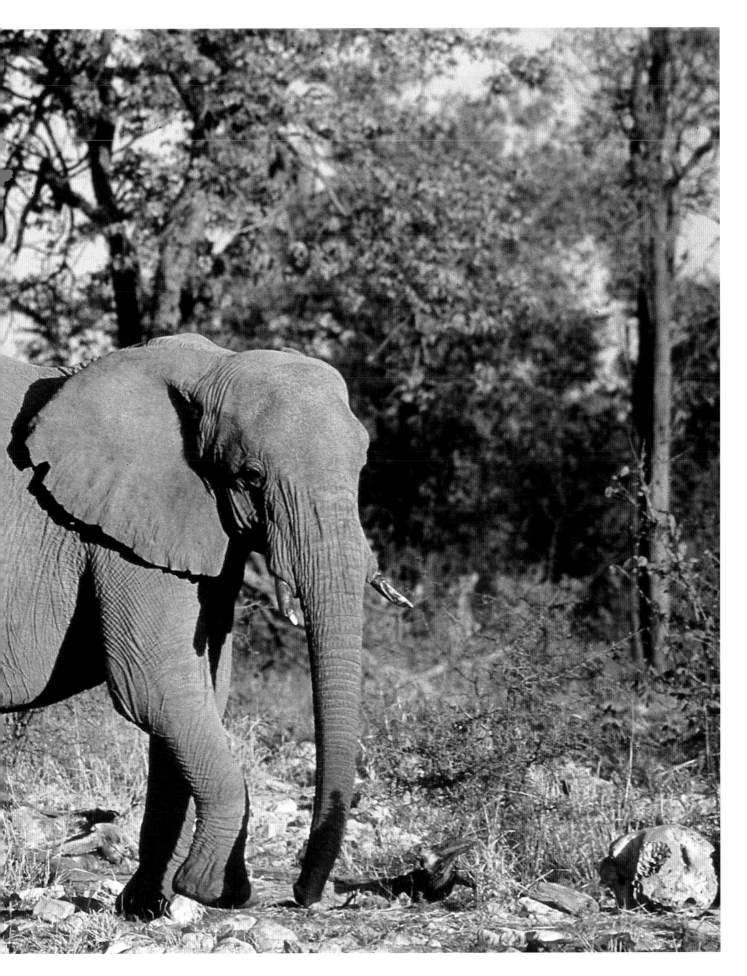

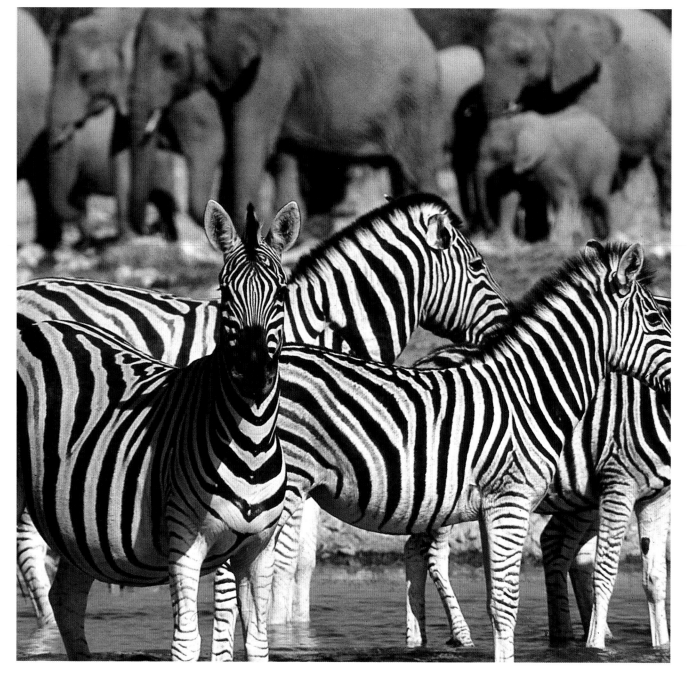

issue from its base. The park's wildlife include introduced white rhino, buffalo, eland, hartebeest and other antelope species. Notable among the avifauna are Cape vultures. Another reserve in the eastern plateau country is Hardap Nature Reserve, near Mariental, about 130 miles (210km) south-east of Windhoek. Essentially a recreation resort, it enables visitors make close contact with black rhino and other game.

Namibia's largest reserve is the immense Namib/Naukluft Park, which is 19,200 square miles (49,730km²) in area. It lies to the east and south of the port of Swakopmund, extending as far south as the Naukluft mountains. The park is within the ancient Namib desert:

much of the landscape in the west consists of vast areas of sand dunes; elsewhere there are extensive gravel plains, cut through here and there by occasionally tree-lined but almost always dry river beds. The wildlife in the few places within reach of reliably perennial waterholes includes ostrich, several antelope species, bat-eared fox, black-backed jackal, leopard and hyena.

Previous Page: An elephant and her young follow the line of a dry river bed in search of water in Etosha National Park.

Above: These elephants are luckier, but they have to wait their turn while a party of Chapman's zebra drink at Etosha's Kalkheuwel waterhole.

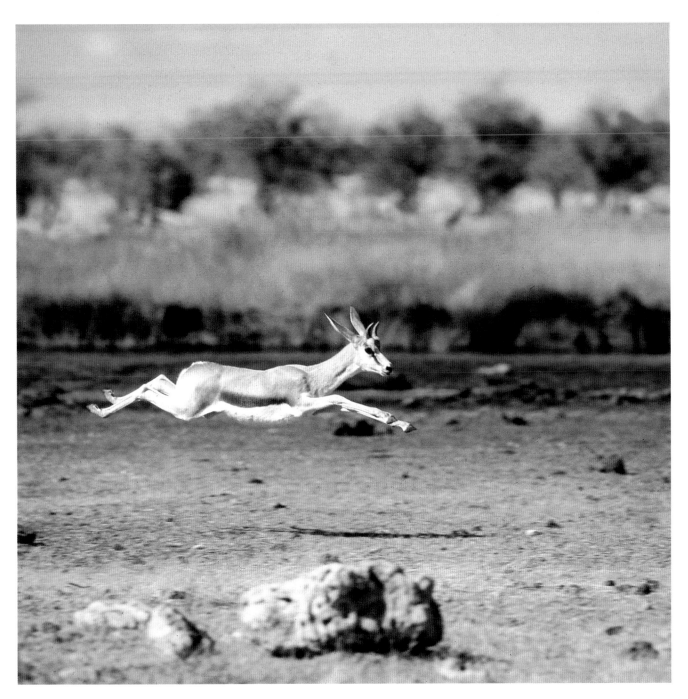

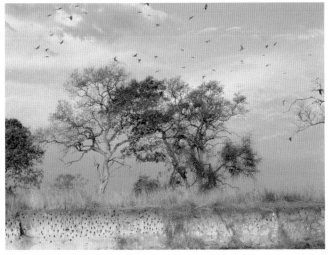

Top: A springbok leaps in Etosha National Park. It is July and the vegetation, still green at the water's edge, is beginning to dry out in the bushy scrub beyond the river.

Left: Carmine bee-eaters flying above their nest holes in a sandy bank in the Caprivi Strip, in the north-eastern corner of Namibia.

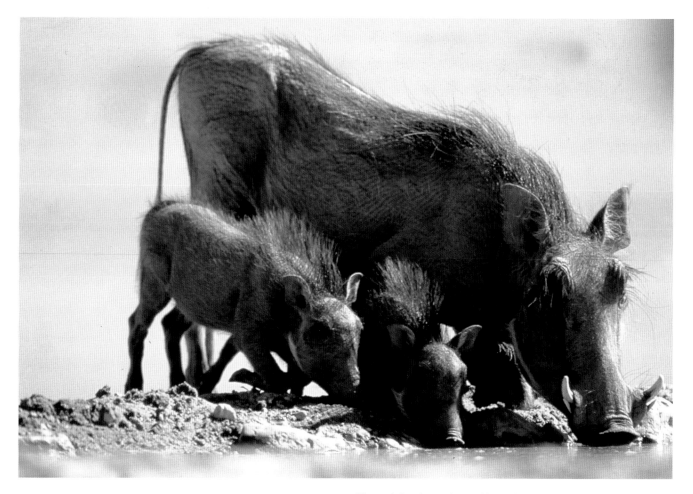

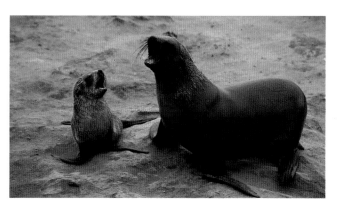

Above: A female warthog and her piglets quench their thirst at a muddy waterhole in the Caprivi Strip.

Left: The Cape fox is native to southern Angola, Namibia, Botswana and much of South Africa and is found mainly in dry grassland and semi-desert scrub. A nocturnal hunter, it eats mainly rodents and invertebrates.

Below Left: Cape seals frequent the shore of Namibia's Skeleton Coast, where they sometimes fall prey to spotted hyenas. This adult and young are on a beach at Cape Cross, north of Swakopmund.

Below: The sociable weaver builds the most elaborate communal nest of any bird species. Each nest, built of twigs infilled with large quantities of straw, contains enough chambers (each with an entrance tunnel) for several hundred birds.

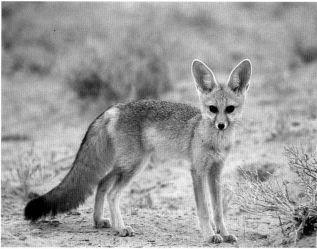

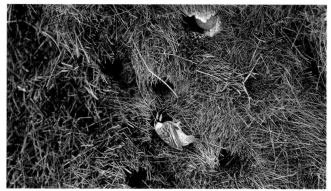

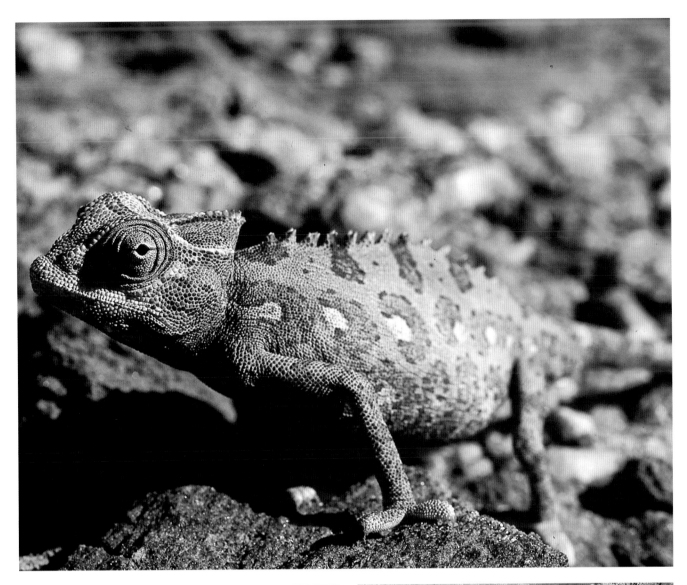

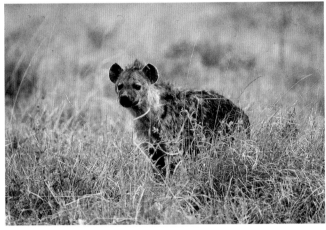

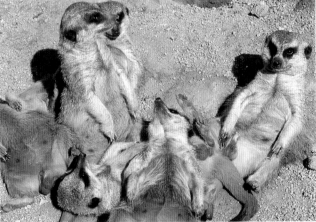

Top: For a naraqua chameleon dull greyish brown colours provide good camouflage against gravel-strewn scrub in north-eastern Namibia.

Above: The huge Namib/Naukluft Park consists mainly of sand dunes in the west and extensive gravel plains and dry river beds, but visitors can often see large predators such as this spotted hyena, as well as many ungulates, near the park's perennial water holes.

Above: The suricate (also known as meerkat) lives in drier and more open country than other mongooses. This small pack are lolling about in the sun near an entrance to their burrow. They are hunted by jackals, birds of prey and other predators.

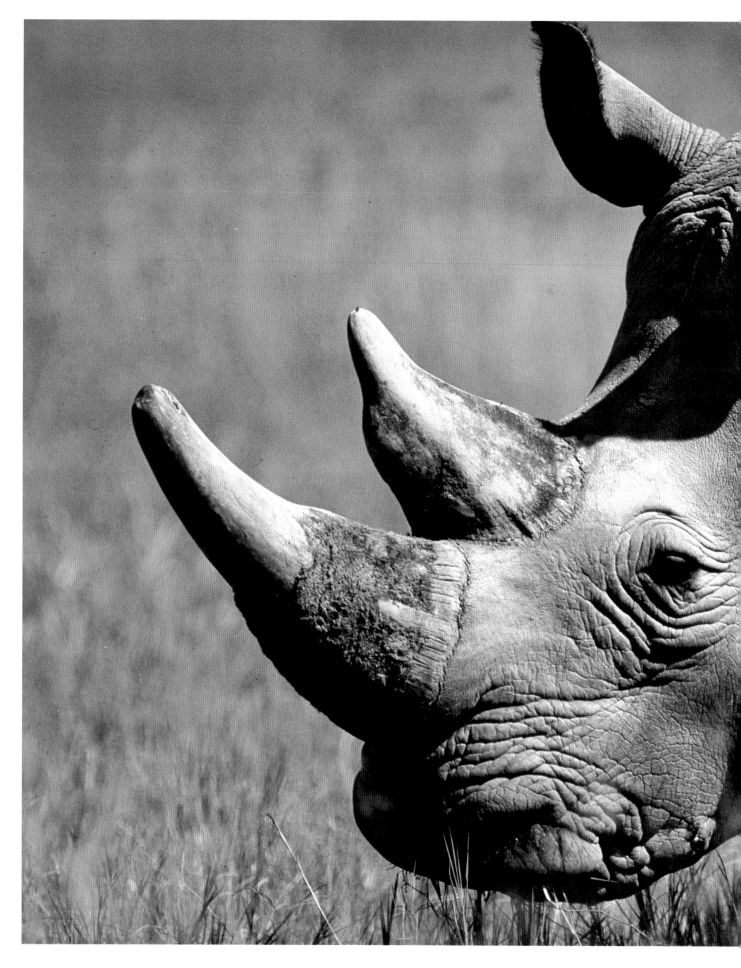

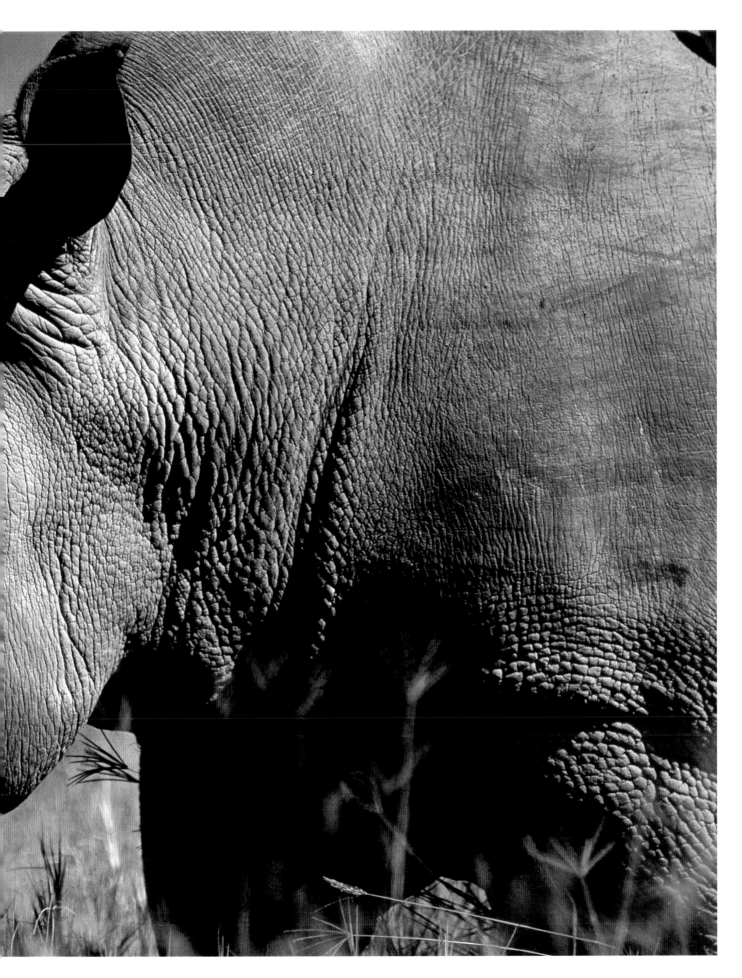

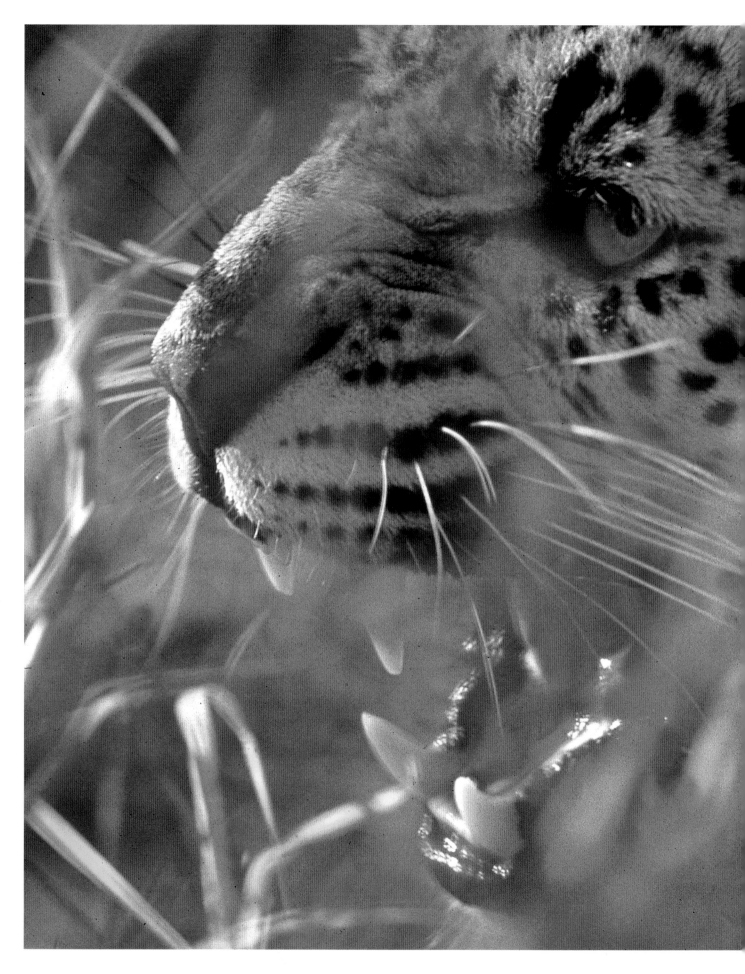

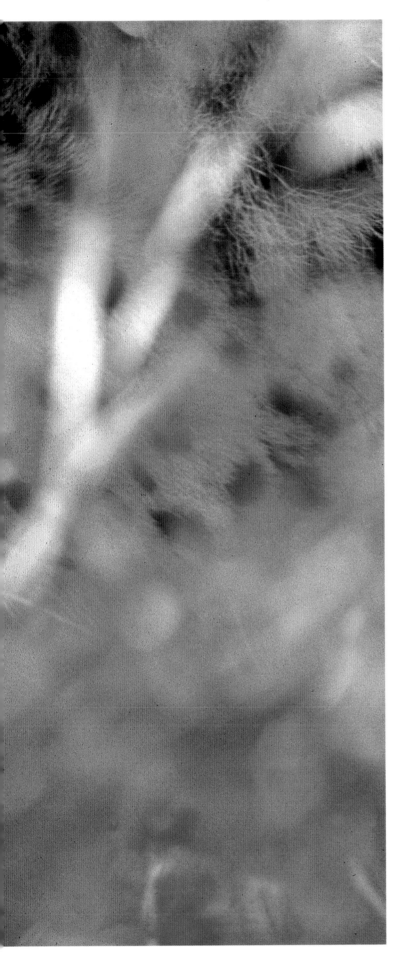

Swaziland

Tucked between the southern extremity of Mozambique to the east, Transvaal to the west and KwaZulu-Natal to the south, Swaziland has a total area of 6,705 square miles (17,366km^2)—only a fraction of that of some of the great national parks elsewhere in Africa. In the highveld (cooler upland grassland) of the north-west, Malolotja Nature Reserve can claim to be the last remaining area of true wilderness in the country and features the 330ft (100m) Malolotja Falls and deep-cut river gorges as well as grassy plains. Wildlife includes reedbuck, rhebok, oribi, klipspringer, and other antelopes, zebra, warthog, and predators such as leopard, jackal, the hyena-like aardwolf, and caracal. South of the capital, Mbabane, Mlilwane Wildlife Sanctuary has hippo, white rhino and many antelope species. To the south-east, the lowveld (wooded grassland) of Mkhaya Nature Reserve has elephant, black and white rhino, giraffe, zebra, ostrich, and several antelope species. Finally, in the north-east, Mlawula Nature Reserve, in a mixture of lowveld and upland terrain, and including areas of moist woodland, hosts hippo, zebra, white rhino, many species of antelope, leopard and spotted hyena; samango monkey can be seen in the woodland. Hlane National Park, immediately to the west, also includes vultures and jackals.

Lesotho

Most of this small landlocked kingdom, enclosed on the north by Orange Free State, on the east by KwaZulu-Natal and on the south and west by Cape Province, lies at more than 6,000feet (1,830m) above sea-level. It sits astride the highest part of the Drakensberg range and the dominant terrain includes mountains with jagged peaks and steep-sided canyons. The Sehlabathebe National Park is in the south-east on the edge of the escarpment, and resident wildlife includes baboon, several species of antelope and rare birds such as the bearded vulture, orange-breasted rockjumper, and bald ibis.

Previous Page: The white rhino is one of the main attractions at three of Swaziland's wildlife reserves.

Left: Leopards roam the lowveld grassland and woodlands of north-eastern Swaziland's Mlawula Nature Reserve.

South Africa

The republic has more national parks and nature and/or game reserves than any other African country, and their wildlife conservation and protection record is second to none. There is space here to consider only a few of the finest in each province; moreover, there are hundreds of protected areas in addition to the parks and reserves.

Transvaal

Kruger National Park, in the lowveld along the Mozambique border, stretches from Zimbabwe in the north almost to Swaziland in the south and dates its origins from the much smaller Sabie Game Reserve, founded in this area in 1898. Today the park has an area of 7,520 square miles (19,480km²). The northern region consists mainly of dry, wooded savanna of the type known as "mopane" woodland; the drier southern region has more open grassland dotted with isolated acacia trees; the south-western margins of the park in the upper Sabie valley west of Skukuza are higher and have lusher grazing than elsewhere. Many antelope species, buffalo, leopard, wild dog and warthog are found in most areas of the park; elephant, eland and roan are mostly in the north; giraffe, black rhino, impala and lion are mostly in the south; white rhino and several antelope species graze in the south-west. Hippo and crocodile inhabit the rivers, congregating in natural and maintained pools in the dry season. Tourists can visit six private reserves on the western margins of the park.

To the west of the southern part of Kruger National Park, spectacular Blyde River Canyon Nature Reserve has a mixture of subtropical evergreen forest, protea (shrub) forest, and highveld grassland enclosing swift-flowing rivers, rapids and waterfalls. Wildlife includes hippo, rhebok, oribi, grysbok, klipspringer, and other antelope, and baboon, samango and vervet monkeys, as well as bushbabies; the forest areas have a rich highland avifauna. Among several other reserves in the area are Blydeberg Nature Reserve, Tshukudu Game Reserve, and Mohlabetsi Game Reserve.

In western Transvaal, north-west of Rustenburg and close to the resort of Sun City, Pilanesberg National Park (founded only in 1979) is set in a huge volcano crater. The natural vegetation is a mixture of arid Kalahari thornveld and wetter sour bushveld. Massive reintroduction schemes have ensured a thriving resident population of black and white rhino, elephant, buffalo, giraffe, zebra, hippo, leopard,

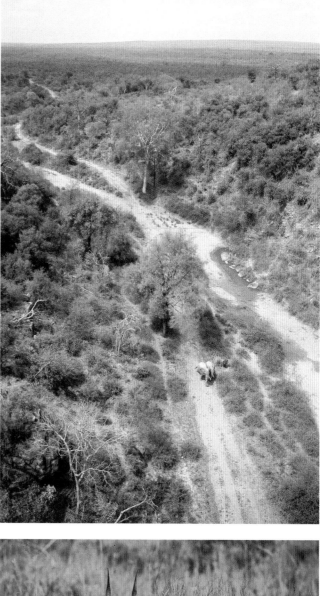

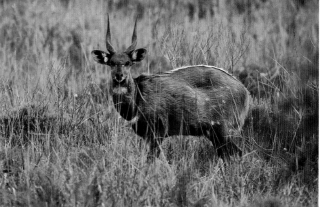

Top: Elephants on a dirt road beside a dry river bed in the mopane woodland of Transvaal's famous Kruger National Park.

Above: The southern race of bushbuck are plentiful in the riverine woodlands in the south of Kruger National Park.

Above Right: White rhinos are found mainly in the lush grassland of the south-western area of Kruger National Park.

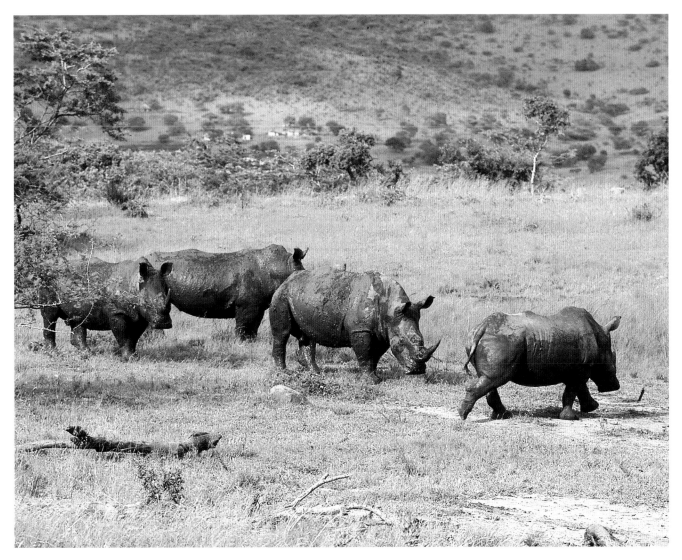

brown hyena, cheetah, and many antelope species. The abundant avifauna includes about 30 bird-of-prey species. In the south-western corner of the province, north-east of Delareyville, Barberspan Nature Reserve is the country's leading sanctuary (and an important research centre) for waterbirds. Among more than 300 species of regular visitors to the pan are flamingo, night heron and egret. The grassland areas surrounding the pan have wildebeest, springbok, blesbok, zebra and ostrich.

Orange Free State

Bounded largely by three rivers—the Orange in the south and south-west, the Vaal in the north-west and the Klip in the north-east—the Orange Free State is in the highveld and once consisted of grassland savanna that stretched uninterrupted from horizon to horizon. As in the Serengeti plains of Tanzania, it was formerly inhabited by enormous herds of migrating herbivores. Today the countryside is mostly given over to arable farming, but many of the species that once roamed its plains have been re-introduced to reserves. The largest of these, Qwaqwa Conservation Area, is in the eastern corner of the province where its borders with Lesotho and KwaZulu-Natal meet, south-west of Harrismith. It is located high in the Maluti mountains and Drakensbergs, where the main vegetation is short grasses and protea scrub, with occasional patches of forest. The rather elusive wildlife includes baboon and grey rhebok, and birds such as bearded and Cape vultures, bald ibis and wattled crane. Golden Gate Highlands National Park is next door, set in the foothills of the Maluti range. The park's herbivores include Burchell's zebra, mountain reedbuck, oribi, grey rhebok, blesbok and several other antelope species. Willem Pretorius Game Reserve, surrounding Allemanskraal dam in central Orange Free State, north-east of Bloemfontein, has white rhino, zebra, giraffe, black wildebeest, red hartebeest, reedbuck, eland, springbok and kudu, while fish eagles

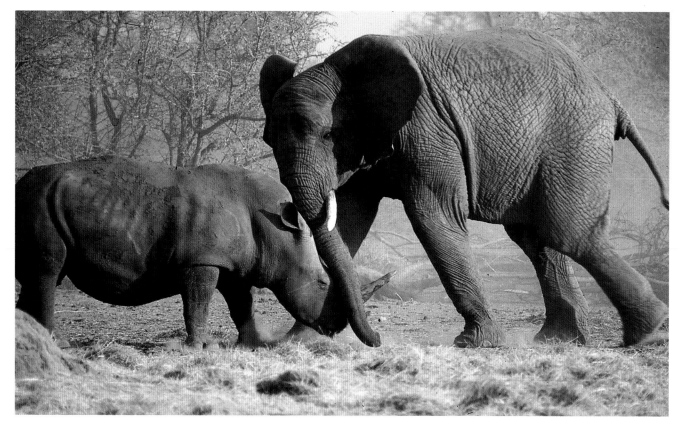

and martial eagles breed here. Erfenis Dam Nature Reserve, with a similar range of ungulates, is a few miles to the south-west. Finally, in the far south, Tussen-die-Riviere Game Farm, around the point at which the Orange and Caledon rivers meet, features white rhino, zebra, wildebeest, blesbok, springbok, gemsbok, reedbuck, kudu, eland, ostrich, aardwolf, and bat-eared fox.

KwaZulu Natal

Hluhluwe Game Reserve celebrated its centenary in 1997 and is one of the oldest in Africa. It one of several excellent reserves in the north-eastern (KwaZulu) region of the province. It is linked by a corridor of land, allowing free passage of game, with Umfolozi Game Reserve, both reserves are north-west of Mtubatuba. To the north-east lies Mkuzi Game Reserve, notable for its game-viewing hides located at the waterholes. All three reserves feature black and white rhino, hippo, giraffe, leopard, zebra, warthog, over a dozen species of antelope plus baboons and other primates. To the east, on the estuary, St. Lucia Wetland Reserve offers one of the best places to view hippo (more than 600 of them) and crocodiles as well as pelican, heron and fish eagle. On the province's Pongolo river border with Transvaal at Louwsburg, Itala Game Reserve lies

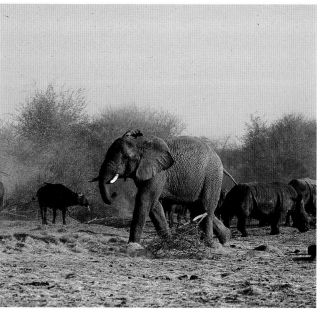

Top and Above: Cape buffalo, bush elephant and white rhino graze peacefully together (above) in the lowveld woodland acres of Tshukudu Game Reserve, to the west of Kruger National Park. Minor quarrels occasionally occur between the larger animals: this young male elephant in Tshukludu seems to think the white rhino is standing in his space (top).

Right: This 10-month-old lioness cub is a member of a small but thriving population of Tshukudu lions preying on kudu, wildebeest and other ungulates in the reserve.

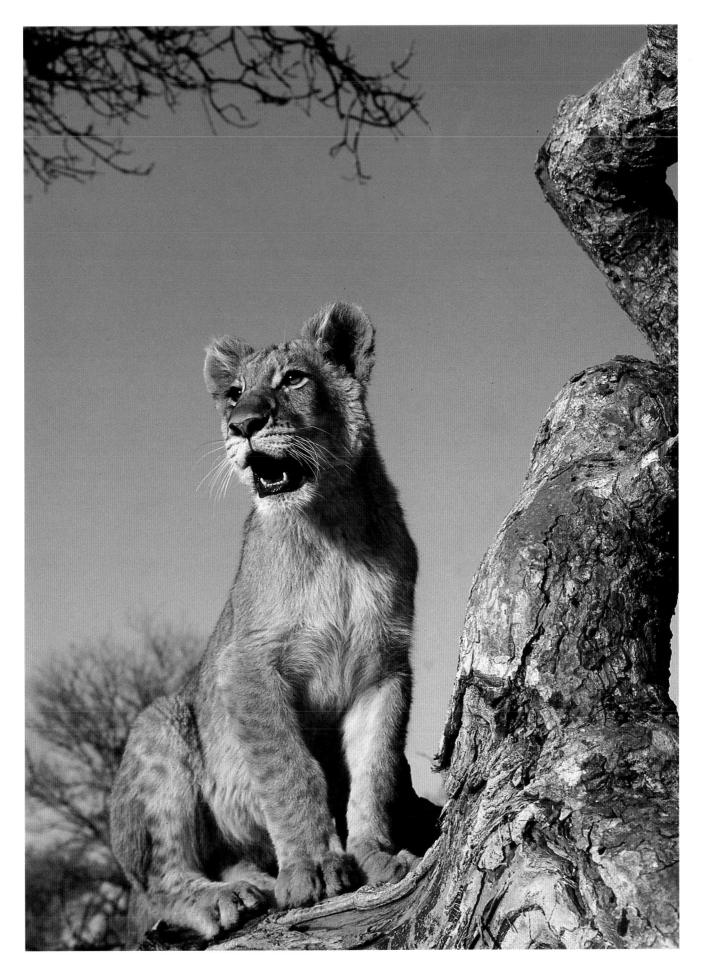

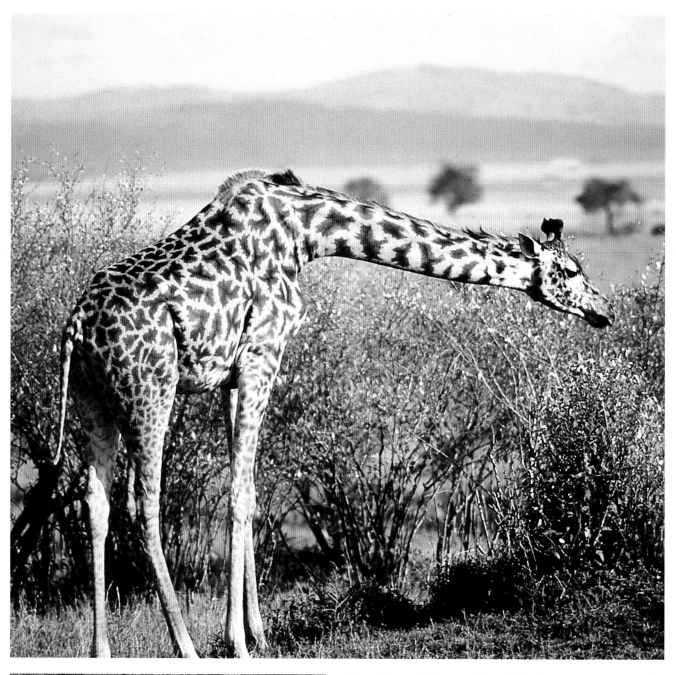

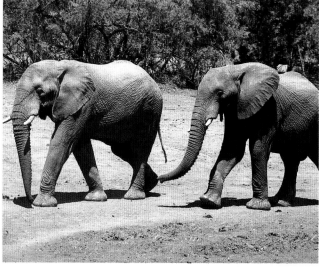

Above: Transvaal's Pilanesberg National Park has thriving populations of ungulates, including giraffes, as well as their major predators.

Left: A pair of young elephants stroll through Pilanesberg. The park's ambitious reintroduction program includes a wide range of large mammals.

Above Right: Transvaal's Barberspan Nature Reserve, an important avifauna research centre, attracts many species of waterbirds. This greater flamingo is typical of regular visitors to the pan.

Right: The plains zebra is resident among the ungulate populations of several reserves in the Orange Free State.

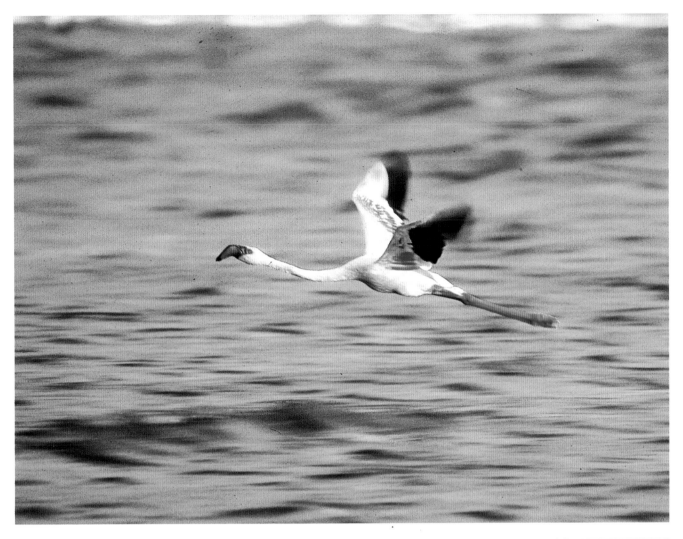

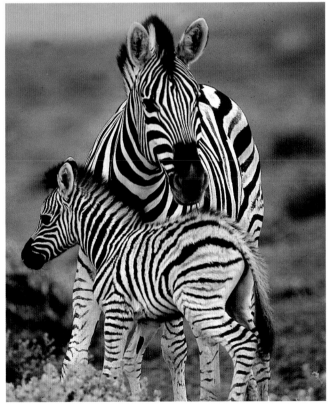

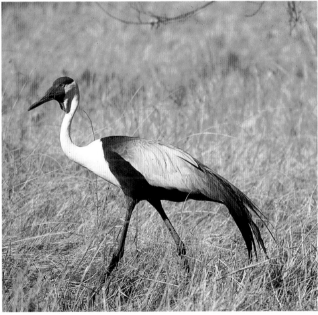

Above: Among the larger resident birds of Qwaqwa Conservation
Area, in eastern Orange Free State, is the endangered wattled crane.
A bird of wetlands and grasslands, it is sometimes found among herds
of grazing ungulates.

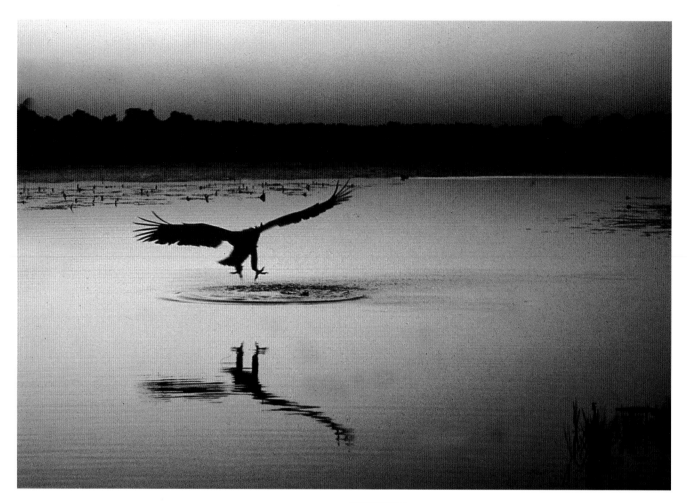

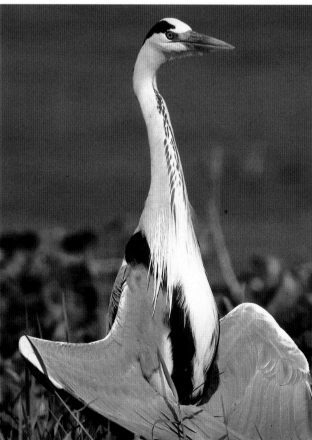

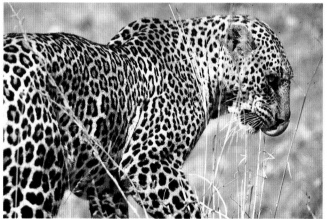

Top: The lake formed by the Allemanskraal dam in the Free State's Willem Pretorius Game Reserve attracts large numbers of game birds, including fish-eagles. This one is about to snatch a large fish swimming near the surface.

Above: The leopard is the only naturally occurring large predator among some 75 native or introduced mammal species in the Itala Game Reserve in northern KwaZulu-Natal.

Left: A visitor to Willem Pretorius reserve is this blacksmith plover, whose repeated "klink-klink-klink" call warns all animals in the vicinity of approaching predators.

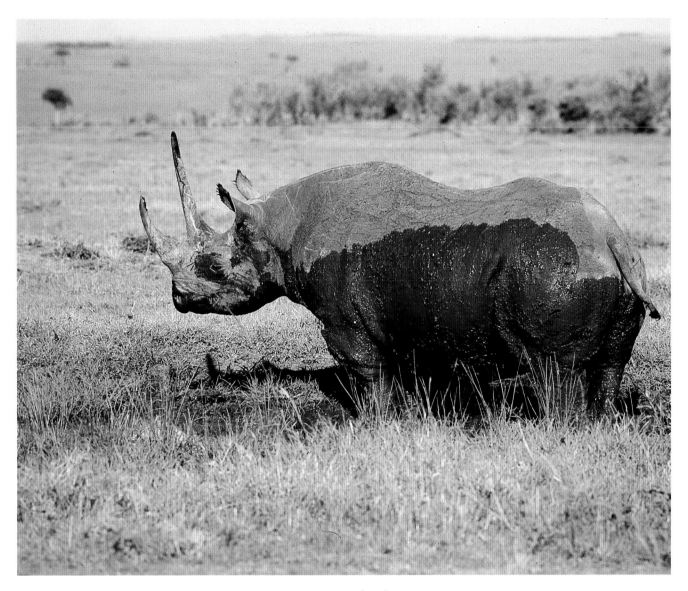

in an area of grassy hills, steep-sided river valleys and bushveld (open woodland savanna). Resident (native or introduced) wildlife includes, black and white rhino, many antelope species, zebra, giraffe, crocodile, leopard, cheetah and brown hyena.

In the west the province is dominated by the eastern escarpment of the Drakensberg range. In the foothills near Bergville, south-west of the city of Ladysmith, Spioenkop Reserve on the Tugela river has a good variety of introduced species, including white rhino, giraffe, zebra, wildebeest, hartebeest, reedbuck, kudu, impala, blesbok, eland and other antelope. Royal Natal National Park, to the north-west, includes lofty Mont-aux-Sources (10,822ft/3,299m), the crescent-shaped rock face of the Amphitheatre and the dramatic Tugela Falls. Wildlife here, and in Rugged Glen Nature Reserve next door, includes klipspringer, mountain reedbuck, duiker, grey rhebok, bush-buck, as well as baboon.

Cape Province

The province's largest (and most remote) reserve is the Kalahari Gemsbok National Park in the far north, (now formally combined with Botswana's even larger Gemsbok National Park), and game moves freely between the two across the usually dry Nossob river; on the west the park is bounded by the Namibia border. The terrain is a mixture of semi-desert, with low sand ridges, and dry savanna grassland. The park witnesses the seasonal migrations of ungulates from February to May, including eland, blue wildebeest, gemsbok, red hartebeest, steenbok and springbok. Carnivores include lion, leopard, cheetah, brown and spotted hyena, black-backed jackal, Cape fox and suricate (meerkat); and the rich

Above: KwaZulu-Natal has several reserves in which black rhinos are one of the chief attractions for visitors.

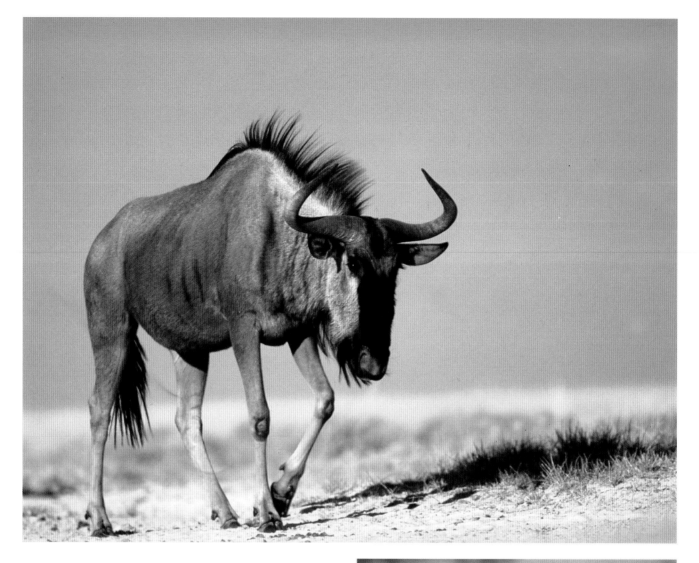

avifauna includes ostrich, lappet-faced vulture, pygmy falcon, and the sociable weaver with its extensive colonies of communal nests. Some 150 miles (240km) due south, a few miles east of where the south-marching Namibia border hits the Orange river, Augrabies Falls National Park sits astride the river, which hereabouts flows over a succession of rapids and through a narrow gorge before tumbling 184 feet (56m) over Bridal Falls. The largest animal in the park is the black rhino, reintroduced in 1985; resident wildlife includes springbok, steenbok and klipspringer, leopard, black-backed jackal, caracal, bat-eared fox, and baboon and vervet monkey; smaller mammals such as rock hyrax (commonly known as dassie in South Africa) feed within close range of tourists. In the far north-west corner of the province, Goegap Nature Reserve, east of the village of Springbok, is set in a harsh, arid landscape featuring domed outcrops of granite; the vegetation is mainly low-growing shrubs, succulents and the aloe tree known as kokerboom. The chief wildlife

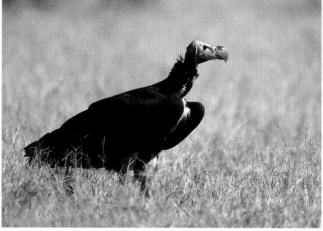

Top: North-western Cape Province's Kalahari Gemsbok National Park is one of southern Africa's best places to witness the seasonal migration of ungulates. One of the main protagonists of this mass movement is the wildebeest—in this region the so-called blue subspecies.

Above: As in East Africa, the migration attracts all the main ungulate predators—followed by vultures, such as this lappet-faced species, and other scavengers hoping to pick up scraps left by the big cats and hyenas.

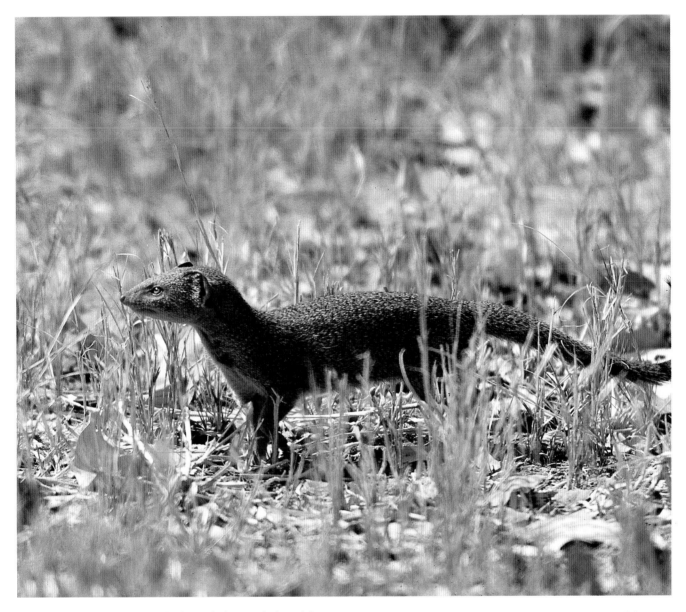

residents are mountain zebra, eland, gemsbok, springbok, rock hyrax and yellow mongoose.

Cedarberg Wilderness, near Clanwilliam (about 120 miles/193km north-east of Cape Town), lies in an area of montane fynbos (shrubby, heath-like vegetation). The main mammal residents are smaller antelope species—duiker, Cape grysbok, grey rhebok, klipspringer and others—together with baboon, rock hyrax and grey mongoose. Due east of Cape Town, near Swellendam, Bontebok National Park, along the northern bank of the Breede river, was founded in 1931 to protect the world's last 22 remaining bonteboks (a subspecies of the blesbok). Today it has several hundred bonteboks (and many have also been relocated to other reserves) as well as grey rhebok, Cape grysbok, duiker and Cape mountain zebra. Karroo National Park is set around the gorges and dry river beds of the Nuwefeld

Above: The slender, or black-tipped, mongoose is more arboreal than most other mongooses (it readily eats fruit), but it also preys on rodents and reptiles.

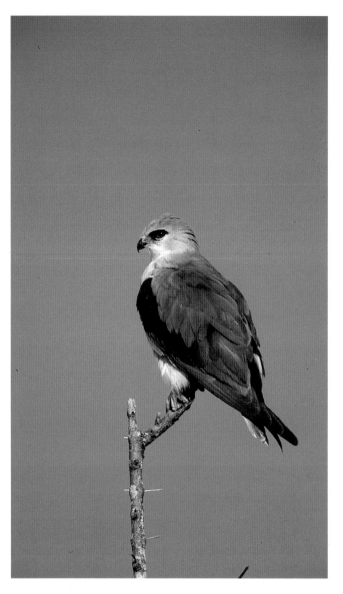

mountains north of Beaufort West. Among its wildlife residents are Cape mountain zebra, red hartebeest, black wildebeest, springbok and many smaller antelope species as well as rock hyrax, Cape and bat-eared fox and caracal. To the east, Karroo Nature Reserve encircles the town of Graaff-Reinet in rugged, hilly country dominated in the south by several peaks. Wildlife includes Cape mountain zebra, red hartebeest, black wildebeest, eland, blesbok and springbok. Similar game animals, as well as several species of eagles, can be seen in Mountain Zebra National Park, between Graaff-Reinet and Cradock, to the east. East again, and bigger game are resident at Addo Elephant National Park, which is enclosed by an elephant-proof fence and is set in hilly country with dense evergreen bush.

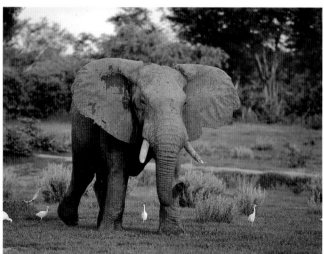

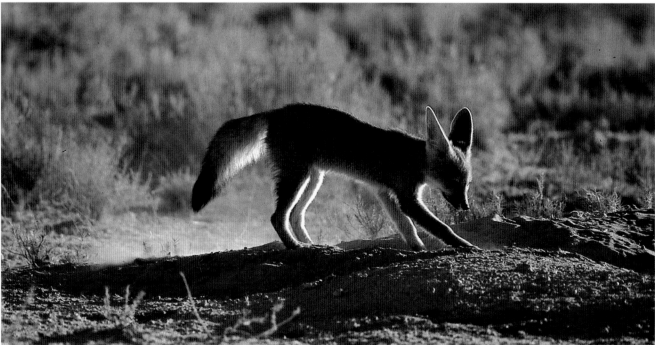

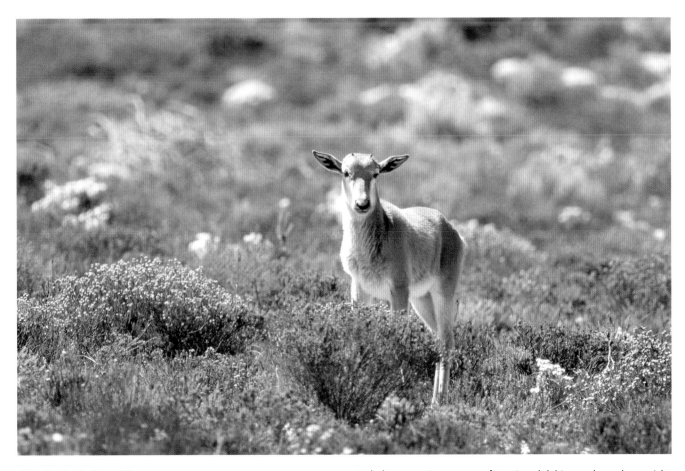

Cape Province's Coastal Reserves

Some 130 miles (210km) west of Port Elizabeth, Tsitsikamma Coastal National Park is a wonderfully scenic strip of coast that stretches for 44 miles (70km) eastward from Plettenberg Bay. It consists of a narrow coastal plain that ends in steep cliffs at the shore's edge, backed by deep and narrow river valleys descending from the Tsitsikamma range. The vegetation is a mixture of fynbos and patches of indigenous forest. The wildlife includes duiker, bushbuck, baboon, and vervet monkey, rock hyrax and Cape clawless otter. A few miles to the west, between Krysna and George, Wilderness National Park is formed around a series of lakes and linking waterways. Although waterbirds are the main attraction here—more than 80 species can be watched from hides—the park also has some duiker, bushbuck, and Cape grysbok. West again, De Hoop Nature Reserve, a few miles south of Bontebok National Park, protects the province's largest remaining area of fynbos; the terrain also includes rocky and sandy beaches, vlei (seasonal marsh or pan) and the Potberg hills. The park has the world's largest community of bonteboks, as well as eland, grey rhebok, Cape grysbok, duiker, rock hyrax and Cape clawless otter. De Hoop also includes a marine reserve featuring dolphins and southern right whales. Cape of Good Hope Nature Reserve, at the end of Cape Peninsula south of Simonstown, consists of a ridge of hills in the east running along the coast of False Bay, and flatlands that gently rise and fall towards the Atlantic coast in the west. The game population includes chacma baboon, Cape fox, rock hyrax and caracal as well as bontebok, Cape mountain zebra, Cape grysbok, grey rhebok, eland, duiker, and red hartebeest. Finally, the West Coast National Park, about 75 miles (120km) north-west of Cape Town, between

Above: A bontebok calf on the fynbos (heath) in the hilly eastern side of the Cape reserve. The bontebok (found only in south-western Cape Province) and the blesbok (which occurs from eastern Cape Province to northern KwaZulu-Natal) are two races of the same species.

Above Far Left: A skilful predator of rodents is this black-shouldered kite, seen here in Cape Province. It also has a taste for locusts.

Above Left: The main residents of Addo Elephant National Park are prevented by fencing from straying onto neighbouring agricultural land.

Left: The Cape fox is found in many of Cape Province's national parks, favouring grassland, scrub and semi-desert habitats. It is largely nocturnal and feeds mainly on small rodents and invertebrates.

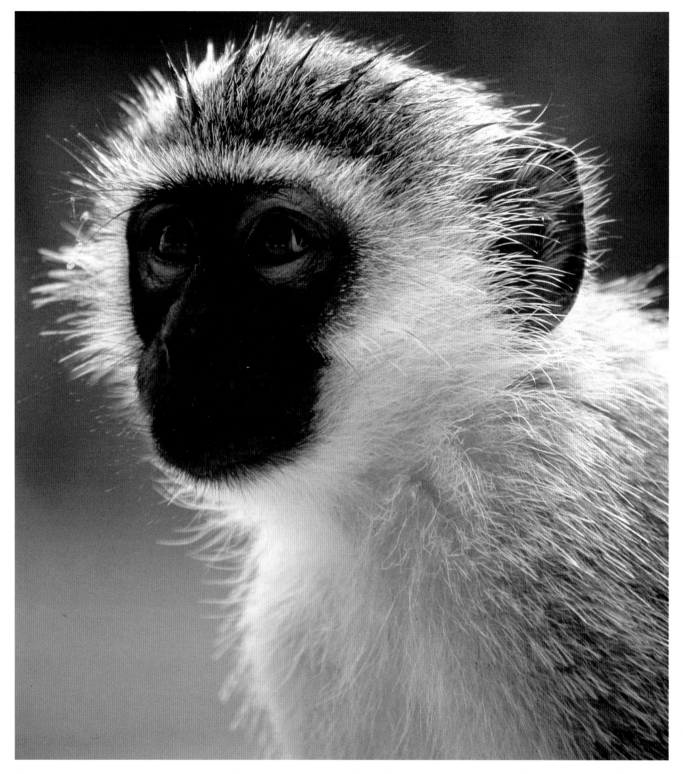

Ysterfontein and Langebaan, includes sandveld and fynbos areas enclosing a lagoon and several islands in a bay at the head of the lagoon. Marshes around the edge of the lagoon attract waders; the islands have nesting colonies of gannets and gulls; the fynbos on the eastern side of the lagoon is home to black wildebeest, eland, and bontebok.

Above: The vervet monkey, a feature of Tsirsikamma Coastal National Park, lives mainly in the park's small areas of forest. More than 20 races of vervet monkey have been described; some are known as grivets, others as green monkeys.

Right: Cape of Good Hope Nature Reserve occupies most of Cape Peninsula south of the port of Simonstown. This photograph shows the southernmost part of the reserve, with Cape Point at the bottom of the picture.

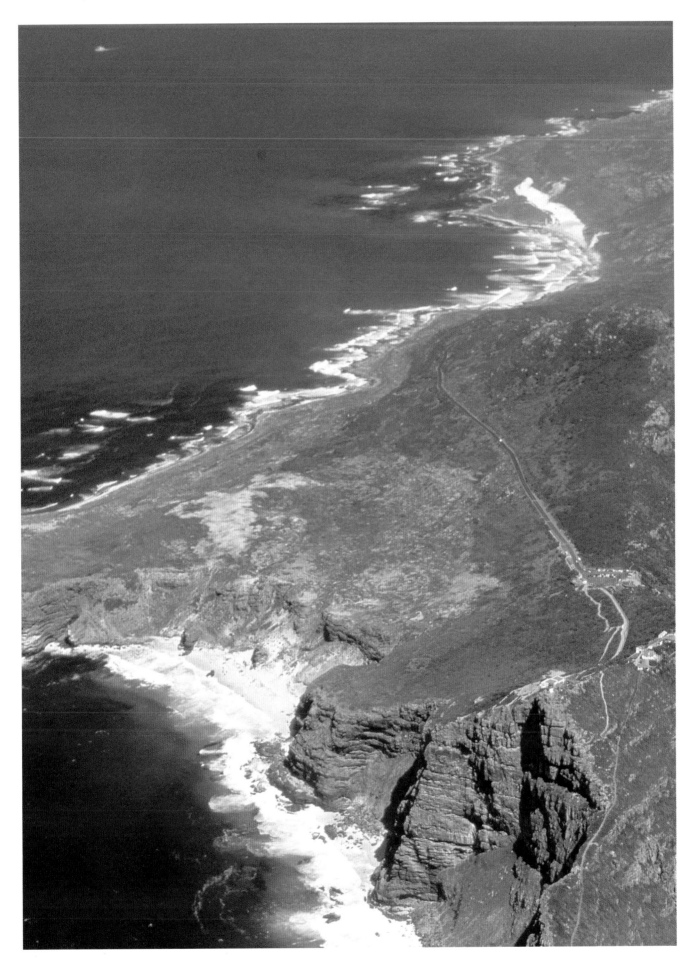

UNGULATES: THE HOOFED MAMMALS

Ungulates are mammals with hooves as opposed to claws. As might be expected in animals such as horses, antelopes and gazelles, hooves are an evolutionary adaptation to aid running at speed—their chief resource in evading predators such as the lion, leopard, hyena and wild dog. Ungulates fall into two groups: odd-toed (the Perissodactyla), with either one or three toes on each foot, and even-toed (Artiodactyla), with two or four toes. The odd-toed ungulates are rhinos, zebras, tapirs, horses and asses; the even-toed include hippos, pigs and hogs, giraffes, antelopes and wild cattle. The geographical distribution and range specified for each animal in the following chapters refer to its natural habitats, not to where it may nowadays be found in national parks and reserves.

Right: Plains, or Burchell's, zebra: with wildebeest at Mara river, Tanzania.

Overleaf: Black rhino head: note hooked upper lip, which aids browsing.

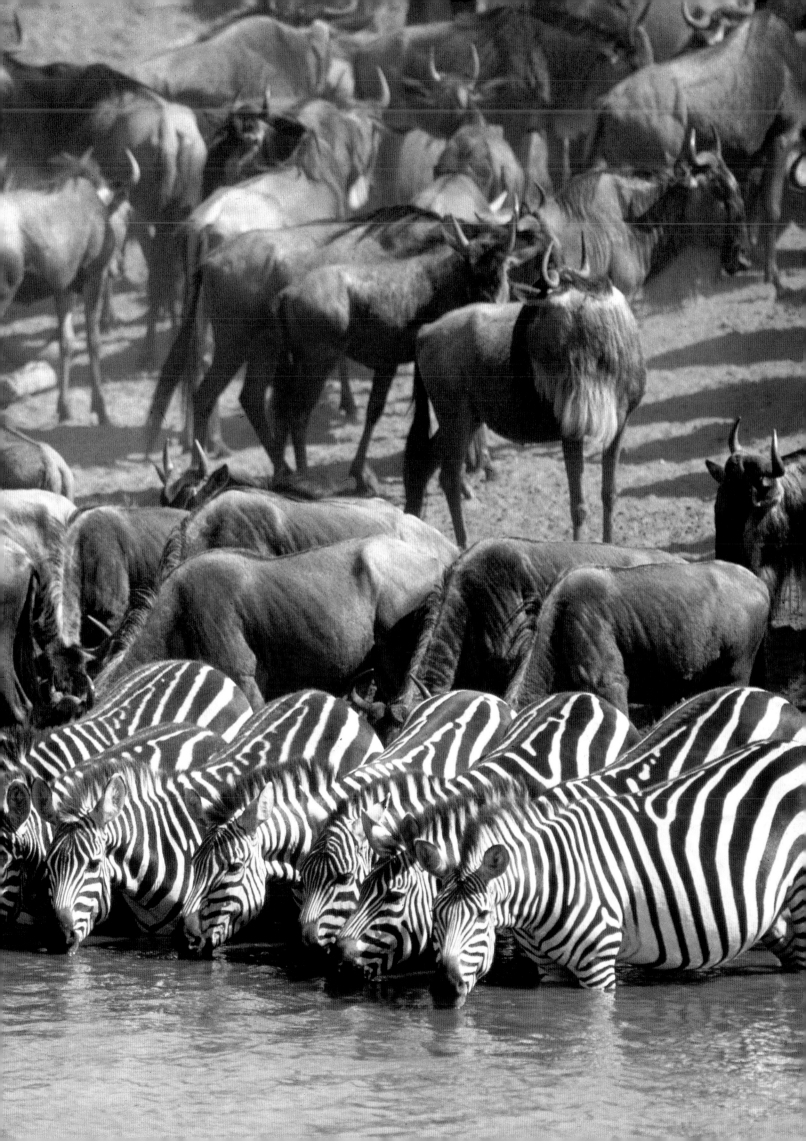

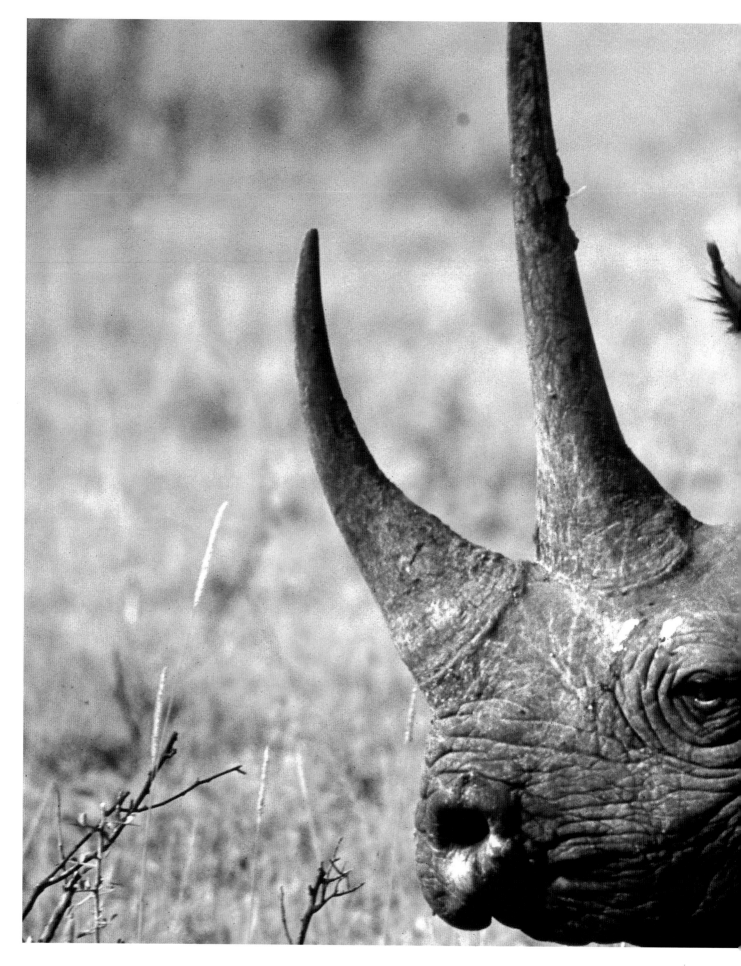

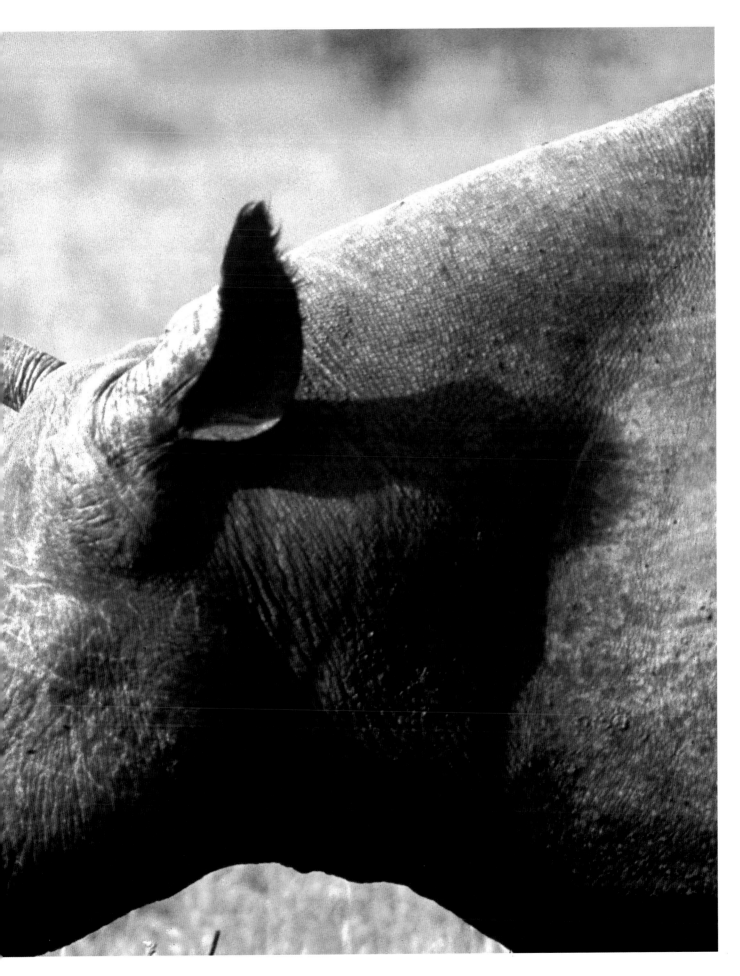

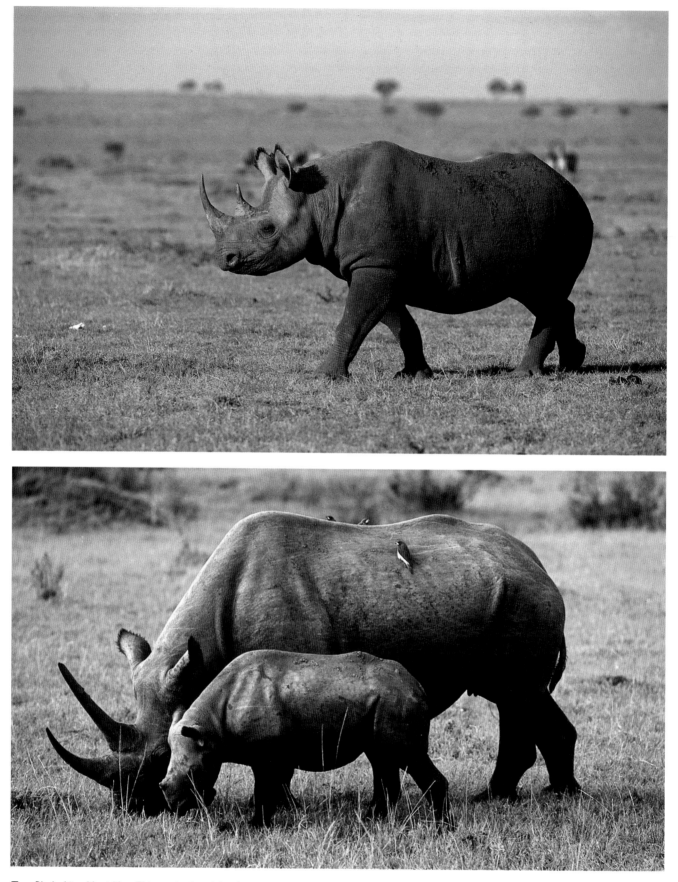

Top: Black rhino: Masai Mara. This species is mainly a browser.

Above: Black rhino with calf: Masai Mara.

Right: Plains zebras, showing stripe pattern: Amboseli National Park. The bird is a yellow oxpecker which feeds on ticks on the hides of ungulates.

Odd-toed Ungulates

There are two African species of rhinoceros: the black or browse rhino (*Diceros bicornis*) and the white or grass rhino (*Ceratotherium simum*). Males and females of both species have two horns. The black rhino is in fact dark grey in colour, the areas of thickest skin forming inflexible plates over shoulders, sides and haunches. Its upper lip is hooked and pointed to aid its browsing technique. Notably unpredictable in temperament, the black rhino is the more likely to charge if disturbed—and a full-grown male can make up to 30mph (48km/h). As its other common name implies, the black rhino is a browser of foliage, so is mainly found in dense or open woodland. More than 20 subspecies have been recognised. The white rhino is the largest land animal after the elephant, males weighing up to 7,700lb (3,500kg). It has a larger, wider mouth than the black and its upper lip is not hooked; its neck forms a hump when the head is raised. Its preferred habitat is grassland savanna with shade-giving trees and water holes offering muddy places in which to wallow. There are northern and southern subspecies. Today, both species of rhino are found only in reserves.

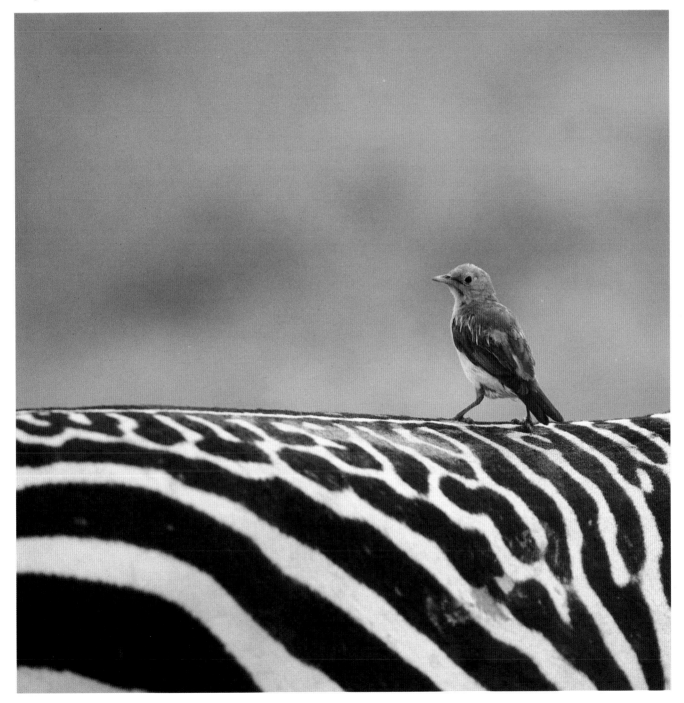

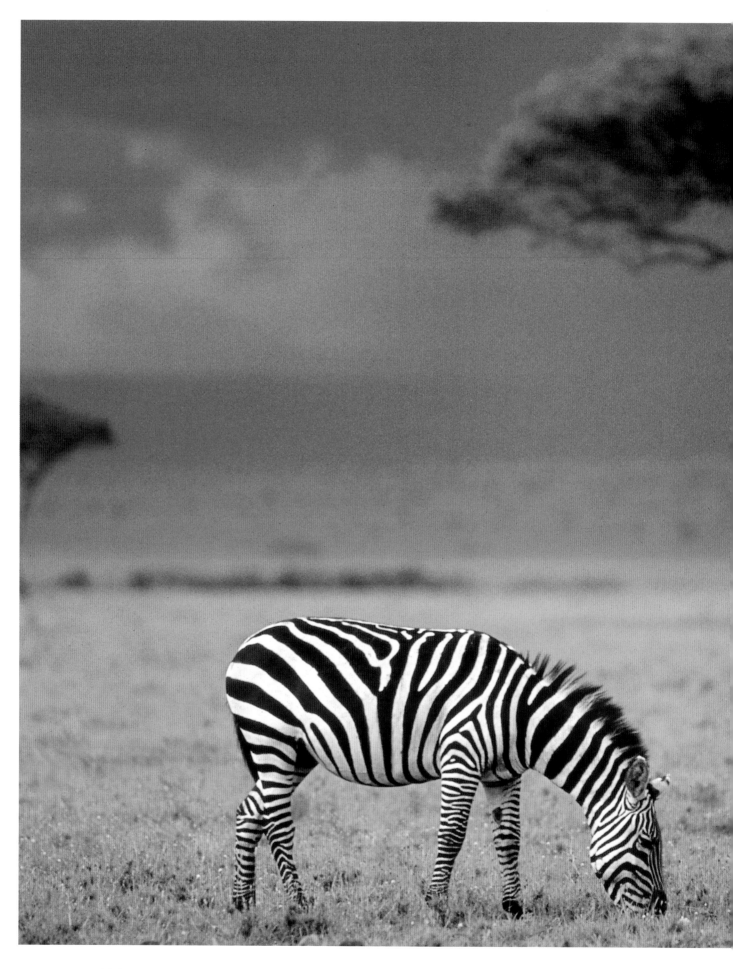

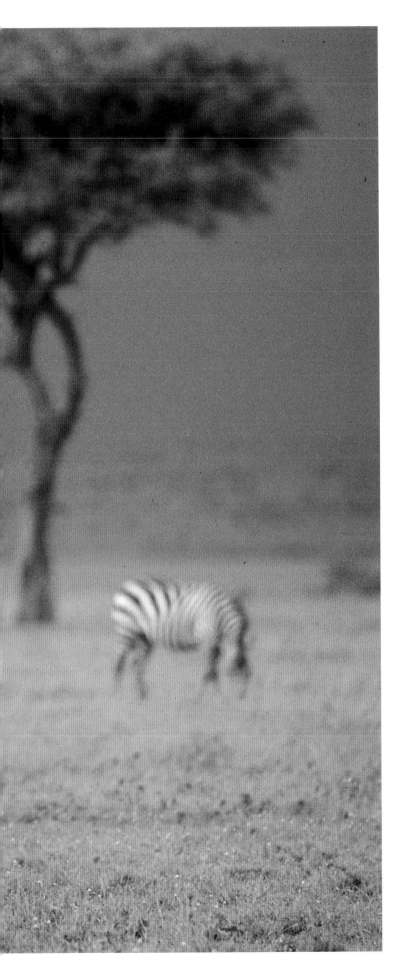

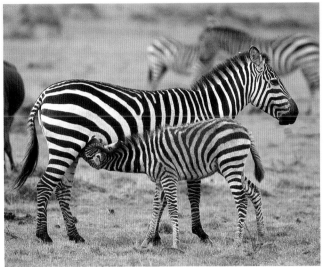

There are three species of African zebra: the plains zebra, the mountain zebra, and Grevy's zebra. The plains zebra (*Equus burchellii*), also known as Burchell's zebra or common zebra, is more stocky than the others, with a rather short neck; it stands 50-56in (1.27-1.4m) at the shoulder. Its short coat has black or brown stripes extending some way under the belly against a white or light sand ground colour. It is a species of the rich grasses of the open savanna and wooded savanna. There are three main subspecies: Boehm's (also known as Grant's) zebra of south-eastern Sudan and East Africa south to Zambia; Selous' zebra of Zambia, Malawi, Zimbabwe and Mozambique; and Chapman's zebra of Angola, Namibia, Botswana, Transvaal and KwaZulu-Natal. The stripe patterns and ground colour vary from region to region; in some southern populations narrow, lighter-coloured "shadow" stripes appear between the broader, darker ones. The mountain zebra (*Equus zebra*) is more slender and taller than its plains cousin; its stripes do not go under the belly and they are much thicker and wider-spaced on the hindquarters, while the bridge of its nose is orange-brown. There are two subspecies: Cape mountain zebra of South Africa and

Above: Boehm's zebra with young: Serengeti plains.

Left: Boehm's (also known as Grant's) zebra: Masai Mara.

Overleaf: Chapman's zebra: Etosha National Park, Namibia. Note the shadow stripes.

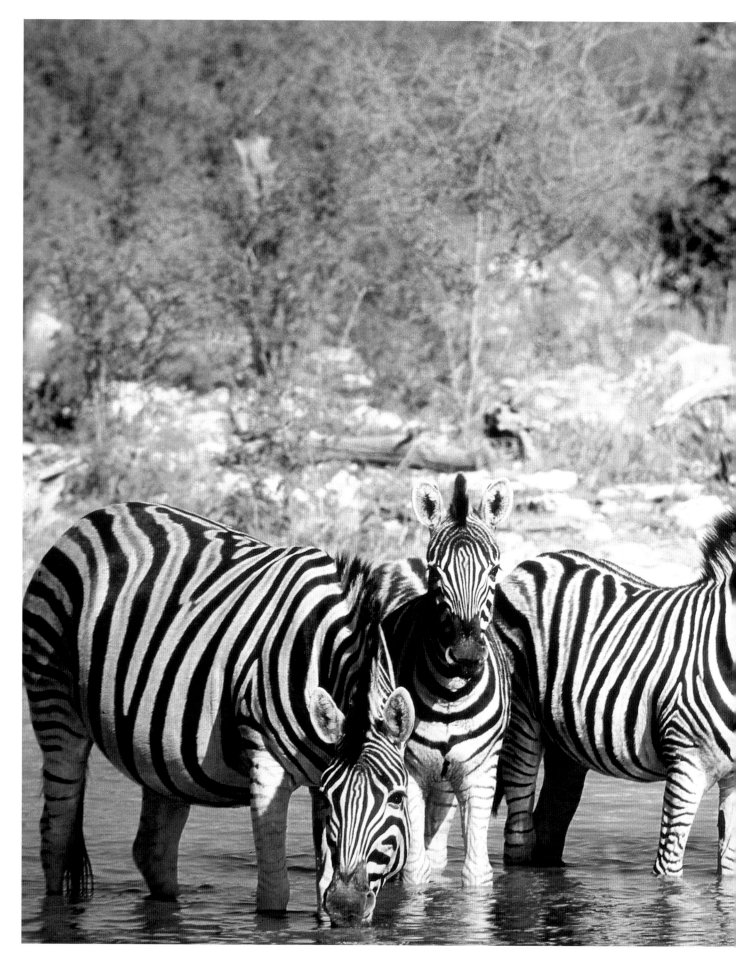

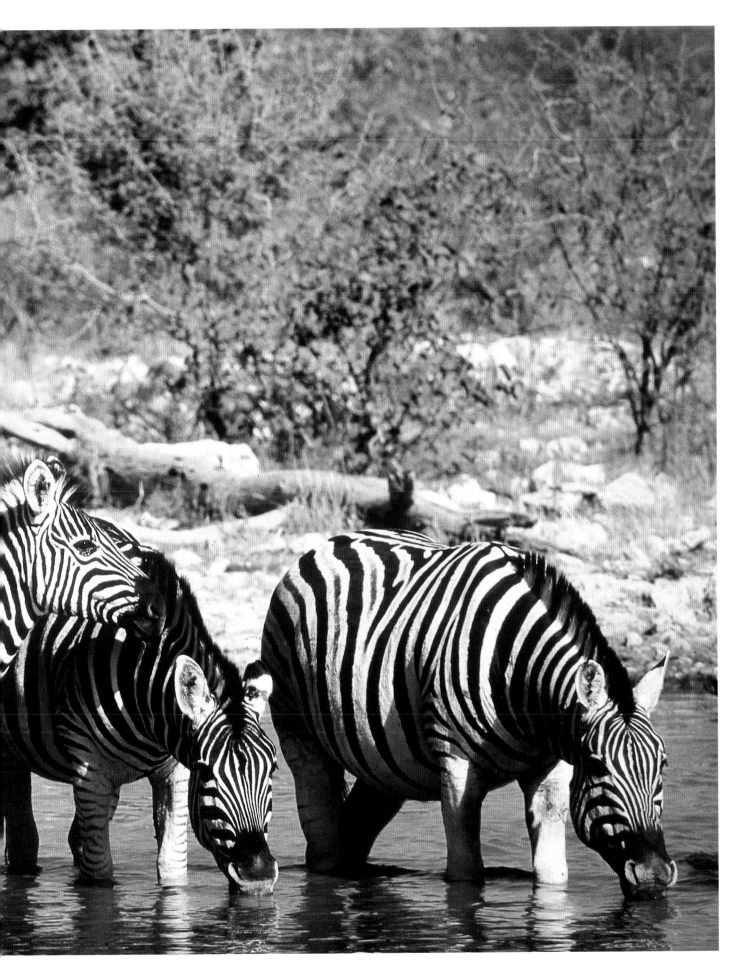

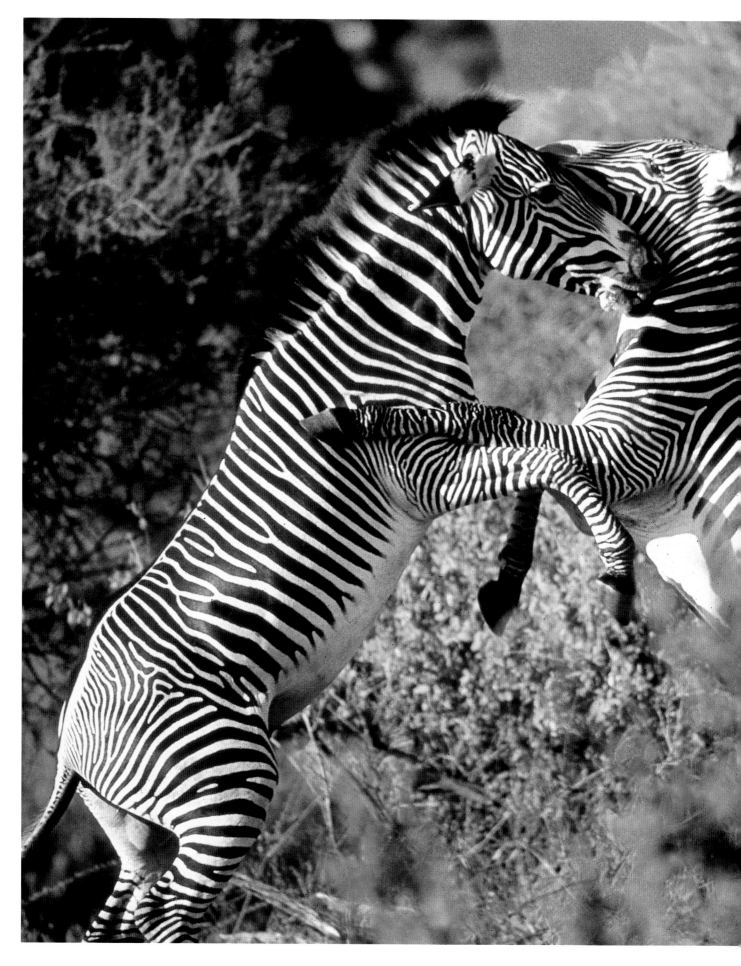

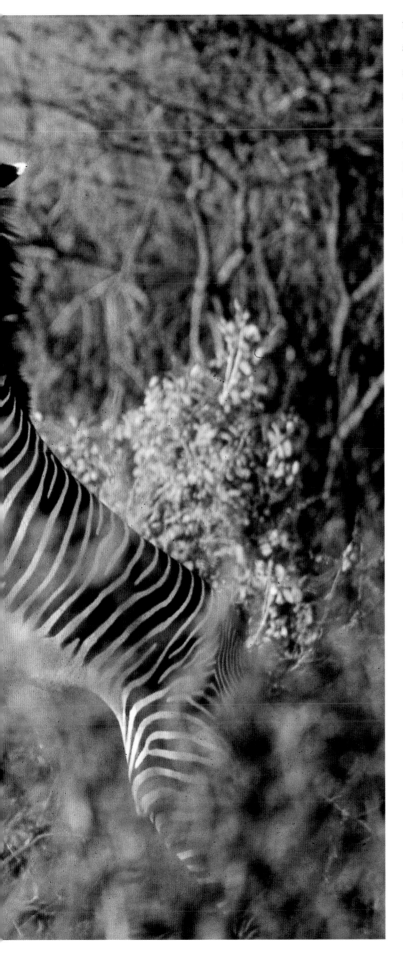

the slightly larger Hartmann's mountain zebra of western Angola and Namibia. Grevy's zebra (*Equus grevyi*), the largest of the three species, has a large head and ears and an upstanding mane. The stripes are of similar width overall (though the width varies from one individual to the next), and there is a broad dark stripe along the spine. Its range is southern Ethiopia and Somalia and northern Kenya. Its natural habitat is somewhat drier than the plains zebra's: arid grasslands and acacia savanna. Like the plains species it is seasonally migratory. Zebras are essentially grazers but all species, especially Grevy's, top up their diet with browse.

Grevy's zebras fighting: Samburu National Park, Kenya.

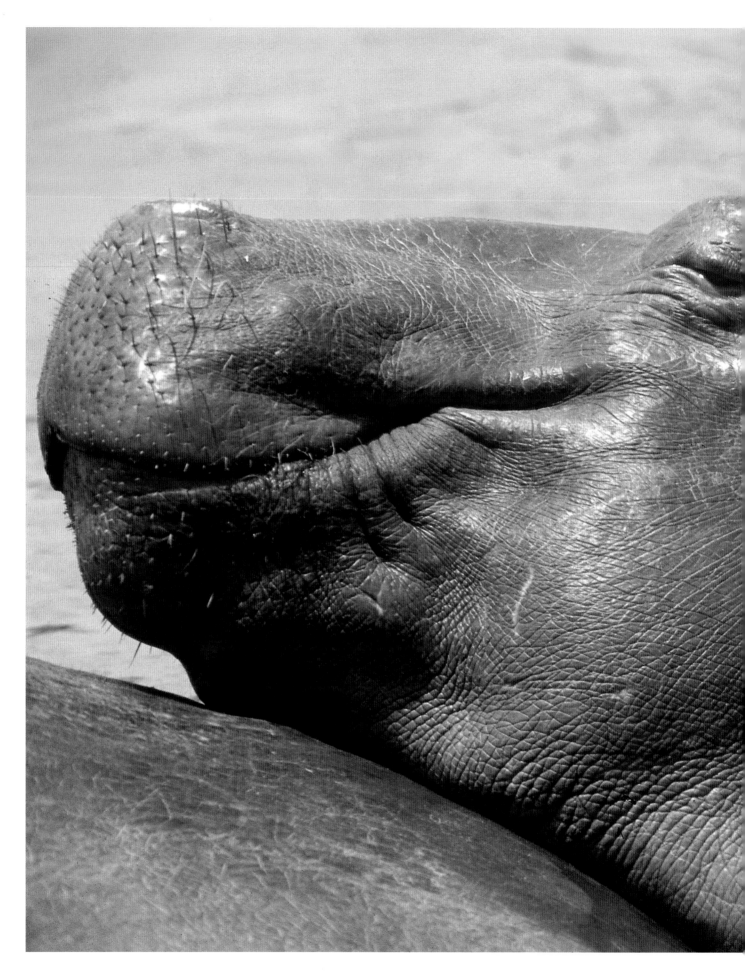

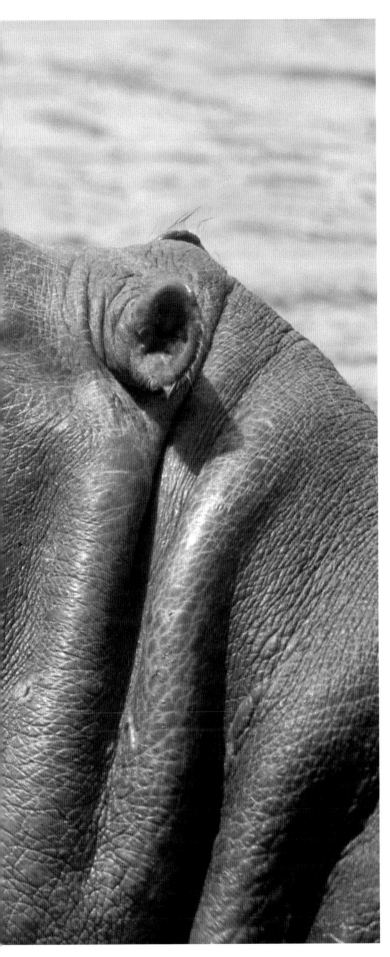

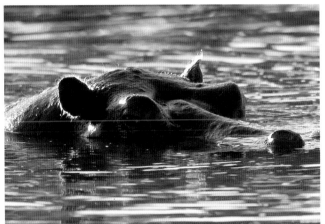

Even-toed Ungulates

The common hippopotamus (*Hippopotamus amphibius*) is the largest of the even-toed ungulates, with a massive barrel-shaped body on stubby legs, and huge head with a very wide muzzle; the adult males may weigh more than 7,000lb (3,175kg). Hippos have smooth skin, generally grey-black in colour but often with a pinkish tinge on the underparts. They secrete through their pores a reddish fluid that protects their hairless skin against the heat of the sun and may also have antibiotic properties. Hippos are semi-aquatic, spending most of the day in water but frequently basking on mudbanks. Their river, waterhole, lake or whatever must be deep enough for the largest member of the herd to submerge completely. At night they emerge to graze on rich but preferably short grasses at feeding grounds that may be several miles from their favourite river site. They are native to all the major rivers, lakes and swamps south of the Sahara, and there are large populations in northern Zambia, Uganda and eastern Zaïre. Bull hippos and cow hippos with young are, if provoked, probably the most dangerous animals in Africa.

The adult pygmy hippopotamus (*Hexoprotodon liberiensis*) closely resembles the young of the common hippo, weighing at most 600lb (272kg); but it has much less protruding eyes. It is a forest animal of West Africa, living beside rivers and swamps in dense lowland forests, mainly in Liberia and Ivory Coast. It has a more varied diet than the common hippo: it eats roots, tubers, foliage and fallen fruit as well as grass.

Above: Hippo half submerged: Botswana.

Left: Hippo calf: Tanzania.

Wild pigs and hogs belong to the Suidae family, which in Africa includes the warthog, bushpig, red river hog and giant forest hog. All these species are omnivores and have evolved efficient rooting techniques, a practice aided by the shape of their snouts, which are tipped with tough cartilage. The warthog (*Phacochoerus africanus*), pig-like in appearance, is uniformly grey in colour, largely hairless except for an erectile mane on the neck and back and tufts of light-coloured whiskers along the cheeks. Both sexes have curved upper tusks, but these formidable weapons are much thicker and longer in the male. The warthog has much the largest range of any African pig: it found in arid savanna (including the Sahel on the southern fringe of the Sahara), moist savanna in West, East and southern Africa and floodplains in many regions, though it is absent from lowland and montane rainforest. It stands about 28in (70cm) at the shoulder and weighs up to 230lb (104kg).

The bushpig (*Potamochoerus larvatus*) has a more rounded body and shorter legs than the warthog. Its coat is often extremely shaggy and varicoloured, including brown, brownish grey and brownish

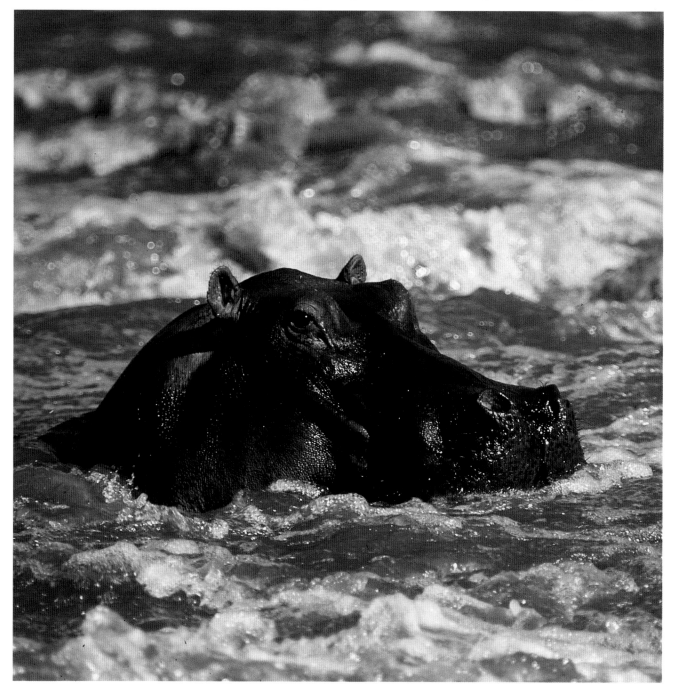

Above: Hippo in river rapids: Kenya.

Right: Hippo yawning: waterhole, Masai Mara.

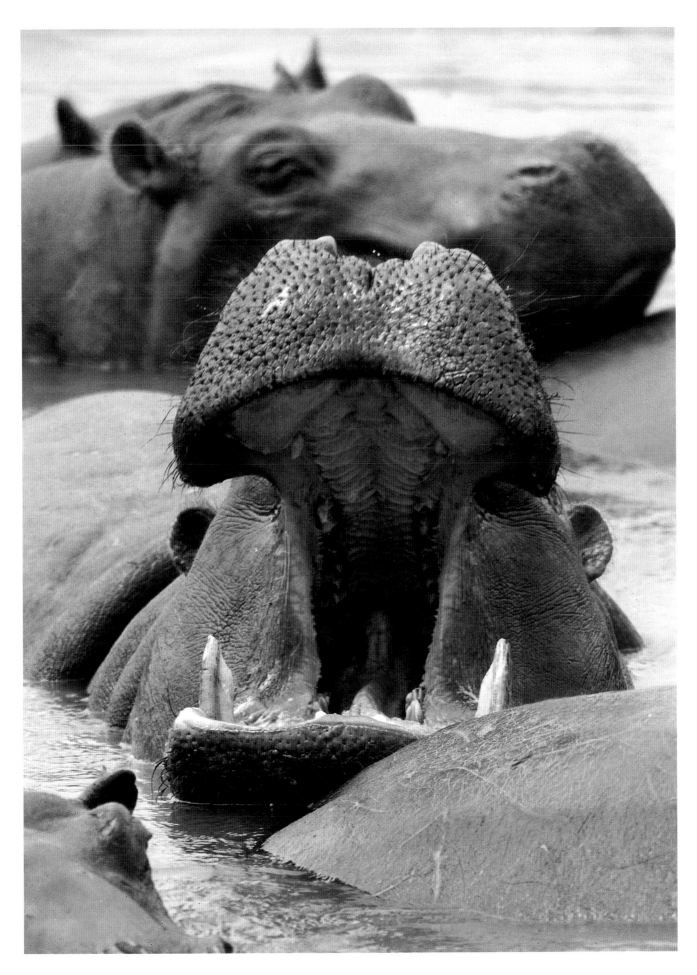

233

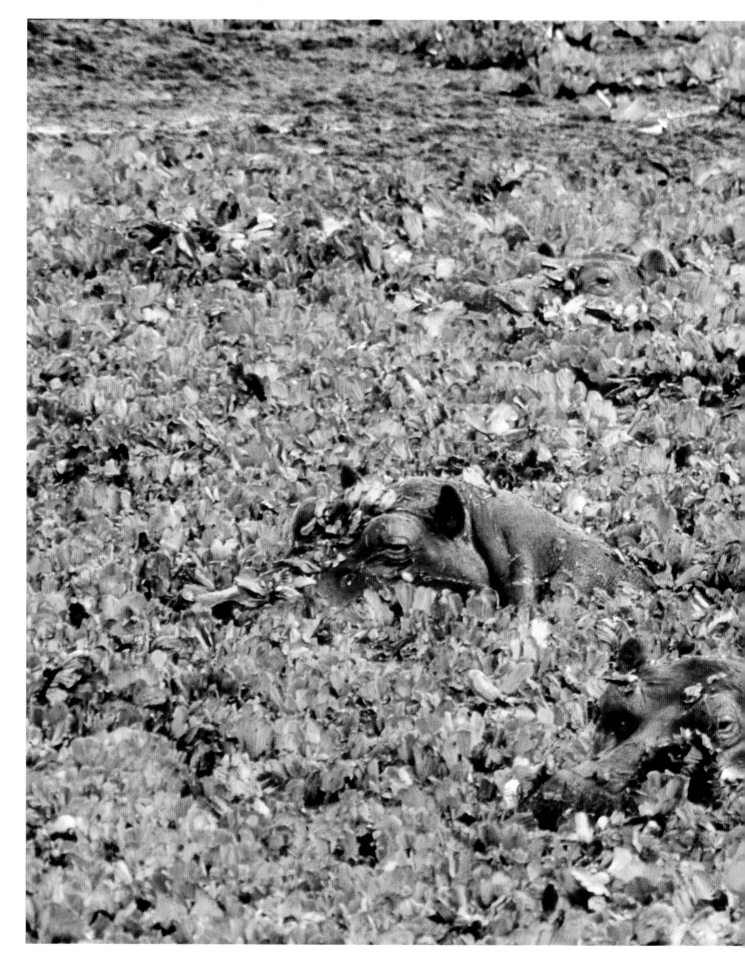

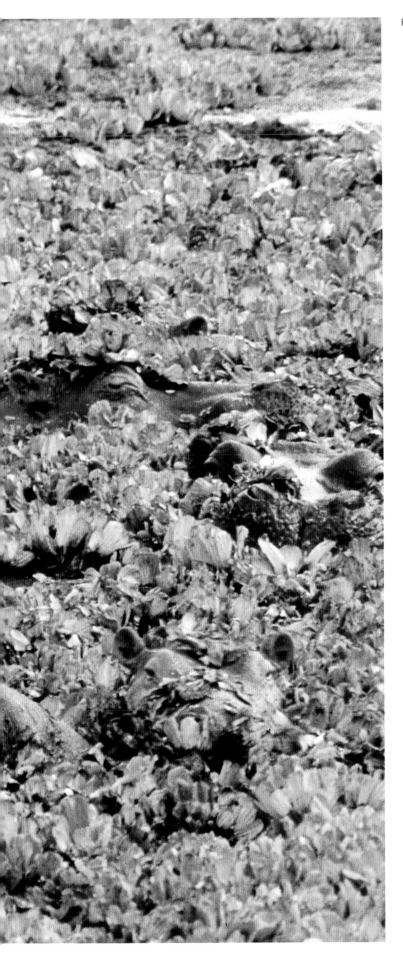

Hippos in swamp with aquatic plants: Masai Mara.

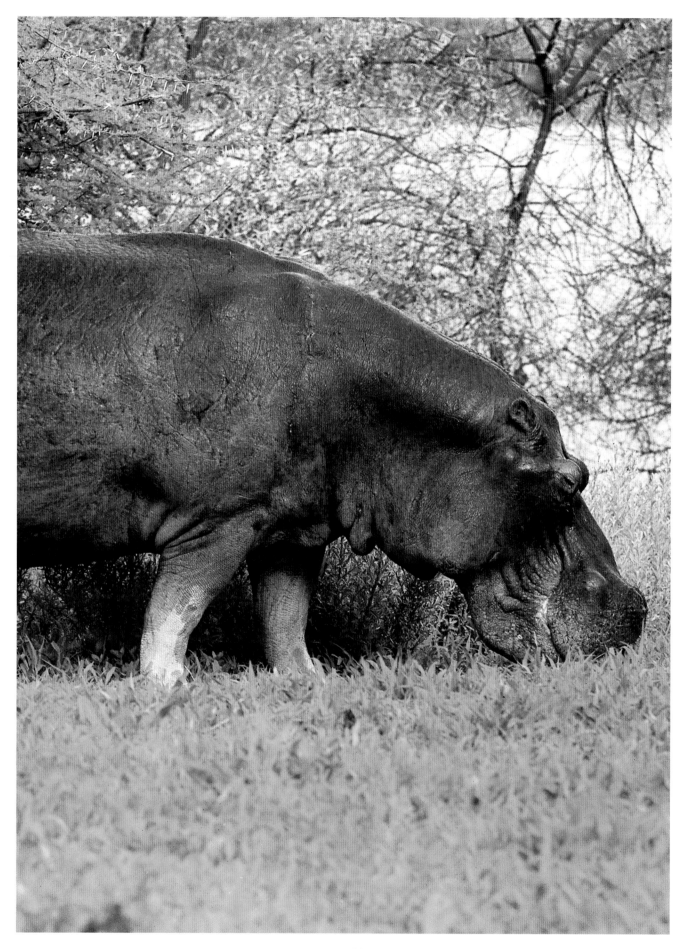

Above: Hippo grazing at feeding grounds: Zimbabwe.

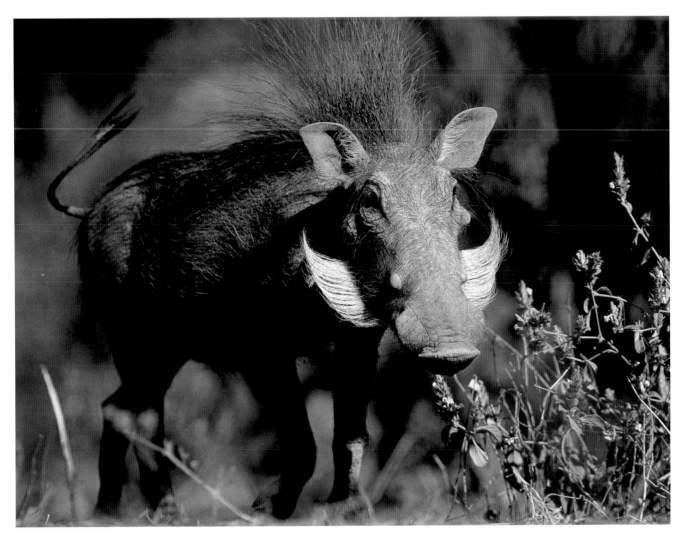

black; the erectile mane is lighter in colour. The upper tusks barely extend beyond the lips, but the lower ones are longer and extremely sharp. Highly sociable, the females and young live in groups of a dozen or more. The bushpig inhabits montane forests (up to 4,000ft/1,220m), moist woodlands, grasslands and swamps throughout much of East Africa, the range extending from Ethiopia and southern Sudan to South Africa, and westward into southern Zaïre and eastern Angola. Its close cousin the red river hog (*P. porcus*), also called the forest bushpig, has an almost brick-red coat and is less shaggy than *P. larvatus*.

The giant forest hog (*Hylochoerus meinertzhageni*) is the largest member of the tribe, standing up to 40in (100cm) at the shoulder and weighing as much as 600lb (272kg). Its greyish brown skin is covered by long bristly hairs, longest on the neck and back. The massive head has large, hairless swellings around the eyes and above the tusks, and in the male the outward-flaring upper tusks may be up to 12in (31cm) long. It lives in lowland and montane forests and neigh-

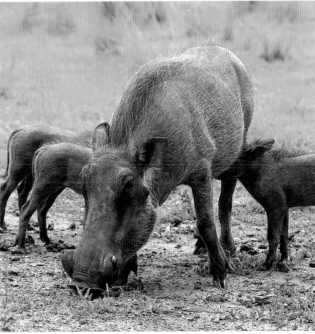

Top: Female warthog: Zambia. Note elaborate cheek whiskers.

Above: Female warthog with young: South Africa.

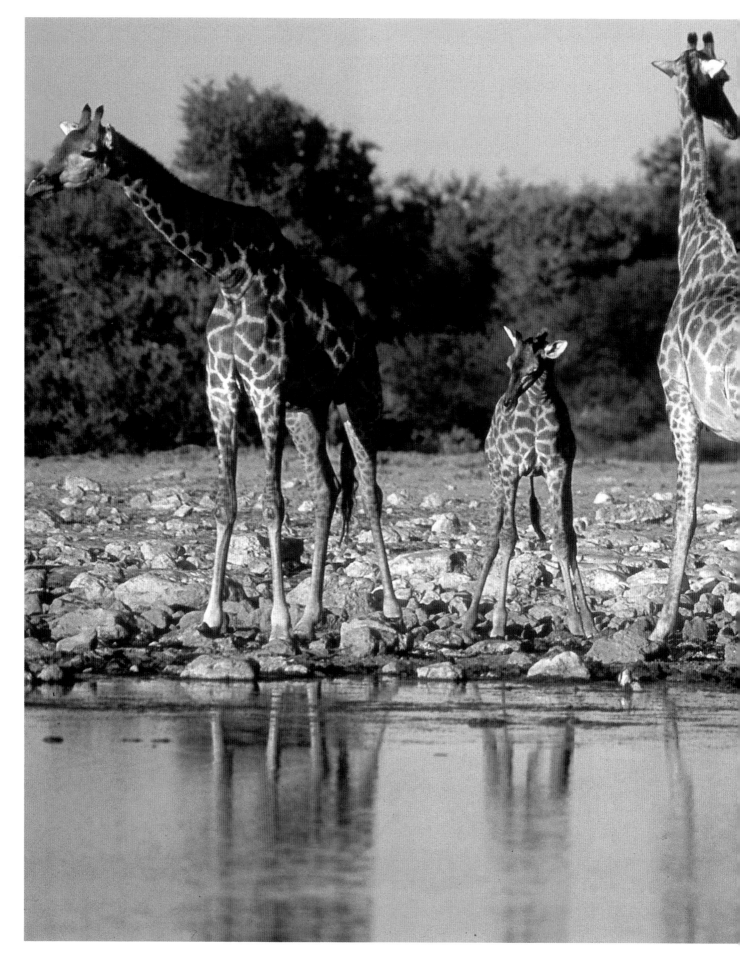

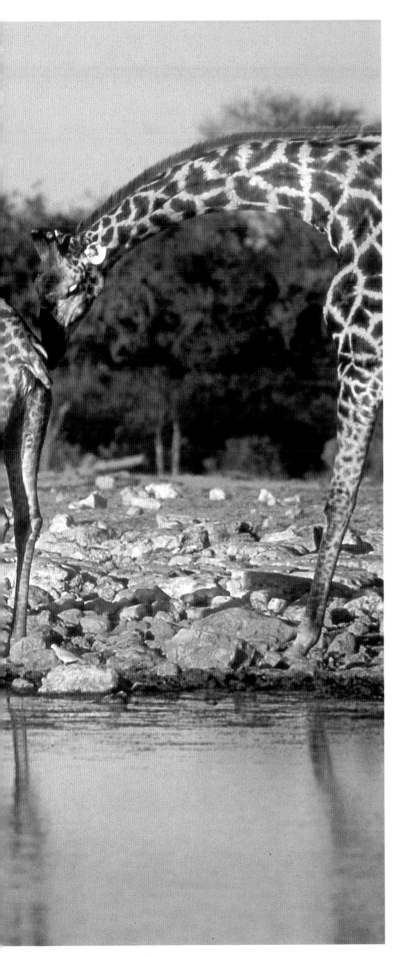

bouring grassland in West and central Africa north of the Congo river and as far east as the western arm of the Rift Valley.

The giraffe is comfortably the tallest mammal in the world, with exceptionally long legs and neck: a large male may be up to 11ft 6in (3.5m) high at the shoulder and 18ft (5.5m) high at the top of the head; and he may weigh more than 3,000lb (1,365kg). All giraffes belong to a single species, *Giraffa camelopardalis*, but there are a number of subspecies that are distinguished by the colour, size and shape of their coat markings. The most readily recognisable subspecies is the reticulated giraffe of southern Ethiopia and northern Kenya, with a coat that resembles neatly cut, rich brown crazy paving separated by a "mortar" of narrow white or cream lines. In contrast, the Masai giraffe farther south has a somewhat darker ground colour and irregularly shaped brown patches with jagged edges. In some areas, individuals or whole populations may be darker or lighter in colour than elsewhere; and old males tend to be darker than females or young. Both sexes have a pair of short, bony horns; older males may have one or more additional ones. The

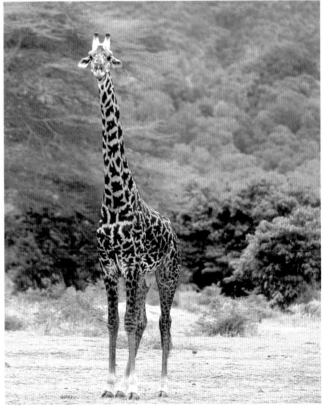

Above: Masai-race giraffe: Manyara National Park, Tanzania.

Left: A southern-race giraffe family at waterhole: Etosha National Park, Namibia.

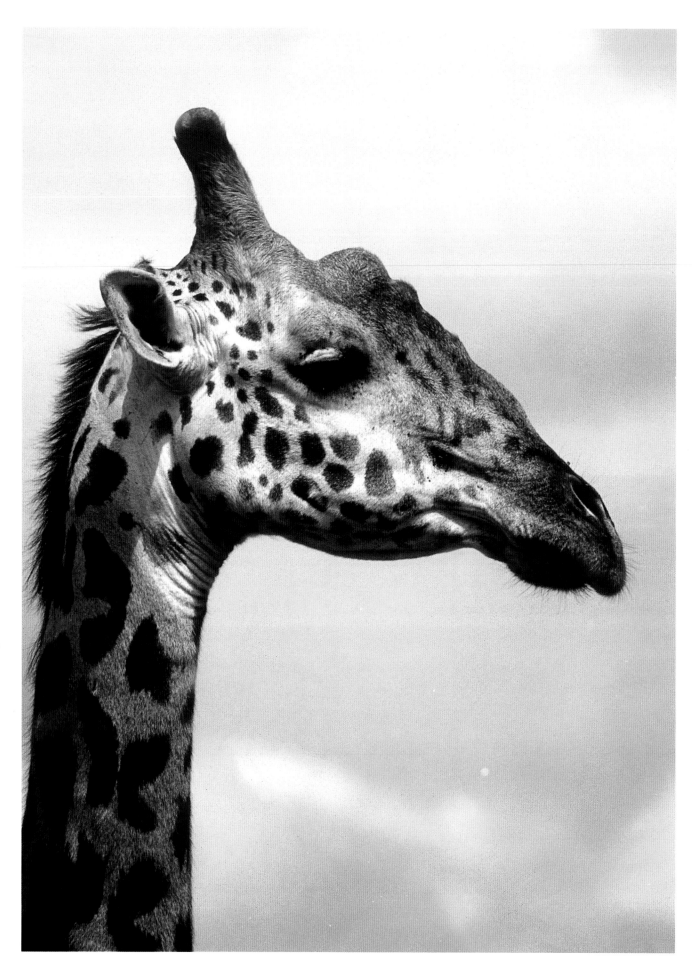

giraffe's height enables it to feed on foliage and shoots beyond the reach of other browsers; the food is stripped from trees by its powerful lips and 18in (450mm) long tongue. Giraffes live mainly in dry savanna woodland; they prefer deciduous tree and bush species but will browse on riverine evergreens in the dry season. Their natural range is south of the Sahara as far as northern areas of Namibia and Botswana. The only other member of the Giraffidae family is the Okapi (*Okapia johnstoni*), which was discovered by naturalists less than 100 years ago. Sometimes called the forest giraffe, it is found only in northern and north-eastern Zaire, from the Ubangi river

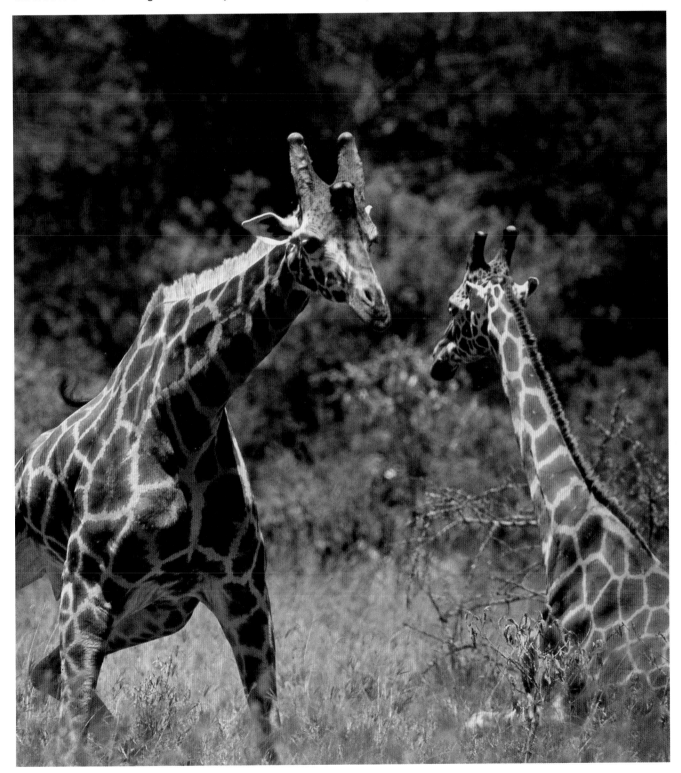

Left: Head of giraffe, Masai-race.

Above: Rothschild's, or Baringo, giraffe rises to its feet: Nakuru National Park, Kenya.

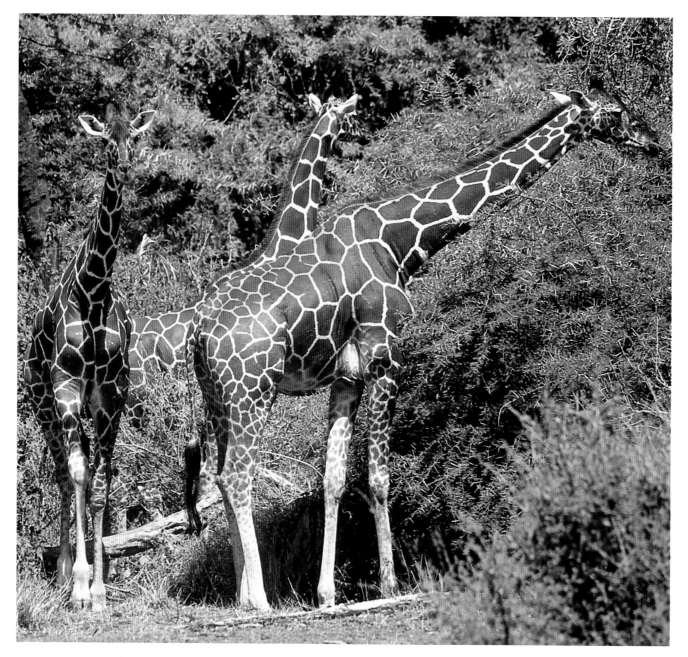

eastward almost to the Uganda border. Long-necked and long in limb, the okapi has a soft, velvety chocolate-brown coat, with the upper parts of the legs and the rump marked with black and white transverse stripes. The males and females are similar in size, reaching about 5ft 3in (1.6m) at the shoulder. Mainly browsers, okapi feed on the forest understory, occasionally also eating fruits and fungi.

Bovids (Bovidae) are the family of ruminants (cud-chewing herbivores) that have permanent, hollow, unbranched horns. In Africa this means, essentially, the buffalo and the antelopes among the indigenous wild species. There are 86 antelope species across the world: all but 13 of them are native to Africa. The African buffalo (*Syncerus caffer*) occurs in two distinct subspecies: the Cape,

or savanna, buffalo; and the forest, or red, buffalo. The Cape buffalo is much the larger: it has a short-necked, heavily built, black or dark brown body, with large, hair-fringed ears below massive, outward-flaring horns. The forest buffalo is smaller and slighter, with a reddish or red-brown coat that is darker on the head and legs. The Cape buffalo is highly gregarious, congregating in herds of up to several thousand mainly in the open savanna grasslands from Sudan and Ethiopia in the north to Angola, Zambia, Zimbabwe and northern South Africa in the south. The forest buffalo is found in lowland

Top: Reticulated giraffes browsing: Buffalo Springs National Reserve. Kenya.

Right: Reticulated giraffe: Samburu National Reserve, Kenya.

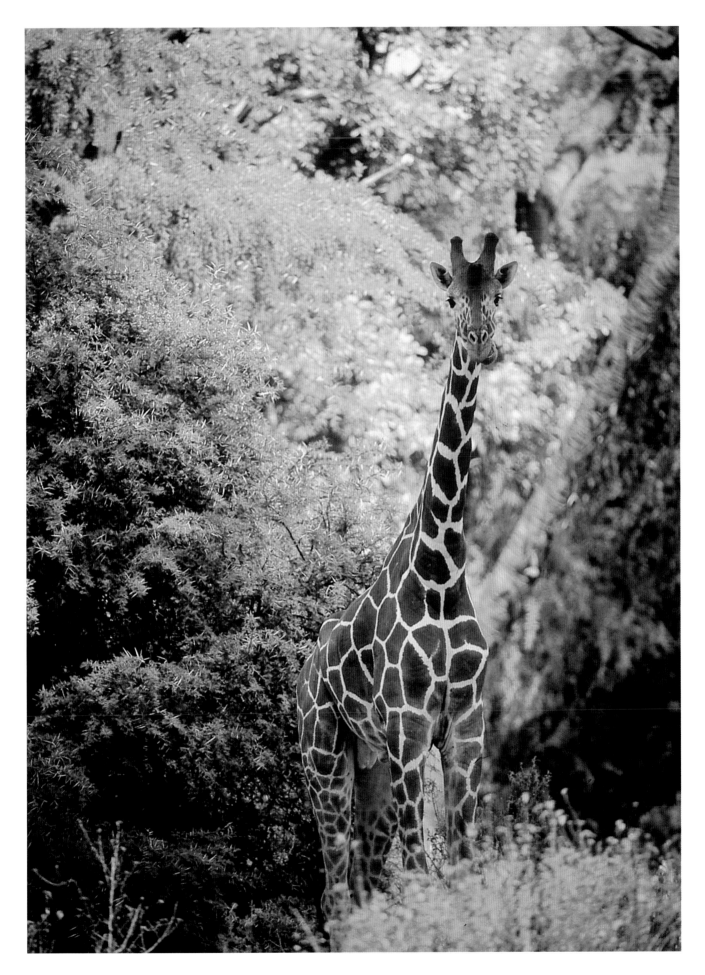

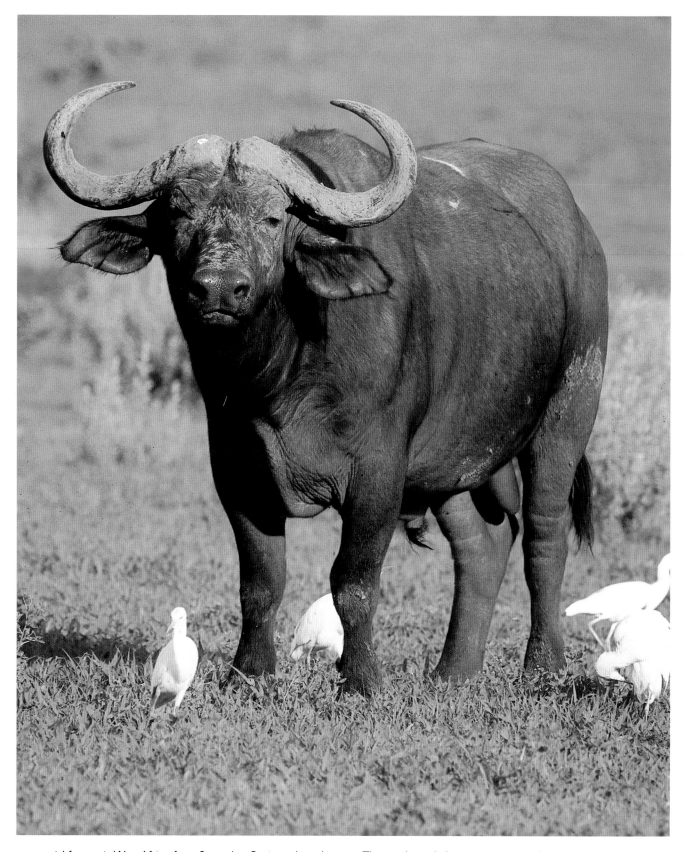

equatorial forests in West Africa, from Senegal to Benin, and south-wards as far as Angola. The Cape subspecies, which may weigh more than 1,550lb (700kg), can be a formidable foe of predators, and it has also taken a heavy toll of human hunters.

The antelopes belong to various subfamilies of the Bovidae. The Tragelaphinae subfamily of spiral-horned antelope includes eland, bongo, kudu, nyala, sitatunga and bushbuck, all of which belong to the genus *Tragelaphus*. They are mainly browsers of forest or

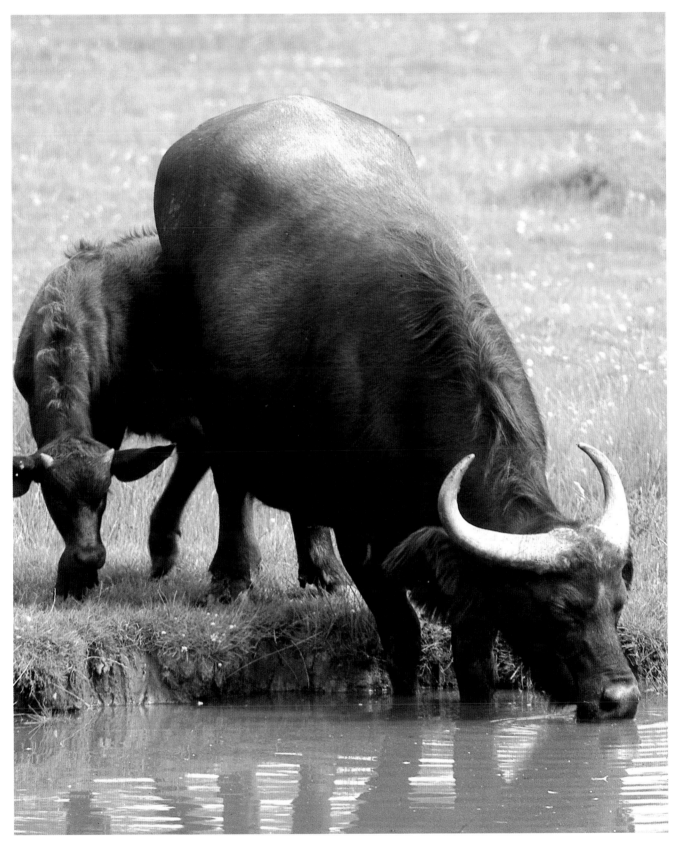

woodland, though some also graze. Their horns' spiral pattern varies between species from tightly bound to open corkscrew. The eland is Africa's largest antelope. There are two species: common (or southern) eland (*T. oryx*) and Derby (or giant) eland (*T. derbianus*).

Above: Cape buffalo and calf at waterhole: South Africa.

Above Left: Cape buffalo: Matusadona Nationa; Park, Zimbabwe.

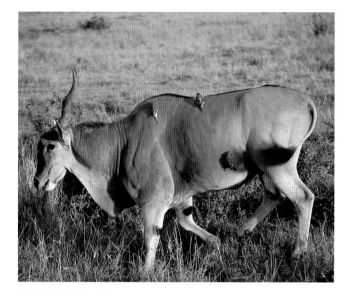

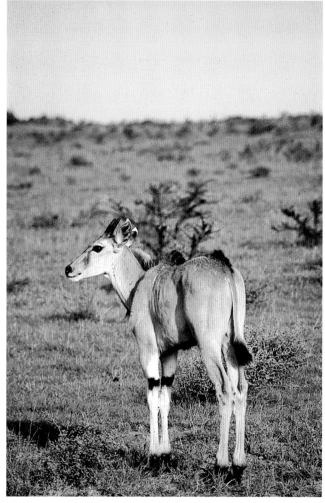

Top: Common eland cow: Masai Mara.

Above: Common eland calf: the tail tuft is larger and darker than that of Derby eland.

Right: Common eland cow: the horns are longer and thinner in the cow than in the bull.

Both are massive, somewhat ox-like in appearance, with a raised shoulder hump and large pendulous dewlap on the throat. The common eland is mainly fawn in colour, with a short, dark mane on the back of the neck. The Derby is of a richer brown colour, with thin white stripes on the upper body between fore and hind legs. The largest male Derbys are slightly the taller—about 6ft (1.8m) at the shoulder, while the largest common males, at about 2,050lb (930kg), are a little heavier. The common eland's range is from southern Ethiopia to KwaZulu-Natal in the east and from southern Zaïre to southern Angola in the west. The Derby eland occurs in fragmented ranges of mainly broadleaved savanna from Senegal in West Africa eastward to southern Sudan and northern Uganda.

The bongo (*T. euryceros*) is large and stocky, its rich reddish brown coat marked with up to 16 thin vertical white stripes down each side. A stiff brown crest (white where the stripes intervene) runs along the spine from the shoulders to the base of the tail. Both sexes have heavy, smooth, white-tipped horns, black and white markings on the legs and, usually, two white spots on the sides of the face. Adult males may be a little over four foot (1.25m) at the shoulder and weigh up to 660lb (300kg). The bongo lives in lowland rainforest in West Africa, Cameroon, Gabon and eastwards in the Congo basin and western Uganda, and in montane forest in Kenya's highlands.

The greater kudu (*T. strepsiceros*), a large, long-legged antelope, is brown with white torso stripes, usually with a greyer neck, and a maned hump; there is a white chevron between the eyes and white cheek spots. Only the male has horns—long with deep, open spiral—above the very large ears. It stands up to five foot (1.5m) at the shoulders, and weighs up to 220lb (100kg). Mainly a browser, it lives in woodlands and more open country with shrubby thickets, from Chad to Ethiopia and Somalia, south through central and southern Africa; it avoids open savanna plains. The lesser kudu (*T. imberbis*) is smaller, with similar horn shape, but with more torso stripes and with a more greyish brown coat colour. It has two large white marks, one above the other, on the throat. Almost solely a browser, it favours acacia woodland and dense scrub, and is found in south-eastern Ethiopia, Somalia, and parts of Kenya and Tanzania.

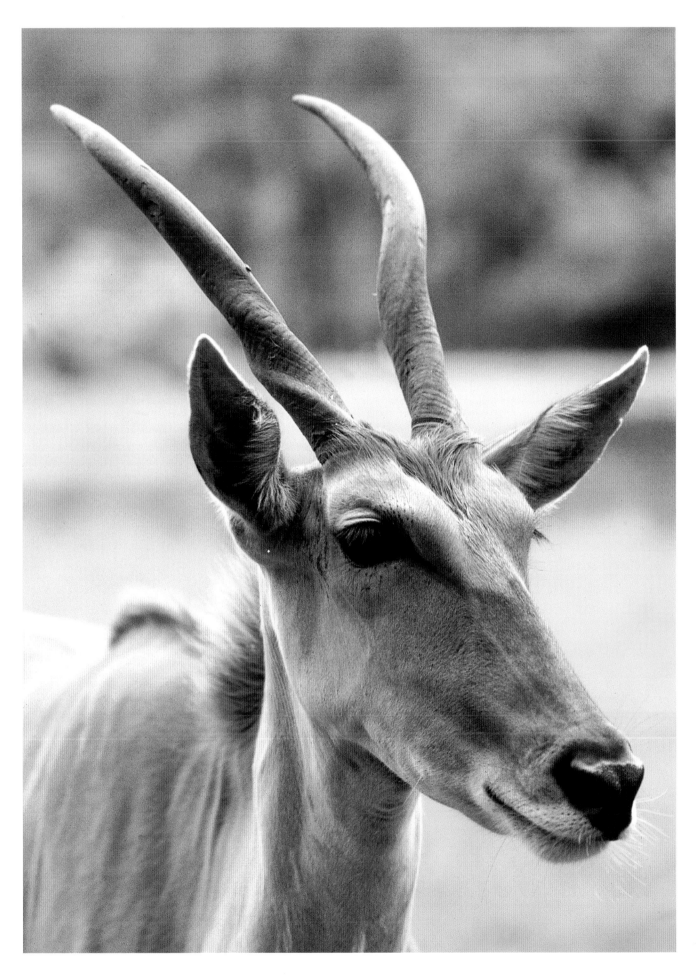

Greater kudu male: Botswana. Note the size and coiling of the horns, the large ears, and the white chevron between his eyes.

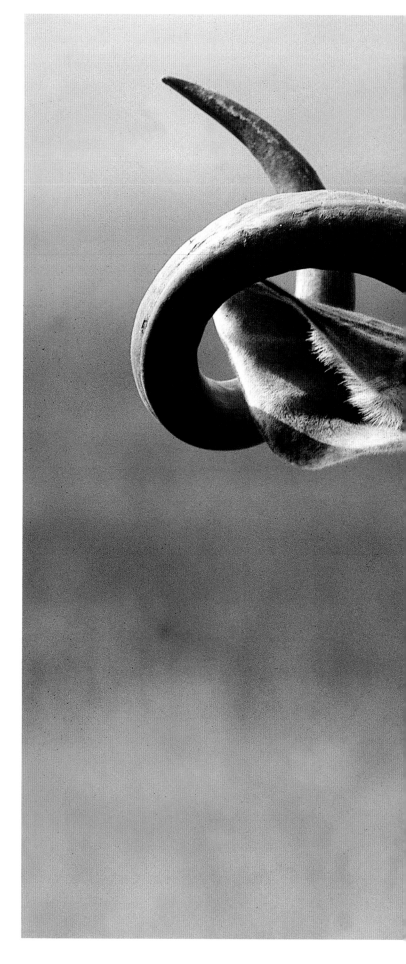

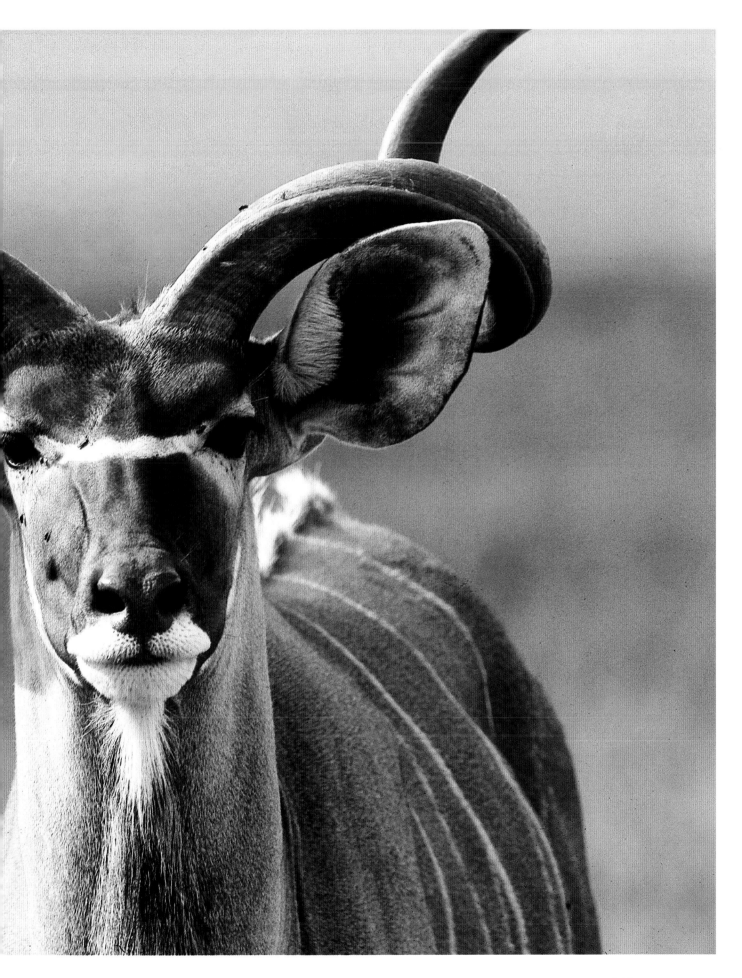

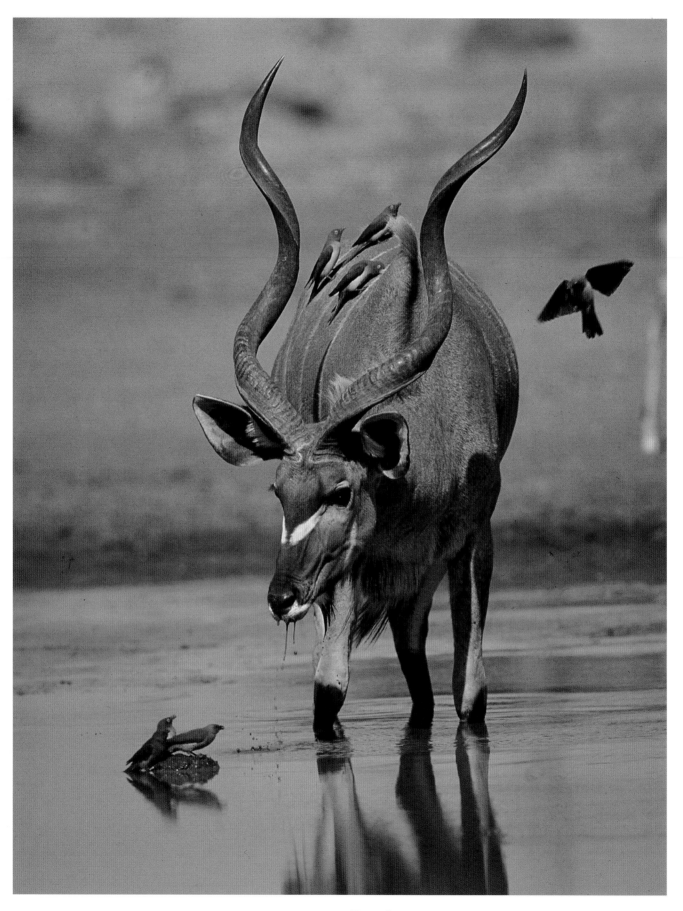

Above: Greater kudu male: Botswana. The attendant birds are red-billed oxpeckers.

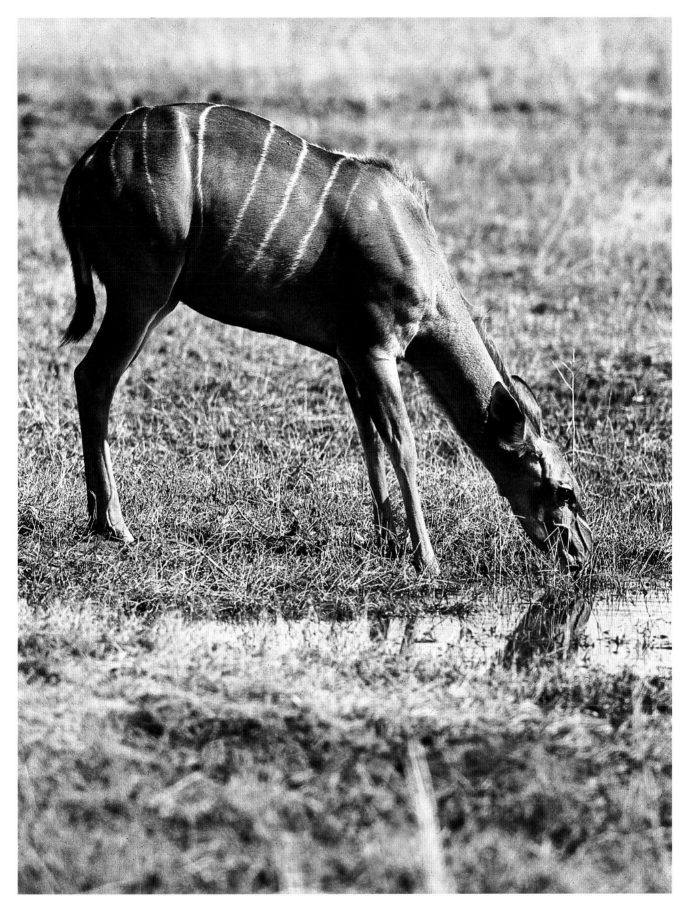

Above: Greater kudu female: Botswana. Note her brown coat (the male's is bluish grey) and small head.

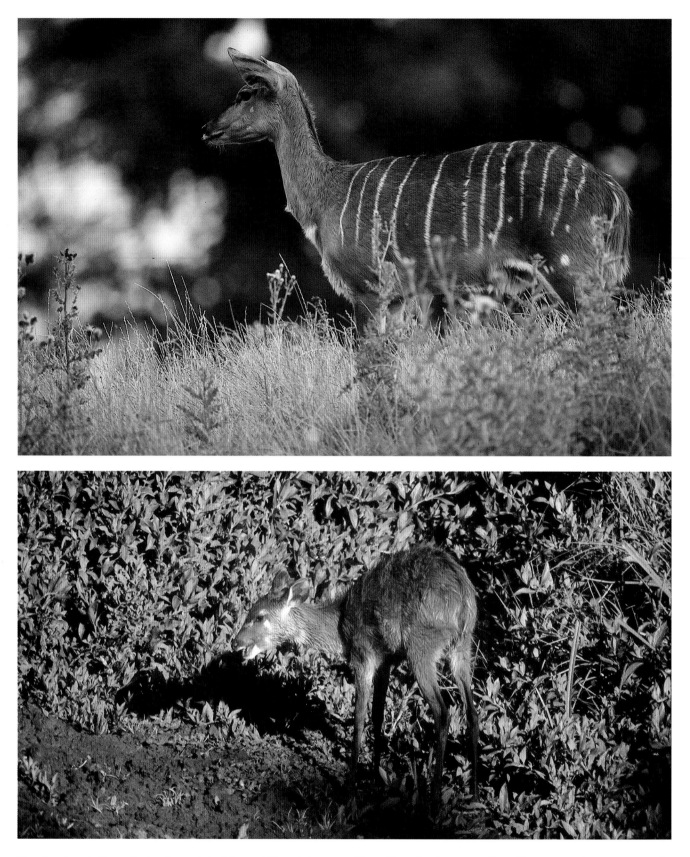

Top: Female nyala: Kenya. She has the species' minimum of 12 vertical white stripes. The male's coat is charcoal grey and much shaggier.

Above: Young female sitatunga: Kenya. This species is the most aquatic of all the antelopes.

Above Right: Female bushbuck: Kenya. Similar in build but smaller than the closely related nyala and sitatunga. Note the white spots on her side.

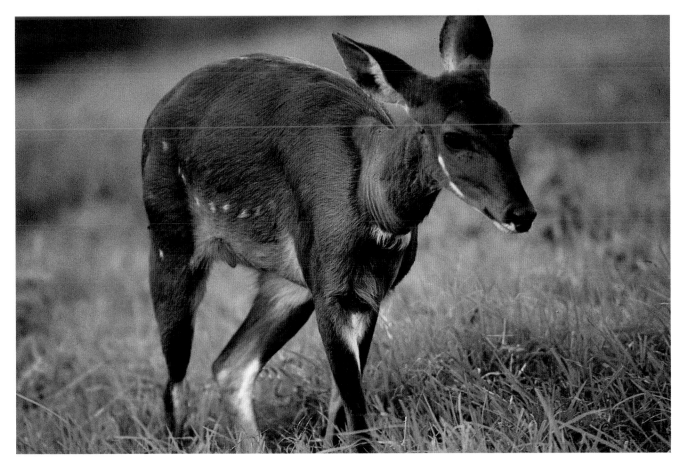

Somewhat larger than the lesser kudu, the nyala (*T. angasi*) has striking differences in appearance between the sexes: the male is dark brown to greyish brown in colour, with up to 14 narrow white vertical stripes; it has a long mane along the length of the back and a long fringe hanging under the body from throat to hind legs; the lower legs are mid-brown. The female is chestnut or yellowish brown in body colour, with up to 18 white stripes, and lacks the long shaggy hair. Both sexes have a shallow white chevron between the eyes and one or more spots on the cheek. Only the male has horns—long, upward-curving with shallow spirals. A mixed, mainly nocturnal feeder, the nyala occurs in dry savanna woodland and riverine woods from southern Malawi to KwaZulu-Natal. The much larger mountain nyala (*T. buxtoni*), which may weigh up to 660lb (300kg), is sandy, or sometimes greyish, brown with four faint stripes on each side, a spinal crest from nape to tail, a white chevron between the eyes and two white patches on the throat. Mainly a browser, it is confined to the central highlands of Ethiopia to the east of the Rift Valley.

There are several races of the semi-aquatic sitatunga (*T. spekei*): in the northern race the males are grey-brown with faint white markings and the females are bright chestnut; in the western race the males are dark brown with clearer markings, and the females are red-brown; in the southern race both sexes are dull grey-brown with few white marks. The coats of all races are long and shaggy, especially in the males, and their hooves are long and slender. Only the males are horned. The sitatunga lives in swamps and dense reedbeds, feeding on papyrus and other aquatic plants and occasionally on floodplain grasses. The northern race occurs in Chad and southern Sudan southwards to Kenya; the western in Togo, Senegal and Gambia; the southern from central Africa south to Botswana.

The smallest member of this subfamily, the bushbuck (*T. scriptus*) is no more than 32in (80cm) high at the shoulder, with a maximum weight of 100lb (45kg). More than 25 subspecies have been proposed, and there is considerable variation in coat colour and markings over its very extensive range. The coats vary from almost black to golden brown; white markings are abundant in some races and almost invisible in others. The male carries relatively short, almost straight horns. A shy, woodland species, the bushbuck feeds mainly on leaves but also shoots, flowers, fruits and grass and in some

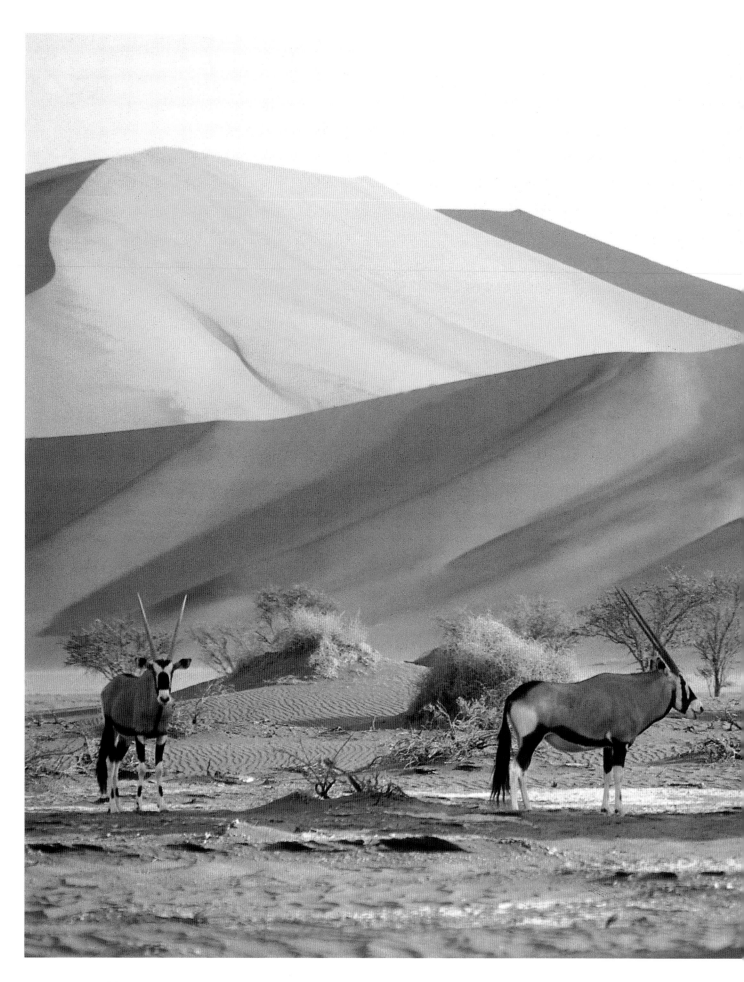

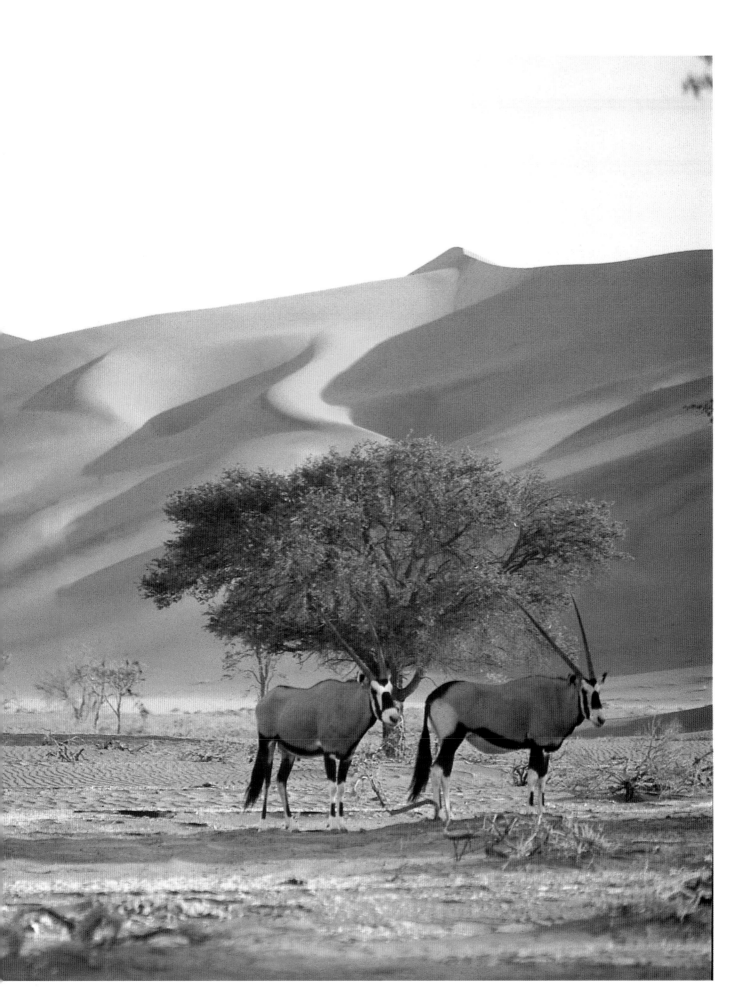

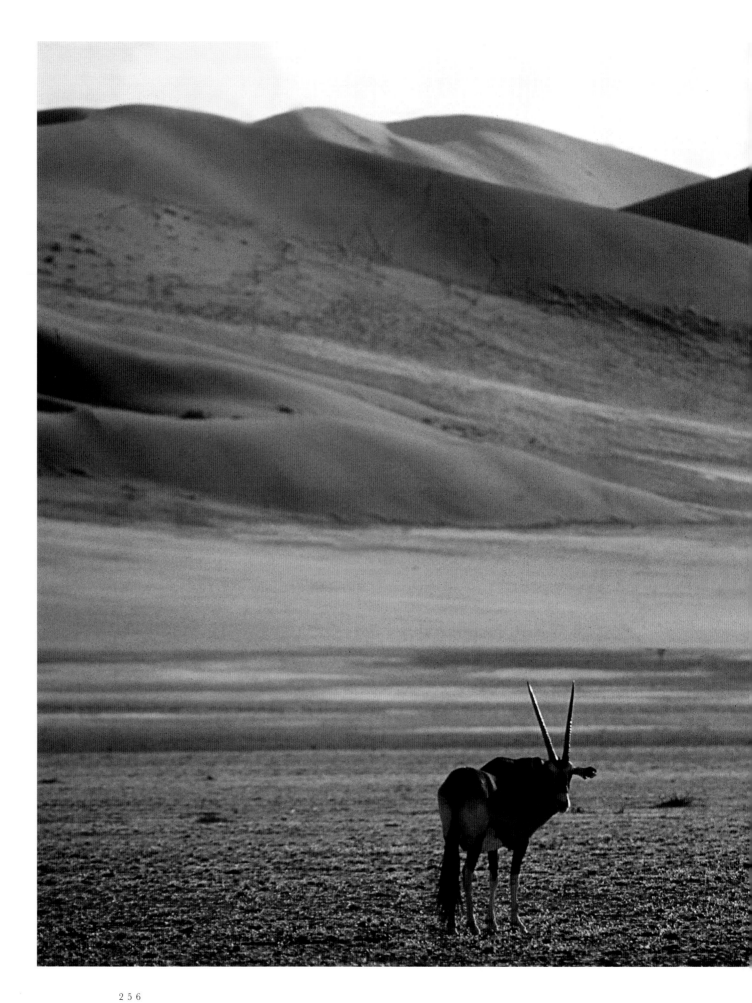

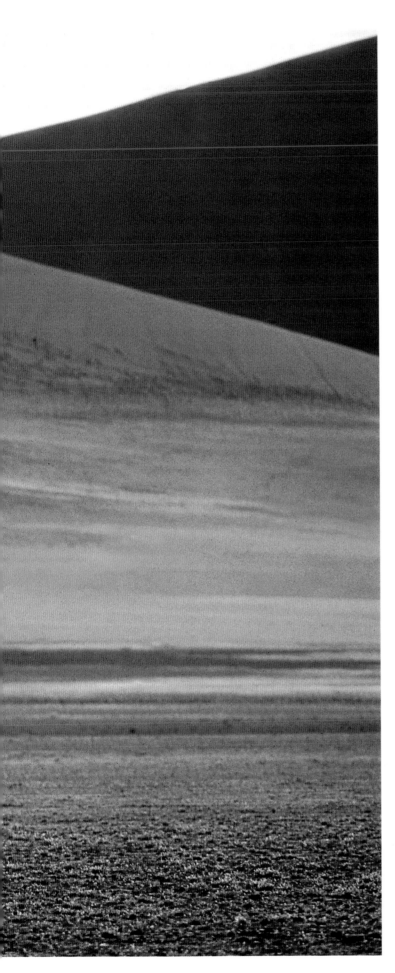

regions is regarded as a pest by farmers and gardeners. It has the biggest range of the tragelophines: from Senegal eastwards to Ethiopia then southwards through east Africa and the eastern Congo basin to Botswana and Cape Province.

The subfamily Hippotraginae, or horse antelopes, consists of the roan, sable, oryx and addax—large, powerfully built antelopes with striking face-markings and magnificent horns carried by both sexes. The largest of this group, the roan (*Hippotragus equinus*), lives in the rich savanna grasslands to the north and south of the lowland equatorial rainforest zone: in the north its range extends from Senegal to south-eastern Sudan; from there it swings through the Rift Valley, then west to Angola and Namibia and south to Botswana and Transvaal. Powerfully built, with a short thick neck, through most of its range the roan's coat is greyish brown, but the West African race has a reddish tinge. It has a black and white face "mask", long, narrow ears with end tufts, and heavily ridged, swept-back horns in both male and female. It is mainly a grazer of short and medium grasses. Second in size only to the eland among the antelopes, it is up to five feet (1.5m) at the shoulder and weighs up to 660lb (600kg).

The sable (*H. niger*), another large antelope, exhibits gender dimorphism in main body colours. The adult male is jet black except for white underparts and black and white face markings; the female and sub-adults are usually reddish brown, again with white underparts and black and white face mask. Both sexes have a broad black blaze from forehead to nose, and a mane extending from the top of the neck to beyond the shoulders. Both sexes have horns, the adult male's being especially fine, backward-sweeping, deeply ridged and up to 5ft 6in (168cm) long. Sables live in dry, open woodland from Kenya south to Tanzania, Zambia and Zimbabwe. Small numbers of giant sable (*H.n. variani*), with even longer horns, live in reserves in central Angola.

Previous Page: Gemsbok: Namib desert. This is the southern race of the oryx: note the black patches on its upper hindlegs. The black and white face markings differ from those of the beisa oryx.

Left: Gemsbok on gravel plains: Namib desert. Oryxes and gemsboks thrive in more arid habitats than any other African antelope.

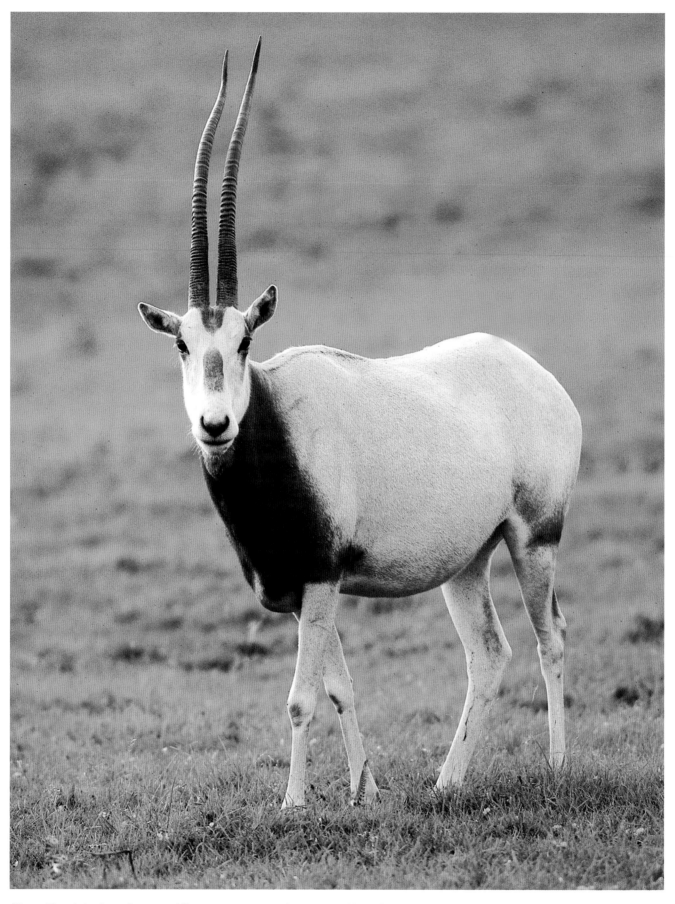

Above: The scimitar-horned oryx is a different species, native to, but now vanished from, the Sahel, where it once grazed on the edge of the Sahara.

Above Right: A pair of Coke's hartebeest: Masai Mara. Note the white rump and inner surfaces of the legs.

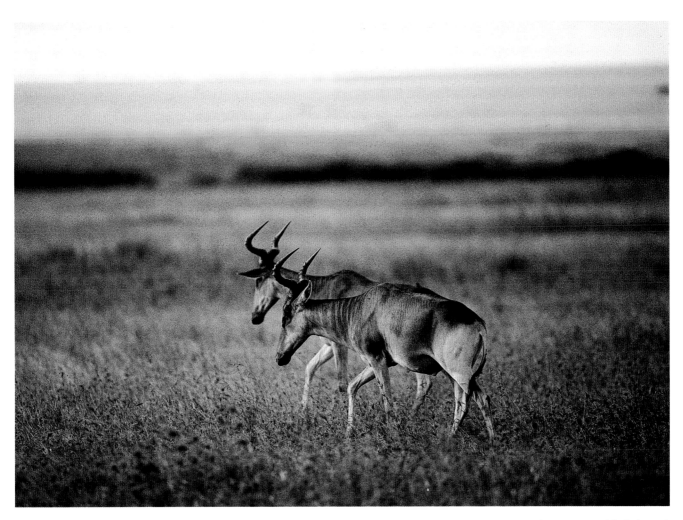

The oryx (*Oryx gazella*) exists in three main subspecies: the beisa oryx (*O. g. beisa*) of Ethiopia to the Tana river in south-east Kenya; the fringe-eared oryx (*O. g. callotis*), found from the Tana river to central Tanzania; and the gemsbok (*O. g. gazella*), which ranges from southern Angola and southern Zimbabwe through Botswana and Namibia to Cape Province. All races have distinctive black and white facial markings. The southern race's main body colour is greyish fawn, with a broad black stripe separating its upper body colour from its white underparts; it also has black "bandages" on its upper legs, and black patches on rump. The northern race's upper body colour is less grey, the black body stripe is narrower, and the bandages are on the forelegs only. The superb transversely ridged horns of both sexes are only slightly curved. Oryxes are primarily grazers living in habitats ranging from dry acacia savanna through gravel plains to deserts. The scimitar-horned oryx (*O. dammah*) and the somewhat smaller addax (*Addax nasomaculatus*) once roamed the Sahel semi-desert of Chad and Niger; both exist now only in reserves.

The Alcelaphinae subfamily—hartebeests, topi, blesbok and wildebeests—are medium-sized nomadic or migratory grazers of open grasslands. Long-legged, and higher at the shoulder than at the rump—adaptations for effortless loping over long distances—they have long, pointed heads and narrow faces; both sexes have horns.

The hartebeest (*Alcelaphus buselaphus*) exists in at least six recognised subspecies: the western race (*A. b. major*) of West Africa from Senegal to Chad, is of tan colour, but darker on front of legs; the Lelwel race (*A. b. lelwel*), from Chad to Sudan, Uganda and western Kenya, reddish brown all over, with V-shaped horns; dark brown Swayne's hartebeest (*A. b. swaynei*), of Somalia, and Coke's hartebeest (*A. b. cokei*), of Kenya and Tanzania, tan with a white rump, are the smallest races; the red hartebeest (*A. b. caama*), of Botswana, Namibia and Cape Province, is reddish brown with white rump and black on sides and front of upper legs. The western race is the largest, measuring up to 4ft 9in (1.5m) at the shoulder and weighing up to 500lb (227kg). Hartebeests are mainly grazers and in

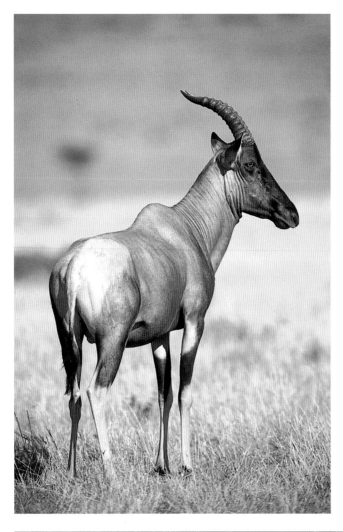

arid areas will travel great distances in search of grass. Lichtenstein's hartebeest, although at present assigned to a different genus (*Sigmoceros lichtensteini*), is regarded by many experts as another subspecies of *Alcelaphus buselaphus*: not only is it similar in appearance to the other hartebeests, it also forms a geographical link between their northern and southern races, being native to south-eastern Zaïre, Tanzania, Zimbabwe and eastern Angola. Its general colour is yellowish fawn, sometimes with a reddish tinge with a darker area stretching from shoulders to rump. The tips of the horns slope sharply back. Its habitat is the margin between woodland and savanna grassland.

The topi (*Damaliscus lunatus*) and its various named subspecies resemble hartebeests in general appearance (deep chest, shoulders higher than rump, long legs; long, narrow head with dark blaze on face). Their coats are noticeably glossy, and usually lighter on rump and back than on underparts. The four recognised subspecies are: korrigum (*D. l. korrigum*), bright reddish, in isolated pockets from Ivory Coast to Cameroon; tiang (*D. l. tiang*), bright reddish, from northern Cameroon to Ethiopia; topi (*D. l. jimela*), dark reddish brown with purplish sheen, between east and west arms of Rift Valley in Uganda, Rwanda, Kenya and Tanzania; tsessebe

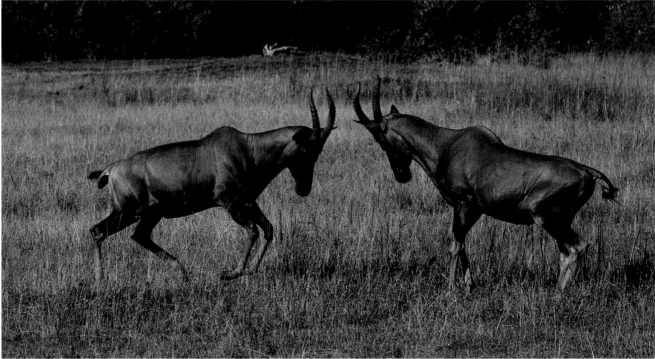

Top: Topi (*jimela* race): Kenya. Note purple blotches on face and upper limbs.

Above: Pair of topi males fighting: Masai Mara.

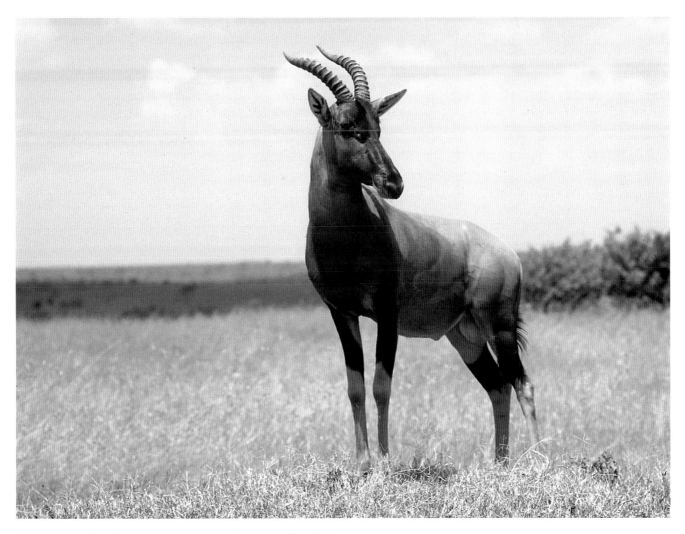

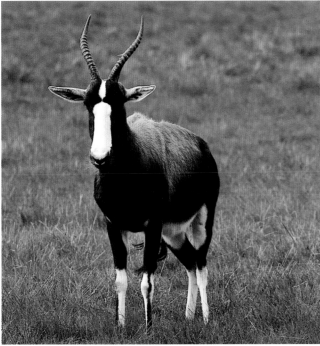

Top: Tsessebe: Zambia. Note the reddish coat and rather short horns.

Above: Bontebok: South Africa.

(*D. l. lunatus*), reddish, shorter horns than the others, in Zambia, eastern Angola, northern Botswana. Topis are purely grazers of short to medium long grasses of savanna plains and open woodland. The largest are about 4ft (1.2m) high at the shoulder and weigh up to 310lb (140kg). A closely related species, the hirola (*D. hunteri*), also known as Hunter's hartebeest, is uniformly tawny in colour, with no face blaze but a white chevron between the eyes.

Another close relative of the hartebeests is the blesbok (*Damaliscus dorcas phillipsi*), of north-eastern Cape Province, Orange Free State and KwaZulu-Natal. It is reddish brown in colour with white underparts, white on lower legs and white blaze on face. Close kin is the bontebok (*D. d. dorcas*), of south-western Cape Province, which is very similar in appearance but darker in colour, with a large white rump patch and base of tail, and with wholly white lower legs. Both these antelopes are smaller than the hartebeests, with the blesbok (the larger) weighing no more than about 185lb (84kg).

The last members of this group are the wildebeests, also known as gnu. The blue wildebeest (*Connochaetes taurinus*) has robust shoulders and chest and more lightly built hindquarters. The head is large, with characteristic convex face profile, and ends in a wide snout. Their overall colour is dark grey or brownish grey, with darker vertical stripes on neck and chest. There are long hairs along the throat forming a fringe, which varies in colour according to subspecies, and a generally dark mane of hair along the back of the neck. The main subspecies are the western white-bearded (*C. t. mearnsi*) of the Masai Mara, Serengeti plains and Ngorongoro crater; the eastern white-bearded (*C. t. albojubatus*) of southern Kenya and Tanzania east of the eastern rift; Johnston's (*C. t. johnstoni*) of southern Tanzania to Mozambique; and the blue (*C. t. taurinus*) of southern Tanzania to Zambia, south-eastern Angola, Botswana and northern South Africa. The biggest members of the species are up to five foot (1.5m) high at the shoulders, and may weigh 600lb (272kg). As many as 1.5 million of the two white-bearded races are involved in the vast seasonal migrations through the Serengeti and Masai Mara.

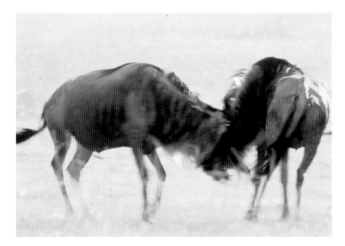

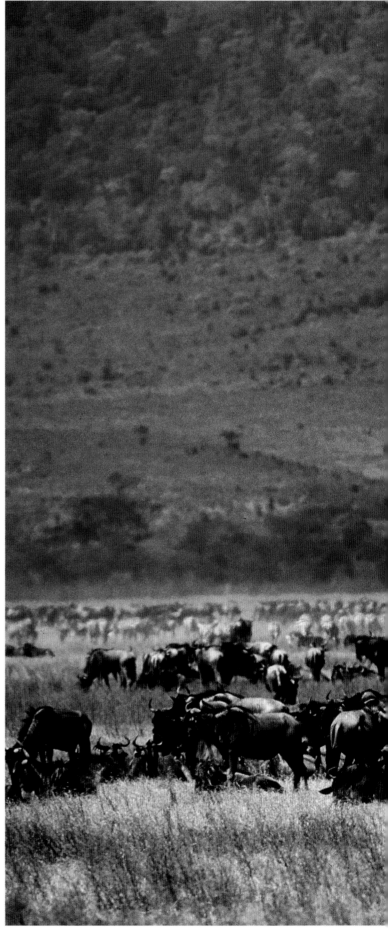

Above: Two male white-bearded wildebeest fighting: Serengeti plains.

Right: White-bearded wildebeest on migration through the Ngorongoro Crater.

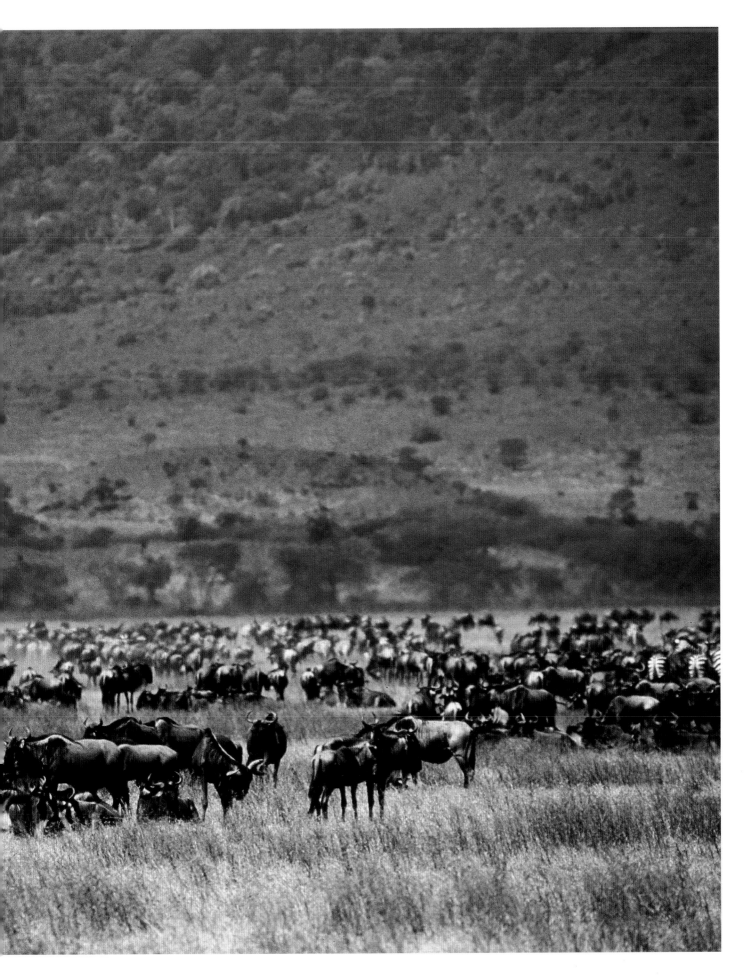

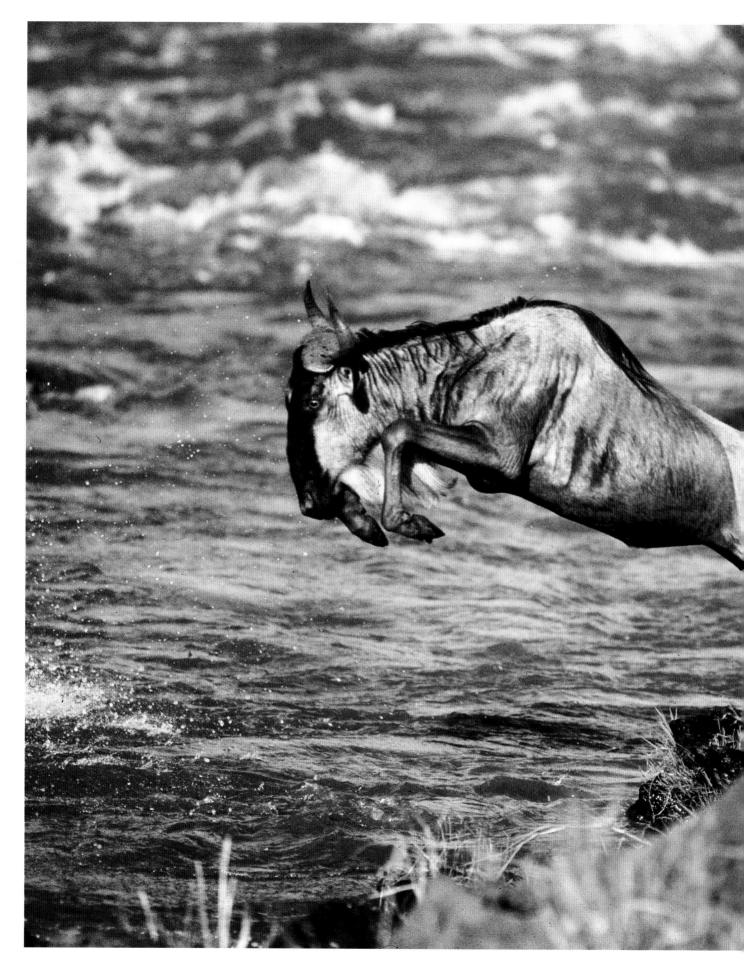

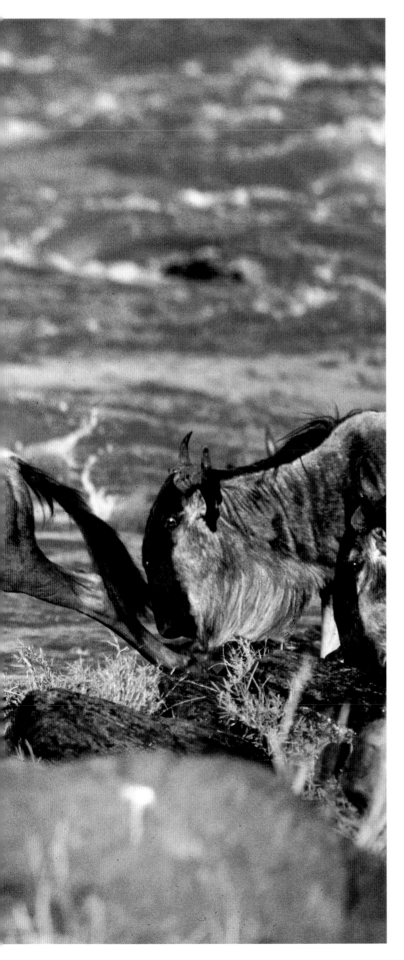

Smaller than is blue cousin, the black wildebeest (*C. gnou*), or white-tailed gnu, is in fact dark brown, though with a blackish head. The face is mostly covered with dark, brush-like tufts of hairs, and there are more hairs on the throat and chest. Its horns, massive at the base, slope down and forward, then sharply upward like hooks. It has a long, white or cream tail similar in appearance to a horse's. A grazer (and occasional browser), it is now confined to reserves in South Africa's highveld and the Karoo.

The Aepycerotinae subfamily is represented solely by the impala (*Aepyceros melampus*), an elegantly formed medium-sized antelope with a long neck and legs. The main colours of its short, glossy coat are reddish fawn on the upper parts lightening to light tan on the sides and limbs. The belly, underside of tail, inner sides of thighs, throat, lips and inside of ears are white; the face has a black blaze, the ear tips are black, and each buttock has a vertical black stripe. Only the male has the lyre-shaped, deeply ridged horns, which in some individuals may be more than 30in (76cm) long. There are several races: the East African subspecies (*A. m. swara* and *A. m. rendilis*) are found in Uganda, Kenya and much of Tanzania; the southern impala is found from Tanzania and Zambia southwards to South Africa; the black-faced impala (*A. m petersi*) is native to the Angola-Namibia borderlands, including Etosha National Park. Impalas are mixed feeders, preferring savanna woodland with access to drinking water. They stand up to 3ft (90cm) high at the shoulder and weigh up to 110lb (50kg).

White-beared wildebeest jumping into the Mara river, Tanzania, during seasonal migration.

White-bearded wildebeest towards the end of their migration: dawn in
Amboseli National Park, Kenya.

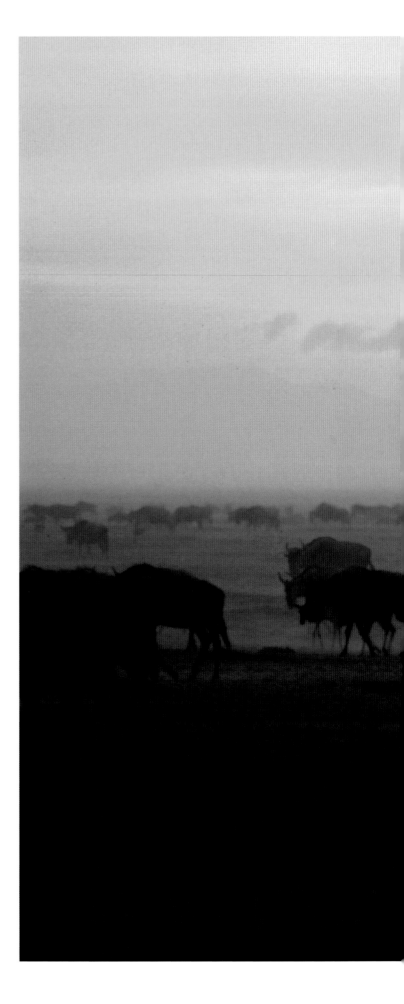

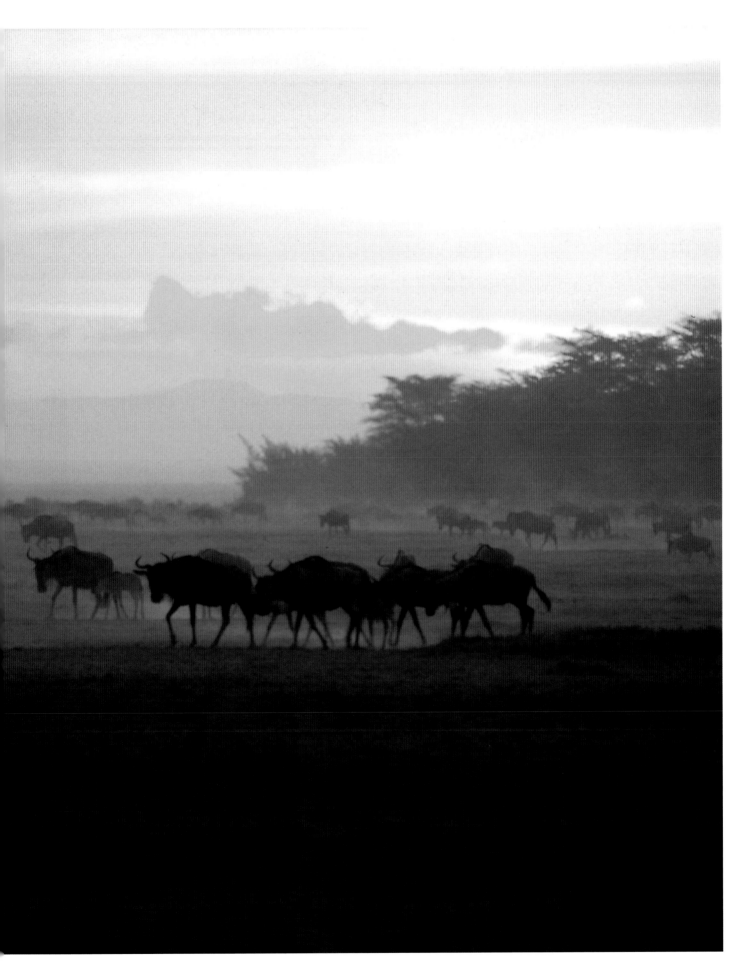

Herd of blue wildebeest at almost-dry waterhole: central Botswana.

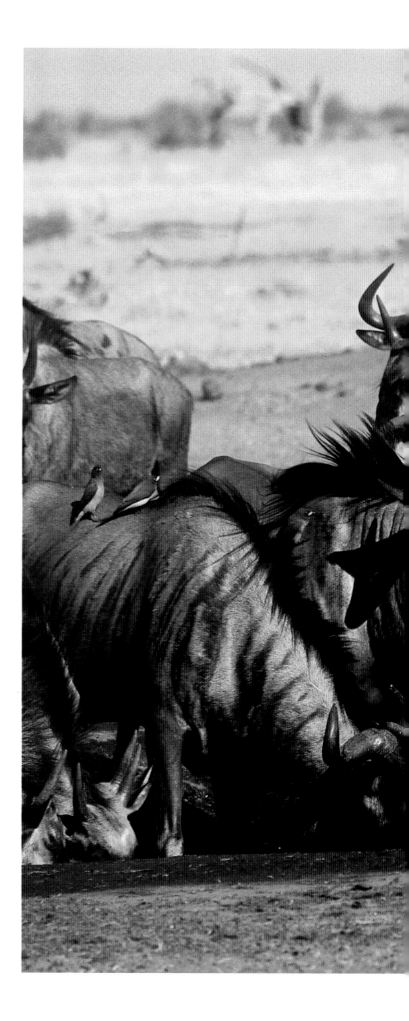

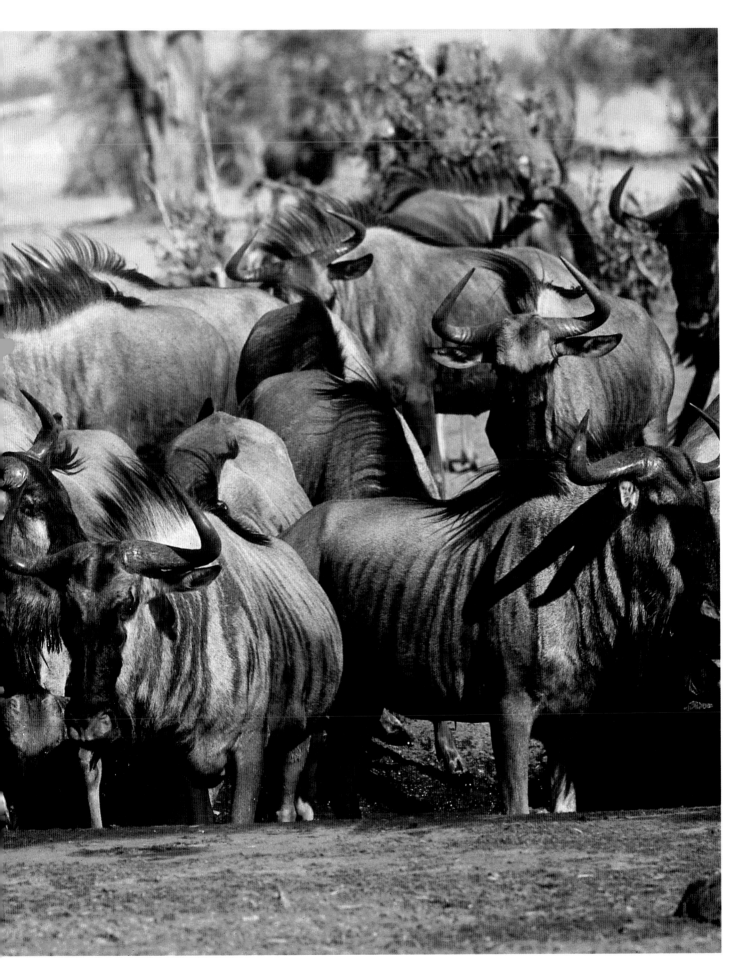

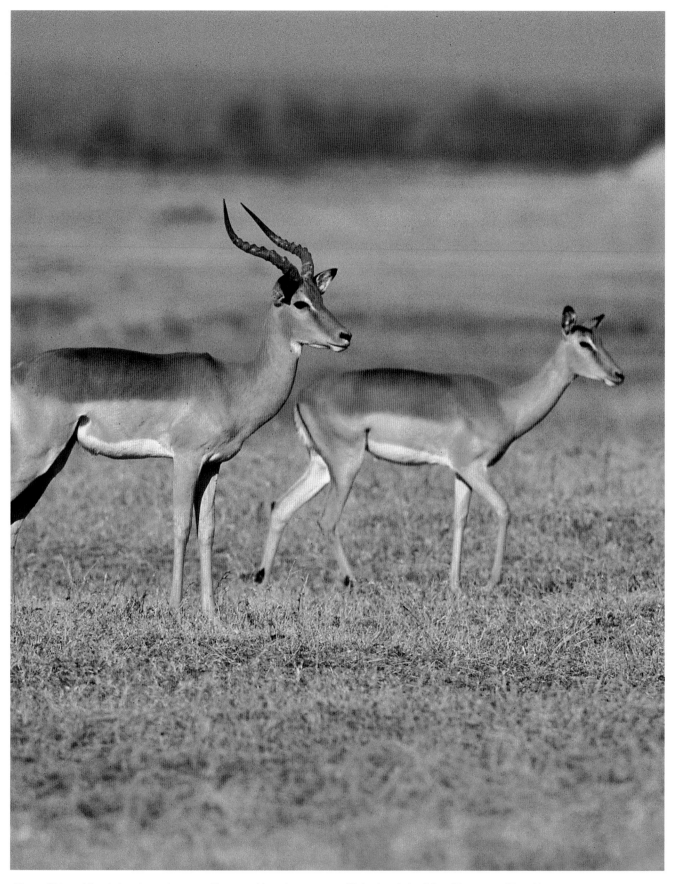

Above: Male and female impala, southern race: Botswana. Note the two-tone colour of the torso.

Right: Impala herd, East African race: Masai Mara.

Overleaf: Group of female impala: Lake Manyara National Park, Tanzania.

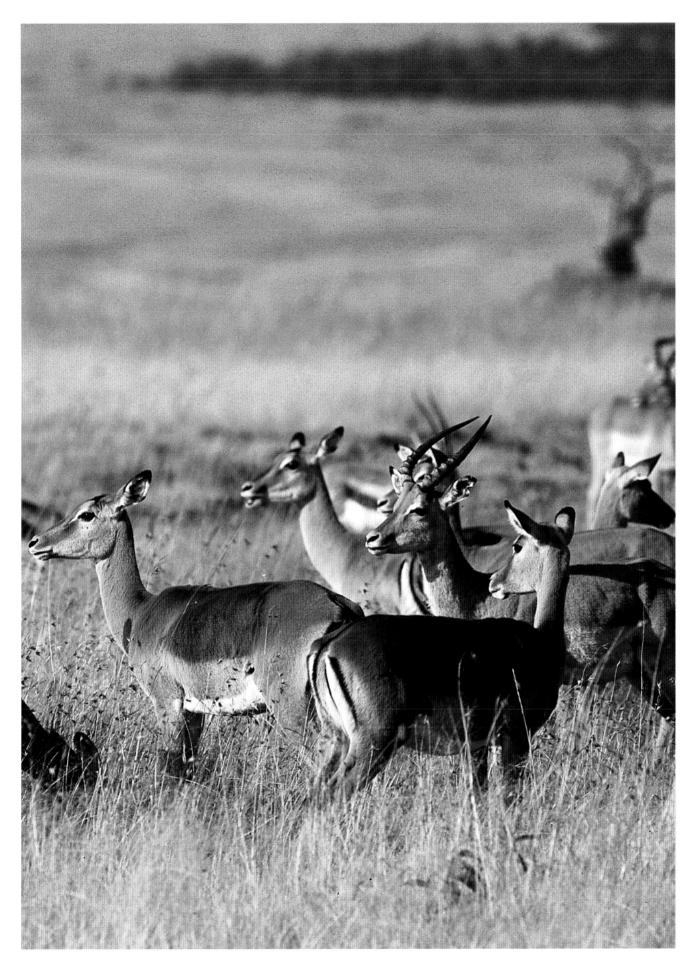

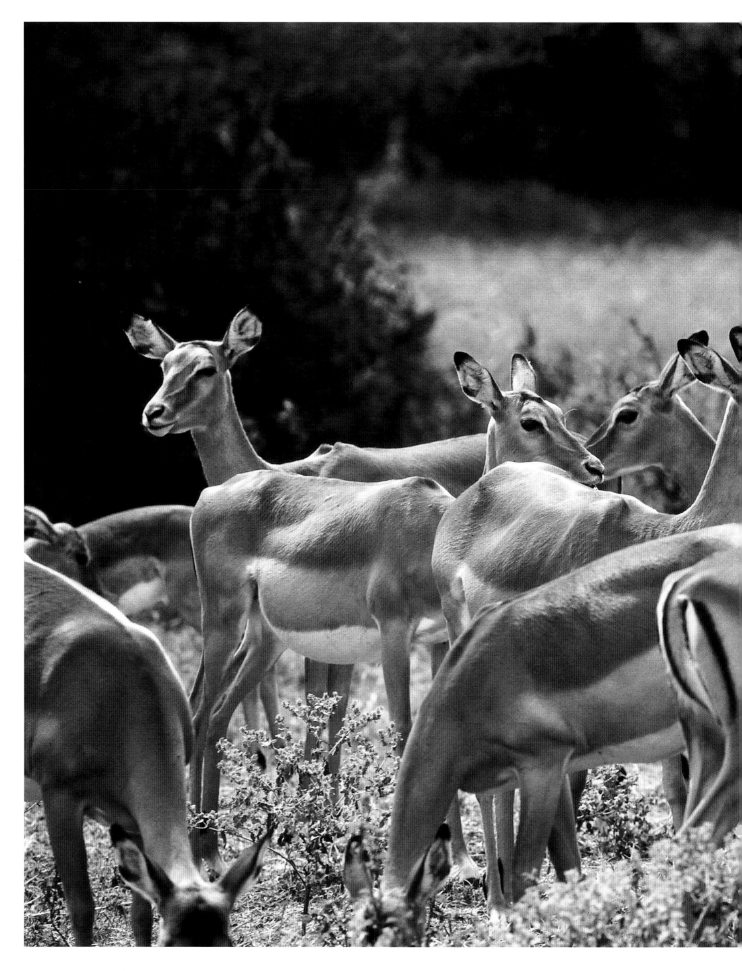

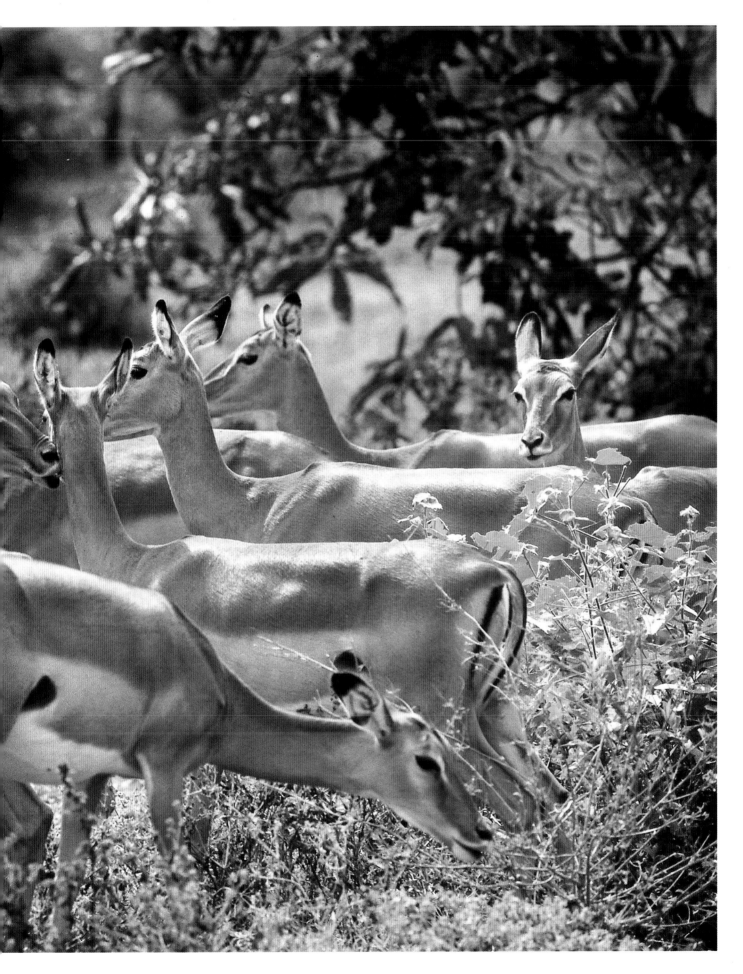

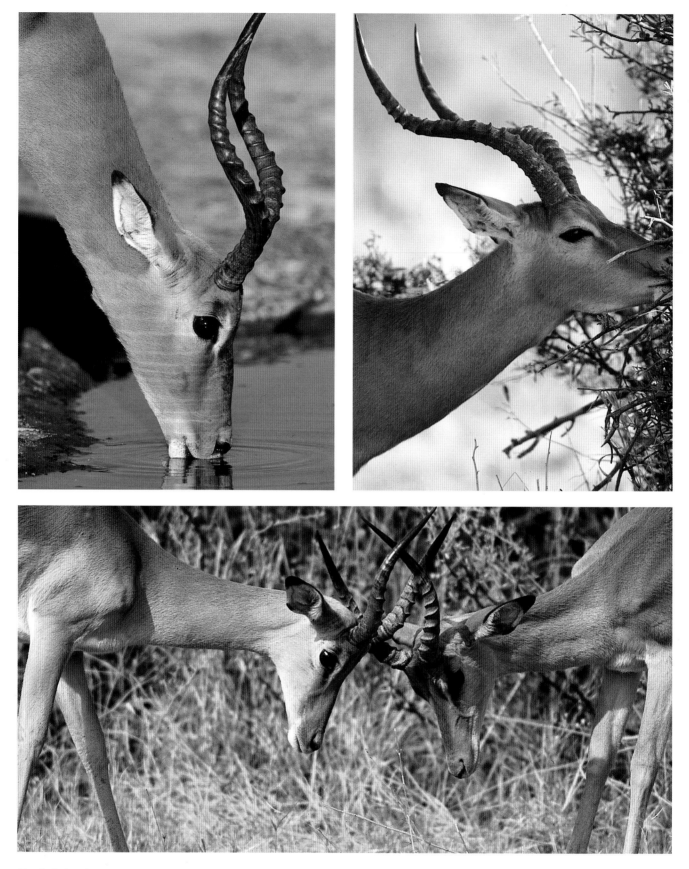

Top Left: Impala at a waterhole, Botswana. Only the male has horns.

Above: Two male impala locking horns: Botswana.

Top Right: Male impala nibbling bush foliage: Botswana. Impala are mixed feeders, browsing as well as grazing.

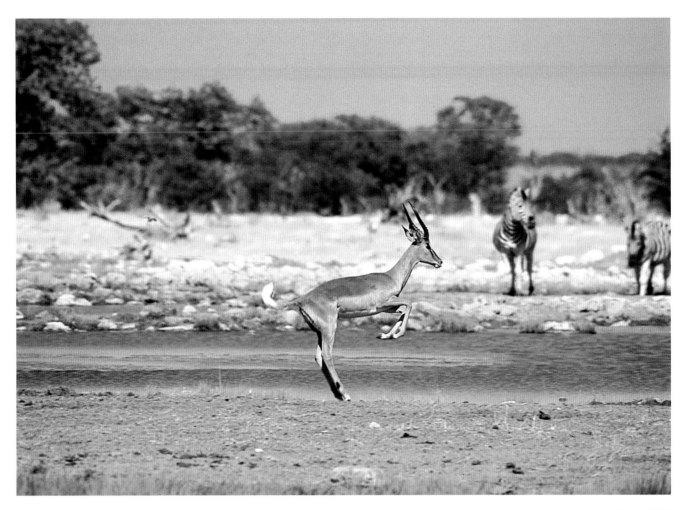

The Reduncinae subfamily is made up of the waterbuck, kob, puku, lechwe and reedbuck—small, medium-sized and large grazers that roam savannas within easy reach of water. Only the males are horned. The common waterbuck (*Kobus ellipsiprymnus ellipsiprymnus*), the largest of this group, has a coarse, shaggy coat (the hair usually longer at throat) usually greyish brown. It has white "eyebrows", a white muzzle and throat, white inside the ears, and white on buttocks. The horns are long, heavily ridged and forward-curving towards the top. Its close cousin, the defassa waterbuck (*K. e. defassa*) has a reddish tinge to its coat and more clearly defined white on buttocks. Both waterbucks stand 50in (1.25m) at the shoulder and weigh up to 575lb (260kg). They prefer riverine areas with reedbeds and tall grasses as well as open woodland. The common waterbuck occurs in eastern Kenya and southwards to Botswana and eastern Transvaal; the defassa ranges from Senegal eastwards to southern Sudan and southwards, west of the eastern arm of the Rift Valley, as far as Zambia.

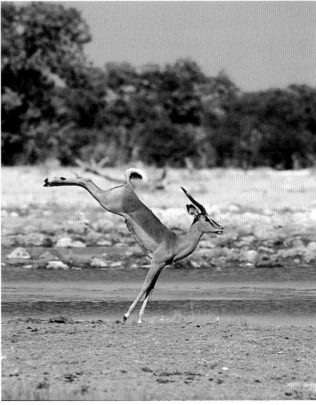

Top and Above: Black-faced impala leaping: Etosha National Park, Namibia.

The kob (*Kobus kob*) is a medium-sized antelope, sturdily built, with thick, deeply ridged, lyre-shaped horns, occurring in three races: Buffon's kob (*K. k. kob*), found in the moist savanna zone from Senegal eastward to Sudan; the Uganda kob (*K. k. thomasi*), of western Uganda, north-eastern Zaïre, and southern Sudan; and the white-eared kob (*K. k. leucotis*), confined to south-eastern Sudan and neighbouring areas of Ethiopia. Buffon's is the smallest, with a bright yellowish brown coat; the white-eared has a very dark brown coat with white underparts, white throat patch and white rings around the eyes; the Uganda is dark reddish brown with similar white markings. The two larger races are up to 36in (92cm) high at the shoulder and weigh up to 265lb (120kg).

Rather similar in appearance to the kob but smaller, the kudu (*Kobus vardoni*) is generally a deep golden yellow with somewhat paler sides and with off-white underparts and areas around the eyes and under the chin; the horns are shorter but thicker than the kob's. It is found close to rivers in eastern Angola, north-western and south-western Zambia, south-eastern Zaïre, and western Tanzania.

Slightly larger—up to 220lb (100kg) in weight—the lechwe (*K. leche*), unlike the kob, is noticeably higher at the rump than at the shoulders, and it has longer horns. The coat colour is chestnut (sometimes darker in the male) with white underparts, throat, chin and mouth. There are three main subspecies: red lechwe (*K. l. leche*) of western Zambia, south-eastern Angola and northern Botswana; Kafue lechwe (*K. l. kafuensis*) of central Zambia; and the very dark black lechwe (*K. l. smithemani*) of north-eastern Zambia around the swamps of Lake Bangweulu. The Nile lechwe (*K. megaceros*), of similar size and build, is also of similar colour in the ewe and juveniles, but the male is almost black in colour, with a white stripe along nape of neck and shoulders and short throat mane. It is native to the Sudd marshes of southern Sudan and similar marshes in western Ethiopia.

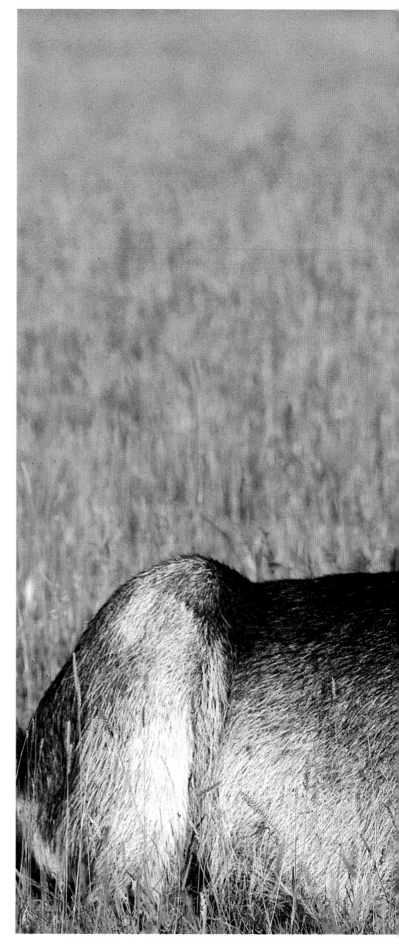

Female defassa waterbuck: Zambia.

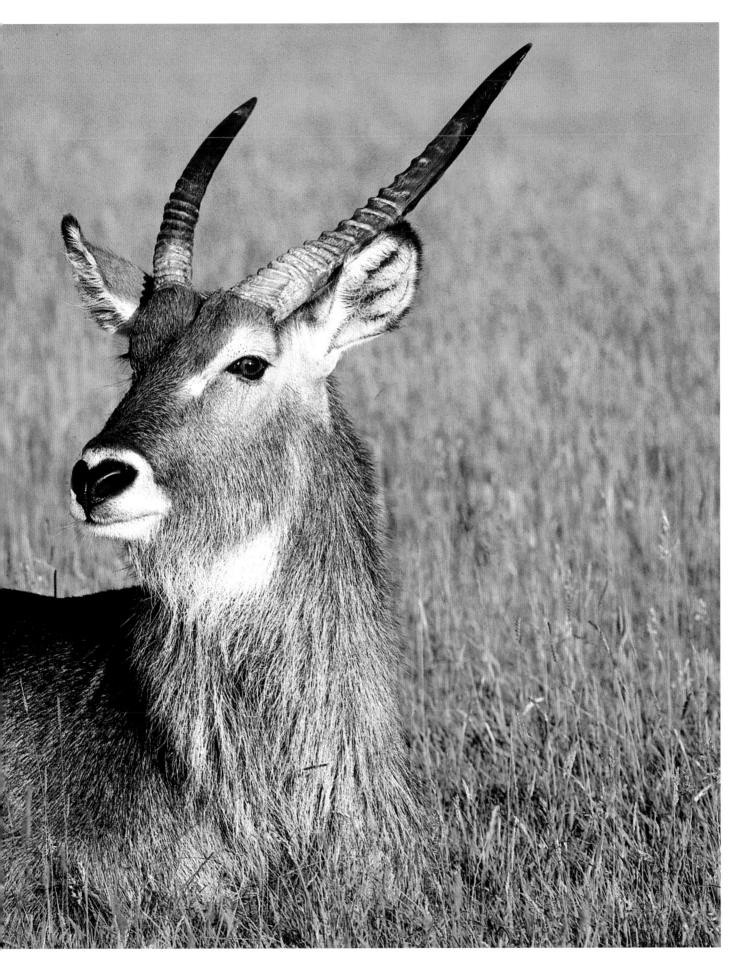

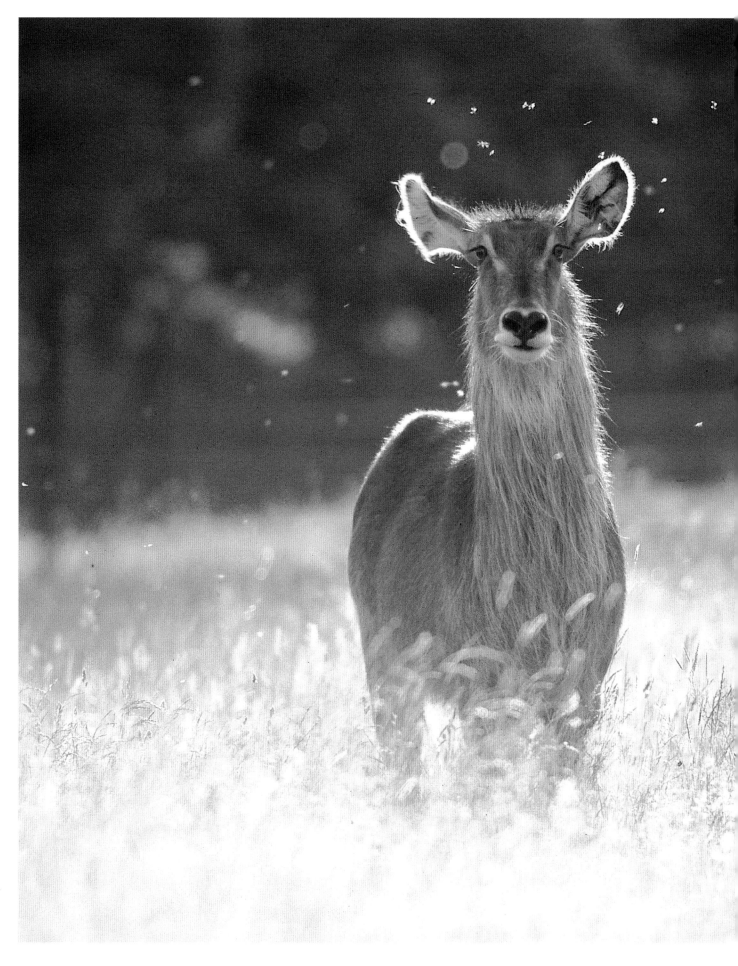

The horns of the reedbucks are shorter than those of other members of this subfamily and are hooked forward; the tails are notably bushy. The common or southern reedbuck (*Redunca arundinum*), the largest, has greyish fawn upperparts, head and outer sides of legs, white or cream underparts, chin and throat, and the underside of the tail. It occurs throughout most of central Africa from southern Zaïre and Tanzania to South Africa. The bohor reedbuck (*R. redunca*) has yellowish brown (sometimes red-tinged) upperparts and paler underparts. It lives in floodplain grasslands and reedbeds from Senegal eastward to Ethiopia and southward into Tanzania. The mountain reedbuck (*R. fulvorufula*) is smaller than the others, with grey-fawn upperparts and white underparts. Its southern race (*R. f. fulvorufula*) is confined to the mountains of South Africa, Lesotho and Swaziland; the northern race, Chanler's mountain reedbuck (*R. f. chanleri*), exists in isolated pockets of the Kenya and Ethiopian highlands.

Sole representative of the Peleinae subfamily, the small grey rhebok (*Pelea capreolus*), with long neck and graceful limbs, has a noticeably thick, woolly coat that is grey on the upperparts, paler below. The horns (confined to the male) are slender and rise almost vertically from above the eyes. About 30in (75cm) high at the shoulder, the male rarely weighs more than 44lb (20kg). It prefers short plateau grasses, and is confined mainly to highlands above 3,000ft (900m) in South Africa and Lesotho.

A male common waterbuck: Kenya. Note the shaggy coat and white throat bib.

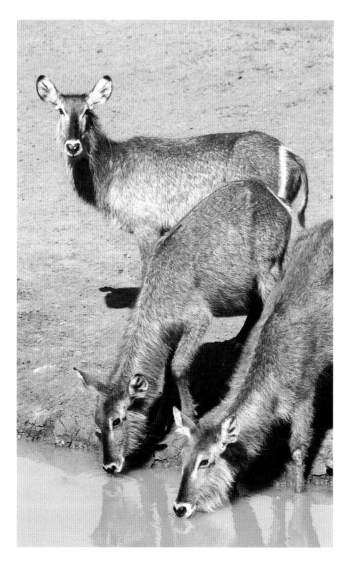

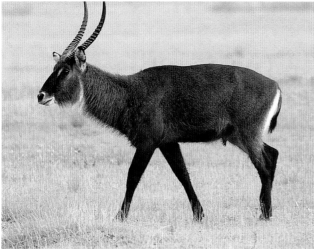

Top: Female common waterbuck at waterhole: Botswana. Note the white rump ring on the waterbuck at the rear.

Above: Male common waterbuck: Kenya.

Right: Male red lechwe resting in grass: Botswana.

The final group of antelopes to be considered here is the Antilopinae subfamily—the gazelle and dwarf antelope tribes. Easy to identify, the gerenuk (*Litocranius walleri*) has a very long, thin neck and legs, short head and large rounded ears. Its upperparts are reddish brown in colour, with a light edging giving way to buff-coloured sides and legs, and white underparts. Only the male has horns—lyre-shaped and heavily ringed. The gerenuk is strictly a browser and can stand erect on its hind legs when feeding on new leaf and flowers. It is native to eastern and southern Ethiopia, Somalia, Kenya and northern Tanzania. It stands about 40in (100cm) at the shoulder and weighs up to 110lb (50kg). The dibatag (*Ammodorcas clarkei*) is similar but smaller, with a somewhat shorter neck, and greyer upperparts. It shares the northern part of the gerenuk's range.

The dama gazelle (*Gazella dama*) is a long-necked native of the Sahel in Mali, Niger and Chad. Its coat is reddish brown above and white below. It is primarily a browser but also takes many herbaceous plants and fresh grass. Soemmering's gazelle (*G. soemmeringi*) of southern and eastern Ethiopia and Somalia, is a mixed feeder of semi-arid savanna grassland. Its coat is a rich chestnut, with white underparts and buttocks, and a black blaze between white patches on the face. Somewhat larger—weighing up to 175lb (80kg)—Grant's gazelle (*G. granti*) is most numerous in the savanna plains of Kenya and Tanzania but is also found in Uganda and southern Ethiopia. Fawn-coloured with white underparts, it has white buttocks bordered on each side by a black stripe. Its superb horns, up to 30in (76cm) long, are heavily ridged and point forward at the tips. Much smaller, Thomson's gazelle (*G. thomsoni*) is native to the same region. Its general body colour is yellowish fawn, with white chest, belly, inside legs and buttocks. It has a broad black stripe along its side and a black tail. It stands about 25in (65cm) at the shoulder and weighs up to 55lb (25kg). Of similar size and weight, Speke's gazelle (*G. spekei*) is restricted to open plains and upland plateaus in the Horn of Africa.

The springbok (*Antidorcas marsupialis*) is the only gazelle native to southern Africa, occurring in dry savanna and semi-deserts in the extreme south of Angola, Namibia, Botswana and South Africa. (Today it is found in South Africa only in reserves and on farms: it is

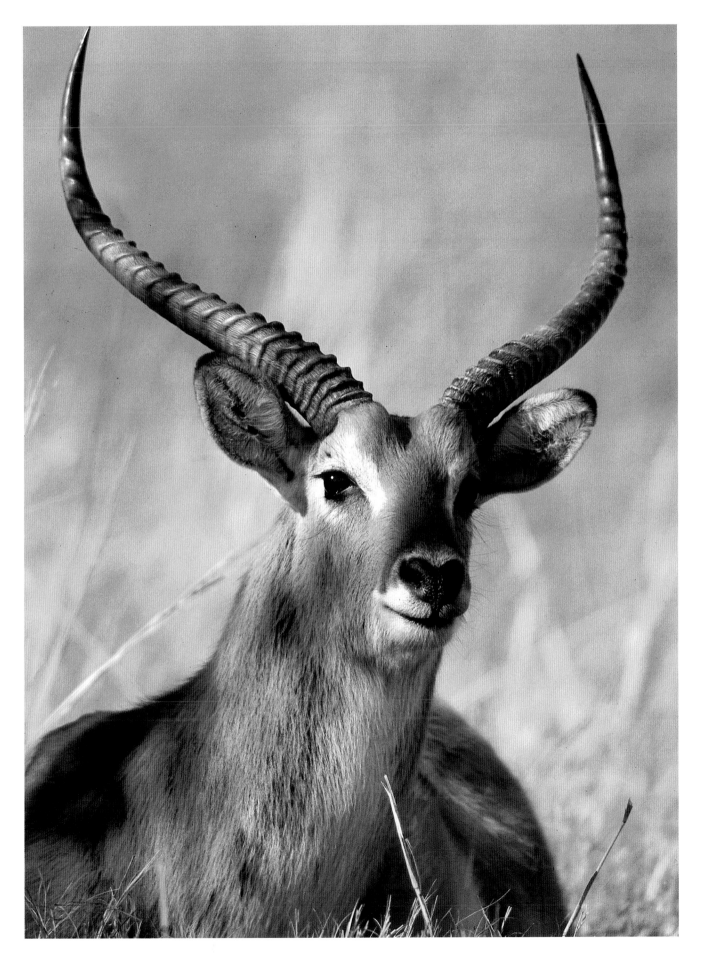

a major source of venison.) The fawn-brown upperparts are separated from white underparts by a dark brown band along the sides; the white head has a brown stripe running from the eye to the corner of the mouth; there is a white crest of erectile hairs from mid-back to rump, and the rump has a broad white patch. The springbok both grazes and browses, and will also dig for roots. It stands about 30in (75cm) at the shoulder and weighs up to 90lb (41kg). The springbok is the greatest adept of "pronking" among antelopes, leaping stiff-legged and with arched back as much as 10ft (3m) into the air—an action often triggered by the presence of predators.

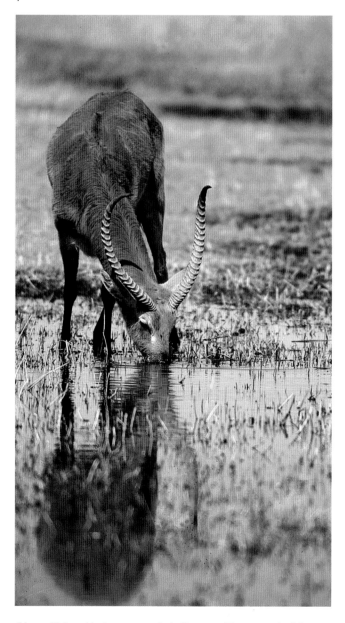

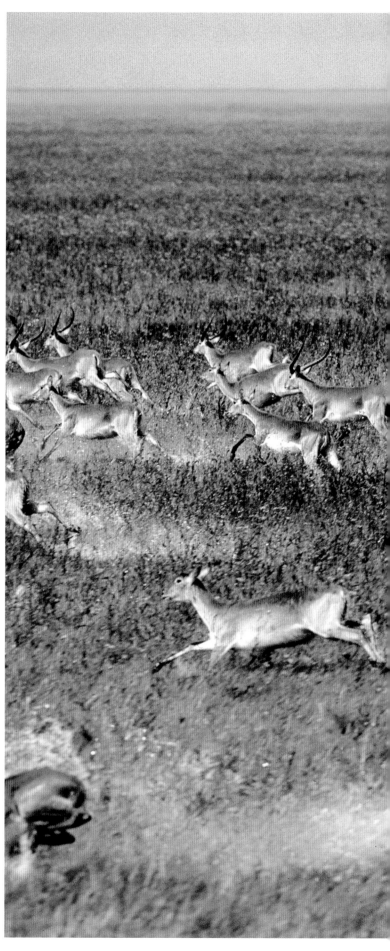

Above: Male red lechwe at waterhole: Botswana. Note swept-back horns.

Right: Red lechwe herd running through swamp: Zambia.

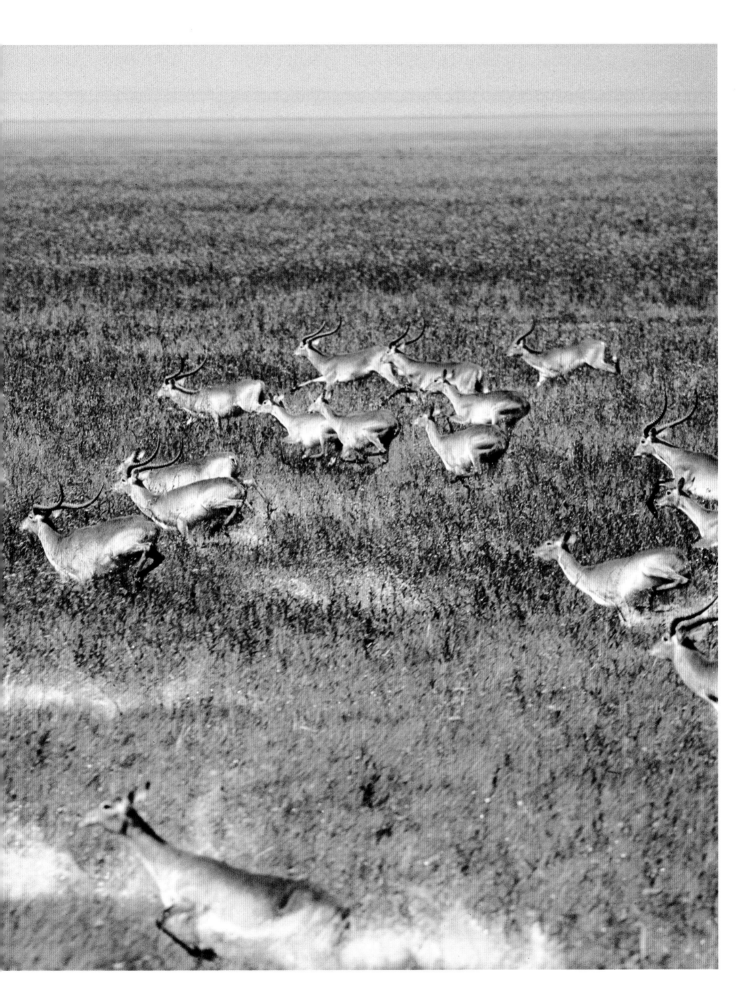

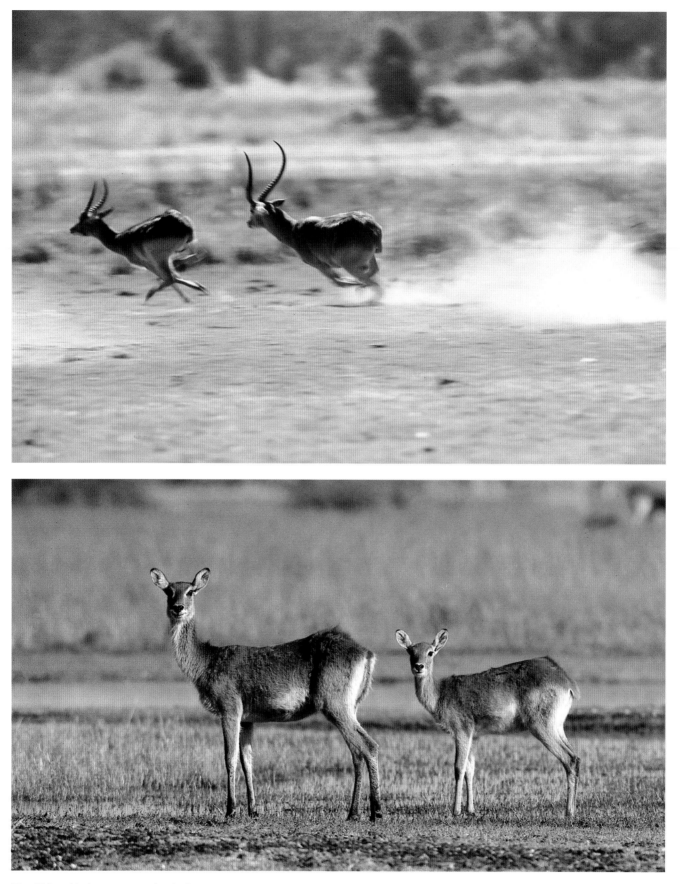

Top: Male red lechwe pursuing a female: Botswana.

Above: Female red lechwe and young: Botswana.

Right: Male gerenuk browsing on foliage: Samburu National Reserve, Kenya. Note length of neck and impala-like two-tone torso colours.

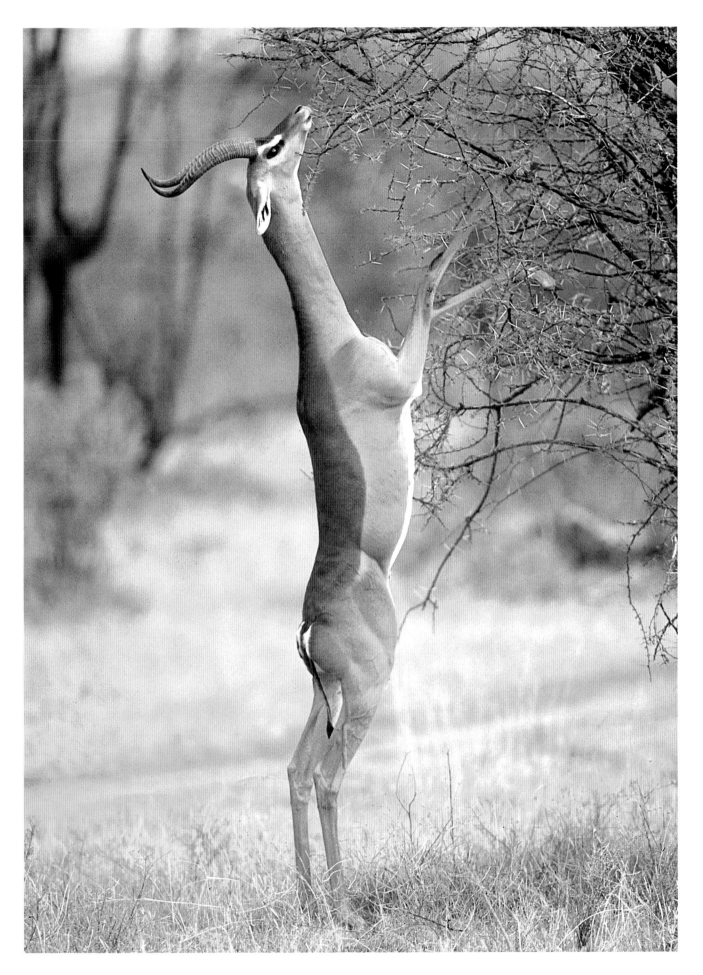

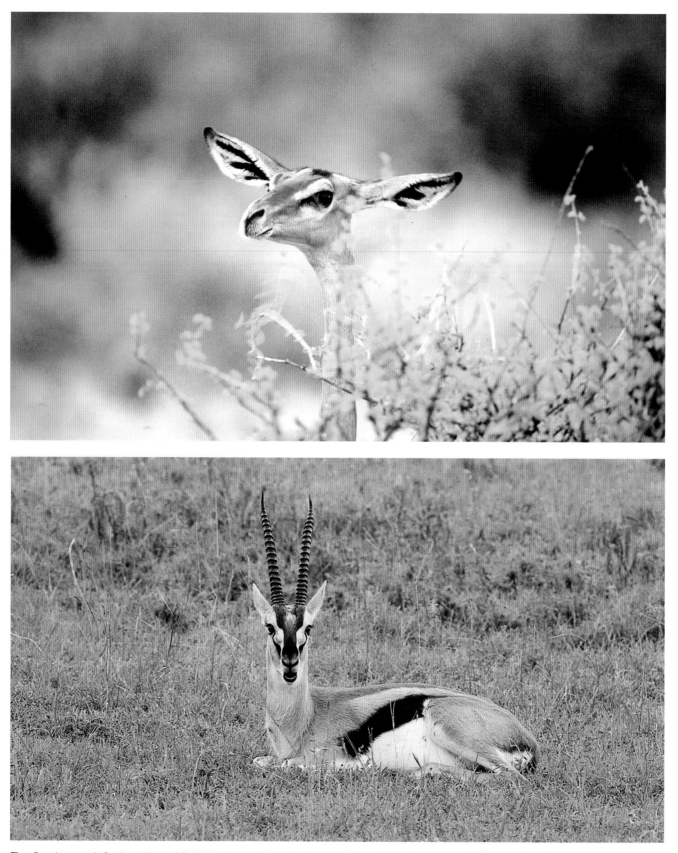

Top: Female gerenuk: Samburu National Park. Note her small head and the black/white pattern on inside of her ears.

Above: Male Thomson's gazelle: Masai Mara. Note his horns (much larger in the male), and black and white face markings.

Above Right: Two young male Thomson's gazelles jousting: Masai Mara. Note the black side stripe and white buttocks, chest, belly and inner legs.

Above Far Right: Two springbok males sparring: Etosha National Park, Namibia. Note the dark brown stripe on their sides and cheeks.

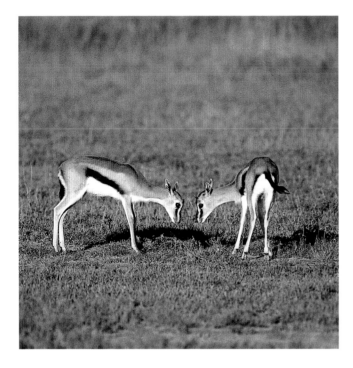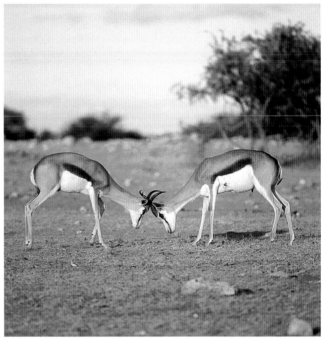

The Neotragini tribe of dwarf antelopes consists of 13 species, most of which inhabit woodlands or more open country with tall grasses or dense thickets to provide cover and are mainly browsers or mixed feeders. Two noticeable characteristics of the tribe in general are high, rounded hindquarters and, in the males, short, straight horns. Smallest of all the tribe are the royal antelope (*Neotragus pygmaeus*), which is no more than 11in (28cm) high at the shoulder and weighs six pounds (2.8kg) at most, and lives in West African rainforests; and Bates's pygmy antelope (*N. batesi*), a rain-forest dweller in Cameroon and north-eastern Zaïre. Almost as small are the four, or possibly five, species of dik-dik (genus *Madoqua*), with their elongated, slightly "swollen" noses, which inhabit the drier savannas of north-eastern Africa.

Other dwarf antelopes include the suni (*Neotragus moschatus*), of eastern Africa from north-eastern Kenya to KwaZulu-Natal; oribi (*Ourebia ourebi*), of the moist savannas of West and East Africa, Angola and Zambia, Mozambique and eastern South Africa; steenbok (*Raphicerus campestris*), of the dry savannas of Kenya and Tanzania and Africa south of Angola and the Zambezi; Sharpe's grysbok (*R. sharpei*), of moist woodlands from south-eastern Zaïre and Tanzania to north-eastern Transvaal; Cape grysbok (*R. melanotis*), restricted to the coastal belt of Cape Province; and the greyish yellow, coarse-haired klipspringer (*Oreotragus oreotragus*), which inhabits rocky terrain in hills and mountains (up to 14,750ft/4500m) from the Horn of Africa to the Cape of Good Hope; also in Namibia and southern Angola.

The last subfamily is the Cephalophinae—the duikers, a group of 17 rainforest antelopes of small to medium size, long-necked, short-legged, and with high, rounded hindquarters and short horns. They are unique among antelopes in including animal food (mainly invertebrates, frogs and carrion) in their diets as well as their preferred wild fruits, leaves, flowers and fungi. The following are representative. The blue duiker (*Cephalophus monticola*), the smallest and most abundant, is slate grey in colour tinged with brown, with paler underparts, and lives in lowland and montane rainforests mainly in central Africa from Cameroon south to Angola and southern Zaïre. The slightly larger bay duiker (*C. dorsalis*) and the similar Peters' duiker (*C. callipygus*) inhabit montane forests, dense bush and forest-savanna mosaic regions of central and West Africa. The zebra or banded duiker (*C. zebra*) has ten or more black transverse stripes from shoulders to rump against a light reddish brown ground colour; it is native to lowland rainforests in Sierra Leone, Liberia and Ivory Coast. Something of an exception to the above species is the common or grey duiker (*Sylvicapra grimmia*), with longer legs, less-rounded hindquarters and longer ears than the others. It is the most widespread of all the duikers, being found in most habitats south of the Sahara except for lowland rainforest; its coat colour varies from light grey to red-tinged brown, depending on the region.

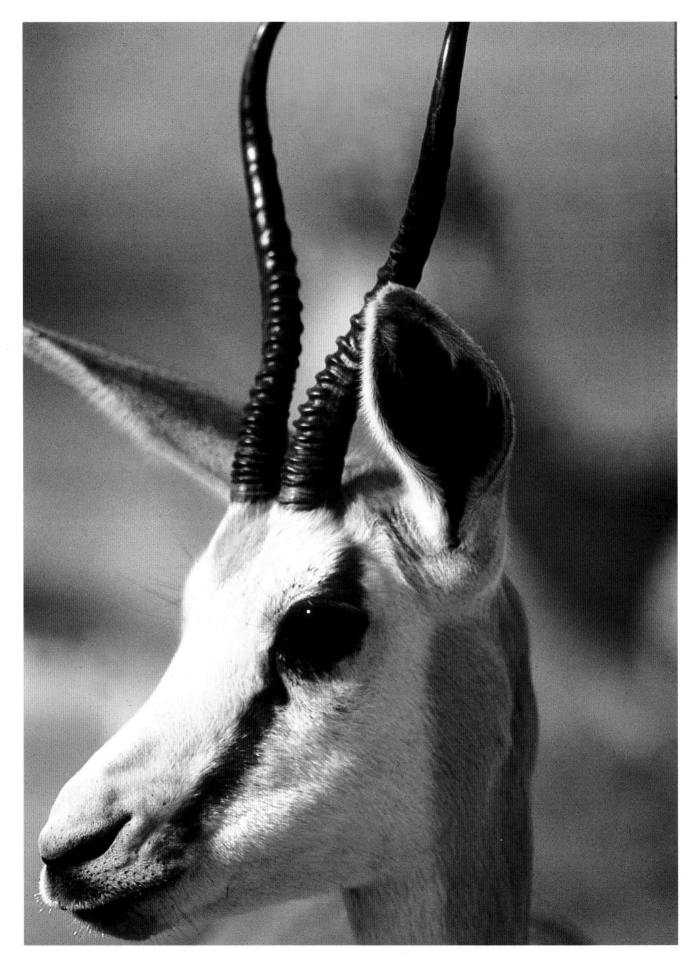

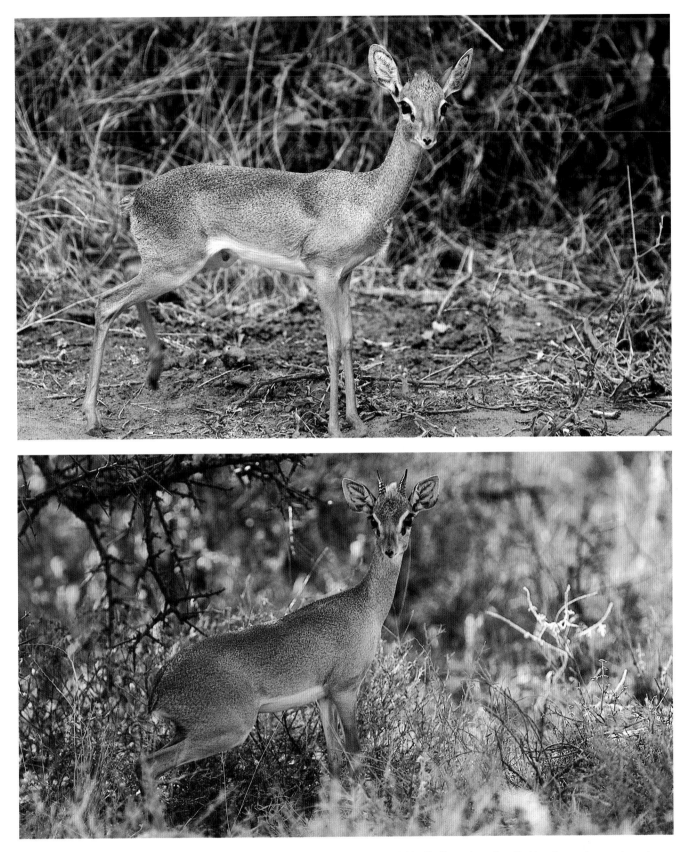

Left: Male springbok: Etosha National Park. Note the strong ridging of his horns, which have inward-hooking tips.

Above: Kirk's dik-dik: southern Somalia. Note its good protective colouring for browsing in thornbush and woodland.

Top: Kirk's dik-dik: northern Namibia. Note the white eye ring and underparts.

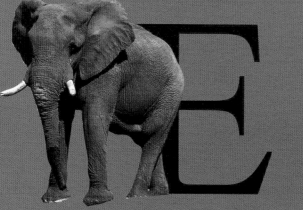

ELEPHANTS

The African elephant is by some margin the largest land mammal. Some five or six million years ago its evolutionary ancestor split into three main lines that would eventually become the mammoth (*Mammuthus*), the Indian elephant (*Elephas indicus*) and the African elephant (*Loxodonta africana*). Fossil evidence suggests that the Indian species was abundant in Africa as well as India for several million years but that it died out in Africa some 20,000 years ago. Their extinction was almost certainly due in large measure to the activities of human farmers and hunters—and a similar fate may well overtake the modern species over the next few decades.

Right: A party of elephants, with young of various ages, in Amboseli National Park, Kenya In the background is cloud-wrapped Kilimanjaro.

Overleaf: A bull elephant on lush grassland: Ngorongoro Crater. In the distance loom the huge enclosing walls of the crater.

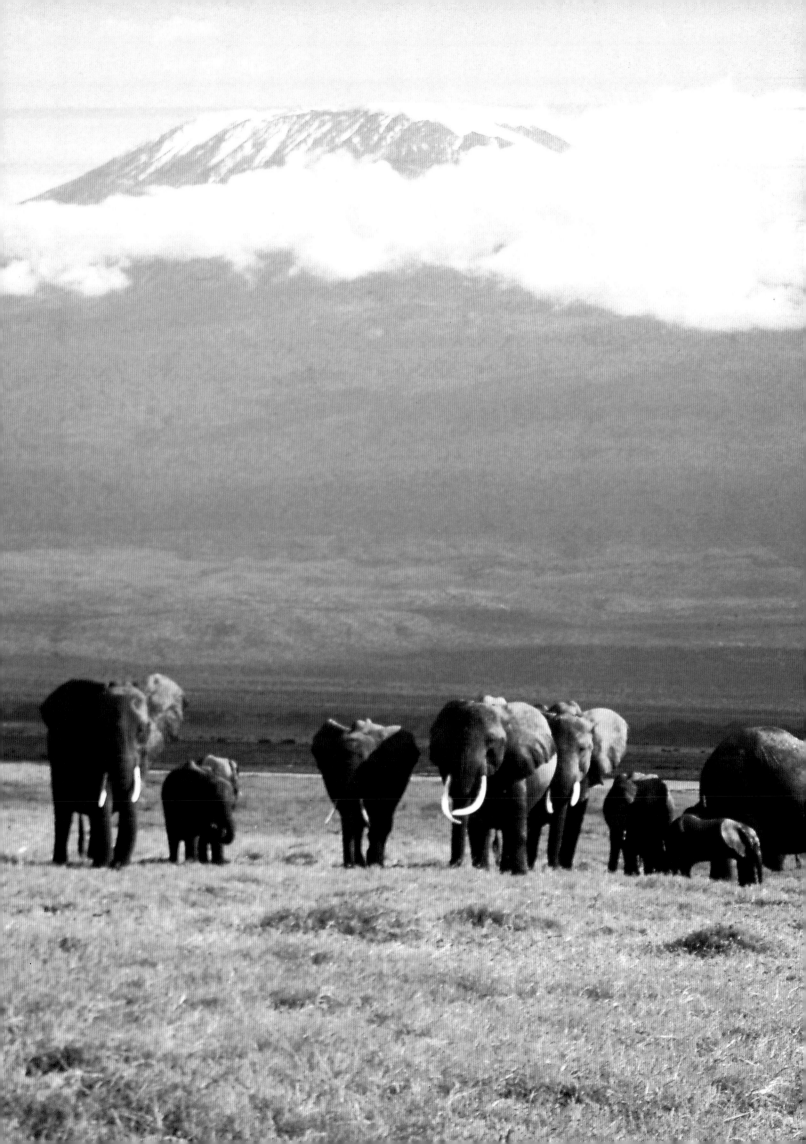

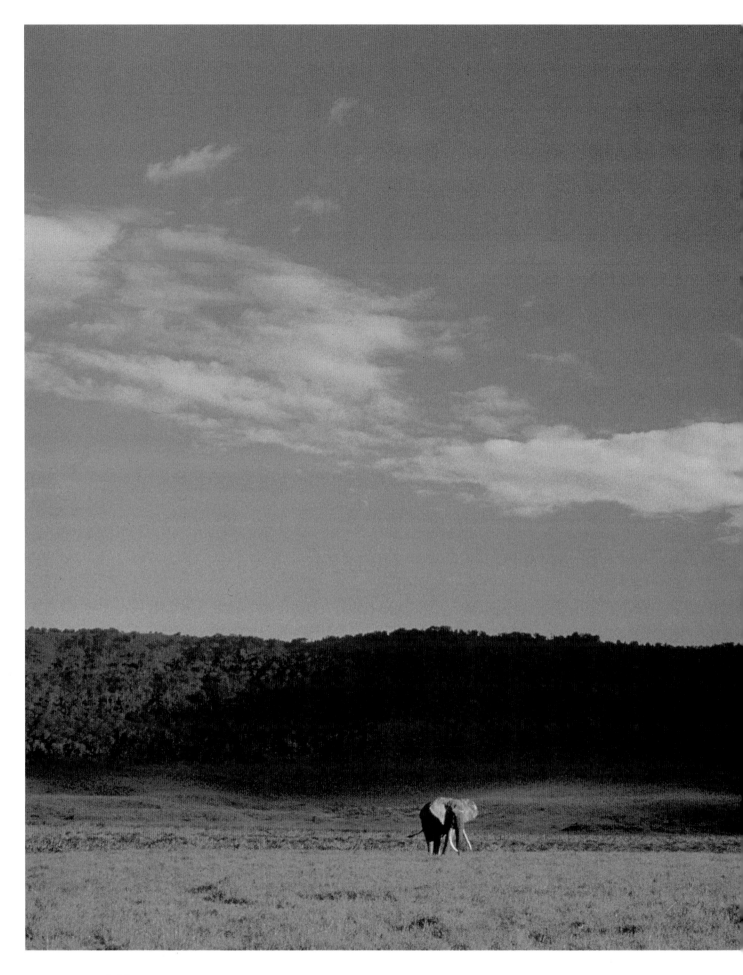

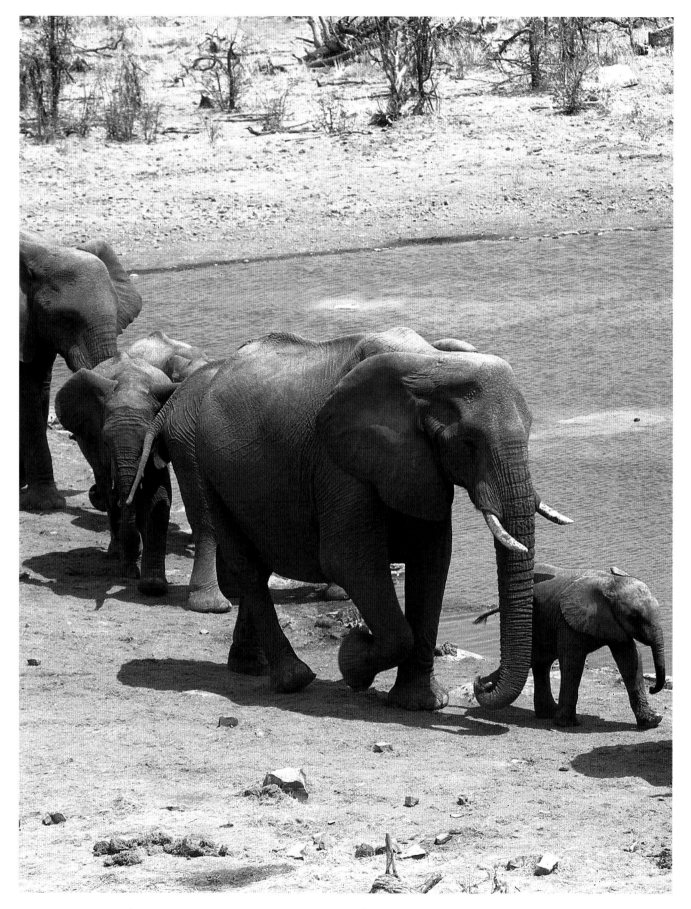

Above: Elephants at a waterhole in the otherwise parched Etosha National Park, Namibia.

The African elephant occurs in two subspecies: the bush or savanna elephant (*L. a. africana*) and the much rarer and more elusive forest or pygmy elephant (*L. a. cyclotis*). The bush elephant is much the larger: an adult male may stand 13ft (4m) at the shoulder and weigh up to 14,000lb (6,350kg); equivalent figures for the forest elephant are 9ft (2.8m) and 7,700lb (3,500kg).

The elephant's most noticeable features, apart from its sheer size, are its trunk, its tusks, its large ears and its massive, column-shaped legs. Its trunk is an astonishingly versatile organ: it is, of course, used for breathing (and acts as a snorkel when the animal swims or fords deep rivers); it can squirt powerful jets of water or mud; it is an immensely strong tool for gathering food and transferring it to the mouth; it gives the animal a formidable reach, enabling an adult to pluck foliage or fruit more than 20 feet (6m) above the ground; it is also an extremely delicate instrument, with a small finger-like projection at its tip that enables it to pick up objects as small as a berry; and it is an important vocal tool. The tusks, which may be present in both sexes and continue to grow throughout an elephant's life, are modified incisors of the upper jaw. Those of the bush elephant are longer, thicker, slightly splayed and curve forwards; those of the

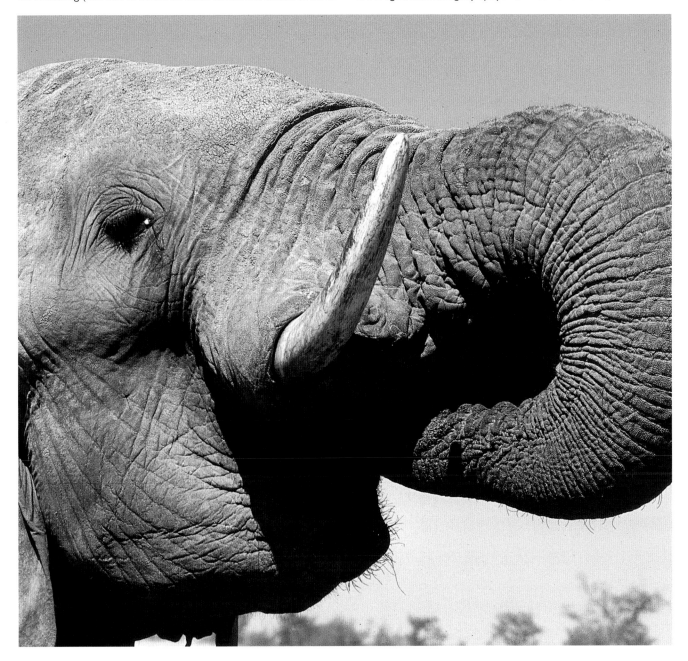

Above: An elephant sprays water into its mouth: Etosha National Park.

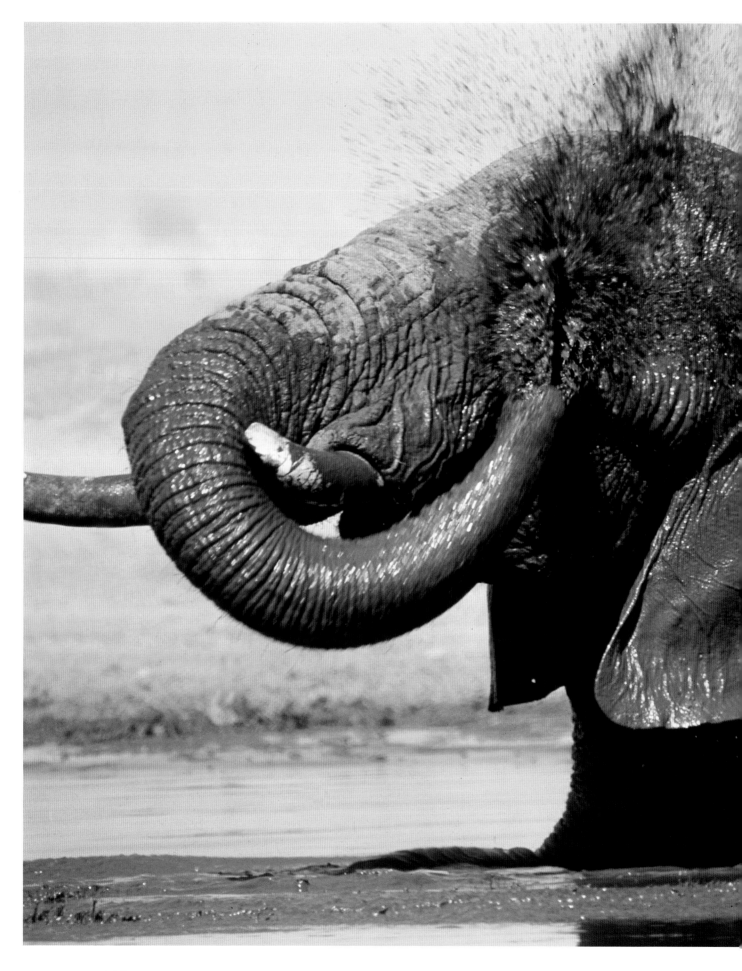

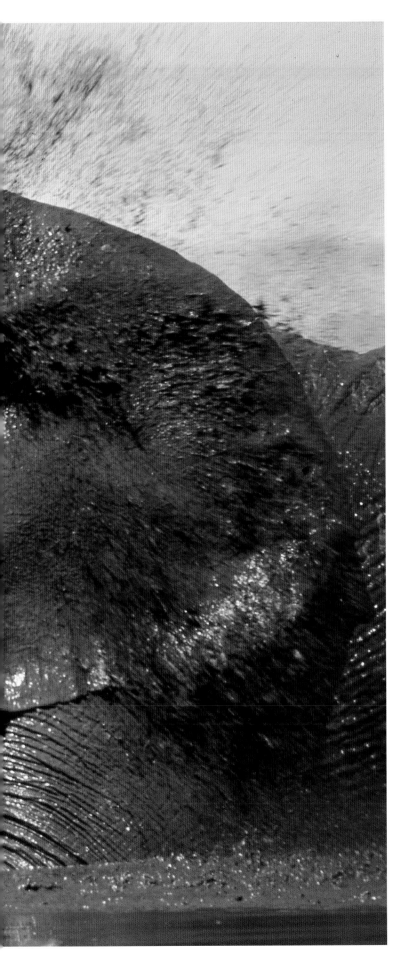

forest elephant are straighter, parallel and point downwards. (Not all adult elephants have tusks, however, and there are populations of bush elephants in some regions where there seems to be a much higher proportion of tuskless individuals than in other regions—perhaps an evolutionary adaptation to local conditions.)

The sail-like ears are not only mobile sound-catching "dishes" and indicators of mood, but also help to regulate body temperature: the backs of the ears have a dense network of blood vessels that acts like a radiator when the elephant fans its ears in hot weather. The bush elephant's ears are massive, and the lower lobe comes to a point; the forest elephant's are smaller in proportion and more circular in shape.

Elephants have five toes, and their feet are underlain by a thick cushion of elastic tissue over smooth footpads. The pads—more or less circular on the forefeet, more elongated but smaller on the hindfeet—have a network of surface cracks that leave individually identifiable tracks. The adult elephant's thick skin is almost hairless except for bristles on the chin, trunk and the end of the tail. Its colour is greyish brown, although the animal's frequent and obviously enjoyable recourse to dust or mud baths means that for much of the time it is the colour of the soil in its home range.

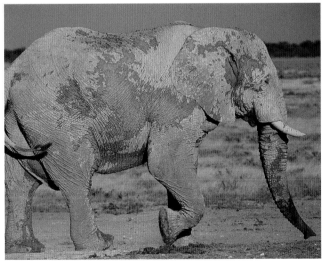

Above: An elephant completely covered by a mud layer; the dark patches are where mud is still damp.

Left: Mudbaths help an elephant to keep its skin free of parasites and protect it against sunburn. This mudpack is being applied in Savuti swamp, Botswana.

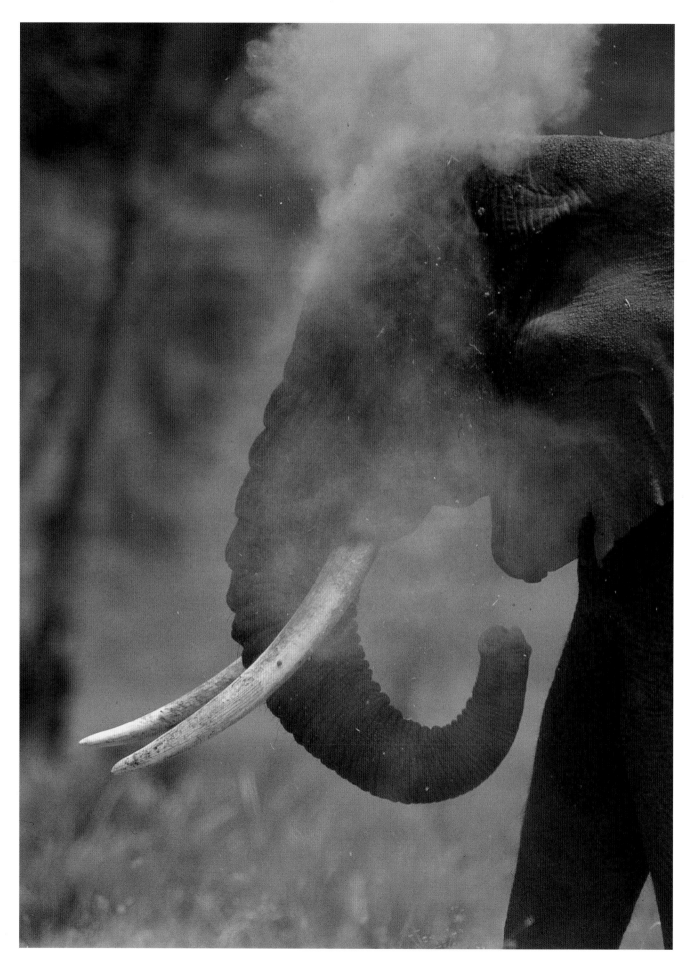

Elephant society is based on the mother and her offspring. A female is unable to become pregnant until she is at least eight years old. A well-established herd might consist of ten females and their young, but there is never a rigid dominance structure, the "matriarch" of a herd will normally be the oldest, largest and healthiest. When the herd has grown substantially larger—to, say, 15 related females and their young—it will split into two or more smaller units, which may remain in the same area and continue to associate amicably, sometimes combining, in areas where there is plenty of food and water, to form larger temporary herds.

Adult females come into oestrus at intervals that may be up to nine years apart. Normally quite vociferous animals, with an impressive repertoire of roars, snorts, trumpetings and squeaks, the females communicate their readiness to mate in a highly specific manner—by emitting a series of signals in infrasound at a frequency that is inaudible to the human ear but perceptible to other elephants at a range of two miles (3.2km) or more. The signals are attractive to all adult male elephants, but especially to those in the state of heightened sexual readiness known as "musth". While the males become sexually competitive at about 25 years of age, matings are dominated by the biggest males of 35 years and more.

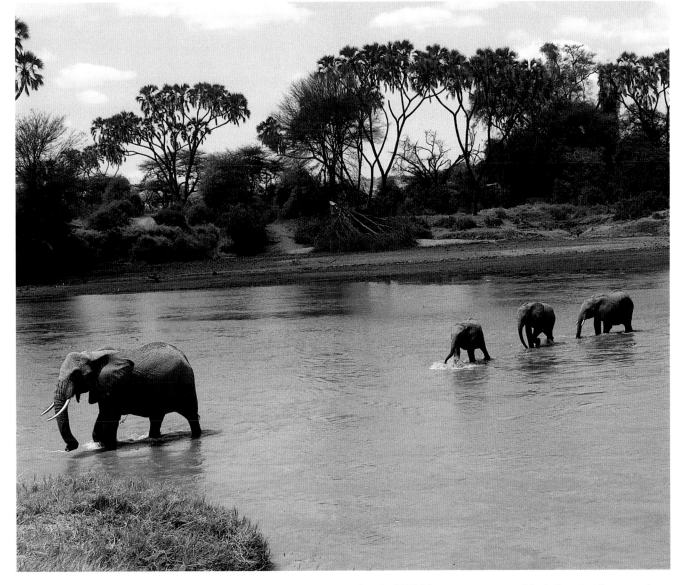

Above: Elephants quench their thirst while fording the Ewaso N'giro river in Buffalo Springs National Reserve, Kenya.

Overleaf: Wildlife contrast: a mature adult elephant dwarfs a party of impala with which its shares a waterhole near Savuti.

Left: When mud is not available, an elephant makes do with a sandbath.

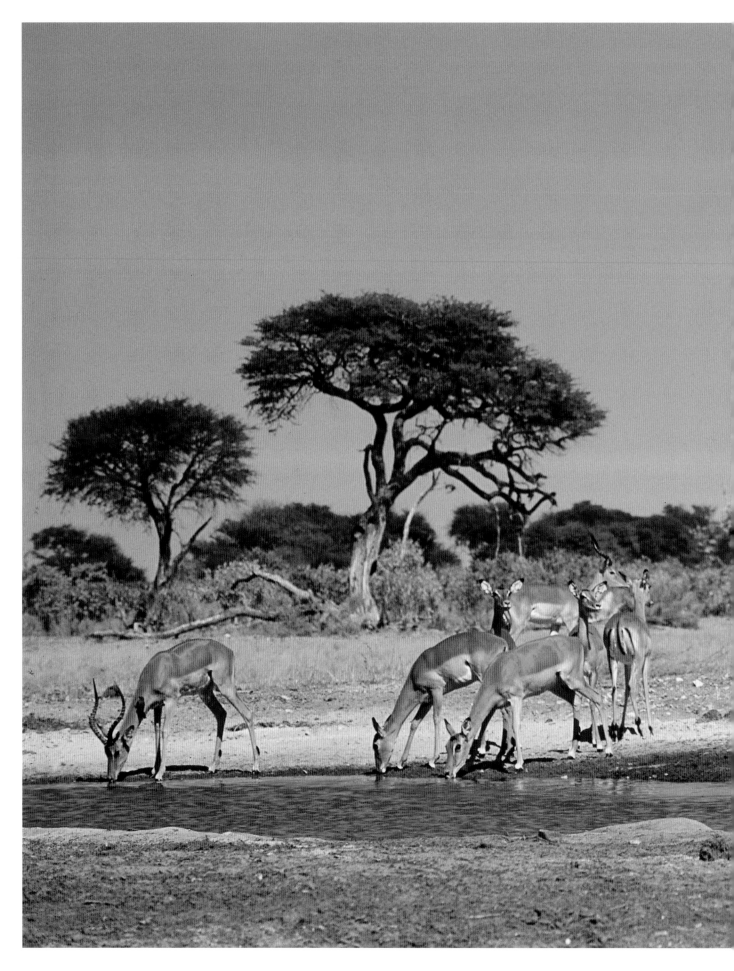

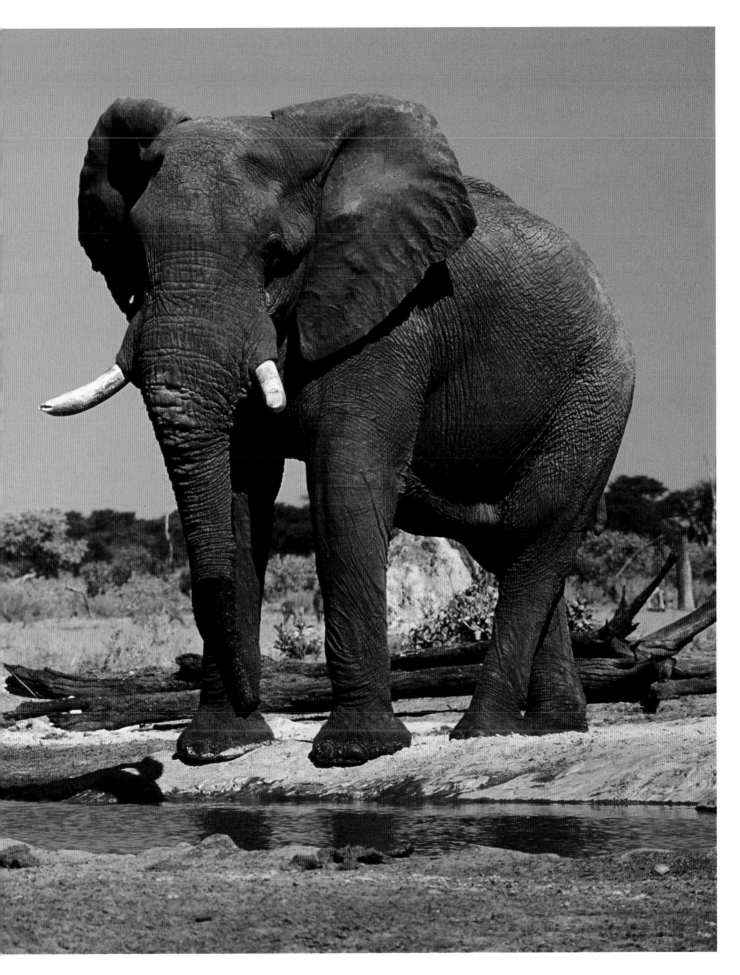

Right: A party of adults surrounds a youngster on a walkabout in Tsavo West National Park, Kenya.

Below: This baby elephant was one day old when caught on camera in Amboseli National Park.

Bottom: A few weeks old, this baby elephant has just taken perhaps its first mudbath: Masai Mara.

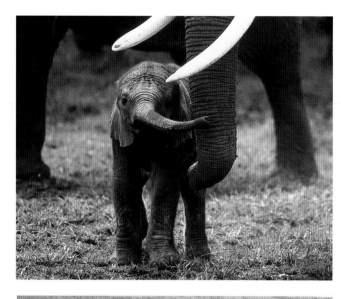

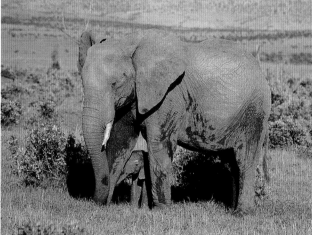

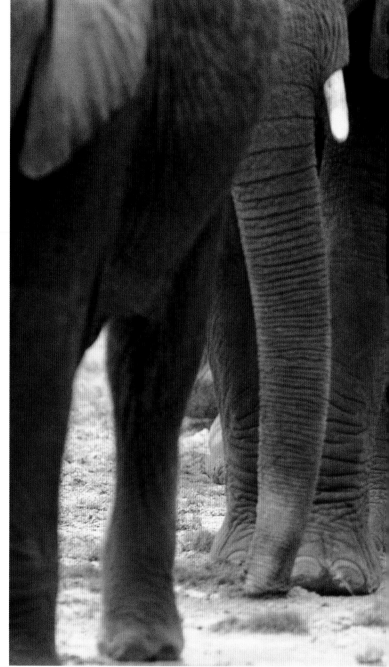

The females give birth to one (or occasionally two) young after a gestation of about 650 days. The young do not become fully mobile for three or four weeks, and it is during this critical period that they are at risk to predation by lions and hyenas. All adult females in the group will help defend the young against predators. While the calves may not be weaned for at least four years, they will be eating solid food long before that. They may not become fully independent feeders for ten years or more and the young cows will remain with their birth group until they break away to form their own groups. The young bulls remain until they reach puberty at about 12 years of age, when they leave (or are forced out) and will then join groups of other males or lead a partly solitary life. In favourable circumstances elephants will live for 60 to 65 years; in fact, about half of all elephants die before they reach 15 years of age, due mainly to human predation.

Matriarchal (family) groups move about ranges that vary considerably in size depending on the availability of food and water, which in many of their habitats depends in turn on the season. A small family group in favourable circumstances has a home range of anything from 10 to 20 square miles (26-52km²); those of adult

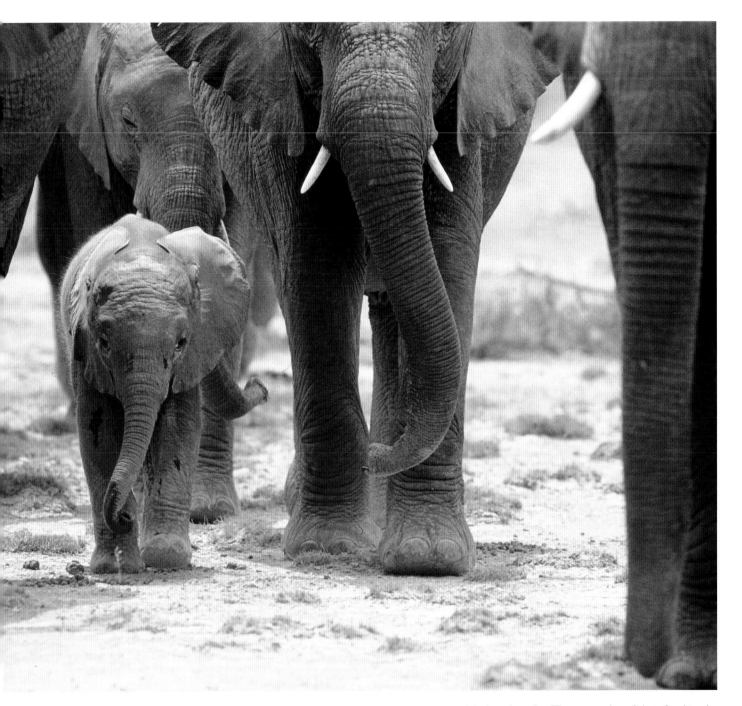

males may be 20 times as big, since they move freely among several matriarchal groups. Bush elephants live in every kind of habitat from rainforest and montane forest, through open woodland and savanna grassland to semi-desert; in Namibia they may sometimes be seen walking in dry river beds between the vast dunes of the Namib desert in search of water. Their diet consists of a wide range of plants. In the wet season, grass accounts for almost three quarters of their food intake, and low browse (shrubs and young trees up to about elbow height) for about one fifth; in the dry season low browse accounts for about two fifths

and grass slightly less than that. The remainder of their food intake consists of higher browse, including canopy foliage and fruit. An adult eats 350-650lb (160-300kg) of food a day (if available) and drinks anything from 20 to 50 gallons (90-230 litres) of water. Forest elephants occur in small isolated groups in areas of mainly rainforest from Senegal in the west to eastern Zaïre. Their diet is less varied but more reliable than that of the bush elephant. Where the habitats of the two subspecies coincide—in areas of forest and woodland mosaic—the herds mingle and there is considerable interbreeding.

The future prospects of *Loxodonta africana* are a matter of anxious speculation. It has been estimated that the elephant population of some ten million in 1930 had by the early 1990s declined to about half a million. The cause of the decline is not just the evil international trade in ivory: rapid increases in the human population, with a consequent need to bring more and more land into cultivation, for food or cash crops or for managed pastures, has also led to drastic reductions in the elephant's open woodland and savanna grassland habitats. The hope for the future lies in national parks and game reserves, where the land cannot simply be commandeered by local farmers and where greater control can be kept over the ivory hunters. Even so the prospects for these magnificent beasts are not good.

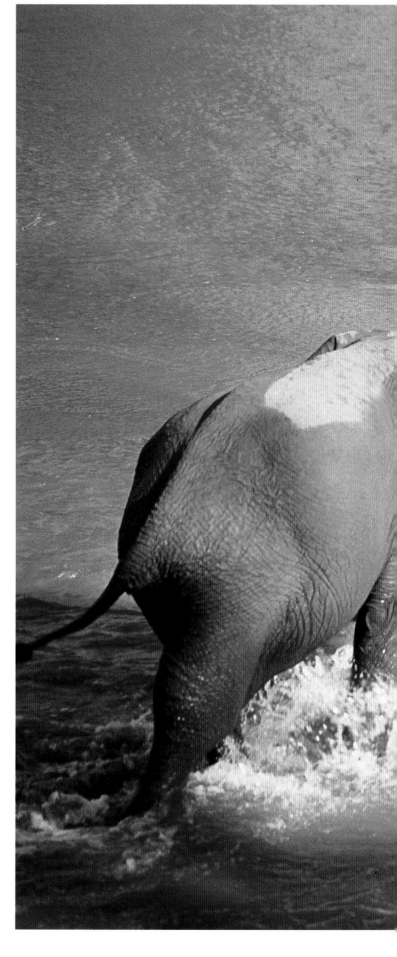

Two juvenile elephants, five or six years old, paddle in a stream in Samburu National Reserve, Kenya.

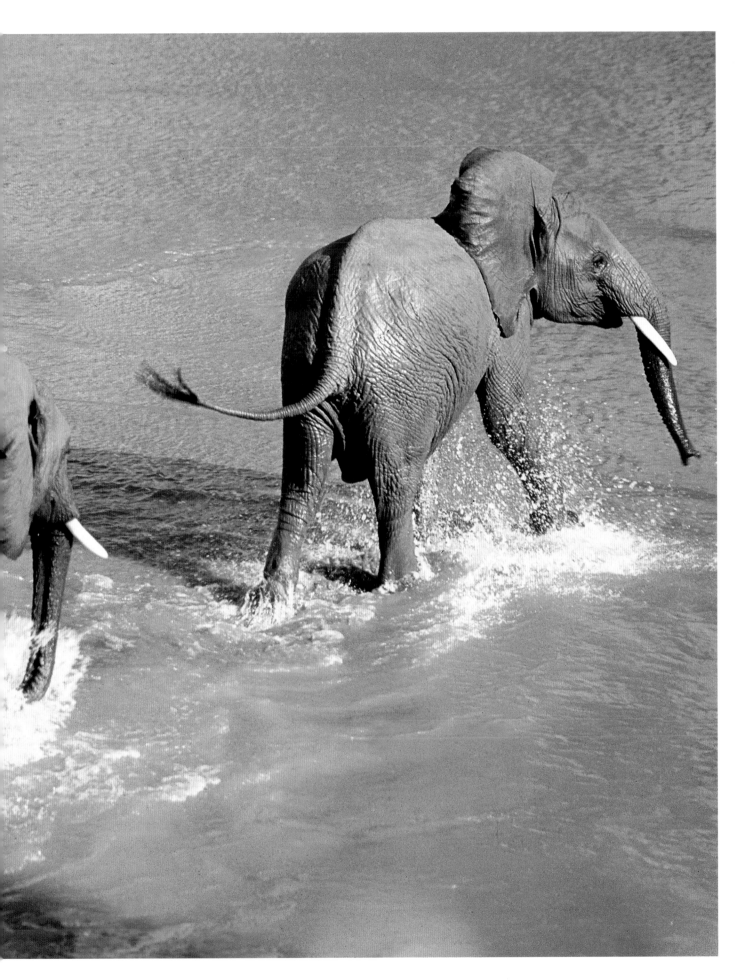

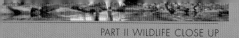

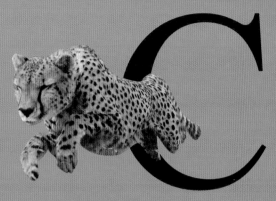

CARNIVORES

Of the 235 carnivore species throughout the world, more than 70 are native to Africa. The carnivores are divided into two major divisions or sub-orders: the feliforms and the caniforms. The feliforms consist of the cats, hyenas, civets, genets and mongooses; the caniforms consist of the dogs, weasels, raccoons and bears, of which only the raccoons and bears are absent from Africa.

The term carnivore means "meat-eater"—but the term covers a very wide range of prey. Even the leopard, one of nature's most powerful predators of big game, will not disdain to catch and eat a large insect if the opportunity occurs. On the other hand, the caracal, a wild cat that rarely weighs more than 40lb (18kg), will prey on springbok larger than itself. In short, carnivores may attack and eat any form of animal life that is to their liking and within their capacity to kill. At the same time, by evolutionary necessity or for other reasons, many carnivores became omnivorous, eating meat when animal prey was available but topping up their diet with fruit or other vegetable matter when it was not. We begin this chapter with some of the feliforms.

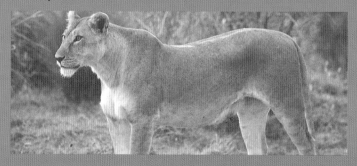

Above: An adult lioness is about four fifths the weight of the male. This one is on the lookout for game on the Masai Mara.

Right: King of the African savanna: an adult male in prime condition, Etosha National Park, Namibia.

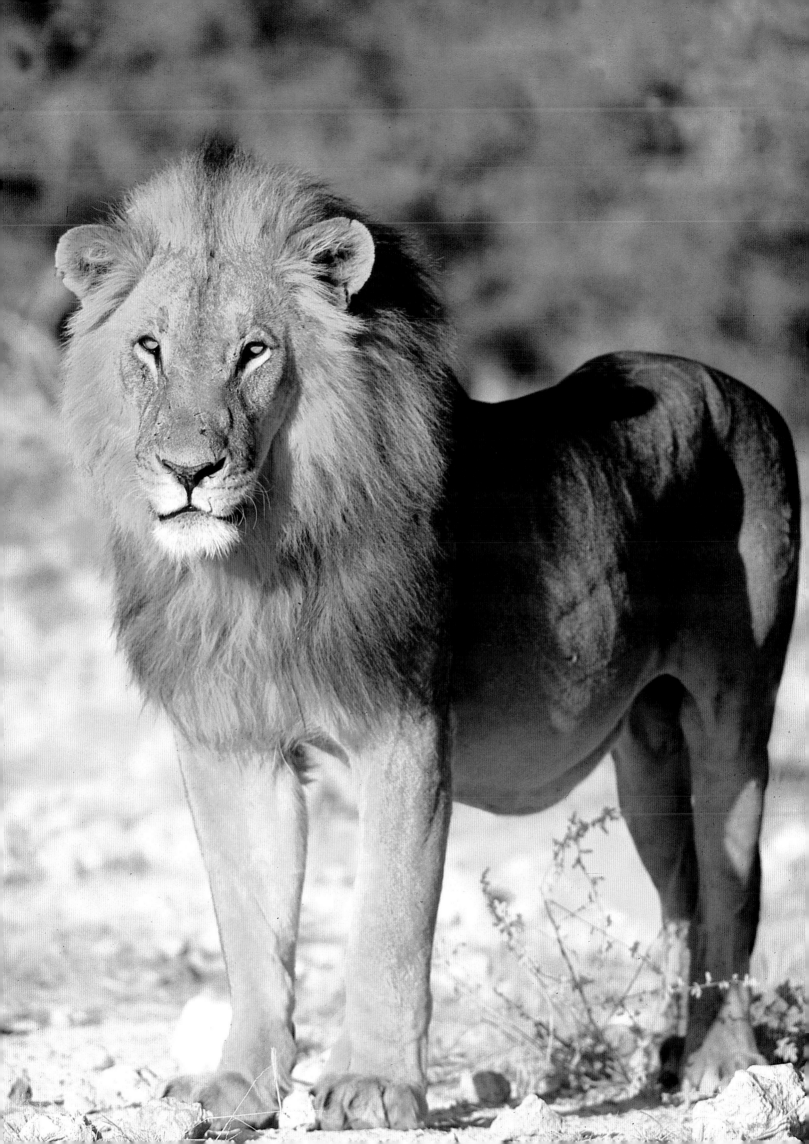

THE BIG CATS

Lion (Panthera leo)

The lion belongs to the same genus, *Panthera*, as the other four largest cats: the tiger of Asia, the leopard of Africa and Asia, the jaguar of the Americas and the snow leopard of the mountain fastnesses of Central Asia. The lion once inhabited the whole of Africa and all the lands eastwards from Egypt to the Bay of Bengal. Today it is found, in greatly reduced numbers, south of the Sahara in open grasslands, savanna woodlands and dense bush, from Senegal in the west to Ethiopia and Somalia in the east; in most of East Africa; and in Angola, northern Namibia and Botswana eastward to northern Transvaal and Mozambique. (The only lions roaming free outside Africa are a few hundred in the Gir Forest reserve in the western Indian state of Gujarat.)

The four great cats, as they are called—the lion, tiger, leopard and jaguar—have one physiological feature that separates them from all other felines: the special structure of the hyoid bones that support and anchor the throat and tongue. In the great cats these bones are connected by a large, elastic ligament that, when stretched, opens up the air passage and enables the cats to emit that deep, terrifying roar. No other cats are capable of roaring in this way. (Incidentally, the young of the four great cats are called cubs; those of the other felids, large or small, are called kittens.)

The basic light brown colour of the adult's coat varies considerably not only from region to region, and between different types of habitat: it may also vary between individuals in the same local population. The colours can range from cream to darkish brown with a slightly reddish tinge; the undersides of the body are of a lighter

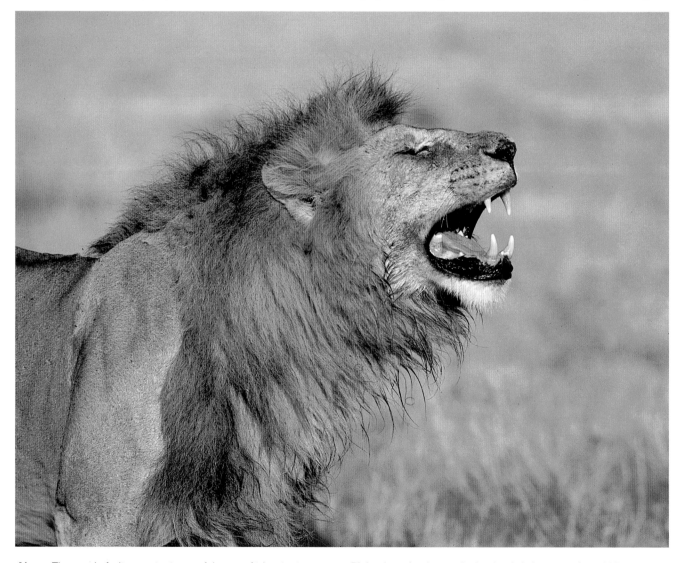

Above: The sound of a lion roaring is one of the most frightening in nature. This lion is giving voice on the Serengeti plains.

Right: A snarling lioness displays her lethal weapons: formidable upper and lower canine teeth.

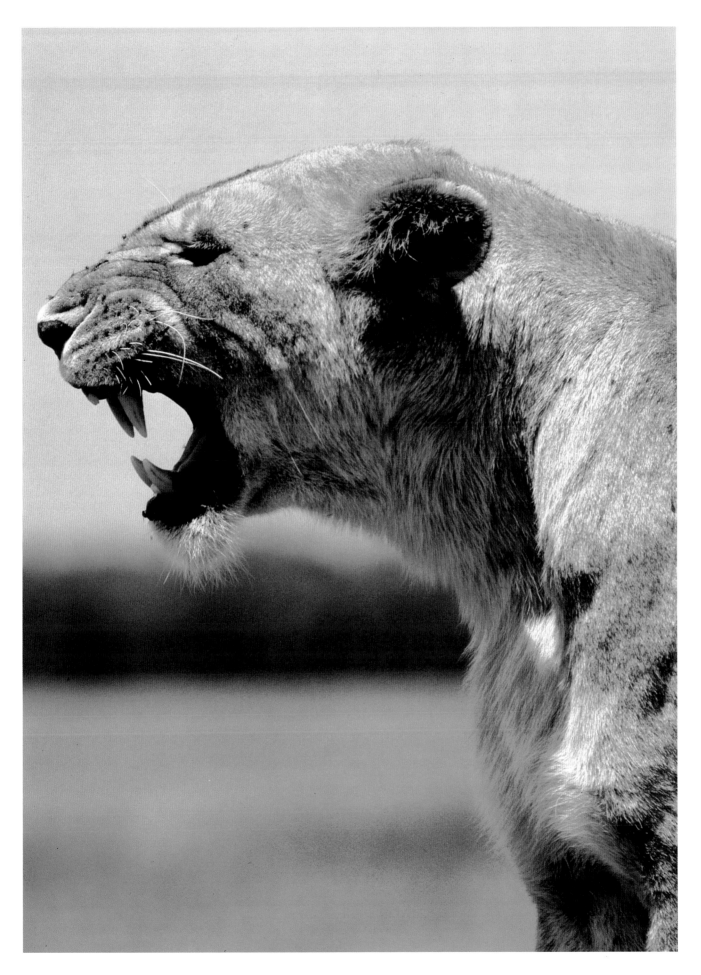

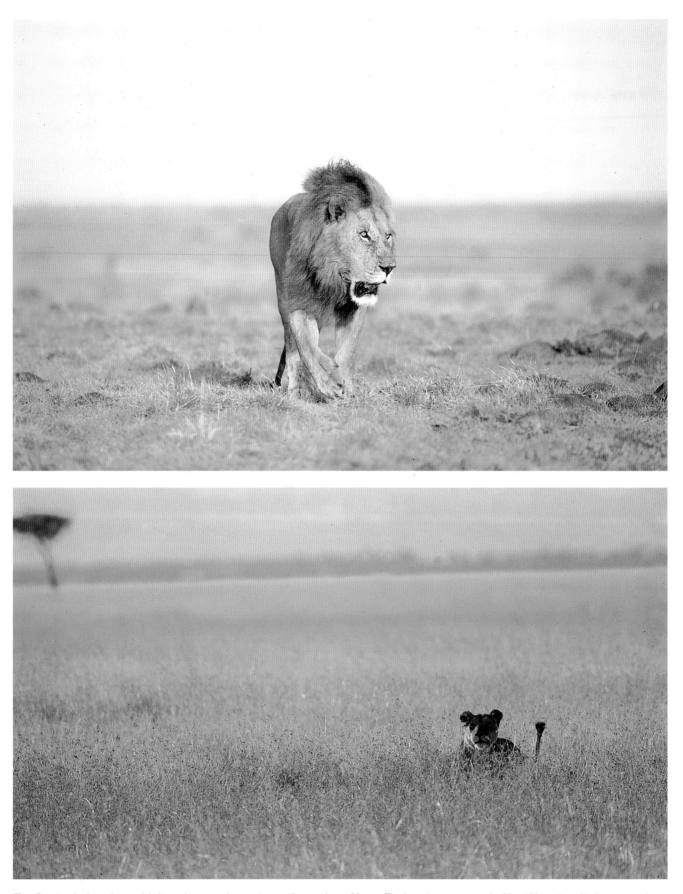

Top: Beating the bounds: an adult lion takes an early morning stroll around his territory. He will assert his claim to it by spraying urine at convenient points around its margins.

Above: The hunt: long grass on the Masai Mara gives this lioness good cover as she looks for prey.

colour. Differences in overall body colour, as well differences in overall size, mane size and mane colour have led to as many as 20 different subspecies of *Panthera leo* being proposed, although many, if not all, of these are of dubious taxonomic validity. Most experts agree that the subspecific title *P. l. leo* adequately covers all the lions at present in Africa. In general, however, the lions of southern Africa tend to be slightly larger than those of East Africa, and lions in captivity tend to have slightly darker coats than those in the wild.

Only the male lion has a mane, the rich growth of longer hair on the sides of the face, the neck, chest and shoulders. Its development becomes noticeable when the lion is between 30 and 36 months old; at that time it is usually much the same colour as the rest of the coat, but it will gradually darken with age and may eventually be very dark brown or even black. Some observers have reported that the lions of the Masai Mara and Serengeti plains have somewhat darker manes than those elsewhere. Lions inhabiting cool upland regions usually have more luxuriant manes than those living in drier, warmer regions. The only other departure from the overall body colour is in the characteristic tassel at the tip of the tail, which is dark brown or black.

The lion is by far the largest of Africa's cats, and the male is considerably larger than the female. The male may be up to 10ft (3m) in length, including the tail, stand 4ft (1.2m) at the shoulder, and typically weigh up to 450lb (204kg); the figures for the female are 9ft (2.7m), 3ft 9in (1.1m), and 360lb (164kg) respectively.

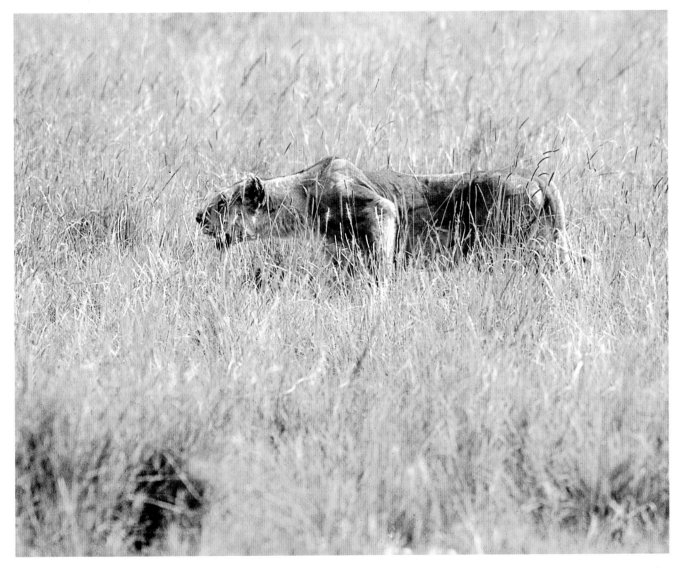

Above: Prey sighted: a lioness (with other female members of her pride) begins a stealthy approach to the quarry, using whatever cover is available on the Mara.

Lions are the most sociable of all the cats, living in groups, called prides, that number anything from three to as many as 30 individuals, depending partly on the local density of the lion population and partly on the availability of prey. A pride consists of several females and their cubs and one or more males who live and hunt in a particular area. Lionesses, related as mothers and daughters or as siblings, constitute the core of the pride, entry to which is barred to any unrelated females. The genetic health of the pride is validated by the male pride-leaders, who may be related to each other but are unrelated to the females with whom they mate. Moreover, as the male cubs become sexually mature, they are expelled from the pride by the adult males. The gene pool may also be freshened by some females mating with males who are not members of their pride. Males seize leadership of a pride by killing or driving off the previous leaders and by killing any cubs that the latter have fathered. Such leadership may last for a few months or a few years: it ends, almost invariably, with the arrival of younger, more aggressive males on the lookout for vulnerable pride-leaders.

Lionesses have their first cubs when they are about four years old. There is no breeding season but, interestingly, all the adult females in the pride come into œstrus at the same time; sometimes

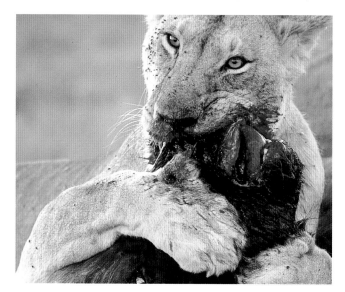

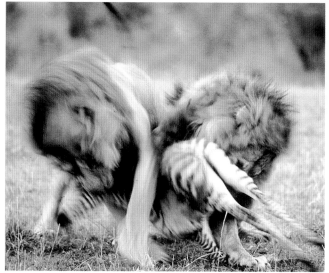

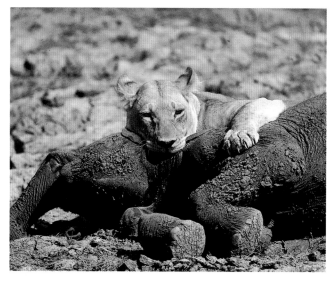

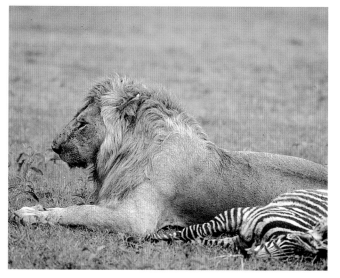

Top: The killing: this lioness and her sisters have killed a big Cape buffalo—a formidable task requiring three or more big cats.

Above: This baby elephant—possibly one already weakened by disease—has succumbed in Chobe National Park, Botswana.

Top and Above: Rather less strength was needed by these two adult males to kill a young plains zebra on the Masai Mara, and the more dominant of the pair then laid claim to the victim.

this is triggered when new pride leaders kill off cubs of the former leaders which are still being suckled by the lionesses. Cubs are born after a gestation period of about 110 days. There are usually two to four in a litter, weighing about 3lb (1.5kg). The cub's coat has brownish spots for the first three months or so. One advantage of all the cubs in the pride being born at the same time is that they can suckle from any of the several lionesses that are lactating.

The cubs remain dependent on the pride for food for as long as two years. One reason for this is that they need time to learn how to live within a pride. In particular, they have to be schooled in the skills of hunting in a group—skills that are unique to the lion among the big cats and which are fully developed towards the end of the young cats' fourth year. By this time, the young males will have been expelled from the pride by the dominant males and will usually pursue a nomadic life together until or unless they succeed in taking over another pride.

Catching and killing prey is mainly the work of the lionesses: they are not only faster but more skilful hunters than the males, who nonetheless will often participate in the hunt (and, of course, the nomadic bands of young adults hunt as all-male groups) The degree to which a pride's lionesses act cooperatively in the hunt is

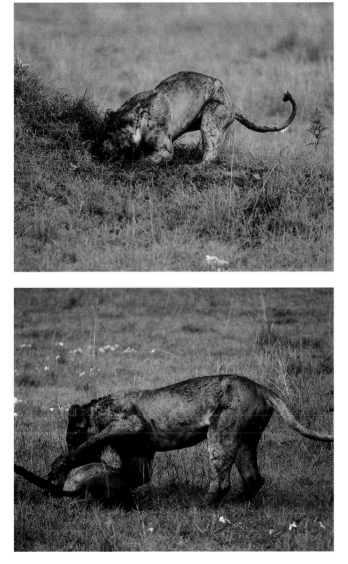

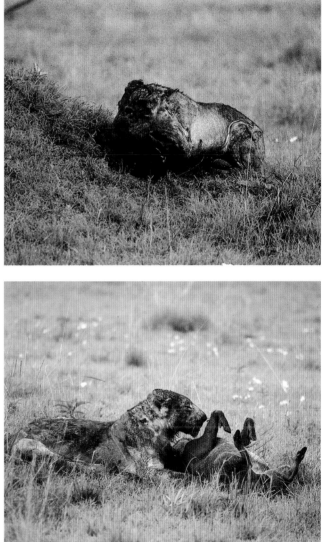

Top: Death on the Serengeti plains. A lioness digs into the burrow of a warthog.

Top Right: She kills her victim by sinking her teeth into its neck and breaking its spinal cord.

Above Left: She drags the dead warthog clear of the burrow.

Above: She prepares to enjoy her meal.

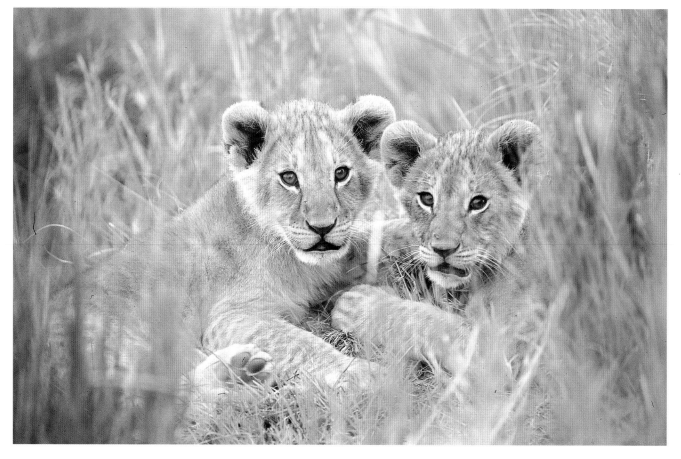

remarkable. Typically, they will split into two groups, one group seeking to round up their quarry and drive them toward the second group, which is waiting concealed behind any available cover. Once caught, the prey is felled and one lioness will usually seize it by the neck or throat and snap its spinal cord. The largest prey will be attacked by several lionesses at a time; these victims may include bull giraffes and Cape buffalo, while other favoured prey include the larger antelopes, zebra, warthog and the young of elephant and hippo.

One of the drawbacks of living in a pride, of course, is that all its members will have a good meal after the hunt only if the prey is of a substantial size. In spite of the fact that they do most of the killing, the lionesses are often the last to eat. The dominant males enjoy the first "sitting", and they will then often allow the cubs to eat before leaving the carcass to the lionesses. The hierarchy within the pride is evident in much of its social behaviour. Individuals spend much time on their own or with a couple of companions; but when such groups reunite, as after a kill, the subordinate adults and juveniles indulge in "appeasement" behaviour, such as cheek-to-cheek rubbing and licking of the dominant members of the pride.

Old or sick males are usually driven out of the pride, and when this happens their prospects of survival are slim. They may manage for a while to exist on a modest diet of reptiles, rodents and other small prey, but as soon as they visibly begin to weaken they almost inevitably fall victim to packs of hyenas.

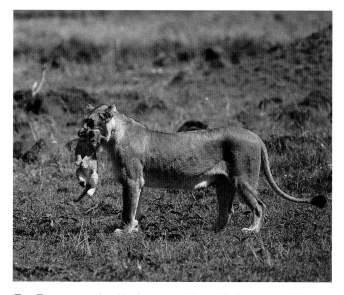

Top: Two two-months-old cubs rest together in the long grass of the Masai Mara.

Above: A lioness carries her month-old cub by the scruff of its neck.

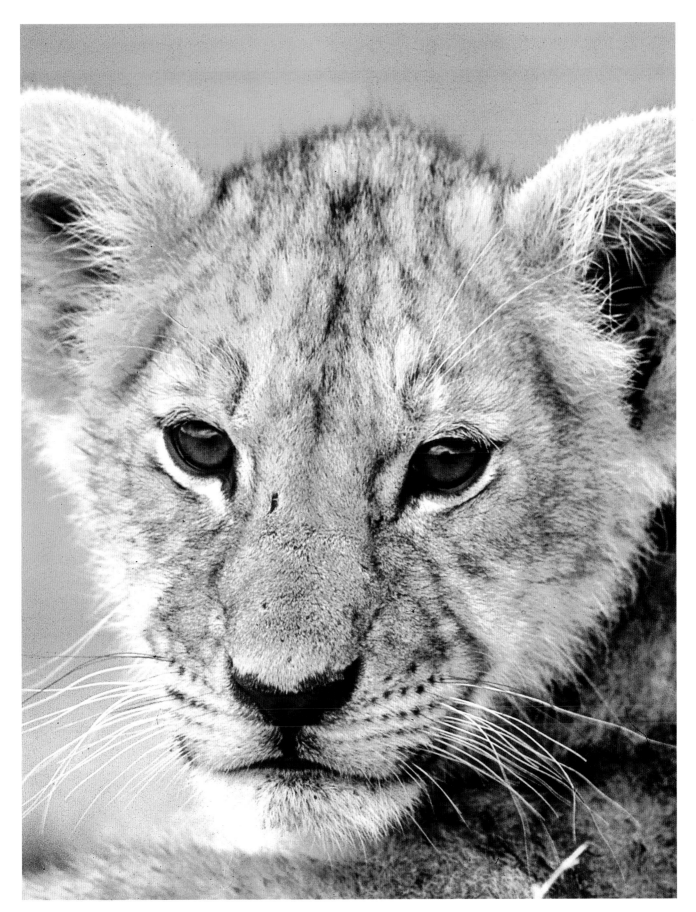

Above: Cubs have brownish spots on their coats for the first three to
four months after birth.

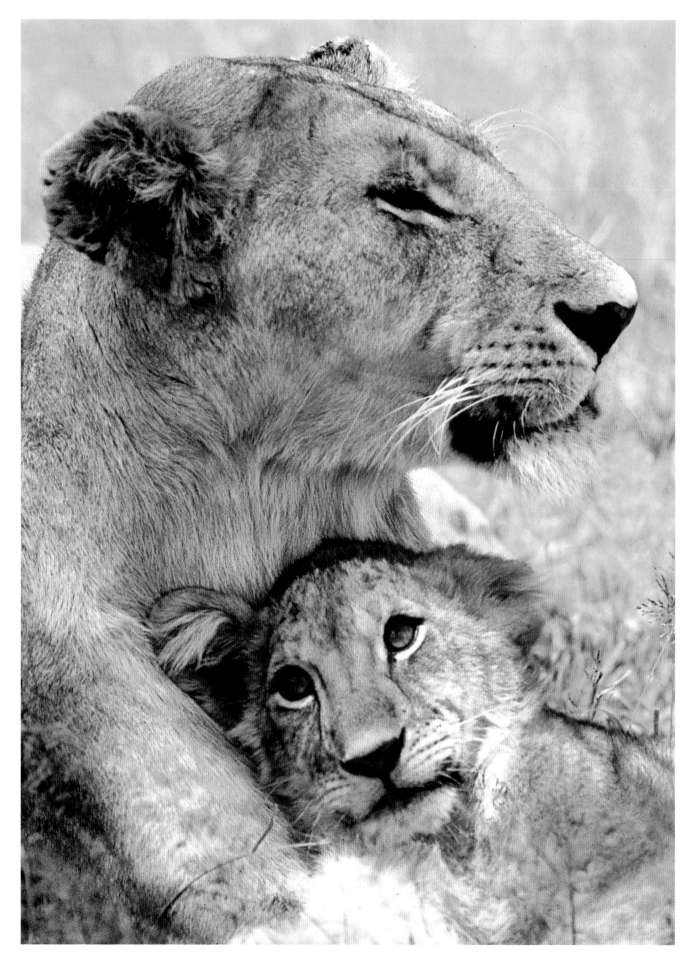

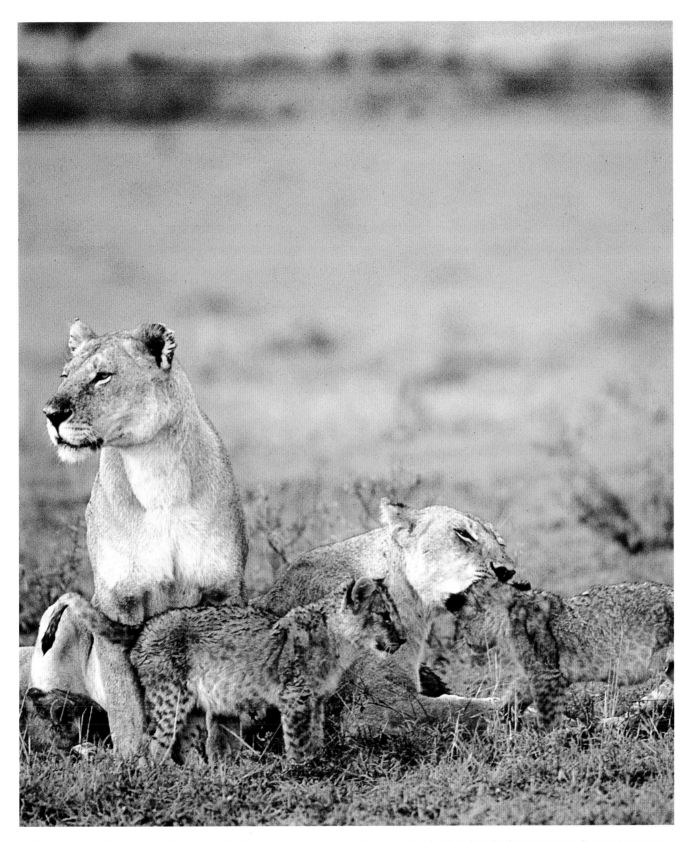

Left: A cub rests with its mother after being suckled.

Above: Family life. All the breeding lionesses in a pride come into œstrus at the same time, so all the cubs of a new generation are born at the same time and can suckle from any of several lionesses that are lactating. This photograph hints at the powerful bond that develops between cubs, their mother and their various "aunts" in the pride. The cubs seen here may well be the progeny of only one of the lionesses.

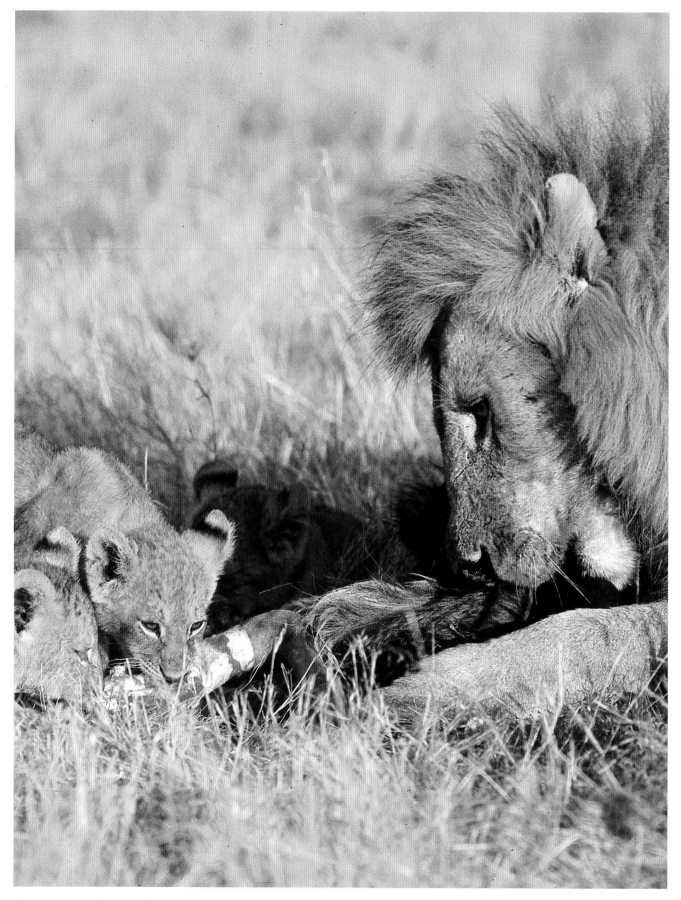

Above: A pride leader on the Masai Mara allows two of his cubs to share
his wildebeest carcass.

Lions, like other big cats, have a well-documented record as man-eaters. One of the best-known episodes of man-eating over a sustained period began in 1932 and involved a pride living near the Tanzanian town of Njombe, some 60 miles (97km) north-east of the northern end of Lake Nyasa (now Lake Malawi). Fifteen years later, when 15 lions of the latest generation were shot dead, the pride had accounted for more than 1,000 people.

Although the lion is not in such grievous danger of extinction as the tiger, its prospects in the long term are not good and its only chance of survival will be to live in the protected reserves, mainly in eastern and southern Africa. The problem centres on the competition for land between animals and man. As human populations rise, and they are doing so in most of the lion's African range, the demand for land becomes ever more acute. On the grassland savannas in many regions ungulates are being killed or driven off in their thousands to make way for the domestic animals on which rural economies depend. The lion (and other species that prey on ungulates) resort to killing cattle and sheep in order to survive, and so are hunted as pests.

Today, Africa's total lion population is unknown, but it is likely that at least half lives in reserves rather than in the wild. The vast open plains of the Serengeti and Masai Mara reserves are home to several thousand lions. In southern Africa something over 4,000 live in reserves, the largest concentrations being in Zimbabwe's Hwange National Park, Transvaal's Kruger National Park and Namibia's Etosha Game Reserve. In many other reserves, and especially those in West Africa, apparently prosperous lion populations may in fact be too small to guarantee their genetic health in the long term—a problem that also applies to zoos that attempt to operate lion-breeding programmes from too restricted a gene pool.

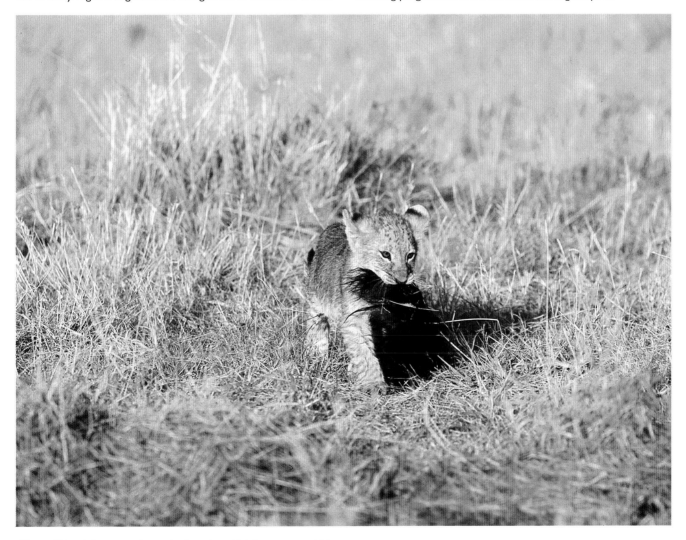

Above: This cub has secured a trophy from the pride's hunt—a mouthful of wildebeest hair.

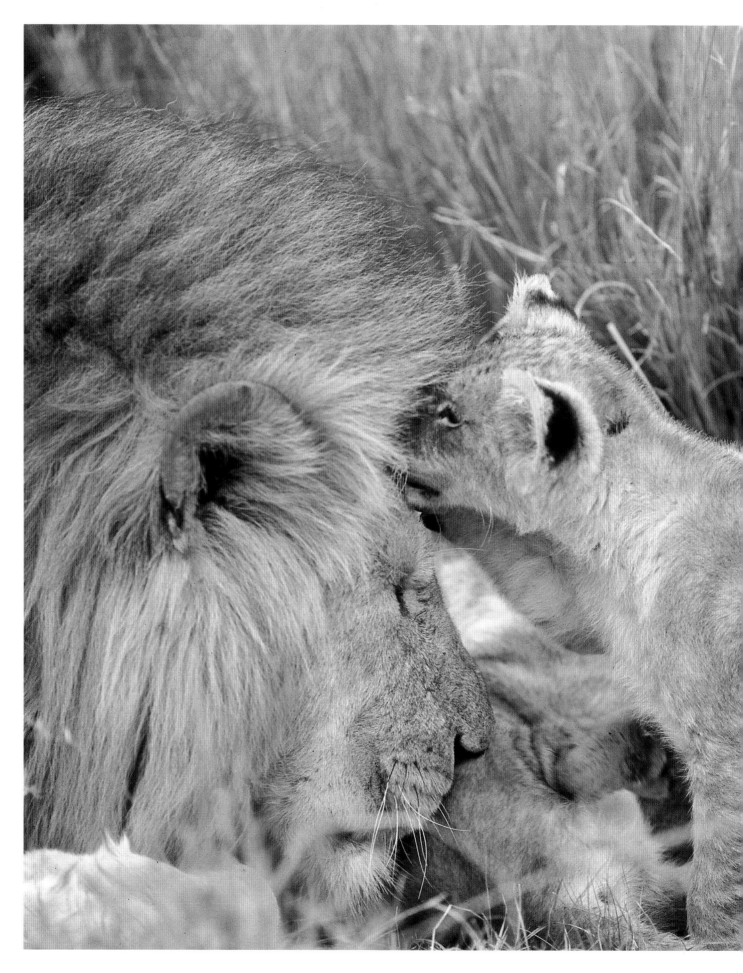

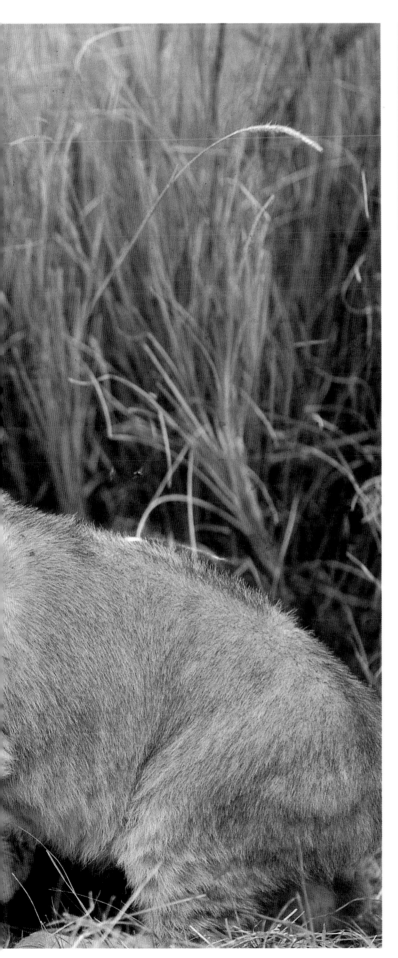

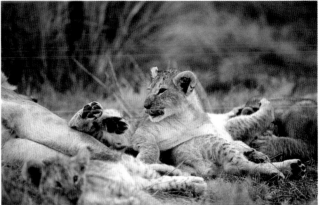

Above: The young cubs indulge in boisterous play-fighting, eventually collapsing in an exhausted heap.

Left: A four-month-old cub attempts to rouse its sleeping father.

Overleaf: Having reached sexual maturity, these male lions have been driven out by the pride leader. They may combine with outcasts from other prides to form roving gangs, each of whose members will hope to wrest control of a pride from an aging leader.

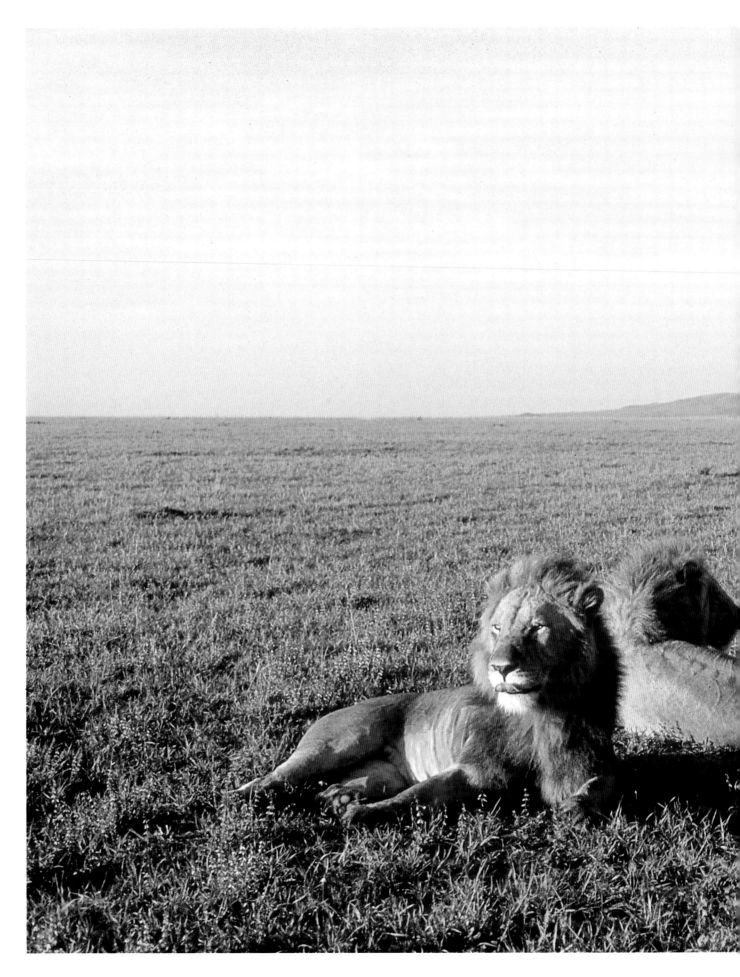

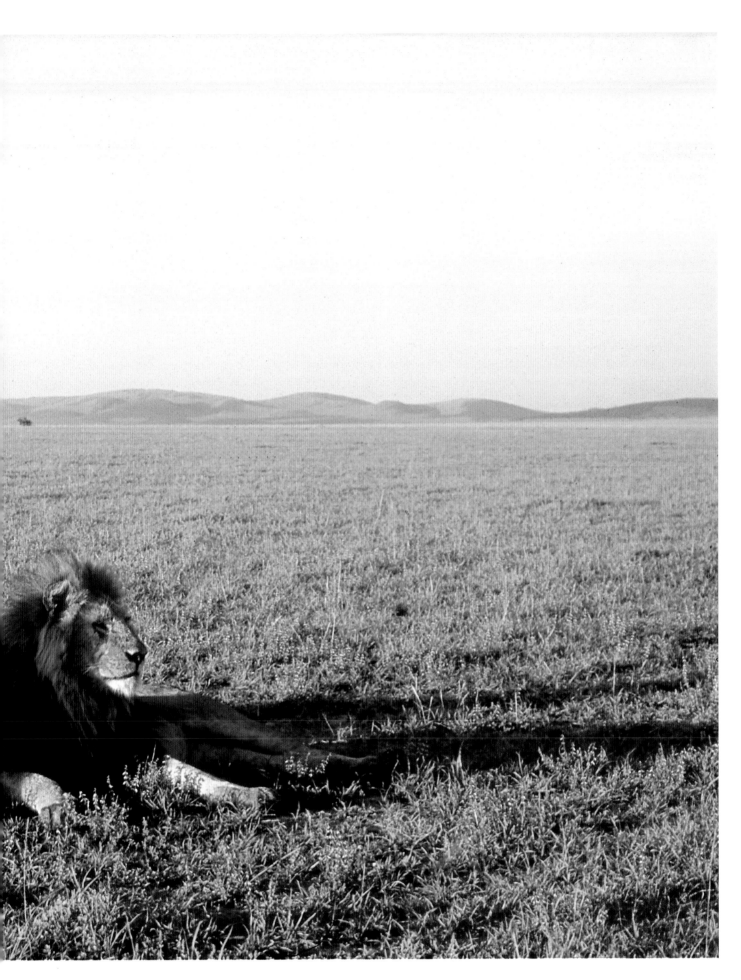

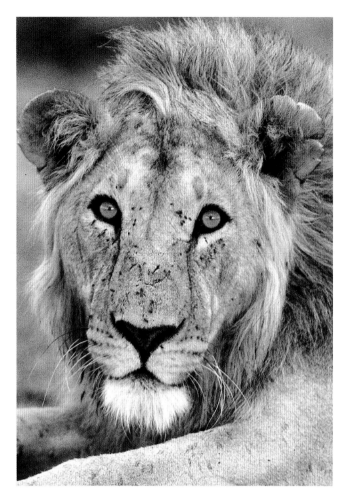

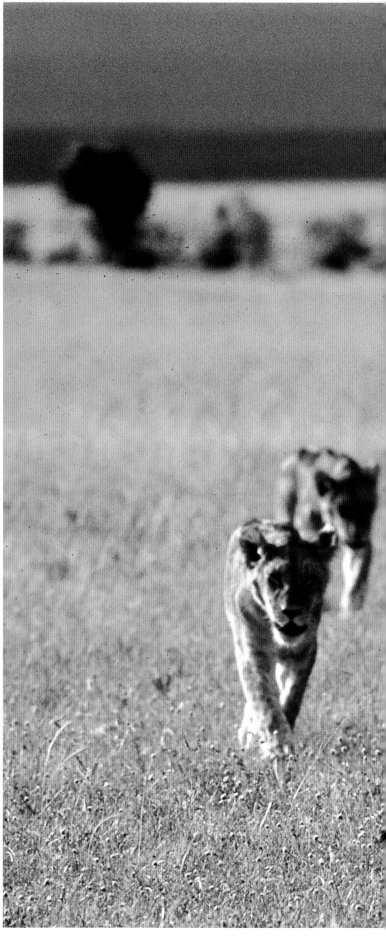

Above: The vanquished pride leader, like this old male, will be condemned to a solitary existence that is likely to be cut short by marauding hyenas.

Right: These cubs are just beginning the long and complicated process of learning the basics of hunting on the Masai Mara. It will be at least another two years before they cease to be dependent on the pride for food.

Overleaf: A pride leader greets the start of another day on the Masai Mara.

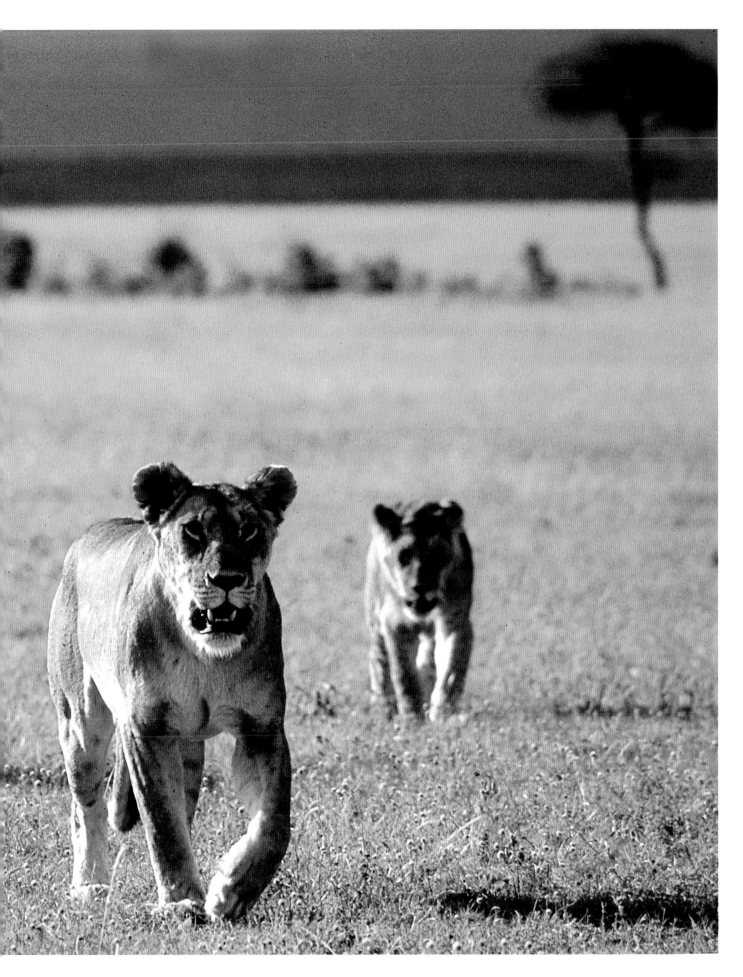

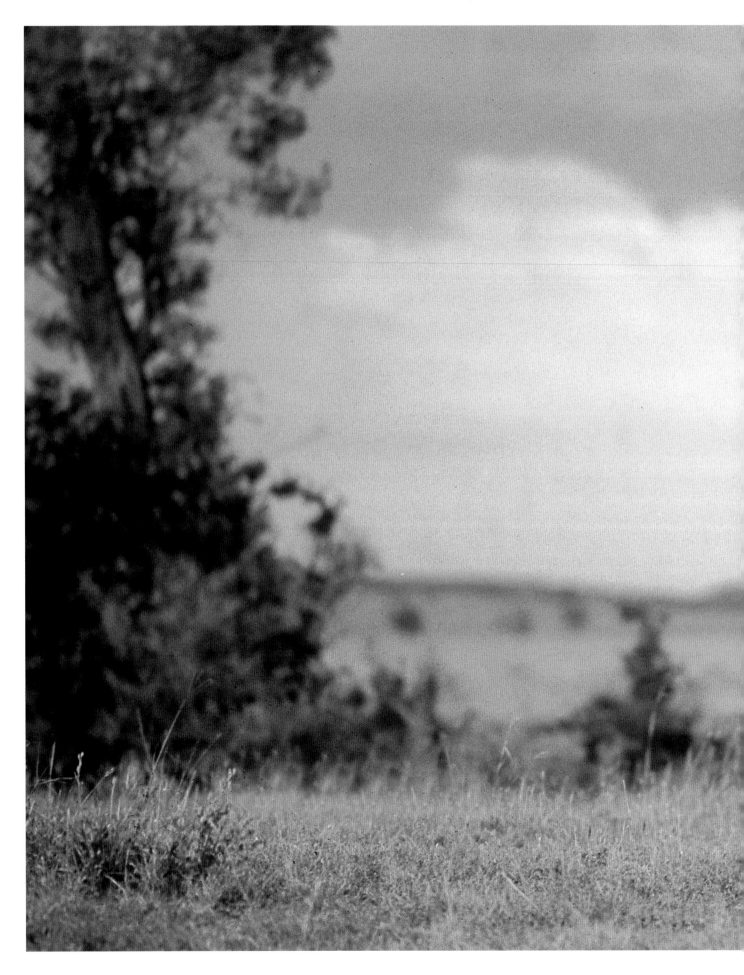

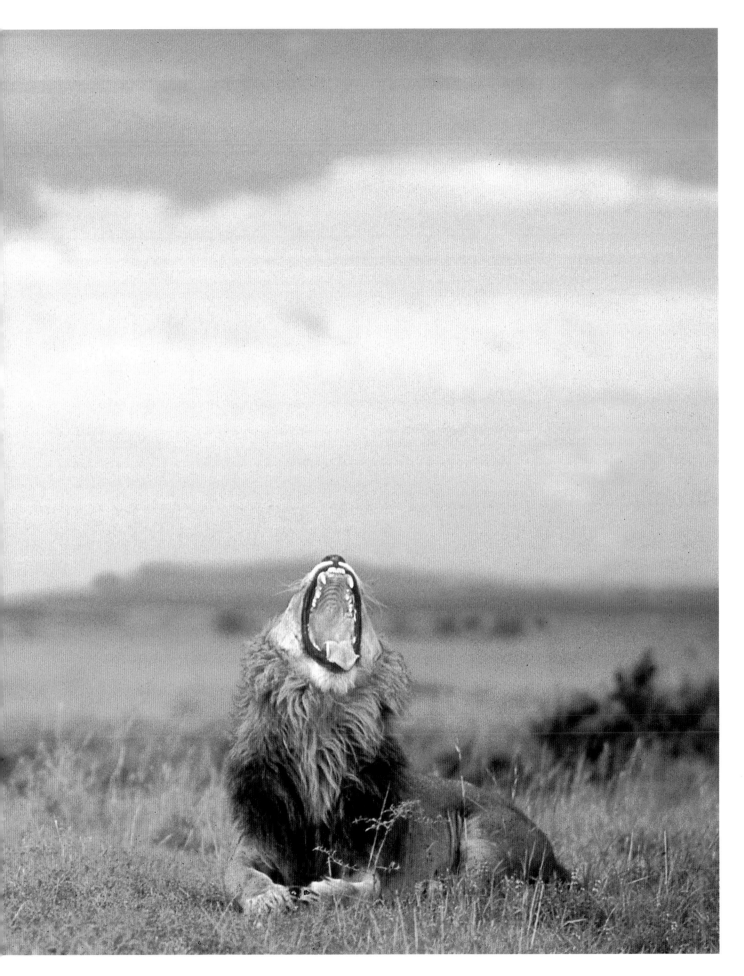

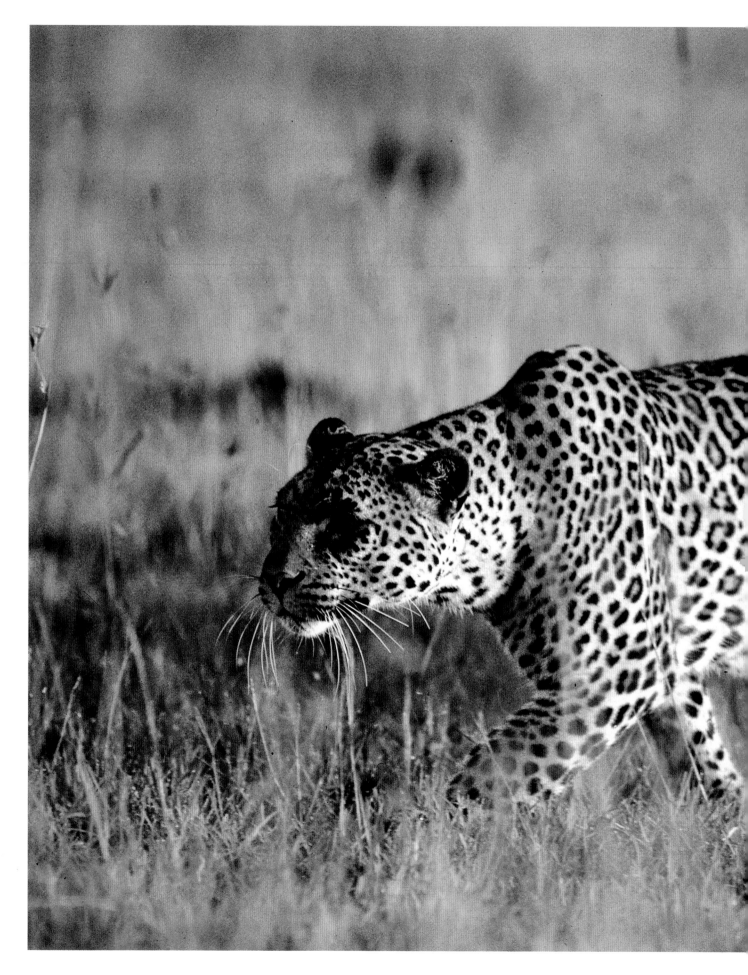

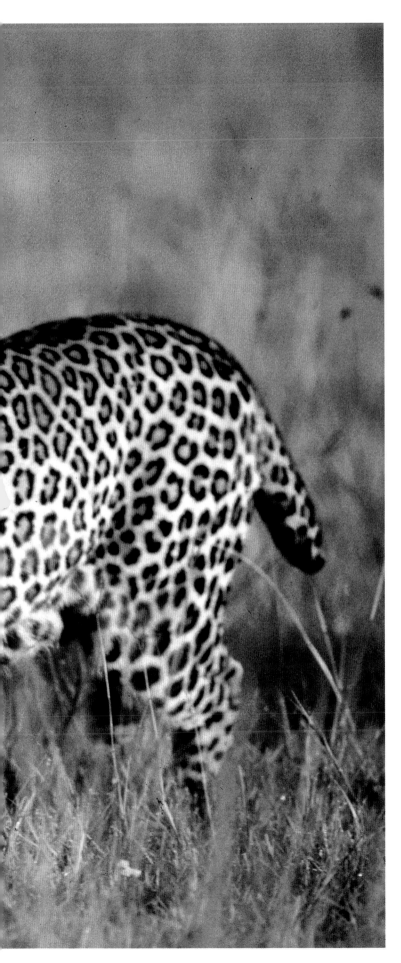

Leopard (Panthera pardus)

Leopards are found in a varied range of habitats (excluding true desert) in most of Africa south of the Sahara as well as eastwards through much of southern and eastern Asia as far as Korea and Indonesia. In Africa (as elsewhere) their size depends greatly on the nature of the habitat: the largest races occur in savanna and mountain regions, the smallest in forests and sub-deserts. The critical factor here is the difference in sizes of the leopard's prey animals, which are larger in the savanna and montane grasslands than in the forests and more arid areas. Adult males range in size from about 5ft 3in to 8ft 3in (1.6-2.5m) including the tail, and stand as much as 2ft 9in (84cm) at the shoulder; they may weigh anything from 60 to 200lb (27-91kg). Adult females are little more than two thirds the size of the males.

The leopard's coat is highly distinctive. The ground colour varies greatly from region to region, from pale straw darkening, with greyish or reddish tinges, to mid-brown; the ground colour of the Ethiopian race is among the darkest. In most races, the ground colour is noticeably paler on the undersides. The leopard's dark spots are, on much of the back, sides and upper legs, in the form of rosettes—clusters of (usually) four or five dark brown or black dots arranged into a rough square or circular shape. Unlike the rather similar rosettes of the jaguar, the leopard's do not have an additional dot in the middle of each cluster. Not surprisingly in view of its variations in size and coat colour in different regions, a very large number of subspecies have been proposed, but the so-called African leopard, *Panthera pardus pardus*, is by far the most important subspecies numerically.

A male leopard stalks prey on the Masai Mara in the early evening. Leopards have been observed approaching prey from downwind so that their victims do not catch their scent until it is too late.

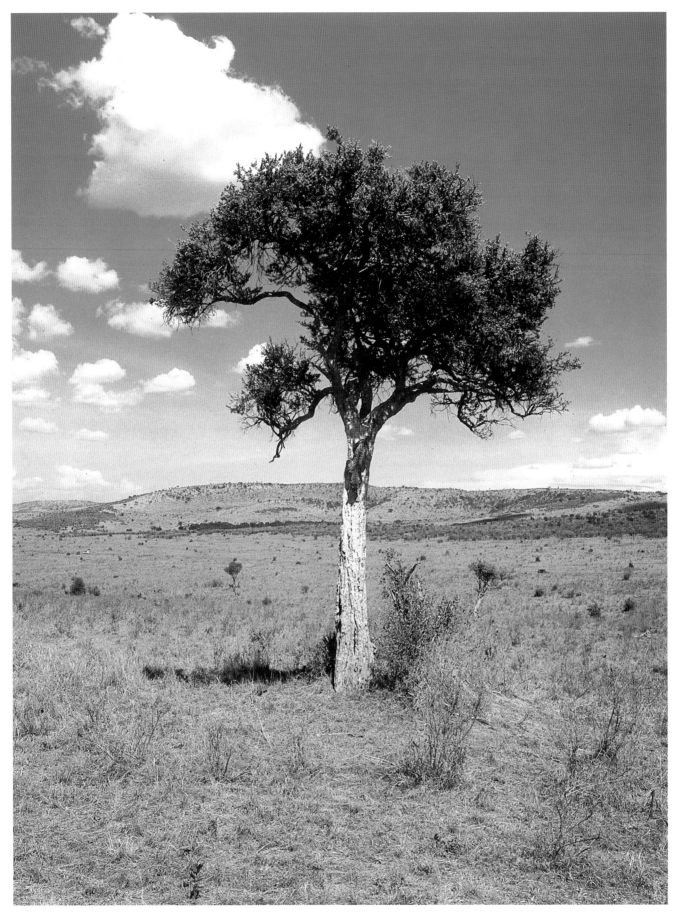

Above: A leopard descends from a tree on the Masai Mara.

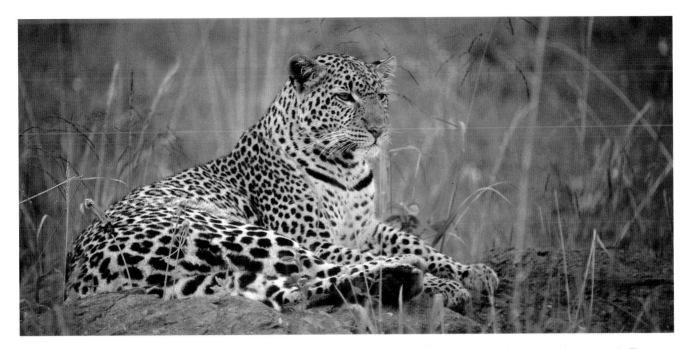

The leopard makes a living in a wider range of habitats than any other big cat. On the dry savannas (in both true wilderness as well as in game reserves) it shares its habitat with the lion; but although the lion (and packs of hyenas) will kill leopards and their young if given the chance, in general the two big cats avoid competing with each other for territory.

Females give birth to one to six cubs after a gestation period of anything from 90 to 115 days. Pairings between adult leopards are brief, and the males take no part in nurturing or defending the young. Breeding occurs all the year round, but most cubs are born during the rainy season (which varies in habitats north and south of the equator). The young are born in a den, a cave, a thicket or a burrow, and do not emerge for more than a month. They are weaned after about three months, by which time they are taking meat brought to them by their mother. They mature sexually at the age of two years, by which time they live independently. Cubs have a high mortality rate at the hands of predators, especially hyenas, but healthy adults may live for 20 years or more.

The leopard's adaptability to a wide range of habitats is reflected in its feeding habits: it will catch and eat large insects, rodents, reptiles, many different kinds of birds including ostrich, fish, warthogs, baboons, ungulates (some much larger than itself), and other carnivores such as jackals. It hunts mainly at night, when there is less competition for prey from other large carnivores. But it will

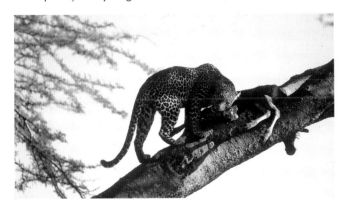

Top: A leopard rests after an unsuccessful chase. Most elusive of Africa's big cats, leopards do most of their hunting at night.

Above: A leopard hauls its ungulate victim along the branch of a tree. Immensely strong, leopards can carry prey larger than themselves for considerable distances.

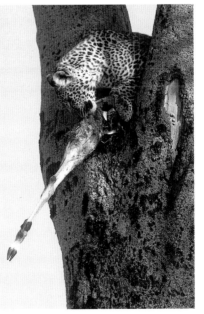

Left: Leopards cache large prey up trees so that they will be out of reach of lions and hyenas.

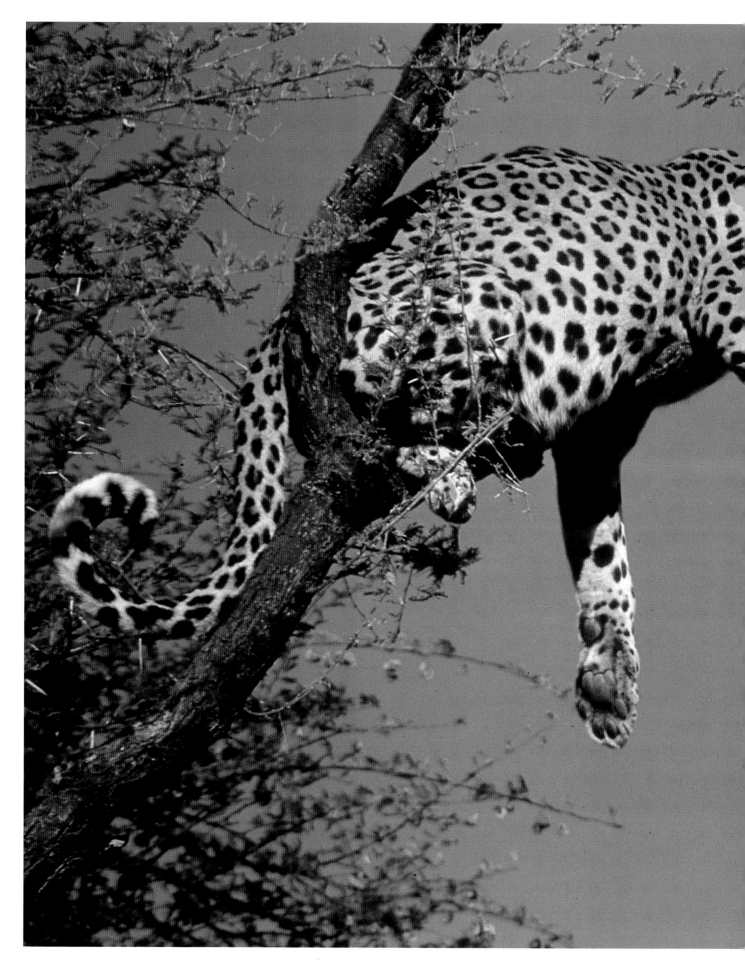

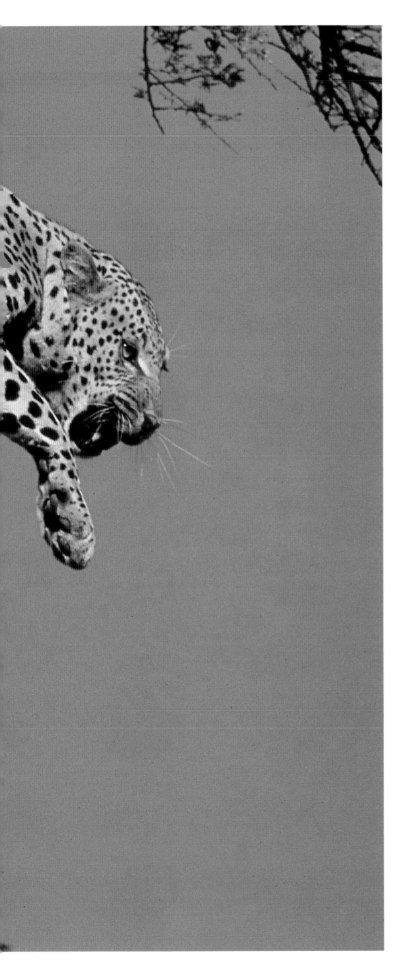

also hunt during the day, especially when in the sort of cover where dappled sunlight can render its coat almost invisible at a distance of more than a few feet. In more open terrain on the dry savanna it reveals itself as the most resourceful stalker of all the big cats, patiently tracking prey for several miles. Some observers have reported that leopards deliberately approach prey from downwind so that their quarry cannot catch their scent before it is too late.

Leopards are remarkably agile tree climbers. One of the most memorable sights of the East African savanna is of a leopard taking its ease in a solitary acacia tree, its legs dangling from either side of a stout branch. The enormous strength of an adult leopard is displayed by the ease with which it will carry the carcass of a large antelope high into a tree and wedge it into the fork formed by two branches—out of the reach of lions, hyenas or wild dogs. A leopard can make swift progress through the canopy of large trees, which is where it catches many of its baboon prey.

Because of their nocturnal habits and their gifts for concealment, leopards are able to live quite close to human settlements without being spotted. As yet the African leopard has not acquired the truly fearsome reputation as a man-eater enjoyed by its cousin in parts of India, and there are probably several hundred thousand leopards in sub-Sahara Africa as a whole.

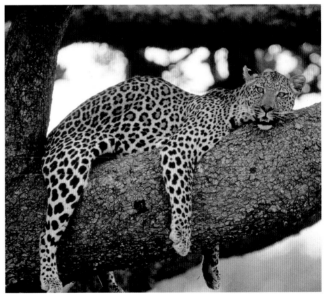

Above: Leopards spend much of the day napping in trees. This one has just finished gorging on its tree-cached prey.

Left: A leopard leaps from a tree on prey passing below. Superbly agile climbers, leopards catch many of their baboon prey in the tree canopy.

Cheetah (Acinonyx jubatus)

The cheetah's name comes from the Sanskrit word *chitra*, which means "speckled"—a reminder that this cat is native to extensive areas of Asia as well as to Africa. Today, the cheetah's African range extends, in a discontinuous series of scattered populations, from southern Mali and Nigeria in the west to south-western Ethiopia in the east, and then throughout eastern Africa from Kenya to Mozambique and northernmost South Africa; it is also found in Angola and Namibia. The most numerous and most generally recognised race is the type subspecies, *A. j. jubatus*. The well-attested and, for conservationsts, worrying lack of genetic diversity in the cheetah population throughout its range in Africa and Asia calls into question the taxonomic value of the subspeciation of several local populations of cheetah that have been proposed and quite widely accepted.

The adult cheetah has a typical body length of 4ft to 4ft 9in (1.2-1.5m); the tail is up to 2ft 8in (81cm) long; and the shoulder height is about 2ft 8in (81cm). It weighs from about 100 to 135lb (45-61kg). The are only small differences in size between adult males and females. The coat has a cream or slightly silvery fawn ground colour, sometimes with a slightly tawny cast, with underparts and the inside of the legs a lighter shade. The dots are dark brown or black, mostly circular or oval, and of varying size. The underparts have fewer dots and the lower chest sometimes has none at all. About halfway along the tail the dots become rings, and the tip of the tail is black. The face is immediately distinguishable from other big cats by the dot-coloured "tear stripe" that runs from the inner corner of each eye to the corner of the mouth. The new-born kittens have much darker fur on the belly and a light-coloured mantle of long hair extending from the top of the head along the back. The mantle gradually disappears when the kittens begin to acquire adult colouring from the age of three months onwards.

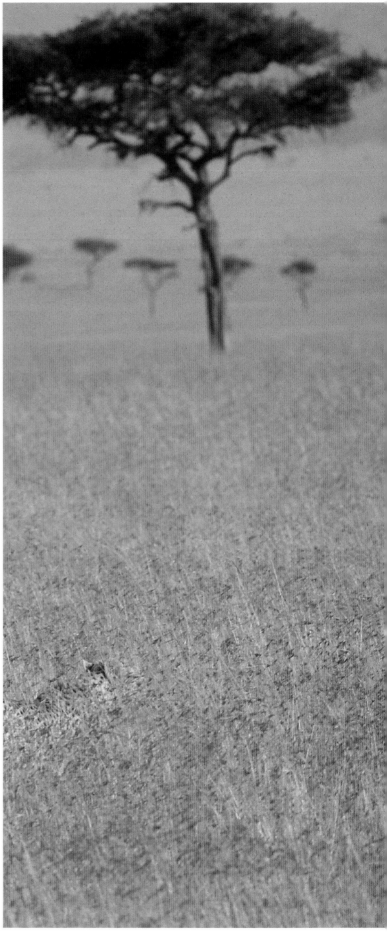

A cheetah is almost hidden by the golden grasses of the Masai Mara as she stalks game.

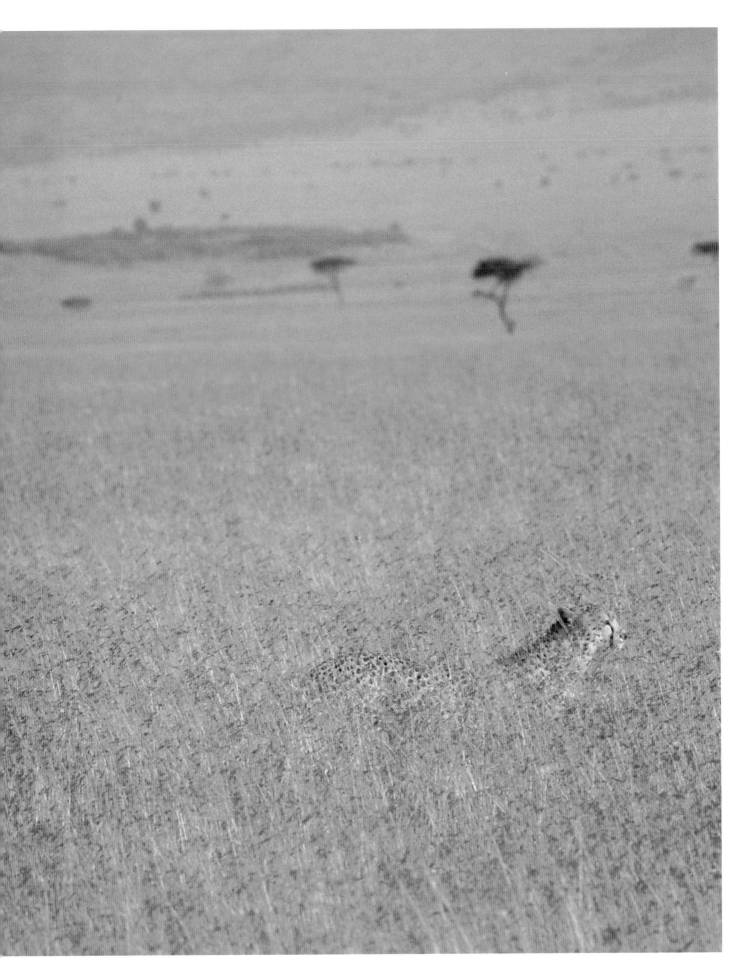

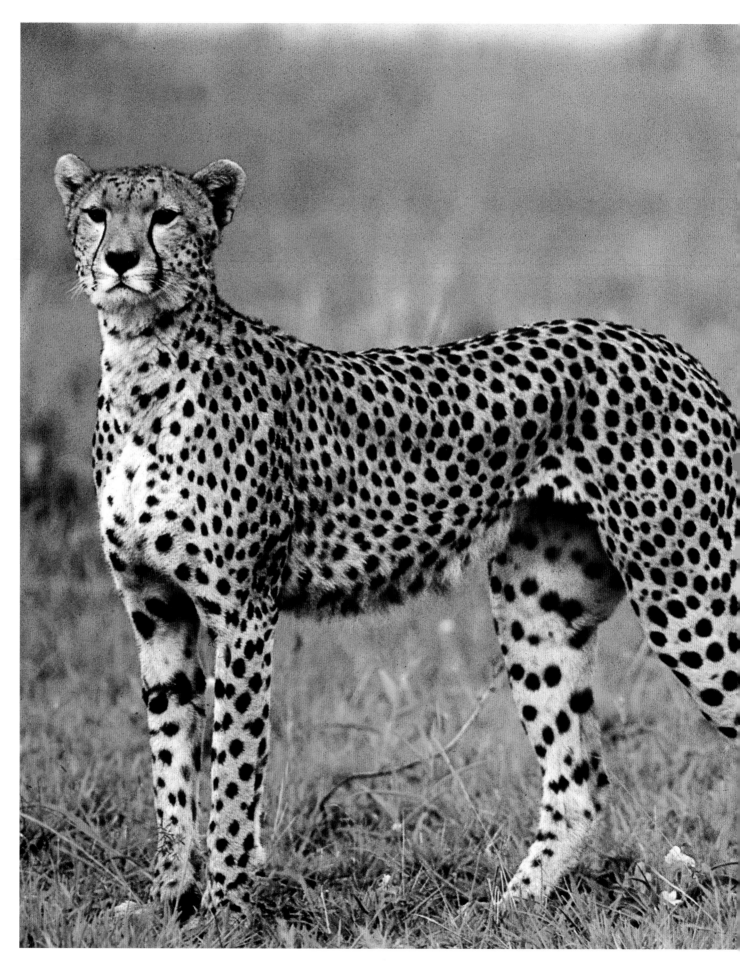

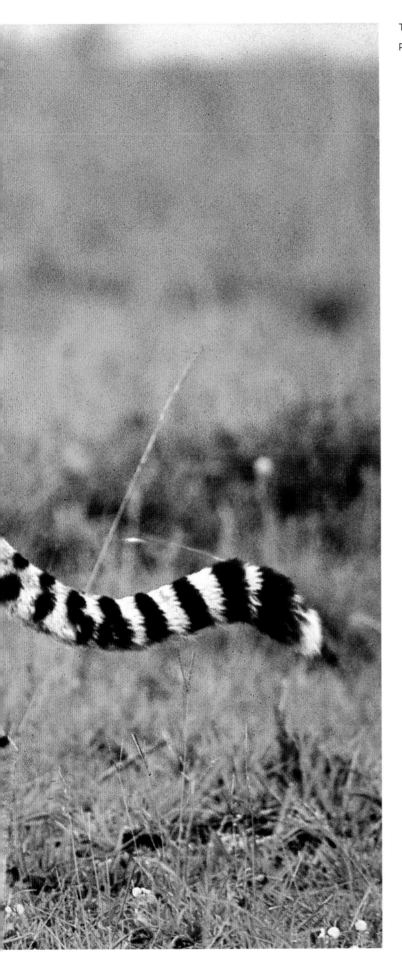

The cheetah is built for speed: slim, deep-chested and with long and powerful hind legs.

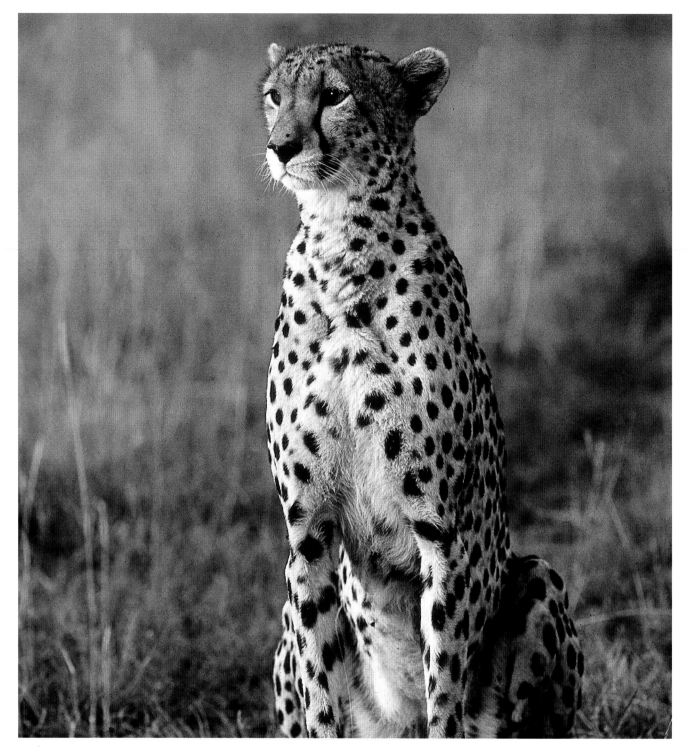

Cheetahs are sexually mature at about two years of age. Essentially solitary animals, male and female adults come together only to mate. The female spends most of her adult life rearing kittens and hunting for food: the departure of the survivors of a litter from the family group seems to be the trigger that brings her into œstrus once more. After a three-month gestation, she gives birth to up to eight kittens—a larger litter than that of any other of the big cats—which offers at least some natural insurance against the very high mortality rate among kittens during their first three months. The inherent genetic weakness in the species gives rise to problems with the immune system that leaves adults and, espec-ially, the kittens prey to a variety of feline infectious diseases. Moreover, until they are at least three months old and can run fast, they are defenceless against predation by lions, leopards, hyenas or wild dogs. Indeed, the mother constantly moves her young from one hid-ing place to another during these early weeks of their lives.

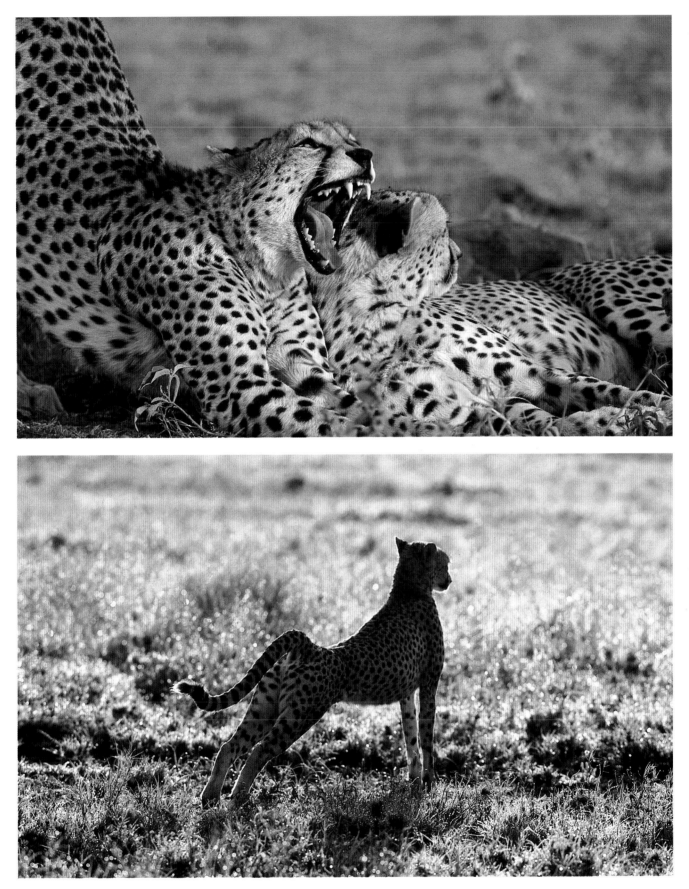

Above Left: The cheetah's upright, rather dog-like sitting posture is a reminder that Indian princes once used cheetahs as hunting dogs.

Top and Above: Cheetahs stretch in the evening sun on the Serengeti plains. The remarkable flexibility of the animal's spine enables it to take enormous strides when it runs at full speed.

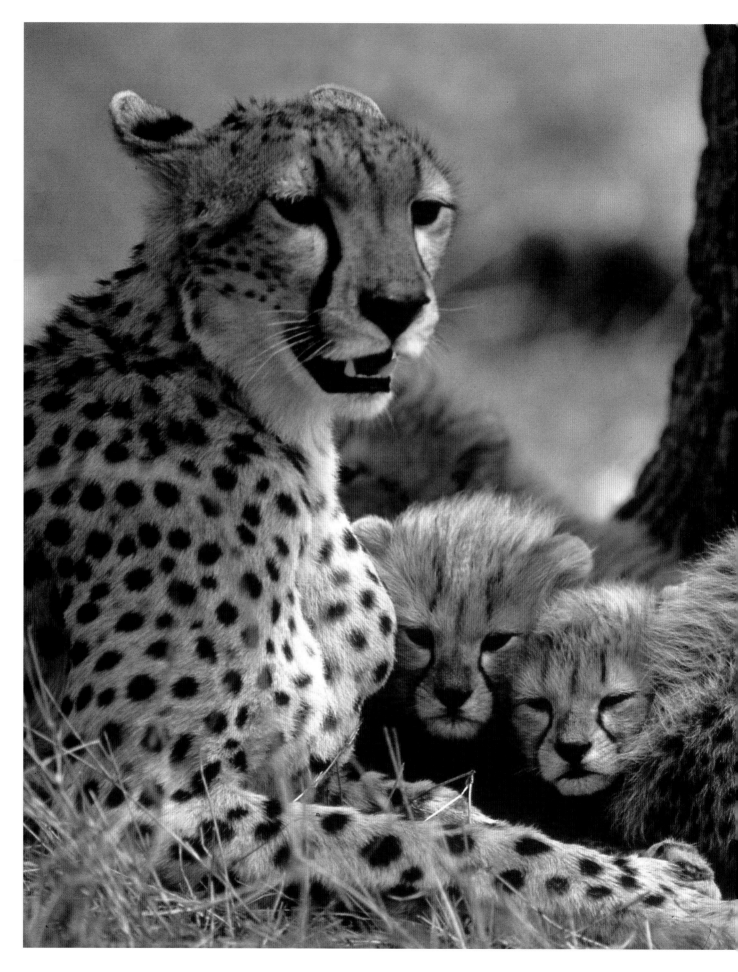

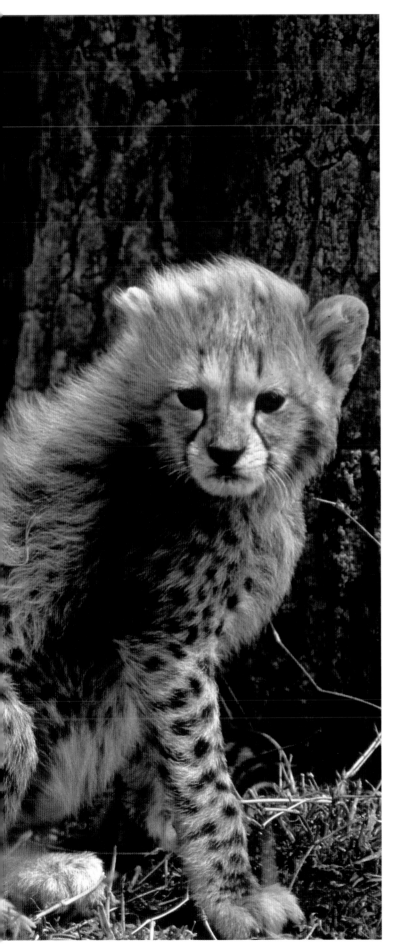

The young are sufficiently large and fleet-footed to accompany their mother in the hunt from the age of eight or nine months, but it will be some time before they acquire sufficient expertise to be of much help to her. By the time they are between 15 and 18 months old, however, they will be capable of providing for themselves. Most leave their mother at that stage, although others will stay with her until they are two years old. On leaving the family group, young males (usually, but not always, siblings) may form groups of two or three and remain together for a few months before striking out on their own to establish their individual territories; those of siblings may overlap. A typical size for such a territory is about 25 square miles ($65km^2$), but the home range of an adult cheetah—that is, the area over which it regularly hunts for food—may be anything from 40 to 375 square miles ($104-970km^2$), depending on the local abundance of both prey and predators.

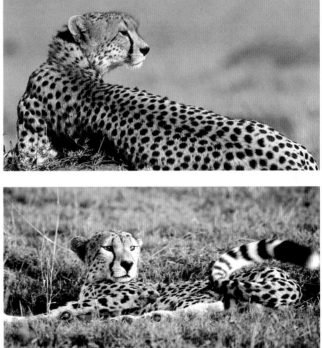

Top: The cheetah's coat has a silvery fawn ground colour, usually darker along the spine, and lighter on the underparts. The slightly fluffy spots are dark brown or black and vary in size.

Above: The cheetah's tail is spotted for the first half of its length and ringed in the other half. In some individuals, as here, the two rings nearest the tip coalesce to become a broad band.

Left: A female cheetah with her kittens. For the first three months of their life the kittens have a mantle of long hair extending from the top of the head along the back.

Although the cheetah shares its savanna grassland and open woodland habitat with the lion and leopard, and preys on at least some of the same species of ungulate, it avoids contact with these larger predators by hunting at different times: in the late morning, long after the leopard has finished his night's hunting; and in the early afternoon, well before the lions set out on their early evening hunt. The cheetah's principal prey are Thomson's and Grant's gazelles, impala, springbok, topi, reedbuck, puku and the young of kudu, wildebeest and zebra. If these are unavailable it will go after smaller animals, such as jackal and hare, and birds such as ostrich.

The sight of a cheetah at full tilt after prey is one of the most exhilarating in nature. The animal is built for speed: small-headed, deep-chested, slim-waisted and long-legged, it is the fastest-running four-legged animal on earth by a comfortable margin. On several occasions cheetahs have been reliably timed at speeds of up to

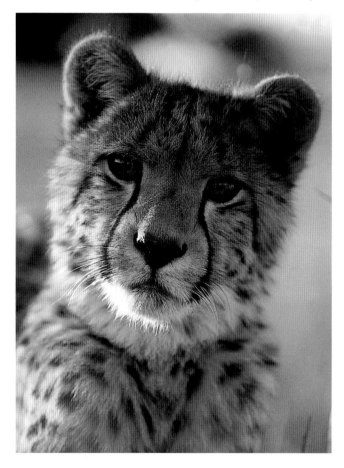

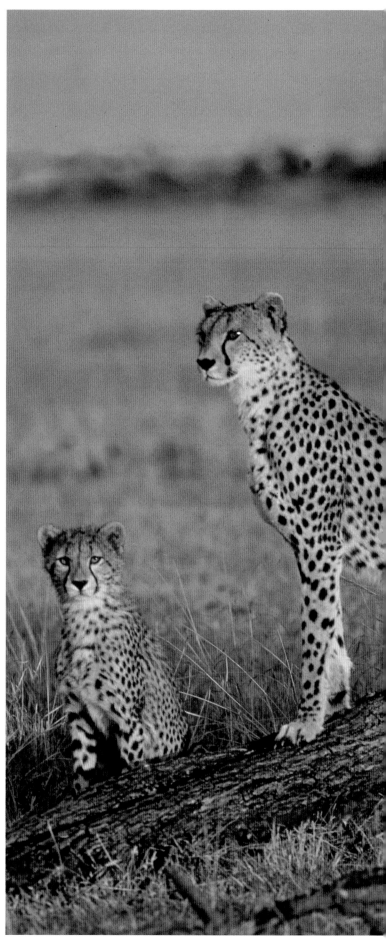

Above: A cheetah kitten at about five months of age. The species' characteristic dark "tear-stripe" running from the inner corner of each eye to the corner of the mouth is already clearly marked.

Right: These six-month-old kittens with their mother can now run fast enough to avoid predation by lions or hyenas.

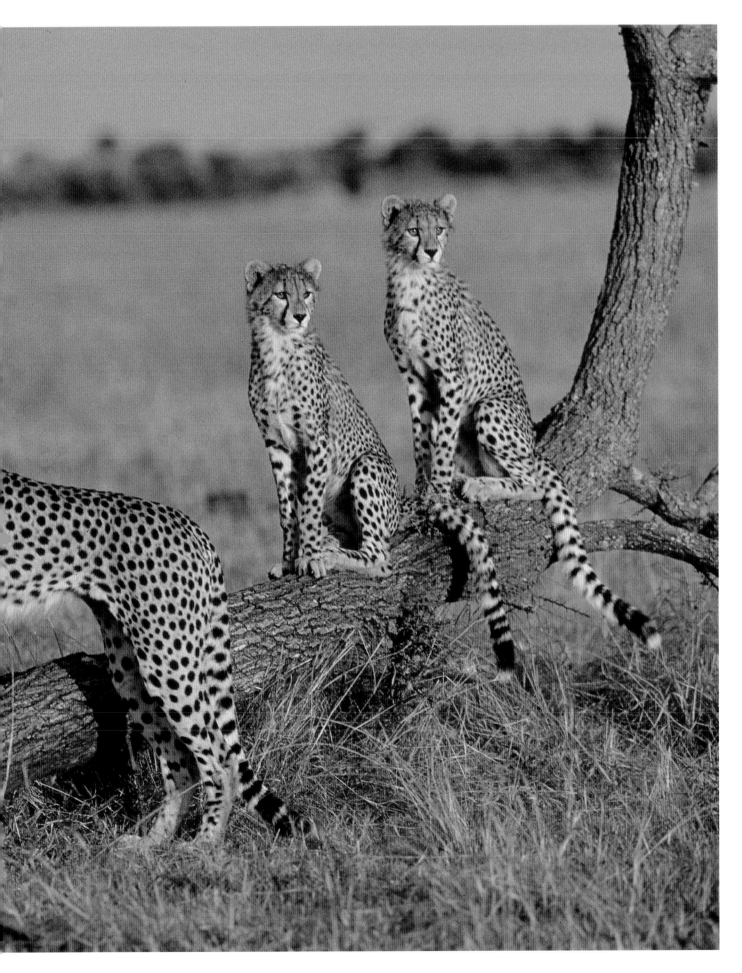

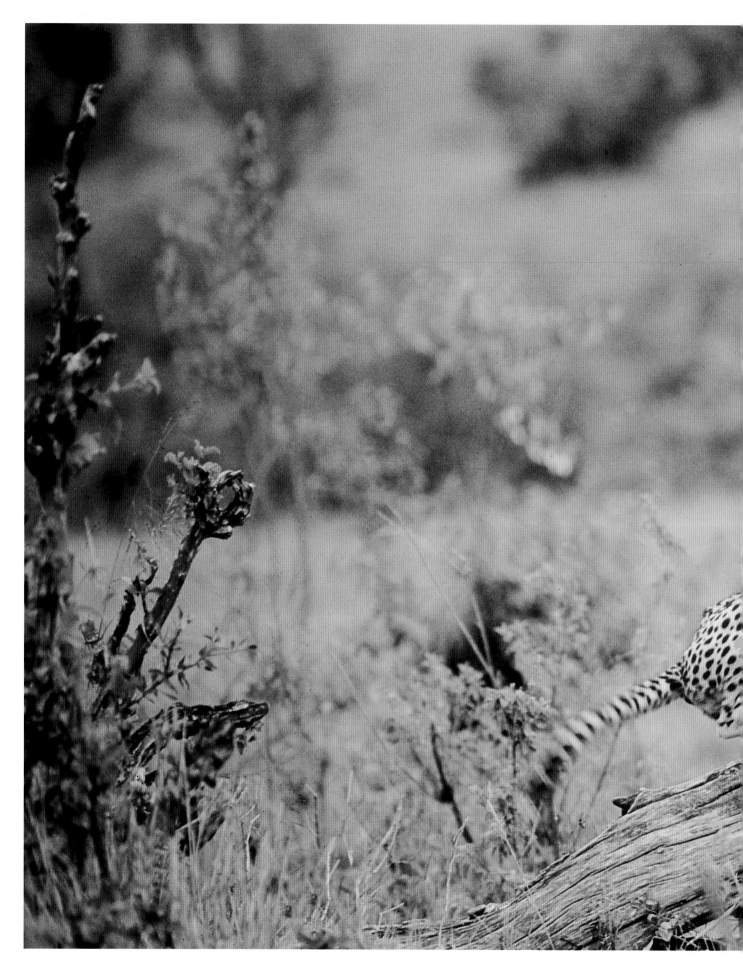

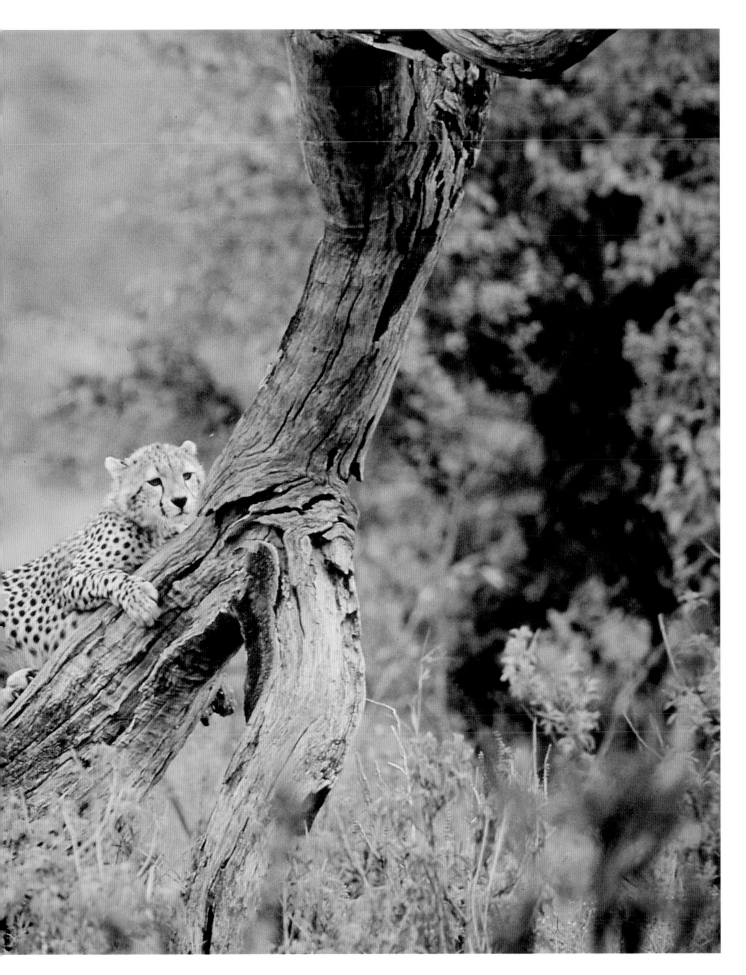

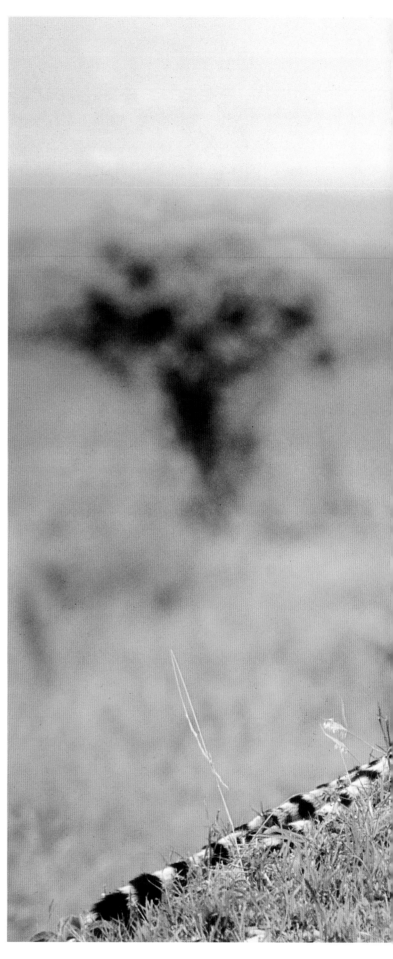

70mph (113km/h) for brief periods. The animal owes its speed primarily to the extraordinary flexibility of its spine, which enables it to take three strides up to 22ft (6.7m) long every second when at full speed.

When it has selected its quarry—perhaps a small group of impala—the cheetah will usually approach at an easy lope. Unless it is able to make its approach behind some kind of cover the cheetah is unlikely to be able to get closer to the impala than about 150 yards (137m), at which point they will take flight. The cheetah invariably selects as its prey the first impala to flee, and it will not be deflected from this even though it may overtake other, easier targets during the chase. The cheetah keeps pace with the fleeing group as they accelerate away but does not seem to be gaining on its prey for a hundred yards or so. Then suddenly, as if a switch has been thrown, the cheetah surges forward at top speed and over-takes its quarry in a few seconds. In spite of the speed at which it is running the cheetah homes in inexorably on the impala, instantly answering its desperate lurches to left or right. Once it reaches its prey the cheetah will attempt to knock it over or, if its is too big, trip it up by striking at its hind legs. As soon as it falls, the cheetah pounces, seizing it by the throat in a stranglehold.

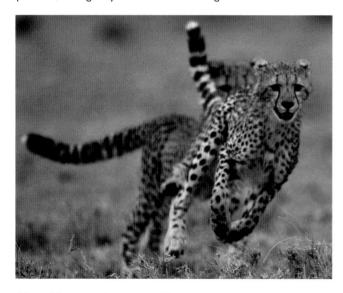

Above: These juveniles are now old enough and quick enough to join their mother in the hunt—but for a while yet they are likely to be more of a hindrance than a help when the mother is trying to approach prey unobserved.

Right: A mother (rear, left) and her three juveniles find this grassy mound on the Masai Mara a good lookout point for spotting distant herds of ungulates.

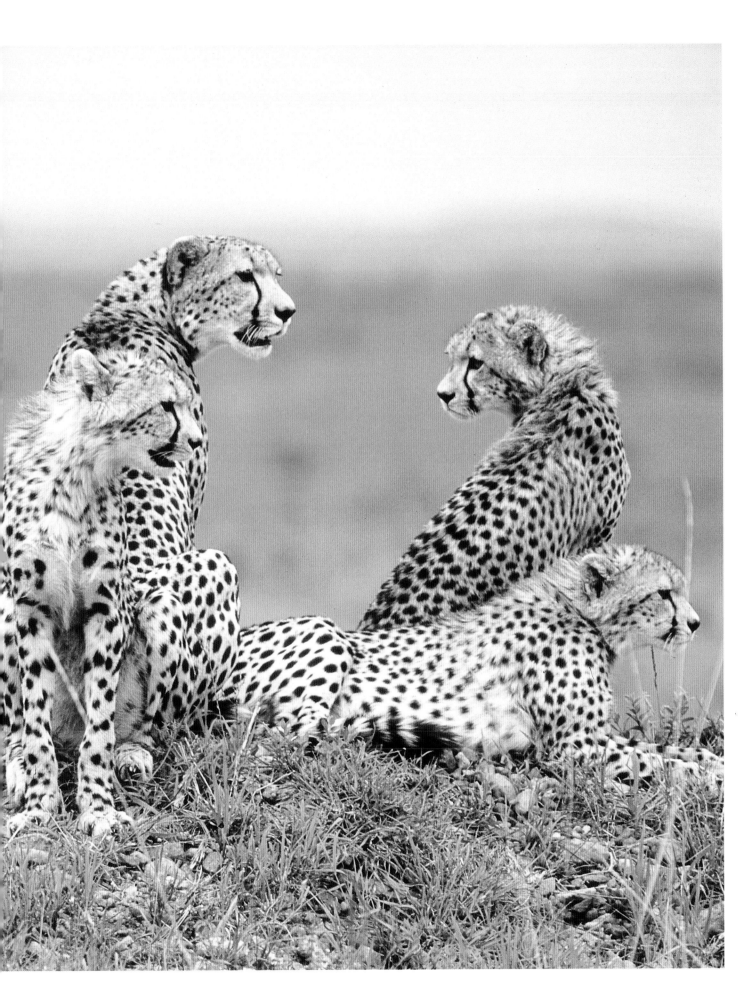

Those who witness the lightning drama of a cheetah and its quarry for the first time are invariably puzzled by the length of time the predator seems to need to kill its victim: it will not usually loosen its stranglehold for at least 15 minutes. In fact, the victim will

have died within a minute or so: the cheetah is recovering from the enormous physical demands of the chase. Over a dash of several hundred yards the cheetah experiences a potentially lethal level of oxygen debt and rise in body temperature, and after it has caught

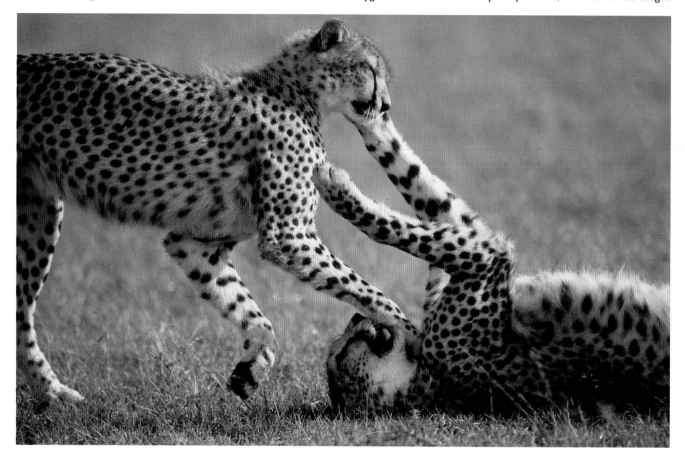

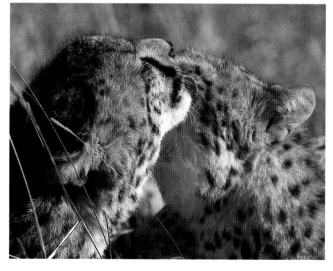

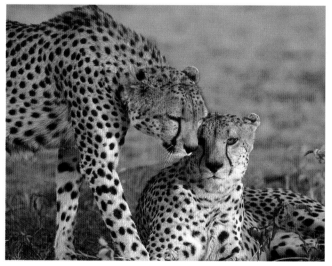

Top, Above and Above Left: About one year old, these two cheetahs are still attached to their mother, and after bouts of rough and energetic play they will usually indulge in head rubbing, mutual grooming and other acts that reinforce the family bond.

Right, above: Meanwhile, the boundaries of their joint territory have to be marked out with urine and glandular secretions.

Right, below: Book-ends: two 18-month-old males who have left their mother but are remaining together for a few months before each establishes his own territory.

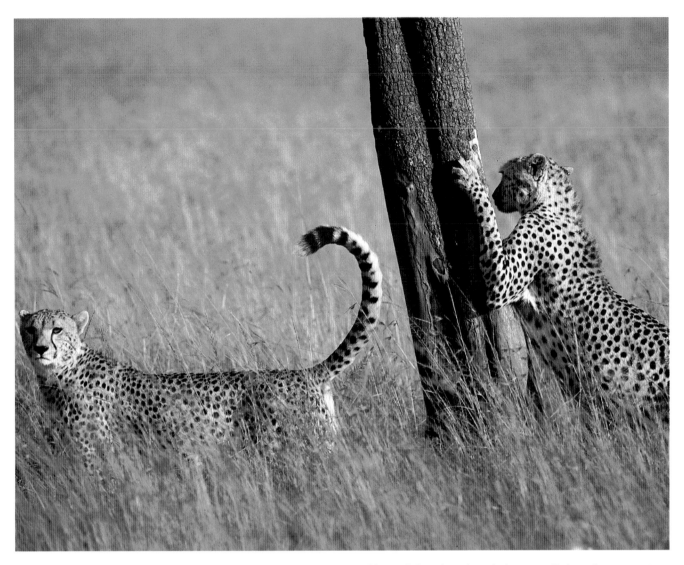

After a kill a cheetah with kittens will drag the carcass into whatever cover is available. After she and the kittens have eaten as much as they can they will not attempt to cache the carcass, as other big cats do. Cheetahs eat only freshly killed prey—and they are quite often chased away from a kill by larger predators before they have had a chance to assuage their hunger.

The cheetah population is under threat in many of its habitats. One of the main reasons for this lies in the lack of genetic diversity in the cheetah population as a whole. One legacy of this is an exceptionally low conception rate in adult females, attributable to the very low sperm count in the males. Many zoos and some private reserves around the world have instituted breeding programmes with little success. In any case, the limited numbers of cheetahs involved in such schemes at any one place simply amplifies the already intractable problem of the lack of genetic diversity that threatens the cheetah population as a whole.

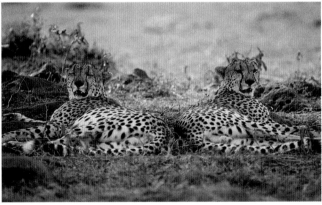

its quarry it needs 15 to 20 minutes to catch its breath and allow its temperature to return to normal. A cheetah can manage a high-sped dash for no more than 450 to 500 yards (410-460m). If it has failed to catch its prey by then, it must give up the race and take time off to recuperate. Now, if the cheetah is a mother with cubs to feed, she will be hunting at least once a day: and every time she hunts she is quite literally putting her life on the line.

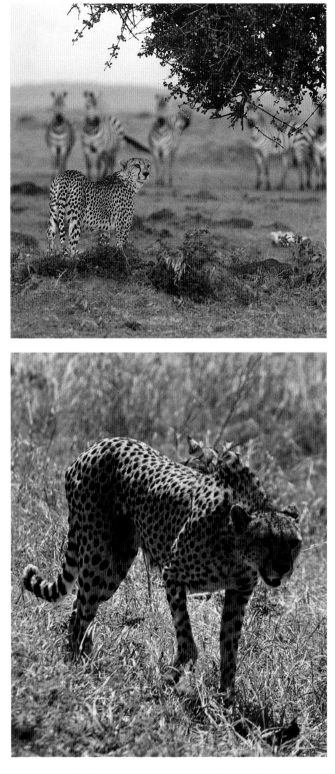

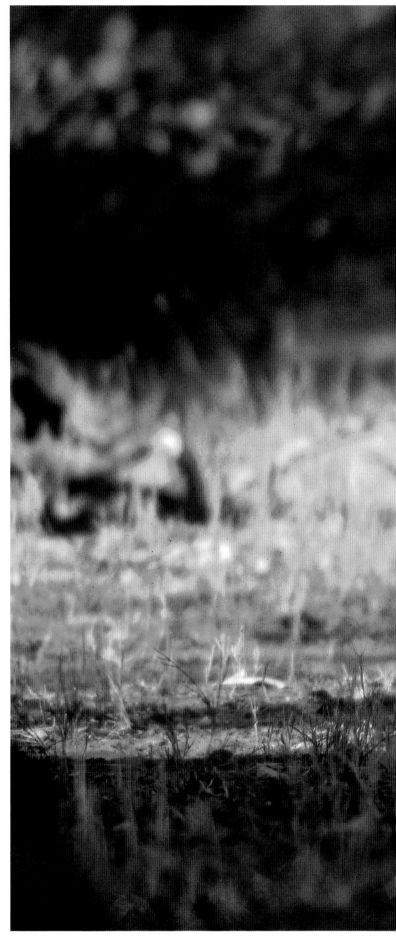

Top: A party of plains zebras watch as a female cheetah sniffs the air for the scent of prey. Adult zebras are too big to interest her, but she would go for a young foal if the opportunity arose.

Above: This female has caught the scent of prey and is approaching stealthily.

Right: She uses whatever cover is available to get as close to her quarry as possible before beginning the chase.

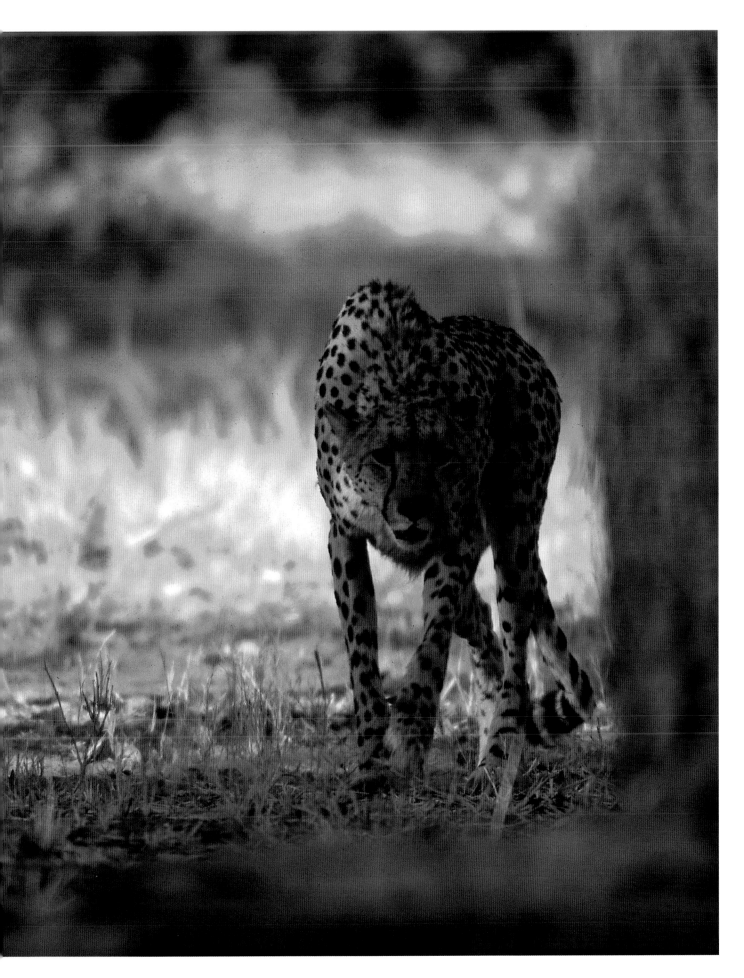

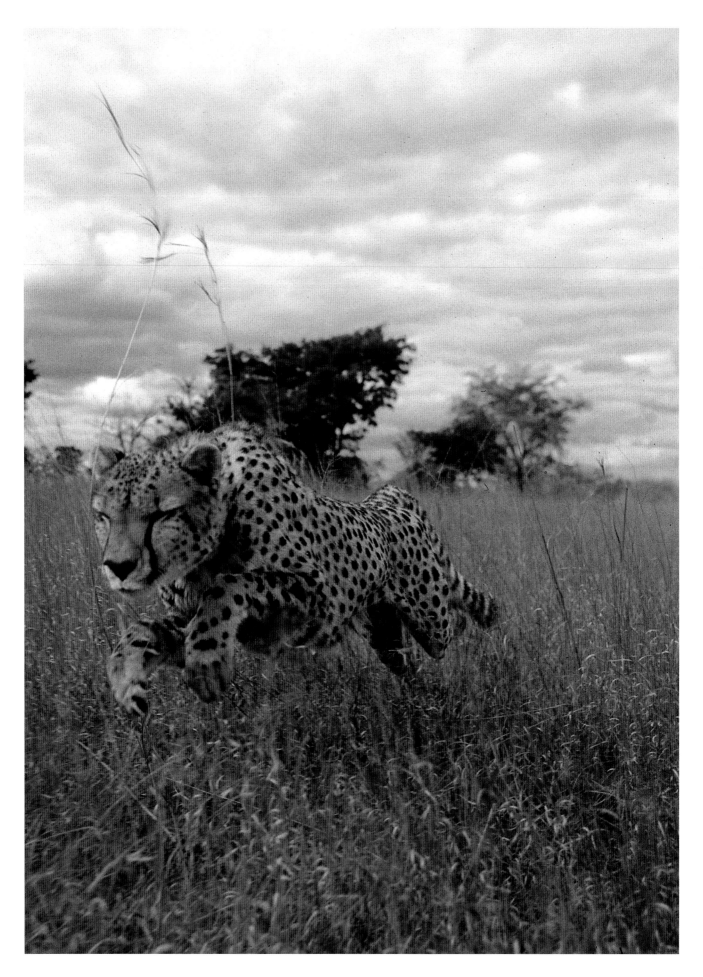

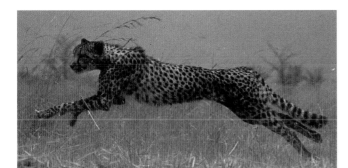

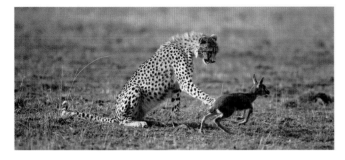

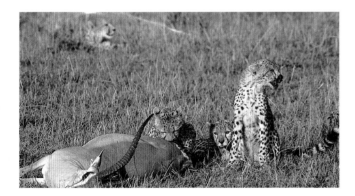

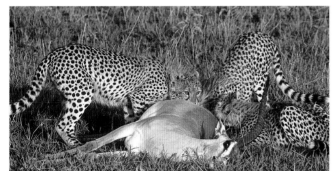

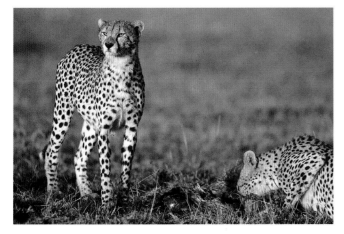

Far Left: She is in the open now and begins to pick up speed as the ungulate herd she is pursuing stampedes.

Left, Top: She has selected her target individual and is now running at full tilt. She will pursue only her selected quarry even though other members of the ungulate herd may be within easier reach.

Second From Top: She has caught up with her Thomson's gazelle victim and knocks it over with a paw before taking its throat in her jaws and snapping its spinal cord. Other, larger ungulate prey will be throttled by the same method.

Third From Top: This family is gorging on a considerably larger kill—a Grant's gazelle, which will provide them all with a good meal.

Fourth From Top: The young continue to feast while their mother (in the background) keeps a lookout for predators or scavengers—even a flock of vultures may chase cheetahs away from a kill.

Bottom: Once they have eaten their fill, cheetahs will abandon a carcass: they will eat only freshly killed prey. A mother with a large litter will therefore need to hunt every day if her kittens are to survive.

SMALLER CATS

Most of the seven smaller African cats belong to the genus *Felis* (to which one much larger cat, the puma of the Americas, also belongs). They are much like smaller versions of the *Panthera* species, with similar dentition (including long, powerful canine teeth), lightning-fast reflexes, rapid acceleration from a standing start, excellent jumping and tree-climbing abilities, and the gifts of stealth and cunning in the hunting of prey. Two species are considered here.

The serval (*Felis serval*; synonym *Leptailurus serval*) is a slender, long-legged cat with large, rounded, erect ears and rather short tail. The ground colour of its coat is dull white to reddish fawn, with lighter underparts. Dark brown or black longitudinal stripes on its nape and shoulders give way to spots elsewhere on the body and legs, and to rings along the dark-tipped tail; there is a black patch and a white patch on the back of the ears. It stands up to 24in (60cm) at the shoulder and weighs a maximum of 42lb (19kg). The serval ranges throughout the moist savanna zones, from Senegal in the west to Somalia in the east, and thence south through East Africa to KwaZulu-Natal; and from south-western Zaïre to Angola and northern Namibia. It prefers areas with water, tall grasses or reedbeds; it also frequents the fringes of forests. Mainly nocturnal, it exploits its exceptionally keen sense of hearing to locate its mainly rodent prey; it will also take birds, reptiles and invertebrates.

The caracal (*Felis caracal*) has been assigned by some experts to its own, unique genus (*Caracal*) and by others to genus *Lynx*; it certainly has the short tail and, most notably, the prominent ear tufts characteristic of the lynxes. It is a strongly built cat with long legs and with powerful hindquarters slightly higher than the shoulders. Its short, dense coat is monocoloured, but may vary from fawn to almost brick-red, with underparts lighter in tone; the ears are white inside, with the outsides and tufts black. It stands about 18in (45cm) at the shoulder and weighs up to 42lb (19kg). For its size it is one of the most formidable feline predators, well able to kill antelope as large as springbok (and it preys on sheep and goats in parts of southern Africa). It is also capable of prodigious jumps and uses this ability to knock down low-flying birds such as peafowl.

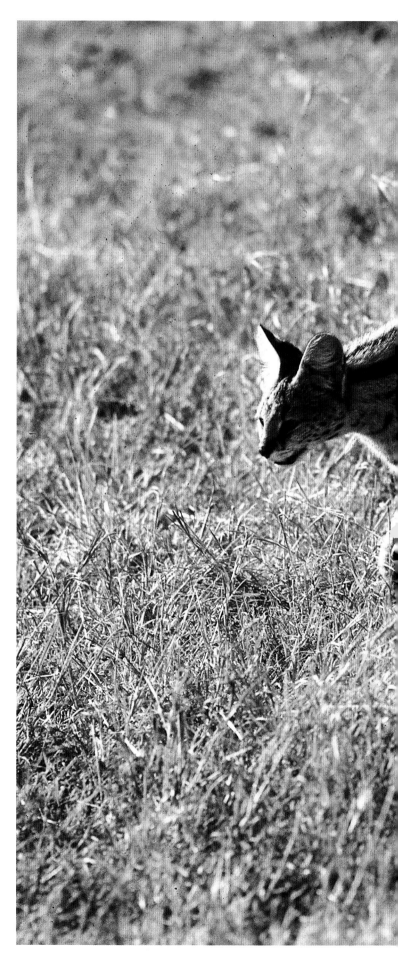

The long-legged serval (this one is from Kenya) has dark stripes on neck and shoulders and spots over rest of body.

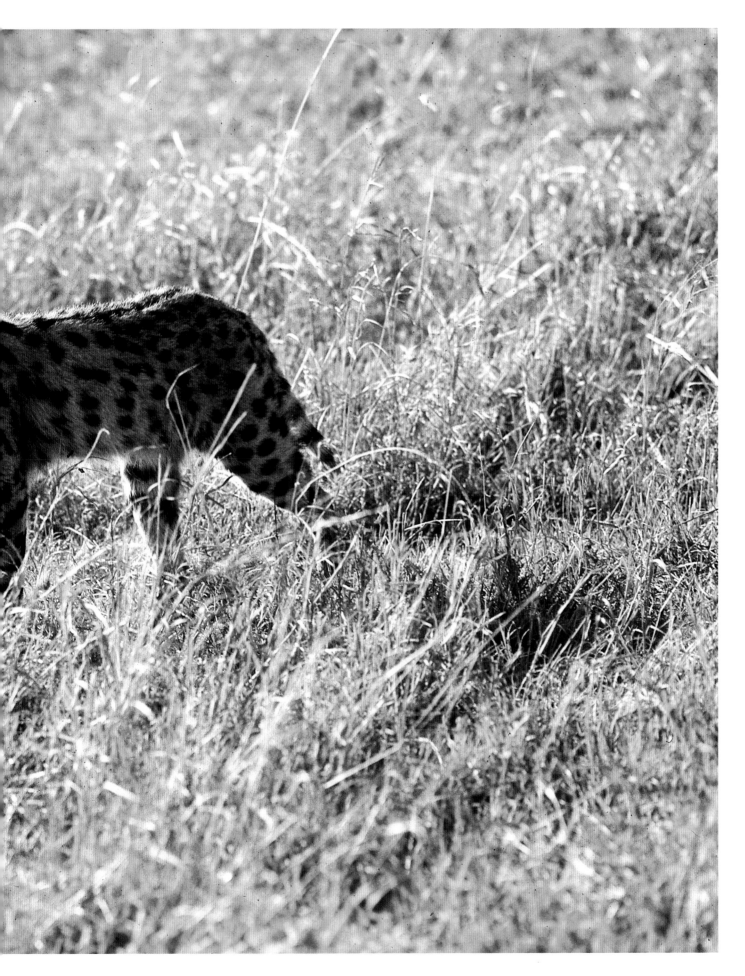

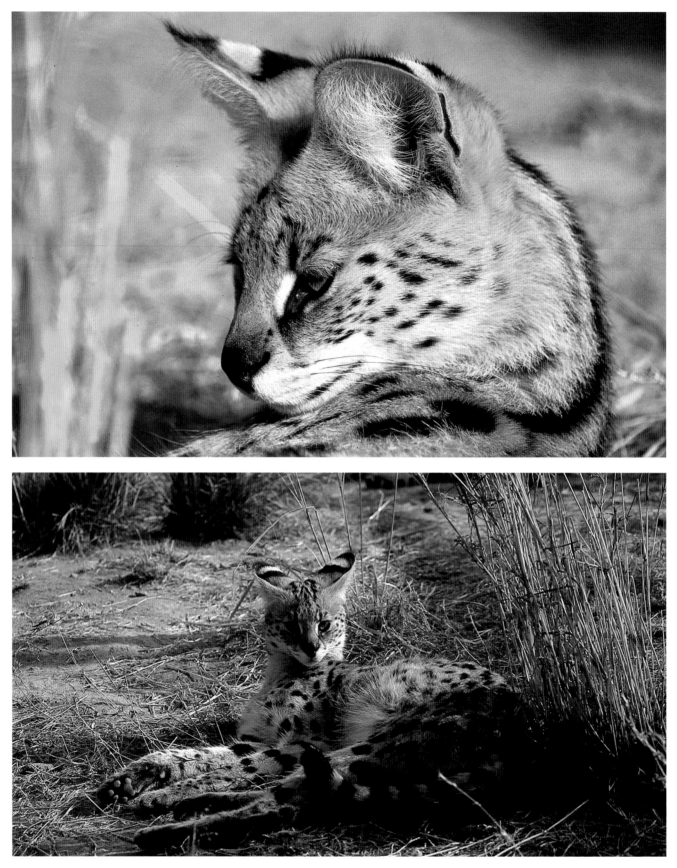

Top: The serval's usually greyish white ground colour has a tawny tinge in some populations, as in this male from South Africa. Note the dark necklace stripe and characteristic black-white-black bars on the backs of the large oval ears

Above: A serval at rest in Tshukudu Game Reserve, South Africa. Note the dark/light ring pattern on its tail.

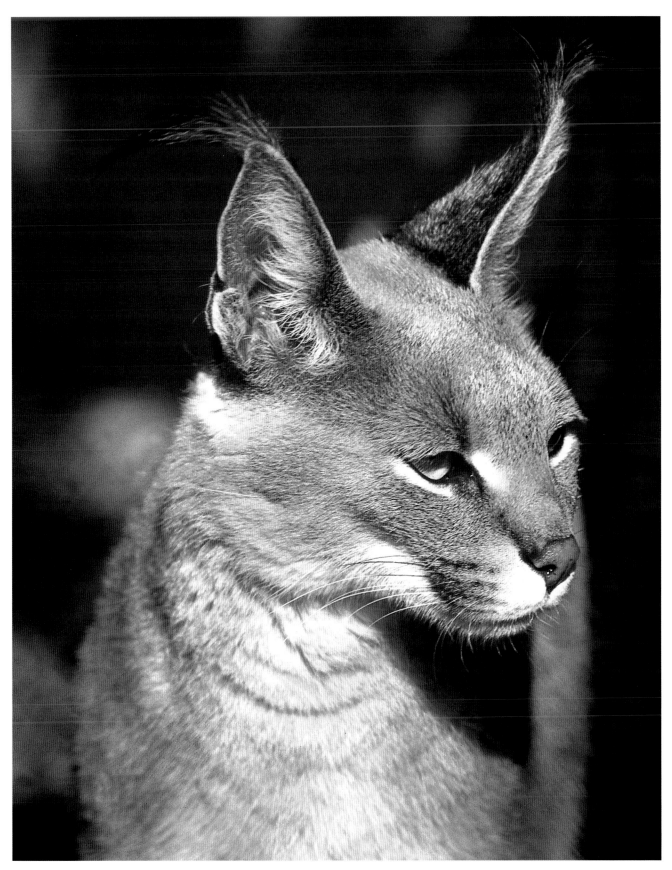

Above: The caracal, the most formidable hunter of Africa's smaller cats, is found in most of sub-Sahara Africa except for rainforests.

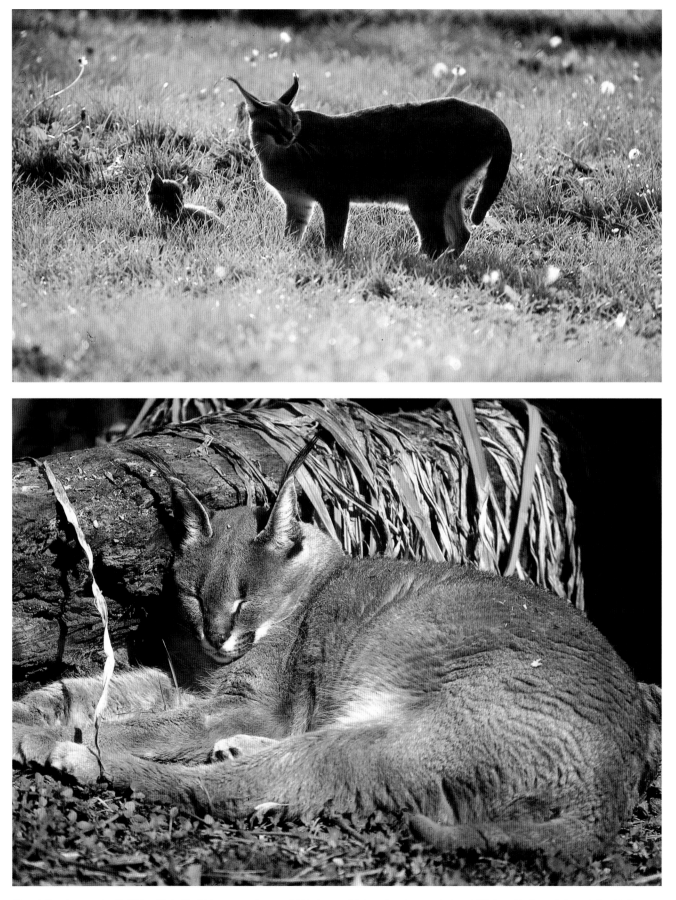

Top: A female caracal with kitten. Note the high rump and powerful hind legs, which hint at her remarkable jumping ability

Above: A male caracal at rest. His long black ear-tufts and short tail suggest he is closely related to the lynx.

HYENAS

The Hyaenidae family consists of four species from three genera—three hyenas and the aardwolf. Although somewhat dog-like in appearance, the hyenas are more closely related to civets and to mongooses than to the canids. They share with civets a digestive system that is able to break down tough and complex organic materials such as bone and chitin, and true hyenas will commonly eat the entire carcass of a prey animal, including hide, hooves, bones and teeth, digesting even the most massive bones in a few hours. All members of the family are long-necked and tall at the shoulder, with the back sloping downward towards a rather short tale.

Formerly ranging over most of non-forested Africa apart from true deserts, the spotted hyena (*Crocuta crocuta*) has been subject to eradication programmes over most of its range—programmes that continue to this day. Its preferred habitat is open savanna, dry and moist grasslands, and mountain moorlands—anywhere with

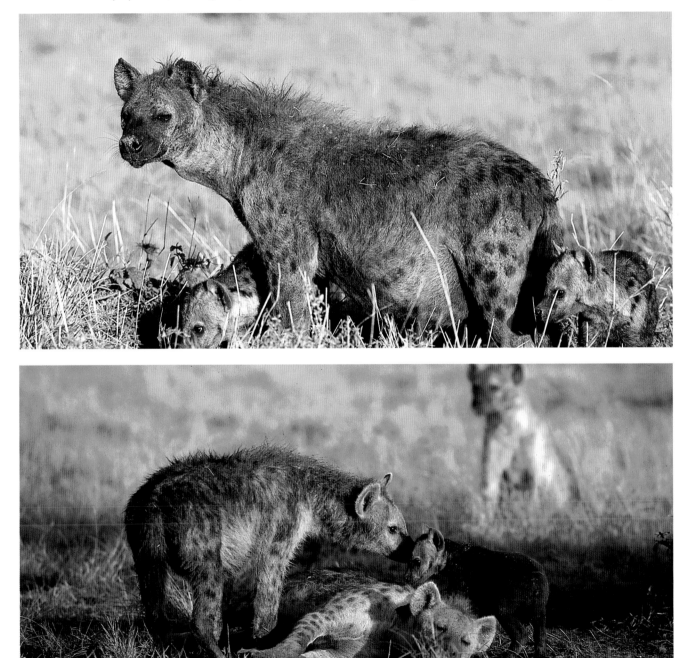

Top: A heavily pregnant female spotted hyena at the clan's den with two four-month-old pups of another female. Note the adult's characteristic brown spots and black muzzle.

Above: An adult female spotted hyena playing with pups on the Masai Mara. Although the alpha female is leader and most powerful member of the clan, other females in the clan also produce young.

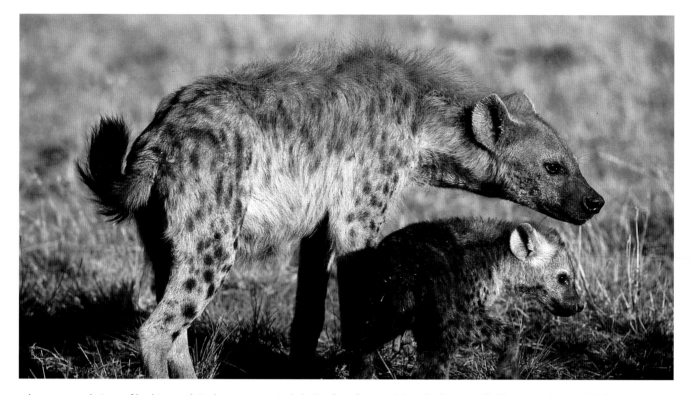

adequate populations of herbivores. It is the most massively built of all the hyenas and is in fact Africa's largest carnivore after the lion. The adult coat colour is a variable shade of brown, becoming paler and tawny with age. The neck, body and legs have darker, irregular spots and blotches which, again, become paler with age. The muzzle is dark brown or black. Unusually, the adult female is between 12 and 14 per cent heavier than the male, weighing up to 200lb (91kg). She is up to 6ft (1.8m) long including the short tail and stands up to 36in (91cm) at the shoulder.

The spotted hyena is highly opportunistic in its feeding habits, scavenging food by forcing other carnivores (even individual lions) to abandon their kills and, in game parks, raiding campsite dumps.

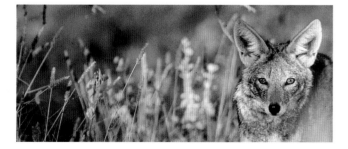

Top: A female spotted hyena and pup. The pups are dark brown or black for their first three months; thereafter their coats lighten in ground colour and the characteristic spots begin to appear.

Above: A female with pups. There are rarely more than two pups in a litter and those shown here are from three litters.

But an adult individual is well able to run down and kill a wildebeest, while hyenas hunting collectively prey on the largest antelopes, zebra and even buffalo. Once they have made a kill, the spotted hyenas' massive jaws and formidable teeth—especially the huge, bone-crushing premolars—enable a hunting group to deal with the carcass in short order, each individual gorging as if competing with its fellows.

The collective name for a hyena group is "clan". In areas of abundant food a clan may consist of more than 100 members, one third to three quarters of which will be adults. Clans have an established hierarchy of related females and their offspring. The clan head, or alpha female, has testosterone levels that may exceed those of the males: she is not only the dominant member of the clan but is even more aggressive than the fiercest males and she is able to deter males from attacking her cubs. She gives birth to up to four cubs after a gestation period of four months. They grow fast and are able to join in the feeding frenzy at a kill when they are eight months old. Remarkably, however, the mother continues to suckle them for up to 18 months. (Incidentally, the alpha female's high testosterone levels presumably account for her "hermaphroditic" sex organs—the development of growths that mimic the male's genitalia.)

The spotted hyena's long-distance call, an echoing whoop repeated a number of times, carries for up to 3 miles (5km). The species is also known as the laughing hyena, which derives from its repertoire of appeasement calls that include groans, grunts, whines and maniacal giggles.

The striped hyena (*Hyaena hyaena*) is much less massive than the spotted, rarely weighing more than 100lb (45kg). It has larger, more pointed ears and nose. Bold black transverse stripes stand out against the tan or grey ground colour of the body and legs. A light-coloured mane runs from its nape to its tail; when raised in defensive posture the mane increases the apparent size of the hyena by about one third. It inhabits sub-deserts and dry savannas on the southern margins of the Sahara and in East Africa is found as far south as central Tanzania. Its diet includes carrion, rodents, insects and fruit as well as smaller antelope. The closely related brown hyena (*Hyaena brunnea*) is similar in form to the striped hyena but

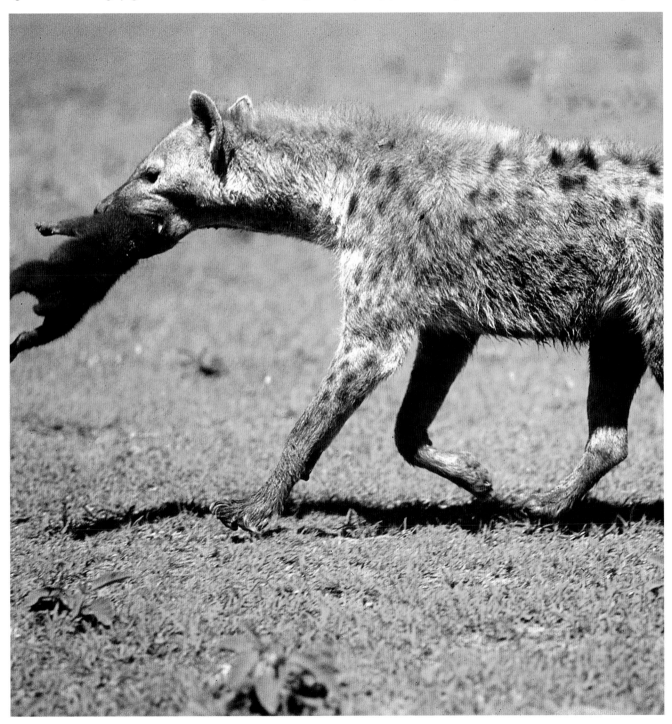

Above: A female carries her young pup, who has strayed from the den. Adult male spotted hyenas play no part in looking after the pups.

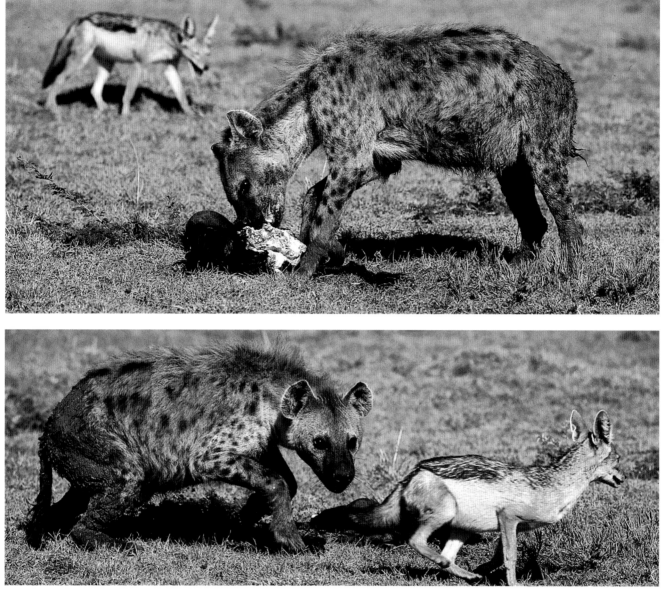

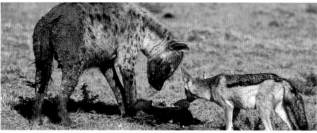

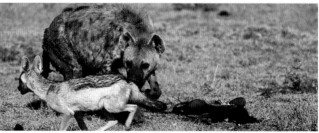

Top: A spotted hyena has dug up some cached portion of a carcass and has attracted the attention of a black-backed jackal.

Centre: The jackal circles the hyena looking for the chance to grab a share.

Above: The jackal closes in, waiting for its chance.

Above Right: The hyena loses patience and lunges at the jackal, who retreats—prepared to try again in a little while.

Top Right: The grisly sequel to a successful attack on a wildebeest by a spotted hyena clan. The hyenas begin to gorge while their victim is still alive.

Above Right: A large clan will make short work of a wildebeest. This is all that remains of a recently killed adult—even its largest bones have been crushed in the hyenas' powerful jaws, swallowed and digested.

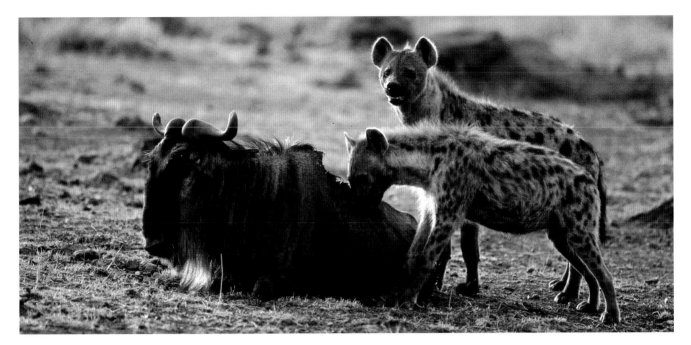

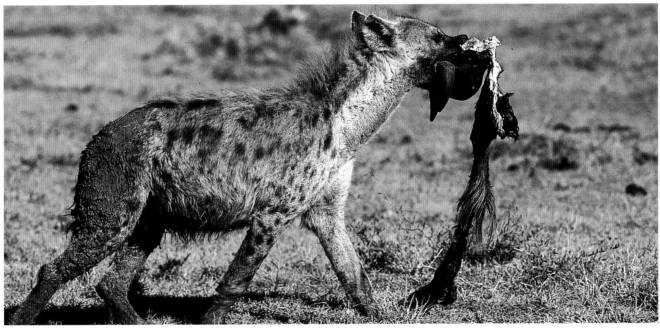

has a mantle of light coloured hair overlying its dark brown torso and a cream-coloured throat. It, too, is a creature of sub-deserts and dry savannas but its range is south of the Zambezi in Zimbabwe, Botswana, south-west Angola, Namibia, north-west Cape Province and northern Transvaal. Mainly nocturnal, it relies on carrion and abandoned ungulate carcasses for much of its food but also feeds on small mammals, invertebrates and fruit; in Namibia it scavenges for dead sea-lions along the shore of the Skeleton Coast.

The aardwolf (*Proteles cristatus*)—the name comes from the Afrikaans *aard* (earth)—resembles a striped hyena but is much smaller, up to 20in (50cm) at the shoulder and rarely more than 25lb (11kg) in weight. The ground colour of its coat is more tawny than the striped hyena's, but it has similar dark brown stripes on the torso and legs and an erectile mane from nape to tail. Its habitat is dry grasslands and sandy plains in East Africa, southern Angola, and most of Africa south of Zambia. Although it eats carrion, birds and small rodents, the aardwolf's main diet is harvester termites, which it laps up with its long, sticky tongue when the termites emerge above ground at night. The aardwolf is unrelated to the elusive ant- and termite-eating aardvark (*Orycteropus afer*), which is found throughout sub-Sahara Africa apart from the Namib desert.

WILD CANIDS

The African members of the Canidae family of carnivores include foxes, jackals, the Ethiopian wolf and the wild dog. The sub-Sahara foxes consist of the Cape fox, the pale fox, and the bat-eared fox. The Cape fox (*Vulpes chama*) is a close relative of the larger red fox (*V. vulpes*) of Eurasia and North America. It is the only true fox of southern Africa and is found in grasslands, fynbos (Cape Province heathland), scrub and semi-desert areas of southern Angola, Namibia, Botswana and most of South Africa. The ground colour of its coat is reddish fawn but its back and upper sides are grizzled silvery-grey; the bushy tail has dark brown or black "stippling" that makes it look darker than the rest of the coat. It stands about 14in (36cm) at the shoulder and weighs up to 9lb (4kg). Males and females pair up but hunt alone, mainly at night. It eats a wide range of food, including rodents, hares, insects, reptiles and birds. Its close relative, the pale fox (*V. pallida*), is found throughout the Sahel (dry, stony savanna) belt from the Atlantic to the Red Sea. The basic coat colour is fawn, with lighter underparts, but the legs and back are reddish tinged in some individuals; the bushy tail has a black tip. It is mainly nocturnal and its diet consists of small mammals, invertebrates, fruit and berries. A mated pair excavate underground dens in which to raise their young. Slightly larger than either of the above, the bat-eared fox (*Otocyon megalotis*) is notable for its enormous oval, black-edged ears; it uses its acute hearing to locate insects. Its general coat colour is greyish buff, which over the back and sides is grizzled with black-tipped white hairs; its legs and tail tip are black. It fore feet have very long nails ideal for excavating its own burrow and for digging into the nests of harvester termites, its main source of food along with dung beetles. It has two separate populations: one extends from southern Ethiopia and Somalia southward into Tanzania; the other extends southward from Angola and Zambia through Namibia and Botswana to most of central and western South Africa.

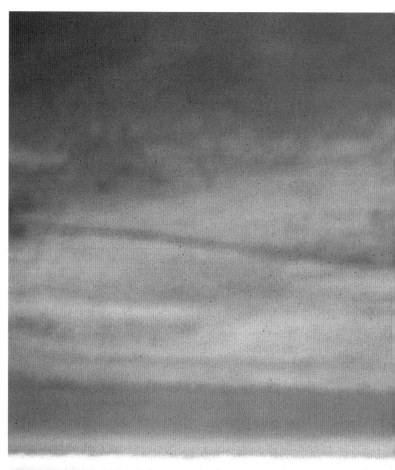

The golden jackal is found throughout most of the northern half of Africa, including the Sahara desert. This one, near the southern limit of its range, is trekking across a dried-up lake bed in Ngorongoro Crater, Tanzania.

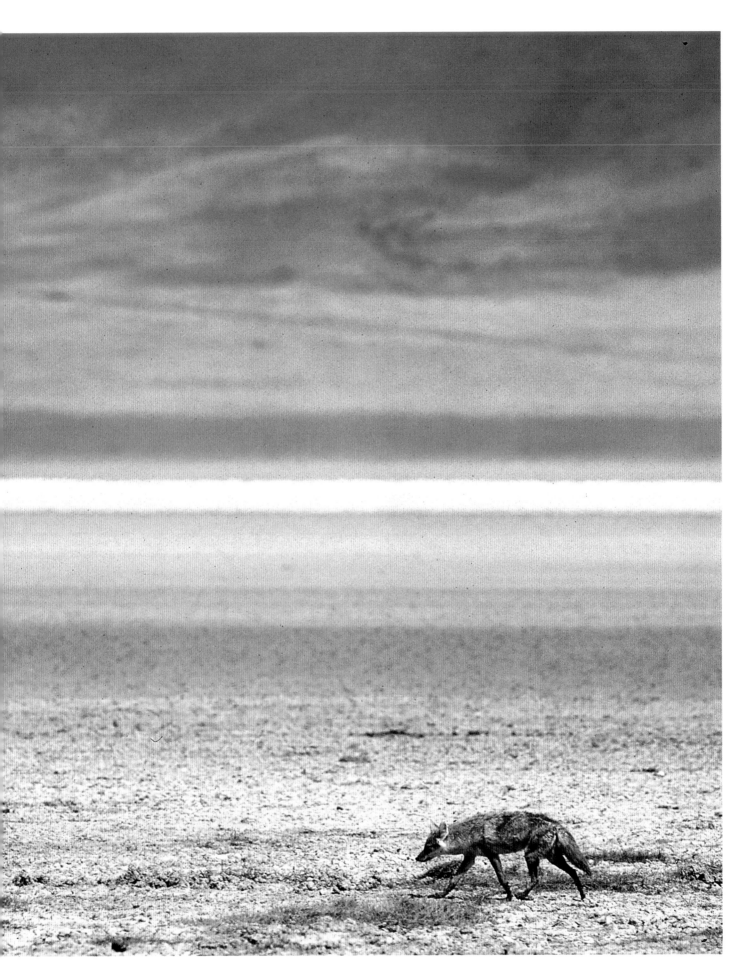

The jackals, which are native to Africa, are the Old World cousins of the coyote of North America: like it, they are members of the genus *Canis*. The largest species is the golden jackal (*Canis aureus*), which stands about 20in (50cm) at the shoulder and weighs up to 33lb (15kg). It is found throughout the northern half of Africa, in the west as far south as southern Mali and northern Zaire, in the east extending from Ethiopia and Somalia southwards through the eastern and western branches of the Rift Valley as far as the southern limits of the Serengeti Plains: it is equally at home in open savannas, dry grasslands, and deserts. It is an opportunistic scavenger, eats carrion, and will hunt down small mammals, including the young of the smaller antelopes, especially Thomson's gazelle fawns, which in the Serengeti are born at the same time (January and February) as the jackal pups. Pairs mate for life, and family groups often include sub-adults of the previous litter, which help to feed and care for newborn young. Golden jackals howl, and family groups give vent to memorable choruses of high-pitched wails, usually at dusk.

The black-backed jackal (*Canis mesomelas*), which is slightly smaller, has two separate populations distributed in much the same regions as those of the bat-eared fox, except that the southern range includes the whole of South Africa. It takes its common name from its characteristic black "saddle" of hairs, broad at the shoulder and narrow at the base of the tail. This species' other name is silver-backed jackal: in many populations the saddle has a generous sprinkling of white or silvery hairs. Its flanks, legs and face are reddish brown, lighter in some populations, darker in others, while the throat, chest and underparts are generally paler. Its family life and diet are generally similar to that of the golden jackal, but the black-backed—a bold scavenger—is usually in close attendance at hyena and lion kills in both its ranges.

The side-striped jackal (*Canis adustus*), of similar size and weight, is overall grey in colour when seen from a distance; close-up, a band of white hair, fringed with black, is visible along each flank (whence its name); on the legs the grey is often slightly red-tinged; the underparts are generally lighter; the bushy tail has a white tip. Its range

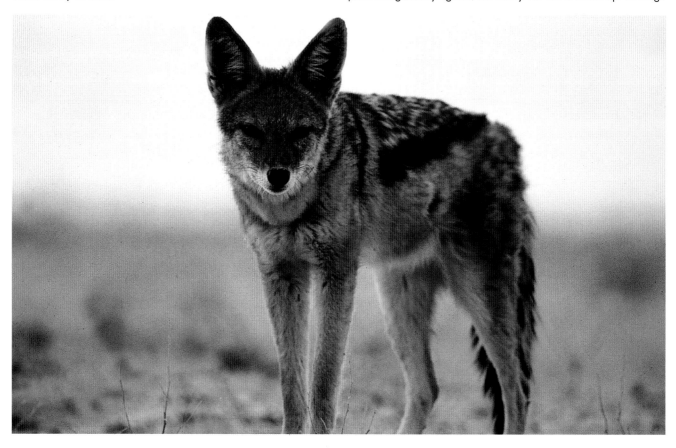

Above: A black-backed jackal from the northern range, where it is a creature of the dry, acacia savanna—in this case the Lake Manyara region in north-eastern Tanzania.

extends from northern Nigeria eastwards to Ethiopia, then southwards from Kenya to KwaZulu-Natal; and in the west from southern Gabon and southern Zaïre to north-eastern Namibia. It is a creature of moist savannas, marshlands, open woodland, and mountains to an altitude of 9,000ft (2,750m), and feeds on a wide range of items, including small mammals, reptiles, birds, insects and carrion. It does not howl but sometimes emits a series of high-pitched yaps. Like the other two species, adult side-striped jackals pair for life and family groups sometimes include sub-adults.

The Ethiopian wolf (*Canis simensis*), also known as the Simien jackal or Simien fox, has in recent years been recognised as a close relative of the grey wolf (*C. lupus*) of Eurasia and North America, although its behaviour is more akin to a jackal's. Larger than any of the jackals, it stands about 25in (62cm) at the shoulder and weighs up to 42lb (19kg). It is a native of, and confined solely to, the Ethiopian highlands at altitudes between 10,000 and 13,000ft (3,050 and 3,960m). It is found mainly in the Simen mountains in the north and in Balé Mountain National Park near the southern end of the

highlands to the east of the Rift Valley. It is the largest African member of the genus *Canis*, standing as much as 25in (64cm) at the shoulder and weighing up to 42lb (19kg). A handsome, long-legged canid with a long, fox-like muzzle, it is a bright reddish brown on the head, face, back, sides and outside of legs; the insides of the ears, lower jaw, throat, lower chest and underparts are white, as is the first half of the tail, which then bushes out with black hairs overlying red. The Ethiopian wolf inhabits montane and plateau grasslands, moors, heaths and boglands, where it preys on small mammals—mainly mole rats and swamp rats, but also hares and, occasionally, the young of mountain nyala and reedbuck. It is in extreme peril of extinction, partly because it is hunted by farmers who regard it (erroneously) as a predator of their sheep and goats, and partly through hybridization with feral and domestic dogs. There are probably no more than 500 individuals alive today.

The African wild dog (*Lycaon pictus*), also known as the Cape hunting dog, is a creature of semi-deserts, moist and dry savannas, montane grasslands and moorlands up to an altitude of 9,500ft

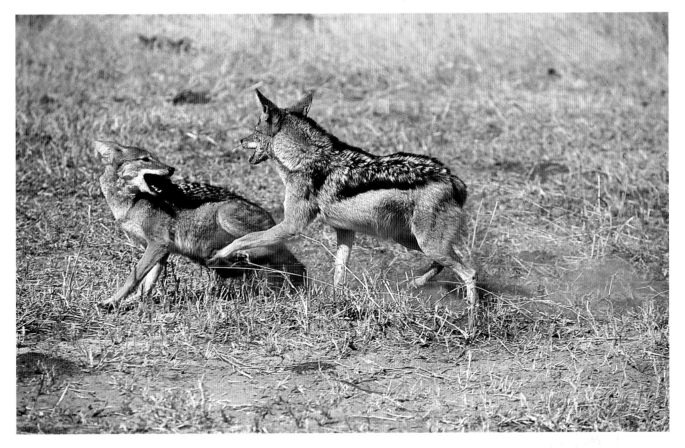

Above: Two sub-adult black-backed jackals at play. Hunting parties often include older offspring, who continue to live in the territory of their parents for a while before striking out on their own.

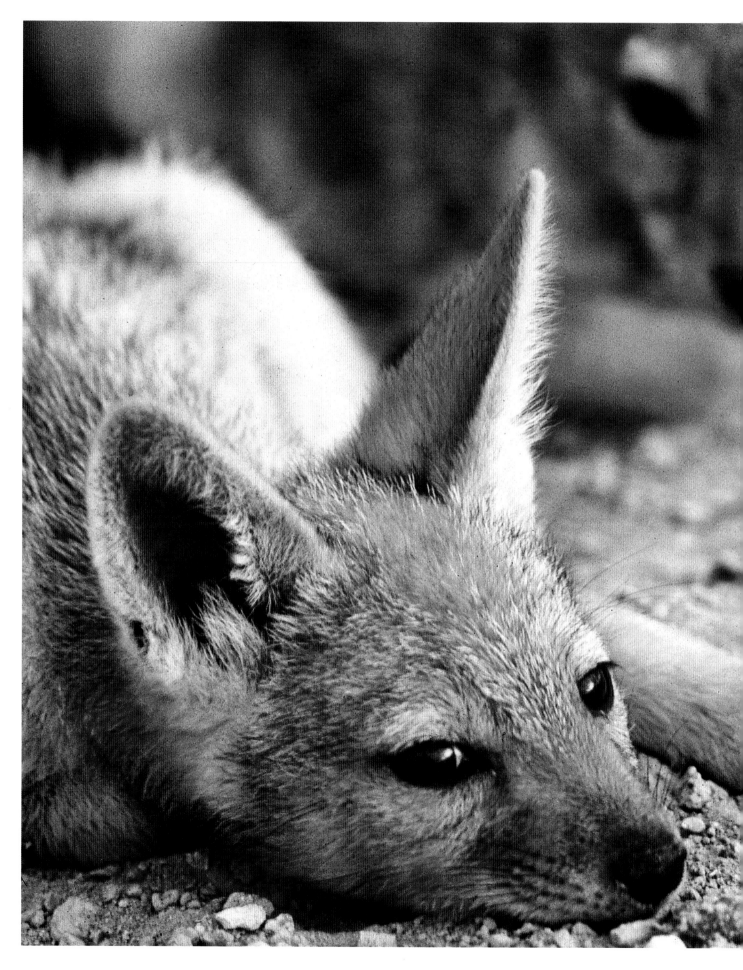

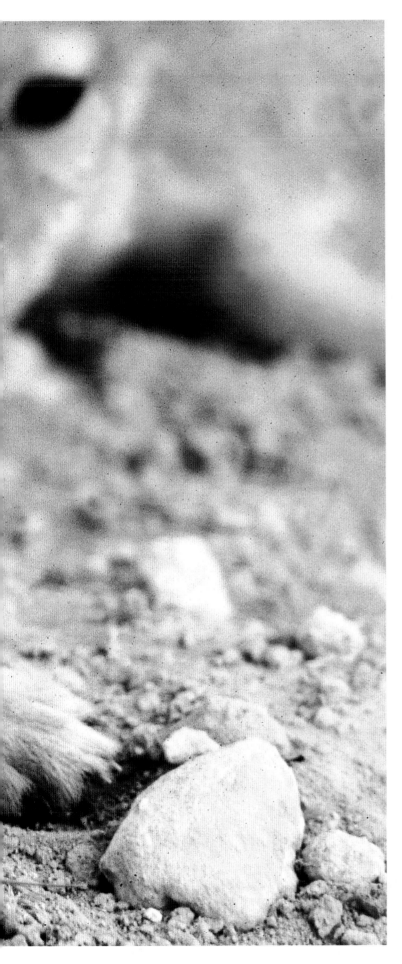

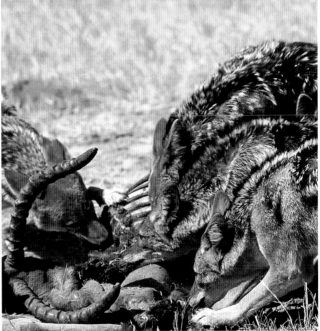

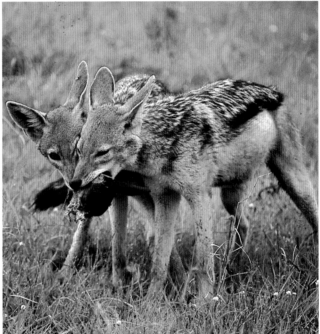

Top: Black-backed jackals are patient and resourceful scavengers, often to be seen at lion and hyena kills. This family party gorges on the abandoned carcass of a medium-sized ungulate.

Above: Black-backed are also good hunters, preying on young antelope, rodents, hares, reptiles and birds. These two debate ownership of the remains of a kill on the Masai Mara.

Left: A pair of black-backed jackal pups. Young adults of the previous season's litter will help their parents defend the pups against predators.

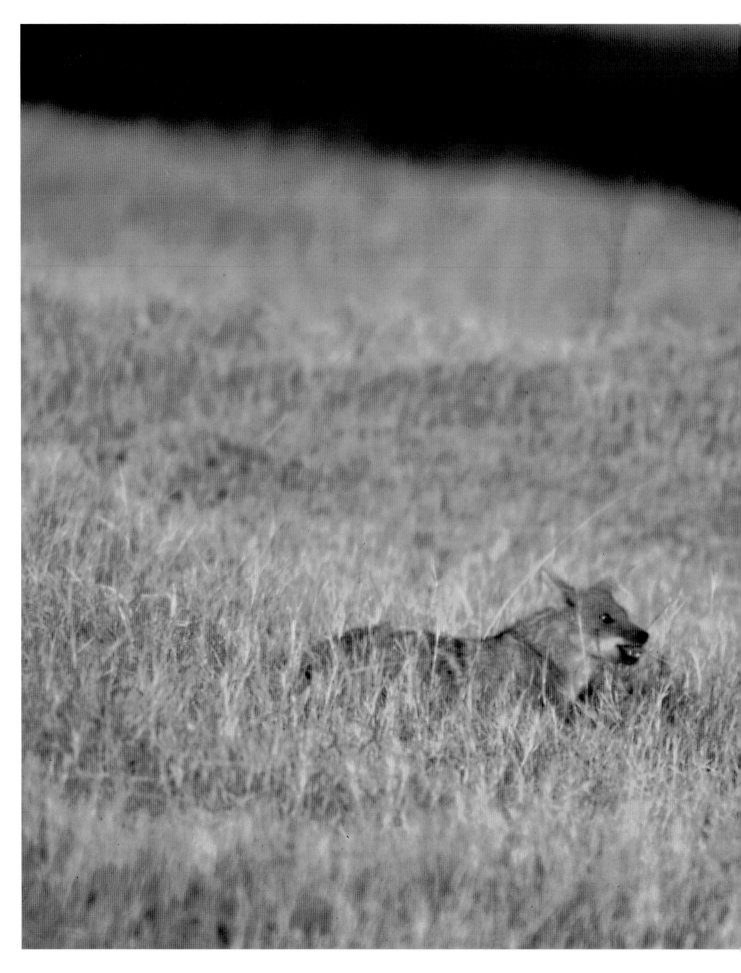

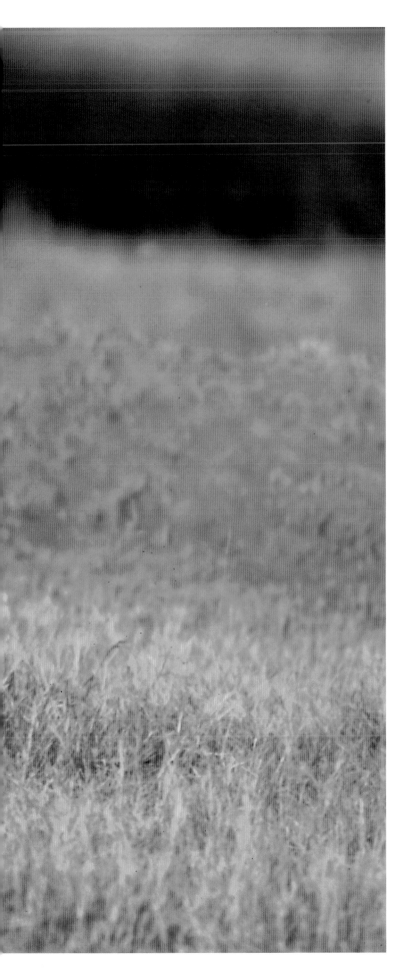

(2,900m). Once found throughout sub-Sahara Africa outside the forests, it now survives (mainly in parks and reserves) only in Kenya, Tanzania, Zambia, Zimbabwe, Botswana and Transvaal (Kruger National Park). Tall and lanky, the wild dog has a coat consisting of randomly shaped patches of black, various browns and (often) white. The face from eyes to snout is black, the forehead brown (sometimes with a black "parting"); the ears are large, rounded and dark; the tail is brown at the base, then black, then white and bushy. Highly social, the wild dog lives in packs of 10 to 15 (sometimes more) adults and sub-adults, including several adult males and one or more adult females, the latter of a different lineage from the males. Only the dominant (alpha) female produces new members for the pack: she kills all young produced by the other, subordinate females, who will usually leave the pack when they are between 18 months and two years old to form packs of their own. The alpha female, who is effectively the leader of the pack, produces litters of 12 or more pups, but there is a high mortality rate.

Wild dog packs are the most efficient hunting units of the savanna, far exceeding the kill rates of the lions, leopards, cheetahs or hyenas with which they share many of their habitats; they will chase fleeing prey for several miles and can sustain speeds of up to 30mph (48km/h) for minutes on end. Their prey includes mainly medium-sized ungulates such as wildebeest, impala, and springbok, but they can and will take young buffalo, zebra and eland on occasion. The wild dog has been subject to extermination campaigns throughout its range for many years and the persecution continues today.

A side-striped jackal finds perfect cover in grassland in southern Zambia.

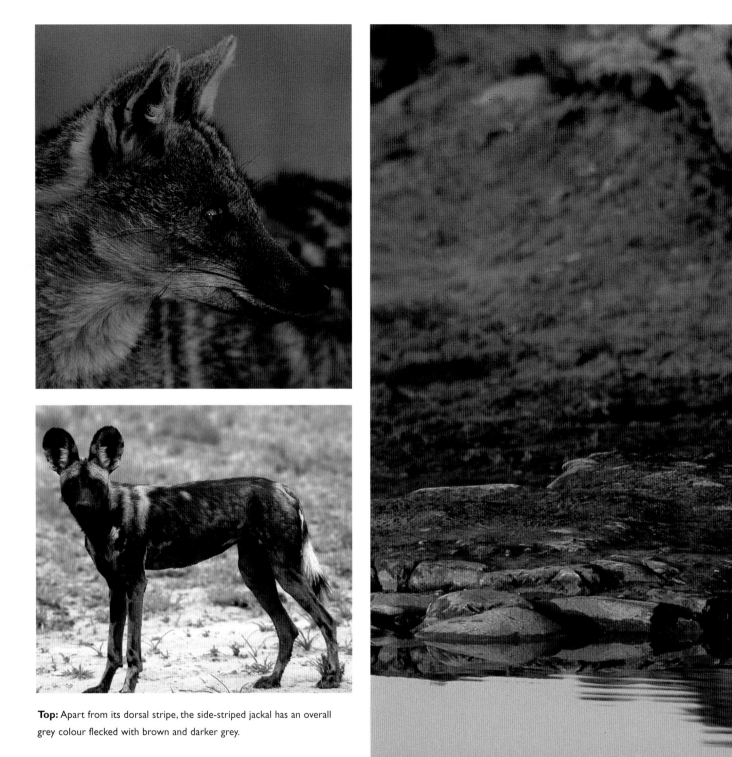

Top: Apart from its dorsal stripe, the side-striped jackal has an overall grey colour flecked with brown and darker grey.

Above: The lanky African wild dog's coat is a patchwork of dark brown, black and usually some greyish white. Note the black face, fawn forehead with black "parting", and huge oval ears.

Right: A black-backed jackal at a Botswana waterhole at sunset. Jackals frequently hunt at night.

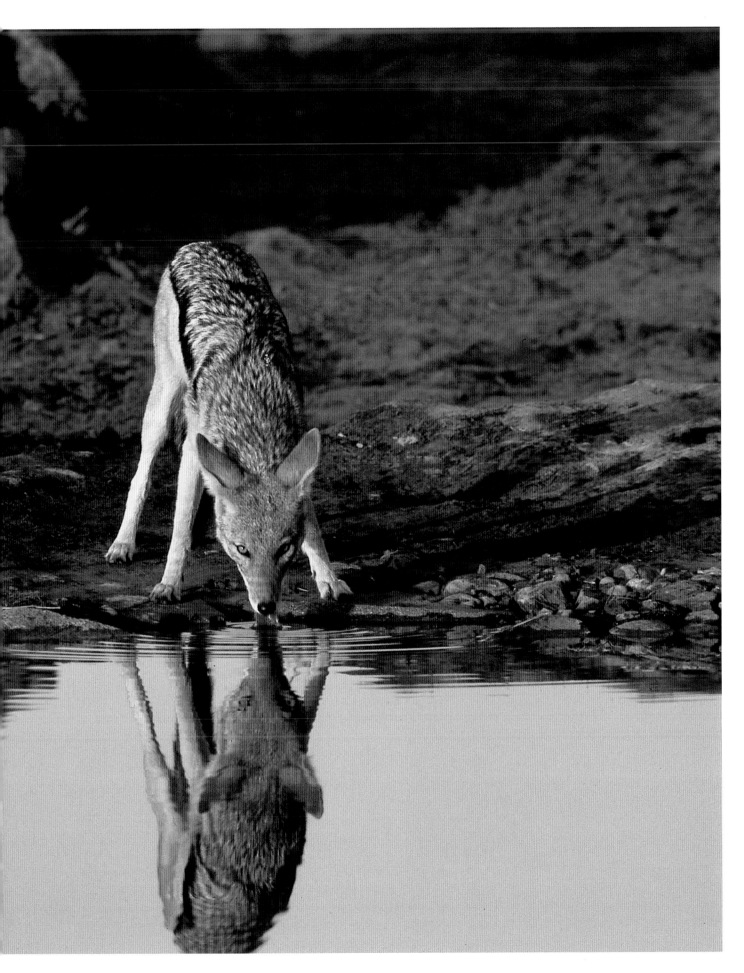

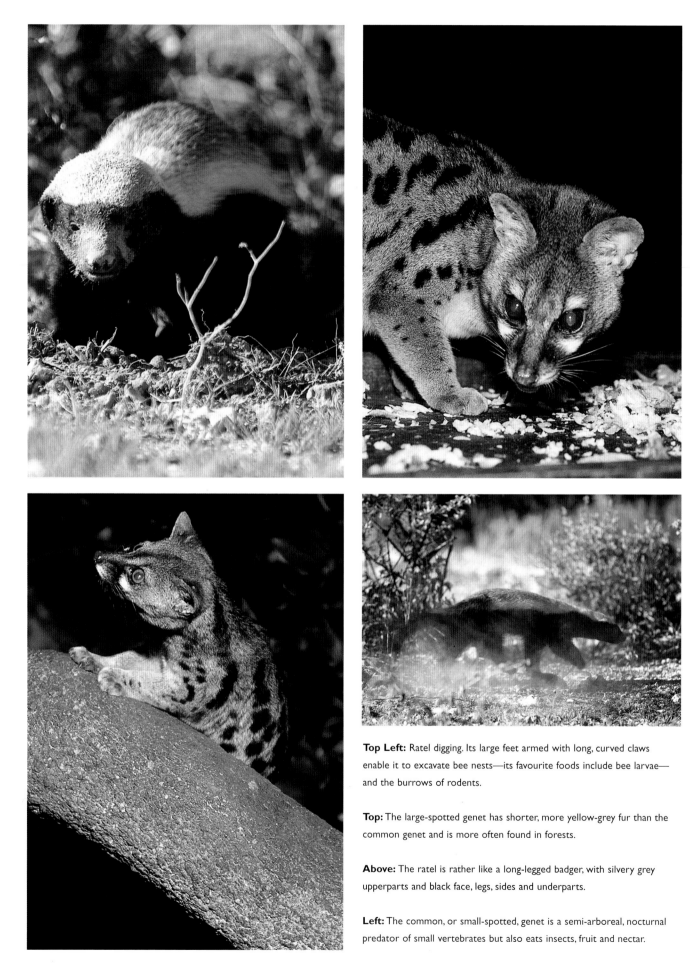

Top Left: Ratel digging. Its large feet armed with long, curved claws enable it to excavate bee nests—its favourite foods include bee larvae—and the burrows of rodents.

Top: The large-spotted genet has shorter, more yellow-grey fur than the common genet and is more often found in forests.

Above: The ratel is rather like a long-legged badger, with silvery grey upperparts and black face, legs, sides and underparts.

Left: The common, or small-spotted, genet is a semi-arboreal, nocturnal predator of small vertebrates but also eats insects, fruit and nectar.

MUSTELIDS

Among the seven African members of the Mustelidae family (the otters, weasels and polecats), one of the largest is the ratel or honey badger (*Mellivora capensis*), which ranges throughout sub-Sahara Africa apart from true deserts; it is rare in tropical lowland forests and is absent from the Orange Free State. Similar in form to a badger, its coarse black coat has a grey mantle that runs from the top of its forehead to the tip of its short, stubby tail; often whitish fur separates the mantle from the black fur on its face, sides, legs and underparts. It stands about 10in (25cm) at the shoulders and weighs up to 30lb (14kg). With thick skin, powerful jaws and long, curving claws it is formidably armed, its defensive armoury being supplemented by a foul-smelling liquid it ejects from anal sacs. Strong and aggressive, it has been known to attack animals as large as buffalo when threatened. It takes one of its common names from its favoured food—bee larvae and honey—but it also eats rodents, reptiles, birds and carrion.

GENETS AND CIVETS

The family Viverridae to which genets and civets belong is believed to represent the modern form of the ancient ancestral stock from which most of the carnivores have evolved. The genets, which are mainly arboreal, have semi-retractable claws and soft fur and may resemble the forerunners of the cats. The civets, essentially terrestrial, have shorter footpads, non-retractable blunt claws and coarser fur, and may be representative of the early canid line.

The common genet (*Genetta genetta*) ranges over dry savannas and subdeserts in most regions of sub-Sahara Africa. Its longish fur, which is coarser than that of other genets, is light grey to brownish grey (lighter on the undersides). It has a dark brown to black dorsal stripe with a distinctive crest. Its dark brown, often elongated spots on the torso are in five rows on each side of the spine and also appear on the neck and upper legs; the face has a dark mask below the eyes; the very long tail has nine or ten black rings. Its body length is up to 20in (50cm), its tail perhaps one inch (2.5cm) less, and it weighs up to five pounds (2.3kg). Essentially nocturnal, it eats small vertebrates, insects, fruit and nectar.

There are seven other African *Genetta* species, most with broadly similar coat markings and dorsal crests, and also the more distantly related aquatic genet (*Osbornictis piscivora*), a fish-eating species of the upper Congo basin in Zaïre, mainly deep reddish brown in colour with a black, bushy tail.

The African civet (*Civettictis civetta*) is a sturdily built, somewhat raccoon-like animal with a complex pattern of black or dark brown bands against a ground colour that is generally light brown but sometimes almost white on the neck and face. The lower halves of the legs are black, the muzzle is white and the face has black eye patches. The coat hair is coarse, and a black crest extends from the forehead to the tip of the tail. Much larger than the genets, this species is up to 16in (40cm) high at the shoulders and may weigh as much as 44lb (20kg). Found throughout most of sub-Sahara Africa other than Somalia, Botswana, Namibia and western South Africa, it inhabits dense forests, woodland-savanna mosaics (especially dense woodland along rivers), marshy areas and farmlands. A solitary animal, hostile to others of its species except when breeding, it feeds mainly on vertebrates (including dangerous snakes) and fruit.

MONGOOSES

Of the 37 species of the mongoose family, the Herpestidae, all but seven are native to Africa. Of these only seven species are true carnivores, the others being mainly insectivorous. The carnivorous ones are long-bodied and short-legged and are expert stalkers of snakes, rodents and birds. Typical of these is the ichneumon or Egyptian mongoose (*Herpestes ichneumon*), with its slender, pointed snout and long, tapered tail ending in a black tassel. Its long-haired coat is grizzled grey over light or reddish brown; the legs, with much shorter hair, are darker and greyer. Its forepaws have long claws well adapted for digging. The species' common name, from the Greek word *ichneumon* (tracker), refers to its expertise in hunting down prey, which also includes fish, crabs, crayfish and frogs (it is an accomplished swimmer). The ichneumon is found all over Africa except in deserts and rainforests. It is up to 24in (60cm) long, with the tail almost as long again, and weighs about nine pounds (4kg). Much smaller, weighing no more than 30oz (850g), is the slender or black-tipped mongoose (*H. sanguineus*), grey-fawn to chestnut in

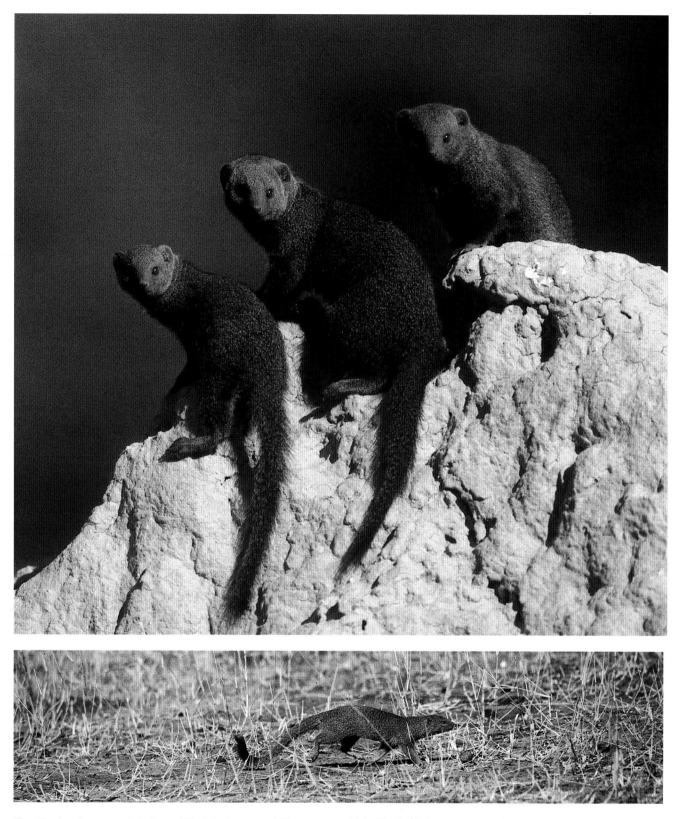

Top: The dwarf mongoose is highly sociable, living in groups of 10 or more on the drier savannas; it eats mainly invertebrates, and small reptiles and rodents.

Right: The banded mongoose, which lives in packs of up to 40, has 10 or 12 dark brown transverse bands across its greyish brown coat. This group lives on a termite mound in Kenya.

Above: The slender mongoose—this one is from Botswana—has a grey-fawn to rich brown coat depending on region and is recognisable by the black tassel at the tip of its long tail.

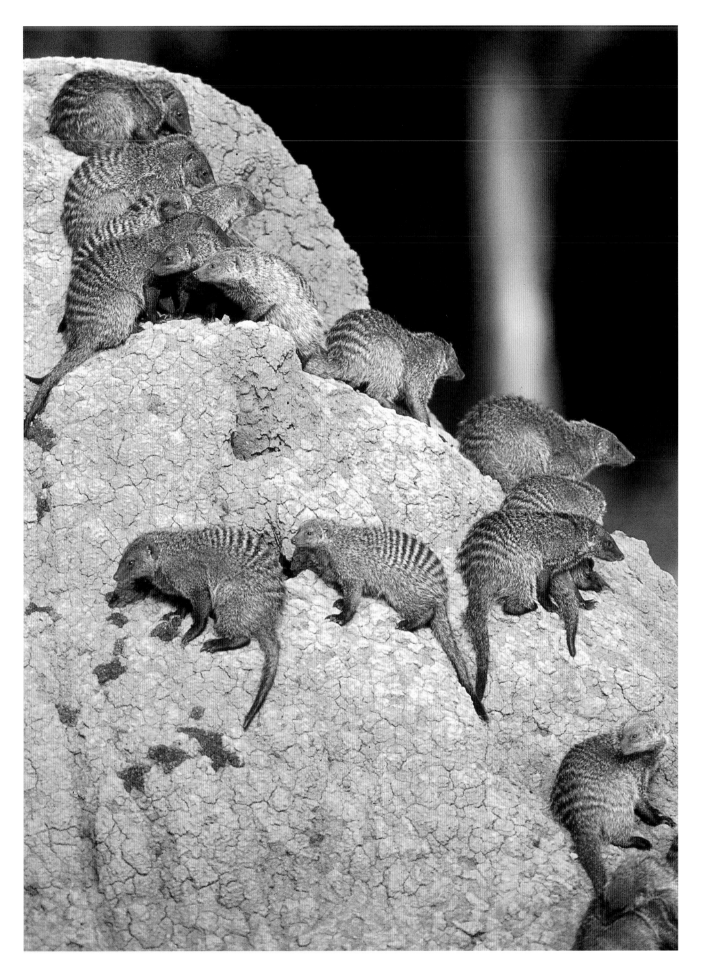

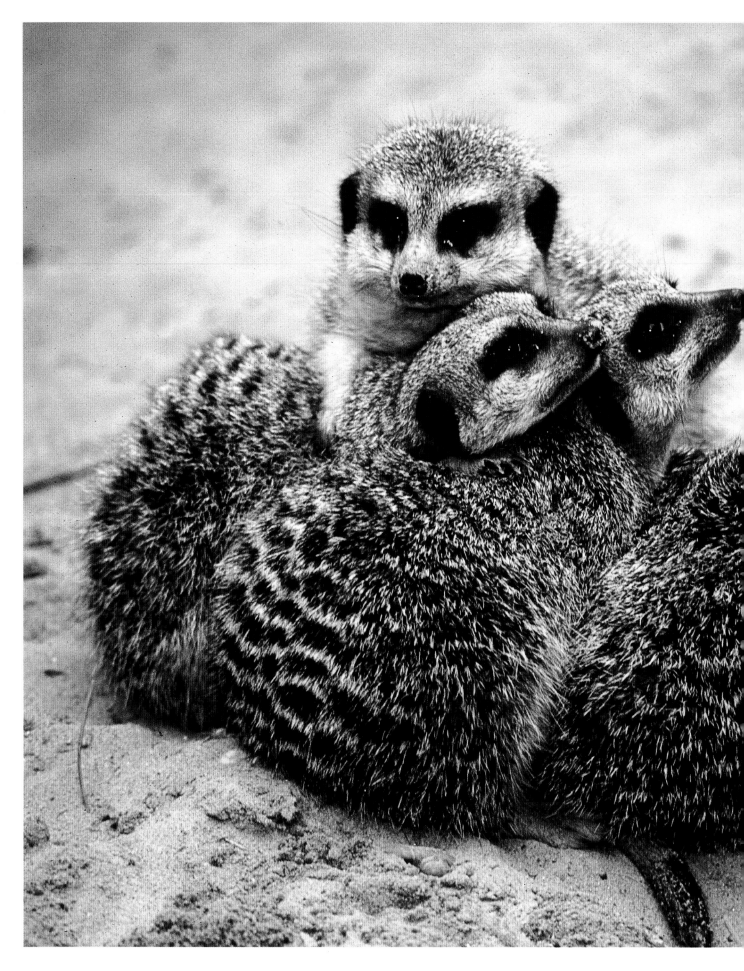

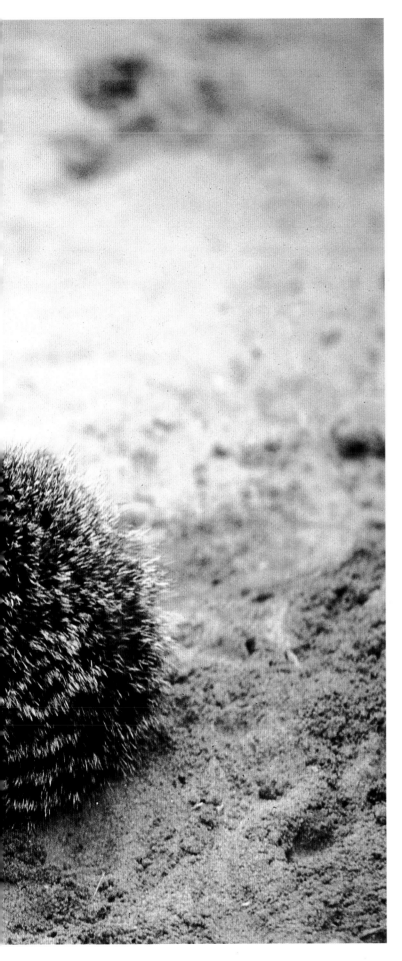

The suricate, or meerkat, replaces the banded mongoose in harsher, sub-desert regions of southern Africa. It too has transverse bands on the back, though broken and less distinct than those of its cousin. This trio huddles together on a typical area of hardpan outside their burrow.

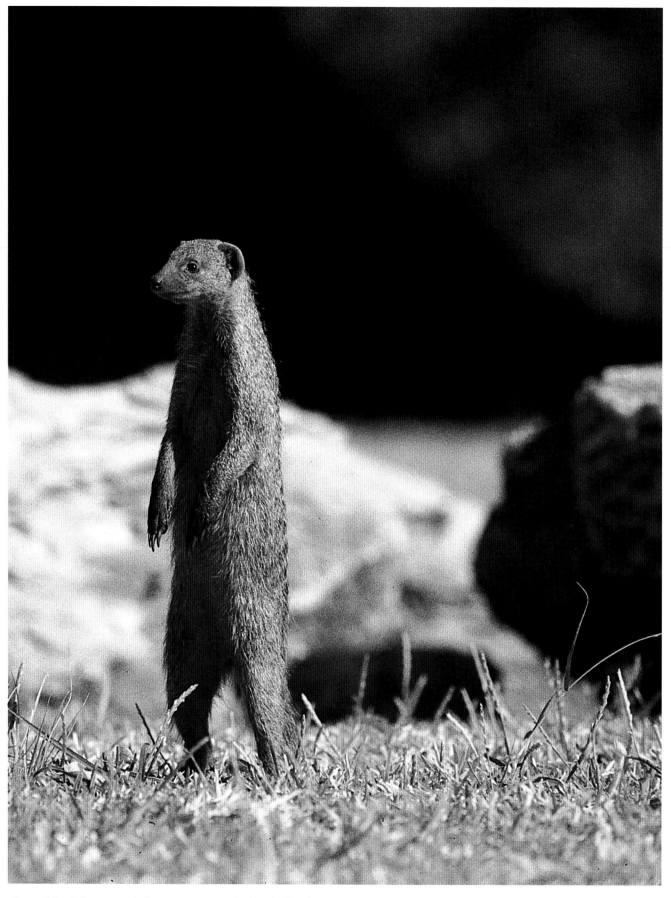

Above: A banded mongoose in Botswana gets on its hind legs looking for predators.

colour depending on region, and with reddish amber eyes, has much the same mammal and reptile diet as the ichneumon but is also has a squirrel-like ability as a tree climber. Two mongooses that include the odd small mammal or reptile in their mainly invertebrate diets are the dwarf mongoose (*Helogale parvula*), Africa's smallest carnivore—it weighs no more than 14oz (400g)—and the banded mongoose (*Mungos mungo*), with its striking dark brown transverse stripes on its greyish brown coat.

Of the essentially insectivorous mongooses, one of the most attractive is the suricate or meerkat (*Suricata suricata*), which is superficially like a smaller, lighter-coloured banded mongoose. It has dark eye patches and ears and an almost hairless belly. It is a native of southern Africa, from southern Angola through Namibia and Botswana to the highveld and Karroo of Cape Province. Its habitat is typified by the acacia bushland of the Kalahari: it favours open country with sparse vegetation grazed by wild or domestic ungulates. Highly sociable, the suricate lives in packs of up to 30 animals which may include more than one breeding pair. There is no obvious hierarchical structure within the pack and there are few displays of aggression except towards trespassing neighbours, who will be fiercely ousted from their territory. The pack lives in a warren dug in hard soil close to waterholes; they quite frequently move to, or build, new warrens when local food sources are exhausted. Outside the warren suricates are constantly on guard against predators, mainly birds of prey and jackals, and pack members take turn as sentries, standing on the top of mounds, boulders or bushes. A sharp alarm bark will send the pack dashing into the warren. The adults threaten smaller mammal predators by fluffing up their coats, snapping, and jumping up and down in unison. In favourable areas suricates sometimes amicably share a cluster of well-established warrens with South African ground squirrels (*Geosciurus inauris*) and colonies of yellow mongoose (*Cynictis penicillata*).

Right: Poorly defined brownish transverse stripes are visible on this suricate against the mainly grey ground colour. The lower chest and belly have very little hair.

Overleaf: A domed forehead, dark eye-patches and ears, and thin, rather fluffy hair around the shoulders are useful recognition features of the suricate. This one is from the Kalahari desert.

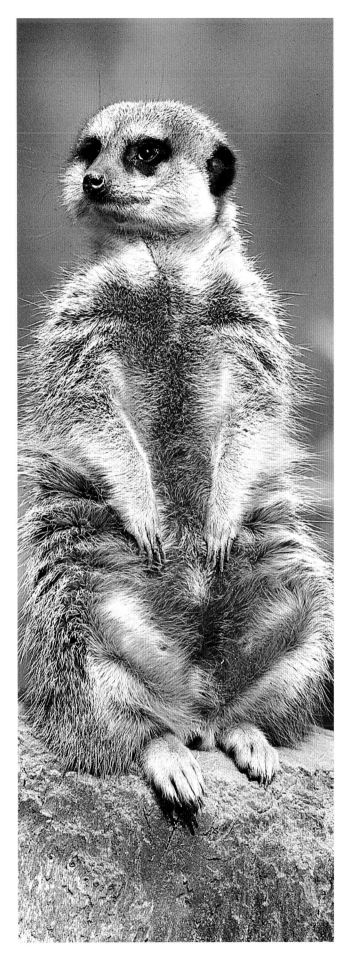

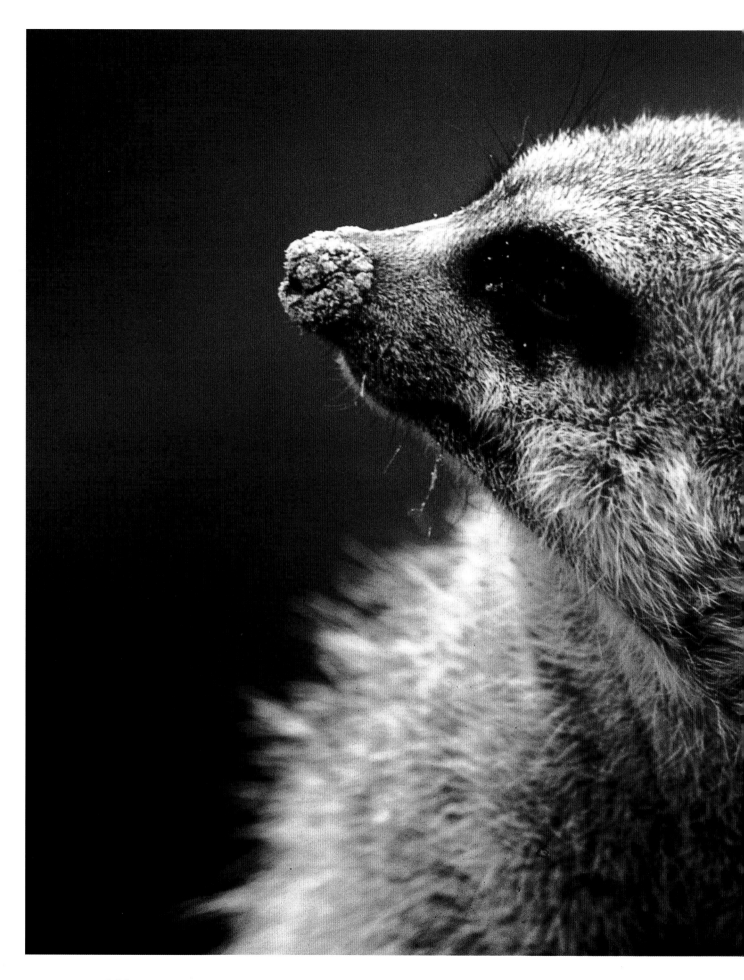

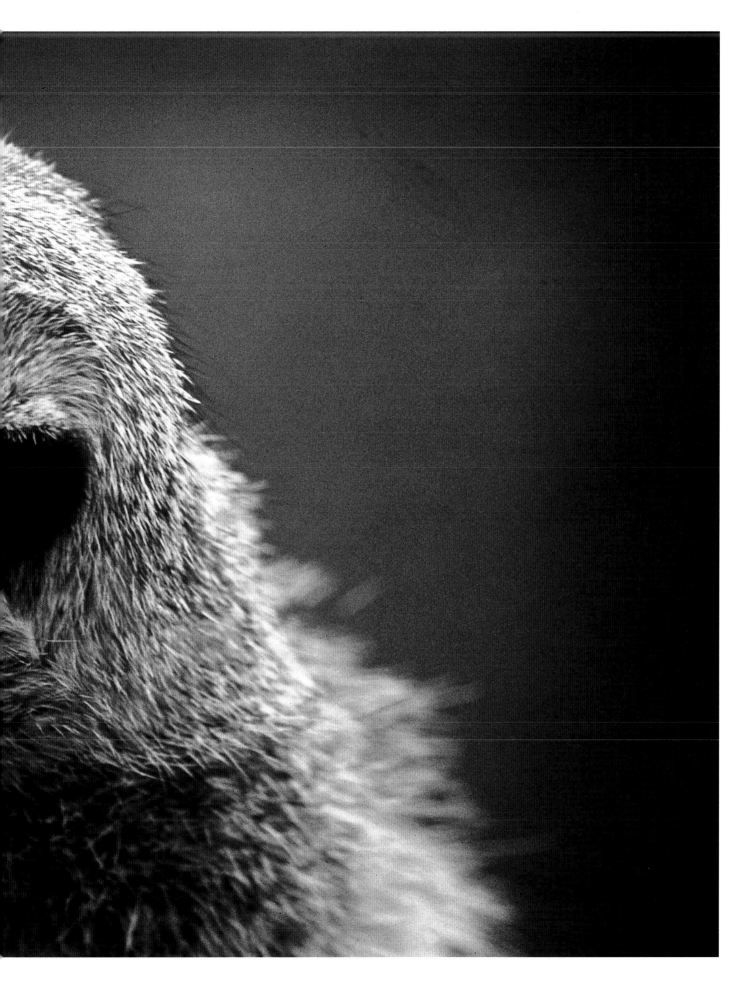

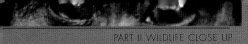

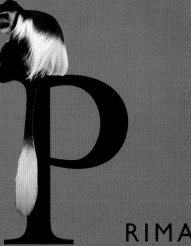

P RIMATES

The Primate order comprises two main groups: the prosimians, or lower primates, consisting of the galagonid and lorid families; and the monkeys and apes, or higher primates. Of 225 primate species in the world, more than 50 are native to mainland Africa. Here we shall look briefly at some representatives of the main families.

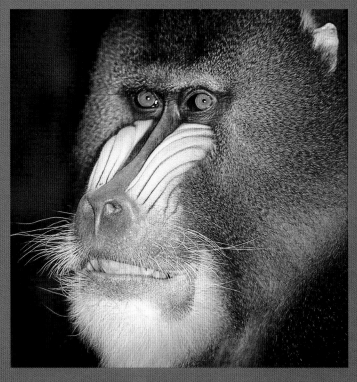

Above: The extraordinary facial markings of the adult male mandrill mark it distinctly against any other species. A fully grown male such as this is twice the size of the female. Like its close cousin the drill, it is widely hunted and is an endangered species.

Right: Red colobus monkeys are at home in the trees—their light weight allows them to go further out on the branches than other, heavier species. This gives them access to fresher leaves, their main food. Note the absence of thumbs on their hands.

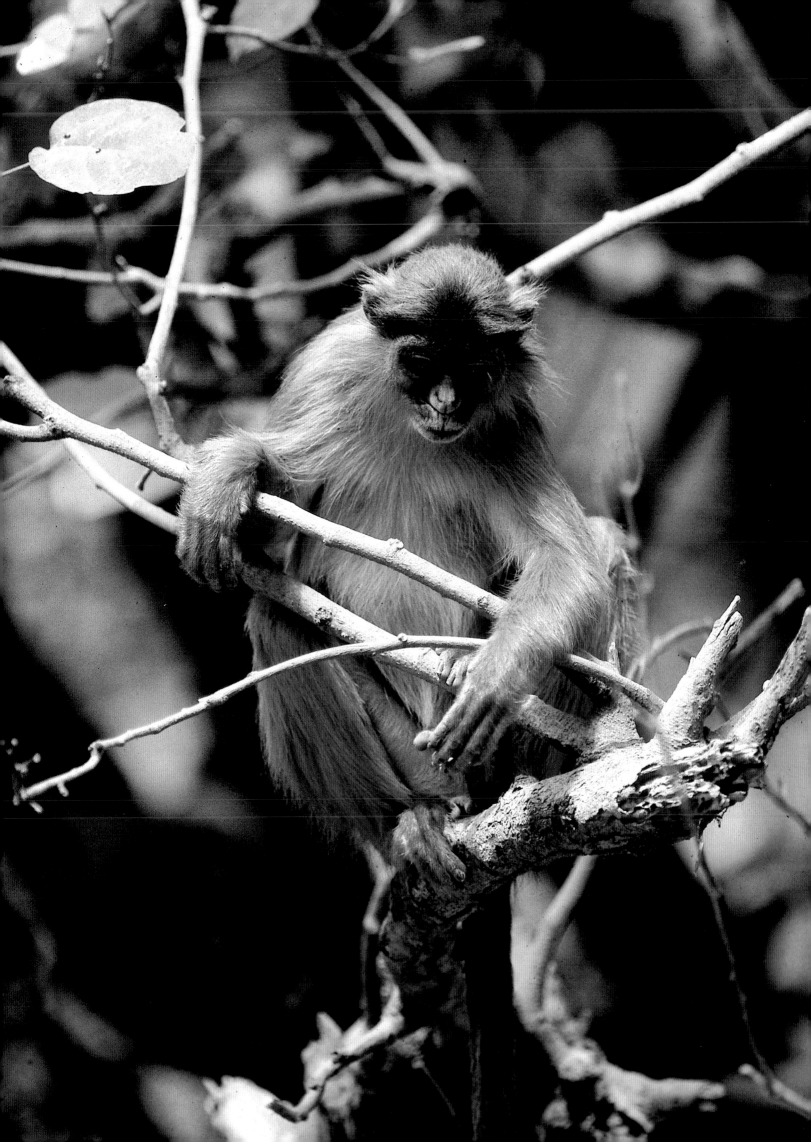

GALGONIDS

Bushbabies, which are found only in Africa, are small, nocturnal species with very long hind legs and a furry tail, longer than their body, that contributes to their astonishing feats of balancing as they leap through the trees of their forest habitats. Their long, slender hands and feet have opposing thumb and big toe. Their heads are rounded, with forward-facing eyes that have excellent night vision, and furless ears that can retract and fold flat. Their body fur helps to hold and diffuse a variety of scents secreted by several scent glands that play an important role in the social life of these species.

The thick-tailed bushbaby (*Galago crassicaudatus*), also known as the greater galago, is the largest African bushbaby—cat-sized and weighing up to 4½lb (2,000g). Its coat colour varies from light grey to brownish or reddish grey depending on region; its ears are relatively large; there are dark areas around the eyes. It walks or runs along branches. Like other galagos, it likes the gum from acacia and some other trees; it also eats fruits, flowers and seeds, as well as slugs, insects, reptiles and birds. Its range is from southern Kenya and Tanzania, westwards through Rwanda and southern Zaïre to Angola and southwards through Zambia as far as KwaZulu-Natal. Its habitat is mainly dense evergreen lowland or montane forest and bush. The thick-tailed bushbaby's vocal repertoire includes the high-pitched wail that has earned the galagos their common name. Other galago species include the lesser bushbaby (*G. senegalensis*), weighing little more than half a pound (250g), found in much of sub-Sahara Africa in acacia savannas and gallery forests from Senegal to Somalia and south to Mozambique; and the greater bushbaby or small-eared galago (*Galago garnettii*), found in East African coastal regions and the Kenya highlands. There are also a number of even smaller dwarf species. (Certain species of the genus *Galago* are assigned by some naturalists to the genus *Otolemur*.)

LORIDS

The Loridae family consists of three pottos and three lorises (the latter native to south-east Asia). The potto (*Perodicticus potto*) is a small, very slow-climbing animal that will remain stock still for minutes on end at the slightest disturbance. It is about 14in (36cm) long and weighs up to three pounds (1.6kg). Its long, slender body and

limbs are given a somewhat teddy-bear-like shape by its thick, soft fur, which is reddish brown or dark brown, with lighter undersides. It has small ears and a stumpy tail. Its neck and shoulders have a mass of bone, muscle and thick skin that offer a protective shield beneath the thick fur. Like galagos, the potto depends on gums for part of its diet, the rest consisting mainly of fruits, snails, eggs, fungi and insects. It lives mainly in lowland rain forests, coastal scrublands, and montane forests from Sierra Leone to western Kenya.

The angwantibo or golden potto (*Arctocebus aureus*), is smaller, rarely weighing more than 9oz (255g), has only a vestigial tail, hairless ears and large eyes. Its coat colour is as likely to be a rich

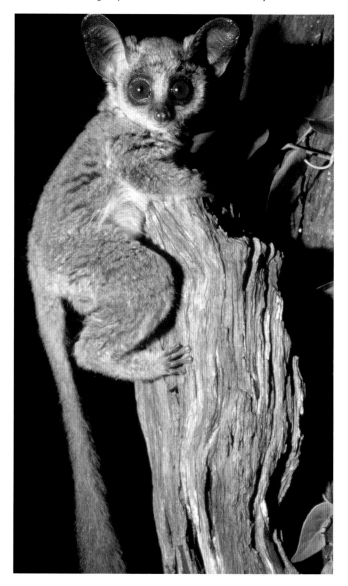

Above: The thick-tailed bushbaby's long tail helps it to balance while running and jumping through the trees. This combined with powerful hind legs and excellent night vision, makes it superbly adapted for a nocturnal life in its evergreen forest habitat.

russet as golden, and it has creamy undersides. Fine guard hairs on the shoulders, back and haunches give the coat a frosty sheen. In this species and the one below the second finger is lost and the third is little more than a stump. It is confined to dense lowland evergreen rainforests from the Sanaga river (Cameroon) in the west to the Oubangui river (the Congo's main southward-flowing tributary) in the east. Its close relative, the Calabar angwantibo (*A. calabarensis*), is somewhat larger at about one pound (454g) in weight, has a soft light brown coat with white underparts and inside legs. Its range, smaller than that of the golden species, is in localised communities in lowland rainforest from the Sanaga river westwards to the Niger.

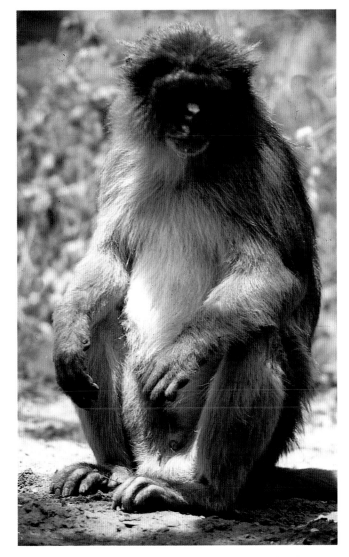

Above: The gentle colobus monkeys inhabit large areas of Africa. This individual is a red colobus monkey. They are hunted not only by humans but also by chimpanzees, which go on regular monkey hunts, catching and killing them almost as much for pleasure as for food.

MONKEYS

Of the 74 species of Old World monkeys, 39 are native to Africa and the rest to Asia. The main African groups include the baboons, the guenons (forest monkeys), the mangabeys, and the colobus monkeys. These primates are basically narrow-bodied, with deep chests and slim waists; they mostly move and stand on all four legs, but they sit (and sleep) on buttocks that are padded with callouses. All but the colobus monkeys have sacs (pouches) behind each cheek.

The five species of baboon are all native to Africa. They are large, with fore and hind limbs of similar length and with shorter tails than forest monkeys. They spend much of the day on the ground, and at night they sleep in trees or on cliffs. They have characteristically dog-like muzzles and closely set eyes under a prominent brow ridge. They have relatively short fingers but fully opposable thumb and forefinger. The female has a pad of naked skin on each buttock which distends hugely during œstrus. The adult male, which is up to twice the size of the female, has a powerful physique and long fangs. The common or savanna baboon (*Papio cynocephalus*) is the subject of some taxonomic confusion. It has been given different common names in different parts of its very extensive range: western or Guinea baboon (Mauretania to Sierra Leone); olive baboon (Gambia to Somalia); yellow baboon (Somalia through Tanzania, and Angola through Zambia and Malawi to Mozambique); chacma baboon (southern Africa from Angola and Zambia to Cape of Good Hope). All these are best regarded as races or subspecies of the savanna baboon. It is the largest baboon, and the fourth largest primate after the gorilla, chimpanzee and bonobo: the male stands as much as 30in (75cm) when on all fours and typically weighs up to 75lb (34kg), though much heavier males have been reported; the female up to 40lb (18kg). The tail is carried high in an inverted "U" shape, with a pronounced "kink" at the top—a convenient feature for identifying the species. The coat colours vary from race to race and are generally as follows: western baboon, reddish brown; olive baboon, greenish olive; yellow baboon, yellowish brown or grey, lighter underparts; chacma baboon, dark grey to greyish brown, with blackish mane.

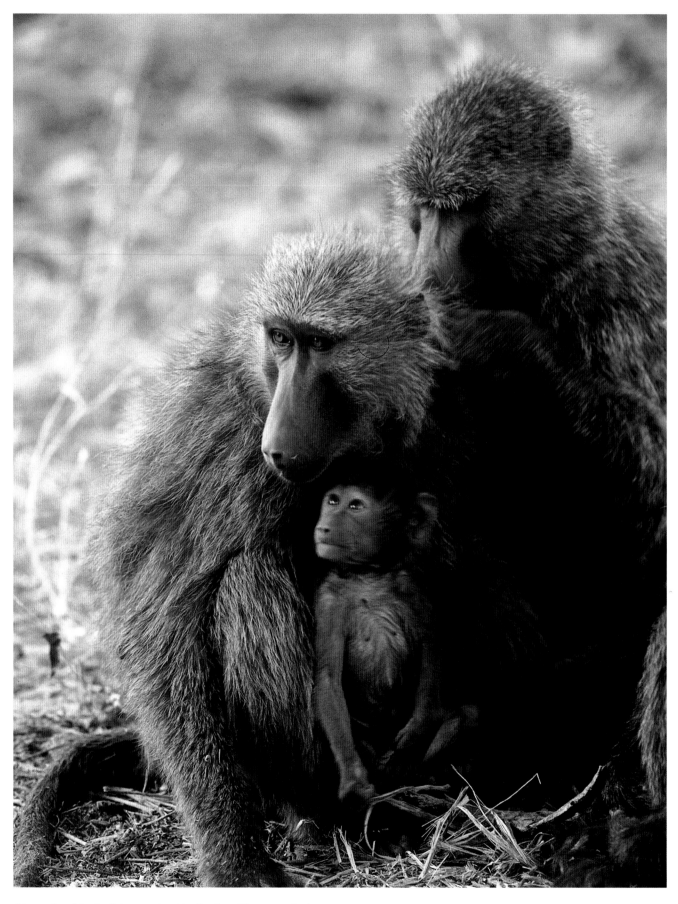

Above: An adult olive baboon male with a female and her young: Samburu
National Reserve, Kenya.

The savanna baboon is organised socially into family groups of females and their young together with several sexually mature males, one of which (usually at least five years old) will be dominant over both females and other males. These groups coalesce into larger congregations, called troops, numbering 150 individuals and more. Baboons are non-territorial, so the ranges of different troops often overlap, sometimes leading to violent conflict. The savanna baboon's habitat includes dry and moist savanna grasslands and scrub, open woodland and the margins of forests, including montane forests up to 10,000ft (3,000m). It is omnivorous, its diet including seeds, fruits, resin, leaves, roots, invertebrates and (if available) young antelope, hare, rodents, birds and reptiles.

The hamadryas or sacred baboon (*P. hamadryas*) is the smallest of the baboons, the adult male standing no more than 24in (60cm) at the shoulders (which are higher than the rump when the animal is on all fours) and weighing up to 44lb (20kg). The male's coat is a slightly grizzled ash grey; he has a heavy cape of fur and bushy cheek tufts usually of a slightly paler shade, and large, hairless muzzle and buttocks of bright reddish pink. The females are much smaller, lack the cape, and are greyish brown or olive brown in colour.

Hamadryas baboons live in more hierarchical groups than their savanna cousins. The basic social unit is the harem, a group of up to ten females and their young controlled by an adult male. The male assembles his harem over a period of several years by luring or abducting juvenile females from their mothers' group and guarding them until they are of an age to breed. Thus the dominant male's band will usually consist of females from many different harems, which no doubt helps to maintain variety in the gene pool of a local population. Males and their harems form into troops which for sleeping purposes at night may on occasion total more than 700 individuals. The sleeping quarters are on cliffs or rocky outcrops within reach of drinking water. The hamadryas is found only in Ethiopia, living in acacia savannas and both grassy and rocky plateau areas. It prefers the lower mountain slopes, but is also found in the Simen range at up to 10,000ft (3,000m). It feeds mainly on plant seeds, roots, bulbs and fruit and also on invertebrates and other animal food.

The closely related mandrill (*Papio sphinx*), smaller and stockier than the savanna baboon, and with a tiny tail, has the most extravagant colouring of all the primates (see page 384), especially the male. Its long muzzle has longitudinal silvery blue or grey ridges running from the eyes to the nose; the central ridge of the muzzle and the nose are bright red, as is the skin around the genitalia. The female has a dark muzzle and hind parts except for pink calluses on the buttocks. The basic colour of the male's coat, which is densely furred, is olive brown; there is a darker crest, and a light brown area about the throat and chest, while the underparts are yellowish grey. The mandrill male weighs up to 55lb (25kg), the female less than half as much. The species is mainly terrestrial, though all members of a troop sleep in trees. The species' diet includes fruits, nuts and foliage, as well as termites and ants. The somewhat smaller drill (*P. leucophaeus*) has less colourful markings: a shorter, black muzzle with a whitish ruff and a greyish brown coat. The adult male has a scarlet lower lip and blue, violet and red markings on the buttocks; the female develops pink swellings on her buttocks during œstrus. The drill's diet is similar to that of the mandrill. The social organisation of both species is based, like that of the hamadryas, on the harem, several of which may associate for limited periods in troops of up to 200 individuals. Both species are essentially forest dwellers, the mandrill being found in both montane and lowland rain forests, while the drill is confined to lowland, coastal and riverine forests. The two species' ranges are adjacent but do not overlap. The mandrill's range extends southward from the Sanaga river in Cameroon, through Gabon to the Congo river. The drill's smaller range is from the south-eastern corner of Nigeria eastwards to (but not south of) the Sanaga river and also nearby Bioko island (formerly Fernando Poo) in the Gulf of Guinea.

The gelada (*Theropithecus gelada*) is a close cousin of the baboons, about the size of the drill, and in general terms similar to them in appearance. Its dark, elongated muzzle is ridged longitudinally but its small, upturned nostrils are set much higher on the face, and below the mouth the chin is deep and rounded. The male has an extensive mane on the neck and shoulders and backward-flaring whiskers. The body colour is basically greyish brown or dark brown. Both sexes have bright red hairless throat and chest patches; in the male,

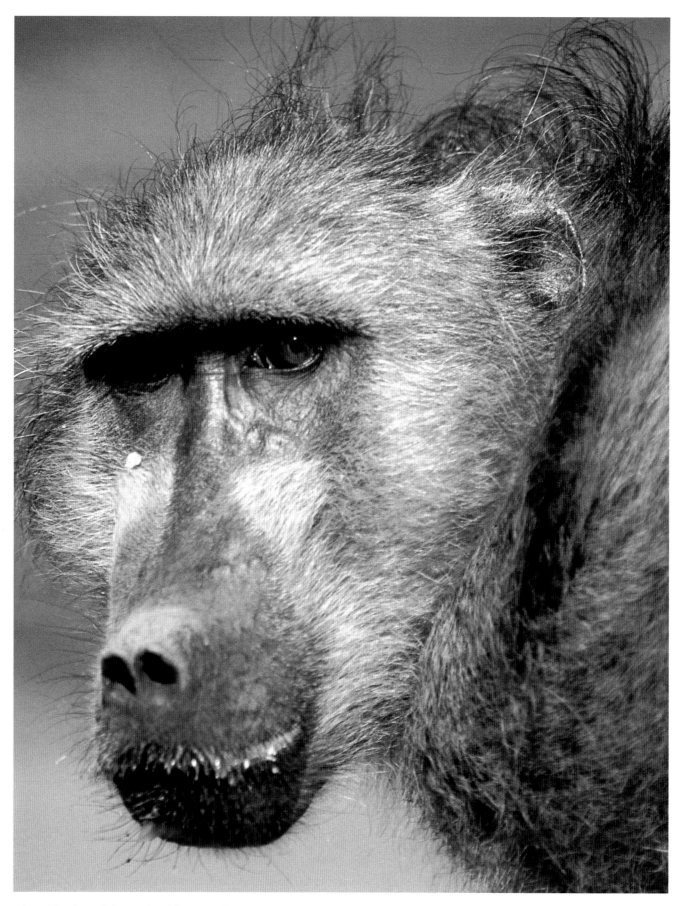

Above: The chacma baboon is found from central Angola and Zambia southward to the Cape. This one is from the Okavango Delta, Botswana.

Above Right: This adult male chacma lives in Chobe National Park, Botswana. Note his bright pink eyelids.

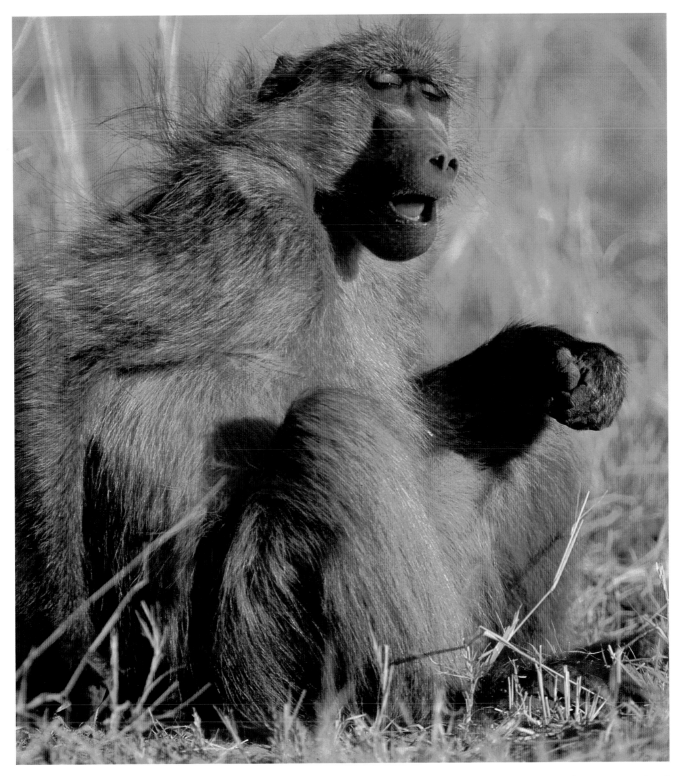

especially, the two are linked by a vertical line, giving the whole the appearance of a bright red hourglass. Gelada communities are based on harems of closely related females and associated groups of bachelor males. The harem is led not by a male but by a dominant female suckling young. Geladas rarely venture into trees, spending most of their day within a small area, shuffling about and digging up grass shoots and roots and rhizomes. They are found only in the Ethiopian highlands, mainly on high grassy plateaus in the area around and eastward of the Blue Nile gorges; they rarely venture far from the edges of escarpments, where they retreat to if alarmed and where they sleep at night.

The mangabeys are also closely related to the drill and baboons. There are eight African species, six members of the genus *Cercocebus* (the drill mangabeys) and two of the genus *Lophocebus*

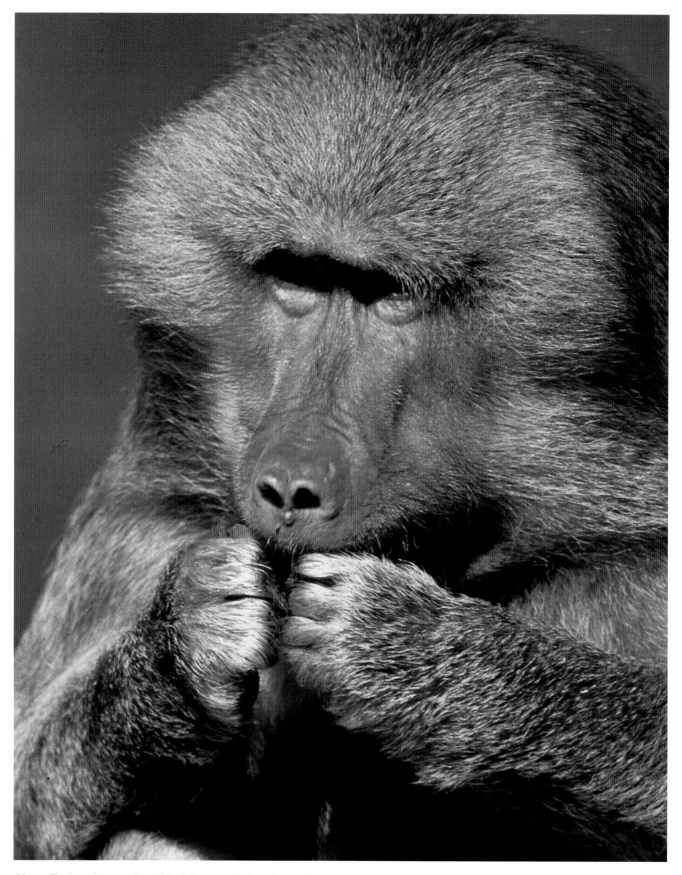

Above: The hamadryas, smallest of the baboon species, has a bare, red-skinned face. The male, as here, has a silver-grey cape of fur over the shoulders; the female's coat is brown.

(the baboon mangabeys), and all live in tropical rainforests. Although their connection with baboons is not obvious in their appearance, it is clearly evident in their behaviour: their vocal and postural repertoires are similar, they too spend much time on their haunches, and their social organization and mating patterns have much in common with their larger cousins.

The drill mangabeys are also known as "eyelid monkeys" owing to the high visibility of their white eyelids. Typical is the Tana mangabey (*Cercocebus galeritus*), which is found only in forests along the floodplain of the Tana river in south-eastern Kenya. The main colour of its rather shaggy coat is grizzled, pale yellowish brown, with paler fur on the temples, chest and underparts and an off-white tip to the tufted tail. The hands and feet are dark brown. The eyelids stand out in the black face. During the dry season it is semi-terrestrial and its diet includes a proportion of insects, lizards and frogs. Its main diet, however, consists of fruits, of which figs are most important. Closely related, and sometimes classified as a subspecies of the Tana, the Sanje mangabey (*C. sanjei*) is confined to valley forests on the wet eastern side of the Uzungwa mountains in south-central Tanzania. Its stand-up crown fur, back and sides, limbs and tail are a grizzled ash grey, with dark grey hands and feet; its belly and chest are pale orange; the buttocks are bluish grey with chevron-shaped pink callouses. Fruits and foliage make up most of its diet. Both these monkeys are in danger of extinction owing mainly to human encroachment on and development of their already restricted ranges. Other drill mangabeys include the olive-grey agile mangabey (*C. agilis*), found mainly in Zaïre in regions north of the Congo river; the red-capped mangabey (*C. torquatus*), a slate-grey monkey with white underparts and a russet crown, found from the Cross river in south-eastern Nigeria eastwards to the Oubangui river; and the golden-bellied mangabey (*C. chrysogaster*), which has a violet-coloured rump, a grizzled dark olive-brown crown, back and outer limbs, pale underparts except for an orange lower belly, and lives south of the Congo river in Zaïre.

The two baboon mangabeys are more wholly arboreal than the drill mangabeys; they are confined mainly to rainforest, especially swamp forest. The grey-cheeked mangabey (*Lophocebus albigena*) includes several different races found, variously, from the Cross

river eastwards (north of the Congo river) to Uganda. All the races have a dark brown coat, a long tail, stand-up crown fur, and a black face. The striking shoulder cape of long hair is pale but varies in shade between races. The black mangabey (*L. aterrimus*) is black or charcoal throughout; it has a pointed head crest and upswept cheek whiskers. It is found in lowland swamp forests south of the Congo river in central Zaïre. Both these baboon mangabeys live on a variety of fruit and nuts—breadfruit, dates, oil-palm, false nutmeg—and also extract insects from bark and rotten wood.

The guenons consist of 23 related species, mostly of the genus *Cercopithecus*. Small to medium-sized—few weigh more than 20lb (9kg)—they are graceful, long-tailed monkeys with soft coats of varying colours, often grizzled on backs and limbs. Some species have striking "moustaches", sideburns, nose-spots, or bright colour markings on various parts of the body. The guenons are essentially arboreal and only rarely descend to the ground. Each species mixes amicably with other species of guenons as well as with mangabeys and colobus monkeys in its range, and each has an extensive and unique repertoire of calls. They eat a variety of plant species,

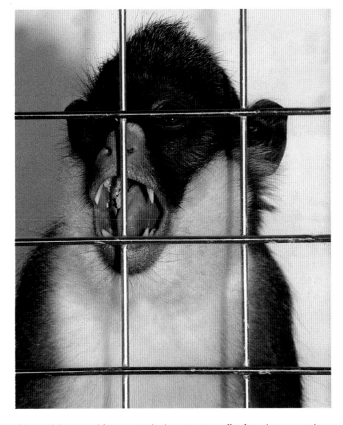

Above: Like many African animals the primates suffer from human predation. This spot-nosed guenon has been captured for sale.

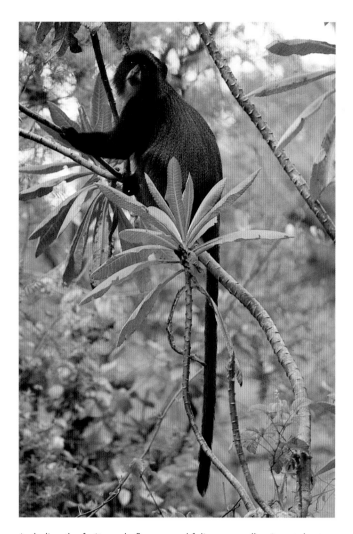

A monkey that shares evergreen forest habitats with, and associates with, the red-tailed guenon over large parts of its range is the similar-sized gentle monkey (*C. mitis*), which is subject to some taxonomic confusion: no fewer than 25 subspecies have been proposed, many of them with radically different basic coat colours and markings. These include the blue monkeys (which range from the eastern Congo basin to western Kenya and north-western Tanzania); the mitis monkeys (widely scattered relict populations in central Africa); the white-throated races (eastern Congo basin; also riverine forests from Somalia to southern Mozambique); and the silver monkeys (mainly in the western arm of the Rift Valley, especially the Lake Kivu region).

The moustached guenon (*C. cephus*) is so-called after the broad white chevron on its upper lip; above the chevron and around the eyes the face is light blue; in overall appearance and coat colour it resembles the red-tailed guenon. It is the most abundant monkey in Gabon and the lower Congo and, where their ranges overlap, it associates peaceably with several other guenon species. The red-eared guenon (*C. erythrotis*) is similar but lacks the white chevron; it is confined to small areas of south-eastern Nigeria, western Cameroon and the island of Bioko and is an endangered species.

A group of guenons that live outside the rainforest regions are the so-called savanna monkeys, which inhabit dry and moist savanna, woodland-grassland mosaics, dry montane forests, and alpine moorlands up to 14,000ft (4,250m). All are small, typically weighing in the range of 9-20lb (4-9kg). Several of them have overlapping ranges, and because they are mutually fertile and frequently crossbreed, some taxonomists treat them as races or subspecies of a single species. The vervet (*C. pygerythrus*) has the largest range of any African monkey, extending from southern Ethiopia and Somalia to south-eastern South Africa. It has a black face enclosed by whitish forehead and side whiskers; the hands and feet are black; the general coat colour varies from region to region (there are several races), greyish or olive green in the south, brownish grey in the north. In the extreme north of its range it hybridizes with the Balé guenon (*C. djamdjamendis*), a native of Balé Mountain National Park and neighbouring plateau areas in the south-eastern highlands of Ethiopia, whose thick, long coat is a grizzled, yellowish deep brown

including the fruit, seeds, flowers and foliage, as well as invertebrates. They live mainly in tropical rainforest, although some species are also found in dense riverine forests. One of the species with the most extensive range is the red-tailed guenon (*Cercopithecus ascanius*), which may weigh anything from 4 to 12lb (1.8-5.5kg), and which is also known as the black-cheeked white-nosed monkey. It does indeed have a deep orange-red tail from half way to the tip; also white cheek-whiskers with a black stripe, and a white heart-shaped nose spot on an otherwise dark face. It has a mainly dark brown coat with a rufous tinge on its upper parts and white or cream underparts. It is found throughout the tropical forests of Zaïre, northwards into the Central African Republic, east into western Uganda and western Kenya, and southwards into the northern margins of Angola and Zambia. The rather similar lesser spot-nosed guenon (*C. petaurista*), found in the West Africa lowland forests from Senegal to Togo, also has a white nose spot and white cheek fur with a black stripe below the ear, and white underside to the tail.

on the crown and torso, grey on the legs, and off-white on the underparts; the face is black, the chin and cheek ruffs white. This species' northern range overlaps with that of the grevet (*C. aethiops*), with which it also interbreeds. This guenon has grizzled, rich brown or olive brown fur on crown and torso, greyish lower limbs and tail, a black face with long-furred white sideburns, and white feet. It has two races: one occurs from southern Sudan eastwards to Eritrea; the other (which hybridizes with the Balé race) in the Ethiopian highlands west of the Rift.

The savanna guenon with the second largest range is the tantalus monkey (*C. tantalus*), whose eastern race, which hybridizes with the vervet in the area to the north of Lake Victoria, extends from Uganda westwards to the Oubangui river; the western race occurs from the Oubangui westwards through Cameroon and Nigeria to Ghana; in the north its range extends almost as far as Lake Chad and the most northerly reach of the Niger valley. It is the largest of the savanna guenons, with a greenish gold back, sides, upper limbs and tail and white undersides; the face is black. Finally, the long-legged callithrix monkey (*C. sabaeus*), whose range extends from Ghana to north-western Senegal, is found in a wide range of habitats that include mangrove swamps in the far west, rainforest margins in the centre, and very dry woodlands in the Sahel regions of the north. The coat is golden green on the crown, back, sides and upper parts of the limbs. The hands and feet are pale grey and the undersides are white; the cheek ruffs are yellowish white, the face is black, and the end of the tail is pale orange.

The colobus monkeys take their common name from the Greek *colobus*, which means mutilated or crippled, and refers to the fact that monkeys of the Colobidae family have no thumb. They are wholly arboreal, and their specialized stomachs and digestive systems enable them to live almost wholly on leaves and unripe fruit, many of which would be toxic to other monkey species. The absence of a thumb partly explains their usual method of feeding: they use their fingers and palms not to pick leaves or fruit but to hook around tree branches, which are pulled to the mouth so that the food can be bitten directly off the tree. There is great confusion in the taxonomy of this family, but three genera are widely recognised: *Procolobus*, *Piliocolobus* and *Colobus*.

The olive colobus (*Procolobus verus*), also known as Van Beneden's colobus, is the smallest in the family, rarely weighing more than 10lb (4.5kg). Its coat colour is greenish brown or olive on the back with dull grey undersides. The small head has a short crest and there are two grey patches on the forehead. The species lives mainly in swamp and palm forests in a series of separate populations stretching from southern Sierra Leone in the west to the Cross river on Nigeria's south-eastern border.

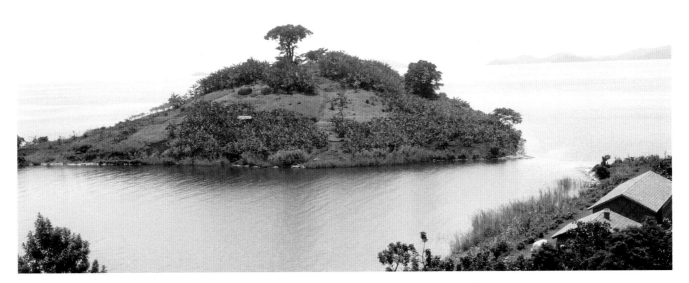

Above Left: There are more than 20 species of guenon in Africa, including several well-known species of the genus *Cercopithecus*. They have long tails, glossy coats in a variety of colours, and are brilliant arboreal athletes.

Above: A view of Lake Kivu, in the western rift, from the densely forested eastern shore. Guenons such as silver monkeys are found in this region.

The name red colobus covers no fewer than eight species (or, according to some experts, subspecies) of the genus *Piliocolobus* whose collective range extends from Senegal in the west to Zanzibar in the east, mainly in equatorial forests close to permanent water. They are medium-sized monkeys, adult males weighing in the range 20-29lb (9-13kg) All have small heads on longish, rather pot-bellied bodies, and have long limbs (the legs longer than the arms). All have black or dark grey faces, although some have a pink nose and lips. Their fur colours are mostly various combinations of red, black, white, brown and grey. The western red colobus (*Piliocolobus badius*), found in West Africa from Senegal to Ghana, has a pink, turned-up nose, pink lips and eye rings, red whiskers, black or charcoal crest, back, tail and upper limbs, and bright red or orange underparts and lower limbs. Pennant's or eastern red colobus (*P. pennantii*) is found in the Niger delta, on Bioko island, and in two communities near the west bank of the Congo between Brazzaville in the south and the confluence with the Oubangui in the north. Its coat is dark reddish grey above and lighter red on underparts and legs; it has a white neck ruff. It is regarded as an endangered species. The central African red colobus (*P. ousteleti*) has by far the most extensive range, from west of the Oubangui river eastwards (always north of the Congo river) into Uganda and western Kenya and Tanzania. Local populations vary in coat colours and markings; most have a red crest or cap, reddish torso with lighter underparts, and black hands and feet; those living in mountains areas often have a heavy shoulder cape. The Tana river red colobus (*P. rufomitratus*), a small monkey with a red cap, dull brown body, paler, greyish limbs and whitish undersides, occupies a tiny habitat near the deltas of the Tana river in south-eastern Kenya. A few years ago it was reported to be highly endangered and it may now be extinct—a victim of

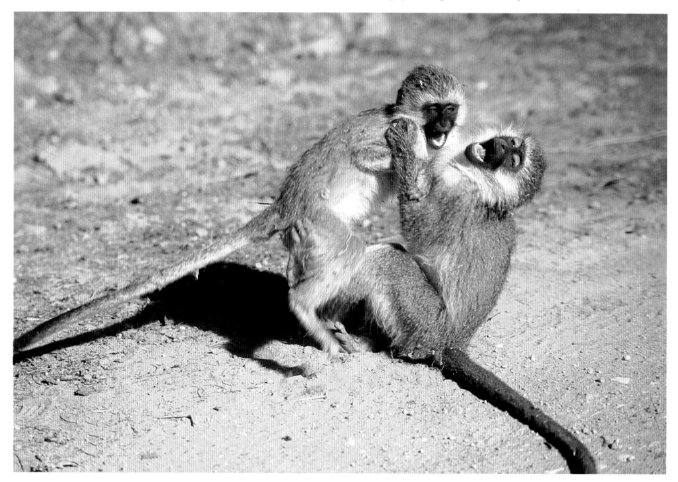

Above: These two juvenile grivets are play-fighting in southern Somalia. Adult grivets develop luxuriant side whiskers.

Above Right: The vervet, close kin to the grivet, has similar colours of coat and face but has a much more extensive range.

Above Far Right: The guereza, or eastern black-and-white colobus, is abundant in the montane forests of the East African highlands, living arboreally in troops of eight to a dozen led by an adult male.

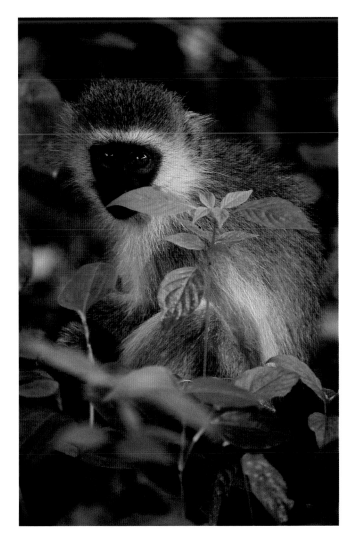

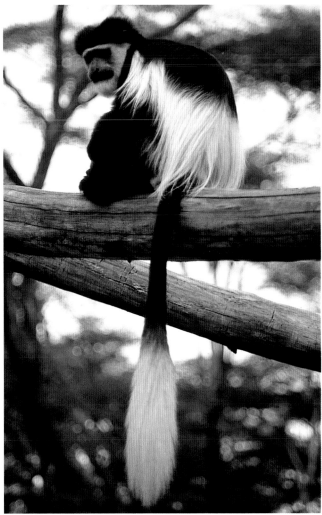

river-damming and irrigation schemes together with forest clearance. Finally, the Zanzibar red colobus (*P. kirkii*) has a long, rather wispy-haired coat, black on the upper back, shoulders and outer arms, red on the lower back and part of tail, and greyish white on the underparts, legs and inner arms; the black face has pink lips and nose. This species, found only in small communities in southern and eastern parts of Zanzibar, is also in extreme danger of extinction.

The five pied colobus species belong to the genus *Colobus*. Their collective name refers to the fact that their coat colours are various mixtures of black and white—with the exception of one species that is wholly black. They are found in tropical and subtropical forests (including some montane forests) across the continent, from the Atlantic to the Indian Ocean. Social groups are particularly vocal in their tree-top threat displays, jumping about, shaking branches, and giving vent to raucous croaking calls. The black colobus (*C. satanus*), which is wholly black and without shoulder cape, lives in high-canopy forests from south-western

Cameroon eastwards to the Congo river, and also on Bioko island. It is an endangered species. The Angola pied colobus (*C. angolensis*) has a very large main range extending from the lower Congo basin to the Ruwenzori mountains in the Western Rift, and smaller ranges dotted about the coastal forests of Kenya and Tanzania. It is black-bodied except for a white ruff and very long white "epaulettes" that hang down the arms from the shoulders. Finally, the Guereza colobus (*C. guereza*) has two distinct forms: a lowland race and an eastern highland race. Both forms have black cap, upper back and limbs, with longer white fur on the flanks and rump, and black face with white cheeks and throat. The lowland race is found in much of the Congo valley except for the Lualaba section and also in Uganda and western Kenya; its mainly black tail has thicker, pale brown fur towards the tip. The highland race (often classified as a subspecies, *C. g. abyssinicus*) occurs mainly in the Ethiopian highlands. Its coat is heavier and longer than that of the lowland race, and its tail is white and bushy throughout most of its length.

GREAT APES

The apes and humans are closely related members of a group called the hominids. They all have compact, tail-less bodies, large heads and brains, a hairless, flat face, and small nose, and their genetic make-up is almost identical. There are three African ape species, the chimpanzee, bonobo and gorilla (a fourth, the orangutan, is native to Borneo and Sumatra). Apes, which belong to the family Pongidae, have wide mouths, broad chests, long arms and relatively short legs, and long hands with opposable thumbs and feet with opposable great toes: both hands and feet are capable of grasping objects. Apes commonly walk or run on all fours, using the whole of the feet and the knuckles of the hands, but they can also walk upright, on the feet only; all are capable climbers.

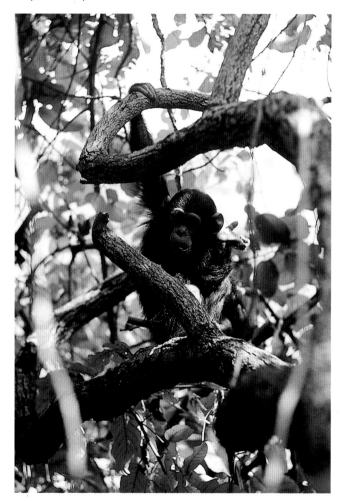

Above: Even young chimpanzees may be remarkably self-sufficient. This juvenile is content to pass the time lazing in a tree in western Tanzania.

Right: A veteran alpha male chimpanzee. He is at the head of a complex social hierarchy and may be involved in violent battles in defence of his territory and harem of females.

The chimpanzee (*Pan troglodytes*) is a robustly built ape, the adult male as much as 5ft 10in (178cm) tall when standing upright and weighing up to 120lb (55kg). Its wide mouth is set well below the nostrils; its teeth are larger than man's, and the adult male has big canines. The coat is usually black or charcoal, but some individuals have dark brown or reddish brown fur. The skin is of varying colours from black or slate grey to sandy yellow; in some races the mouth, nose, brow ridge and ears are a light shade, the rest of the face dark. The adult female's sexual skin becomes swollen and bright pink when she is in œstrus.

Chimpanzees live mainly in rainforests—including mixed montane forests up to about 6,000ft (1,825m)—and gallery forests merging with woodland savanna. They have three main ranges: the western race is found mainly in Sierra Leone and Guinea; the central African race from the Cross river (Nigeria) to the Oubangui river region north of the Congo (Zaïre); and the eastern race from the Oubangui to Uganda and north-western Tanzania. Chimpanzees are omnivorous and their diet varies considerably from region to region and from season to season. Fruit, such as figs, forms about half their diet; leaves, stems and bark are also eaten along with animal foods such as termites, birds eggs and small mammals.

Chimpanzees live in communities of anything from 15 to 120 individuals in large, fiercely defended territories. Generally, however, these communities consist of small parties—some all-male, some single mothers with offspring, some mixed groups; and within such groups, individuals may wander alone in search of food. At other times, a whole community may converge on, say, a grove of trees with ripening fruit. Within a community dominance structures exist, with competition between those seeking to become alpha males. Males remain in their community for most or all their lives; they are thus related and they combine to defend their territory, and its females and young, against incursions by their neighbours. On the other hand, adolescent females of about ten years of age emigrate and are eventually accepted into other communities, usually at a time when they come into œstrus. Both sexes have a repertoire of at least 30 calls they use to communicate such things as emotional mood, dominance, danger, sexual arousal, and the discovery of a source of food.

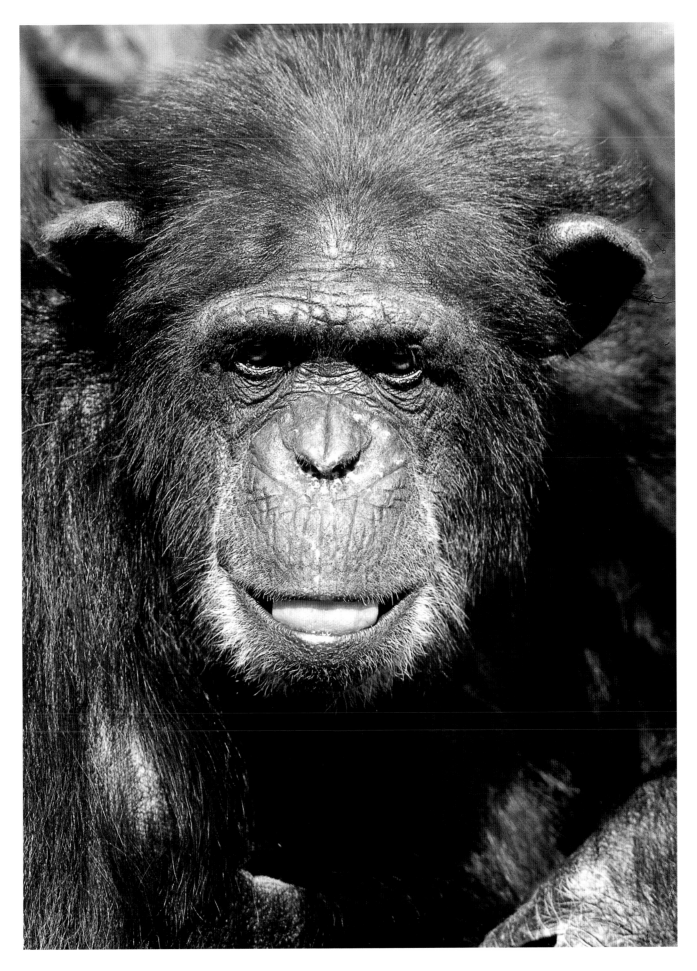

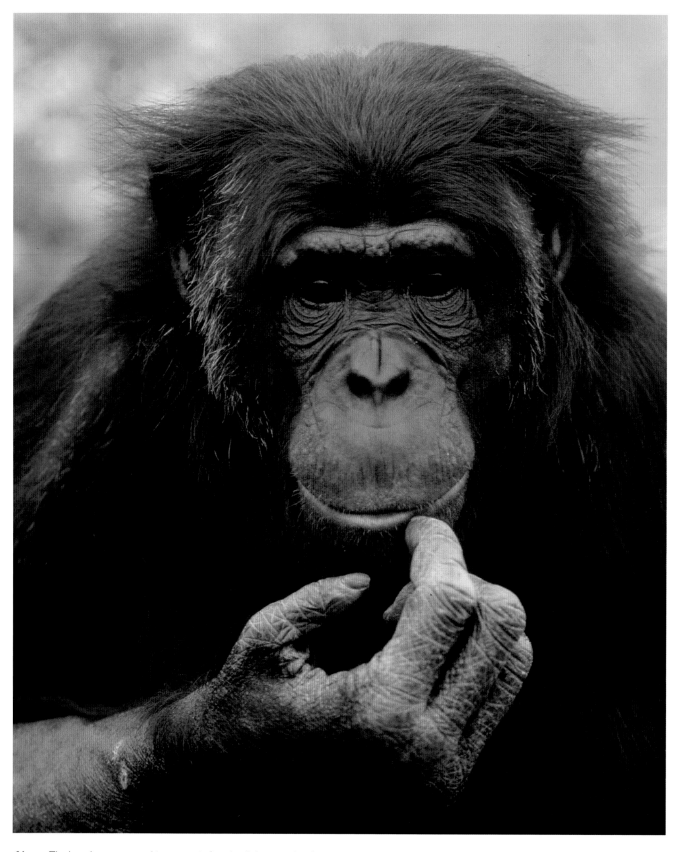

Above: The bonobo, or pygmy chimpanzee, is found only in a restricted area of rainforest south of the Congo river in Zaïre.

Right: A captive female bonobo. The species is about the same height as the chimpanzee but of lighter build.

Far Right: A male western lowland gorilla, western Zaïre. This subspecies is the smallest race of gorilla but the most numerous.

The bonobo (*P. paniscus*) is sometimes called the pygmy chimpanzee: it is a close cousin, and the male can be just as tall as the chimpanzee, but it is of more slender build, rarely weighing more than 85lb (39kg), and with longer legs. The face is completely black, the nostrils are somewhat more pronounced, and there is a smaller gap between nose and mouth. The bonobo inhabits a mosaic of lowland rainforests and swamp forests between the Congo river in the north, the Lualaba river in the east and the Kasai river in the west, and especially the region between Kisangani in the east and Mbandaka in the west. More arboreal than the chimpanzee, the bonobo can be highly acrobatic in the tree canopy. Its diet includes fruit, seeds and other parts of plants as well as fungi, invertebrates, honey and birds' eggs. The basic social unit among bonobos is the adult female with offspring, including sub-adult sons, and communities consist of aggregations of such groups together with smaller all-male groups; there is much less male aggression shown towards females than in chimpanzee communities.

The gorilla (*Gorilla gorilla*) is a massive, barrel-chested, pot-bellied ape with a naked black face and chest, and heavily muscled arms and legs; the hands and feet are broad, with thick, stubby fingers and toes. The head is large, the male's topped by a dome of muscle. The eyes are deep-set under a single prominent brow bar; the large nostrils face upwards; the powerful jaws have large teeth, the adult male's canines being especially impressive. The coat is black or charcoal, but the mature adult males have a broad, silvery grey "saddle" on the back (whence the term "silverback" for dominant males). The largest males are up to six feet (1.8m) tall when standing upright and weigh up to 470lb (215kg).

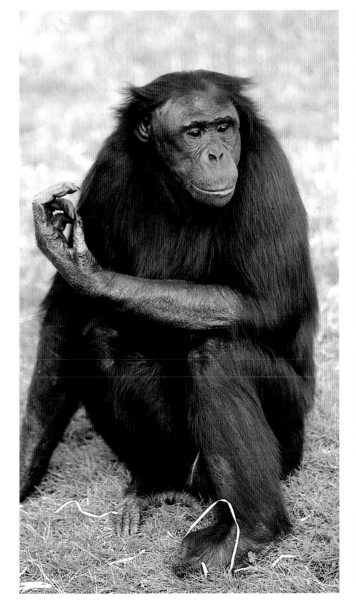

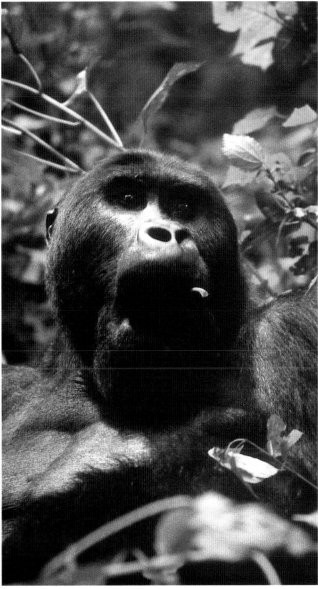

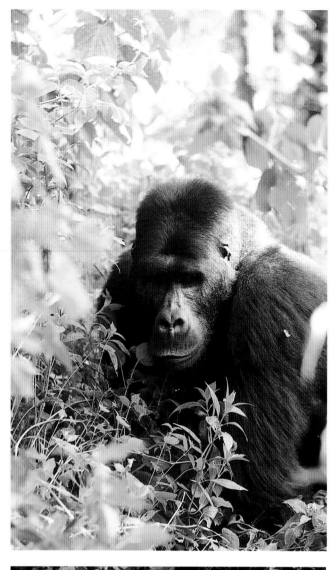

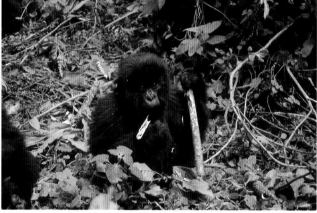

Top: A male eastern lowland gorilla in lush undergrowth on the edge of a forest in south-western Uganda.

Above: A juvenile mountain gorilla chewing a dry stick in montane forest in the Virunga range, Rwanda.

Right: A juvenile mountain gorilla in Bwindi forest, Uganda. Both the hair and skin of all gorilla species are black.

There are three subspecies of gorilla living in quite separate regions: the western lowland gorilla (*G. g. gorilla*), the eastern lowland gorilla (*G. g. graueri*) and the mountain gorilla (*G. g. beringei*). The western lowland race is both the smallest and by far the most numerous: some 35,000 or more inhabit mixed lowland tropical forest from the Cross river (Nigeria) in the west almost to the Oubangui river in the east and with discontinuous pockets of communities southwards through Gabon almost to the Congo estuary. The eastern lowland race exists in isolated pockets of rainforest in a region bounded by the Lualaba river (eastern Zaïre) in the west, the south-western corner of Uganda in the north, and Lake Tanganyika in the south, taking in escarpments of the western arm of the Rift Valley. There are perhaps 4,000 to 6,000 of this race. The mountain gorilla, with longer, thicker fur than the others, lives at altitudes of 9,000 to 11,000ft (2,750 to 3,350m) in the cloud-forested slopes of the volcanic Virunga range on the Zaïre/Rwanda border north-east of Lake Kivu. This race is on the very cusp of extinction: fewer than 350 survive today. The eastern lowland race is officially listed as endangered.

Gorillas live in small, non-territorial harems averaging five to ten mature females presided over by a single silverback. Offspring (both male and female) born into the harem leave it when they reach maturity. Such a female may join another harem; on the other hand she may join up with a solitary adult male. Such a pair, forming a powerful bond, represents the core of what in time will become a harem. On the other hand, any attempt by a mature male to abduct a harem female in œstrus will be furiously resisted by the harem's silverback.

Gorillas eat mainly a range of herb, shrub and vine leaves and also invertebrates such as termites (whose mounds they break open with powerful blows of their hands). The mountain race is particularly partial to vines and wild celery. The western lowland race eats more fruits than the others, as well as wild ginger. Although their diet requires fairly intensive foraging, gorillas spend long periods of the day resting and sunning. They sleep in nests built in trees or on the ground.

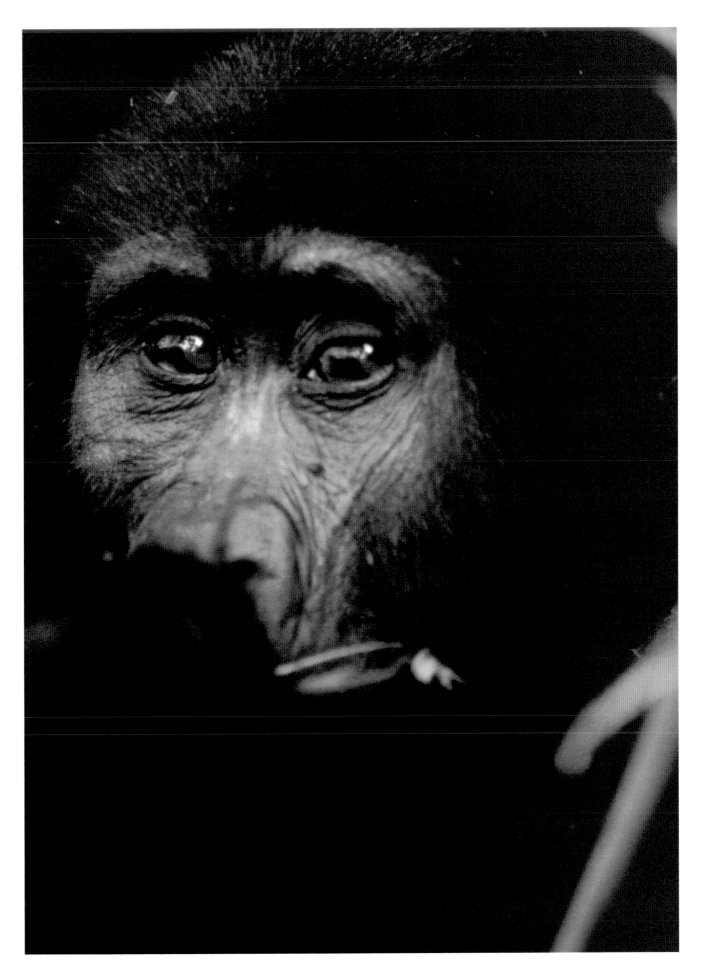

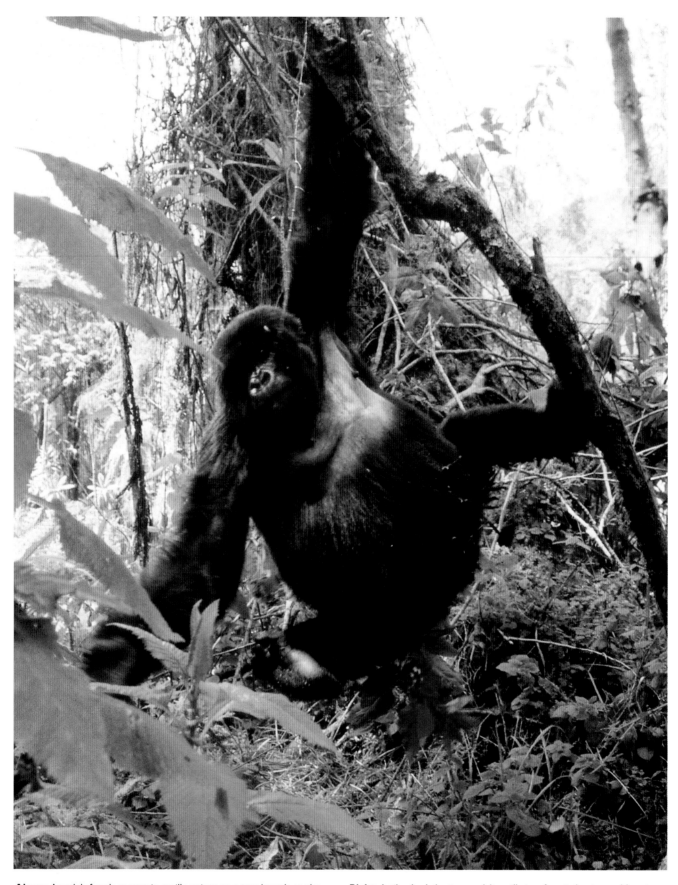

Above: An adult female mountain gorilla swings on a tree branch on the slopes of the Virunga range, Rwanda. Like adult males and females of all gorilla species, she is pot-bellied.

Right: A silverback (mature male) gorilla in a forest clearing on Mount Visoke, Rwanda. Mountain gorillas have thicker and longer hair than the lowland species.

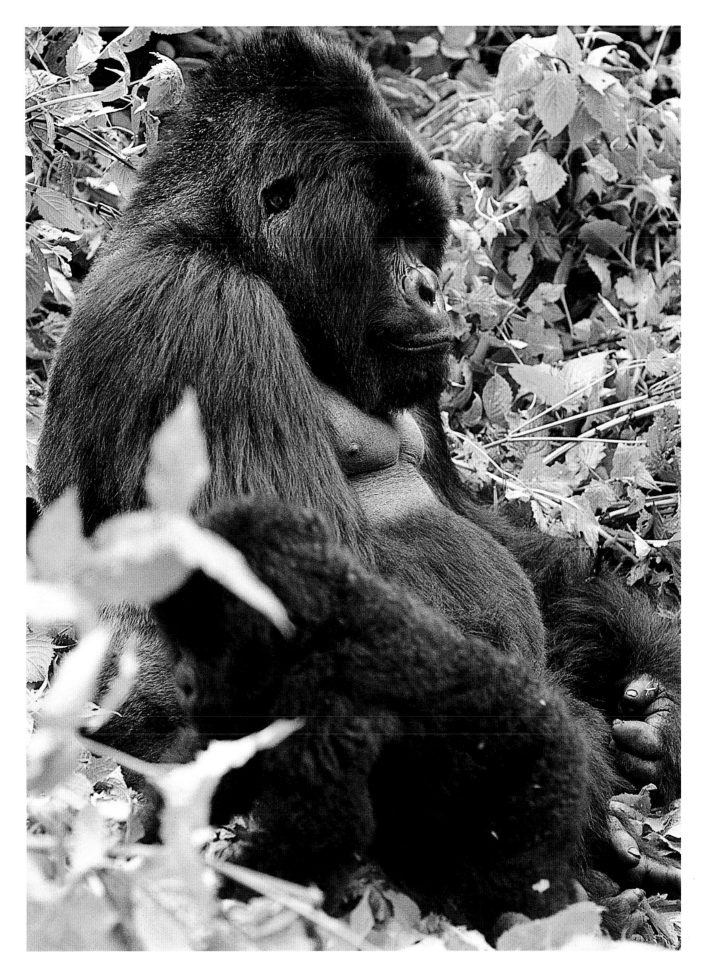

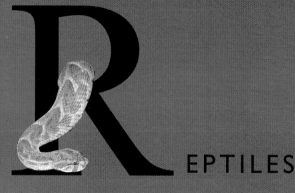R EPTILES

In one sense, reptiles are survivors of a bygone age: it is from them that all birds and mammals evolved, and the ancestors of many modern reptiles roamed the Earth with dinosaurs more than 100 million years ago. Unlike mammals, reptiles do not possess internal mechanisms to control their blood temperature, and much of their daily life is concerned with keeping their temperature at optimum levels—by moving in or out of shade, for instance, or by slipping in or out of water (many reptiles are fully or semi-aquatic). Reptiles' skin is covered by water-retentive scales or plates, which helps them deal with problems of dehydration in some of their dryer habitats. Most reptiles lay eggs, but they do not feed, nor can they suckle, the hatched young. We deal here mainly with crocodiles, snakes and a few other reptiles.

Right: The Nile crocodile, largest of the three African species, is found in rivers, lakes and swamps in much of the sub-Sahara continent except for South Africa.

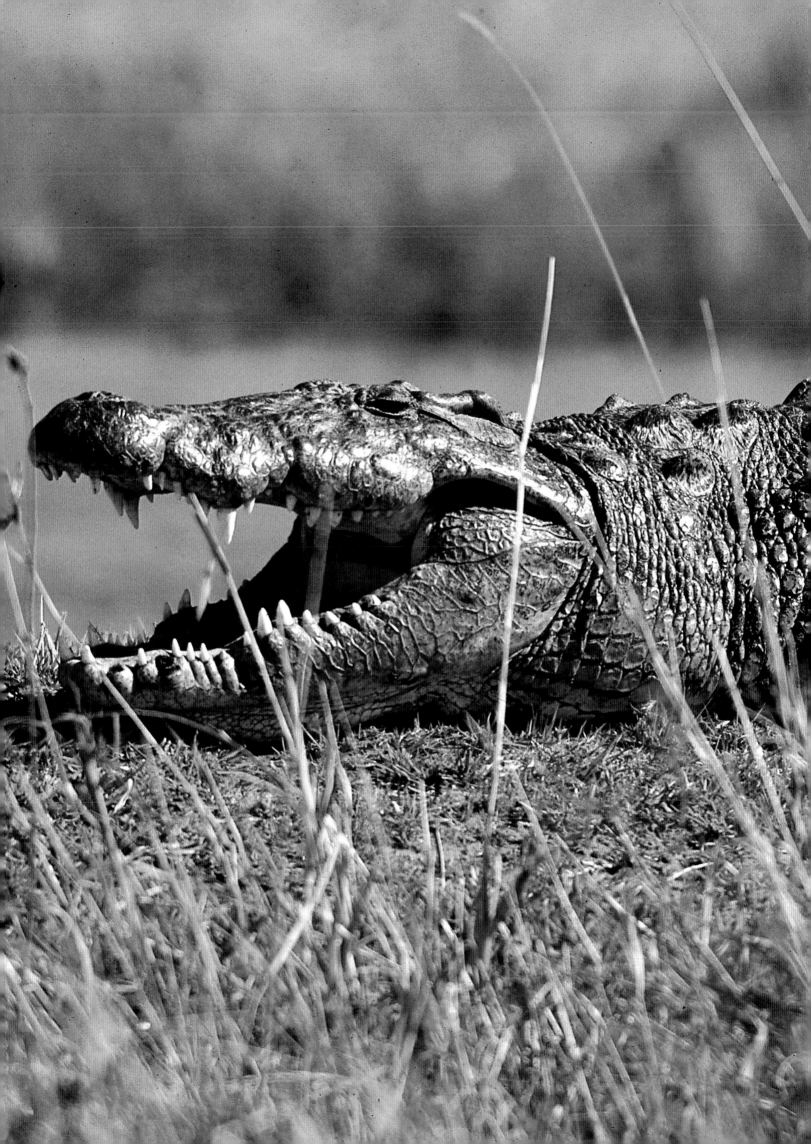

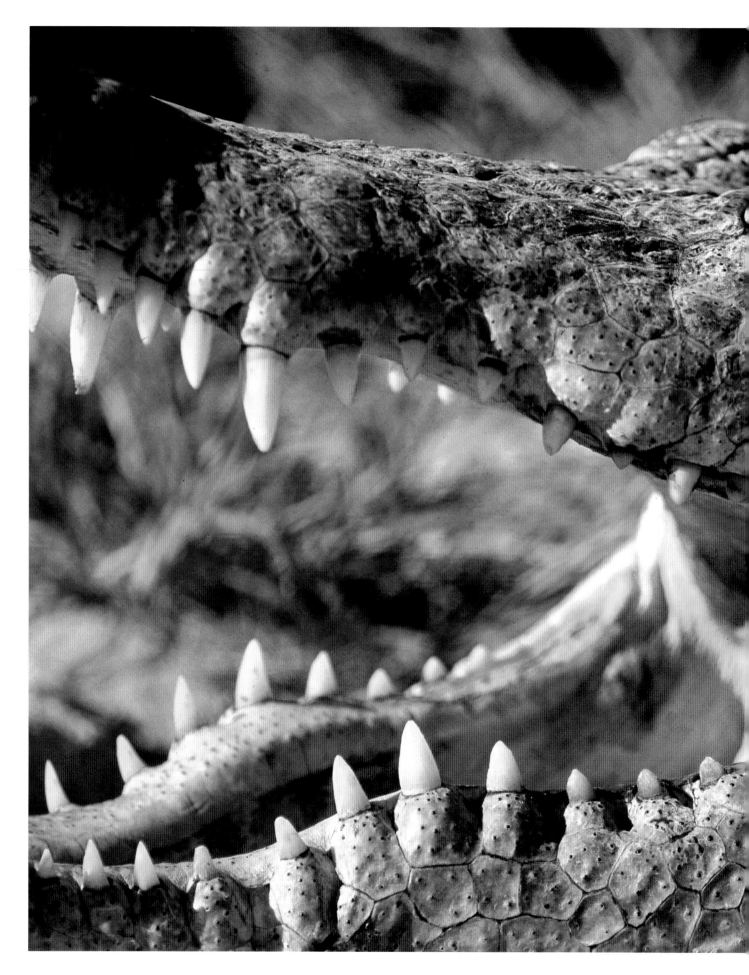

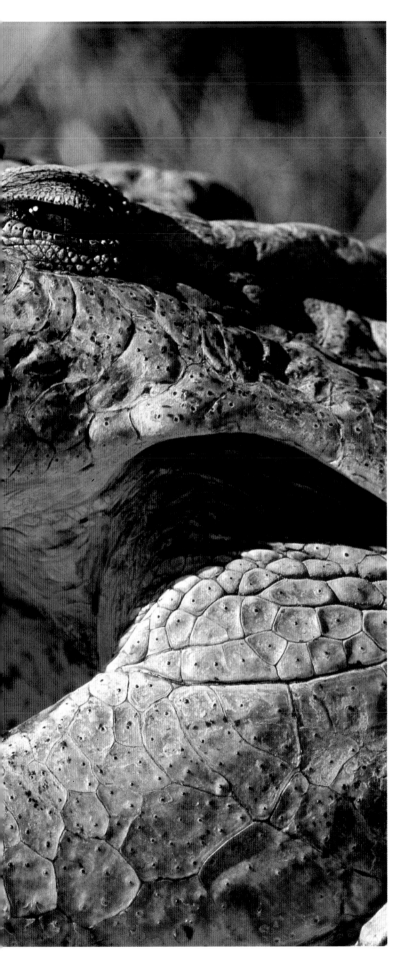

CROCODILES

Looking rather like giant lizards, crocodiles have thick, plated skin, hard and ridged on the back and shoulders but softer on the belly. Their long, wide-opening jaws have formidable conical teeth. They have short legs, their feet have webbed toes ending in claws, and their long, powerful tails propel them at speed in water.

The Nile crocodile (*Crocodylus niloticus*) is the largest of the three African species, some individuals attaining a length of more than 20ft (6m) and weighing as much as 2,200lb (1,000kg). Its body is covered in horny plates, notably six large, ridged plates behind the head; the long tail has two ridges along most of its length. It is found in rivers and lakes and also in coastal estuaries and mangrove swamps. Its range runs from Senegal in the west to Ethiopia in the east, then southward throughout central Africa as far as northern Botswana and, in the east, northern KwaZulu-Natal. They particularly favour rivers with sandbars, where they can bask undisturbed when not on the lookout for food. The crocodile mates in water. The female lays about 45 hard-shelled eggs in a waterside hole she has dug out with her hind legs, then covers the eggs with soil or sand, guarding the site until the eggs hatch. (Many eggs are lost through predation by Nile monitors and water mongooses.) She then gathers the young into her mouth and introduces them into their aquatic environment. The young will remain together as a group for three or four months.

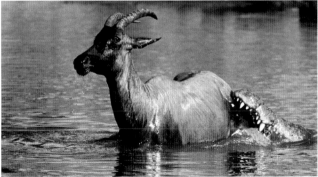

Above: A Nile crocodile attacks a jimela-race Topi fording a river in Kenya. Crocodiles take a huge toll of migrating antelopes in the rivers of the East African savannas.

Left: Its huge jaws and conical teeth make the Nile crocodile a formidable predator in water and on land.

Overleaf: Captive crocodiles bred for leather and meat at a farm near the Victoria Falls, Zimbabwe.

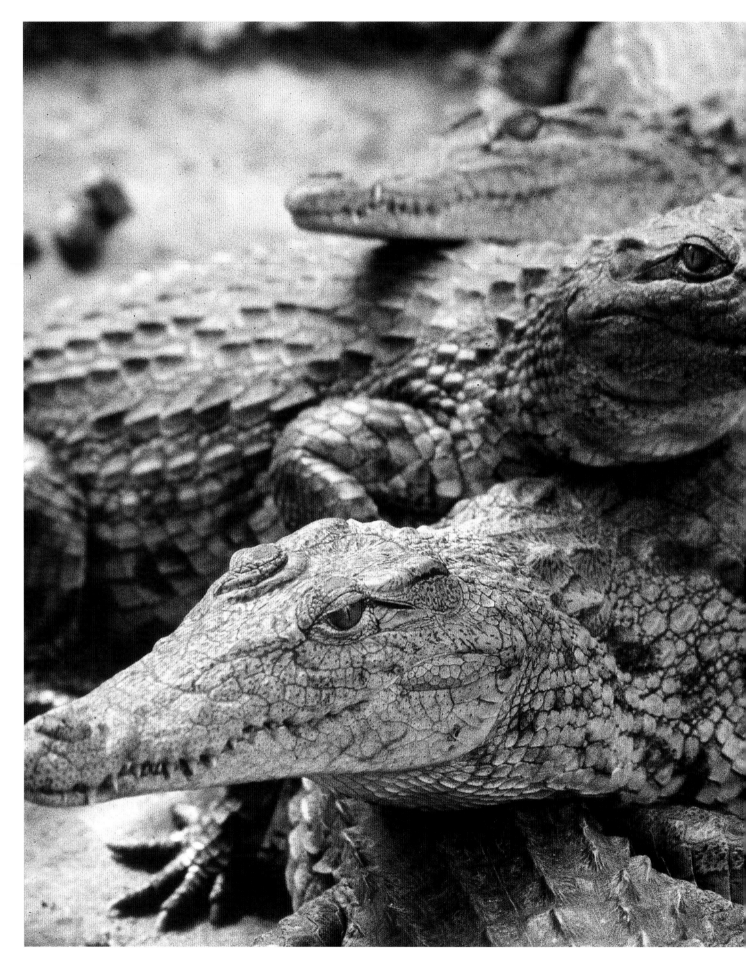

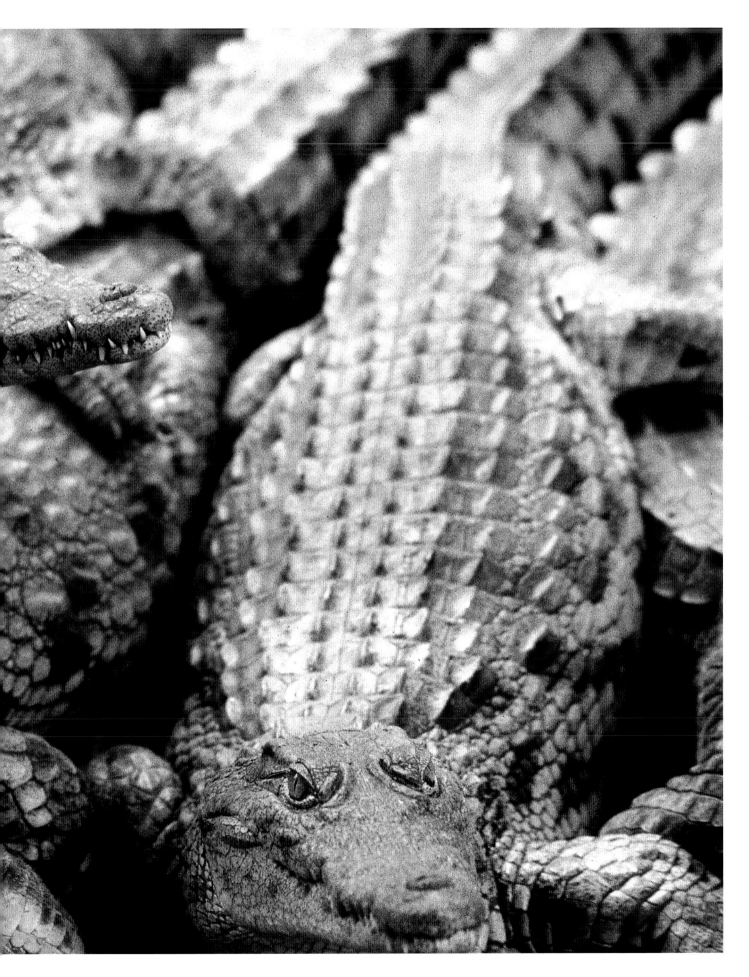

The juvenile crocodile feeds mainly on small mammals, fish, birds, terrapins and frogs. It reaches maturity at about 14 years, by which time it preys on larger game, ambushing ungulates coming to the waterside to drink. It approaches its victim underwater, or gliding like a log just below the surface. Even if its victim sees it as it emerges from the water, the crocodile's remarkable speed ashore over a short distance often enables it to make a kill. The Nile crocodile takes a fearful toll of the hordes of wildebeest which are forced to cross rivers on the Serengeti and Masai Mara on their annual migrations. Although hunted relentlessly for its skin, and eliminated from large parts of its natural range, it is still abundant in many regions. Among the best places for tourists to see it are the Ewaso N'giro river in Kenya's Samburu National Reserve; the Kazinga Channel linking lakes Edward and George in Ruwenzori National Park (Uganda); and the Okavango Delta in Botswana.

The long-snouted crocodile (*C. cataphractus*), also known as the slender-snouted crocodile, is well-named: its snout is much less massive than the Nile species and is about three times as long as it is broad. It is well suited to the species' eating habits: it seeks out fish hiding in waterside tree roots and other protected sites, and it also feeds on water snakes, crabs, shrimps and frogs. Ther species attains a maximum length of about 13ft (4m). It is found in fresh-water rivers, streams and lakes and also in coastal estuaries and lagoons from Senegal eastwards to the Central African Republic and southward to Gabon, Zaïre, and western Tanzania. More elusive than the Nile crocodile, it is also becoming rarer as hunters take an ever-increasing toll (it is valued for food as well as for its skin).

The African dwarf crocodile (*Osteolaemnus tetraspis*), which rarely exceeds six feet (1.8m) in length, has a short, wide snout. By far the shyest (and least studied) of the African crocodiles, it occurs in regions of rainforest and swamp forest from Senegal eastwards to the Zaïre-Uganda border, and southwards through much of the Congo basin to northern Angola. Although found in small streams and swamps, the dwarf crocodile is less aquatic than the other African species, and hunts for food (small mammals and reptiles) mainly at night on the forest floor.

LIZARDS & SNAKES

One of the commonest lizards of tropical and East Africa, the red-headed or common agama (*Agama agama*) has a somewhat spiky appearance owing to its ridged scales; it has a triangular head, a long tail, round eyes, and may be up to 15in (38cm) long. It is somewhat chameleon-like in its coloration. During the day a dominant male's body and limbs are blue and its head and tail are red; but at night it changes to a brownish grey colour overall—the same as the permanent colour of the female and subordinate male. Its habitat is rocky outcrops, such as the kopjes on the Tanzanian savanna, cliffs, and savanna scrublands, but it is also found on farms and in domestic buildings. At night it roosts communally in rock crevasses. Its range is from Senegal in the west to Ethiopia in the east, and southward through central Africa through the western arm of the Rift Valley and Zaïre to Zambia and northern Angola. A dominant male will mate with anything up to ten females, each of which lay up to 12 soft-shelled eggs in a hole in the ground, usually after heavy rain has led to an abundance of insects. The agama a fast runner (sometimes on only its back feet), and feeds mainly on termites, beetles and other invertebrates. There are over 30 African species of agama, some larger than the red-headed, and in many the head and/or tail colours of dominant males are different from those of the body.

Chameleons are a group of somewhat torpid, largely arboreal lizards, more than 100 species of which live in Africa. The one thing about chameleons that is not slow is the speed with which they shoot out their immensely long telescopic tongues to snatch insects. Their long prehensile tails are often employed as an extra limb for grasping branches or twigs. A remarkable physiological feature of the chameleon concerns its eyes, which are able to move completely independently of each other, enabling the animal to look out for prey (or predators) in two different directions at once. Many chameleons have a basic colour of green or brown, some-times plain, sometimes spotted, but they are able to produce temporarily other colours or shades to enable them to blend in with their surroundings; more vivid colours may appear if the chameleon is excited. The males of some species, such as Jackson's chameleon (*Chamaeleo jacksonii*), are horned; this species has three horns, two projecting from its forehead, the other from its snout.

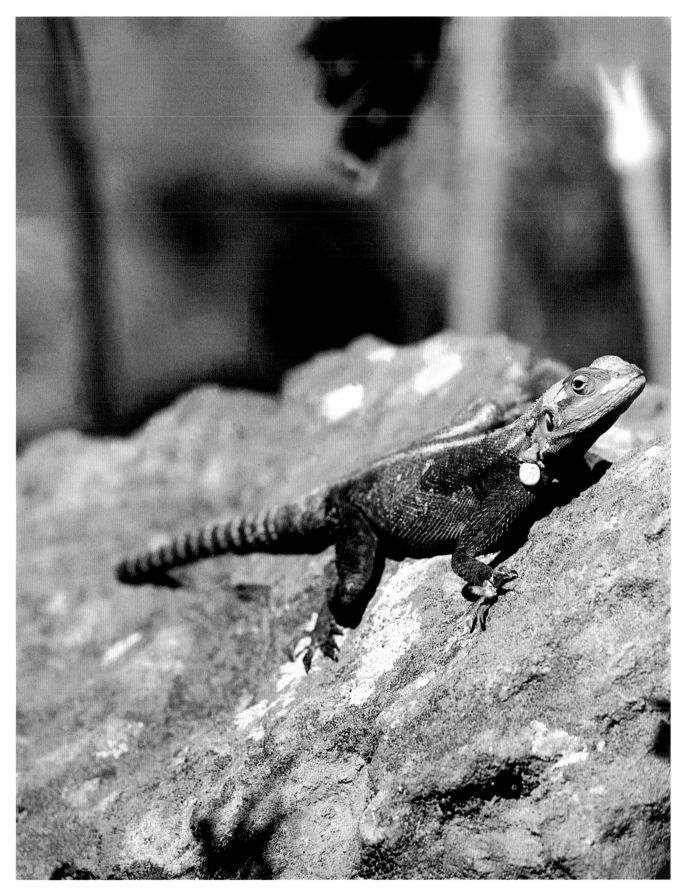

Above: Red-headed agama: Nakuru, Kenya. Common throughout equatorial Africa, it often chases invertebrates by running only on its back feet.

The largest African lizards are the monitors. The Nile monitor lizard (*Varanus niloticus*) is commonly up to 4ft 6in (1.4m) long, although much larger ones have been recorded. Its rather stout, thick-skinned, greyish brown or olive-brown body is covered with bead-like scales, and it has a long head and powerful limbs with strong claws; the tail is longer than the body. Like snakes, the monitor has a long forked tongue with which it tests the air and ground for scents. This species lives in rivers, lakes and marshes and in neighbouring woodland. Its very large range extends from Senegal eastwards to Sudan and Ethiopia, and southwards throughout central Africa and as far south as Angola in the west and eastern Cape Province in the east. As mentioned above, this monitor raids unguarded crocodile nests and also includes fish, frogs, crabs, mussels and water birds in its diet.

The savanna monitor lizard (*V. exanthematicus*) has a shorter, more bulbous snout than the Nile species; its dark greyish brown or black body has yellow-grey patches. It has a heavier build than the Nile monitor, but its tail is shorter and its overall length rarely exceeds four feet (1.2m). It is very much a land animal, a creature of dry savanna grasslands, savanna mosaics, and rocky localities in both grassland and semi-desert. Its range extends from Senegal eastwards to Eritrea and Somalia, then southwards through East Africa all the way to Cape Province, and in the west taking in Zambia, southern Angola and Namibia and much of Botswana. Its diet includes young tortoises, snails, a variety of larger insects, birds and birds' eggs, and carrion. The female makes a nest in soft, moist soil and lays up to 36 eggs, which do not hatch for a year. Outside the breeding season, an adult savanna monitor will often use the ventilation "chimney" of one of the larger termite mounds as sleeping quarters.

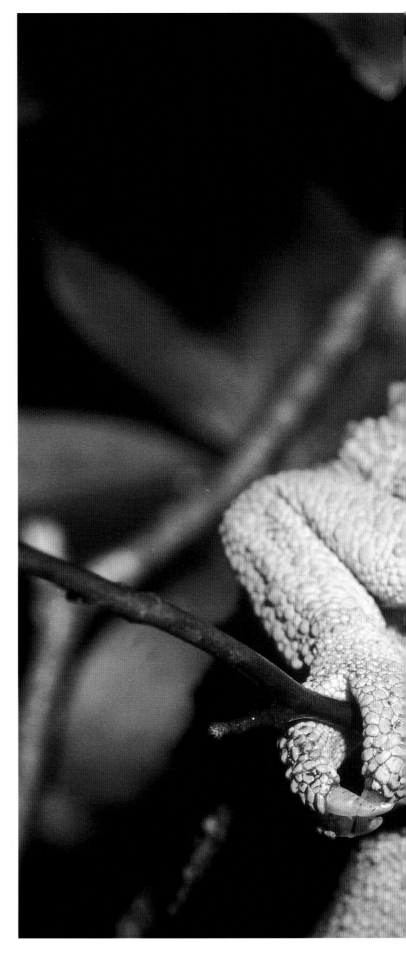

Jackson's chameleon, also known as the Kikuyu three-horned chameleon, is found from the Kenya highlands to north-eastern Tanzania.

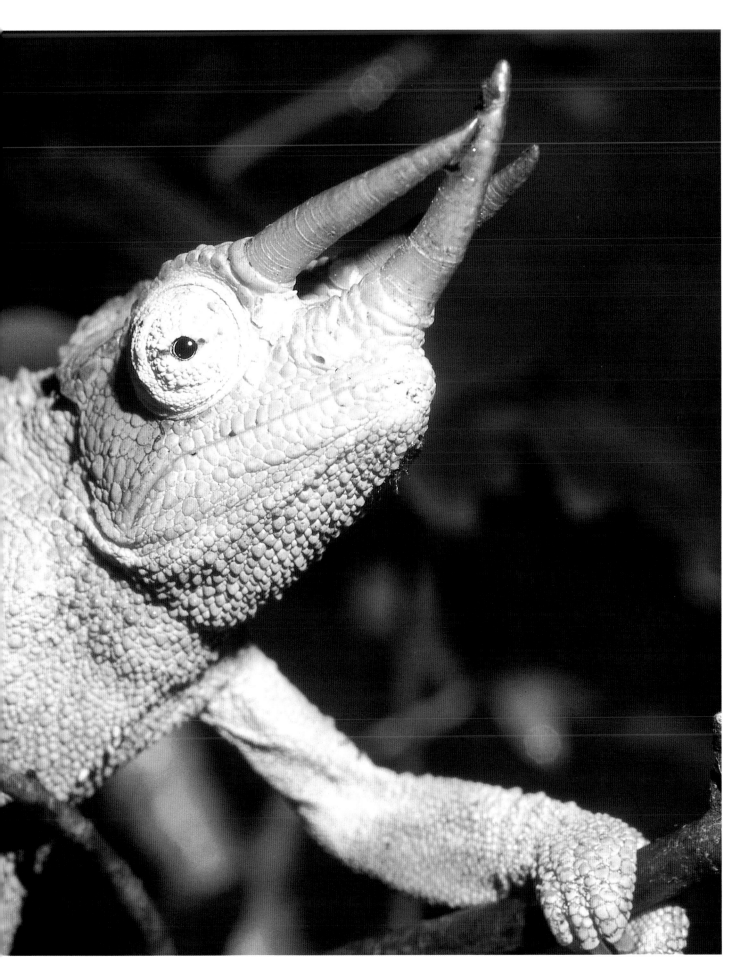

There are no fewer than 450 species of snakes in Africa, of many different types and sizes. The largest of all is the rock python (*Python sebae*), which is not only long—more than 20ft (6m) in rare cases—but enormously fat. It has a triangular head and its jaws have a for-midable array of teeth for holding on to prey. The body colours are a mixture of reddish brown, dull brown, greenish grey and beige-yellow; the top of the head has a dark brown "arrow-head" mark outlined in beige. It inhabits savanna woodlands and grasslands, riverine forests and rocky areas from Senegal eastwards to Ethiopia and southwards as far as central Namibia and KwaZulu-Natal. The rock python preys on the smaller antelopes, jackals, monitor lizards, monkeys, water birds and smaller mammals such as hyraxes and hares. It will also attack crocodiles, sometimes succumbing to the latter's jaws, sometimes making a successful kill. Its usual method of attack is to take hold of its victim in its jaws, then coil itself round it and constrict it to the point of suffocation.

The boomslang (*Dispholidus typus*) is a much more slender snake reaching a maximum length of about 6ft 8in (2m). The colour of the male varies radically from race to race: some are bright green, some yellow, or red or blue; the adult female is usually light brown or olive brown. The boomslang has one of the most toxic venoms of any of the world's snakes—a venom that attacks the nervous system and prevents the blood from clotting. It is essentially arboreal, moving swiftly among the branches of trees to attack its favoured prey—birds (especially weaver-birds in their huge communal nests), chameleons and other lizards. In spite of its venom it is not consid-ered to be dangerous to man since it is shy and generally avoids contact with humans. It inhabits open bush and savanna mosaics throughout most of sub-Sahara Africa apart from southern Namibia and north-western Cape Province.

The black mamba (*Dendroaspis polylepis*), which grows up to eight feet (2.4m) or more in length, is considered to be the most dan-gerous of Africa's large venomous snakes: an extremely fast mover, it is capable of chasing and catching game birds and some small mammals. It is olive brown or pewter grey on its upper half, and lighter below. The female lays about a dozen eggs in a rock crevice, hollow log or, occasionally, a hole burrowed into a termite mound by an aardvark. The species is found mainly in bushy savannas, grass-land-woodland mosaics and scrublands from central and East Africa southwards to Namibia and Mozambique. Its mainly arboreal cousin, the eastern green mamba (*D. angusticeps*), inhabits evergreen riverine, coastal and montane forests in East and south-eastern Africa, preying on small mammals, birds and their eggs and lizards. Its venom is less toxic than the black mamba's.

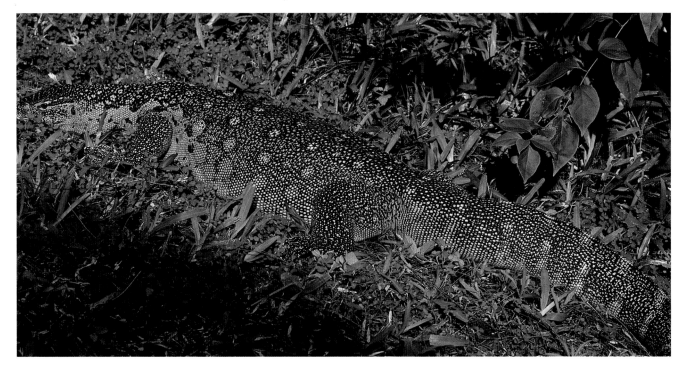

Above: Largest of the three African monitors, the Nile monitor lizard is tough-skinned and has strong limbs and claws.

Right: The rock python, Africa's largest snake, is quite fat enough to swallow this young impala and other small antelopes.

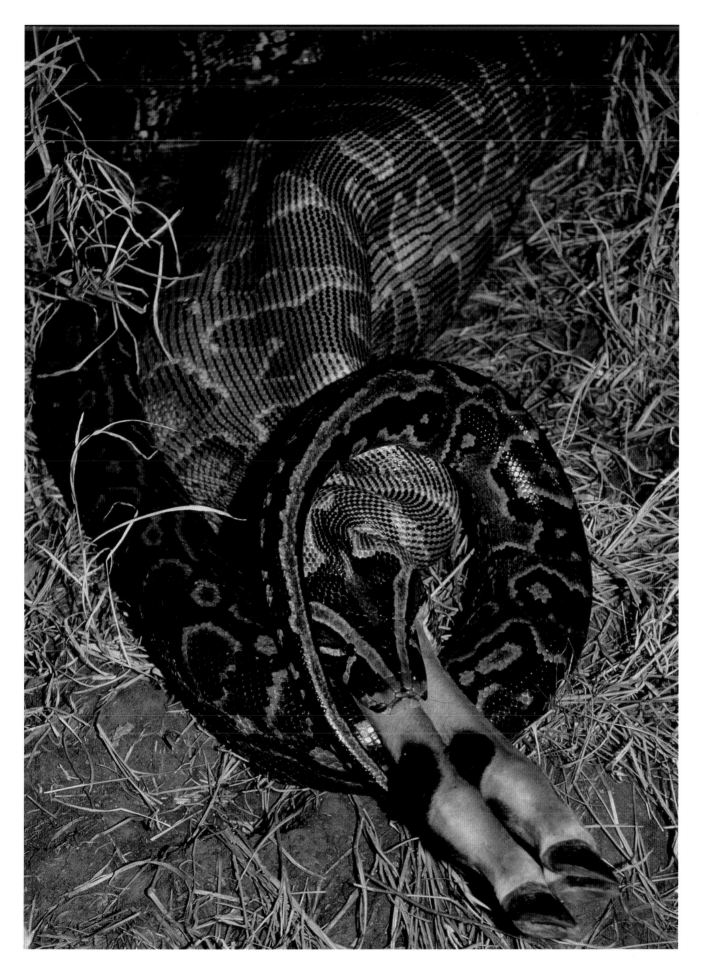

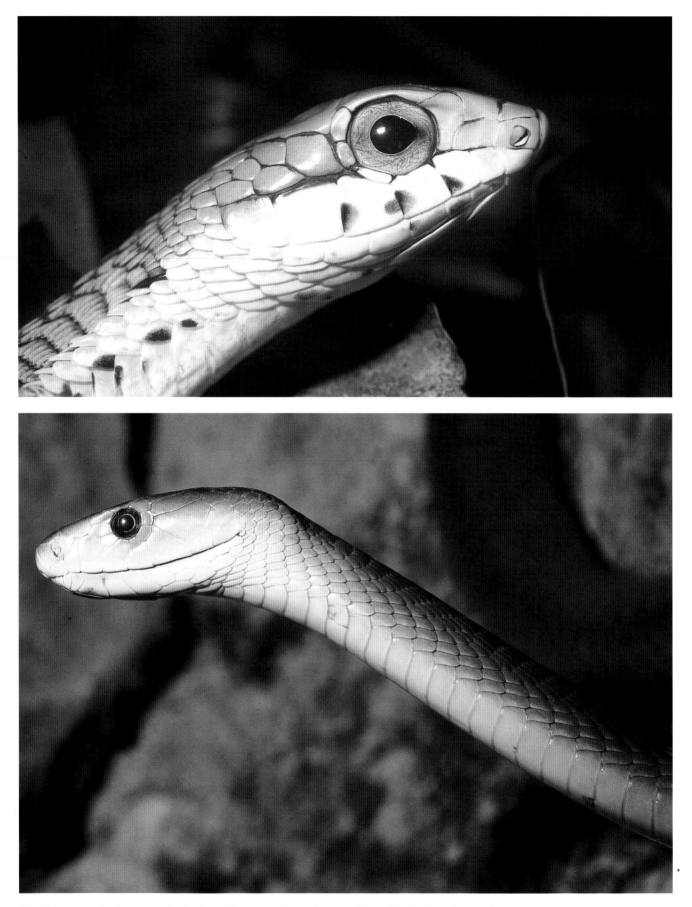

Top: Yellow ground colour, black-edged scales and large eyes identify the boomslang, whose venom is among the most toxic of all snakes.

Above: The black mamba, very fast and very dangerous, is in fact not black but gun-metal grey on top and pale grey on the underside.

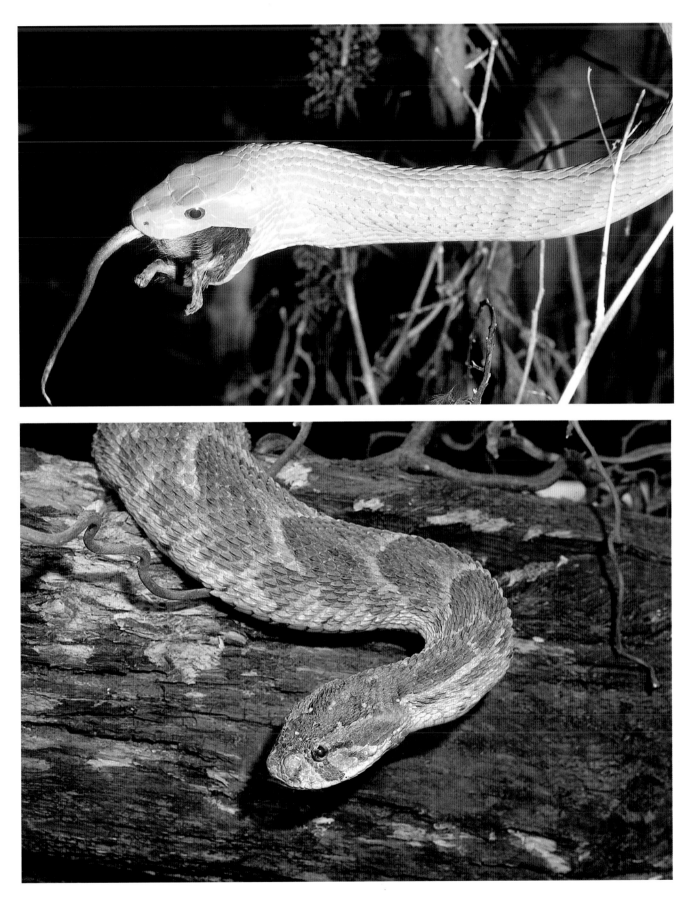

Top: The green mamba lives in evergreen tropical and montane forests.

Above: A puff adder emerges from its hiding place behind a log in pursuit of a rodent or ground bird. The puff adder's prolonged hiss is the sound most people associate with snakes in general.

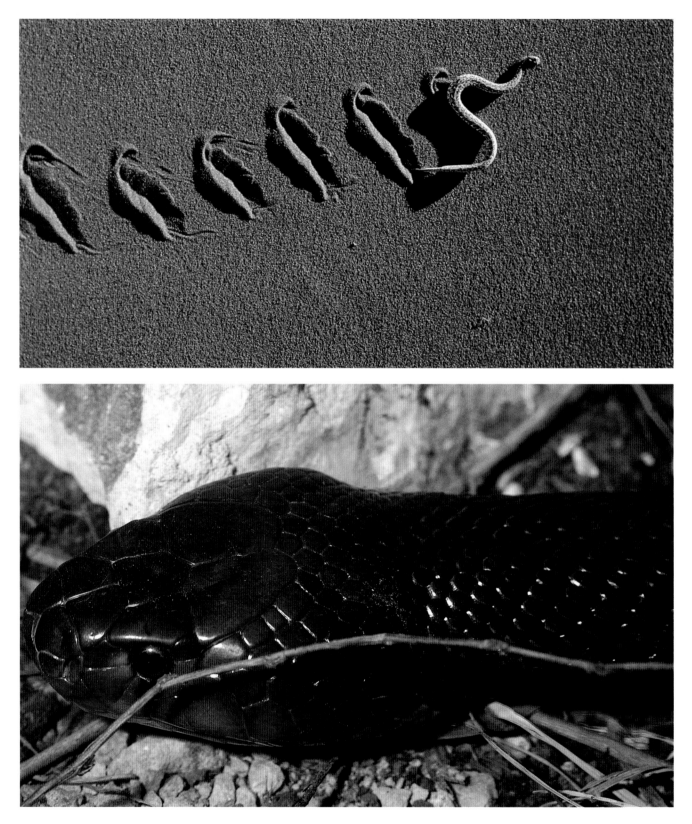

Top: In contrast to the puff adder's caterpillar-like locomotion, the sidewinder—seen here speeding across the face of a Namib desert sand dune—adopts a rapid version of the sideways movement used by most snakes.

Above: The spitting cobra (there are four African species) can spit venom from its fangs a distance of up to ten feet (3m).

Right: The leopard tortoise, found in woodland and grassland savannas and thorn scrub in East and most of southern Africa, has dark brown or black geometric patterns and spots against a carapace ground colour of tan or reddish yellow.

The puff adder (*Bitis arietans*), a fat dark brown snake with pale chevron or bar markings and large, round head, grows to a length of about 5ft 9in (1.75m). Mainly nocturnal, it preys on rodents and other small mammals as well as birds. It is found in almost every habitat except for true deserts and above the snowline on mountains and ranges all over sub-Sahara Africa except for parts of the Angolan and Namibian coasts. In motion it is instantly recognisable: it moves rather like a caterpillar does, raising the centre section of its body and drawing the end section forwards, rather than twisting its body from side to side. The puff adder accounts for more snake-bite deaths among humans than any other African species.

Other dangerously venomous African snakes include the Egyptian cobra (*Naja haje*) and its southern African cousin, the Cape cobra (*N. nivea*); and the spitting cobras (*Naja* species). All of these are creatures of the savanna grasslands, scrub woodlands and, occasionally, semi-desert areas. The spitting cobras have modified fangs that enable them to shoot streams of venom at their prey. Aimed at the eyes, the venom causes temporary blindness and extreme pain, although it is relatively harmless if it merely hits the skin.

TORTOISES

These reptiles are members of the order Testudinata, which also includes their salt-water cousins, the turtles, and their fresh-water cousins, the terrapins. In all three groups, the most striking physical feature is the shell, which may be soft or leathery or hard. The upper shell (to which the spine and ribs are fused) is called the carapace and the lower shell is the plastron; the individual plates that make up the carapace are called scutes. Most tortoises have parrot-like beaks and powerfully clawed feet.

The leopard tortoise (*Geochelone pardalis*) is found in much of East and southern Africa apart from western Cape Province and southern Namibia. The largest race is in eastern Cape Province, where it may weigh more than 80lb (36kg). It lives in dry and open woodland, grasslands, around kopjes on the Serengeti plains and in thorn scrub. It has a high carapace with steep-sloping side and a distinctive notch at the front. The basic colour of the carapace is usually reddish or yellowish brown with darker spots—whence the species' common name. The leopard tortoise likes to remain in thick vegetation, browsing on foods with a high water content—

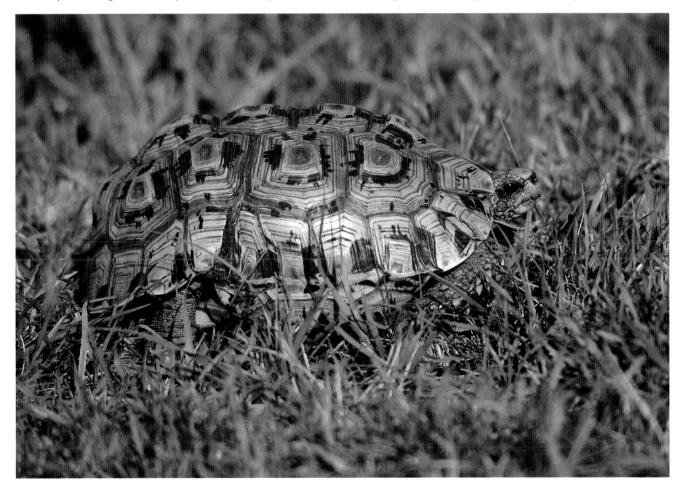

lush grasses, thistles, prickly pear (cacti), and ripe fruit fallen from trees. Its close relative, the spurred tortoise (*G. sulcata*), lives in the dry wooded grassland and Sahel belt stretching from the Atlantic to Ethiopia. Whereas other tortoises escape the heat of noonday by burrowing under the sand, this species cools its head, neck and forelegs with its own saliva.

One of the most attractive southern African species is the geometric tortoise (*Psammobates geometricus*), with black or very dark brown carapace marked with yellow "wheel-and-spokes" patterns. It lives in the extreme south-western corner of Cape Province but, because of its striking appearance it is eagerly sought by collectors and is likely to become extinct quite soon. Its close relative, the starred tortoise (*P. oculifer*), is one of several species that inhabit the drylands of Namibia, although they are absent from the harsh interior of the Namib desert; others include the tent tortoise (*P. tentorius*) and the speckled tortoise (*Homopus signatus*).

Finally, we must mention the tortoises of the genus *Kinixys*, whose long, steep-sided carapaces have a movable rear hinge that allows them to cover their tail and hind limbs at the approach of a predator. One of these tortoises, Bell's hinge-backed tortoise (*K. belliana*), inhabits savanna woodlands and grasslands, from Senegal eastwards to Eritrea and southwards to Transvaal and Mozambique. It eats insects, snails, fruit, foliage, grasses and fungi. Another member of this genus, the serrated-hinged tortoise (*K. erosa*), lives in lowland rainforests. Remarkably for a tortoise, it dives and swims in forest streams in search of food.

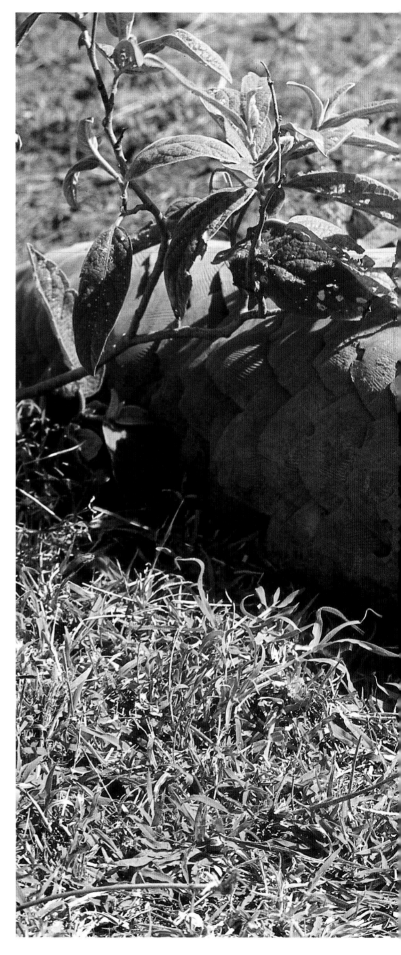

The giant pangolin (*Manis gigantea*) is a scale-covered ground-dwelling insectivore living mainly on ants and termites, which it catches with its long, sticky tongue. Pangolins are unique to one family of the order Pholidota; there are three other African species (two of them tree-dwellers) living in much of sub-Sahara Africa's moist and dry savannas.

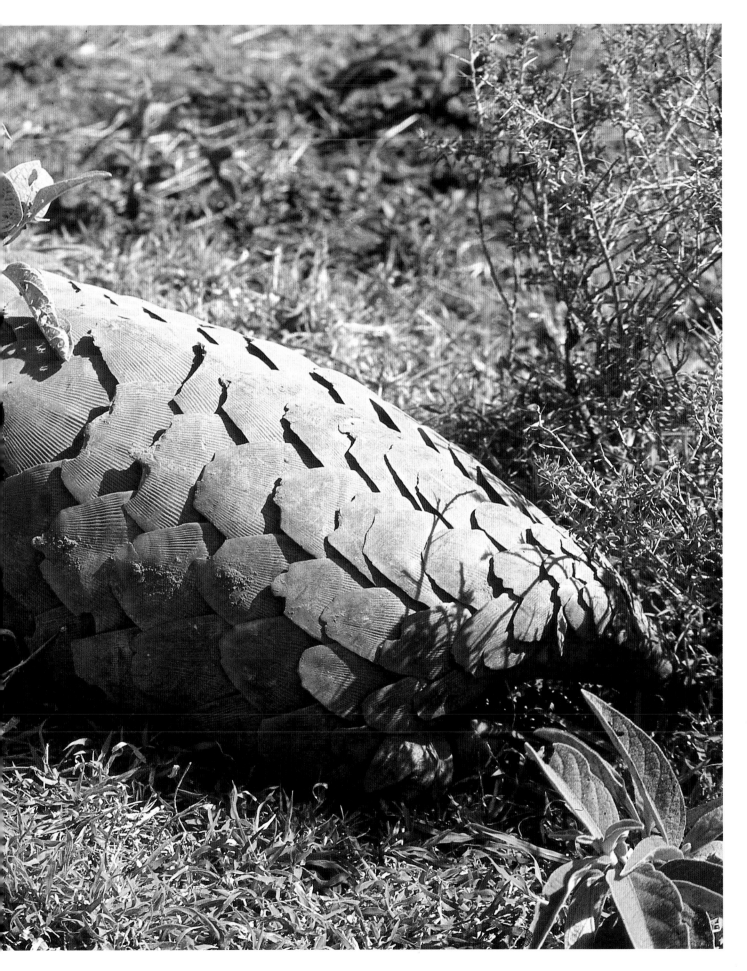

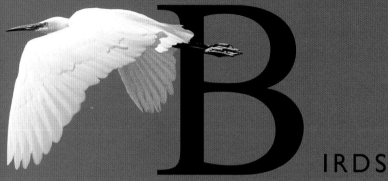

Birds

More than 2,000 species of birds have been recorded in Africa, and given the continent's great range of habitats it is not surprising that its avifauna is wonderfully rich and varied. Here we introduce a few of the most interesting and spectacular.

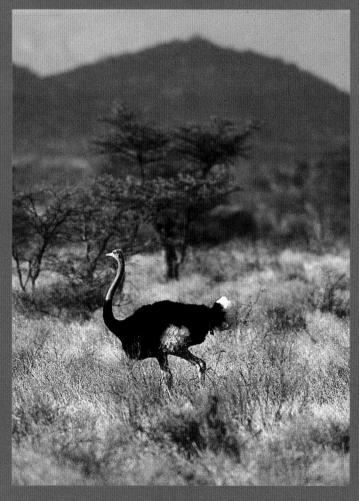

Above: Male ostrich in wooded savanna: Kenya.

Right: Ostrich pair, with male on the left: Masai Mara, Kenya. A territorial male often has several hens, some of whom may lay their eggs in the same nest.

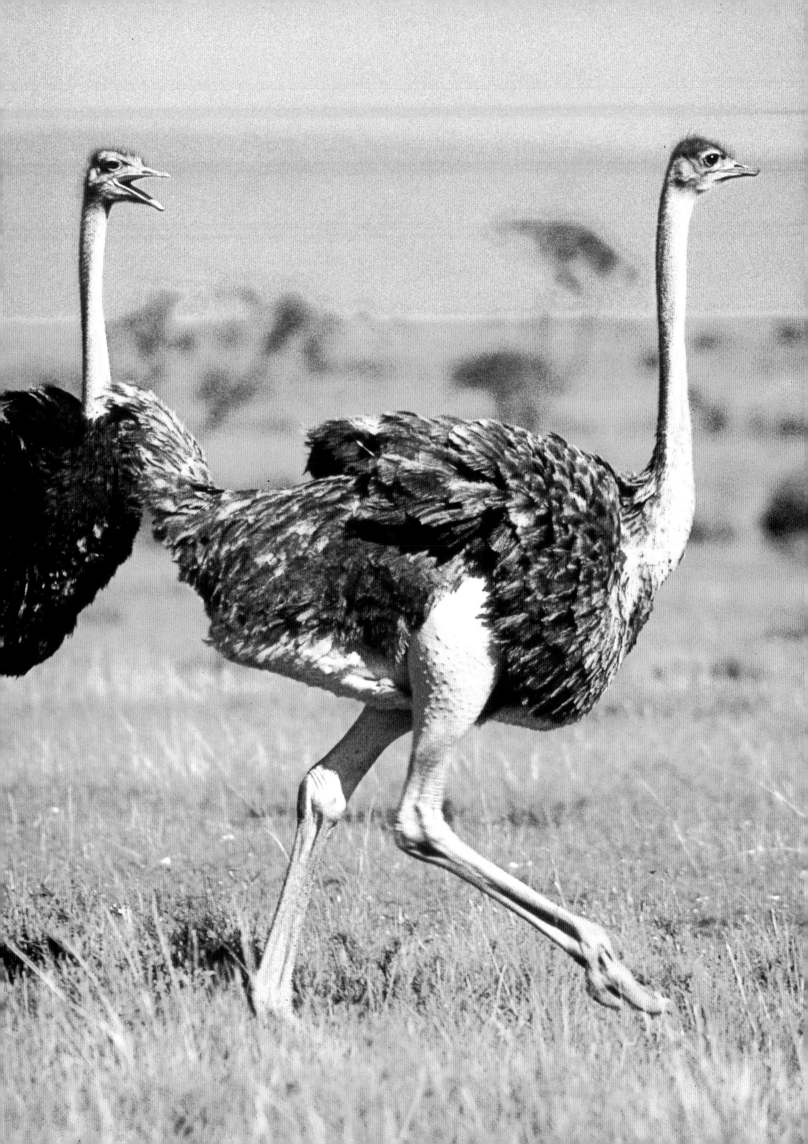

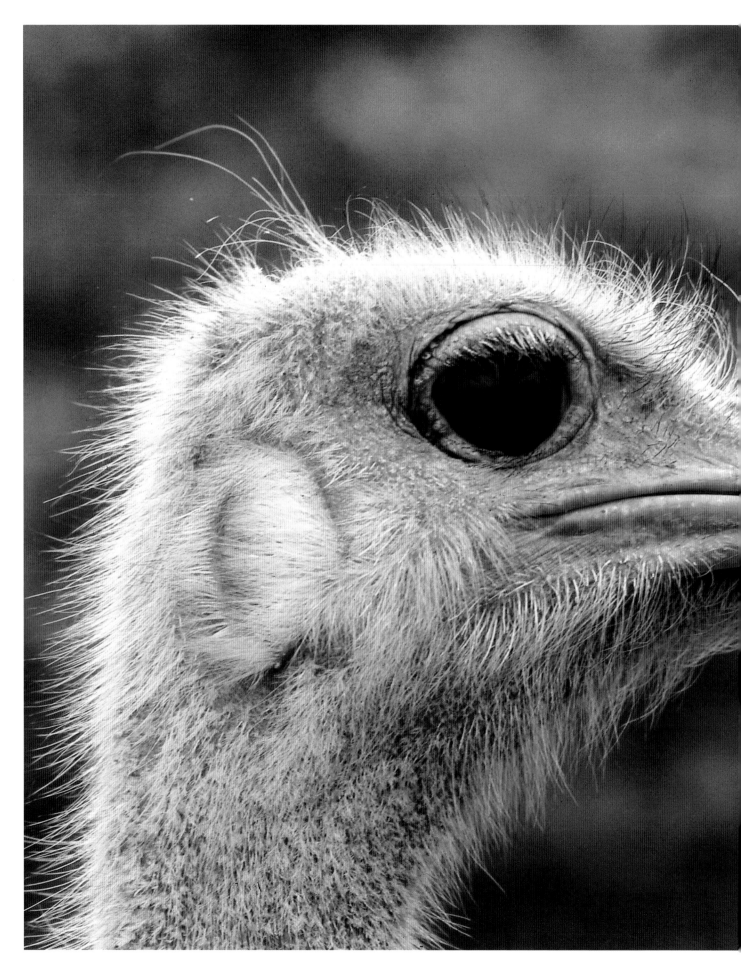

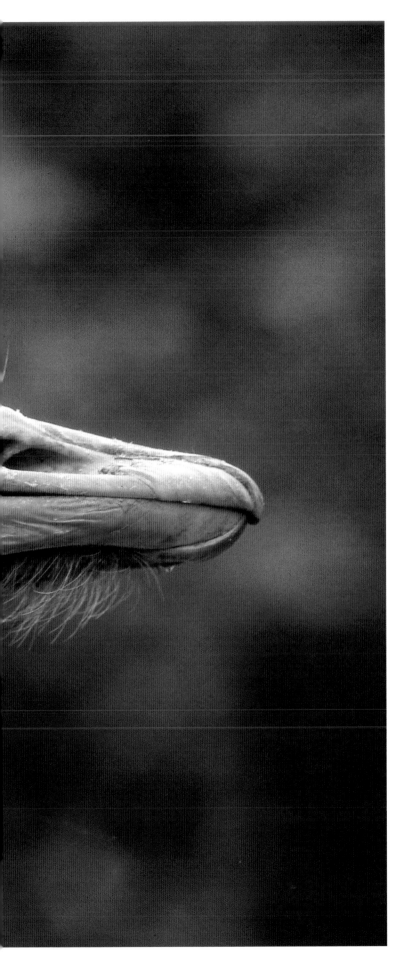

OSTRICH

Largest of all birds, the flightless ostrich (*Struthio camelus*) is unique—the only member of its order and family—and occurs only in Africa. It is one of the characteristic sights of the open savannas and drylands, where its keen sight and its fleetness of foot—it can run at more than 30mph (50km/h) for half an hour or so—give it good survival prospects against predators. Groups of ostriches often mingle with herds of plains zebra and blue wildebeest: the ungulates' keen sense of smell and the bird's acute vision combining to confer some extra security against predation.

The ostrich has a long, featherless neck and legs, which in the adult male are pink or red in some races, blue in others. The male has black plumage with white wings and tail feathers. The female is mainly brown with greyish white wings and tail. The ostrich is the only bird with two toes on each leg, the inner one being much the larger. The adult male is up to nine feet (2.7m) high (the female is considerably smaller) and may weigh up to 280lb (127kg). The breeding male may have several hens. Eggs are laid on the open savanna in a crude scrape that may be used by more than one of the hens. Seldom seen in the Sahel plains immediately south of the Sahara, the ostrich is found throughout the open plains of East Africa from Sudan to southern Tanzania, and in southern Africa from south of the Zambezi river in the east and southern Angola in the west.

The head of a female ostrich. Note the fine hairs on her featherless head and neck.

A female ostrich with a family of juveniles on the Masai Mara.

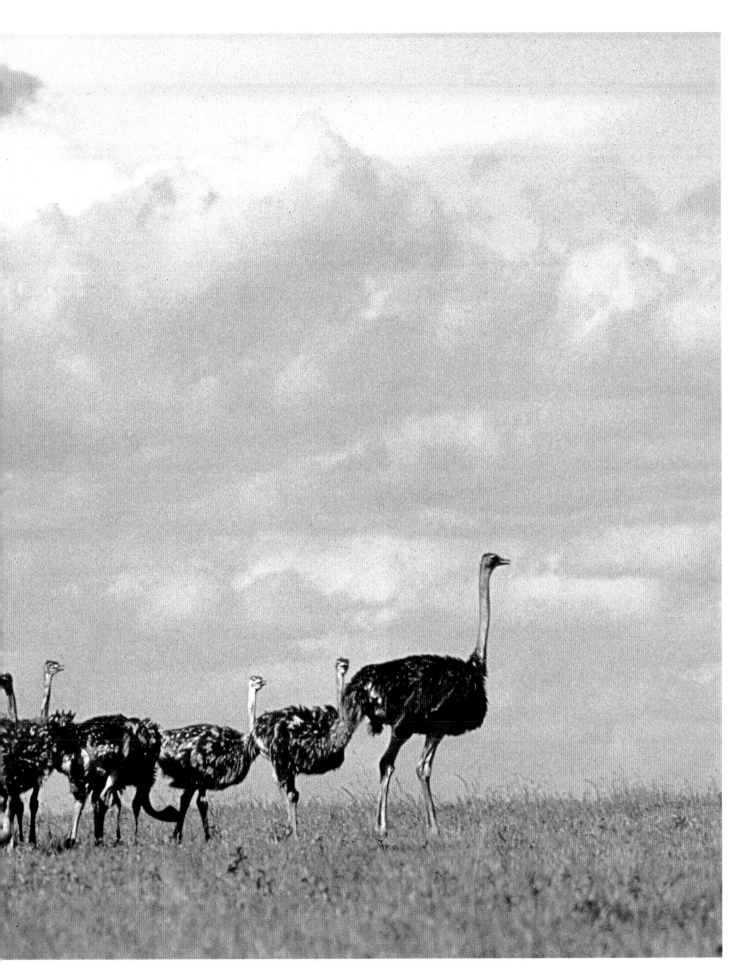

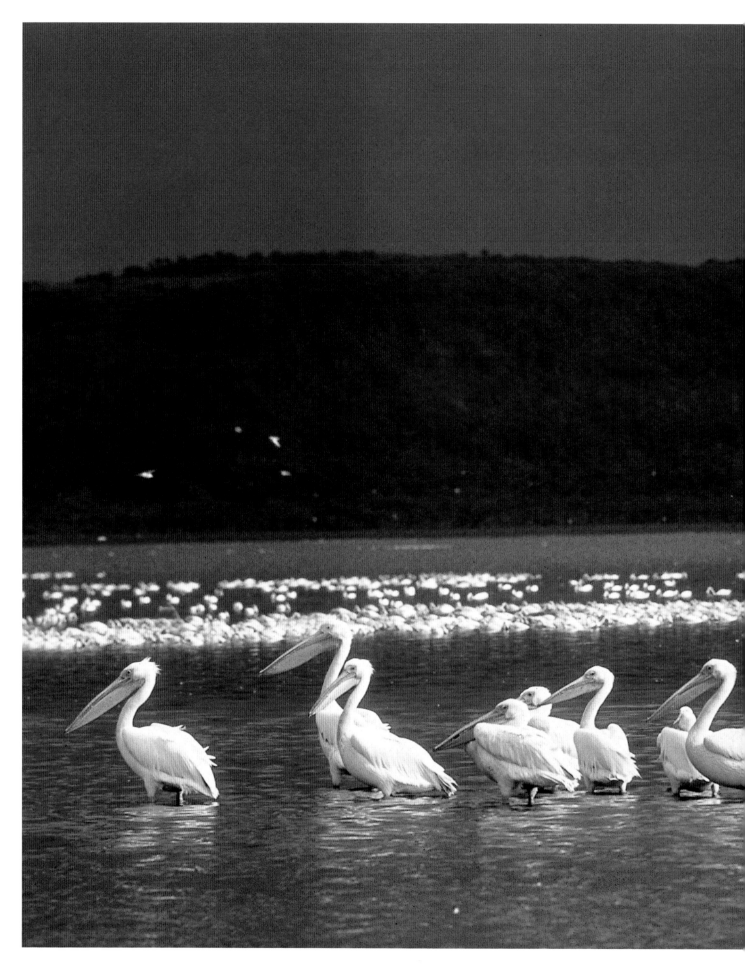

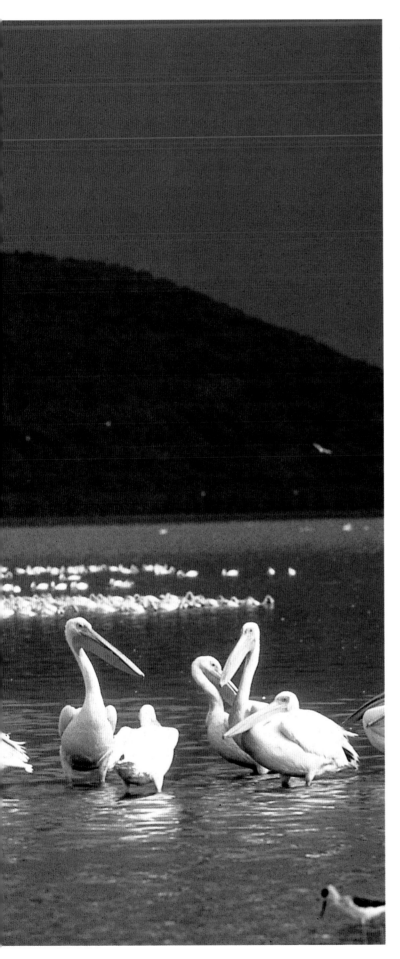

PELICANS & CORMORANTS

The Pelicaniformes order of mainly fish-eaters includes seabirds such as the gannet and tropicbirds as well as the pelicans and cormorants found in rivers and lakes. All have four forward-facing toes with connecting webs.

The pelicans are Africa's largest flying birds. Apart from their size, their most striking physical attribute is their lower mandible which contains an elastic, muscular pouch that is vital to their method of catching food; the rigid upper mandible has a hook at the tip. The great white pelican (*Pelecanus onocrotalus*), the larger of the two African species, has a wing-span of up to 12ft (3.6m). The tip of its upper mandible is red and its pouch is yellow. Normally white in colour, its plumage is tinted pink and yellow in the breeding season; its flight feathers, however, are black. Its facial skin is bare and usually pink or yellow. It congregates in huge colonies of many thousands during the breeding season, nesting on the ground, often at the same site year after year. It is found in much of sub-Sahara Africa in both fresh- and salt-water lakes and around the coasts of South Africa and Mauretania. Its method of catching fish is to swim forward with its bill open under water. It can move with some speed, propelled by its huge webbed feet. Among the best places to see it are the alkaline lakes in Kenya's eastern rift, notably lakes Baringo and Nakuru. Its smaller cousin, the pink-backed pelican (*P. rufescens*), is silvery grey with dark grey flight feathers and with pink bill and pouch; its beak tip is pink or yellow. At breeding time the pouch turns yellow, the feet red and a black marking encircles the eye. It

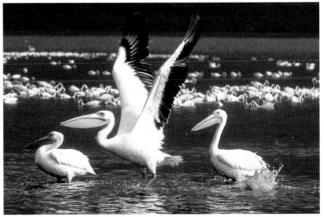

Above: Great white pelicans: Lake Nakuru, Kenya. Note the black flight feathers and yellow beak.

Left: Great white pelicans: Lake Nakuru.

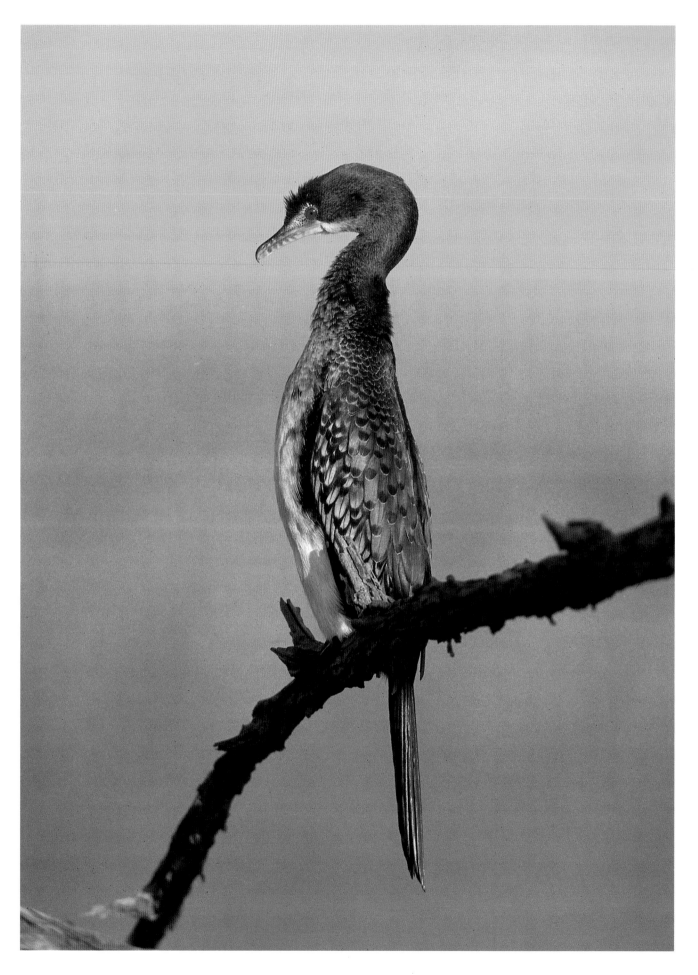

has a wing span of nine to ten feet (2.7-3m). It nests in trees in colonies of up to 450 pairs, often in the company of storks and herons. It is found in most of sub-Sahara Africa except for Namibia, the Kalahari desert and Cape Province. It favours fresh-water lakes and rivers, but is also found in salt lakes and lagoons.

The most ubiquitous of Africa's cormorants is the reed or long-tailed cormorant (*Phalacrocorax africanus*), which is found throughout sub-Sahara Africa and also in Madagascar. Smaller than most of its cousins, its breeding colour is glossy black (dark brown at other times), and it has a red eye. Its wing-span is about three feet (92cm). It is found in fresh-water lakes and rivers and also estuaries and mangrove swamps. It eats mainly small fish. The white-breasted cormorant (*P. lucidus*) is much larger, with a wing-span of more than five feet (1.5m). Apart from its white face and breast it is mainly black. It has a patch of yellow skin below its blue eye. It tolerates fresh or salt water, and is found throughout East Africa and south-wards to Botswana, Namibia and South Africa. It nests in large colonies, often with the reed cormorant and herons.

LONG-LEGGED WADERS

These three-toed waders include herons, egrets, storks, ibises, flamingos and others. In all, there are 43 species native to Africa.

The goliath heron (*Ardea goliath*), the biggest heron of all, stands some 4ft 9in (1.45m) tall on its very long legs which, like its bill, are black. Its head and neck are darkish orange, its eye yellow, and its throat white. It has black and white marks at the front of its neck, red shoulders, belly and upper legs, and grey back and upper wings. It is mainly a bird of fresh-water lakes and rivers offering good shrub or tree cover at the water's edge; it is also found in mangrove swamps. Its range is throughout sub-Sahara Africa apart from Namibia, Botswana and western Cape Province. It feeds on large fish, frogs, crabs and aquatic snakes. It often nests in groups with other heron species. The grey heron (*A. cinerea*) is indeed mainly grey but it has a white crown, black and white stripes on its lower neck, black shoulders and a black eyebrow that lengthens into a trailing crest. Its long legs are yellow, as is its bill. A solitary bird, it patrols the banks and shallows of rivers, lakes and ponds, and is also

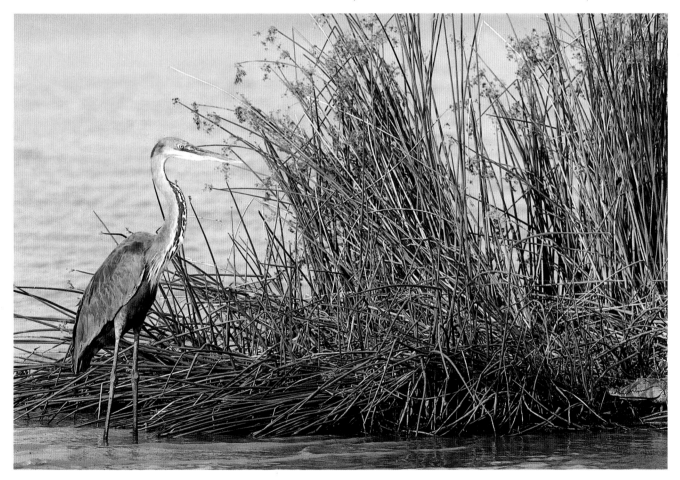

Left: Reed cormorant: South Africa.

Above: Goliath heron: Lake Baringo, Kenya.

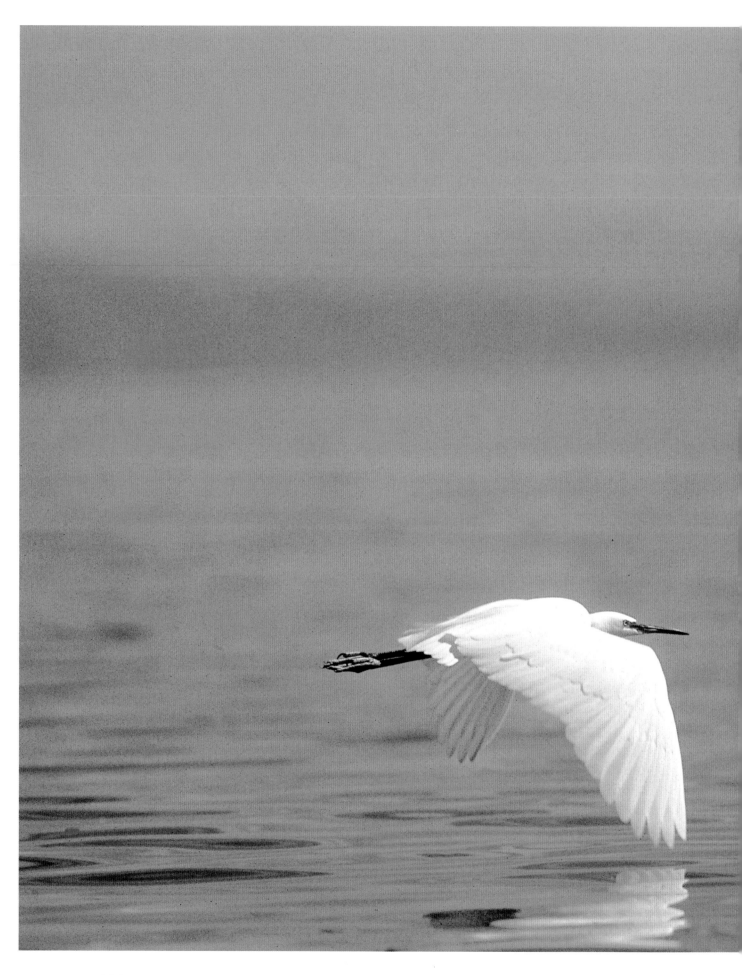

found in coastal marshes. Its diet includes fish, crustaceans, amphibians, snakes, rodents, waterbirds such as ducks and grebes. It builds its nest out of substantial twigs, often sharing a tree with other large waders.

Other herons ranging over most of sub-Sahara Africa include the black-headed heron (*A. melanocephala*), a bird of open woodlands and savanna grasslands; the squacco heron (*Ardeola ralloides*), with brown body and white wings; and the black heron or black egret (*Egretta ardesiaca*), which has the remarkable fishing technique of standing in shallow water, fanning its wings to form a feather canopy just above the surface, and wriggling its red toes to attract fish into its shadowy trap. Its cousin, the little egret (*E. garzetta*), has almost all white plumage but long black legs (with yellow feet) and a straight black bill. It is a native of lakes and marshes south of the Sahara, and also of coastal reefs. Its subspecies, the western reef egret (*E. g. gularis*) is found on coasts from Mauretania to Gabon and also on the Red Sea coast.

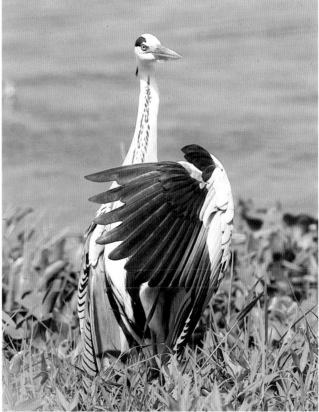

Above: Grey heron: Lake Kariba, Zimbabwe. Note the long black "eyebrow" and the orange-red (breeding-season) colour of its bill.

Left: Little egret flying low over Lake Naivasha, Kenya. Note the long, thin black bill and black legs.

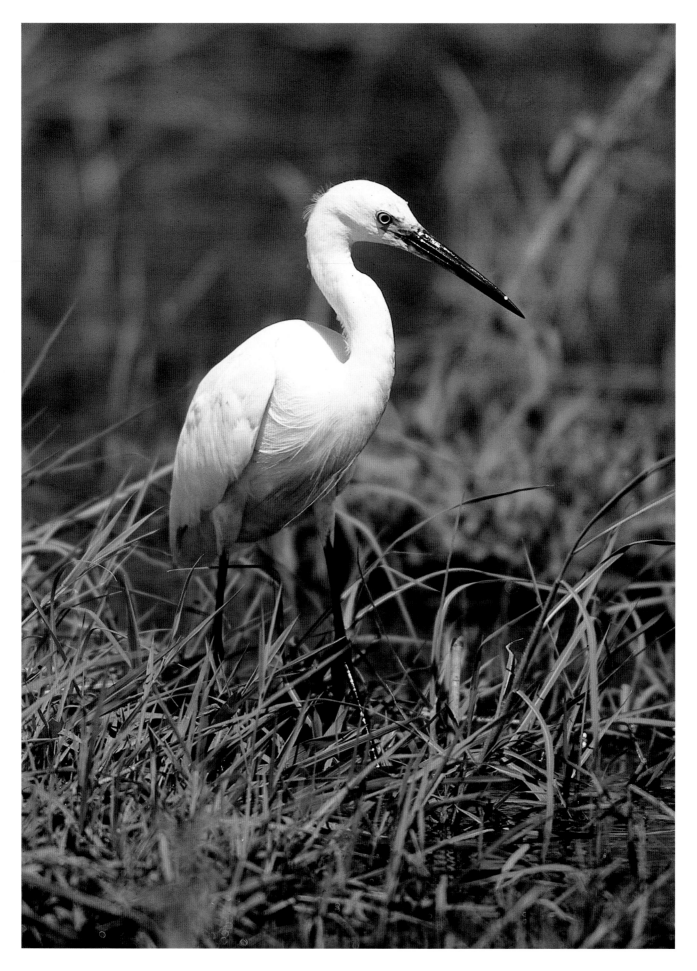

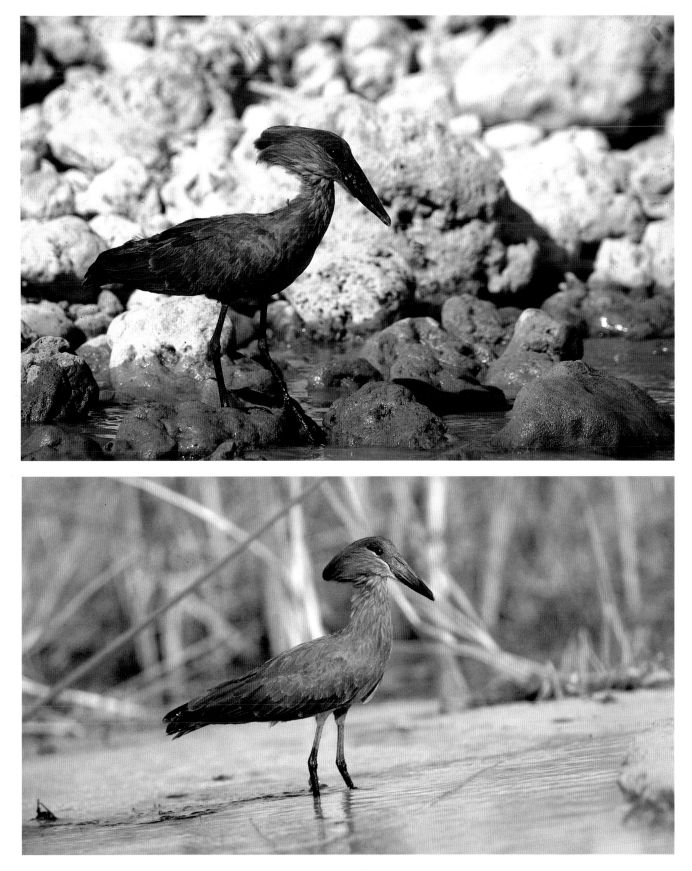

Left: Little egret wading in grassy shallows: Savuti marshes, Botswana.

Top: A hammerkop looks for frogs in shallows on the edge of Lake Baringo. Note the hammer-shaped head formed by rear-facing plumage.

Above: Hammerkop in the marshes of Okavango Delta, Botswana.

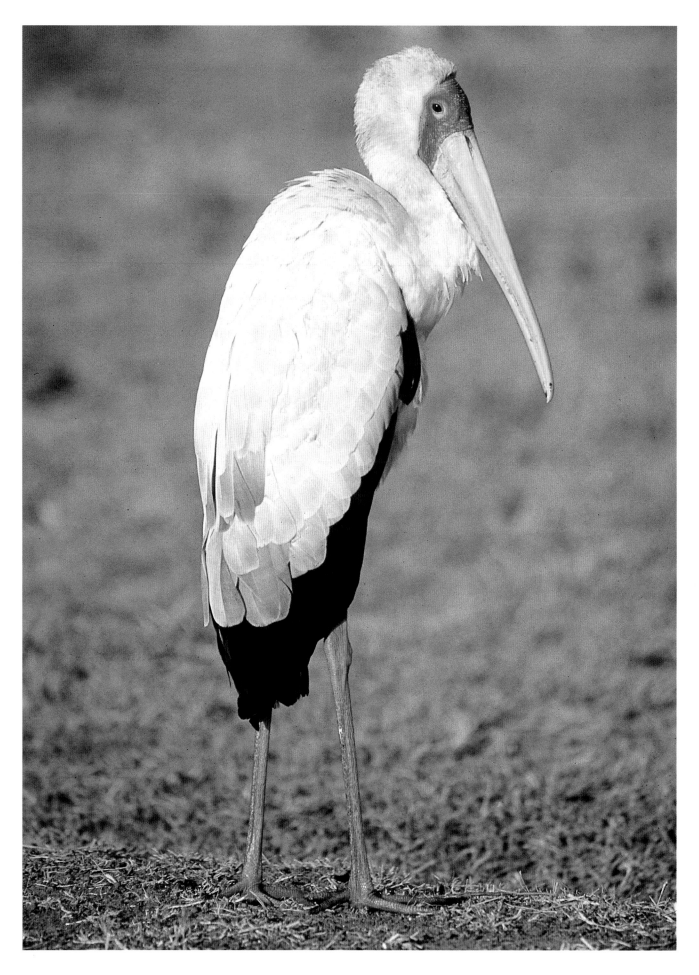

The hammerkop (*Scopus umbretta*) is brown with a very large hammer-shaped head (the common name is Afrikaans for "hammerhead") and a thick black bill. It is found throughout sub-Sahara Africa except for the Kalahari desert, its habitat being rivers, ponds and marshes. Its main food is frogs and tadpoles. It builds a huge, usually spherical and fully enclosed nest with a downward-facing entrance, which is usually colonised by other birds when the hammerkop has finished with it.

The yellow-billed stork (*Mycteria ibis*) has white plumage (which turns a rosy pink in the breeding season) with black tail and flight feathers, and red face and legs. Its long yellow bill bends downwards at the end. It lives on the shores and marshes of fresh-water and saline coasts, rivers and lakes in most of Africa south of the Sahara. The huge saddle-billed stork (*Ephippiorhynchus seneghalensis*), which has a wing-span of nine feet (2.7m), has a black head and neck and wings that seem black when folded but show white shoulders and mainly white flight feathers. Its massive, upturned bill is red with a black band across the middle. The male has a yellow wattle and a black eye, the female a yellow eye. It lives on marshes around the shores of fresh-water and saline lakes in most of sub-Sahara Africa

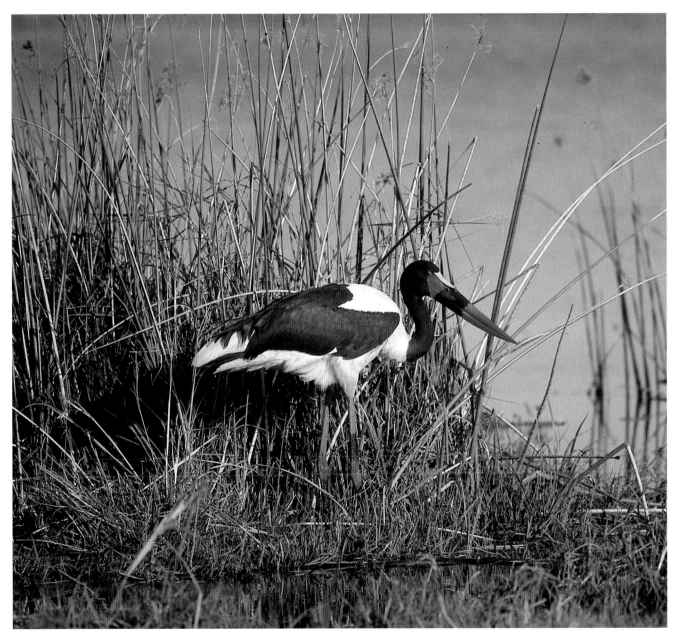

Left: Yellow-billed stork: Nairobi National Park, Kenya. Note the long yellow bill, bright red face and black flight feathers.

Above: Saddle-billed stork wading in marshes: Okavango Delta, Botswana. This is the tallest African bird after the ostrich. Note the wide black band in the middle of its red bill.

except for Namibia, southern Botswana and south-western South Africa. Its diet includes fish, lizards, frogs, locusts and other large invertebrates. Larger still is the marabou stork (*Leptoptilos crumeniferus*), with a maximum wingspan of almost 11ft (3.4m), a dark grey bird with white marks on the wings, a white collar and white underparts. The bald head is red with black mottling and the neck is pink. One of its characteristic calls is a mooing sound. It inhabits mixed woodland and grassland savannas and also coastal areas in most of Africa south of the Sahara except for rainforests and true deserts. It nests in colonies that may number several thousand birds.

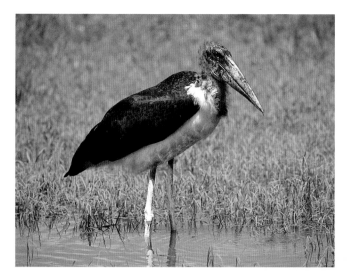

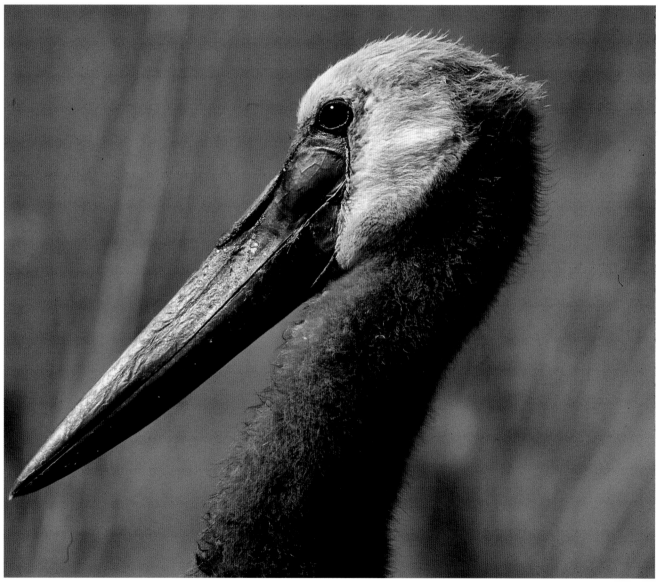

Top: Marabou storks rival vultures as scavengers. This one stands in a pond on the Masai Mara.

Right: A marabou stork preening its feathers.

Above: Immature saddle-billed stork: Botswana.

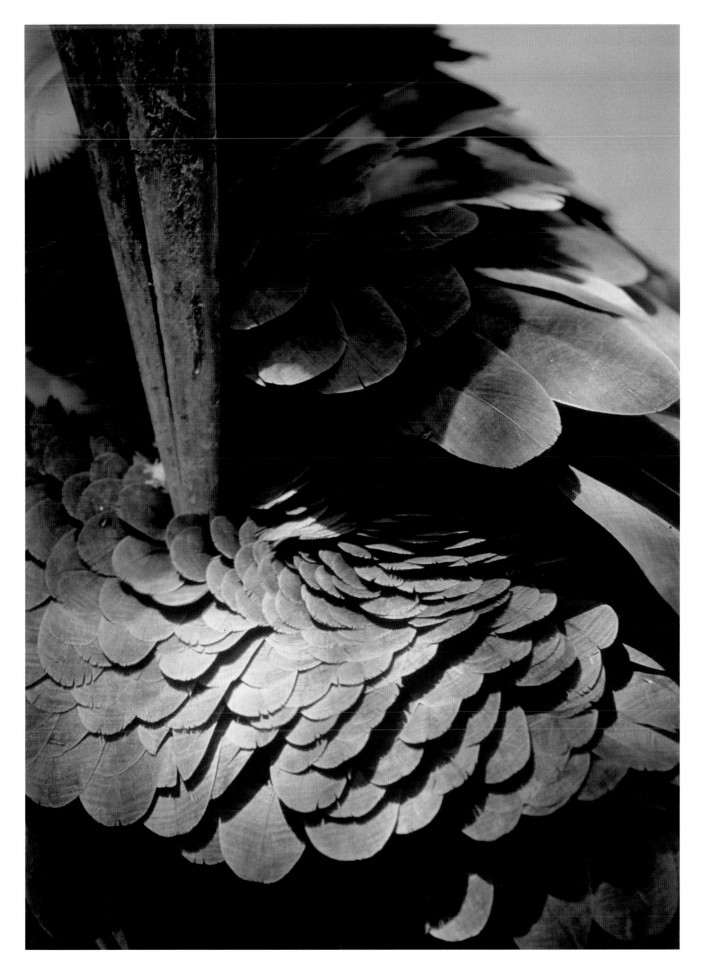

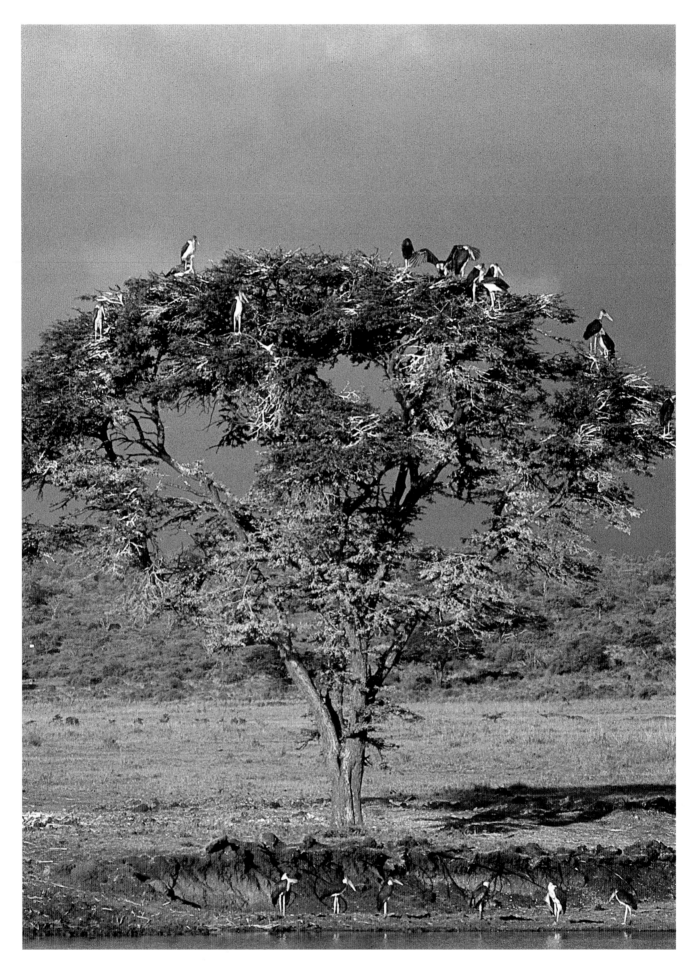

The Hadada ibis (*Bostrychia hagedash*; syn. *Hagedashia hagedash*) is overall dark brown but with a purplish gloss on the wings and a white moustache at the base of its head. Its thick black bill has a red stripe on the upper mandible. It is found in grasslands and open woodlands and is often attracted to farms and large gardens. Much less gregarious than most waders, it builds a solitary tree nest quite close to the ground. It is widespread throughout sub-Sahara Africa except for Angola, Namibia, Botswana and north-western Cape Province. The sacred ibis (*Threskiornis aethiopica*), which is similarly widespread in range, has a white body and wings, a naked black head and a thick, black, downward curving bill. A much more gregarious bird, it builds a large, rather flat nest of sticks in a tree that may be part of a colony of several thousand waders of various species.

Flamingos have immensely long necks and legs relative to their body size. In the air they are instantly recognisable: they fly with extended necks and with their legs trailing behind their body. The lesser flamingo (*Phoeniconaias minor*), which stands about three feet (91cm) high, is white with a slight pink tinge which intensifies to a deep pink at breeding time. Its flight feathers are black and its legs dark red. The bill is very dark red. It lives in areas of alkaline or fresh-water lakes and coastal lagoons. It occurs in the greatest numbers in Rift Valley lakes from Ethiopia to Tanzania, but large flocks also gather farther south when salt pans are seasonally flooded in Botswana, Namibia and elsewhere. It builds mud nests in inaccessible areas on mud- or salt-flats, one of the most important breeding sites being the highly alkaline Lake Natron, in Tanzania. The greater flamingo (*P. ruber*) is much larger, up to five feet (1.5m) tall and with

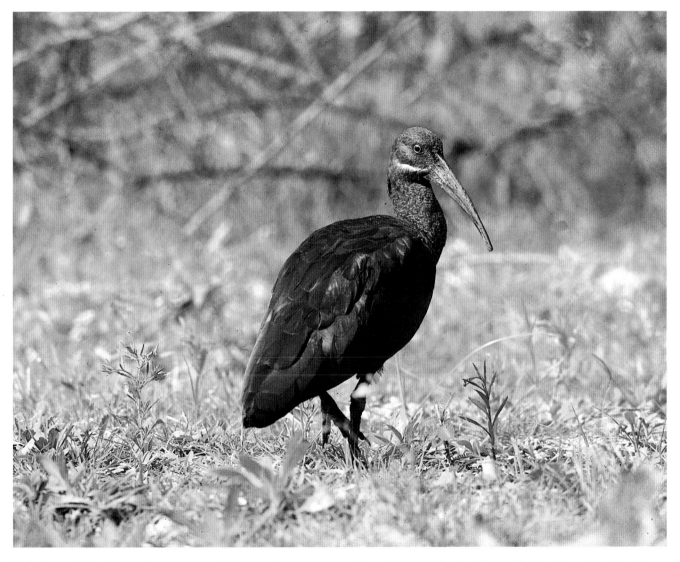

Left: A crowd of marabou storks use a tree as lookout post by a waterhole in Nairobi National Reserve. Others stand by the water's edge.

Above: Hadada ibis: Samburu National Reserve, Kenya. Note the white "moustache" at base of its head.

a wing span of 65in (1.7m) or more. It is readily distinguishable from its smaller cousin not only by its size but also by its S-shaped neck. It is white or very pale pink, with red shoulders and black flight feathers. Its rather short, pale pink bill droops at the end and its long legs are pale pink. It breeds mainly in the East Africa Rift Valley lakes, but also in Tunisia and South Africa. The lesser flamingo is herbivorous, feeding on blue-green algae and diatoms growing near the surface in shallow water. It is more tolerant of highly alkaline water than the greater flamingo. The latter is omnivorous, but feeds mainly on lake-fly larvae, copepods and other animal matter, which it catches by filtering mud and water through its bill bristles. The best places to see both species—they often congregate together— are in Kenya's Rift Valley lakes, especially fresh-water lakes Naivasha and Baringo and alkaline Lake Bogoria. Vast hordes numbering in the hundreds of thousands gather at these sites to feed and drink or simply to rest, the lesser flamingo usually outnumbering the greater by at least 20 to one.

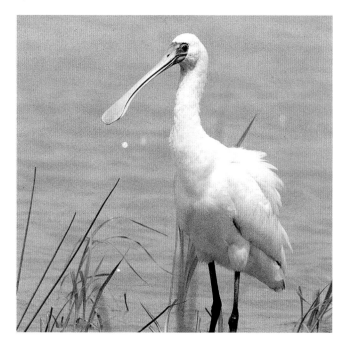

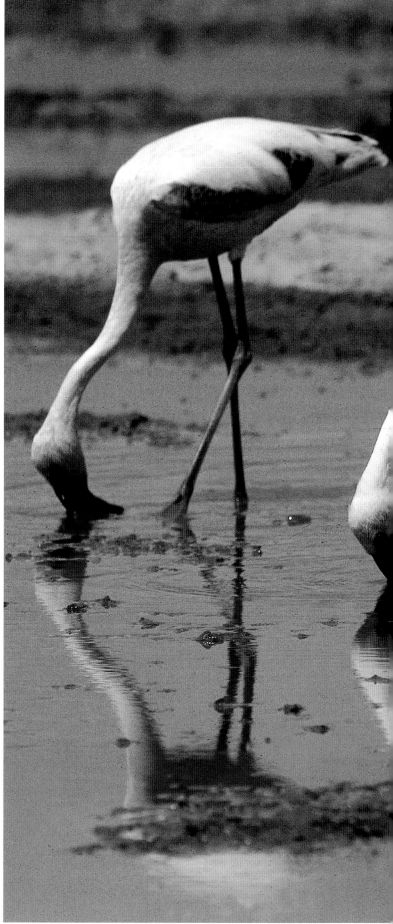

Above: The African spoonbill, though resembling an egret, is closer kin to the ibises. Note the flattened spoon-shaped end to its bill, which helps it to catch small fish and frogs. This one patrols the shallows of Lake Baringo.

Right: Three lesser flamingos feeding in Lake Naivasha, Kenya. Its dark red legs and dark bill distinguish this species from the much larger greater flamingo.

Overleaf: Close-up of the deep pink breeding plumage of the lesser flamingo.

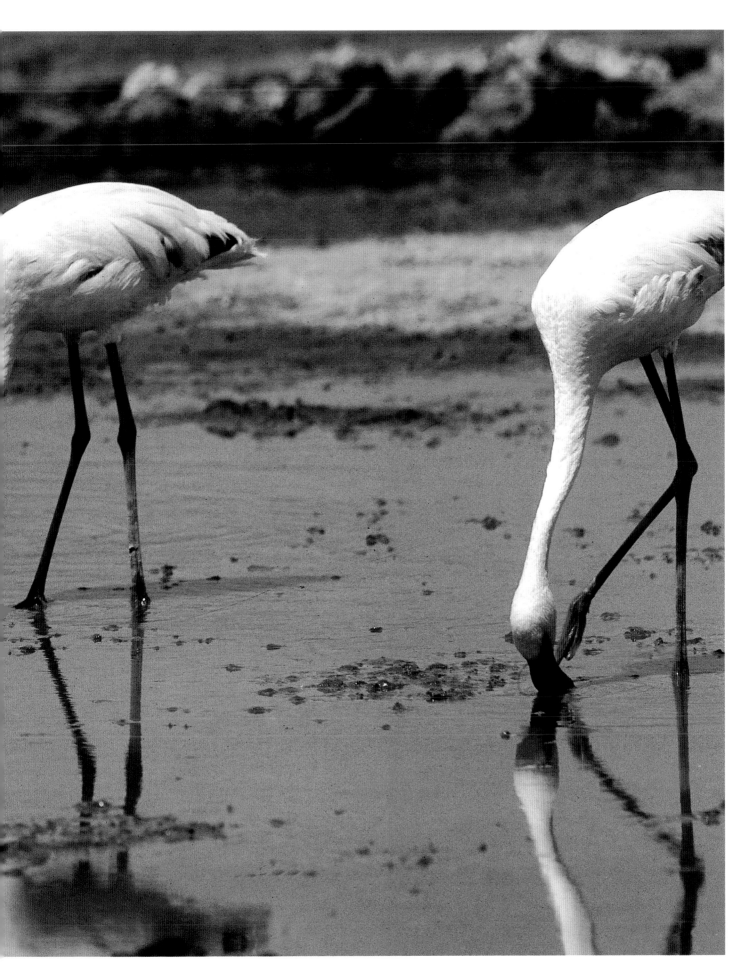

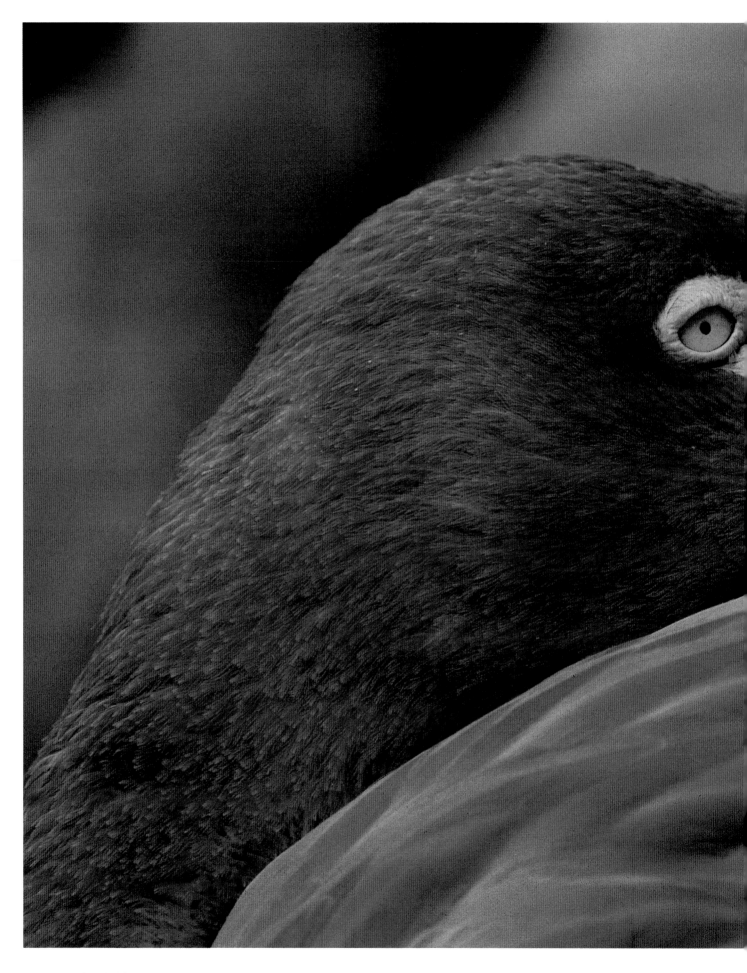

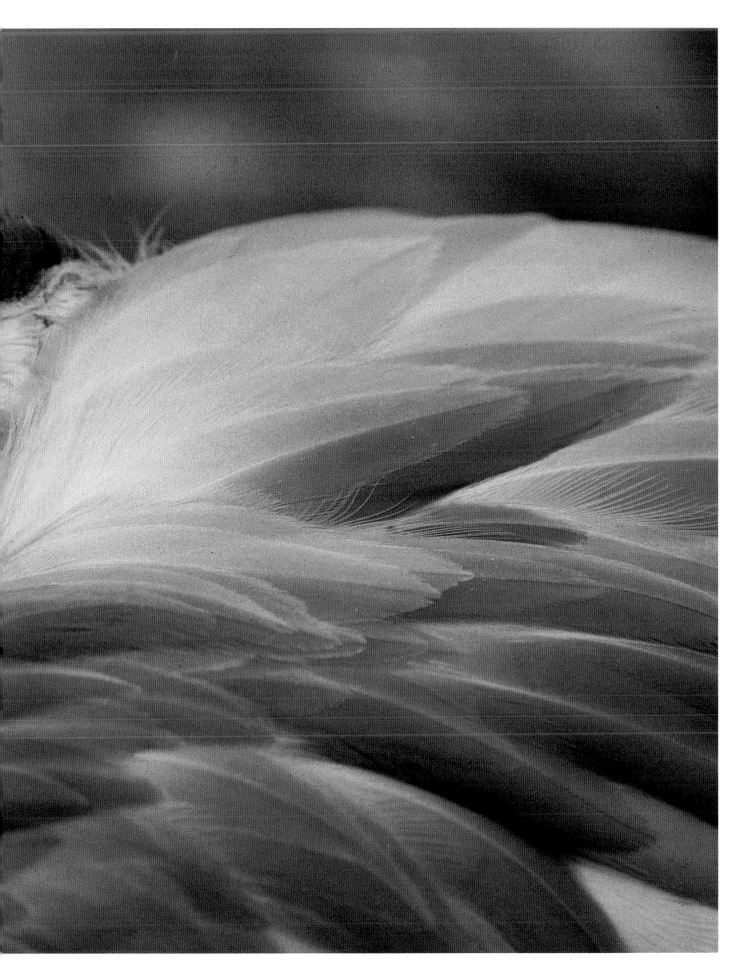

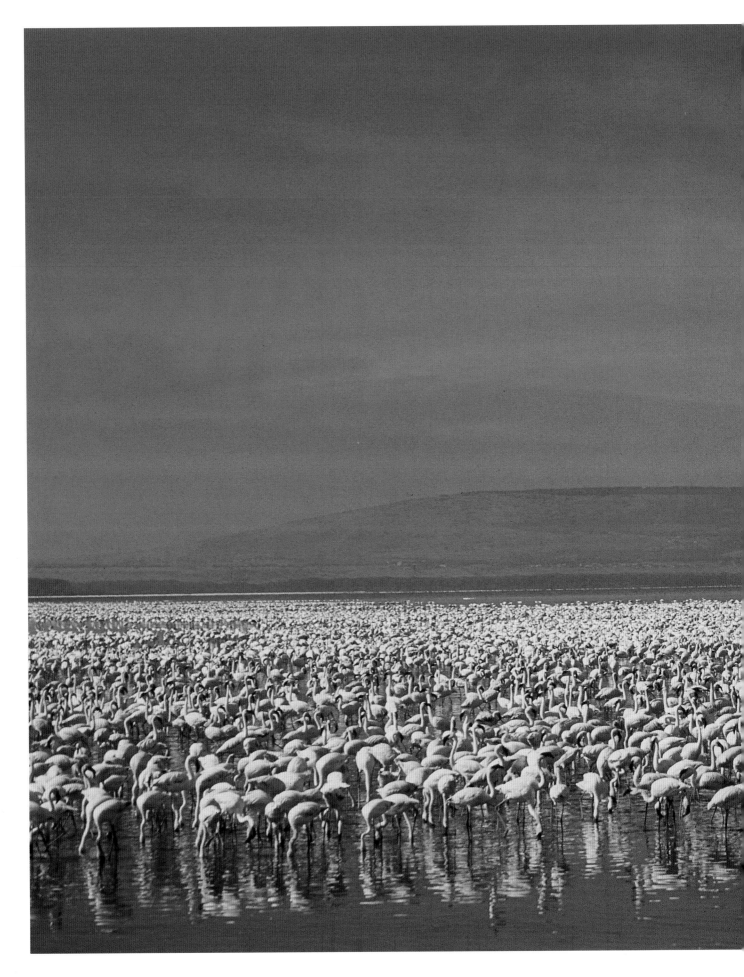

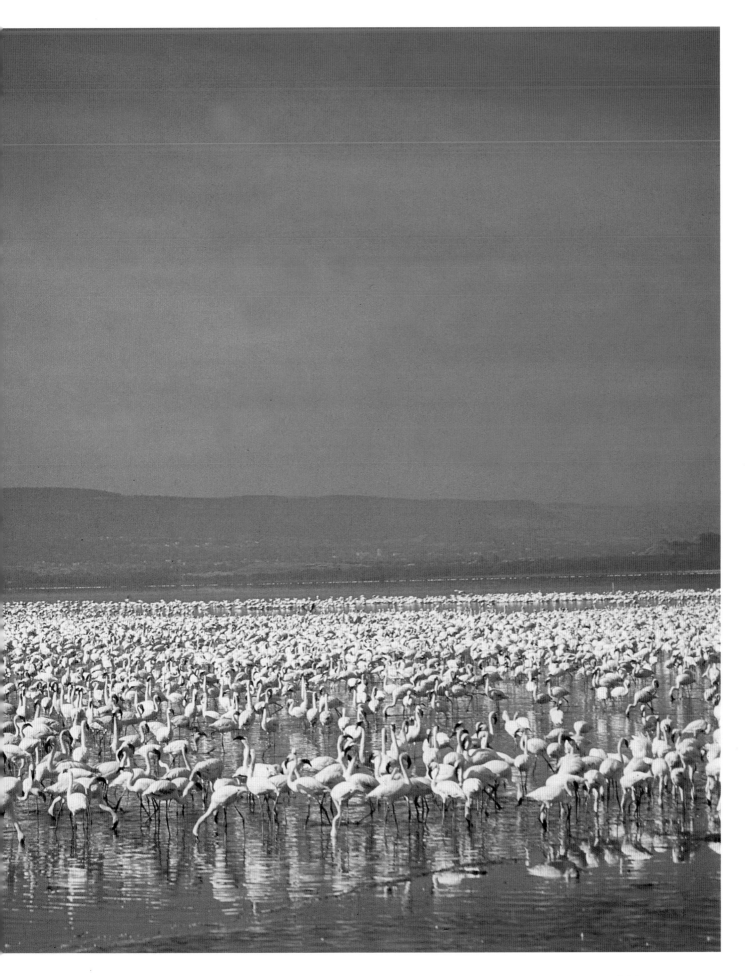

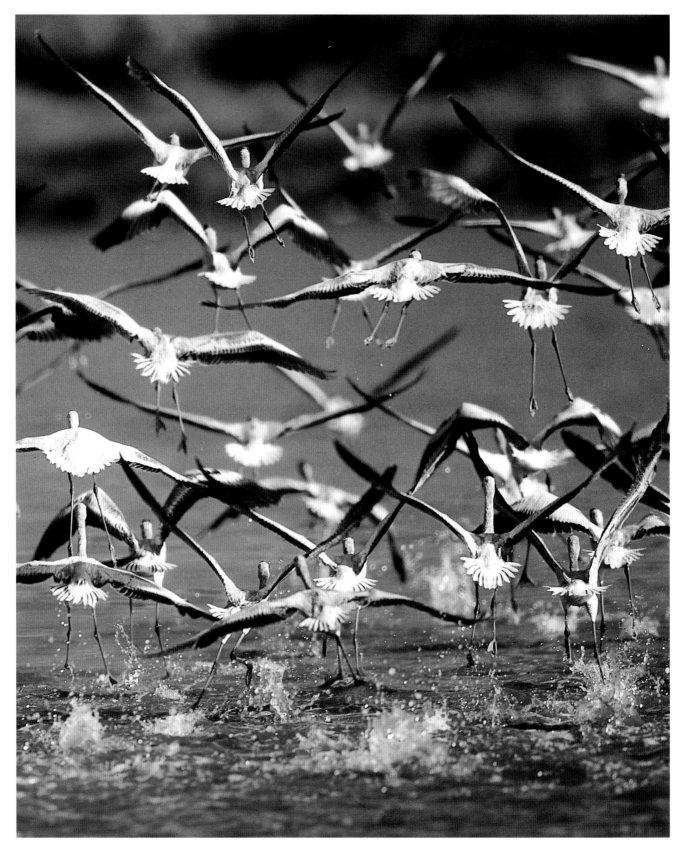

Above: A flock of lesser flamingos takes to the air from a lake in Arusha National Park, Tanzania.

Right: Lesser flamingos in their breeding plumage fly over Walfish Bay, Namibia.

Previous Page: A stupendous gathering of lesser and greater flamingos on Lake Bogoria, Kenya.

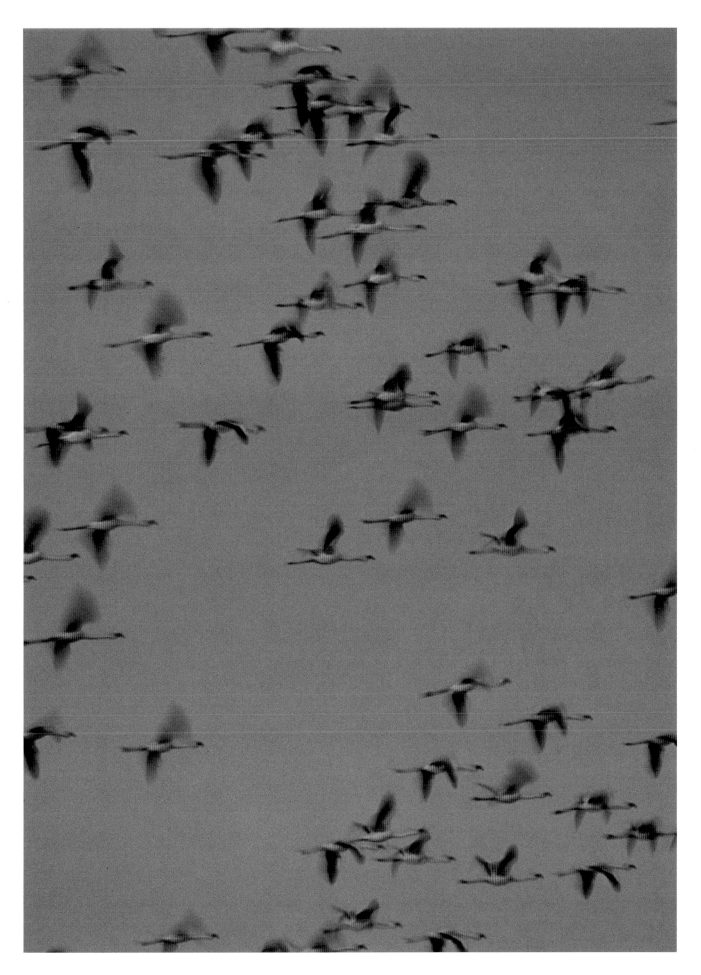

CRANES AND BUSTARDS

The large, long-legged cranes of the family Gruidae are notable, among other things, for their wonderfully elaborate courtship dances, each species having evolved its own distinctive choreography. The blue crane (*Anthropoides paradisea*), the national bird of South Africa, is in fact blue-grey in colour, with a white-capped head and a short pink bill. Its very long black secondary wing feathers seem to droop to the ground when the bird is standing still. It is a native of open grasslands, marshes, ponds and streams, but nowadays is often found in grainfields. It eats seedheads and tubers as well as locusts and other invertebrates, crabs and frogs. Ranging through most of South Africa except western Cape Province, the blue crane is also found in Namibia's Etosha National Park. Its courtship dance includes running in circles, jumping up and down flapping its wings and tossing tufts of grass into the air.

The slightly larger wattled crane (*Bugeranus carunculatus*), about four feet (1.2m) tall, has light grey wings and back, black underside and legs, long white neck, black cap, red face skin and a white, feathered wattle. It lives in grasslands and open marshlands in the Ethiopian highlands and in a large region that takes in south-western Tanzania, Zambia, Angola, the Okavango Delta (Botswana), and upland KwaZulu-Natal. Its courtship dance includes high jumps and grass tossing and also bowing.

The grey crowned crane (*Balearica regulorum*) has a dark grey back and underpart, black legs and feet, white and pale yellow wing patches, golden crown feathers, pale grey neck and red throat wattle. It inhabits grasslands, marshes and floodplains from Uganda and Kenya southwards to KwaZulu-Natal and south-westwards to north-eastern Namibia. Its courtship involves bowing, jumping, running in circles and tossing various handy objects into the air.

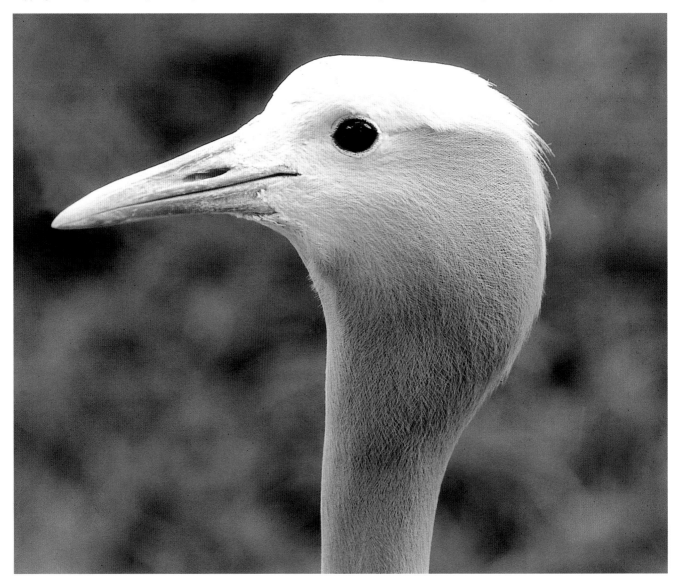

Bustards resemble oversized, long-necked chickens in general shape. They are rather awkward flyers and usually keep to within a few feet of the ground. By far the largest is the kori bustard (*Ardeotis kori*), a huge bird measuring up to 4ft 9in (1.5m) from beak to tail. It is brown on the back, with white underpart and black-and-white-speckled shoulders, and long yellow legs; the face and neck are grey. It inhabits open savanna grassland, open woodland, and semi-desert in East Africa from southern Ethiopia to Tanzania, and most of Africa south of the Zambezi. The black-bellied bustard (*Eupodotis melanogaster*) and the white-bellied bustard (*E. senegalensis*) are much smaller, neither of them more than two feet (61cm) long. Both of them are found from Senegal eastwards to Ethiopia and southwards all the way to South Africa, where bustards are commonly known by the Afrikaans term *korhaan*.

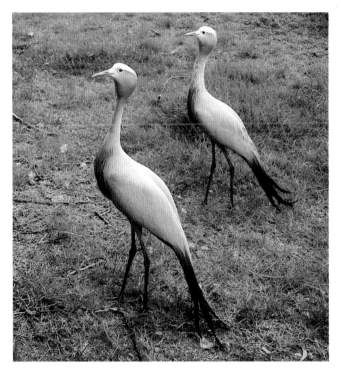

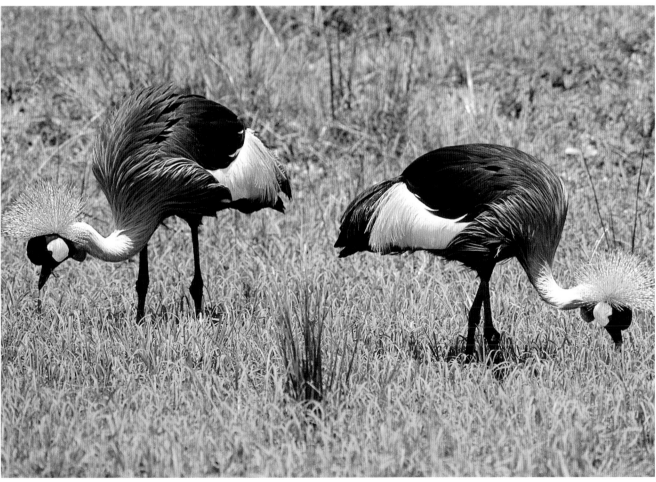

Top: The blue crane, national bird of South Africa, is confined to that country and Etosha National Park, Namibia.

Above: The spectacular plumage of the grey crowned crane, one of the most colourful of Africa's birds.

Left: Blue crane: South Africa. Note the white cap to its head.

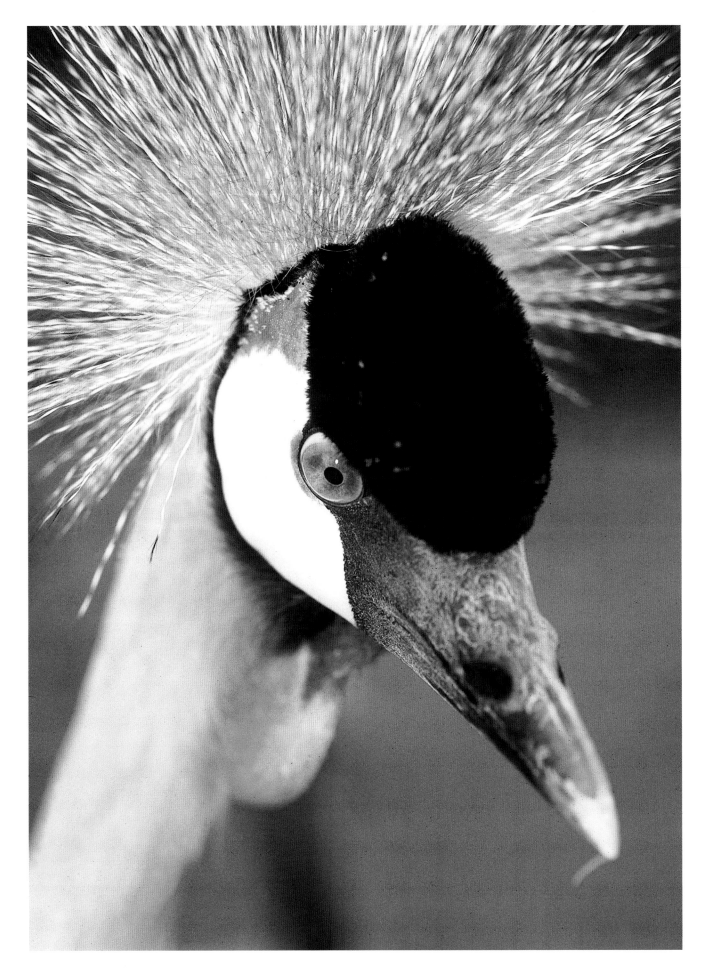

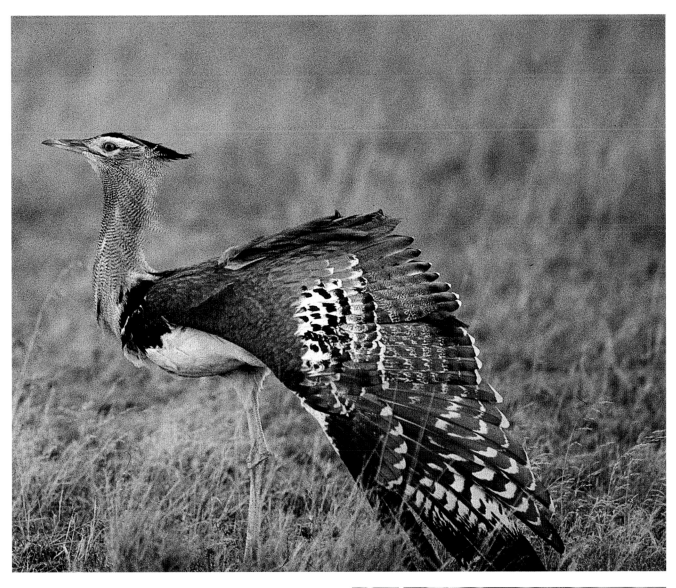

Above: Kori bustard with wings spread: Serengeti National Park, Tanzania. This is the largest bustard species.

Right: Three-day-old grey crowned crane chicks.

Left: Head of grey crowned crane: Masai Mara. Note the golden spray of feathers on its crown, the black fore-crown, the large patch of bare white skin on the side of its head with the small red patch above it, and the red throat wattle.

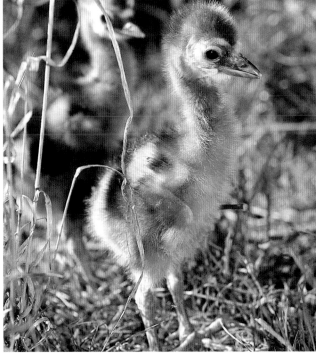

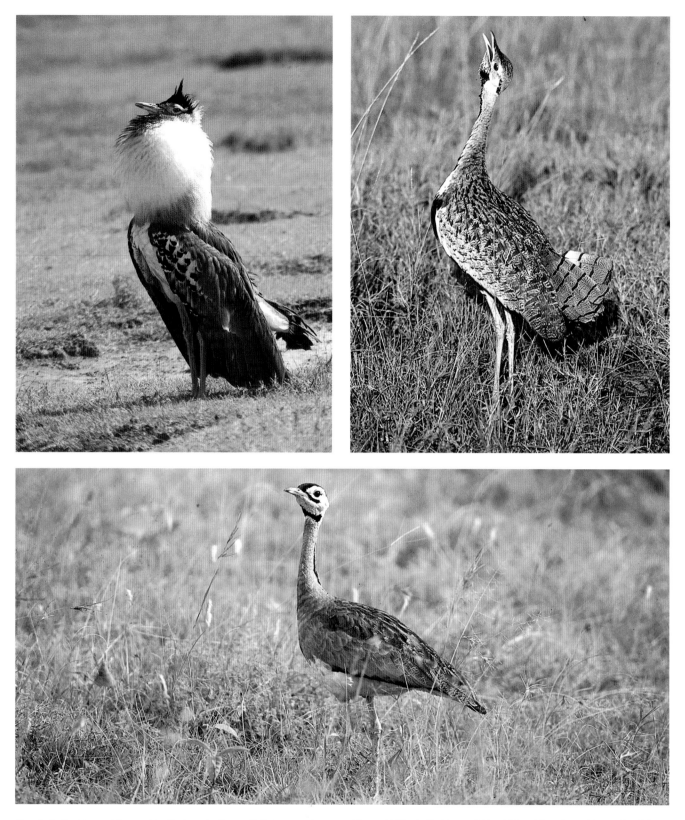

Top Left: Kori bustard in coutship display: raised crest, fluffed out neck feathers and much strutting about making clucking calls.

Top Right: The female black-bellied bustard lacks the male's black underparts.

Above: White-bellied bustard: Masai Mara. Note the red base of its bill and white face with black cap, "moustache" and neckband.

Above Right: Pair of African fish-eagles perched on the branch of a dead tree in the Okavango Delta. Note the rich chestnut underparts, black flight feathers, white chest, neck and head, and the large black-tipped yellow beak.

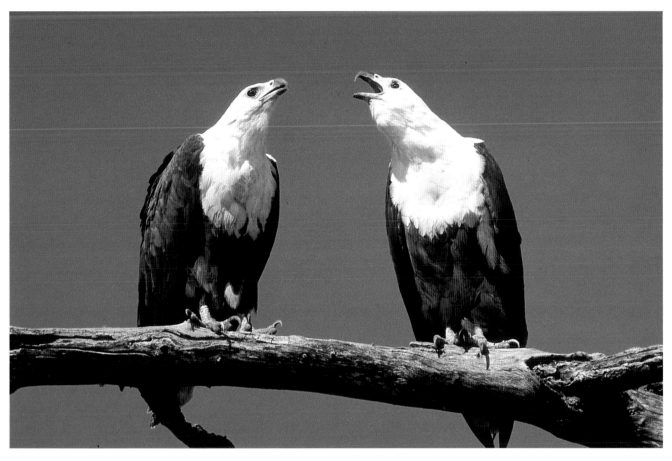

RAPTORS

This term covers birds of prey such as eagles, hawks, falcons, kites, vultures and some others. All these birds have large eyes (and very keen vision), hooked beaks and powerful feet with hooked talons. Almost without exception among these birds, the female is larger than the male, in some species by almost one third.

The African fish-eagle (*Haliaeetus vocifer*) is a large eagle with a wing span of seven feet (2.1m) and more. Its vivid white head, neck, chest and back give way on ther lower chest, underpart and thighs to a rich milk-chocolate brown; the flight feathers are black; the beak is dark grey or black with a yellow base; the feet are yellow. It is resident by rivers, lakes and reservoirs, and also saline creeks near coasts, throughout sub-Sahara Africa. The fish-eagle scans areas of water from lofty perches—treetops, cliffs or man-made structures—rather than by hoveriong at height. It looks mainly for large fish swimming near the surface, which it takes by gliding down to the water and seizing the prey in its talons. It also preys on young flamingoes and other waders, newly hatched crocodiles, turtles and even monitor lizards, and will not hesitate to steal fish from other birds.

Verreaux's eagle (*Aquila verreauxii*), sometimes called the black eagle, is the largest of Africa's native eagles, with a wing span of up to 8ft 6in (2.6m). It is deep black all over except for white at the base of its primary feathers (visible only when in flight) and a white rump patch; the beak is mainly ash-grey. There is a thin white or pale yellow line around the eye; the feet are yellow. It is a denizen of open mountain slopes, gorges and escarpments and is commonly seen at altitudes up to 16,000ft (4,900m); its range includes the Red Sea and southwards through the East African highlands, onwards to South Africa and round to Namibia's Skeleton Coast. Its diet includes hyraxes (dassies), as well as small antelopes, hares, and guineafowl.

The African hawk-eagle (*Hieraaetus spilogaster*), with a wing span of five feet (1.5m), is black on the upper areas, white on the underpart. When viewed in flight from below, the wings are vivid white with black leading and trailing edges, the flared tail feathers are white with black at the tips, and the chest white with black streaks and spots. Its habitat is wooded mountain slopes, wooded savanna and riverine forests from Senegal eastwards to Ethiopia, then southwards throughout the Rift Valley and on to northern Namibia and

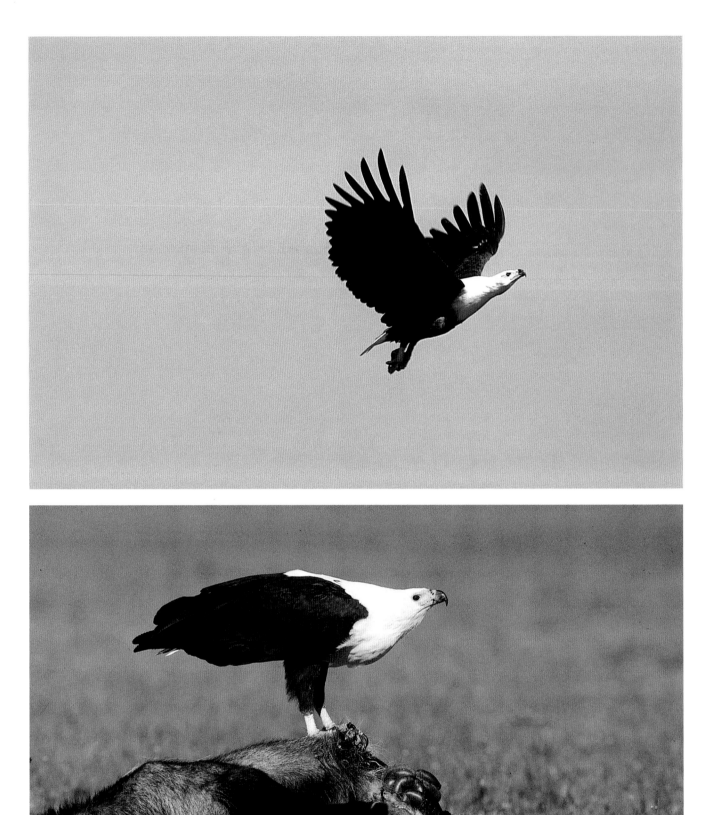

Top: A fish-eagle in flight over the Serengeti plains, Tanzania.

Above: A fish-eagle inspects the abandoned carcass of a waterbuck near Lake Naivasha.

Right: Verreaux's eagle in flight over Matobo National Park in western Zimbabwe. It is big and powerful enough to prey on small antelopes.

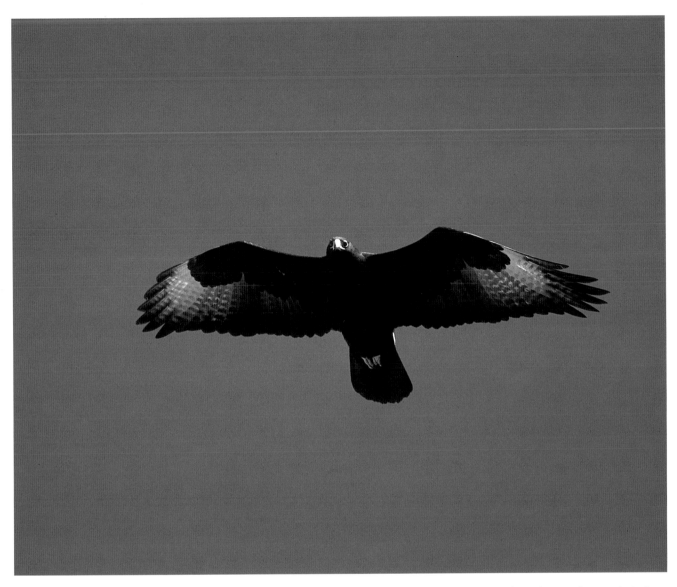

Botswana and the Drakensberg range in Swaziland. Its diet includes birds, small antelopes, hyraxes, hares and mongooses. It is relentless in pursuit of its prey, and a pair often hunts cooperatively.

The bateleur (*Terathopius ecaudatus*)—its common name is French for a tightrope walker who uses a balance-pole, a reference to the bird's side-to-side dipping motion in flight—has a massive head and heavy, orange-yellow beak and face. It has mostly jet-black plumage, but greyish brown shoulders and rich brown back. The short legs are bright red. In flight, the undersides of the wings are white with a black trailing edge. It hunts mainly in open, deciduous woodlands, grassy savannas and semi-desert over much the same range as the hawk eagle; it can also be seen patrolling the skies over Mount Kenya and neighbouring highlands. Its diet includes small antelopes, hares, birds (including bustards), and monitor lizards as well as carrion.

The black kite (*Milvus migrans*) is also—and more logically—called the yellow-billed kite: none of the various races of this species, which is found throughout sub-Sahara Africa, is black. Most have yellow beaks, and most have mid- to dark-brown plumage, while some have underparts streaked with reddish brown. It is long-winged, and the long tail feathers are deeply notched. It is native to savannas and sub-desert regions and is also found along coasts and rivers and close to human settlements. It feeds on small birds, lizards, rats, fish and insects and scavenges for domestic waste in villages and towns.

The secretary bird (*Sagittarius serpentarius*) looks rather like a cross between a crane and an eagle, with its long legs and slim but hawk-like profile. As large as many true eagles, it has a wing span of up to seven feet (2.1m). It derives its common name from the supposed resemblance of the black feathers on the nape of its neck to quill pens parked behind the ears. Its overall colour is whitish grey. Its tail feathers, including the two very long central ones, are pale grey with black and white tips, and the flight feathers are black as are the long thigh feathers above the red legs. The hooked beak is grey, but its base and the bare skin around the eyes may be yellowish orange or red. It is mainly a bird of the savannas—open woodland, grassland and semi-desert—from Senegal to Somalia and most regions to the south apart from Zaïre, Cameroon and Gabon. It hunts mainly on foot rather from the air, frequently stamping on the ground to flush out insects or rodents. Snakes often feature in its diet; it also eats nesting birds and lizards. When fires periodically sweep through the tinder-dry grass of the savanna, the secretarybird is often seen pouncing on the snakes and small mammals fleeing before the advancing flames.

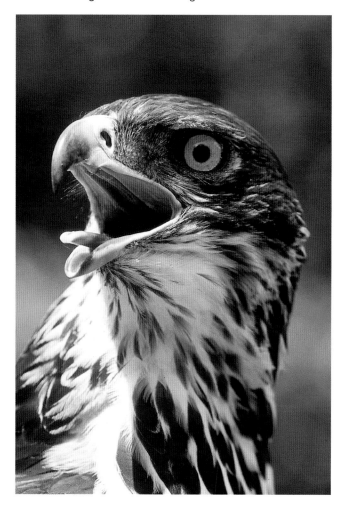

Above: African hawk-eagle: Matusadona National Park, Zimbabwe. A very fast flier, it often hunts cooperatively with its mate.

Right: The bateleur, seen here in Matobo National Park, preys on small antelopes, birds, monitor lizards and hares.

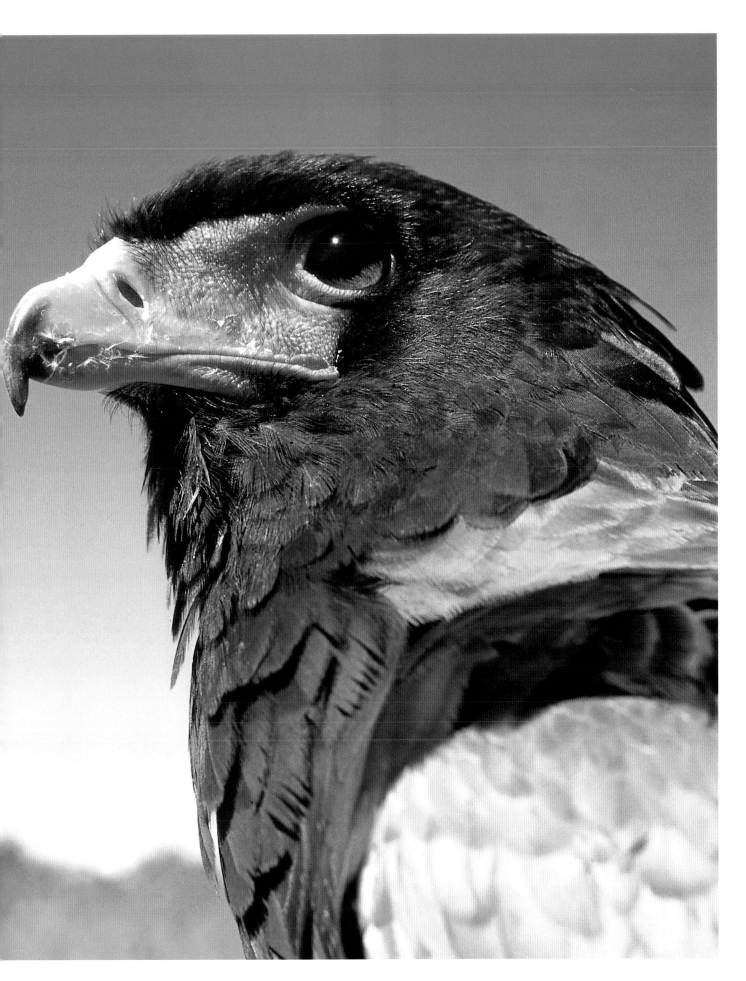

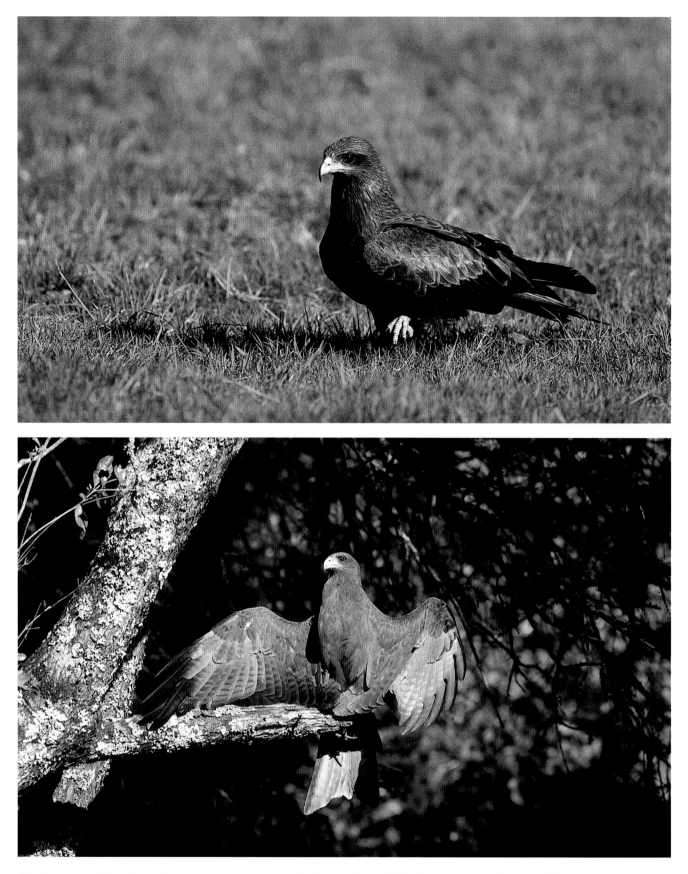

Top: Most races of black kite are in fact various shades of brown. On the ground, as here, they can be recognised by their short yellow legs and feet.

Above: A black kite sunbathing in Nairobi National Park.

Above Right: The augur buzzard is a hawk of highland grasslands and farming country, preying on rodents, hares, hyraxes, snakes and other reptiles.

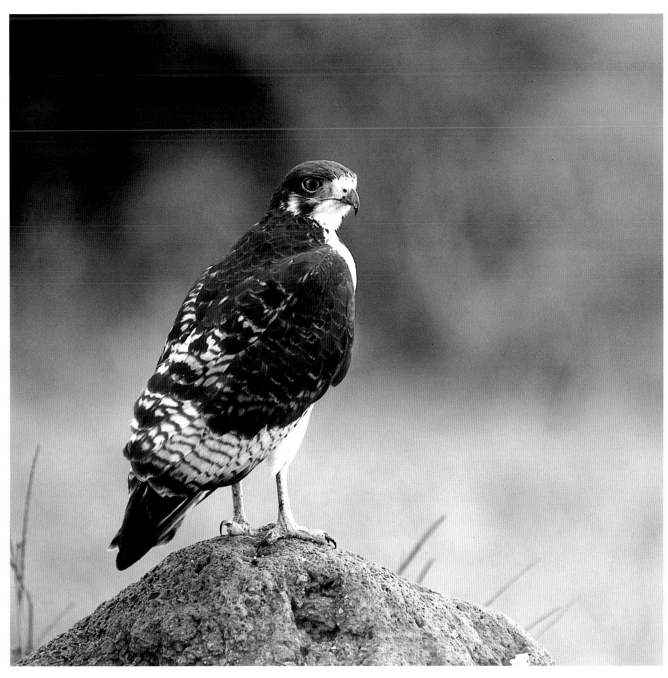

The lappet-faced vulture (*Aegypius tracheliotus*), the largest of the African vultures, has a wing span of up to 9ft 6in (2.9m). Its beak, the largest of any raptor, is yellowish grey. The pink lappets (the term means loosely hanging folds of flesh) somewhat resemble earlobes and hang from each side of the head, which like the neck is also pink. The back and ruff are dark brown, the sides and the thighs are pure white; the underwings are black with a white line by the leading edge. It is a creature of the dry savanna, thorn scrub and semi-desert, ranging from Senegal eastwards through the Sahel to Ethiopia, then southwards through East Africa to Namibia and KwaZulu-Natal. The lappet-faced, like other vultures, is essentially a scavenger, feeding on carcasses of animals abandoned by big cats and other predators. The different vulture species tend to specialise in the particular parts of a large carcass that they prefer to eat. Most other vultures give the lappet-faced precedence at such carcasses, relying on its powerful beak to tear open the hide. It also preys on flamingos and young gazelles.

The white-backed vulture (*Gyps africanus*) is the most numerous of Africa's larger vultures: it is usually this species one sees in wildlife films where hordes of vultures are fighting amongst themselves to get at a large carcass, and afterwards sunning themselves with wings outspread. It is a pale brown colour, with white plumage on the

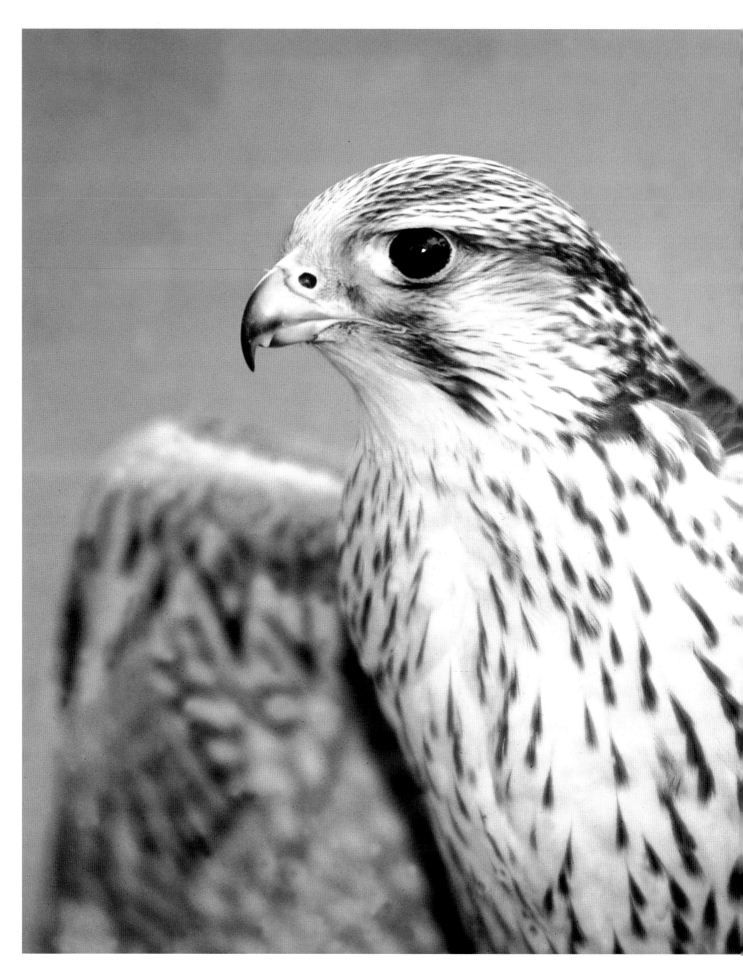

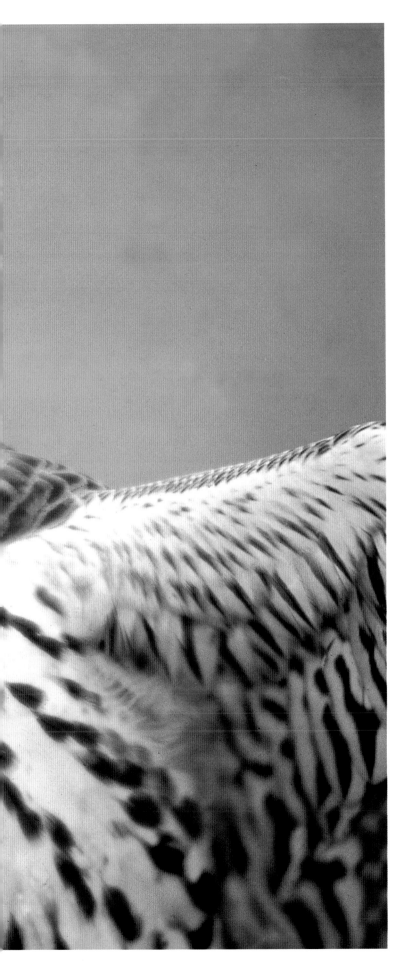

lower back; the face and throat are much darker than the crown; the beak and eye are black. The lining to the underside of the wings, which have a span of up to eight feet (2.4m), is white, the flight feathers black. It has a range very similar to that of the lappet-faced vulture.

Rüppell's griffon vulture (*Gyps rueppelli*) is a creature of mountains and, where it patrols the East African savannas, of the cliffs and escarpments of the Rift Valley. A large vulture, it has a wing span of up to 8ft 6in (2.6m). The plumage is essentially dark brown, but white patches at the ends of the wing and breast feathers produce a marbling effect; while the head and neck are covered only with fine, down-like feathers. Three lines of white feathers towards the leading edge of the underwings are clearly visible when the bird is soaring on thermals. In the Ethiopian highlands it is found at altitudes of up to 14,500ft (4,400m). It roosts on cliffs in colonies that may number several thousand pairs.

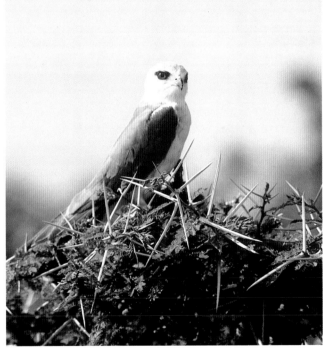

Above: The Black shouldered kite is a fast, acrobatic flier found in most parts of Africa apart from lowland rainforests. It seizes birds in flight and also preys on rodents and lizards.

Left: The African pygmy falcon is no more than eight inches (20cm) long. Its two separate ranges are dependent on those of two species of weaver birds whose nests it commandeers: in East Africa it takes over the thorny nest of the white-headed buffalo-weaver; in Namibia and southern Botswana it moves into a cell in the huge communal structure of the sociable weaver. It preys on reptiles, small birds, rodents and insects.

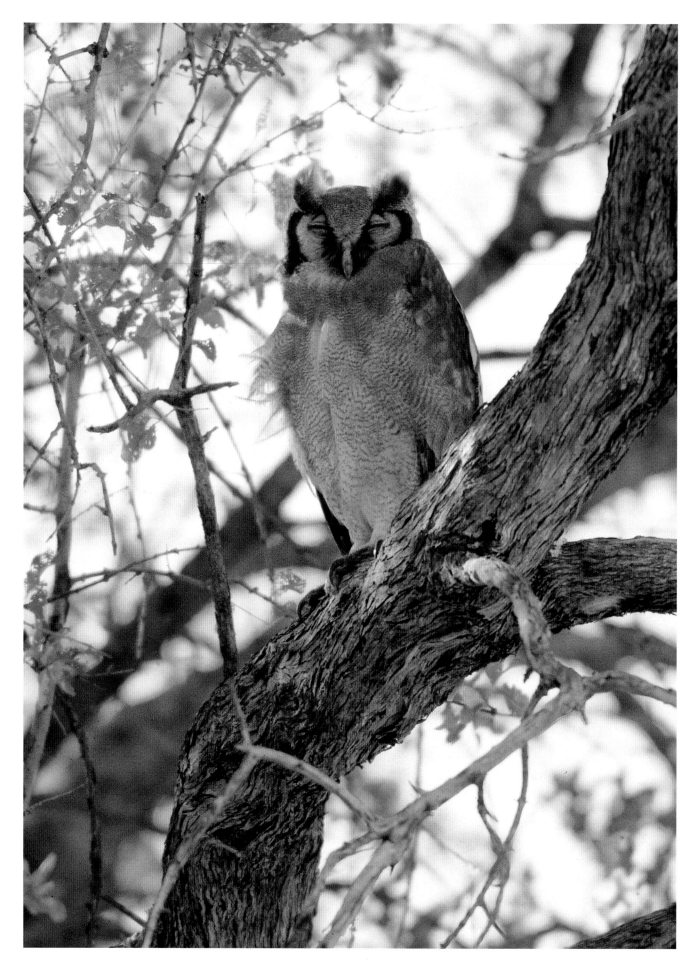

Smallest of the African species, the hooded vulture (*Necrosyrtes monachus*) has a wing span of about 5ft 6in (1.7m). It has a pink or red face and white, downy feathers on its crown, the back of the neck and the crop. The black underwings have a single line of white feathers. Although it ranges through much of West, East and southern Africa, it is absent from the wetter equatorial regions, and from Namibia and most of Botswana and South Africa. It is a scavenger that is found close to human settlements—not only farmsteads but villages and towns in Ghana, Nigeria and Uganda.

The palm-nut vulture (*Gypohierax angolensis*), as its name suggests, is partly vegetarian. Its head, neck, back, underparts and thighs are white; the flight feathers are black; the black tail is white-tipped. The beak is greyish yellow; the bare skin around the eye is pink or red. It has a wing span of up to five feet (1.5m). It is essentially a native of the wet tropics, from Senegal to Angola and including most of the Congo river basin. In the east it is found around the lakes of the western arm of the Rift Valley; also along the Indian Ocean coast from Kenya to KwaZulu-Natal. The largest populations are in West Africa, where the oil palm (wild-growing and cultivated) is most abundant. Its diet also includes wild dates and other fruits, crabs, mollusks, and fish.

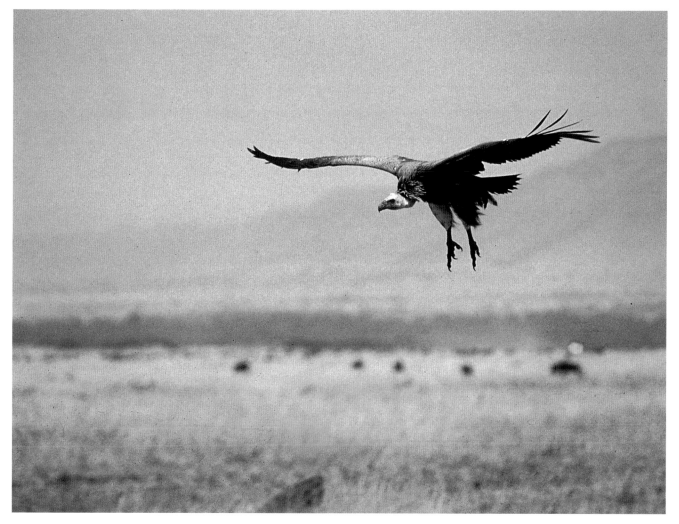

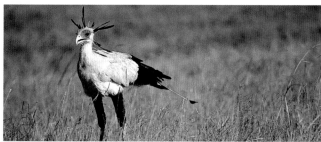

Above: White-headed vulture landing on the Masai Mara.

Far Left: Verreaux's eagle-owl is about 25in (63cm) tall and is found in savannas and woodland throughout East Africa and south to north-eastern South Africa. Note the dark ring around its face and the fluffy ear tufts.

Left: The secretarybird looks like a long-legged eagle. Note the black, erectile, quill-like nape feathers.

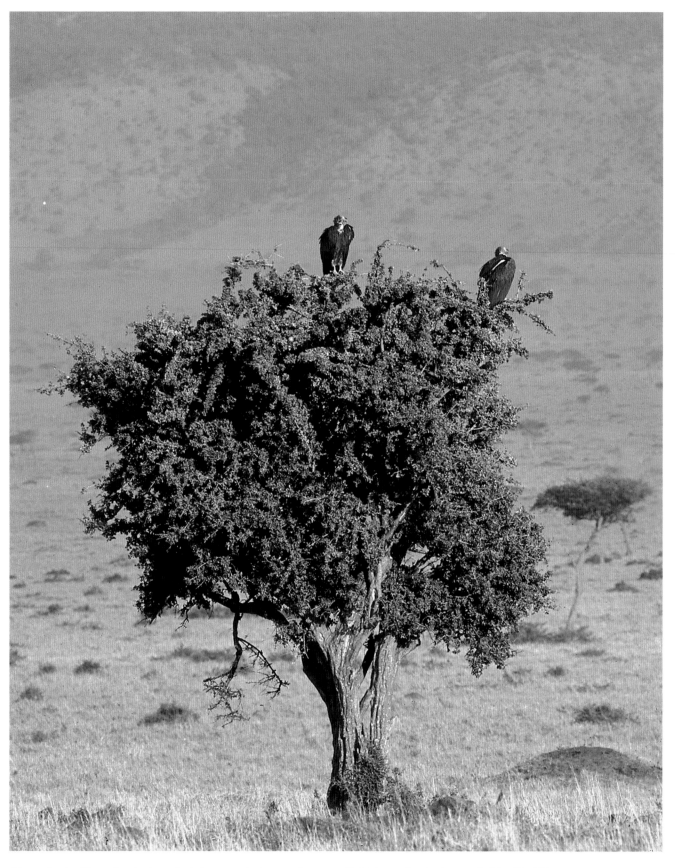

Above: A pair of lappet-faced vultures in their tree-top lookout on the Masai Mara.

Above Right: A lappet-faced vulture preparing to land: Masai Mara.

Right: Lappet-faced vulture sunbathing: Masai Mara.

Overleaf: A head shot of a lappet-faced vulture. Note the pink lappet at the side of its head.

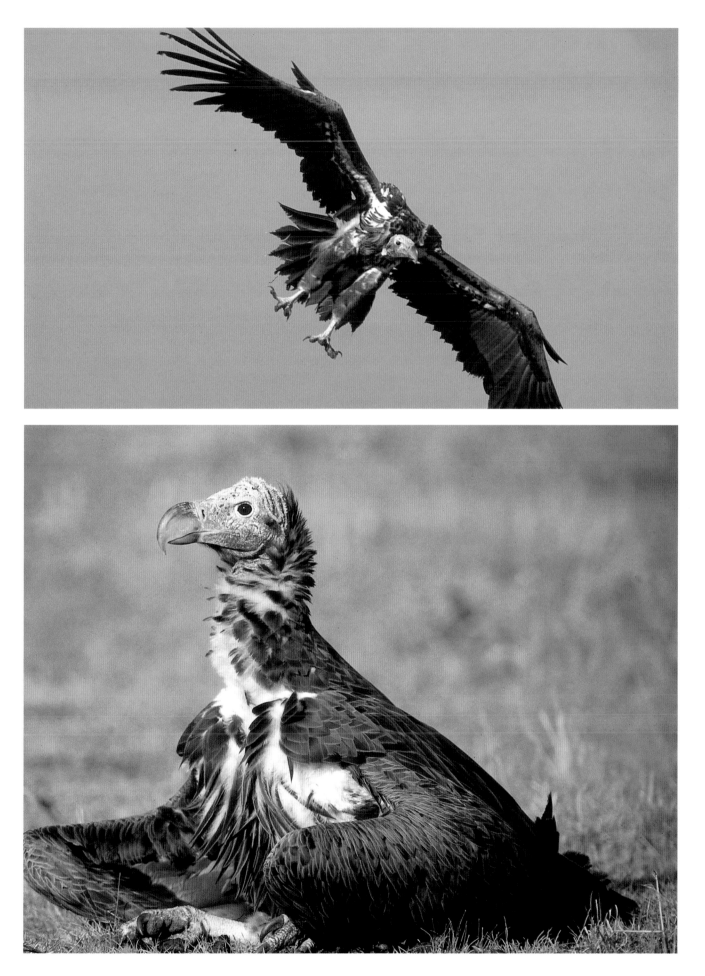

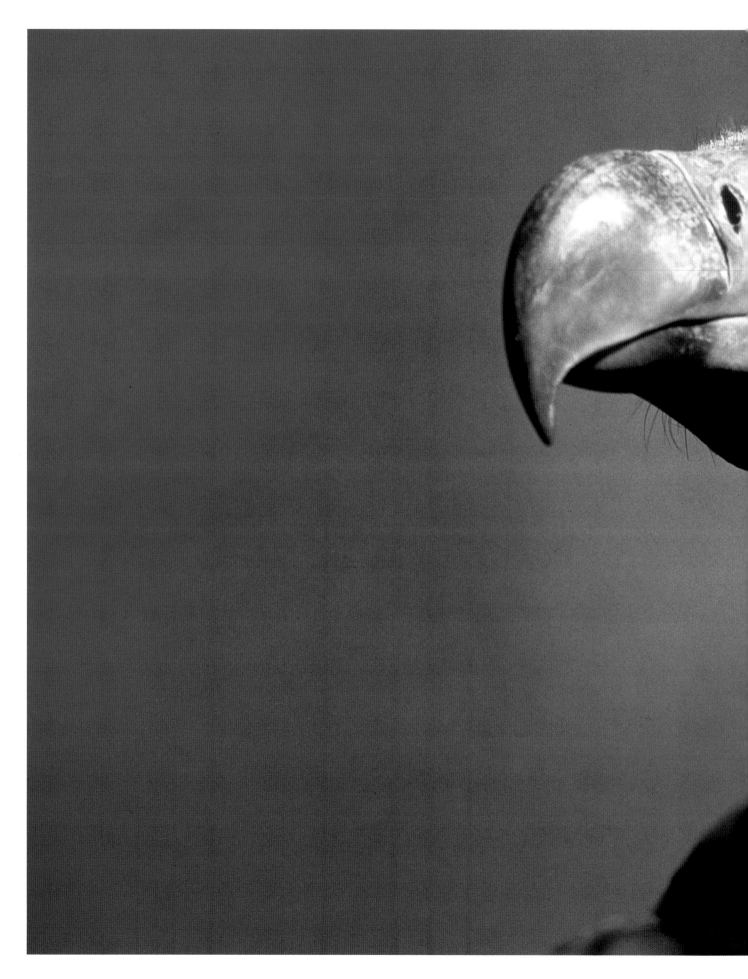

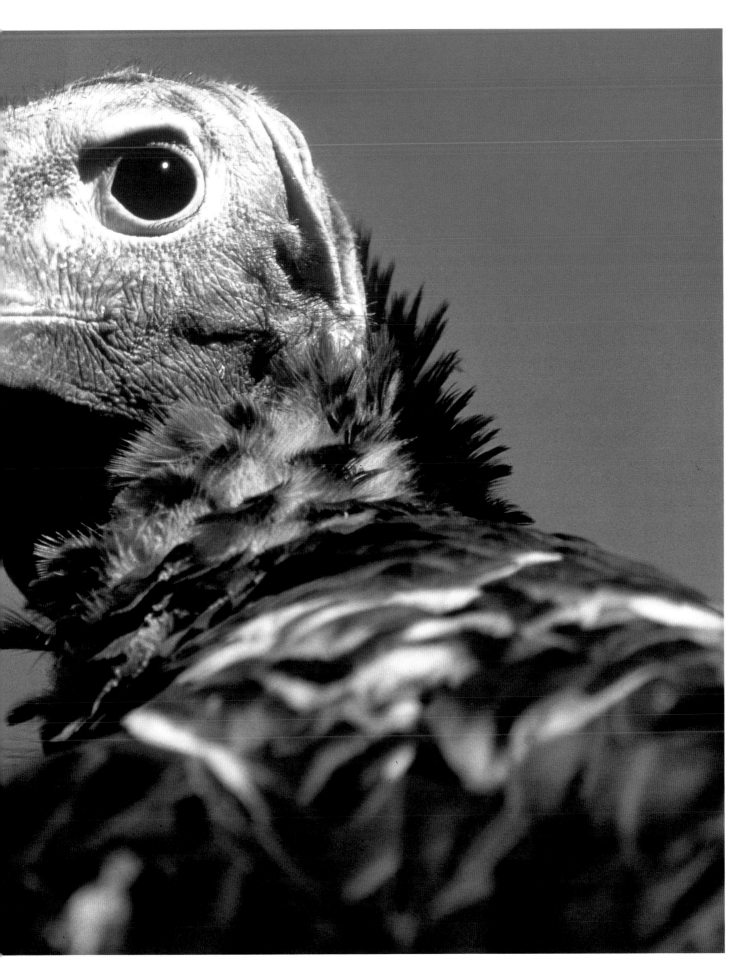

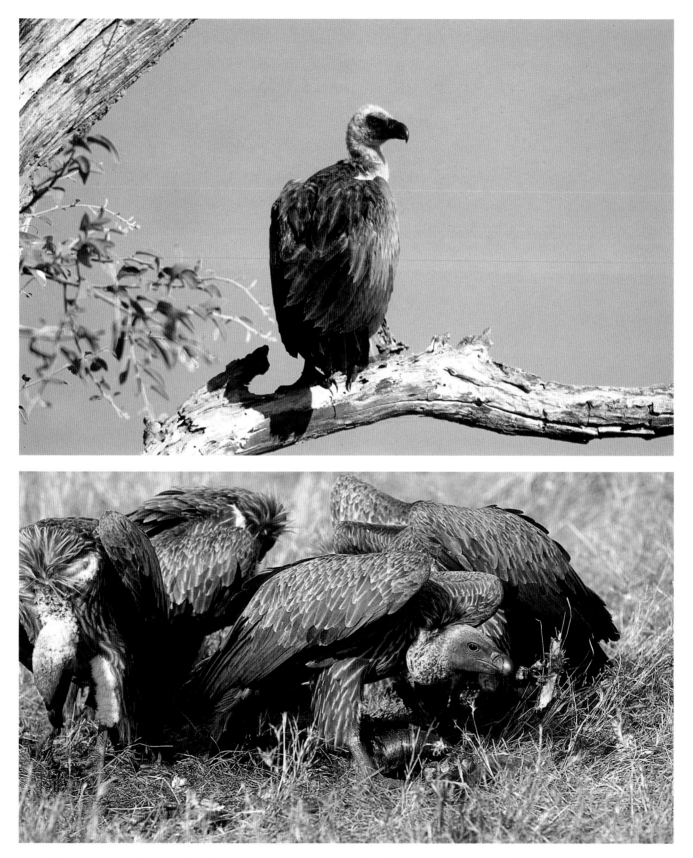

Top: White-backed vulture: Botswana. The white lower-back plumage is concealed.

Above: White-backed vultures pick a carcass completely clean on the Serengeti plains.

Right: White-backed vulture landing: Masai Mara. Note its dark face and throat, the lighter crown and neck.

Overleaf: White-faced vultures at a zebra carcass: Etosha National Park, Namibia.

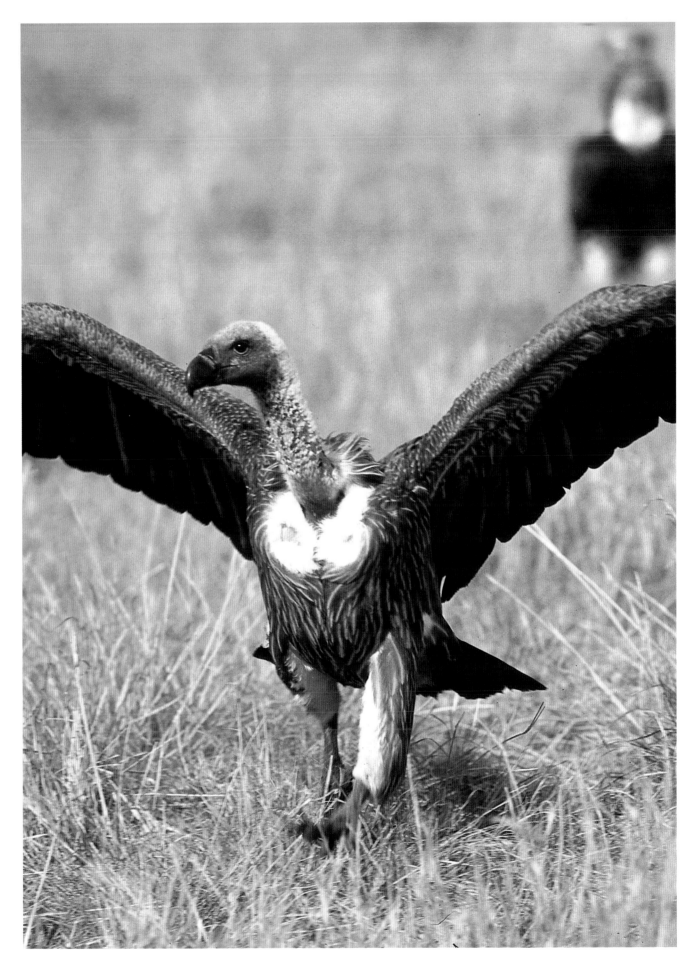

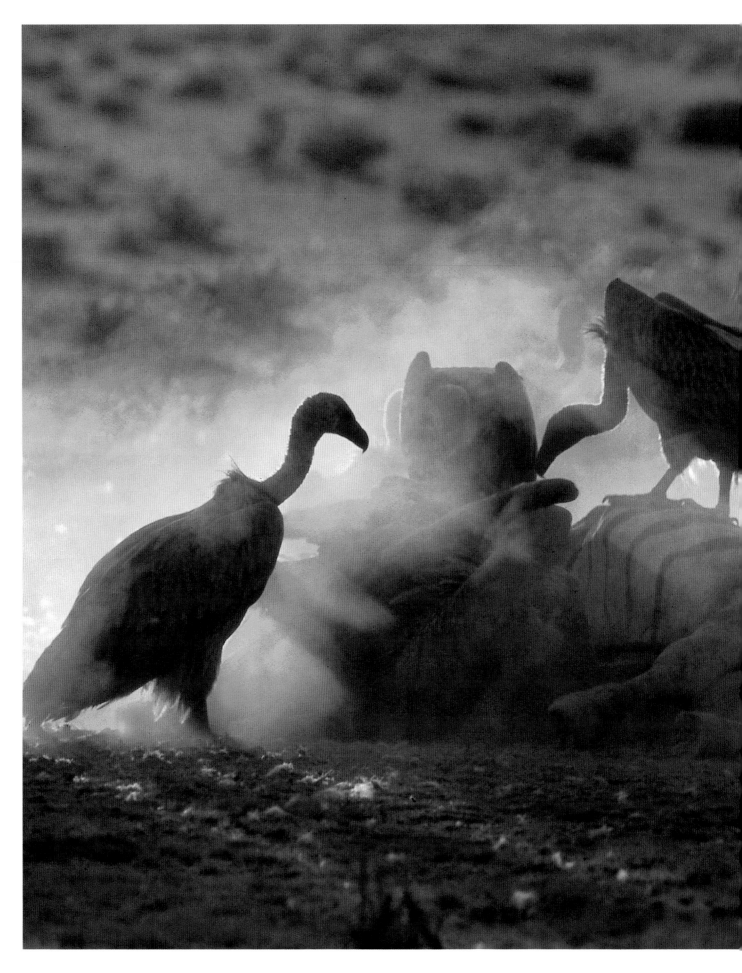

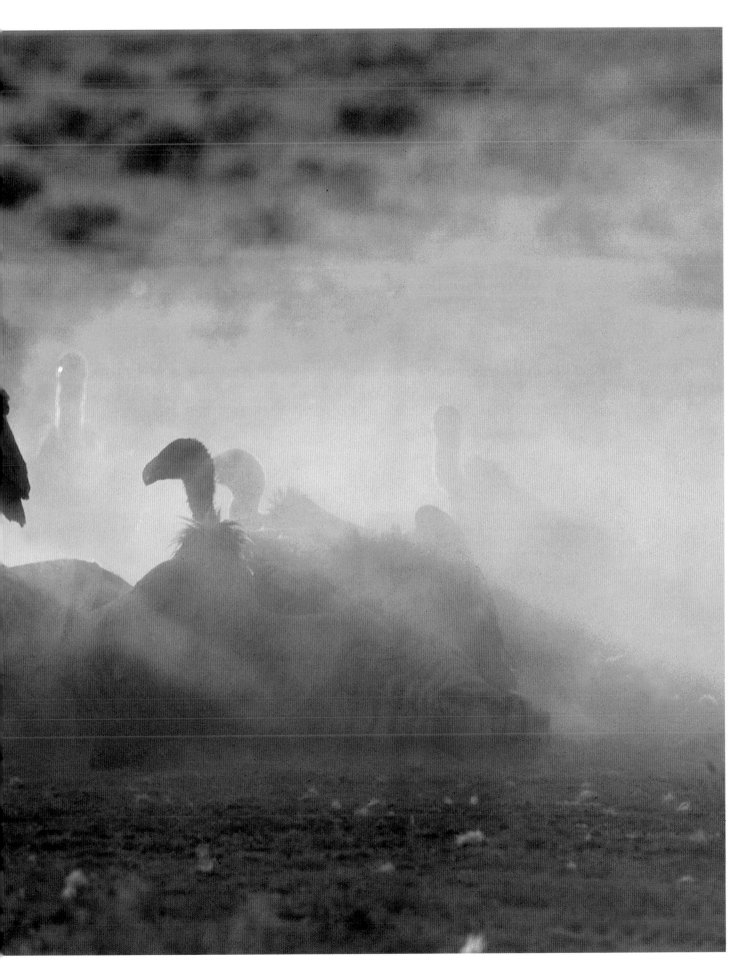

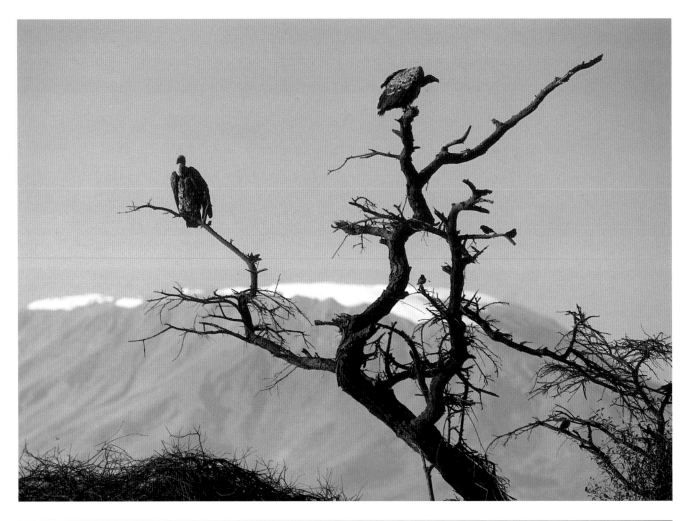

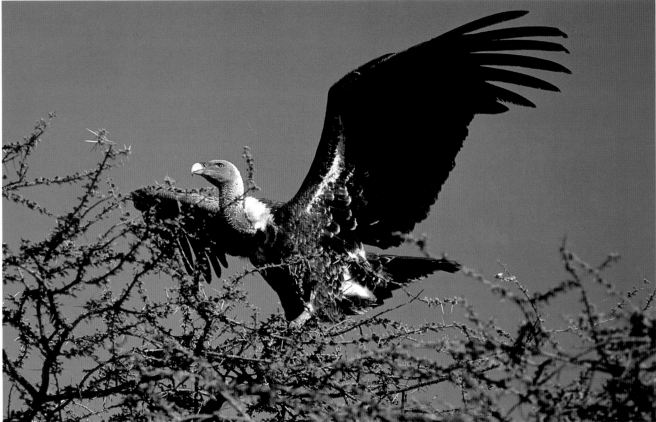

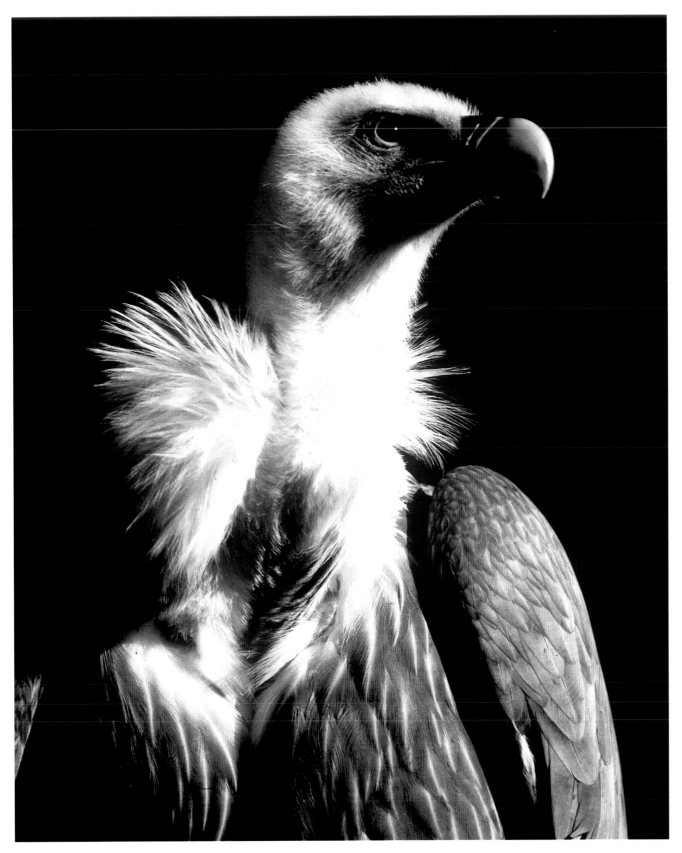

Top Left: Rüppell's griffon vultures on a tree: Amboseli National Park, with Kilimanjaro in background.

Left: Rüppell's griffon vulture alighting on tree, Masai Mara. Note white on underside of wing.

Above: Headshot of Rüppell's griffon vulture. Note white, down-like feathers on neck.

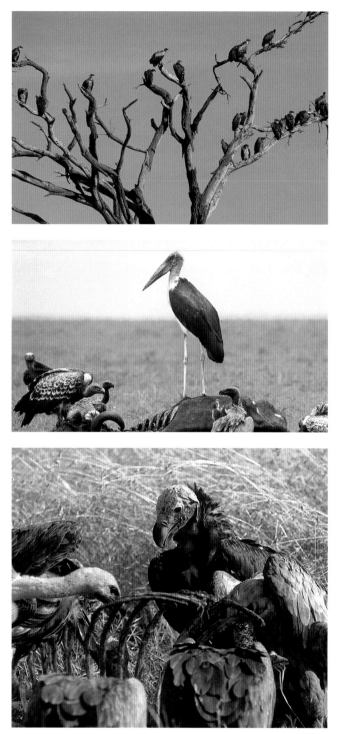

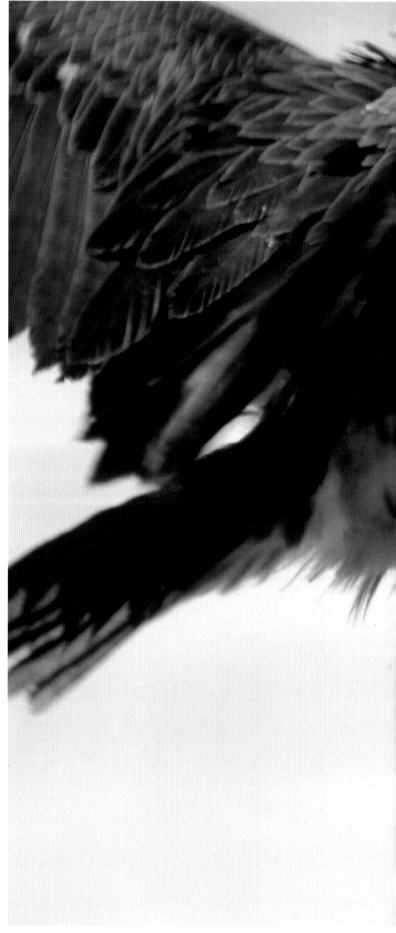

Top: Rüppell's and white-backed vultures gather near a kill in Amboseli National Park.

Centre: Rüppell's griffon vultures at a buffalo carcass on the Masai Mara while a marabou stork prepares to intervene.

Above: White-headed vultures strip bare the carcass of an antelope: Masai Mara.

Right: Two vultures leap into the air in a noisy dispute over a carcass: Etosha National Park.

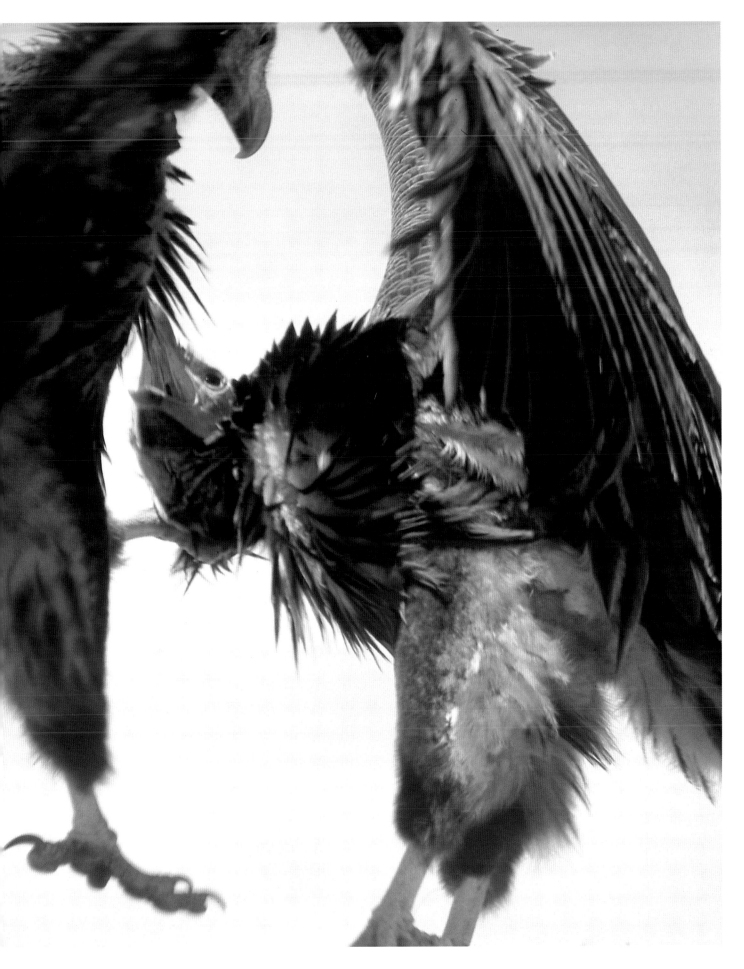

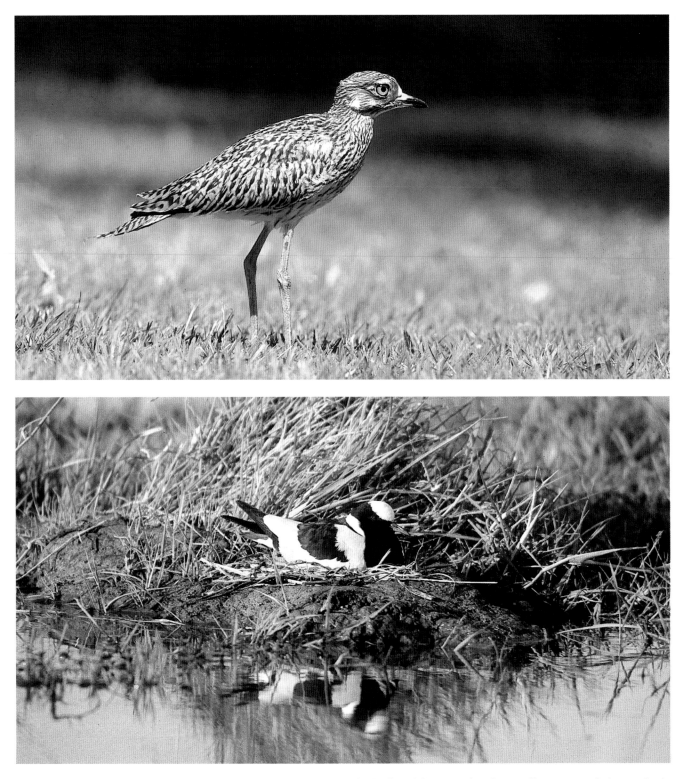

THICK-KNEES

The thick-knees are waders and are also known as stone-curlews, stone-plovers, or dikkops (Afrikaans for "thick-head"); they are related to the oystercatchers. The Cape thick-knee (*Burhinus capensis*), like other members of the genus, is a long-tailed, light brownish grey bird with dark and light stripes about the face and on the crest, and fine black or dark brown stripes and spots on the back and breast; it has large yellow eyes, a dark grey beak, yellow at the base, a white throat, and long, greenish yellow legs with somewhat swollen knees. It is about 16in (40cm) from beak to tail. It is found widely in South Africa around rivers and lakes offering good cover, and also along coasts; in some areas it has become quite tame and can be seen grubbing for insects on the lawns of city parks.

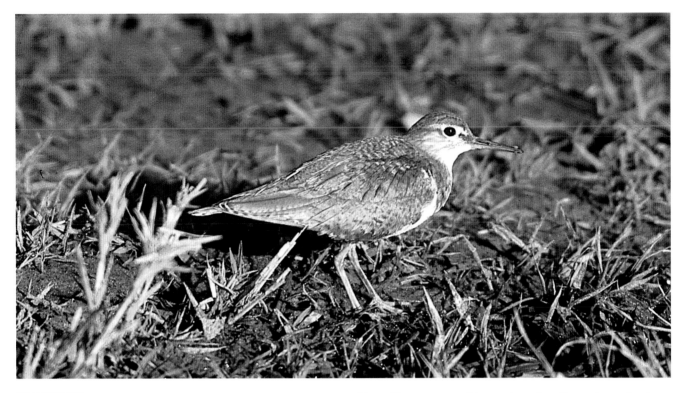

SANDPIPERS

The sandpiper family also includes plover, ruff, curlew, godwit, dowitcher, turnstone and others. The blacksmith plover (*Vanellus armatus*), also known as the blacksmith lapwing, has earned its common name from its loud warning call, a series of rapidly repeated series of metallic "clinks", rather like the sound of a blacksmith's hammer on an anvil. It alerts all animals in the vicinity, not only birds, to the fact that intruders are about. It has a white crown, hind-neck and underpart; a black face, nape, fore-neck, chest and back; and mostly light grey upper surfaces to the wings. It eyes are red, its bill and legs black. It occurs in East Africa's Rift Valley lakes and throughout most of South Africa, living by fresh-water rivers and lakes on dry savanna grasslands and foraging for worms, insects, molluscs and small crustaceans.

The ruff (*Philomachus pugnax*) has a dark brown back on which each feather has white or light brown edging; the underpart is pale brown. The short legs are orange or pinkish yellow. Several million ruffs winter in Africa after breeding in Eurasia; they are found all over Africa (except for the Sahara desert), living on mudflats, by salt- and fresh-water lakes and rivers, and also on grasslands close to permanent water. Its diet includes crustaceans, mollusks, insects and worms.

Above: This common sandpiper, a migrant from Europe, is spending the southern spring and summer in Botswana.

Above Left: Cape thick-knee, or dikkop: Cape Province. Note the yellow base of its beak.

Left: A blacksmith plover on its waterside nest in the Okavango Delta.

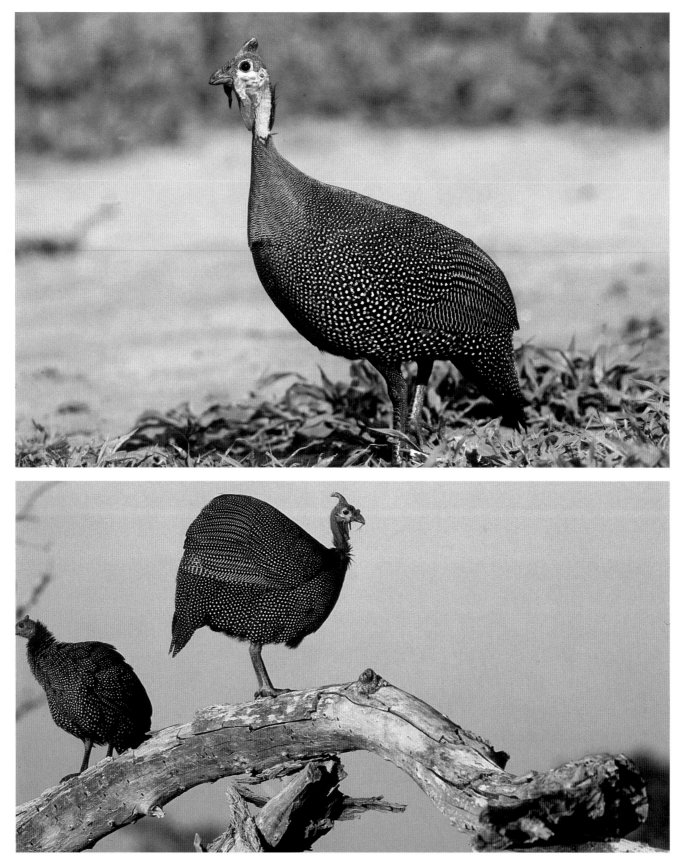

Top: Helmeted guineafowl are found in most of sub-Sahara Africa except for rainforests. This one is from northern Zimbabwe

Right: Grey go-away bird (also known as grey lourie): northern Transvaal.

Above: Pair of helmeted guineafowl on a dead tree: Masai Mara.

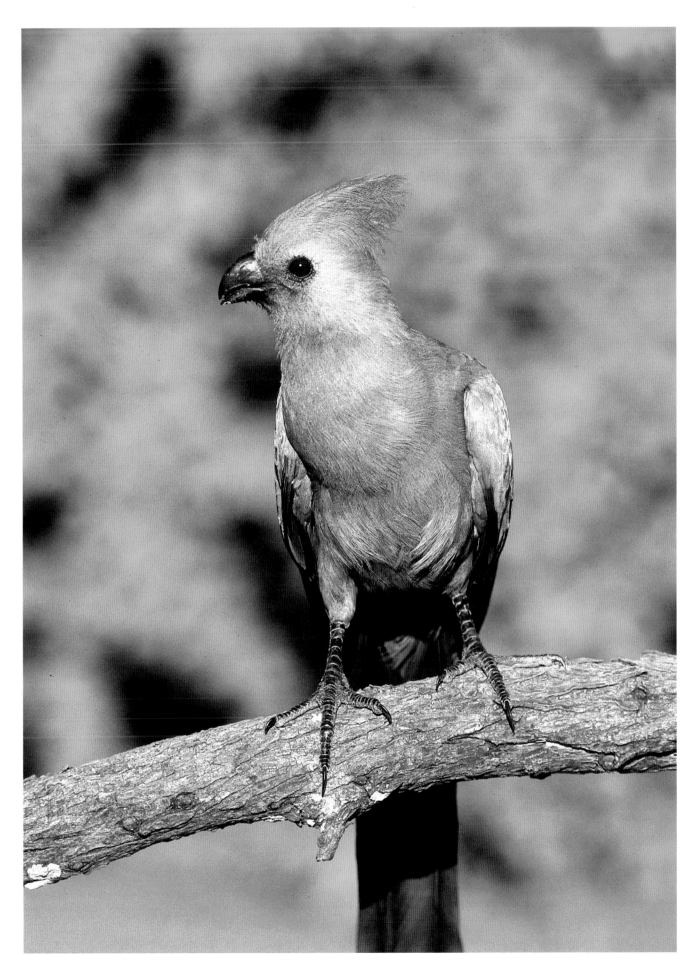

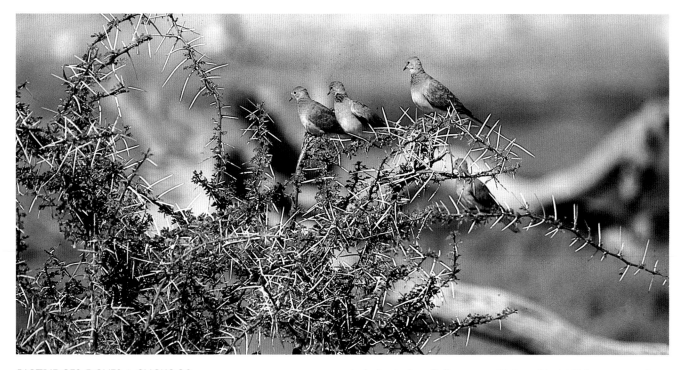

PARTRIDGES, DOVES & CUCKOOS

The African members of the partridge order (Galliformes) include the spurfowls, francolins, stone partridge and guineafowls. The helmeted guineafowl (*Numida meleagris*) is black with hundreds of small white spots distributed evenly over its entire plumage. It has a dark, bony casque on its usually red crown, and usually a blue face and wattles. It occurs in moist and dry savanna woodland and grassland mosaics and also in dryer forests throughout sub-Sahara Africa except for the Namib desert. It roosts in large groups in trees. It feeds mainly on seeds and insects, but also invades cultivated land to eat the seedheads of crops.

The dove family (Columbidae) includes more than 25 pigeons and doves indigenous to Africa. The laughing dove (*Streptopelia senegalensis*) is a close relative of the turtle-dove familiar to the Northern Hemisphere. It has a pale pink head and underpart, a cinnamon-coloured back and bluish leading edges to the wings. It has tiny black spots on the pink front of the neck. It is native to woodland savannas, but it is also found in villages and farms through much of its range, which extends across North Africa, the Sahara oases, and Egypt and all of sub-Sahara Africa except rainforests. It feeds on the seedheads of grasses, herbs and grain crops.

The cuckoo order (Cuculiformes) in Africa includes the turacos, the go-away birds (also known as louries) and the coucals. The grey go-away bird (*Corythaixoides concolor*) is dark smoky grey all over,

including its long fluffy crest, and it has a black bill. It measures about 20in (50cm) from the bill to the end of its long tail. It has earned its common name from the sound of its its rather sneering, nasal call—one of a extensive repertoire of screeches and howls. (Two other go-away species have slightly different versions of the "go-away" call.) It is native to dry and moist savanna woodlands that are close to water; its range is from Tanzania southwards to eastern Transvaal, and south-westwards through Zambia to Angola and Namibia.

Coucals are somewhat clumsy, partly ground-living members of the cuckoo tribe with short, rounded wings and a long, rather ungainly tail. Burchell's coucal (*Centropus burchelli*) has bright reddish brown back and wings, with white and reddish bars on the rump and tail feathers. It is found from eastern Tanzania southward to Cape Province. The rather larger coppery-tailed coucal (*C. cuprecaudus*) has a very long, copper-coloured tail. It ranges from southern Zaïre southwards through Zambia to the Okavango Delta in north-western Botswana. Both species live in moist savannas, swamps, palm groves and on the margins of forests. They build large, globular nests out of grass, leaves, stems and other plant material, close to the ground in dense vegetation. Coucals are not built for speed: on the ground they move listlessly, foraging for insects, frogs, rodents and small snakes; in the air they flap their wings to no great effect and come tumbling back to the ground after a minute or two.

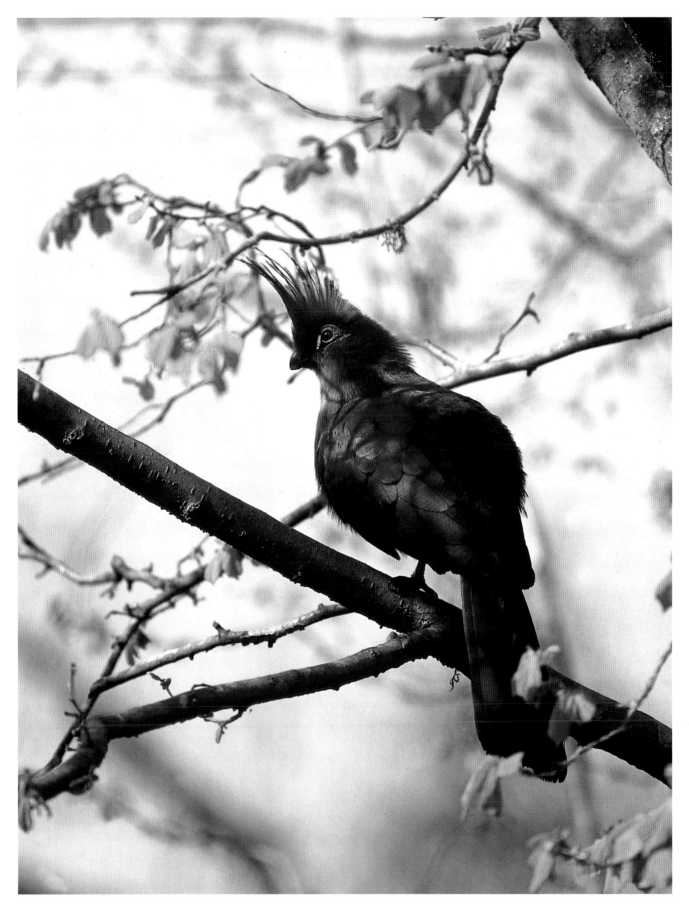

Above Left: The laughing dove gets its common name from the ascending notes of its call. This small group is from Namibia.

Above: Turacos are colourful cousins of the louries, mostly native to montane and rainforests. This is one of the green turacos.

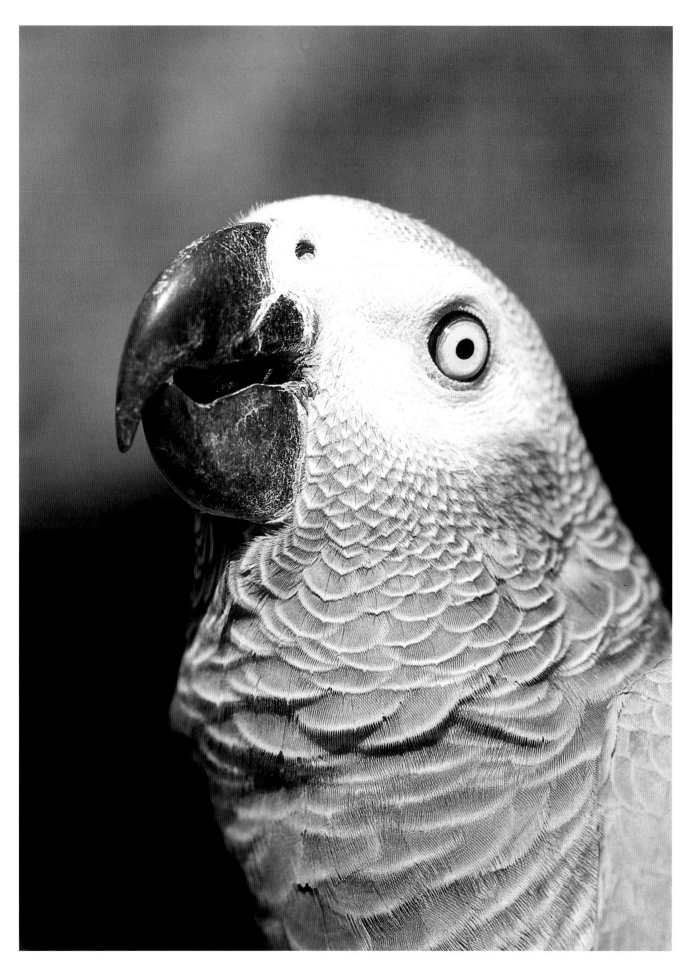

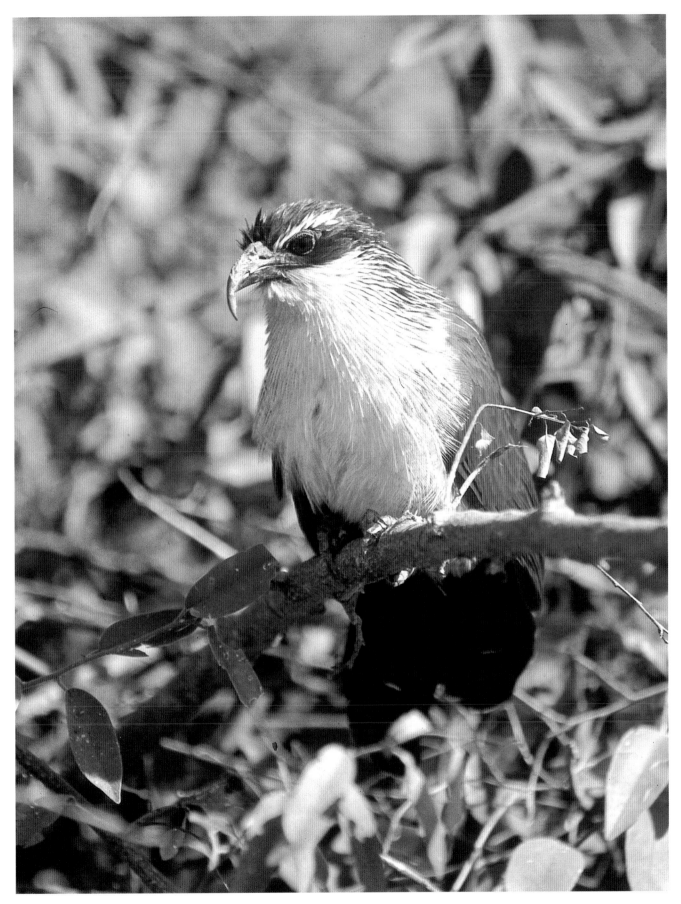

Left: Another native of the rainforest: the grey parrot, largest of the African species and the most accomplished talker.

Above: Burchell's coucal: Botswana.

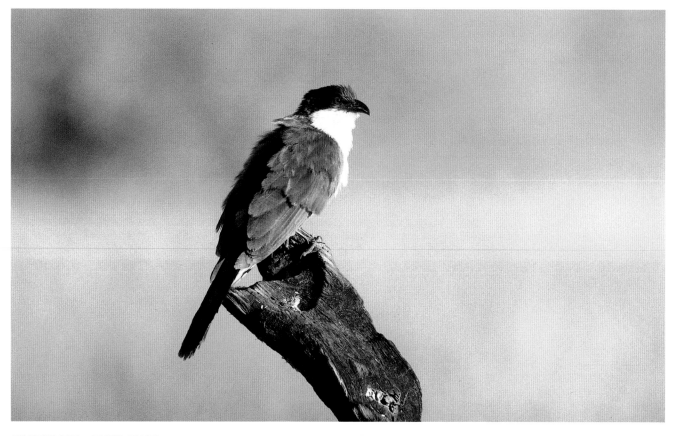

KINGFISHERS & THEIR ALLIES

The kingfisher order (Coraciiformes) also includes the bee-eaters, rollers, hoopoe and hornbills. There are 18 African kingfisher species, of which the following are typical. The pied kingfisher (*Ceryle rudis*) is black on it upper parts, with white spots and feather edges, and white below with two black bands across the breast (one on the female) and on the underside of the tail. It has a flat topped black head with a black crest and a white eyebrow, and a long black bill; like most kingfishers, it has tiny feet. It lives by fresh-water lakes, rivers, floodplains, mangrove swamps and coasts. It is found throughout sub-Sahara Africa except in the Namib and Kalahari deserts; also on the Nile delta. It perches over water—on dead branches, on boats and mooring posts, etc—before flying low over the surface. When it sights a fish it hovers for a moment, then dives vertically into the water, beak open and opaque nictitating membrane (third eyelid) closed. It grasps the fish between its mandibles, and in an instant turns in the water and "rows" to the surface using its wings. It returns to its perch, whacks the fish against a branch until it dies, then swallows it. The smaller, richly coloured malachite kingfisher (*Alcedo cristata*), no more than six inches (15cm) from long red beak to tail, has much the same range, hunting technique and diet.

Contrary to popular belief, not all kingfishers are fish eaters. The following three, for instance, hunt mainly for insects and lizards and do not dive for fish. The grey-headed kingfisher (*Halcyon leucocephala*) has a slightly pinkish grey head and neck, lighter (sometimes white) on throat and chest, and dark orange underpart; the shoulders and back are black, and the flight feathers, lower back and tail are sky blue. The long, heavy beak is red. It inhabits dry savanna woodland and the edge of forests, including montane forest but not rainforest. Its range is from Senegal eastwards to Ethiopia and southwards to eastern Transvaal. In the breeding season it digs out a long hole in a river bank or gully (or sometimes a termite mound) to make its nest. The striped kingfisher (*H. chelicuti*) has a dark brown back with fine, lighter brown stripes on crown and neck, light grey breast and underpart, bright blue on tail and wings. The beak has a black upper mandible and a red lower one. It ranges over the same regions as the grey-headed kingfisher, and lays its eggs in holes in trees. The somewhat larger woodland kingfisher (*H. senegalensis*) has a beak that is red above and black below. Its head and neck are silvery grey, the shoulders and tips of its primaries are black, its back, tail and flight feathers a vivid blue, and its underpart white. It lives in wooded savannas and on the edge of forests, including rainforests, from Senegal eastwards to Ethiopia and southwards to northern Namibia in the west and KwaZulu-Natal in the east.

The bee-eaters are well named: at least 80 per cent of their diet consists of bees, wasps and other stinging insects. All are caught on the wing, then taken back to a perch, where they are held in the beak near the tip of the abdomen, which is rubbed against the perch until the venom is discharged. Bee-eaters have long, slender, downward-curving black bills, red eyes and short legs. Many have as vivid a plumage as the kingfishers, and in most species black feathers either mask or make a line through the eyes. The following are three of 19 species native to Africa.

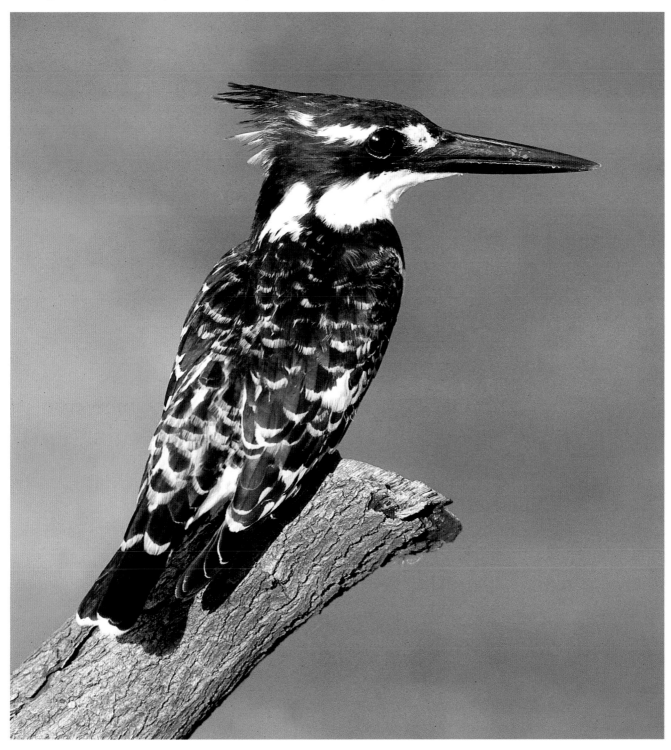

Above Left: The coppery-tailed coucal is larger than Burchell's, and has a longer tail.

Above: Pied kingfisher: South Africa. Note its flat head, black crest and white eyebrow.

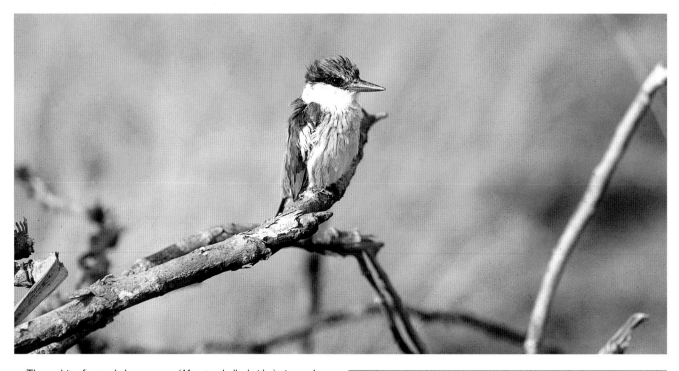

The white-fronted bee-eater (*Merops bullockoides*) is rather confusingly named: it has a white forehead, then a broad black eye mask, below which is a white line, and below that a bright red throat. The breast and nape of the neck are golden fawn, the rump is deep blue, and the back, wings and tail are green. It lives near watercourses and on the margins of montane forests. It digs out a burrow in a cliff in colonies of up to 25 pairs. Smaller groups of pairs within a colony, called clans, are often in and out of each others' burrows but are aggressive towards intruding birds from other clans in the colony. The white-fronted bee-eater is found in the Kenya highlands, in northern Tanzania, in Angola, southern Zaïre, Zambia, Malawi, Zimbabwe, and southwards to eastern Transvaal. The white-throated bee-eater (*M. albicollis*) has a black crown, eye line and "necklace" separated by a white line between crown and eye line and a broad white throat. The nape is light or dark brown, the back, wings and underpart a dusty pale green. The tail, with its long streamers, is blue. It lives in dry, sparsely wooded savanna and semi-desert, often along dry watercourses. It makes its burrow in flat or gently sloping sand in nesting colonies that may number several hundred pairs. Its breeding range is mainly in the Sahel belt that stretches from northern Senegal eastwards (with interruptions) all the way to the Horn of Africa. It winters in the rainforest belt of West Africa and the Congo basin. For much of the year it eschews bees in favour of flying ants and other insects.

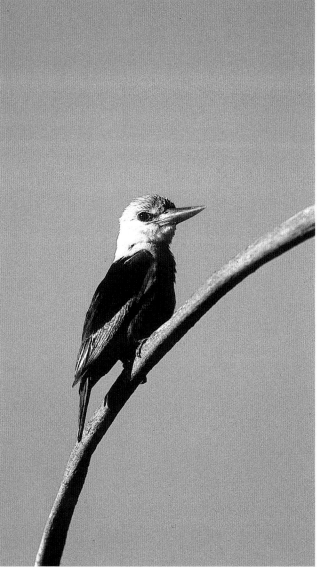

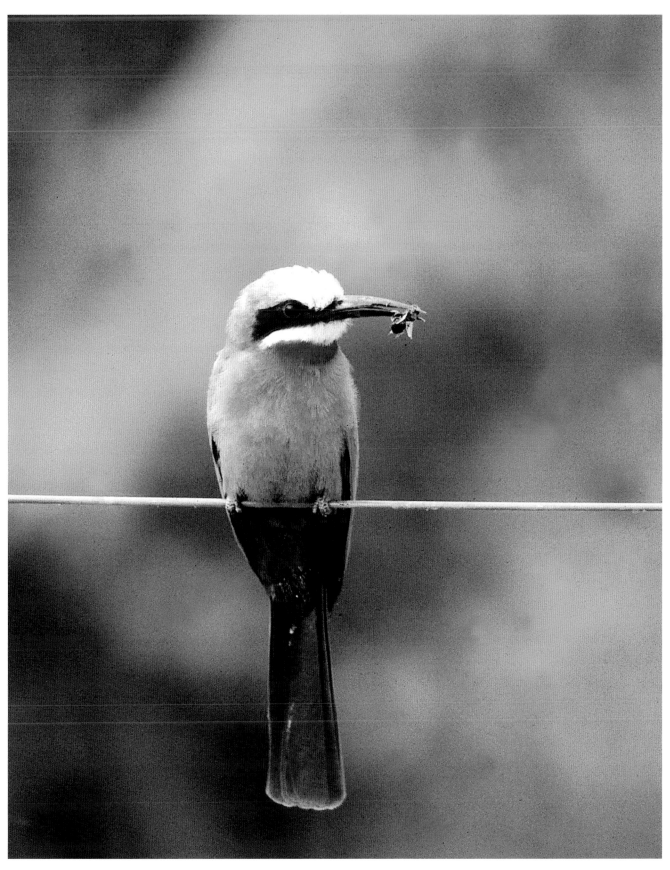

Above Left: Striped kingfisher: Masai Mara. Note the bright blue on tail.

Left: Grey kingfisher: Samburu National Reserve, Kenya. Note the grey cap and red beak.

Above: White-fronted bee-eater: Kenya. In fact, only the fore-crown is white.

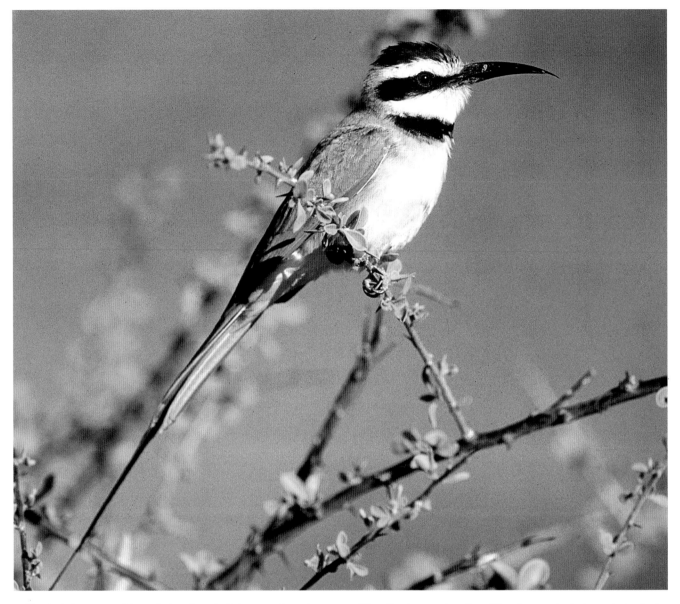

The little bee-eater (*M. pusillus*) is about half the size of its white-throated cousin. It has a green crown, back, wings and tail, a black eye mask, a bright yellow throat, and necklace that is black above and reddish brown below, and rich brownish fawn breast and underpart. It is less gregarious than some other bee-eaters, and solitary pairs build burrows on grassy banks as well as in cliffs. It lives in grassy areas near water in the dry season, and in the wet season moves to open woodland and grassland savanna. It ranges from Senegal eastwards to Somalia, throughout East Africa, and through Angola and Zambia southwards to Botswana and KwaZulu-Natal.

The rollers earned their common name from their remarkable aerobatic displays during courtship and also when defending their territory. Sturdily built, with heavy, slightly hooked beaks, they are also notable in some species for their long tail streamers.

The lilac-breasted roller (*Coracias caudata*) is typical of the Coraciidae family. Measuring about 15in (38cm) from its heavy black bill to its tail, it has a pale green crown and nape, a white eyebrow above a black line through the eye, and a white chin. It has a pinkish lilac throat and chest, a turquoise belly, rump and tail, and dusty cinnamon back. It inhabits woodland and grassland savannas and dry savanna scrubland over most of East Africa and the Rift Valley, southwards to northern Transvaal, and south-westwards to southern Angola, Namibia and Botswana. It eats mainly large insects.

Although quite unlike them in appearance, the hoopoe (*Upupa epops*), the sole member of its family, is quite closely related to the kingfishers, bee-eaters and, especially, the rollers. It takes its common name from its breeding-season call, a soft, low hoop-hoop-hoop, which carries a considerable distance. Its head, neck, back and

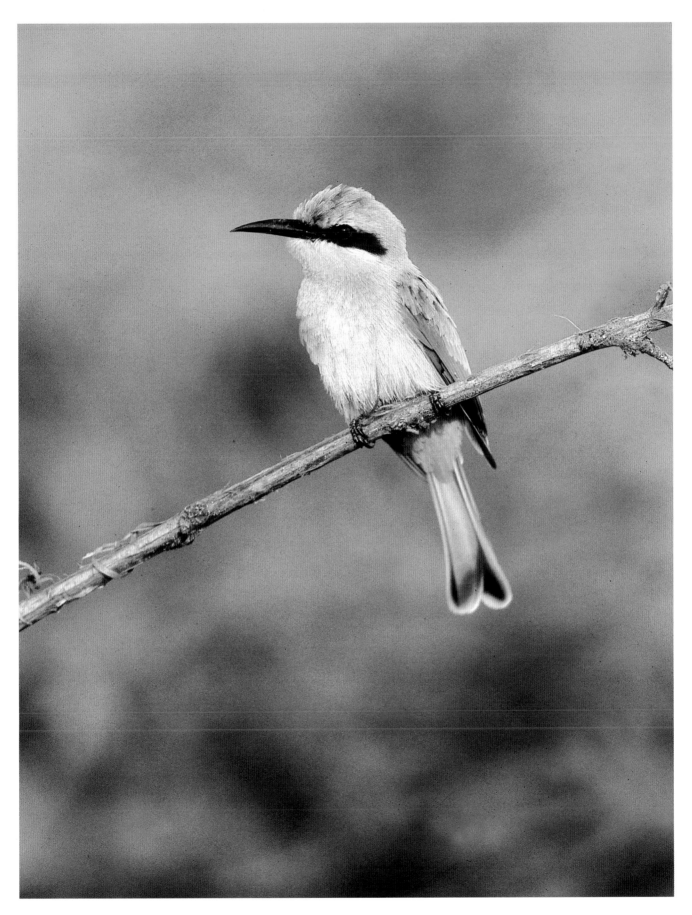

Above Left: White-throated bee-eater: Samburu National Reserve. Note its tail streamers.

Above: Little bee-eater: Zimbabwe. Compare its black eye mask with that of the white-throated species.

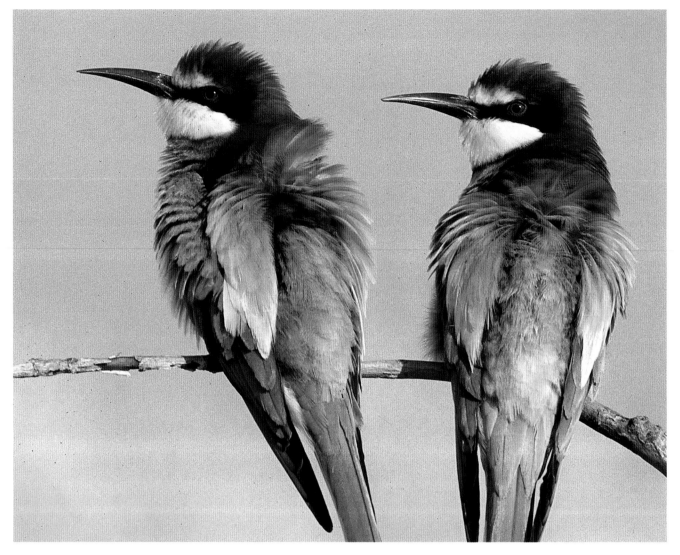

underpart are cinnamon-pink and the black wings and tail are bold-ly patterned in white bars and spots. It has a long, downward-curv-ing bill. Its unusually long crest feathers are black-tipped and can be raised or lowered over the nape. It is about 11in (28cm) long. Like the lilac-crested roller, it usually lays its eggs in a tree cavity or a termite mound. It lives in woodland savanna over much of its range and, in its Algerian and Moroccan habitat, it frequents olive groves in villages and towns. It is also found in most of sub-Sahara Africa excluding rainforests, most of Zaïre and the Horn of Africa. It eats a wide range of insects. (The wood-hoopoes, of the Phoeniculidae family, are a quite distinct group and lack an erectile crest.)

The last members of the Coraciiformes to be considered here are the hornbills, which might seem to have even less in common with the kingfishers than the hoopoe. They are large birds with massive, downward-curving bills and—mainly in the larger birds—a hard casque on top of the bill (whence their common name). Most hornbills have short legs and long tails. Their nesting procedures are fascinating. The nests are built in tree cavities and the female, with her eggs, are walled up inside for several months, the male bringing her and her young food, which is passed through a tiny aperture in the nest wall.

The red-billed hornbill (*Tockus erythrorhynchus*) has a rather narrow red bill and no casque, a white or greyish white head, neck and underpart, black back, secondary flight feathers, and outer tail. There are white spots on the shoulders and secondaries. It inhabits open savanna woodland and thorn scrub, ranging from Senegal east-wards to Ethiopia and southwards through East Africa to KwaZulu-Natal, then westwards to Botswana, northern Namibia and south-ern Angola. It feeds on large insects, scorpions, the young of other birds and dung-beetle larvae, which it excavates with its powerful bill. The southern yellow-billed hornbill (*T. leucomelas*) has a yellow (sometimes orange-tinged) bill and a yellow casque (in the male). It

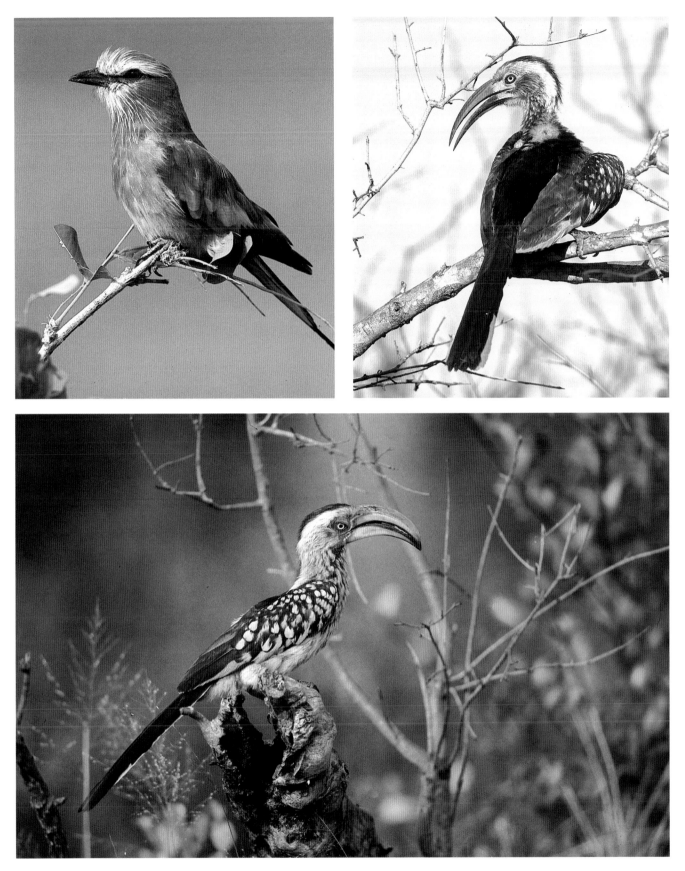

Above Left: Pair of European bee-eaters, which breed in south-western Africa. Note their bright yellow throats.

Top Left: Lilac-breasted roller: Zimbabwe.

Top Right: Red-billed hornbill: KwaZulu-Natal.

Above: Southern yellow-billed hornbill: Transvaal.

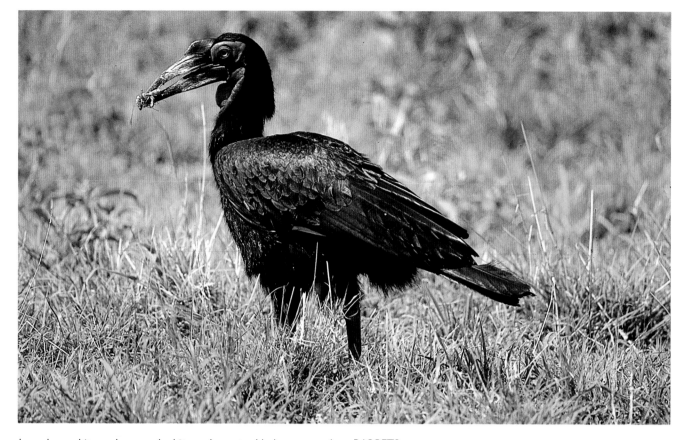

has a long white eyebrow and white underpart, a black crown and back, and large white spots or dashes on the wings. It lives in dry savannas and riverine forests south of the Zambezi river from north-western Namibia through Botswana and Zimbabwe to Transvaal.

The Abyssinian ground hornbill (*Bucorvus abyssinicus*) is a very large black bird, with a long, black, downward curving bill (red or yellow at its base) with a high but short black casque. It has blue facial skin and a large, naked red and blue inflatable throat pouch. Its primary feathers are white. It measures about 3ft 6in (1.07m) from bill to tail. It is a bird of savanna woodlands and grasslands from Senegal to Ethiopia. The rather similar southern ground hornbill (*B. cafer*) has a small, rounded casque, but has bright red skin around the eyes and down the foreneck to the equally red pouch. It is found in open woodland and grassland from central Kenya and southern Zaïre southwards to Zambia and southern Angola, Botswana and eastern South Africa. Both these hornbills spend much more time walking than flying: they amble for miles over savanna plains hunting small mammals, birds, birds' eggs, reptiles and large insects. Like the secretarybird, they are adept at catching a variety of small animals fleeing before the advance of grassland fires.

BARBETS

These small to medium-sized birds are mostly strongly built with large heads and stout, sharp-pointed beaks. Some ornithologists regard them as intermediate between rollers and woodpeckers; they belong to the same order, Piciformes, as the woodpeckers and honeyguides. There are 75 species of barbet worldwide; the 40-odd species native to Africa are found in every kind of habitat from rainforest to semi-desert. Barbets take their common name from the beard-like feathers and bristles that form around the base of the beak.

The red-and-yellow barbet (*Trachyphonus erythrocephalus*) has a red head with a white ear patch and a long red bill. The throat is reddish gold. The nape, back, necklace, wings and tail are black with white spots; the underpart is bright yellow. The male is distinguishable from the female by its black chin stripe (in many other barbet species the sexes have almost identical plumage). It lives in open woodland, dry savanna and arid scrubland from lowland Ethiopia and Somalia to Kenya and north-eastern Tanzania. It forages on the ground, feeding on large insects, fruits and nestlings. It often seeks the company of humans who feed it at the safari lodges at the Ngorongoro Crater and other reserves in the region.

PASSERINES

The order Passeriformes is by far the largest of the avifauna, accounting for more than one third of the existing bird families and more than half of of the living species. Passerines (the word comes from the Latin *passer*, meaning sparrow) are the so-called perching birds, whose feet are adapted to cling to branches or reeds in such a way that the grip tightens as a reflex if the bird begins to topple backwards. Passerines include all the families of birds noted for their singing, so the order as a whole is often referred to as the songbirds. There are 1,276 passerine species in Africa: we have space here to include only a few representative examples.

The gonoleks are members of the bush-shrike subfamily Malaconotidae, which also includes the tchagra and several species of boubou. All the members of this group have long, thick bills that are hooked at the end. They are shy birds, spending most of their time foraging in thickets for insects, invertebrates and fruit. The western gonolek (*Laniarius barbarus*) is similar in appearance to its close cousin, the crimson boubou (*L. atrococcineus*). Both have black bills and have black head, nape, shoulders and back with bright red underparts; but only the gonolek has a yellow crown. Whereas the crimson boubou is confined to south-western Africa (it is the national bird of Namibia), the western gonalek

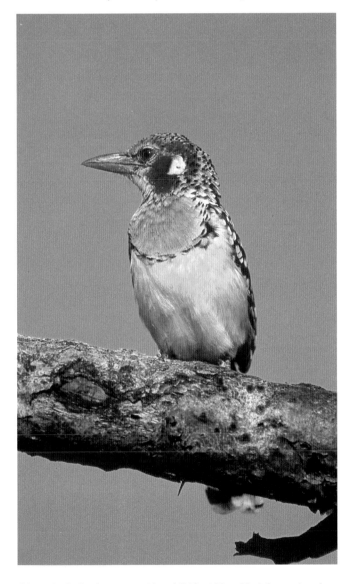

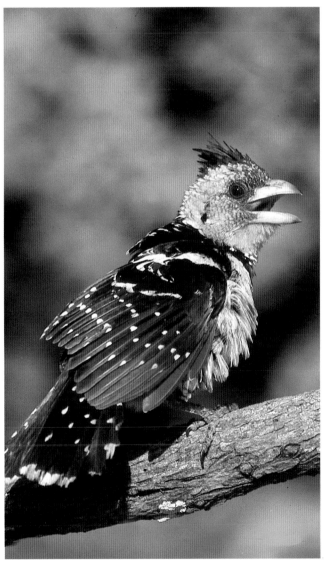

Above Left: Southern ground hornbill: Masai Mara. Much larger than the red- or yellow-billed species, it is mainly a savanna ground-dweller.

Above Left: Red-and-yellow barbet: Samburu National Reserve. Note its black-and-white-spotted necklace.

Above: Crested barbet: Transvaal. Note heavy bill and small black crest.

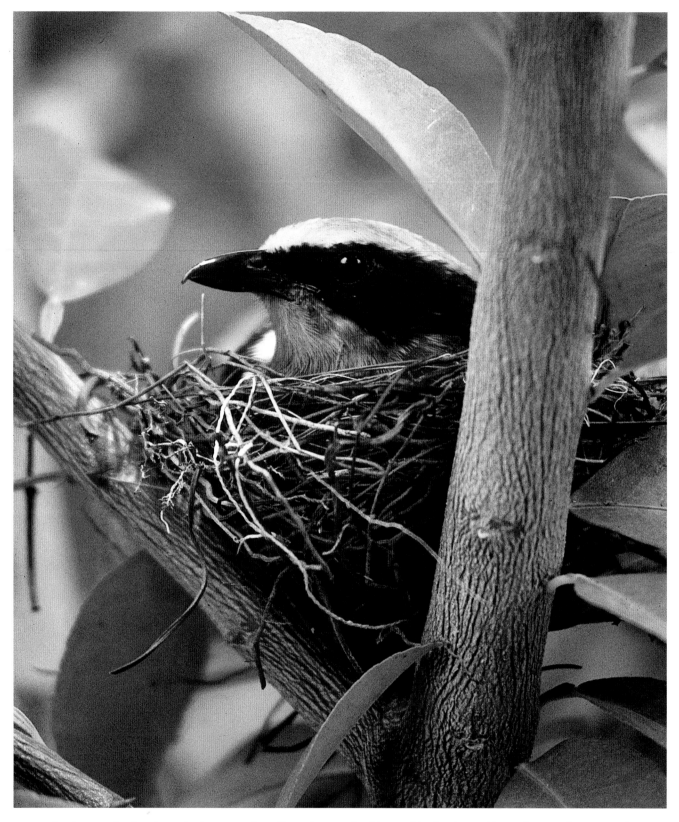

ranges the dry woodland and grassland savannas from Senegal to the Lake Chad region.

The chats are members of the thrush family (Turdidae), medium-sized birds with a fine vocal repertoire. The white-browed robin-chat (*Cossypha heuglini*) has a pale brownish grey crown, neck, shoulders and back, a long white eyebrow, and orange underparts. It inhabits dry savannas from Lake Chad eastwards to Ethiopia, where it is also found on the lower slopes and on the edge of montane forests. Its close cousin, the Cape robin-chat (*C. caffra*), which has orange feathers only at the breast and throat, is a common visitor to gardens in South Africa. Both feed largely on insects and have a liking for caterpillars. The cliff chat (*Thamnolaea cinnamomeiventris*) male has a black head, chest, back, wings and tail, a white flash on the shoulders, and reddish orange underparts. The female replaces the male's black areas with grey. Both sexes have a melodious warbling song; they also imitate other bird's calls.

It has discontinuous ranges in West Africa but is widespread, especially in mountains and hilly areas, from Ethiopia southwards to eastern South Africa. Its preferred habitat is woodlands and scrub, waterside rocks and cliffs, kopjes and farms and villages. It is a spectacularly good flyer. It feeds mainly on insects, spiders and fruit, especially figs.

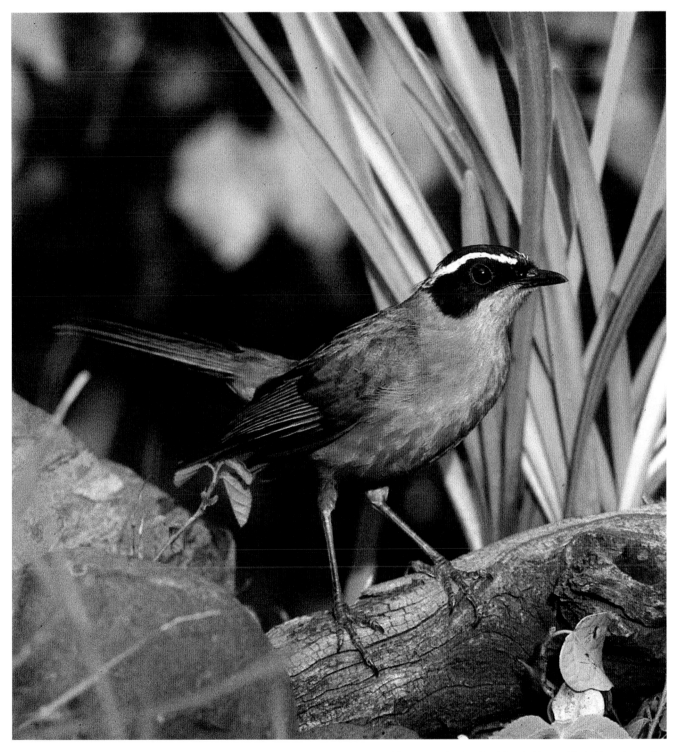

Left: Western gonalek on nest: Gambia. Note its yellow crown.

Above: White-browed robin-chat: Nairobi National Park. Note the bird's white eyebrow—longer than the Cape robin-chat's.

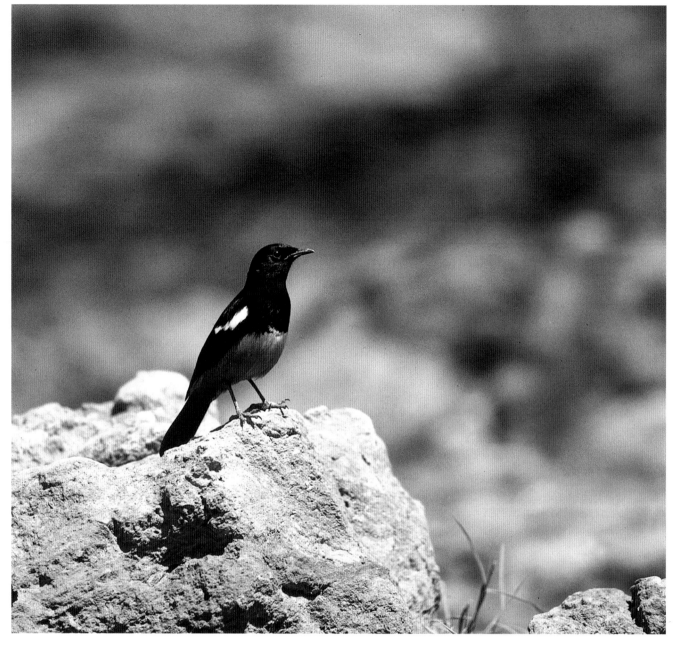

WEAVER FAMILY

This family (Ploceidae) of small to medium-sized mainly seed-eating birds also includes the whydahs, the queleas, the fodys, the widowbirds and the sparrows (although the last are assigned their own family by some taxonomists). The weavers, in particular, are renowned for their beautifully crafted, usually spherical nests made out of a variety of materials depending on the species. By contrast, their close relatives the whydahs do not bother making nests at all, laying their eggs in the nests of birds of quite different species.

The lesser masked weaver (*Ploceus intermedius*) has a black mask on the crown, face and throat, yellow nape, neck and underparts, and greenish olive back with shadowy black streaks. It builds a small grass nest with an entrance funnel and congregates in colonies of several hundred pairs in wooded grasslands and riverine forests. It ranges from Ethiopia southwards to KwaZulu-Natal and as far as northern Namibia and Botswana in the west. The white-headed buffalo weaver (*Dinemellia dinamelli*) has a white head and underparts, a thick black bill and black around the eyes, a black or dark brown back, wings and tail, and a bright red rump. It builds several grass-lined nests made of thorny sticks hung from tree branches. It prefers acacia woodlands and savannas to live in, and ranges from Somalia westwards to northern Uganda and southwards to southern Tanzania.

The village or spotted-backed weaver (*Ploceus cucullatus*) has a very wide range (it is probably the commonest of the weavers), and the male varies considerably in appearance from region to region. In the West and East African and Congo basin races the entire head is black; but only the West African and Congo races have a chestnut band on the nape; in the southern African race the entire crown is yellow. All the races have a yellow back with black spots. It lives in riverine woodland in moist savannas and at the edge of rainforests, and is found in many villages and farms. Its range extends throughout sub-Sahara Africa apart from Namibia, Botswana, and western and central Cape Province in the south and the Horn of Africa in the north. Its nest is immaculately woven of grass or palm fibre, entered via a tunnel from below.

The white-browed sparrow-weaver (*Plocepasser mahali*) has a brown back and white throat and underparts, with a small white patch on the crown and white wing bars. In inhabits dry acacia savannas, often in upland areas to about 5,000ft (1,500m). A rather messy builder, it constructs unkempt-looking nests with two roosting chambers and a funnel entrance for each and also has the unusual habit of building a number of nests that remain unused, perhaps to discourage or mislead possible predators. The northern race ranges from Ethiopia southwards to northern Tanzania; the southern race from south-western Angola eastwards to southern Tanzania, then southwards through Zambia and Botswana to eastern Cape Province. It has a particular liking for harvester termites.

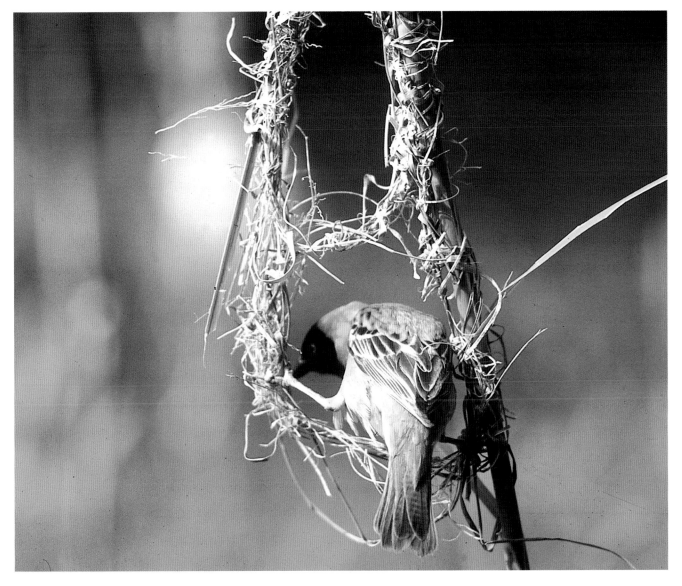

Above Left: Cliff chat: Lake Nakuru National Park, Kenya. Note the white shoulder flash.

Above: Lesser masked weaver building its nest: Lake Baringo, Kenya.

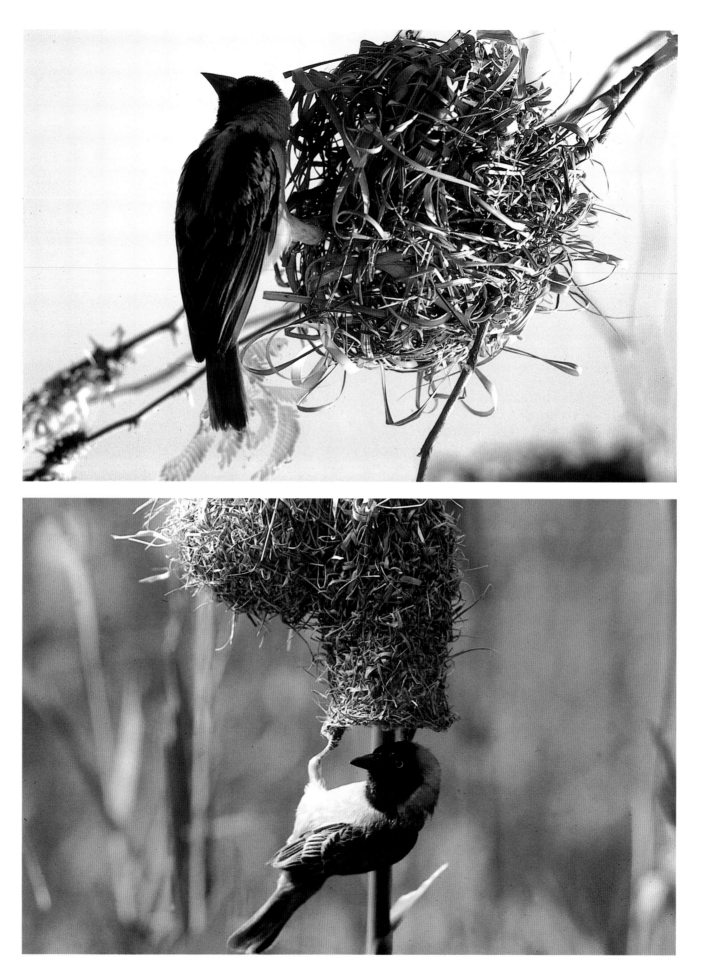

The pin-tailed whydah (*Vidua macroura*) has a bright red beak (male only), a black cap and face, a broad white collar and underparts, a mainly black back with white rump and long white wing martkings; it has very long, black central tail feathers. Inhabiting woods and clearings in forests, it is also attracted to villages and farms. It ranges over most of sub-Sahara Africa except for the Namibia-Angola borderlands, the Namib desert and the Horn of Africa. This species builds no nest, laying a solitary egg in the nest of, usually, a waxbill. The whydah nestling, unlike that of the cuckoo, does not kill or evict the young of the host species.

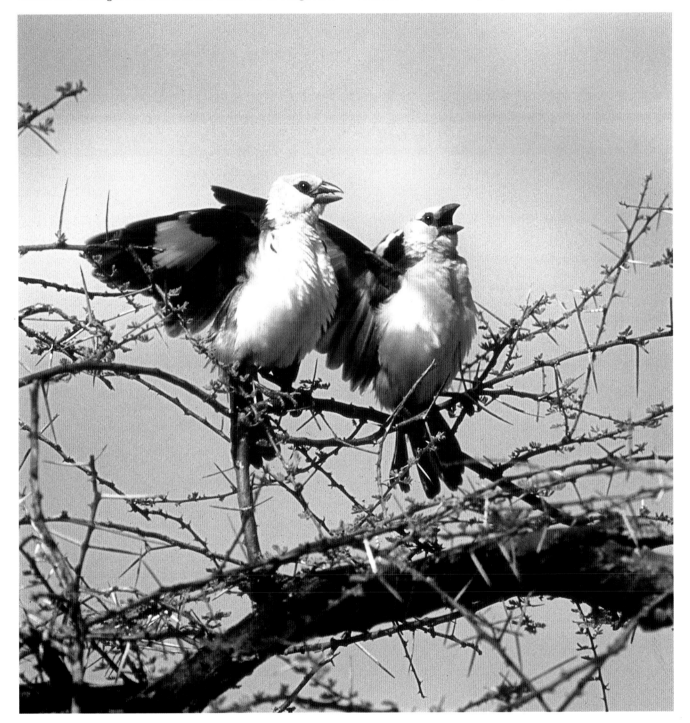

Above Left: Lesser masked weaver with spherical nest almost complete: Lake Baringo.

Left: Lesser masked weaver at completed nest: KwaZulu-Natal. Note the entrance funnel above the bird's head.

Above: A pair of white-headed buffalo weaver: Samburu National Reserve.

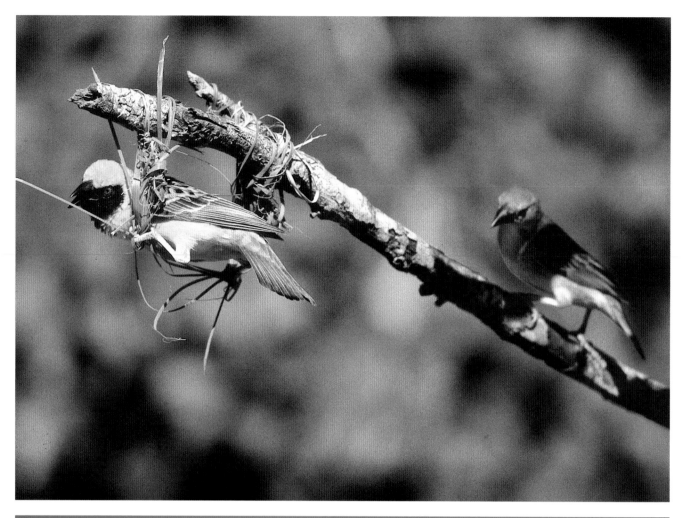

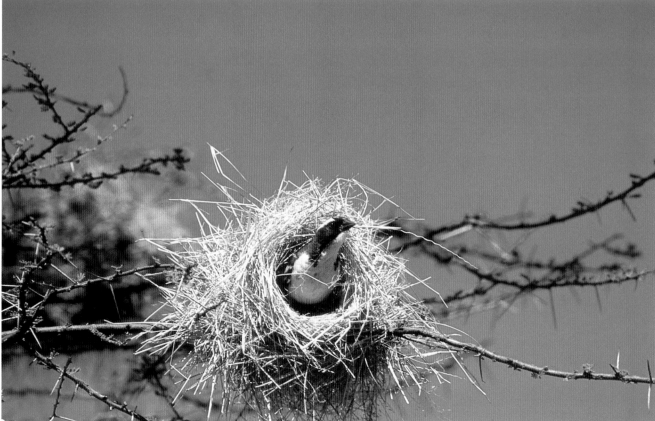

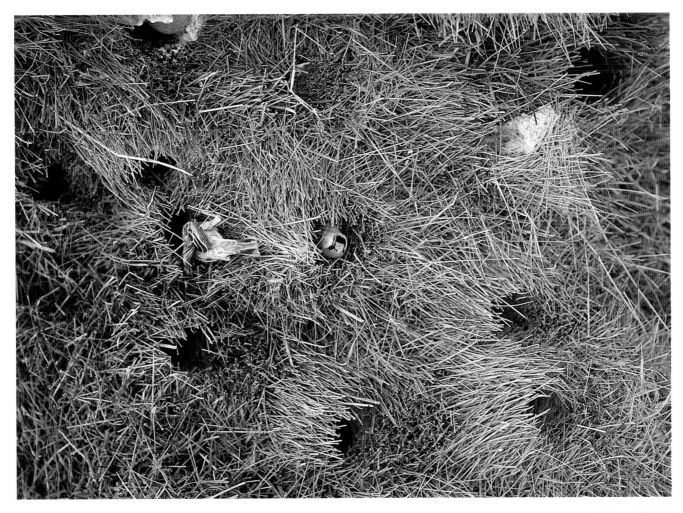

Above: Sociable weavers at their huge communal nest: Namibia. The birds first build a framework of strong twigs across several branches of a tree, then weave masses of straw around the twigs, forming as many as 300 nesting chambers.

Above Left: The village weaver begins to weave its grass nest: eastern Cape Province.

Left: Northern-race white-browed sparrow-weaver: Samburu National Reserve. It often builds several nests that are left unused.

Right: Pin-tailed whydah: KwaZulu-Natal. A close cousin of the weavers, this species does not weave a nest but lays a single egg in the nest of a waxbill or similar species.

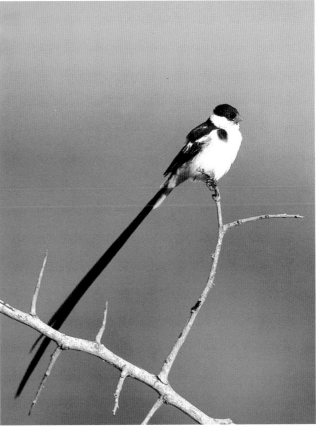

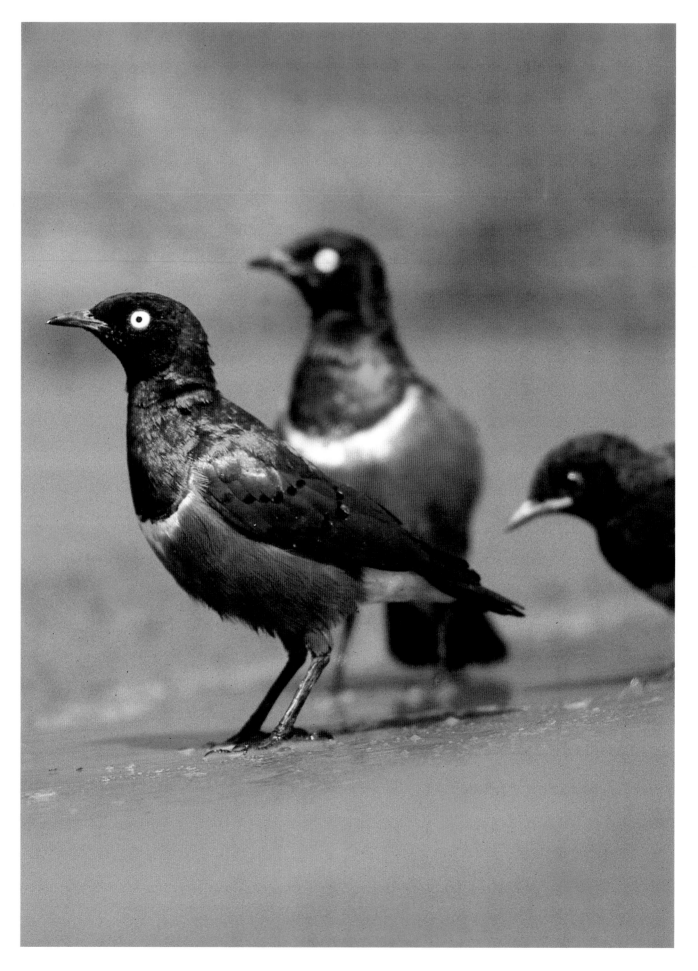

STARLINGS

The Sturnidae family includes the starlings, of which 50 are native to mainland Africa, and the oxpeckers. Starlings are mostly gregarious, sometimes gathering into vast flocks outside the breeding season. The superb starling (*Spreo superbus*) is well named: it has a black head, an iridescent green/blue chest and upperparts divided by a white line from its reddish orange chest and underpart; there are black spots on the wing coverts. It has a typical starling vocal inventory, including a rattling sound and a rather mournful warble; and it is a skilful mimic of other birds' calls. It usually builds a globular nest, like a weaver's, out of twigs and grass; sometimes it uses old nests of other birds. It frequents open woodland and dry savanna grassland from Ethiopia southwards through central Tanzania to Malawi.

Oxpeckers (also known as tick-birds) are unique among birds in living mainly on the parasites, such as ticks and flies, on the bodies of large, short-haired mammals such as buffalo, zebra and giraffe. It is a mutually beneficial association: the oxpecker eats well and regularly, the mammal has its hide, ears and nostrils kept parasite-free. Interestingly, the keen-sighted oxpecker often provides an early warning to its host of the approach of predators. The birds often supplement their diet with insects kicked up by the hooves of their host. The yellow-billed oxpecker (*Buphagus africanus*) is somewhat confusingly named: it does indeed have a large mainly yellow bill, but about one third of the bill at the tip end is a conspicuously bright red. It has a dark brown head and upperparts and rather dusty yellow underparts and rump. It inhabits grasslands, open woodland savanna, riverine or lakeside trees and everywhere that supports large wild (or domestic) herbivores and other grazers. It ranges from Senegal eastwards to western Ethiopia; southwards from Nigeria to southern Angola in the west, and southwards from Ethiopia to northern Botswana in the east. The red-billed oxpecker (*B. erythrorhyncus*) is of similar colours above and below, but has a wholly red bill, a red eye and conspicuous yellow eye ring. It ranges from Eritrea southwards through East Africa to northern KwaZulu-Natal, its range overlapping with its yellow-billed cousin in parts of East Africa.

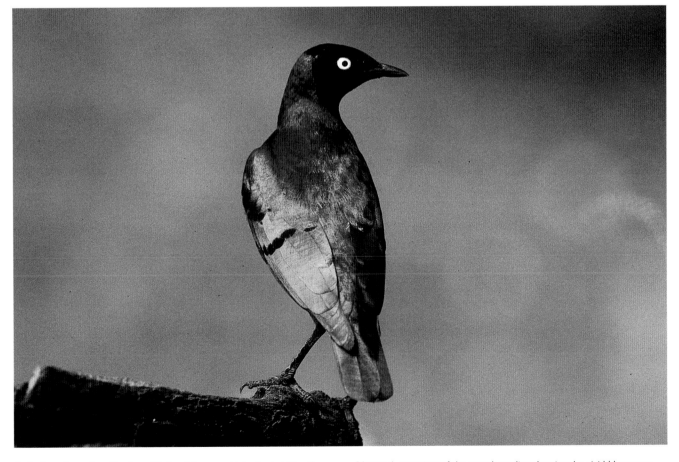

Left: Superb starlings: Samburu National Reserve. Note the bright yellow eye.

Above: A rear view of the superb starling showing the vivid blue-green plumage on its back and wings.

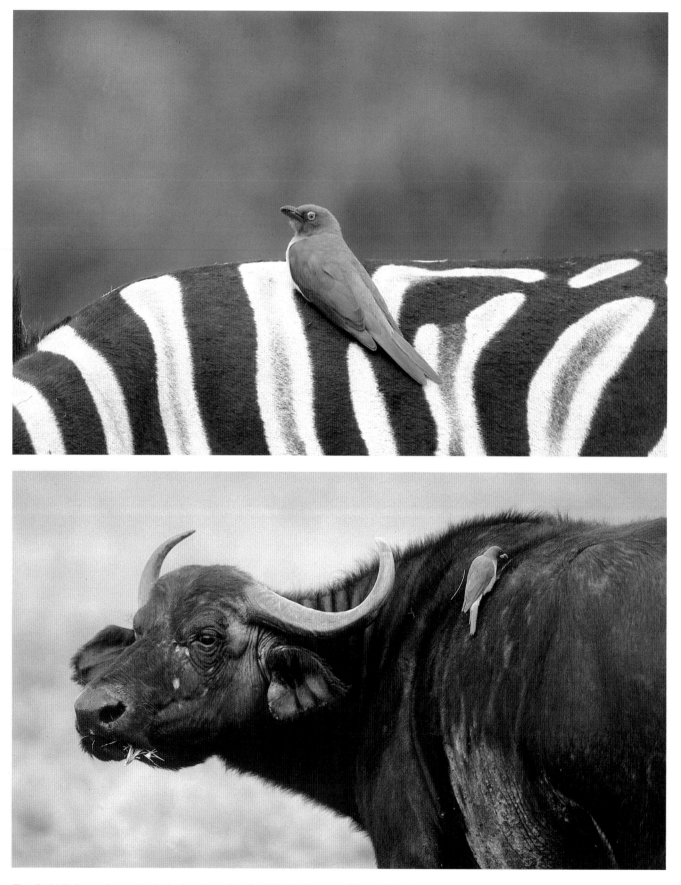

Top: Red-billed oxpecker on the back of a plains zebra: KwaZulu-Natal.

Above Right: Fork-tailed drongo: northern Botswana. Note the bird's glossy plumage.

Above: Yellow-billed oxpecker on shoulder of Cape buffalo: Masai Mara.

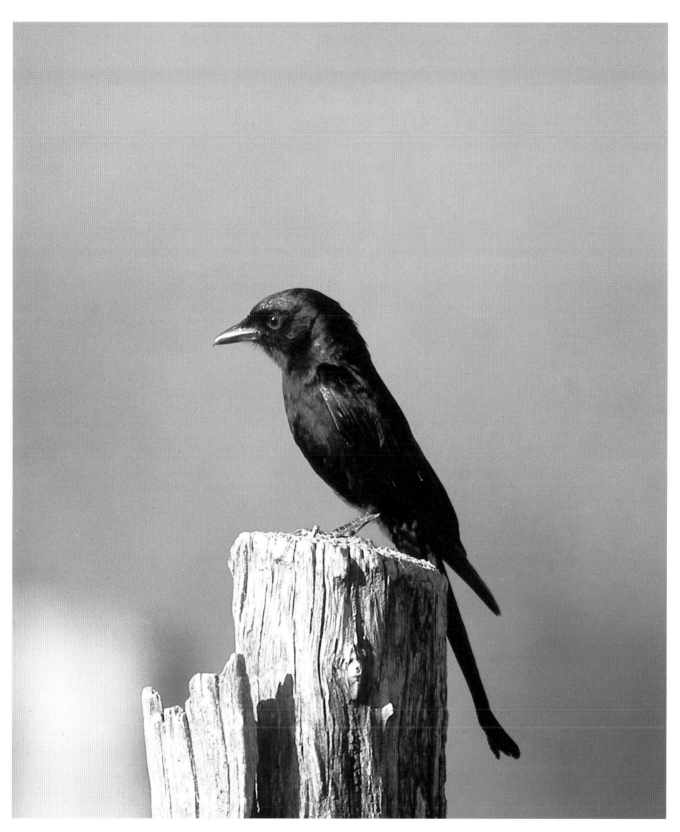

DRONGO

The fork-tailed drongo (*Dicrurus adsimilis*), one of four African members of the family Dicruridae, is an upright-standing, glossy black bird about ten inches (25cm) from its bill to the end of its long, deeply forked tail. It has a red eye. It inhabits open woodland, acacia savannas and cultivated land, including gardens. Its range is most of sub-Sahara Africa apart from rainforests and true desert. It eats mainly insects. A notably aggressive bird, it will chase birds of prey, and it will not hesitate to attack domestic cats and other carnivores of similar size if they approach its nest.

PHOTOGRAPHIC CREDITS:

The publisher wishes to thank the following for kindly supplying the photography for this book:

Pages 2, 36-37, 56(top), 58, 59(bottom), 60(top), 72-73, 74(both), 75(bottom), 76-77(main), 93, 102(bottom), 103(top), 114-115(main), 120(middle), 161(bottom left), 164, 172-173, 174, 178-179, 218(top left corner), 230-231(main), 233, 306(cut-out), 331(bottom right), 342(left), 348(bottom left), 350(bottom left), 352, 409(right), 459 and 460-461(both) courtesy of John Downer/©WILD IMAGES LTD/RSPCA Photolibrary

Pages 4, 38(cut-out), 75(top), 117, 120(bottom), 122-123(main), 128, 138(bottom), 153(bottom), 157, 166-167, 177, 196, 211, 226-227, 243, 256-257, 285, 287(right), 297(right), 302(top left & bottom left), 307, 312(top right), 322-323, 326-327, 332-333(main), 346-347(main), 361, 378-379, 430-431, 451 courtesy of ©Klaus-Peter Wolf /RSPCA Photolibrary

Pages 6(cut-out), 15, 106-107, 130-131, 262(left), 280(bottom), 310(bottom), 413, 437(top), 443, 456(bottom), 467(top), 490(top), 491, 500, 502(top), 508(bottom) courtesy of ©Mr Geoff du Feu/RSPCA Photolibrary

Pages 6(top left corner), 24-25, 38(top left corner), 43(right), 52(top left corner), 119, 136-137(main), 144-145, 146(top), 148-149, 216, 219, 264-265, 292-293, 309, 328-329, 340-341(main), 341(top right), 348(top), 353(upper middle & bottom), 363(top), 377 courtesy of David Breed/©WILD IMAGES LTD/RSPCA Photolibrary

Pages 7, 8(bottom), 28-29, 124-125 courtesy of ©Yann Arthus-Bertrand/CORBIS

Pages 8(top), 16(bottom), 69(bottom), 89, 101, 108, 126, 132-133, 151, 199(bottom left), 248-249, 252(top), 258, 260(bottom), 261(bottom), 266-267, 276-277, 278-79, 289(both), 299, 354-355, 360(bottom), 381, 385, 387, 388, 400, 401(left), 424(main), 426-427, 433, 446-447, 506 courtesy of ©EA Janes/RSPCA Photolibrary

Pages 9, 16(top), 17, 59(top), 69(top), 77(right), 94(top left corner & cut-out), 103(bottom), 104(bottom), 112(left), 118, 120(bottom), 127, 134-135, 142, 143, 150, 154-155, 160, 193(top), 194-195, 197(top), 202-203, 208(top), 209(top), 218(cut-out), 220-221, 222(bottom), 224(main), 228-229, 234-235, 238-239(main), 240, 242, 275(both), 286(top), 288, 311, 312(top left & bottom right), 315, 316, 317, 324-325(main), 336-367, 338, 344-345, 353(middle & lower middle), 382-383, 424(cut-out), 425, 428-29, 431(right), 434-435(main), 438, 440(main), 442, 453(bottom), 456(top right), 467(bottom), 478(middle left), 482(bottom), 484, 492, 496, 497(left), 503, 504(bottom) courtesy of ©Birgit Koch/RSPCA Photolibrary

Pages 10-11, 64, 314(bottom) courtesy of Martin Dohrn/©WILD IMAGES LTD/RSPCA Photolibrary

Pages 12-13, 20(left), 70-71, 102(top), 138(top right), 162-163, 171, 174, 282-283(main), 302-303(main), 331(bottom left), 346(left), 458(top) courtesy of Richard Matthews/©WILD IMAGES LTD /RSPCA Photolibrary

Page 14 courtesy of ©Brian Vikander/CORBIS

Page 18 courtesy of PAPILIO/Paul Franklin

Page 19 courtesy of ©Kennan Ward/CORBIS

Pages 20-21(main), 42-43(main), 60(bottom), 61, 65(top), 68-69(main), 85, 90-91(main), 104(top), 138(top left), 140-141, 146(bottom), 152, 156(both), 158-159, 181(top), 210(bottom right), 222(top), 223, 225(right), 247, 259, 260(top), 261(top), 262-263(main), 271, 272-273, 306(bottom), 308, 310(top), 314(top), 318, 319, 320-321(both), 324(left), 330, 334-335, 339(top), 348(bottom right), 349(both), 350(top left), 359(both), 360(top), 362(top, middle, bottom left), 363(bottom), 364-365, 455(top), 468, 469(both), 472(bottom), 473, 476(top), 478(top left) courtesy of ©Don Davies/RSPCA Photolibrary

Pages 22-23 courtesy of Colin Cradock/©WILD IMAGES LTD/RSPCA Photolibrary

Pages 26, 46-47, 50-51, 52(cut-out), 78-79(main), 83(top right & bottom), 97(top), 191, 192(top), 198(middle), 209(bottom left), 214(bottom), 295, 297(right), 366, 368-369(main), 474-475 courtesy of Claudia Auer/©WILD IMAGES LTD/RSPCA Photolibrary

Page 27 courtesy of PAPILIO/Jane Sweeney

Pages 30-31 courtesy of ©Mark Votier/RSPCA Photolibrary

Pages 32-33(main) courtesy of ©Nik Wheeler/CORBIS

Page 33(right) courtesy of ©Robert Holmes/CORBIS

Pages 34, 217 courtesy of ©Charles O'Rear/CORBIS

Pages 35, 84, 182-183, 204(top) courtesy of ©Peter Johnson/CORBIS

Pages 39, 48-49, 113(bottom), 208(bottom), 254-255, 280(top) courtesy of ©Nick Yates/RSPCA Photolibrary

Pages 40-41 courtesy of ©John Noble/CORBIS

Pages 44-45, 54-55, 63, 88, 109, 110-111, 153(top), 184, 185(top), 186-187, 188-189, 190(left & top right), 193(bottom), 200-201, 212(top), 232, 237(top), 241, 250, 274(top left), 290(top left corner and cut-out), 296-297(main), 300-301, 304-305, 390, 391, 392, 396, 408-409(main), 424(top left corner), 448-449, 457, 470-71, 476(bottom) courtesy of Frank Krahmer/©WILD IMAGES LTD/RSPCA Photolibrary

Page 53 courtesy of ©Karl Ammann/CORBIS

Pages 56(bottom), 129, 313(all), 331(top), 369(bottom right), 397(left) courtesy of ©Cheryl A Ertelt/RSPCA Photolibrary

Page 57(bottom) courtesy of PAPILIO/John Heathcote

Pages 57(top), 91(right), 398, 402(top) courtesy of PAPILIO/Tony Wilson-Bligh

Page 62(bottom) courtesy of ©Anthony Bannister;Gallo Images/CORBIS

Pages 62(top), 339(bottom) courtesy of Alastair MacEwen/©WILD IMAGES LTD /RSPCA Photolibrary

Pages 65(bottom), 78(left), 80-81, 82, 83(top left), 192(bottom), 198(top & bottom right), 199(top), 374(top left & bottom right), 420(top), 478-479(main), 505(top) courtesy of Samantha Purdy/©WILD IMAGES LTD /RSPCA Photolibrary

Pages 66, 100(both), 116, 122(left), 169, 190(bottom right), 209(bottom right), 212(bottom), 213, 231(right), 251, 268-269, 270, 274(top right & bottom), 281, 282(left), 284(both), 306(top left corner), 350-351(main), 367, 369(top right), 370-371, 372(top left), 372-373(main), 376(both), 380, 407, 436, 439, 440(bottom), 466, 472(top), 480(bottom), 481, 487, 488, 509 courtesy of Susan Stockwell/©WILD IMAGES LTD/RSPCA Photolibrary

Pages 67, 114(left), 161(top & bottom right), 246(top & bottom), 252(bottom), 253, 372(bottom left), 374(bottom left), 384(cut-out), 397(right), 401(right) courtesy of PAPILIO/Robert Gill

Pages 86-87 courtesy of ©Diego Lezama Orezzoli/CORBIS

Page 92 courtesy of ©Roger Tidman/CORBIS

Page 95 courtesy of PAPILIO/Jamie Harron

Pages 96, 98-99, 105, 168, 175, 180, 181(bottom), 185(bottom), 199(bottom right), 204(bottom), 205, 210(bottom left), 214(top left & top right), 236, 237(bottom), 244, 245, 312(bottom left), 399, 432, 435(right), 437(bottom), 452, 453(top), 456(top left), 480(top), 482(top), 483, 489, 493, 495(all), 497(right), 504(top), 505(bottom), 508(top) courtesy of ©Mike Lane/RSPCA Photolibrary

Pages 97(bottom), 137(right), 176(top), 286(bottom), 287(left), 291, 458(bottom), 462(both), 490(bottom), 498, 499, 507 courtesy of ©William S Paton/RSPCA Photolibrary

Page 98 courtesy of PAPILIO/John Heathcote

Page 112(right) courtesy of ©Kevin Schafer/CORBIS

Pages 113(top), 357, 358(both), 406(top left corner), 414-415, 418(both), 419(top), 420(bottom), 485 courtesy of PAPILIO/Robert Pickett

Pages 120(top), 333(right), 384(top left corner), 403 courtesy of ©Malie Rich-Griffith/INFOCUS/RSPCA Photolibrary

Pages 121, 165, 206(both), 207, 356(both) courtesy of Cailey Ermer/©WILD IMAGES LTD/RSPCA Photolibrary

Page 139 courtesy of ©Ashley Bennett/RSPCA Photolibrary

Pages 147, 239(right), 298, 450 courtesy of Carlo Falciola/©WILD IMAGES LTD/RSPCA Photolibrary

Pages 170, 444-445(main), 478(bottom left) courtesy of Phillip Harris/©WILD IMAGES LTD/RSPCA Photolibrary

Pages 176(bottom), 198(bottom left), 294 courtesy of ©Jeff Watts /RSPCA Photolibrary

Page 197(bottom) courtesy of ©Gavin G Thomson; Gallo Images/CORBIS

Page 210(top) courtesy of ©Angela Humphery/RSPCA Photolibrary

Page 215 courtesy of ©Eric and David Hosking/CORBIS

Pages 342-343(main) courtesy of RLM Big Cat Diary/©WILD IMAGES LTD/RSPCA Photolibrary

Pages 353(top), 477 courtesy of Philip Sharpe/©WILD IMAGES LTD /RSPCA Photolibrary

Page 362(bottom right) courtesy of ©Dennis Davis/RSPCA Photolibrary

Page 374(top right) courtesy of PAPILIO/William Middleton

Page 384(main) courtesy of ©Vanessa Latford/RSPCA Photolibrary

Page 386 courtesy of ©Clem Haagner, Gallo Images/CORBIS

Page 393 courtesy of ©Richard Thompson/RSPCA Photolibrary

Page 394 courtesy of PAPILIO/Gehan De Silva

Page 395 courtesy of ©Paul Almasy/CORBIS

Pages 402(bottom), 404 courtesy of ©Andrew Routh/RSPCA Photolibrary

Page 405 courtesy of PAPILIO/Paul Franklin

Pages 406(cut-out), 419(bottom) courtesy of ANDREW SHILLABEER/©WILD IMAGES LTD/RSPCA

Page 410-411 courtesy of ©Simon Kench/RSPCA Photolibrary

Page 416 courtesy of PAPILIO/Stephen Coyne

Page 417 courtesy of ©Gus Christie/RSPCA Photolibrary

Page 421 courtesy of PAPILIO/Mike Buxton

Pages 422-423, 463 courtesy of PAPILIO/Dennis Johnson

Page 441 courtesy of Nick Garbutt/©WILD IMAGES LTD/RSPCA Photolibrary

Page 444(left) courtesy of PAPILIO/Pat Jerrold

Pages 454, 455(bottom) courtesy of ©Mr J B Blossom/RSPCA Photolibrary

Pages 464-465(left) courtesy of PAPILIO/Clive Druett

Pages 465(right), 486 courtesy of PAPILIO/John Heathcote

Page 494 courtesy of ©Mark Hamblin/RSPCA Photolibrary

Pages 501, 502(bottom) courtesy of ©Des Cartwright/RSPCA Photolibrary

Please see back flap for jacket credits.